Macroeconomics

Global Economic Watch

Second Edition

William Boyes | Michael Melvin

CENGAGE
Learning™

Australia • Brazil • Japan • Korea • Mexico • Singapore • Spain • United Kingdom • United States

CENGAGE
Learning™

**Macroeconomics: Global Economic
Watch, Second Edition**

Macroeconomics, 8th Edition
William Boyes | Michael Melvin

© 2011 Cengage Learning. All rights reserved.

Global Economic Watch: Impact on Economics, 1st Edition
Global Economics Crisis Resource Center

© 2010 Cengage Learning. All rights reserved.

Executive Editors:
 Maureen Staudt
 Michael Stranz

Senior Project Development Manager:
 Linda deStefano

Marketing Specialist:
 Courtney Sheldon

Senior Production/Manufacturing
Manager:
 Donna M. Brown

PreMedia Manager:
 Joel Brennecke

Sr. Rights Acquisition Account Manager:
 Todd Osborne

Cover Image:
Getty Images*

*Unless otherwise noted, all cover images used by
Custom Solutions, a part of Cengage Learning,
have been supplied courtesy of Getty Images with
the exception of the Earthview cover image, which
has been supplied by the National Aeronautics and
Space Administration (NASA).

For product information and technology assistance, contact us at
Cengage Learning Customer & Sales Support, 1-800-354-9706

For permission to use material from this text or product,
submit all requests online at **cengage.com/permissions**
Further permissions questions can be emailed to
permissionrequest@cengage.com

This book contains select works from existing Cengage Learning resources and
was produced by Cengage Learning Custom Solutions for collegiate use. As such,
those adopting and/or contributing to this work are responsible for editorial
content accuracy, continuity and completeness.

Compilation © 2010 Cengage Learning

ISBN-13: 978-1-111-51854-7

ISBN-10: 1-111-51854-8

Cengage Learning
5191 Natorp Boulevard
Mason, Ohio 45040
USA

Cengage Learning is a leading provider of customized learning solutions with
office locations around the globe, including Singapore, the United Kingdom,
Australia, Mexico, Brazil, and Japan. Locate your local office at:
international.cengage.com/region.

Cengage Learning products are represented in Canada by Nelson Education, Ltd.
For your lifelong learning solutions, visit **www.cengage.com /custom.**
Visit our corporate website at **www.cengage.com.**

Printed in the United States of America

Table of Contents

Global Economic Crisis

Impact on Economics

SOUTH-WESTERN
CENGAGE Learning™

Australia • Brazil • Japan • Korea • Mexico • Singapore • Spain • United Kingdom • United States

SOUTH-WESTERN
CENGAGE Learning

Global Economic Crisis: Impact on Economics

Sr. Art Director: Michelle Kunkler

Cover Design: Rose Alcorn

Cover Images: © Jasony00 / Dreamstime.com

For product information and technology assistance, contact us at
Cengage Learning Customer & Sales Support, 1-800-354-9706

For permission to use material from this text or product,
submit all requests online at **www.cengage.com/permissions**
Further permissions questions can be emailed to
permissionrequest@cengage.com

ISBN-13: 978-1-4240-5968-3
ISBN-10: 1-4240-5968-2

South-Western Cengage Learning
5191 Natorp Boulevard
Mason, OH 45040
USA

Cengage Learning products are represented in Canada by
Nelson Education, Ltd.

For your course and learning solutions, visit www.cengage.com
Purchase any of our products at your local college store or at our
preferred online store **www.ichapters.com**

Printed in the United States of America
1 2 3 4 5 6 7 13 12 11 10 09

Building Up to the Current Crisis

Learning Objectives.

By the end of this chapter, you will be able to:

- Explain the important financial market regulation that came out of the Great Depression of the 1930s.

- Describe why the rise of American consumerism took place after World War II.

- Elaborate on why the Savings and Loan crisis took place.

- Describe why there was a drive for mortgage-backed securities during the first decade of the 21st century.

- Delineate how all of these historical events have led up to the current financial crisis.

In January 2007, everything seemed to be going right for the U.S. economy and, by extension, U.S. financial markets. On January 24, 2007, the Dow Jones Industrial Index ended the day at 12,621. This was the first time ever the Dow had climbed above 12,600[1]. As stock prices continued to increase, the Federal Reserve worried that the U.S. economy might be growing too quickly. The Federal Reserve had raised its target for the Fed Funds Rate from 5.25 percent to 5.50 percent six months earlier, in the hopes of cooling a red hot U.S. economy. Even with the higher interest rates, the economy was growing at faster than 4 percent a year, a rate many economists believed was unsustainable for an economy the size of the United States.

By the fall of 2008, things had changed drastically. By November 12, 2008, the Dow had fallen to 8,282, a 41 percent drop from its high of 14,164 on October 9, 2007. The Federal Reserve had cut its target for the Fed Funds rate to a mere 1 percent, in a desperate attempt to keep the economy from sliding into a deep recession.

What on earth happened? How could such a highly successful economy like that of the United States in January 2007 find itself on the brink of a severe recession a mere few months later? At this point, we must ask ourselves: Where is the U.S. economy headed? As the old saying goes, "If you want to know where you are going, you have to understand where you have been." To learn why the current financial crisis occurred and where the global economy is headed, we need to determine how we got here. In fact, to fully grasp how we got to where we are, we have to travel back over seventy years to the

---

1 See http://www.mdleasing.com/djia.htm.

Great Depression of the 1930s. As the American society was coming to grips with the economic catastrophe of the Great Depression, there was a call for greater regulation of our financial markets. Many of these regulations are still in place, and understanding them helps to frame the structure of the current financial crisis.

From the economic despair of the Great Depression, we moved to the post–World War II economic expansion with its boom in the housing market. One of the main players in this post-war housing boom is the Federal National Mortgage Association and later the Federal Home Loan Mortgage Corporation, or as they are better known, Fannie Mae and Freddie Mac, respectfully. The financial troubles of Fannie and Freddie are a centerpiece of the current financial crisis.

The current financial crisis is not the first crisis to have centered on the American mortgage market. Over twenty years ago, the Savings & Loan crisis also focused on entities that lent money to households to buy their homes. The outfall from the Savings & Loan crisis sets the groundwork for the current global financial crisis. While our current crisis has roots dating back over seven decades ago with the Great Depression of the 1930s, the picture is by no means complete. Updates on this discussion can be found on the web page that accompanies this booklet.

THE EARLY CALL FOR REGULATION OF FINANCIAL MARKETS: THE 1930S

From Flappers to Breadlines

The 1920s was a glamorous decade. The "Roaring '20s," as they were called, saw the rise of American consumerism, with American households buying a wide range of goods and services from new automobiles and household appliances to radios and other electrical devices. Americans were able to buy these consumer goods thanks, in great part, to the booming stock market of the times. The New York Times index of 25 industrial stocks was at 110 in 1924[2]; by June 1929, it had risen to 338, and by September 1929, it stood at 452. Thus, someone buying the index in 1924 would have seen his or her investment grow by over 400 percent by September 1929.[3] The flappers with their trendy dresses, flashy zoot suits, and dancing the Charleston all night long epitomized the carefree decade. However, the good times could not last forever. By the end of the decade, the party that had been the Roaring '20s would collapse into the Great Depression of the 1930s.

---

2 Gary Walton and Hugh Rockoff, "History of the American Economy," South-Western College Publishing, 2004.

3 Charles Kindlegerger, *The World in Depression, 1929–1939*, Berkeley: University of California Press, 1973.

The Depression witnessed the once vibrant American economy seemingly imploding overnight. As the previously dynamic and ever-expanding economy contracted, unemployment across the economy increased dramatically. No sector of the economy seemed to be spared of the growing massive unemployment of the 1930s. The unemployment of unskilled workers, skilled craftsmen, farmers, businesspeople, and even executives increased rapidly. The unemployment rate that stood at only 4 percent for much of the 1920s increased to 25 percent by 1932.

The carefree dancing flappers of the 1920s were replaced with long breadlines and soup kitchens feeding the growing masses of unemployed of the 1930s. The once booming stock market seemed to evaporate and take the rest of the economy with it. The fall in the stock market was so dramatic that stocks lost 40 percent of their value in just two months. The stock market crash caused increased uncertainty over future income and employment translated into a reduction of household spending on durable goods such as automobiles and radios. [4]

The Call for Reform

As the economy contracted and unemployment rose, there were cries from the American people for their elected leaders to "do something" about the economic crisis. The election of President Franklin Delano Roosevelt in 1932 marked a dramatic change in how the federal government would approach the crisis. Roosevelt and his fellow Democrats believed that the Depression and the resulting rise in unemployment was due to the rampant speculation in the stock market and financial markets in general.

Even before Roosevelt was sworn in, Senator Ferdinand Pecora had begun hearings to examine the role the financial markets played in triggering the Depression. The Pecora Hearings, as they became known, resulted in sweeping new regulations of the financial markets. Within weeks of taking office, the Roosevelt Administration called for a bank holiday that would close all of the commercial banks in the country for seven days; passed and signed the Securities Act of 1933; and, perhaps most importantly, passed the Glass-Steagall Act or Banking Act of 1933.

The Glass-Steagall Act accomplished three key things:

- It separated commercial banks (i.e., those entities that take deposits and make loans) from investment banks (i.e., those entities involved with underwriting and selling stocks and bonds).

- It created bank deposit insurance.

- It gave the Federal Reserve the power to limit the interest rates commercial banks could pay on deposits.

The Glass-Steagall Act's separation of commercial and investment banking was based on the premise that if commercial banks were allowed to be involved in the selling of

---

4 Christina Romer, "The Great Crash and the Onset of the Depression," *Quarterly Journal of Economics,* August 1990, Vol. 105, no. 3.

stocks and bonds, a conflict of interest could exist and ultimately make commercial banks less safe.

The creation of deposit insurance was also designed to make commercial banks more stable. With the advent of government deposit insurance, depositors at insured banks could be confident that their savings were secure. Even if an insured bank failed, the government's deposit insurance would be there to ensure that savers would not lose their money. However, in order to make certain that banks were not taking on too much risk, government deposit insurance prompted the need for government regulation or oversight of the banking system.

In addition, Regulation Q of the Glass-Steagall Act was enacted to give the Federal Reserve the power to limit interest rates paid on deposits and to make the banking system more stable by limiting the amount of competition between banks. The drafters of the bill feared that if commercial banks competed for deposits, they would ultimately engage in destructive competitive behavior. Thus, to limit the amount of competition, banks were not allowed to pay interest on demand deposits (checking accounts) and had a cap on what interest rates they could pay on savings accounts.

As time went by, other legislation was passed that increased and expanded the government regulation of U.S. financial markets. The Securities Act of 1933 and the Securities Exchange Act of 1934 created the Securities and Exchange Commission, or the SEC, which is still today the main regulator of the bond and stock markets. In 1938, Congress created the Federal National Mortgage Association, or Fannie Mae, to help stabilize the home mortgage market. See the boxed feature for details.

Fannie Mae & Freddie Mac:
Government Entities to "Semi-Private" Financial Intermediaries

A mortgage loan uses real estate as collateral for the loan. Collateral is the pledge of an asset to ensure repayment by the borrower. Collateral serves as protection for the lender in case of default or nonpayment by the borrower. If a person borrows money and pledges something as collateral and does not repay as promised, the lenders allowed to take the collateral in lieu of the payment. So, a home mortgage loan, or what we will simply refer to as a home mortgage, is when the borrower pledges a house as collateral on a loan. A first mortgage is when a lender agrees to loan money to a family or an individual so that they can purchase a house.

Until the 20th century, mortgages were usually short term, lasting only about five to seven years. During those years, the borrower would have to pay interest on the money borrowed and repay the entire amount at the end of the period. Thus, at the end of the mortgage, the borrower would have to try to find someone or some entity to lend them the money again.

During the Great Depression, many people lost their jobs and could not afford to make their monthly mortgage payment, leaving the borrower to foreclose on them and have the family evicted from their home. With the federal government creation of the Federal National Mortgage Association (i.e., Fannie Mae), borrowers were encouraged to lend money to families over a period of 30 years. Over these 30 years, both interest and the loan principle would be paid. At the end of the 30-year mortgage, the borrower would own the home outright.

To entice lenders to loan money for home mortgages, Fannie Mae would agree to buy certain "qualified" mortgages from banks. Fannie Mae would then either hold the mortgages or sell them to interested investors. In doing so, Fannie Mae would free up funds for the lender to loan on new mortgages.

Due to budget constraints, President Johnson privatized Fannie Mae in 1968. In order to ensure that Fannie Mae did not have a monopoly in the mortgage securitizing business, the federal government created the Federal Home Loan Mortgage Corporation (i.e., Freddie Mac) in 1970.

Since both of these entities were created by the Federal government, many in the financial markets believed that Fannie and Freddie enjoyed a government guarantee against failure. Because of this "implied" government guarantee, Fannie and Freddie could borrow money at very low interest rates in financial markets.

The financial market regulation that came out of the Great Depression seemed to work very well. As the U.S. economy recovered from the Depression, financial markets remained stable and the number of banking failures dropped significantly. During World War II, the U.S. financial markets allowed the government to issue war bonds to finance the wars in Europe and the Pacific.

BUILDING THE AMERICAN DREAM: U.S. HOUSING BOOM IN POST-WAR AMERICA

Pent Up Consumption During World War II

The Second World War was a very hard time for American consumers. While household income increased, household spending decreased significantly. This reduction in household spending was in part necessary, as scarce consumer goods were diverted for the war effort. Many consumer goods, including sugar, meat, gasoline, tires, and even clothes, were rationed during the war. To buy these rationed goods, a family would need not only cash but a government-issued ration coupon. Even having a ration coupon did not guarantee that a consumer could find the good available for sale on store shelves. Shortages of popular goods, especially sugar, were commonplace during the war.

While consumer goods were scarce during the war, one thing was not in short supply: jobs. Workers were needed to build the tanks, ships, and arms that were critical to the war effort. The production of many consumer goods was suspended so that resources could be used for the war effort. For example, there were no new automobiles built in the United States between the end of 1942 and 1946, since the factories that built automobiles were converted into plants for making tanks, aircraft, artillery, etc., for the war. Similarly, no new farm tractors were built during the war, as those factories were likewise converted for the war effort. But these factories needed workers to produce war-related products. Because many young males had joined the military to fight in the war, workers were in short supply. For the first time in U.S. history, large numbers of women entered the labor force.

As employment increased during the war, American households saw their incomes increase. However, with the war rationing in effect, households had very few things on which to spend this new income. Instead, scores of Americans saved their money during the War, waiting and hoping for a better future.

Unleashing American Spending

The end of the Second World War saw a return of American consumerism in grand style. The long years of economic hardship of the Great Depression were behind them, as were the days of sacrifice during World War II. The American consumer had pent up spending power that was being unleashed. For military personnel who were returning from fighting the war overseas as well as those who had "fought the war on the home front," the end of the war created an opportunity to capture the "American Dream." A big part of that post-war "American Dream" was home ownership. In 1940, just 44 percent of families owned their own home; by the end of the 1950s, three out of five families owned their home (according to a U.S. Census). This remarkable increase in homeownership was due, in great part, to the expansion of the Savings and Loan industry.

Savings and Loans are depository institutions that take deposits, mostly from households, and make loans mostly to consumers; these loans are often home mortgages. While the Savings and Loan industry has a long history in the United States going back to the 19th century (the forerunners were called Building & Loans), a number of Savings and Loans failed during the depression. As a result, in 1932, Congress passed the Federal Home Loan Bank Act of 1932, which created the Federal Home Loan Bank Board to lend money to Savings and Loans that found themselves short of funds. In 1934, Congress created the Federal Savings and Loan Insurance Corporation (FSLIC), which would offer government deposit insurance to savers at Savings and Loans.[5]

Expansion of the Savings and Loan Industry

During the post–World War II era, the Savings and Loan industry thrived. The first decade after the Second World War saw the Savings & Loan industry grow at its fastest rate ever. The expansion of American suburbs during the late 1940s and 1950s increased the demand for home mortgages that the Savings and Loans were prepared to offer. In addition, the Savings and Loan trade association worked with the managers of the S&Ls

---

5 David Mason, "From Building and Loans to Bail-outs," Cambridge University Press, 2004.

showing them how to advertise their services and focus on providing a high level of consumer service. As a result, the size and reach of the Savings and Loan industry expanded greatly.

Government regulation of the Savings and Loan industry also played a large role in the industry's expansion. Thanks to Regulation Q, which the Savings and Loans became subject to in 1966, the Savings and Loans faced a cap on their cost of funds. At the same time, government regulations were changing, making it easier for the Savings and Loans to offer even more mortgages and grow even more quickly. These were very successful times for the Savings and Loans. Managers of the Savings and Loans lived by the "3-6-3 Rule," that is, pay 3 percent on deposits, lend the money at 6 percent on mortgages, and be on the golf course by 3:00 pm.

The "3-6-3 Rule" illustrates why the Savings and Loans were so profitable. When a depository institution pays 3 percent for deposits and lends the money out at 6 percent, the difference between the two is what economists call the "interest rate spread." For the Savings and Loans, the 3 percentage point interest rate spread is how they paid their expenses and generated a profit. During the decades after the Second World War, the Savings and Loans were very profitable indeed. These profits allowed existing Savings and Loans to expand and drew in a large number of new S&Ls. By 1965, the Savings and Loan industry held 26 percent of all consumer savings and provided 46 percent of the single-family mortgages in the United States. Unfortunately, the good times would not last forever.

The Savings & Loan Crisis of the 1980s

Inflation and Interest Rates

During the 1970s, the U.S. economy suffered from increased rates of inflation. Inflation is defined as the continuous increase in the general level of prices. A high rate of inflation mean the cost of living for households increases and the cost of operations for firms increase. In addition, as the rate of inflation increases, market interest rates also increase.

To see why this happens, think about how you would feel if you were a lender of money and prices increased. Suppose I ask you to lend me $2 so that I can buy a bottle of diet Coke from a vending machine and agree to repay you tomorrow. . Essentially you are lending me enough resources, the two dollars, to purchase an entire bottle of diet Coke. Now assume the person who refills the vending machine changes the price of a bottle of diet Coke from $2 to $3. Tomorrow comes and I give you $2. You say, "Wait a minute-- I gave you enough resources to buy an entire bottle of diet Coke, and yet you pay me back with resources that can now only buy two-thirds of a bottle of diet Coke!"
Notice what happened: When prices increase, or there is inflation, lenders get paid back in money that simply no longer buys as much. As a result, if lenders think there is going to be inflation, they are going to demand to be compensated for the difference and thus demand a higher interest rate before they will lend their money.

This is what happened during the 1970s. As the inflation rate in the United States increased, market interest rates also increased. Thus, interest rates on Treasury bills, corporate bonds, and other types of debt increased higher and higher as U.S. inflation got worse and worse.

The Problem of Disintermediation

One set of interest rates that did not increase during the 1970s was that paid by the Savings and Loans. Remember that during this time, the Savings and Loans were subject to Regulation Q, the law that stated the maximum interest rate that could be paid on deposits. Thus, while the market interest rates on regular passbook savings accounts could be no higher than 5.5 percent, the yield on a 1-year Treasury bill was over 12 percent by February 1980. As a result of these interest rate differences, savers started to pull their money out of the Savings and Loans in favor of higher paying money market mutual funds. The process of funds moving from one financial intermediary to another is what economists call disintermediation.

To combat disintermediation, the Savings and Loans looked for ways around Regulation Q. One "invention" was the creation of NOW, or negotiable orders of withdrawal. NOW accounts were essentially demand deposits that paid a market rate of interest. Initially the NOW accounts were of questionable legality, since they were violating the premise of Regulation Q that prohibited the paying of interest on demand deposits or checking accounts. But the operators of Savings and Loans thought they had little choice but to offer the NOW accounts. If they did not offer NOW accounts, they would see more and more deposits leave their institutions. If the disintermediation were allowed to go on unchecked, it would lead to a collapse of the Savings and Loan industry, since a depository institution with no deposits simply can not function. Clearly, something needed to change.

DIDMCA: The Solution that Did Not Work

The Savings and Loan industry turned to Washington for help with disintermediation. In response to the growing financial market difficulties, after much debate, Congress passed, and President Carter signed, the Depository Institutions Deregulation and Monetary Control Act (DIDMCA) in 1980. The DIDMCA was the Carter Administration's attempt to bring about some type of financial market reform. Four years earlier, Carter had campaigned on the promise that his administration would bring about such reform, but by 1980, little to nothing had changed in terms of financial market regulation. DIDMCA was about to change all of that.

Two of DIDMCA's major reforms were that it set up for the complete repeal of Regulation Q over six years and it would make it legal for Savings & Loans to offer NOW accounts in order to fend off the disintermediation immediately. While DIDMCA allowed the Savings and Loans to compete with the money market mutual funds for deposits, it created a whole new set of problems. Savings and Loans generated most of their income off the 30-year fixed interest rate mortgages that they had written in the past. The vast majority of these mortgages paid the Savings and Loan a 6 to 8 percent annual rate of interest. When the Savings and Loans were paying 3 to 5.5 percent on deposits, they enjoyed a positive interest rate spread. With the passage of DIDMCA, the Savings and Loans would now be paying upwards of 14 percent on their NOW accounts. That meant that the Savings and Loans would be paying 14 percent for funds while earning only 6 to 8 percent on funds. Thus, the Savings and loans were suffering from a negative interest rate spread.

Garn-St. Germain: Making a Bad Problem Worse

To get relief from their negative interest rate spread, the Savings and Loans returned to Congress in 1981 and 1982 seeking help. In response to the industry's cry for help, Congress passed the Garn-St. Germain Depository Institutions Act of 1982. Garn-St. Germain allowed the Savings and Loans to diversify their lending away from traditional 30-year fixed rate home loans and into shorter term, more profitable business loans. The Act allowed the Savings and Loans to hold up to 40 percent of their assets in commercial mortgages and up to 11 percent of their assets in secured or unsecured commercial loans. In addition, many states, including California and Texas, significantly reduced the amount of regulations on their respective state-chartered Savings and Loans.

As a result of these reduced regulations and a desire to diversify their loan portfolios, the Savings and Loans set off a business lending spree. The Savings and Loans wrote a dizzying array of commercial real estate loans, include loans for high-rise office buildings, massive suburban shopping mall developments, and retail strip mall developments. In addition, many Savings and Loans started lending money for alternative energy development such as windmill farms in the Texas panhandle. One issue with this new lending is that many Savings and Loan lenders had little to no experience in making such loans. As a result, many loans were written where risk was mispriced. Numerous office buildings were built that simply were not needed. Many shopping centers never found enough tenants because they knew shopping centers were not needed. For example, by 1986, nearly one-third of the office space in Houston, Texas, sat unoccupied. As these spaces went unrented, the real estate developers who built these buildings could not pay the loans they had taken out from the Savings and Loans.

The Zombie Savings and Loans

By the late 1980s, the Savings and Loan industry was riddled with insolvent institutions. These institutions had written so many bad loans that they simply did not have enough assets to make good on all of their deposits. These insolvent institutions, sometimes called "Zombie institutions" because they were financially "dead," should have been closed down by their regulators. These regulators, which included the Federal Home Loan Bank and FSLIC, instead chose to suspend the regulatory rules and allowed these Zombie institutions to continue to function. This suspension of the regulatory rules, called "Capital Forbearance," allowed the Zombie institutions to continue in operation and make more and more risky loans.

As the Zombie institutions were allowed to continue in operation, many of the Zombies "infected" the healthy, well run institutions. A Zombie institution would compete with a healthy institution for a loan customer by offering the customer a loan on very favorable terms with a low interest rate and/or easy repayment terms. To compete, the healthy institution would have to offer the loan customer similar terms or face being locked out of the market. Thus, the healthy institution would have to behave like the Zombie institution and essentially "become" a Zombie institution.

One question that has been raised is: why did the regulators allow the Zombie institutions to continue in operation? One answer to this question is that the regulators simply did not have the resources to close all of the Zombie institutions. Closing all of the Zombie institutions would have required perhaps hundreds of billions of dollars to pay insured depositors. Since the regulators did have the resources to close all of these Zombie institutions, they allowed them to continue in operation.

A second potential explanation to why the regulators allowed the Zombie institutions to continue in operation was the political power some of the savings and loan operators wielded. See the box below for one of the more infamous examples of political influence in the savings and loan crisis.

Charles Keating and the Keating 5

One reason many of the Savings and Loan regulators practiced capital forbearance was the political influence of the Savings and Loan operators. An example of this is what became known as the Keating 5. An Arizona real estate developer by the name of Charles Keating was allowed to buy a Savings and Loan in California called Lincoln Savings and Loan. When Lincoln Savings and Loan started to suffer from disintermediation, Keating promised depositors that he could offer them a "special account" that would pay an interest rate much above what money market mutual funds would pay.

Many of Lincoln's depositors were elderly, and they questioned Keating as to the safety of the "special accounts." Keating reassured his elderly customers that the special accounts were fully insured by the federal government. In fact, they were not. The special accounts were actual shares in his real estate development in Arizona.

The regulators of Lincoln Savings and Loan at the Federal Home Bank Board became concerned about the growing riskiness of Lincoln. But Charles Keating did not want the regulators to interfere in his operations. Keating had made large campaign contributions to five key U.S. Senators. Keating now called on these five Senators to intervene with the regulators on his behalf. The five Senators basically did what Keating requested. As a result, Keating was allowed to continue to operate Lincoln Savings and Loan as he saw fit.

In 1989, Lincoln Savings and Loan failed, costing taxpayers $1.3 billion, and more importantly, more than 22,000 depositors/bondholders at Lincoln Savings and Loan lost their savings since they were not in government-insured accounts. Charles Keating eventually was convicted of bank fraud and served four and a half years in prison. What happened to those five Senators known as the Keating 5? Basically, nothing. All were allowed to continue serving in the U.S.

Senate, and two of the Keating 5 went on to run for President of the United States despite their questionable ethical dealings with Charles Keating.

As the 1980s moved on, the Savings and Loan problem grew significantly. In 1988, the FSLIC had closed over 200 Savings and Loans that were insolvent. The problem, however, was that by the end of 1988, over 500 insolvent Savings and Loans continued to operate. Clearly, the current system had failed.

In August 1989, President George H. Bush signed the Financial Institutions Reform Recovery and Enforcement Act. FIRREA was the first dramatic step to resolve the Savings and Loan crisis. Among other things, FIRREA forced the absorption of the FSLIC into the FDIC. In addition, the Federal Home Loan Banks' independence was stripped away and it was taken over by the Office of Thrift Supervision within the Treasury Department. Perhaps most importantly, FIRREA created the Resolution Trust Corporation (RTC), which was to close the insolvent Savings and Loans and sell off their assets.

The once proud Savings and Loan industry that had helped to build the American suburbs after the Second World War was now a mere shadow of itself. The inability or unwillingness of the Savings and Loan operators to measure the riskiness of their loans problem greatly contributed to the industry's demise. The regulators such as the Federal Home Loan Bank and FSLIC arguably did not do their job correctly, and these entities were either stripped of their powers or completely eliminated.

THE SEEKING OF RETURN: 2002–2006

One of the lessons learned from the Savings and Loan crisis is that depository institutions that rely on the interest rate spread between what they earn on long-term loans and what they pay on short-term deposits can suffer greatly when market interest rates increase. The Savings and Loans suffered from negative interest rate spreads throughout the late 1970s and early 1980s, and these negative spreads triggered a series of chain reactions that ultimately led to the current financial crisis.

Banks and Fee Income

In an attempt to avoid a repeat of the Savings and Loan crisis, commercial banks in the United States during the 1990s and throughout the first decade of the 21st century attempted to end their reliance on interest rate spreads. Instead of depending on the spread as a source of profits, commercial banks envisioned themselves as providers of financial services who earned fees for their services. Since fee income was independent of changes in market interest rates, commercial banks saw it as a much more stable source of income and profits.

Commercial banks looked in a variety of places to generate fees. They charged fees for use of ATMs (automated teller machines), for use of the bank lobby, and for printing checks, and they looked at offering new services where they could generate new fees. One expanding market that caught the banks' attention was the home mortgage market. Traditionally, when a depository institution wrote a home mortgage loan, the depository institution would hold the mortgage, collect payment, or service the mortgage for 30 years until the household borrower paid off the mortgage. However, in their desire to earn fees, commercial banks were turning more and more to the securitization of home mortgages.

Securitization

Securitization is the pooling or combining of loans, such as mortgages, into one big bundle. This bundle is then used to create a new financial instrument or bond whose cash flows are the original loans in the pool. For example, the securitization of home mortgages entails the purchase of a large number of home mortgages and the creation of a mortgage-backed security, or MBS. The mortgaged-backed securities are paid the cash flow received from the households as they make their mortgage payments.

Securitization takes place with other loans in addition to home mortgages. Commercial mortgages are also securitized into their own version of securitized securities called Commercial Mortgaged-Backed Assets. Student Loans are also securitized. If you have borrowed money for a student loan, once you signed your promise to repay the loan, the bank or financial institution that lent you the money took your student loan, bundled it with other student loans, and created an Asset-Backed Security, or ABS. In 2006, $79 billion of new student-loan-backed ABS were issued, with the total market size estimated to exceed $350 billion in 2007.

Fannie Mae and Freddie Mac: Their Great Demise

Fannie Mae and Freddie Mac were originally created by Congress to provide liquidity to the mortgage market, and they were very successful. They did so by buying "qualified" mortgages and securitizing them, or bundling them and selling the bundles to investors. The two "government-sponsored entities," or GSEs, came to dominate the mortgage market. Together they hold or guarantee over $5 trillion in mortgages. By comparison, the entire U.S. economy is just over $13 trillion and the total entire outstanding mortgages in the United States amount to $12 trillion.

However, in 2007 and 2008, both Fannie Mae and Freddie Mac ran into a great deal of financial trouble. Both Fannie and Freddie had purchased mortgages without carefully examining the default risks associated with those mortgages. As a result, in 2008, the federal government had to take over both Fannie and Freddie to keep them from failing.

When a commercial bank writes a loan that will be bundled up or securitized, the bank earns a fee from the entity that does the bundling. The "bundler" or securitizer may be an investment bank, a Government-Sponsored Entity (such as Fannie Mae, Freddie Mac, or Sallie Mae--for student loans), or a Special Investment Vehicle, which is created by commercial banks. The bundler then sells the newly created asset, such as a mortgage-backed security, to an institutional investor, such as an insurance company, pension fund, or an endowment.

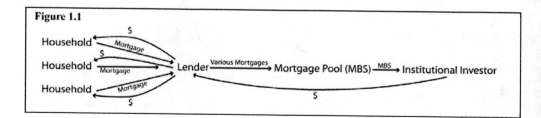

Figure 1.1

Over time, the market for mortgage-backed securities increased. The loan originators, oftentimes commercial banks, liked the process of making mortgage loans and earning a fee and then servicing the mortgage and earning more fees. They could generate fee income and move the long-term mortgages off their balance sheet, so they no longer had to worry about interest rate spreads. The process was appealing too because it enabled the mortgage bundlers to charge a fee for bundling the mortgages together and then selling them to institutional investors.

As time went on, new inventions in the mortgage market came about. One issue that arose was that not all institutional investors had the same desire for risk. Some institutional investors didn't want any risk of default. That is, they wanted to be sure that they received the payments they were expecting. At the same time, other institutional investors were more willing to take on some risk, as long as they were compensated for this increased risk by being paid a higher interest rate.

To meet the differing needs of these institutional investors, the bundlers of Mortgage-Backed Securities decided to slice the MBSs into different pieces. The first slice would be paid first, as the households made their mortgage payments. The next slice would be paid after the first slice was paid, if there was still money left over, meaning if there were only a few or no defaults. Each of the remaining slices would then be paid in descending order. These slices of the MBSs are called *tranches*, from the French word *tranch*, which means slice.

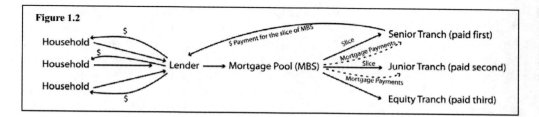

Figure 1.2

In reality, there could be more than just three tranches, but the logic remains the same: the senior tranche gets paid first and so on down the line. Some of the lower tranches, the last to be paid and thus the most risky, the lenders (including commercial banks) held onto the mortgages since they could be very difficult to sell to institutional investors. But, as long as there are no defaults on mortgages, all of the tranches get paid.

Historically, home mortgage defaults were very low, only around 2 percent, so the buyers of the Mortgage-Backed Assets felt fairly safe that they would receive their payments as promised. Thus, the securitized mortgage market grew.

Falling Market Interest Rates

In 2001, in a response to a slowing U.S. economy, the Federal Reserve set out to lower interest rates to stimulate the economy. The collapse of the dot.com boom in 2001 had brought about a significant reduction in the amount of household and business spending. To encourage more borrowing and spending by households and firms, the Federal Reserve cut interest rates throughout 2001, 2002, and 2003. By 2003, market interest rates in the United States were the lowest they had been in forty years.

In response to these falling market interest rates, institutional investors' interest rates in the home mortgage market increased significantly. While other market interest rates had dropped significantly due to the Federal Reserve's actions, the interest rates on home mortgages, and thus the return on mortgage-backed securities, had not fallen as much. Thus, there was a growing interest by institutional investors to buy these mortgage-backed securities.

The mortgage lenders, including commercial banks, were desperate to the meet the growing demand for mortgage-backed assets. But in order to create more mortgage-backed assets, these lenders needed to write more and more mortgages. The problem these lenders faced was that in order to write more mortgages, they would need to go beyond "traditional" borrowers. That is, the lenders needed to lower their lending standards so that more people could qualify for mortgages.

Traditionally, if a family wanted to borrow money to buy a house, they needed to have 20 percent of the purchase price in cash. The family could then borrow the remaining 80 percent of the purchase price of the house via a mortgage. But, as the demand for mortgage-backed assets increased, mortgage lenders began writing "zero-down" mortgages where the borrower puts no money down and borrows 100 percent of the purchase price.

One potential problem with "zero-down" mortgages is that they can result in much higher default rates. In the traditional 20-percent down mortgage, the borrower has some of their own money in the house, or as the saying goes, they have "their skin in the game." If times become financially difficult for the borrower, they would work hard to stay current on their mortgage payments, since defaulting on the mortgage or being foreclosed on would cause the borrower to lose the money they had used to purchase the house. However, with zero-down mortgages, the borrower doesn't have any "skin in the game" or any financial interest in the house. Under this setting, if financial times become difficult, the borrower is much more likely to simply walk away from the house and have the lender foreclose on the house.

Thus, the advent of the zero-down mortgage greatly increased the probability of default by the borrowers. The problem is, many in the financial markets ignored these increasing risks in the mortgage market. Instead, they continued to believe that mortgage default rates would stay exactly as they always had been. In other words, there was a major mispricing of risk occurring in the U.S. mortgage markets.

Heads I Win, Tales the Government Loses

As depository institutions such as Savings and Loans or commercial banks take on more risk, either through writing risky loans or holding risky assets, depositors usually "punish" this behavior by withdrawing their deposits. Depositors do this because if the depository institution fails due to too many of its risky assets failing to pay out as planned, the depositor will lose all of the money they have on deposit. In these cases, the depositors essentially "watch over" the depository institution and help to ensure that Savings and Loans or commercial banks do not engage in excessive risky behavior.

However, deposit insurance changes all of this. With government-sponsored deposit insurance, the depositor knows that even if the depository institution fails, the depositor will not lose any of their money. If the institution fails, all the depositor has to do is go to the government to get a check equal to the amount of the government insurance.

On the other hand, if the depository institution engages in holding risk assets and these risky assets pay off, the institution can "share" these high payoffs with the depositor in the form of higher interest rates on deposits. This is what economists call the "moral hazard" of deposit insurance. A moral hazard is the existence of a contract that can alter behavior by changing incentives.

With the creation of government deposit insurance, the incentives and behavior of depositors change. Depositors no longer "watch over" depository institutions to "keep them safe" and instead have an incentive to push lenders to hold very risky assets. If those risky assets pay off as planned, the depositor benefits, as the institution shares with them the high returns generated by the risky assets. Conversely, if the risky assets fail to pay off as planned and the depository institution fails, the depositor turns to the government to be made whole again. From the point of view of the depositor, government-sponsored deposit insurance creates a situation where the depositor can say "head I win, tails the government loses."

BRINGING IT ALL TOGETHER

The current financial crisis that centers on the home mortgage markets has its roots in the evolution of the U.S. financial markets. Many economists argue that the deposit insurance that was created during the Great Depression of the 1930s may have contributed to the excessive risk taking and the mispricing of risk in the home mortgage market during the first decade of the 21st century. What contributed to this mispricing of risk in the home mortgage market was the rapid expansion of the securitizing of home mortgages, which was an outcome of the Savings and Loan crisis of the 1980s. But this securitization would not have been possible without the rapid expansion of the U.S. housing market in the decades following the Second World War.

But the synopsis of the current financial crisis is not complete. In the next chapter, we will examine in more depth the issues of the current crisis. Updates on the current status of the crisis can be found on the web page www.cengage.com/gec that accompanies this booklet. It will be very interesting and informative to watch this crisis unfold.

The Current Crisis

Chapter Outline

Learning Goals

After reading this chapter, you should be able to answer these questions:
1. Why is there so much uncertainty in financial markets?
2. In what ways is the current financial crisis not limited to just the United States?
3. What issues surround the Wall Street bailout package?
4. What challenges does President Obama face during his first term?

Economic slowdowns and recessions occur for a variety of reasons. Sometimes the economy slows when the central bank raises interest rates to counteract inflation. At other times, the rate of economic growth slows due to a natural disaster or a disruption in the flow of goods and services. The economic recession that began in the United States in December 2007 was triggered by a global financial crisis. Problems in the U.S. home mortgage market set off this widespread financial meltdown. In this chapter, we will examine the current global financial crisis, explain what caused it, and offer potential solutions to resolve it.

As discussed in the previous chapter, the causes of the current financial crisis go back decades. However, the specific events that led to the current financial downturn began in the summer of 2007. One recurring theme in this chapter will be the destructive role that uncertainty has played in pushing the United States into this quagmire. We will see how an entire Wall Street industry, investment banking, has been crippled by it. As policymakers continue to struggle with solutions, we will explore how their past rescue attempts have not worked as planned. Finally, we will look at the economic problems that face the Obama Administration.

The story of the current financial crisis is far from over. Updates to this compelling economic story can be found on the website www.cengage.com/gec that accompanies this chapter.

THE SUMMER OF 2007: THE CRISIS BEGINS

Summer is usually a very slow time for media events in the United States: in Washington, D.C., congress members are on their summer recess; in New York, many people who work in financial markets flee the city for long vacations; and in Europe, financial market activity slows as Europeans take advantage of month-long vacations. But during the late summer of 2007, Washington, New York, and the European financial centers were all a buzz with rumors of what appeared to be a brewing financial storm.

In July 2007, two hedge funds run by investment bank Bear Stearns collapsed, causing an estimated $1.5 billion loss to its investors.[1] The two funds—the High-Grade Structured Credit Strategies Fund and the High-Grade Structured Credit Strategies Enhanced Leveraged Fund—had borrowed huge sums of money to buy a large number of mortgage-backed securities.

In May 2007, as the first wave of mortgage defaults began to be felt, these two funds reported losses much larger than had been anticipated. As a result of these losses and growing uncertainty concerning the future value of the funds under its management, Bear Stearns announced that it would no longer allow investors to withdraw money from these two funds. Commercial banks and investment banks that had loaned money to these funds now demanded more cash as collateral on those loans. Bear Stearns announced on June 26 that it was going to lend the High-Grade Structured Credit Strategies Fund, the more conservative of the two funds, $1.6 billion in an attempt to increase investor confidence. But it was already too late. The market value of the mortgage-backed securities held by these two funds fell so dramatically that by mid-July both funds were essentially worthless.

At the end of July, Federal Reserve Chairman Ben Bernanke told Congress that the losses associated with problems in the mortgage market were "significant" and could approach $100 billion. But, Bernanke said he and the Federal Reserve (the Fed) would remain "alert" and would notify Congress if the problems in the mortgage market posed a threat to the overall economy. Mr. Bernanke did not view the mortgage crisis to be a threat to the overall U.S. economy at that time. Unfortunately for Mr. Bernanke and the Fed, the problems had only begun.

In August 2007, Countrywide Financial Corporation, the largest mortgage lender in the United States, was forced to borrow more than $11 billion from over 40 different

---

1 See Gretchen Morgenson, "Bear Stearns Says Battered Hedge Funds Are Worth Little," *The New York Times*, July 18, 2007.

creditors due to losses on mortgages it had written. Countrywide played a very important role in the U.S. mortgage market. It consistently wrote about 17 percent of all new U.S. mortgages each year; in 2007, it wrote over $400 billion of new mortgages and was servicing about 9 million loans with an estimated value of about $1.5 trillion. The financial troubles at a giant such as Countrywide sent shock waves through the financial markets. People wondered "if Countrywide and Bear Stearns can get into such deep financial troubles, who could be next?"

Who Has What Risk?

One major issue in the current financial crisis is a lack of clarity about *who* has *how much* risk exposure to *what* risk. In a "traditional" mortgage market, the risks are clear: a bank lends money to a household so that the family can purchase a house. The bank holds the mortgage and thus has default risk: the family, for whatever reason, may not be able to make their mortgage payments as promised.

However, with the creation of mortgage-backed securities and payment tranches called **collateralized debt obligations (CDOs)**, it is much more difficult to discern who is holding what portion of what mortgage. Thus, the owner of a CDO might own little slivers of thousands of different mortgages. Determining which of those mortgages is going bad at any point in time is practically impossible. Likewise, during times of financial distress, the value of CDOs can be very difficult to measure because the value of the underlying mortgages or slices of mortgages is unclear. During "good times," holders of CDOs can determine CDO value by looking at the market price of similarly traded CDOs. But when the markets are gripped by uncertainty, as they have been since the summer of 2007, it can become difficult if not impossible to place a market value on those CDOs.

Financial market participants, including bank depositors, hate such uncertainty. People and firms deposit money at commercial banks because they view those banks as safe. However, when those banks have assets, such as CDOs, that are difficult to price, depositors can become worried about their bank's safety. When depositors lose confidence in their bank's security, they can, in mass, attempt to withdrawal their funds all at once. This is called a **bank run**.

In August 2007, the commercial bank division of Countrywide Financial Corporation, called Countrywide Bank, suffered from just such a bank run. Depositors at Countrywide Bank in California feared that since the biggest U.S. mortgage company was in financial trouble that its commercial bank night run out of money.[2] Depositors lined up outside the bank and jammed its phone lines seeking to withdraw their money. Even though all deposits were insured by the FDIC up to $100,000 per account, depositors still wanted to pull their money out of Countrywide Bank "just in case." The uncertainty from the mortgage market and CDOs had now spilled over into the commercial banking market and negatively impacted the expectations and outlook of average depositors.

---

2 See E. Scott Reckard and Annette Haddad "A Rush to Pull out Money," *Los Angeles Times*, August 17, 2007.

The Crisis Goes Global

This inability to correctly price CDOs was also felt around the world. In August 2007, BNP Paribas, the largest bank in France and one of the largest in Europe, ran headlong into the American mortgage crisis. On August 9, BNP Paribas was forced to halt withdrawals from two of its funds because it could not "fairly value" the CDOs it held. BNP said in an August 9 statement:

"The complete evaporation of liquidity in certain market segments of the US securitisation market has made it impossible to value certain assets fairly regardless of their quality or credit rating. The situation is such that it is no longer possible to value fairly the underlying US ABS (Asset Backed Securities) assets ..."[3]

The asset-backed securities to which the statement refers are CDOs and mortgaged-backed securities. Because BNP Paribas could not determine the value of these assets, it could not calculate the balance of any individual investor. Thus, it would not allow investors to sell their shares or halt withdrawals. This was very similar to the problem faced by the two American Bear Stearns' hedge funds three months earlier.

Later in August, German bank Landesbank Sachsen Girzentrale ran into financial trouble due to its exposure to the American mortgage market. Sachsen LB, as it was known, first received a $23 billion loan from a group of regional savings banks in Germany, but even that was not enough. Sachsen LB was sold to a larger rival Landesbank by the end of August.

In September 2008, Northern Rock, the United Kingdom's fifth-largest home lender, suffered a bank run. Northern Rock had borrowed money in the short-term global financial markets, called **money markets**, and then loaned that money out to UK home buyers. Consequently, Northern Rock had relatively fewer depositors than would a traditional commercial bank or an American savings & loan.[4] But, since Northern Rock had been considered stable and reliable, it had been able to borrow money in the money markets at a relatively low interest rate and relend those funds at a higher interest rate in the UK mortgage market. In addition, to support its rate of return on assets, Northern Rock had purchased U.S.-based CDOs.

By the fall of 2008, with CDOs more difficult to price and money market participants no longer willing to lend to any bank that might have exposure to the U.S. mortgage crisis, Northern Rock found it increasingly difficult to borrow money in the money markets. But Northern Rock needed these money market loans in order to have enough cash to meet its depositors' needs. Unable to secure needed funds from the money markets, Northern Rock turned to the UK government for assistance.

---

3 See http://www.bnpparibas.com/en/news/press-releases.

4 Northern Rock at the time had loans and other assets on its balance sheet of £113bn. The value of deposits placed with it by retail customers was £24bn. See

http://news.bbc.co.uk/2/hi/business/6994099.stm.

On September 13, the Bank of England agreed to be the lender of last resort to Northern Rock, but it was already too late. Over the next two days, depositors lined up outside Northern Rock branches and inundated its web site, attempting to withdraw their savings. This lack of confidence in Northern Rock was simply devastating. Even though the Bank of England agreed to guarantee Northern Rock funds, depositors and financial markets had lost confidence in the institution, and its fate was sealed. Northern Rock was eventually taken over by the UK government on February 22, 2008.

The Collapse and Bailout of Wall Street

As the year 2007 drew to a close, it seemed that the fallout from the U.S. mortgage and global financial crisis might not dramatically impact the rest of the U.S. economy. The U.S. stock market was doing well in the fall of 2007, having reached a record high of 14,164 on October 9, 2007. But things were about to take a drastic turn for the worse. In December, President Bush announced a plan to help Americans who were about to lose their homes due to higher market interest rates. In presenting the housing rescue plan, President Bush described the housing downturn as a "serious challenge," but he stated: "The economy is strong, flexible and dynamic enough to weather this storm."[5] So, perhaps the worst of the financial crisis was past. Nothing could have been further from the truth.

Monday, January 21, 2008, was the Martin Luther King, Jr. holiday, which meant U.S. financial markets were closed for the day. But the financial markets across the globe were open, and investors began to panic over the growing problems in the U.S. mortgage market. Stock markets in Asia, Europe, and Latin America fell between 4 and 7 percent during the day's trading. Seemingly in response to the global stock market slide, the Federal Reserve's policymaking group, the Federal Open Market Committee, took the historically unprecedented move of holding an emergency meeting on a Monday night. They decided to drastically cut their interest rate target by 0.75 percent, where most recent changes in interest rates had been by 0.25 percent. This surprise move was thus three times the regular size interest rate change, plus it took place in an emergency meeting. One economic pundit described the Fed's move as a "once in a generation event."[6] Clearly, policymakers were worried that something had gone horribly wrong with financial markets and, by extension, the U.S. economy.

As winter gave way to spring, the problems in the financial markets seemed to get worse. In March 2008, the Federal Reserve announced its biggest move to date: it would make $200 billion of loans available to banks and other financial institutions.[7] The Fed was forced into making these funds available because banks were no longer willing to lend money to one another. Due to the uncertainty in financial markets, banks could not be sure of which other banks were connected to the growing U.S. mortgage crisis. Since banks could not evaluate the creditworthiness of other banks, they simply refused to lend money to one another.

---

5 See http://news.bbc.co.uk/2/hi/business/7129990.stm.

6 See Michael M. Grynbaum and John Holusha, "Fed Cuts Rates 0.75% and Stocks Swing," *The New York Times,* January 22, 2008.

7 See http://news.bbc.co.uk/2/hi/business/7284101.stm.

The lack of bank-to-bank lending caused major problems for other financial markets and the overall economy. If banks are unable to obtain funds from other banks, they will also be unlikely to lend money to nonbank business firms. If businesses are unable to secure loans, they cannot buy much-needed equipment or raw materials nor pay their workers. Thus, banks' refusal to lend to one another can trigger a chain reaction that can cause the entire economy to slow down. This is exactly what was happening in the spring of 2008.

Bear Stearns, JPMorgan Chase, and the Fed

The Fed's emergency lending did not resolve the problem. In March, financial market participants started to lose confidence in Bear Stearns, at the time the fifth-largest investment bank in the country. Investment banks, like commercial banks, depend on their customers' confidence for survival. For 85 years, Bear Stearns' customers had confidence in the big investment bank; it had survived the Great Depression, World War II, and the aftermath of the September 11 terrorist attacks. But it would not survive the current global financial crisis.

Bear Stearns' problems grew to a crisis level in the early days of March, and rumors of its financial distress quickly spread across Wall Street.[8] Only a year earlier, Bear Stearns had been riding a financial high with its stock trading at over $160 a share. But then came the sub-prime mortgage crisis and the failure of two of Bear Stearns' hedge funds. By March 12, the stock price had fallen to only $30 a share, and Bear Stearns' executives took to the airwaves trying in vain to convince the global financial markets that the firm was solvent. This public relations push failed. Bear Stearns needed to borrow huge amounts of money in order to keep up with investors' withdrawals. The bank's executives reportedly called officials at the Fed late in the day of March 13 and asked them to arrange a bailout of the 85-year-old company.

The Fed and Bear Stearns' officials decided to see if JPMorgan Chase would be willing to help the struggling investment bank. JPMorgan Chase had numerous business relationships with Bear Stearns and had much to lose if Bear Stearns failed. But JPMorgan Chase was reluctant to lend money without some type of guarantee of repayment from the Federal Reserve should Bear Stearns eventually fail. The Fed agreed to guarantee the loan from JPMorgan Chase to Bear Stearns, but it was already too little, too late. The financial markets had lost confidence in Bear Stearns. Virtually no one was willing to enter into trades or conduct business with Bear.

Clearly, the Fed-arranged loan was not enough to save Bear Stearns. Over the March 15–16 weekend, the Fed and Bear Stearns' executives worked around the clock to find a buyer for the beleaguered investment bank. Finally, on Sunday March 16, armed with $30 billion of Federal Reserve guarantees of Bear Stearns assets, JPMorgan Chase agreed to buy Bear Stearns at the stunning price of only $2 per share. That price represented a 93 percent discount off the price of a share of Bear Stearns stock on the close of trading on the previous Friday. But the directors of Bear Stearns had little

---

8 See Matthew Goldstein, "Bear Stearns' Big Bailout," *BusinessWeek*, March 14, 2008.

choice. It was either agree to the purchase by JPMorgan Chase at $2 share or face bankruptcy Monday morning at which point the shares would be essentially worthless.

A major uproar from Bear Stearns' employees, who owned one-third of the firm, as well as Bear Stearns' bondholders who would essentially be wiped out by the buyout, forced JPMorgan Chase to raise its offer to $10 per share a week later. Also, sensing a growing rage in Washington at the potential cost to taxpayers of the Fed's guarantee, JPMorgan Chase agreed that it would absorb the first $1 billion loss on Bear Stearns' assets with the Federal Reserve covering the remaining loss.

The Federal Reserve's quasi-bailout of Bear Stearns raised alarm across U.S. financial markets. Questions were being asked from one end of the country to the other: How sick was Wall Street? Who else would the Fed bail out—either indirectly like Bear Stearns or more directly?

Government Takeover of Fannie Mae and Freddie Mac

By the fall of 2008, the two mortgage market giants, Fannie Mae and Freddie Mac, were in deep financial trouble. Although both Fannie and Freddie had been created by the federal government, they were now publically traded corporations. Fannie Mae and Freddie Mac bought mortgages from lenders, repackaged some of these mortgages, and resold them to investors while holding on to other mortgages.

In order to finance this purchasing of mortgages, Fannie and Freddie issued their own bonds that were sold to a wide variety of investors around the world. Because Fannie and Freddie were both formerly part of the U.S. government, many in the financial markets believed that there was an implied government guarantee behind the bonds they issued. That is, people in financial markets believed that if Fannie and Freddie got into financial difficulty and could not repay their debt, the U.S. federal government would step in and make good on those promises to repay. With this "implicit" government guarantee, Fannie and Freddie could borrow money at a very low interest rate. They used these funds to buy mortgages, repackage them, and sell them for a price that resulted in very sizeable profits.

Although the vast majority of Fannie Mae and Freddie Mac mortgages were being repaid as planned, a small portion of them had fallen into default. What made this a significant problem is that both Fannie and Freddie held only a small amount of reserve cash in case of defaults. In other words, if the default rates on their mortgages increased even slightly, both entities would be near financial collapse.

In an attempt to reassure financial markets, Treasury Secretary Henry Paulson took the unusual step of holding a press conference on a Sunday. Standing on the front steps of the Treasury Building in Washington on July 13, Paulson proclaimed that the Treasury would stand behind both Fannie Mae and Freddie Mac.[9] This highly unusual press conference was held right before the financial markets in Asia opened and was designed

---

9 See "The Muddle-through Approach," *The Economist*, July 14, 2008.

to calm fears in Asia over the future of Fannie and Freddie. It was also less than a week after bank regulators had taken over the mortgage lender IndyMac Bancorp, which was the largest bank failure to date in American history. Thus, Secretary Paulson was trying to calm some pretty jittery nerves with his announcement.

Even the Treasury's backing was not enough. In fact, some economists argue[10] that the plan actually backfired. When it became clear that the federal government was taking a larger operational role and part ownership in Fannie and Freddie, no investors were willing to buy shares in Fannie and Freddie. The reason was straightforward: the bailout would essentially make the federal government the "senior" stockholder in both, meaning the government would be paid dividends before private shareholders and would have more say in running Fannie and Freddie than would private shareholders. Thus, investors basically refused to buy the shares of either Fannie or Freddie. The Treasury's plan to stand behind Fannie and Freddie was failing.

In addition, the financial markets simply did not have confidence in the financial viability of Fannie Mae and Freddie Mac. This was a major problem for the two mortgage market giants since they had issued $1.6 trillion of debt, the proceeds of which they had used to buy up mortgages. Without the confidence of financial markets, Fannie and Freddie would have a difficult time issuing new debt and thus could not continue to buy new mortgages. Unable to sell newly written mortgages to Fannie and Freddie, mortgage lenders would simply stop writing new mortgages. This would cause an already troubled housing market to spin even more out of control, and the ripple effects would be felt across the entire economy.

With the failure of the July 13 rescue plan, Secretary Paulson held yet another unprecedented Sunday news conference on September 7. This time, Paulson announced that the Treasury had placed both Fannie Mae and Freddie Mac into **conservatorship**. This basically meant that the Treasury Department, and by extension the U.S. federal government and U.S. taxpayers, were taking over Fannie and Freddie. This represented the largest involvement of the federal government in U.S. financial markets since the Great Depression of the 1930s, but it wouldn't be the last federal move. In fact, it would be the start of what news reports would call "10 days that reshaped U.S. finance."[11]

The Bailout of AIG

American International Group (AIG) is one of the world's largest insurance companies. In addition to offering traditional insurance products such as life insurance and automobile insurance, AIG was one of the biggest sellers of credit default swaps. Credit default swaps essentially provide insurance against the default of a financial asset that is tied to corporate debt or a mortgage-backed security. Since credit default swaps are a type of insurance, an insurance giant such as AIG would naturally sell them.

However, as the number of mortgages in default rose through 2007 and 2008, AIG had to pay out more on credit default swaps than it had anticipated. These huge unexpected

---

10 See http://freakonomics.blogs.nytimes.com/2008/09/18/diamond-and-kashyap-on-the-recent-financial-upheavals.

11 See http://online.wsj.com/article/SB122156561931242905.html.

payouts put a great deal of pressure on AIG, even though its other insurance businesses were doing fine. Things got so bad for AIG that on Monday, September 15, its credit rating was downgraded, which meant that AIG would have to come up with $14.5 billion in cash for collateral on its outstanding debt. While AIG had enough assets that it could sell to raise the $14.5 billion, it could not raise cash fast enough for the financial markets. After having been turned down by a wide variety of banks for an emergency short-term "bridge" loan, AIG turned to the U.S. government for help.

If AIG could not raise the collateral on its outstanding debt, the ripple effect through the U.S. financial markets would be severe. Many financial institutions around the world held debt issued by AIG; a collapse of the insurance giant would badly damage these financial institutions. To prevent such a financial meltdown, the Treasury Department and the Federal Reserve agreed to an $85 billion bailout for AIG. In return for this infusion of cash, the U.S. government would essentially take over the insurance giant. What made this government takeover of AIG even more unusual is that insurance companies such as AIG are not regulated by the federal government; instead, they are regulated by state governments. But the Treasury and the Federal Reserve decided AIG was "too big to fail." The government takeover of AIG represented the end of a 10-day period that saw major changes in U.S. financial markets. From September 6 to September 16, the following events occurred:

- The federal government seized control of Fannie Mae and Freddie Mac.

- Lehman Brothers, a 158-year-old major investment bank, filed for bankruptcy after the Treasury Department refused to help.

- Merrill Lynch, with 60,000 employees and on the verge of collapse, was purchased by Bank of America.

- The federal government took control of AIG.

The day after the AIG takeover—Wednesday, September 16, 2008—the U.S. stock market fell dramatically, with the Dow plummeting more than 446 points. This stock sell-off was due in part to an announcement by Washington Mutual, a major mortgage lender, that it had put itself up for sale due to staggering losses brought on by the troubled U.S. mortgage market. The two remaining investment banks, Goldman Sachs and Morgan Stanley, likewise appeared to be in significant financial trouble. Less than a week later, Goldman Sachs and Morgan Stanley announced that they would seek to become commercial banks and subject themselves to Federal Reserve oversight and regulation. With this move by Goldman Sachs and Morgan Stanley, the financial district in New York saw the end of the investment banking industry as an independent, stand-alone market on Wall Street. All of the major investment banks had failed, been merged into a commercial bank, or evolved into a commercial bank.

The $700 Billion Grasp for a Solution

With no investment banks left standing, Fannie Mae, Freddie Mac, and AIG under government control, banks unwilling to lend to one another, and mortgage default rates increasing, President Bush decided to deliver an address to the nation. On the evening of September 24, 2008, President Bush in a nationally televised speech tried to address the financial crisis by calling on Congress to swiftly pass a $700 billion bailout package for the U.S. financial markets. According to President Bush:

"Financial assets related to home mortgages have lost value during the house decline, and the banks holding these assets have restricted credit. As a result, our entire economy is in danger."

The initial $700 billion bailout bill included very few details on how or when the money would be spent. Under the original three-page plan drafted by the Treasury Department, Secretary Paulson would be given complete discretion over the funds. Paulson could use the money in any way he saw fit, and his use of the money could not be questioned by Congress, the administration, or any court. Thus, Paulson wanted complete control to give $700 billion to anyone he thought needed it in any manner he thought necessary.

Needless to say, many in Congress had serious reservations about the bailout package. To make things even more politically charged, Democrat Speaker of the House of Representatives Nancy Pelosi took to the House floor immediately before a vote on the bailout package and gave a very partisan speech. She blamed the entire financial crisis on Republicans:

"Seven hundred billion dollars, a staggering number, but only a part of the cost of the failed Bush economic policies to our country, policies that were built on budget recklessness. ... For too long this government in 8 years has followed a right-wing ideology ..."

Many Republican House members who planned to vote for the bailout bill on bipartisan terms were greatly put off by Pelosi's partisan speech. Without the Republican votes, the bill could not pass. Speaker Pelosi did little to nothing to calm the angered Republicans, and the bailout bill was rejected by a vote of 228 to 205. The stock market responded negatively to the inability of the politicians in Washington to pass a bailout bill: the Dow plunged 777 points, or 7 percent, in one day. A new bill was quickly introduced and passed by the Senate on October 1 and by the House on October 3. President Bush took the unusual step of signing the bill only two hours later. The $700 billion bailout, officially known as the Emergency Economic Stabilization Act of 2008, gave the Treasury secretary power to purchase any assets from any firm at any price. The $700 billion would be released in stages: $250 billion immediately upon passage, another $100 billion upon White House certification that the funds were necessary, and the remaining $350 billion when the Treasury secretary requested it from Congress.

With the passage of the bailout plan, the Treasury Department established **the Troubled Asset Relief Program (TARP)**, which would be administered through the newly created Office of Financial Stability. The initial purpose of TARP was to buy the difficult-to-price mortgage-backed securities that commercial banks and investment banks held. One of the hardest questions the Treasury Department faced was what price TARP should pay for the mortgage-backed assets it was about to buy from commercial banks and investment banks. This was, perhaps, the most complex finance question to be answered in over 50 years.

To answer this extremely important question, Secretary Paulson, the former CEO of investment bank Goldman Sachs, picked a 35-year-old former underling at Goldman Sachs named Neel Kashkari. In picking Kashkari to run TARP, Paulson passed over many more experienced financial experts such as former Federal Reserve Chairman Paul Volcker. Instead of seeking an experienced hand to run TARP, Paulson picked someone with only a few years of financial market experience.

Kashkari and TARP quickly found that pricing and buying the "troubled" mortgaged-backed securities was in fact very difficult to do. So instead, they decided to do something completely different: buy shares of the troubled financial institutions. In buying shares in these troubled institutions, a process called **recapitalization**, the Treasury hoped that commercial banks would start lending again. There was, of course, no guarantee that they would do so. When the government bought the shares of these banks, or recapitalized them, the banks had complete discretion over what they would do with these new funds. Instead of lending the new funds to customers, the banks could simply hold onto the new funds, pay dividends to their stockholders,[12] buy up other banks,[13] or even pay expenses including executive salaries.

Not surprisingly, a number of prominent economists raised questions about the effectiveness of the TARP program. University of Chicago economist Dr. Luigi Zingales wrote a brief article that circulated widely on the Internet, aptly named "Why Paulson Is Wrong."[14] Dr. Zingales argued that Paulson and the Treasury were going about the bailout with a failed approach. Fellow Chicago economists Anil Kashyap and Doug Diamond similarly raised troubling questions about the wisdom of the TARP.[15] Nobel Prize winner Joseph Stiglitz wrote an article very critical of the conflicts of interest in TARP and argued that the program only addressed some issues of the financial crisis.[16] Criticism of the TARP came from both liberal and conservative economists, and over 100 of them signed a letter of protest.[17]

Finally, on November 12, 2008, Secretary Paulson announced that the TARP would no longer be used to buy troubled assets from financial institutions. Instead, it will be used to offer financial assistance to banks and other firms that issue student, auto, and credit card loans.[18]

From Banks to Autos

As Paulson, Kashkari, and TARP struggled with how to best provide assistance to financial markets, the U.S. auto industry turned to the federal government for financial help. On November 18, the chief executives from the three major American automobile producers asked Congress for $25 billion in emergency loans. In testifying before Congress, Chrysler CEO Robert Nardelli, General Motors CEO Richard Wagoner, Jr.,

---

12 See Binyamin Applebaum, "Banks Continue to Continue Paying Dividends," *Washington Post*, October 30, 2008.

13 See Peter Whoriskey and Zachary A. Goldfarb, "Banks Weighing Other Uses for Bailout Money," *Washington Post*, October 28, 2008.

14 See http://faculty.chicagogsb.edu/luigi.zingales/Why_Paulson_is_wrong.pdf.

15 See http://freakonomics.blogs.nytimes.com/2008/09/18/diamond-and-kashyap-on-the-recent-financial-upheavals/.

16 See Joseph Stiglitz "Henry Paulson's Shell Game," *The Nation*, September 26, 2008.

17 See http://freakonomics.blogs.nytimes.com/2008/09/23/economists-on-the-bailout/.

18 See Peter Whoriskey, David Cho, and Binyamin Applebaum, "Treasury Redefines Its Rescue Program," *Washington Post*, November 12, 2008.

and Ford CEO Alan Mulally all claimed that due to the global financial crisis their companies needed emergency loans from the federal government or else they faced an almost immediate collapse.

A collapse of the U.S. auto industry could significantly impact the entire American economy. Ford, GM, and Chrysler, or The Big 3 as they are known, are the largest purchasers of U.S.-made steel, aluminum, iron, copper, plastics, rubber, and electronic computer chips. The Big 3 employ over 240,000 workers and have suppliers in every one of the 50 states. Thus, the executives argued, a collapse of the Big 3 automakers would dramatically affect the entire country in "days if not hours."

But members of Congress were skeptical about another taxpayer-funded bailout. Since the specific operation of TARP was so vague and had been so ineffective, many in Congress wanted to know, specifically, how the Big 3 would use the taxpayer money. The auto executives could not answer that question. They essentially had no specific plan on how they would use the $25 billion and could only give vague answers as to how they would split the money among the three.

Members of Congress were also upset when they learned that, shortly after receiving a government bailout, the executives at insurance giant AIG had spent $440,000 on a luxury retreat, essentially paid for by the American taxpayers. Likewise, when Congress heard that the executives of the automobile industry had flown to Washington each on their own private corporate jet to ask for taxpayer money, one member of Congress snorted:

"There's a delicious irony in seeing private luxury jets flying into D.C. and people coming off of them with tin cups in their hands … it's almost like seeing guys show up in the soup kitchen in high hat and tuxedo."

Not surprisingly, Congress voted down the auto industry bailout a few days later. Perhaps having learned their lesson, the auto executives returned to Washington two weeks later in automobiles they actually made and with a broad outline of how they would use the government funds.

The auto industry's new plea for help came after quarterly reports indicated the worst sales volume in over 25 years. The executives argued that if they did not get emergency funding within weeks, GM and Chrysler would face dire financial consequences.

PRESIDENT OBAMA'S ECONOMIC CHALLENGES

Upon being sworn in as the 44th president of the United States, Barack Obama will face some daunting economic challenges. Chief among these challenges is how he and his administration will deal with the current global financial crisis. As we have described, one of the main causes of this global downturn is the U.S. home mortgage market. The Obama Administration must find a way to stabilize the mortgage market and that, most likely, will require the stabilization of house prices.

In order to stabilize house prices, the new administration must find a way to deal with borrowers that can no longer afford to make their monthly mortgage payments. Some of these mortgage borrowers undoubtedly are caught up in circumstances beyond their control. Perhaps members of these families have lost their jobs as the economy has slowed. Others may have been duped into mortgages with low initial teaser rates that they did not understand. One could argue that the federal government should assist these types of borrowers.

Clearly, not all mortgage borrowers were innocent victims. Some borrowers sought to make "a quick buck" by purchasing a house and **flipping** the house or selling it at a much higher price in a few months. These borrowers were speculating on the mortgage market, and they lost that speculation. Offering government assistance to these types of borrowers would create what economists call a **moral hazard**.

A moral hazard exists when the creation of a financial contract alters behavior by changing incentives. If the government were to bail out real estate speculators, the government would be sending a clear signal to speculators: *go ahead, undertake risky behavior, because if your bets don't pay off, the government will be there to bail you out*. In such situations, a government bailout would be a type of financial contract that would negatively alter behavior in that it would encourage risky speculation.

Some speculation in markets is fine and even desirable. However, speculators need to suffer losses if they turn out to be wrong. If this is not done, it will encourage an excessive amount of speculation or risky behavior. Therefore, the Obama Administration has to be careful in crafting a program to stabilize house prices: it cannot and should not bail out all home buyers who cannot afford to make their mortgage payments. Arguably, the Obama Administration must find a way to delineate between those home buyers who were caught in a situation that was not of their own making and those that speculated on the housing market and perhaps should have known better.

In addition, the Obama Administration needs to find some way to get banks to start lending and increasing the flow of funds within financial markets. As described above, financial markets depend crucially on trust. If financial market participants do not trust one another, they will not lend to one another nor engage in any other type of financial transaction. The return of trust in financial markets, arguably, depends on transparency or openness. Financial markets need to be able to evaluate the riskiness of various borrowers and entities. As we have seen, the inability to correctly price mortgage-backed securities created major problems in the financial markets. Also, the lack of confidence or trust is what brought on bank runs and created the inability of long-standing firms to borrow money in financial markets.

The Obama Administration must decide what other steps will need to be taken to push the U.S. economy out of its current slowdown. Should the federal government do more to create jobs for the unemployed? As the unemployment rate increases to over 6 percent and the likelihood that firms will be able to borrow money to hire new workers remains slim, where will these unemployed people find work? Also, how will any increase in government spending be paid for? Given that the U.S. government budget deficit is already one of the largest in history, how will any new government programs be funded?

Finally, the Obama Administration will have to reconsider the extent of financial market regulation in the future. While our financial markets have changed dramatically over the past 50 years, the regulation of our markets, both domestically and internationally, has not kept pace. As new financial instruments such as mortgage-backed securities and markets that trade them are created, decisions must be made on who will regulate these markets and what form the regulations should take.

How his administration deals with these and other economic questions will have a significant impact on the success or failure of the Obama presidency. Updates on the current financial crisis and the economic challenges facing the Obama Administration can be found on the website www.cengage.com/gec that accompanies these booklets.

Discussion Questions

1. Assume that you have been appointed as an economic advisor to President Obama. What advice would you give him in terms of how to address the current financial crisis? What should he focus on first and why? Will he be able to get Congress and the American people to go along with what you suggest?

2. What steps could have been taken to prevent this crisis? How can similar crises be avoided in the future?

Key Terms

collateralized debt obligations (CDOs)
bank run
money markets
conservatorship
Troubled Asset Relief Program (TARP)
recapitalization
flipping
moral hazard

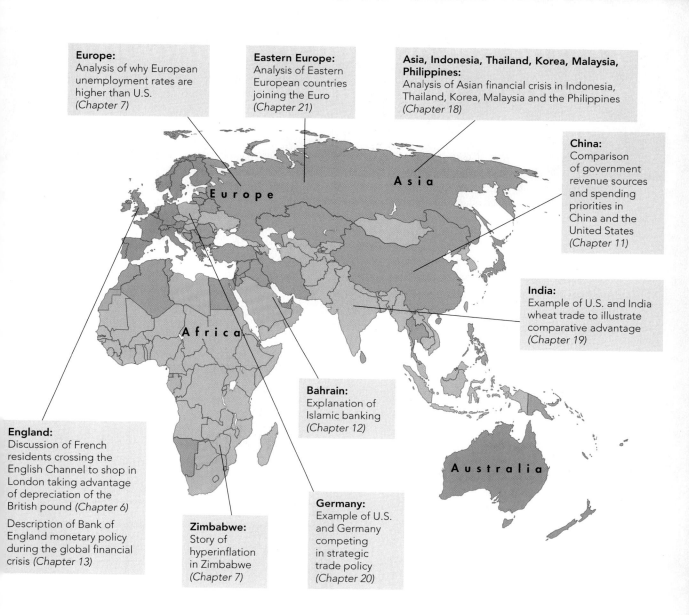

Europe:
Analysis of why European unemployment rates are higher than U.S. *(Chapter 7)*

Eastern Europe:
Analysis of Eastern European countries joining the Euro *(Chapter 21)*

Asia, Indonesia, Thailand, Korea, Malaysia, Philippines:
Analysis of Asian financial crisis in Indonesia, Thailand, Korea, Malaysia and the Philippines *(Chapter 18)*

China:
Comparison of government revenue sources and spending priorities in China and the United States *(Chapter 11)*

India:
Example of U.S. and India wheat trade to illustrate comparative advantage *(Chapter 19)*

England:
Discussion of French residents crossing the English Channel to shop in London taking advantage of depreciation of the British pound *(Chapter 6)*

Description of Bank of England monetary policy during the global financial crisis *(Chapter 13)*

Zimbabwe:
Story of hyperinflation in Zimbabwe *(Chapter 7)*

Bahrain:
Explanation of Islamic banking *(Chapter 12)*

Germany:
Example of U.S. and Germany competing in strategic trade policy *(Chapter 20)*

Let the Boyes/Melvin technology eliminate boundaries —in teaching and in learning!

▪ Aplia™

Founded in 2000 by Economist and Stanford Professor Paul Romer, Aplia is dedicated to improving learning by increasing student effort and engagement. The most successful online product in Economics by far – and most widely used with Mankiw — Aplia has been used by more than 850,000 students at over 850 institutions. Visit www.aplia.com/cengage for more details.

For help, questions, or a live demonstration, please contact Aplia at support@aplia.com.

▪ EconCentral

Multiple resources for learning and reinforcing principles concepts are now available in one place! EconCentral is your one-stop shop for the learning tools and activities to help students succeed.

EconCentral equips students with a portal to a wealth of resources that help them to both study and apply economic concepts. As they read and study the chapters, students can access :

- Video Tutorials
- Flash Cards
- 10 Principles Videos
- Graphing Workshop
- "Ask the Instructor" Videos
- Interactive Quizzing

Ready to apply chapter concepts to the real world? EconCentral gives you ABC News videos, EconNews articles, Economic debates, Links to Economic Data, and more. All the study and application resources in EconCentral are organized by chapter to help your students get the most from the Boyes/Melvin text and from your lectures.

Visit www.cengage.com/economics/econcentral to see the study options available!

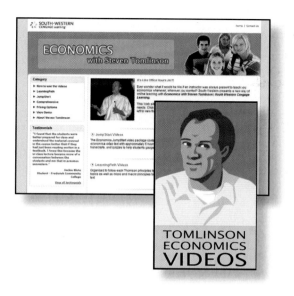

■ Tomlinson Economics Videos

"Like Office Hours 24/7"

Steven Tomlinson (Ph.D. Economics, Stanford) walks you through all of the topics covered in principles of economics in an online video format.

Find out more at www.cengage.com/economics/tomlinson.

■ Cengage Learning's Global Economic Watch

Lessons from real life right now

Cengage Learning's Global Economic Watch helps instructors bring pivotal current events into the classroom — through a powerful, continuously updated online suite of content, discussion forums, testing tools, and more.

The Watch, a first of its kind resource, stimulates discussion and understanding of the global downturn with easy-to-integrate teaching solutions:

CENGAGE LEARNING'S

GLOBAL ECONOMIC WATCH
─── GLOBAL ECONOMIC CRISIS RESOURCE CENTER ───

- A content-rich blog of breaking news, expert analysis and commentary — updated multiple times daily — plus links to many other blogs
- A powerful real-time database of hundreds of relevant and vetted journal, newspaper, and periodical articles, videos, and podcasts — updated four times every day

- A thorough overview and timeline of events leading up to the global economic crisis
- Discussion and testing content, PowerPoint® slides on key topics, sample syllabi, and other teaching resources
- Instructor and student forums for sharing questions, ideas, and opinions

History is happening now. Bring it into your classroom. For more information on how you can enrich your course with The Watch, please visit www.cengage.com/thewatch.

Preface

In the first edition of *Macroeconomics*, we integrated a global perspective with traditional economic principles to give students a framework to understand the globally developing economic world. Events since then have made this approach even more imperative. In the 1990s, the Soviet Union disintegrated and newly independent nations emerged. Much of Latin America was turning toward free markets and away from government controls. But by 2005, several of these nations were turning away from free markets. Hugo Chavez and Evo Morales were guiding Venezuela and Bolivia away from free markets and toward government-run and -controlled economies. Vladimir Putin was driving Russia toward more government control. Other events were making the world seem very small: North Korea was testing nuclear weapons, Somalia was embroiled in a civil war, terrorism was prevalent in nations around the world, and much of Africa remained mired in poverty. In 2007, the interconnectedness of nations was once again highlighted when the world fell into a recession created by the housing collapse in the United States. Students and instructors have embraced the idea that the economies of countries are interrelated and that this should be made clear in the study of economics. *Macroeconomics* gives students the tools they need to make connections between the economic principles they learn and the now-global world they live in.

In this edition, we continue to refine and improve the text as a teaching and learning instrument while expanding its international base by updating and adding examples related to global economics.

Changes in the Eighth Edition

The eighth edition of *Macroeconomics* has been thoroughly updated and refined. A detailed account of all the additions, deletions, and modifications can be found in the Transition Guide in the *Instructor's Resource Manual* (found on the instructor's site at www.cengage.com/economics/boyes and also on the Instructor's Resource CD).

Revised Macroeconomic Coverage

The focus of this new edition has been to ensure that the information and discussion faithfully represent the latest thinking of economists on important macroeconomic phenomena. To this end, many small additions and revisions appear throughout. Larger changes of note include: a reduction of introductory material from five chapters to four; a simplification of the material on real GDP with the deletion of chain-type GDP; many applications to the recent financial crisis and associated recession appear throughout the macro section; a discussion of quantitative easing policies employed by central banks to counter the recent recession and deflation pressures in Chapter 13; the Chapter 14 presentation policymaker credibility now includes a discussion of central bank inflation targeting as a stabilization tool; and Chapter 18 on globalization now includes an extensive new section that explains how the global financial crisis began in the United States but spread globally.

The macroeconomic chapters have all been updated to include the latest available economic statistics. In many chapters, numerical examples have been revised to provide greater clarity in the graphical presentations, and many of the Economically Speaking boxes and commentaries have been revised or replaced with more current examples of economic activity around the wrld.

■ Successful Features Retained from the Seventh Edition

In addition to the considerable updating and revising we've done for the eighth edition, there are several features preserved from the previous edition that we think instructors will find interesting.

Enhanced Student Relevance

With all of the demands on today's students, it's no wonder that they resist spending time on a subject unless they see how the material relates to them and how they will benefit from mastering it. We incorporate features throughout the text that show economics as the relevant and necessary subject we know it to be.

Real-World Examples Students are rarely intrigued by unknown manufacturers or service companies. Our text talks about people and firms that students recognize. We describe business decisions made by McDonald's and Wal-Mart, and by the local video store or café. We discuss standards of living around the world, comparing the poverty of sub-Saharan Africa to the wealth of the industrial nations. We discuss policies applied to real-world economic issues. We talk about political, environmental, and other social issues. These examples grab students' interest. Reviewers have repeatedly praised the use of novel examples to convey economic concepts.

Economic Insight Boxes These brief boxes use contemporary material from current periodicals and journals to illustrate or extend the discussion in the chapter. By reserving interesting but more technical sidelights for boxes, we lessen the likelihood that students will be confused or distracted by issues that are not critical to understanding the chapter. By including excerpts from articles, we help students move from theory to real-world examples. And by including plenty of contemporary issues, we guarantee that students will see how economics relates to their own lives.

Economically Speaking Boxes The objective of the principles course is to teach students how to translate to the real world the predictions that come out of economic models, and to translate real-world events into an economic model in order to analyze and understand what lies behind the events. The Economically Speaking boxes present students with examples of this kind of analysis. Students read an article at the end of each chapter. The commentary that follows shows how the facts and events in the article translate into a specific economic model or idea, thereby demonstrating the relevance of the theory. Nearly two-thirds of the articles and commentaries are new to the eighth edition, and cover such current events as U.S. trade with China, the collapse of consumer confidence during the financial crisis, illegal immigration, Venezuela's redistribution of wealth, high gasoline prices, the impact of the government's bailout of large companies, fair trade coffee, and the change in India's permit raj.

Global Business Insight Boxes These boxes link business events and developments around the world to the economic concepts discussed in the main text of the chapters. Topics include such basic micro- and macroeconomic issues as global competition, resource pricing, and foreign exchange.

An Effective and Proven System of Teaching and Learning Aids

This text is designed to make teaching easier by enhancing student learning. Tested pedagogy motivates students, emphasizes clarity, reinforces relationships, simplifies review, and fosters critical thinking. And, as we have discovered from reviewer and user feedback, this pedagogy works.

In-Text Referencing System Sections are numbered for easy reference and to reinforce hierarchies of ideas. Numbered section heads serve as an outline of the chapter, allowing instructors flexibility in assigning reading and making it easy for students to find topics to review. Each item in the key terms list and summary at the end of the chapter refers students back to the appropriate section number.

The section numbering system appears throughout the Boyes and Melvin ancillary package; *Study Guides* and *Instructor's Manual* are both organized according to the same system.

Fundamental Questions These questions help to organize the chapter and highlight those issues that are critical to understanding. Each fundamental question also appears in the margin next to the related text discussion and, with brief answers, in the chapter summaries. A fuller discussion of and answer to each of these questions may be found in the *Study Guides* that are available as supplements to this text. The fundamental questions also serve as one of several criteria used to categorize questions in the *Test Banks*.

Preview This motivating lead-in sets the stage for the chapter. Much more so than a road map, it helps students identify real-world issues that relate to the concepts that will be presented.

Recaps Briefly listing the main points covered, a recap appears at the end of each major section within a chapter. Students are able to quickly review what they have just read before going on to the next section.

Summary The summary at the end of each chapter is organized along two dimensions. The primary organizational device is the list of fundamental questions. A brief synopsis of the discussion that helps students to answer those questions is arranged by section below each of the questions. Students are encouraged to create their own links among topics as they keep in mind the connections between the big picture and the details that make it up.

Comments Found in the text margins, these comments highlight especially important concepts, point out common mistakes, and warn students of common pitfalls. They alert students to parts of the discussion that they should read with particular care.

Key Terms Key terms appear in bold type in the text. They also appear with their definition in the margin and are listed at the end of the chapter for easy review. All key terms are included in the Glossary at the end of the text.

Friendly Appearance

Macroeconomics can be intimidating; this is why we've tried to keep *Macroeconomics 8th ed.* looking friendly and inviting. The one-column design and ample white space in this text provide an accessible backdrop. More than 150 figures rely on well-developed pedagogy and consistent use of color to reinforce understanding. Striking colors were chosen to enhance readability and provide visual interest. Specific curves were assigned specific colors, and families of curves were assigned related colors.

Annotations on the art point out areas of particular concern or importance. Students can see exactly which part of a graph illustrates a shortage or a surplus, a change in consumption, or a consumer surplus. Tables that provide data from which graphs are plotted are paired with their graphs. Where appropriate, color is used to show correlations between the art and the table, and captions clearly explain what is shown in the figures and link them to the text discussion.

The color photographs not only provide visual images but make the text appealing. These vibrant photos tell stories as well as illustrate concepts, and lengthy captions explain what is in the photos, again drawing connections between the images and the text discussion.

Thoroughly International Coverage

Students understand that they live in a global economy; they can hardly shop, watch the news, or read a newspaper without stumbling upon this basic fact. International examples are presented in every chapter but are not merely added on, as is the case with many other texts. By introducing international effects on demand and supply in Chapter 3 and then describing in a nontechnical manner the basics of the foreign exchange market and the balance of payments in Chapter 6, we are able to incorporate the international sector into the economic models and applications wherever appropriate thereafter. Because the international content is incorporated from the beginning, students develop a far more realistic picture of the national economy; as a result, they don't have to alter their thinking to allow for international factors later on. The three chapters that focus on international topics at the end of the text allow those instructors who desire to delve much more deeply into international issues to do so.

The global applicability of economics is emphasized by *using traditional economic concepts to explain international economic events and using international events to illustrate economic concepts that have traditionally been illustrated with domestic examples.* Instructors need not know the international institutions in order to introduce international examples, since the topics through which they are addressed are familiar; for example, price ceilings, price discrimination, expenditures on resources, marginal productivity theory, and others.

Uniquely international elements of the macroeconomic coverage in the text include:

- The treatment of the international sector as an economic participant and the inclusion of net exports as early as Chapter 4

- The early description of the foreign exchange market and the balance of payments in Chapter 6

- International elements in the development of aggregate demand and supply

- An entire chapter devoted to globalization

Modern Macroeconomic Organization and Content

Macroeconomics is changing and textbooks must reflect that change. We begin with the basics: GDP, unemployment, and inflation. These are the ongoing concerns of any economy, for they have a significant influence on how people feel. These are the issues that don't go away. In addition to these core topics is an easy-to-understand, descriptive introduction to the foreign exchange market and the balance of payments. We provide a critical alternative for those instructors who believe that it is no longer reasonable to relegate this material to the final chapters, where coverage may be rushed.

Armed with these basics, students are ready to delve into the richness of macroeconomic thought. Macro models and approaches have evolved over the years, and they continue to invite exciting theoretical and policy debates. The majority of the instructors we asked voiced frustration with the challenge of pulling this rich and varied material together in class, and stressed that a coherent picture of the aggregate demand and supply model was critical. We have structured the macro portion to allow for many teaching preferences while ensuring a clear delineation of the aggregate demand/aggregate supply model.

To help instructors successfully present a single coherent model, we present aggregate demand and aggregate supply first in Chapter 8, immediately following the chapter on inflation and unemployment. This sequence allows for a smooth transition from business cycle fluctuations to aggregate demand/ aggregate supply (AD/AS). The Keynesian income and expenditures model is presented in full in Chapters 9 and 10 as the fixed-price version of the AD/AS model (with a horizontal aggregate supply curve). Those who want to use the AD/AS model exclusively will have no problem moving from the Chapter 8 presentation to the fiscal policy material in Chapter 11. The policy chapters rely on the AD/AS model for analysis.

The macroeconomic policy chapters begin with a thorough presentation of fiscal policy, money and banking, and monetary policy, with international elements included. Chapter 14 covers contemporary policy issues, and various schools of thought are treated in Chapter 15, when students are ready to appreciate the differences between and can benefit from a discussion of the new Keynesian and new classical models as well as of their precursors.

Part Four, "Economic Growth and Development," brings together the concepts and issues presented in the core macro chapters to explain how economies grow and what factors encourage or discourage growth. Most of the world's population live in poor countries. Growth and development are critical to those people. The material in these chapters also addresses issues of importance to industrial countries, such as the determinants of productivity growth and the benefits and costs of globalization.

Part Five, "Issues in International Trade and Finance," provides a thorough discussion of world trade, international trade restrictions, and exchange rates and links between countries.

■ A Complete Teaching and Learning Package

In today's market no book is complete without a full complement of ancillaries. Those instructors who face huge lecture classes find good PowerPoint slides and a large variety of reliable test questions to be critical instructional tools. Those who teach online in distance or hybrid courses need reliable course management systems with built-in assignments and resource materials. Other instructors want plenty of options available to their students for review, application, and remediation. All of these needs are addressed in the Boyes and Melvin supplements package. And to foster the development of consistent teaching and study strategies, the ancillaries pick up pedagogical features of the text—like the fundamental questions—wherever appropriate.

■ Support for Instructors

Instructor's Manual (IM)

Patricia Diane Nipper has produced a manual that will streamline preparation for both new and experienced faculty. Preliminary sections cover class administration, alternative syllabi, and an introduction to the use of cooperative learning in teaching the principles of economics.

The *IM* also contains a detailed chapter-by-chapter review of all the changes made in the seventh edition. This Transition Guide should help instructors more easily move from the use of the seventh edition to this new edition.

Each chapter of the *IM* contains an Overview that describes the content and unique features of the chapter and the Objectives that students will need to master in order to succeed with later chapters; the chapter's fundamental questions and key terms; a lecture outline with teaching strategies—general techniques and guidelines, essay topics, and other hints to enliven classes; opportunities for discussion; answers to every end-of-chapter exercise; answers to *Study Guide* homework questions; and active learning exercises.

Testing Materials

Printed Test Banks A *Test Bank* for *Macroeconomics,* edited and revised by Mike Ryan of Gainsville State College, is available with the eighth edition of *Macroeconomics*. In all, more than 2,000 test items, approximately 20 percent of which are new to this edition, provide a wealth of material for classroom testing. Features include:

- Multiple choice, true/false, and essay questions in every chapter
- Questions new to this edition marked for easy identification
- An increased number of analytical, applied, and graphical questions
- The identification of all test items according to topic, question type (factual, interpretive, or applied), level of difficulty, and applicable fundamental question

ExamView

This testing software contains all of the questions in the printed test bank. This program is an easy-to-use test creation software compatible with Microsoft Windows. Instructors can add or edit questions, instructions, and answers; and select questions by previewing them on the screen, selecting them randomly, or selecting them by number. Instructors can also create and administer quizzes online, whether over the Internet, a local area network (LAN), or a wide area network (WAN). The ExamView testing software is available on the Instructor's Resource CD.

Instructor Online Resources

The Boyes and Melvin eighth edition provides a rich store of teaching resources for instructors online at www.cengage.com/economics/boyes. Instructors will need to sign up at the site for a username and password to get onto the password-protected parts of the site. This site includes a variety of support materials to help you organize, plan, and deliver your lectures, assign and grade homework, and stay up-to-date with current economics news. Here you'll find a thoroughly updated set of multimedia PowerPoint slides covering key points in each chapter, with graphs, charts, and photos. An online version of the Instructor's Manual contains solutions to end-of-chapter exercises and discussion questions.

Aplia Online Learning Platform

Founded in 2000 by economist and professor Paul Romer in an effort to improve his own economics courses at Stanford, Aplia is the leading online learning platform for economics. Aplia provides a rich online experience that gets students involved and gives instructors the tools and support they need. The integrated Aplia courses offered for Boyes and Melvin include math review/tutorials, news analyses, and online homework assignments correlated to the relevant Boyes and Melvin text. In addition, a digital version of the text is embedded in the course to make it easy for students to access the text when completing assignments. Instructors should consult their South-Western/Cengage Learning sales representative for more information on how to use Aplia with this text.

■ Support for Students

Study Guides

Janet L. Wolcutt and James E. Clark of the Center for Economic Education at Wichita State University have revised the *Macroeconomics Study Guide* to give students the practice they need to master this course. Initially received by students and instructors with great enthusiasm, the guides maintain their warm and lively style to keep students on the right track. Each chapter includes:

- Fundamental questions, answered in one or several paragraphs and the list of Key Terms.
- A Quick Check Quiz, organized by section, so any wrong answers send the student directly to the relevant material in the text.
- Practice Questions and Problems, also organized by section, include a variety of question types to test understanding of concepts and skills.
- Thinking About and Applying uses newspaper headlines or other real-life applications to test students' ability to reason in economic terms.
- A Homework page at the end of each chapter with five questions that can be answered on the sheet and turned in for grading.
- Sample tests consisting of 25 to 50 questions similar to *Test Bank* questions to help students determine whether they are prepared for exams.
- Answers to all questions except the Homework questions. Students are referred back to the relevant sections in the main text for each question.

Student Online Resources

The student companion website, located at www.cengage.com/economics/boyes, lets students continue their learning at their own pace with practice quizzes, chapter summaries, Internet exercises, and flashcards, among other resources.

Acknowledgments

Writing a text of this scope is a challenge that requires the expertise and efforts of many. We are grateful to our friends and colleagues who have so generously given their time, creativity, and insight to help us create a text that best meets the needs of today's students.

We'd especially like to thank the many reviewers of *Macroeconomics* listed on the following pages who weighed in on key issues throughout the development of the eighth edition. Their comments have proved invaluable in revising this text. Unsolicited feedback from current users has also been greatly appreciated.

We would also like to thank James E. Clark and Janet L. Wolcutt of Wichita State University for their continued contributions to the *Study Guides* and Patricia Diane Nipper of Southside Virginia Community College for her work on the seventh and previous editions of the *Instructor's Resource Manual*. Thanks also to Chin-Chyuan Tai of Averett University and Mike Ryan of Gainsville State College for their intensive work on the *Test Banks,* and for their attention to the accuracy of the text. We want to thank the many people at South-Western/Cengage Learning who devoted countless hours to making this text the best it could be, including Steve Scoble, Laura Ansara, Tamborah Moore, and Lindsay Burt (of Macmillan Solutions).

Finally, we wish to thank our families and friends. The inspiration they provided through the conception and development of this book cannot be measured but certainly was essential.

Our students at Arizona State University continue to help us improve the text through each edition; their many questions have given us invaluable insight into how best to present this intriguing subject. It is our hope that this textbook will bring a clear understanding of economic thought to many other students as well. We welcome any feedback for improvements.

W. B. M. M.

■ Reviewers

Okechukwu Dennis Anyamele
Jackson State University
Jackson, MS

David Black
University of Toledo
Toledo, OH

Gary Bogner
Baker College-Muskegon
Muskegon, MI

Rick Boulware
University of South Carolina, Beaufort
Beaufort, SC

Bradley Braun
University of Central Florida
Orlando, FL

William S. Brewer
Genesee Community College
Batavia, NY

Gregory Brown
Martin Community College
Williamston, NC

Kristin Carrico
Umpqua Community College
Roseburg, OR

Jill L. Caviglia
Salisbury State University
Salisbury, MD

Mitch Charkiewicz
Central Connecticut State University
New Britain, CT

Kenny Christianson
Binghamton University
Binghamton, NY

Mike Cohick
Collin County Community College
Plano, TX

Valerie A. Collins
Colorado Mountain College
Glenwood Springs, CO

Wilfrid W. Csaplar, Jr.
Southside Virginia Community College
Keysville, VA

Bob Cunningham
Alma College
Alma, MI

Steven R. Cunningham
University of Connecticut
Storrs, CT

Stephen B. Davis
Valley City State University
Valley City, ND

Lynne Pierson Doti
Chapman University
Orange, CA

Raymond J. Egan
WA (Retired, formerly at Pierce College),
Lakewood, WA

Martha Field
Greenfield Community College
Greenfield, MA

Fred Fisher
Colorado Mountain College
Glenwood Springs, CO

Davis Folsom
University of South Carolina, Beaufort
Beaufort, SC

Kaya V. P. Ford
Northern Virginia Community College
Alexandria, VA

Bradley Garton
Laramie County Community College
Laramie, Wyoming

Omer Gokcekus
North Carolina Central University
Durham, NC

R. W. Hafer
Southern Illinois University
Edwardsville, IL

Michael Harsh
Randolph-Macon College
Ashland, VA

Arleen Hoag
Owens Community College
Toledo, OH

Calvin Hoy
County College of Morris
Randolph, NJ

Miren Ivankovic
Southern Wesleyan University
Central, SC

James Johnson
Black Hawk College
Moline, IL

Jeff Keil
J. Sargeant Reynolds Community College
Richmond, VA

Donna Kish-Goodling
Muhlenberg College
Allentown, PA

Ali Kutan
Southern Illinois University
Edwardsville, IL

Nikiforos Laopodis
Villa Julie College
Stevenson, MD

John D. Lathrop
New Mexico Junior College
Hobbs, NM

Paul Lockard
Black Hawk College
Moline, IL

Glenna Lunday
Western Oklahoma State College
Altus, OK

Leslie Manns
Doane College
Crete, NE

Dan Marburger
Arkansas State University
Jonesboro, AR

Buddy Miller
Carteret Community College
Morehead City, NC

Stan Mitchell
McLennan Community College
Waco, TX

Charles Okeke
Community College of Southern Nevada
Las Vegas, NV

Robert Payne
Baker College
Port Huron, MI

John C. Pharr
Cedar Valley College
Lancaster, TX

Dick Risinit
Reading Area Community College
Reading, PA

Rose M. Rubin
University of Memphis
Memphis, TN

Robert S. Rycroft
Mary Washington College
Fredericksburg, VA

Charles Saccardo
Bentley College
Waltham, MA

Charles Sackrey
Bucknell University
Lewisburg, PA

Rolando Santos
Lakeland Community College
Kirkland, OH

Karen Rapp Schultes
University of Michigan
Dearborn, MI

Gerald Scott
Florida Atlantic University
Boca Raton, FL

J. Richard Sealscott
Northwest State Community College
Archbold, OH

Steve Seteroff
Chapman University College
Silverdale, WA

James R. Shemwell
Mississippi County Community College
Blytheville, AR

Richard Skolnik
SUNY-Oswego
Oswego, NY

Scott F. Smith
University at Albany, State University
   of New York
Albany, NY

Thom Smith
Hill College
Hillsboro, TX

John Somers
Portland Community College, Sylvania
Portland, OR

John P. Speir Jr.
The University of Hartford
West Hartford, CT

John J. Spitzer
State University of New York
   College at Brockport
Brockport, NY

Chin-Chyuan Tai
Averett University
Danville, VA

Rob Verner
Ursuline College
Pepper Pike, OH

Michele T. Villinski
DePauw University
Greencastle, IN

Larry Waldman
University of New Mexico
Albuquerque, NM

Mark E. Wohar
University of Nebraska
Omaha, NE

Edward M. Wolfe
Piedmont College
Athens, GA

Darrel A. Young
University of Texas
Austin, TX

Girma Zelleke
Kutztown University
Kutztown, PA

■ Boyes/Melvin Advisory Board

Chapter 1

© Yuri Arcur/Shutterstock

Economics: The World around You

 Fundamental Questions

1 | **Why study economics?**

2 | **What is economics?**

3 | **What is the economic way of thinking?**

Americans today are more educated than ever before. Today, about 31 percent of Americans aged 25 or older hold a college (bachelor's or associate's) degree, whereas 20 years ago, only 19 percent of Americans held a similar degree. Nearly 15.5 million Americans (5 percent of the population) are currently attending college, and over 50 percent of Americans aged 18 to 22 are currently enrolled in a degree program.

Why is the rate of college attendance so high? College has not gotten any cheaper—indeed, the direct expenses associated with college have risen much more rapidly than average income. Perhaps it is because college is more valuable today than it was in the past. In the 1990s, technological change and increased international trade placed a premium on a college education; more and more jobs required the skills acquired in college. As a result, the wage disparity between college-educated and non-college-educated workers rose fairly rapidly in the 1990s. Those with a college degree could expect to make about 45 percent more than those without a college degree. Since 2001, however, this differential has actually declined. Outsourcing of skilled jobs to China and India may be part of the explanation, and a large supply of college workers may have kept wages from rising. The number of college-trained workers in the United States has grown by 32 percent over the past 10 years, compared with only an 8 percent

Why do the citizens of different countries have different standards of living? Why is the difference between rich and poor much greater in emerging nations than it is in the industrial nations? Answers to questions like these emerge in your study of economics. In this photo, a shantytown is shown next to new, modern apartment buildings and other structures.

© Shutterstock

rise for all other education levels. Still, even though the differential has been declining, college-educated people earn nearly twice as much as people without college degrees over their lifetimes.

Why are you attending college? Perhaps you've never really given it a great deal of thought—your family always just assumed that college was a necessary step after high school; perhaps you analyzed the situation and decided that college was better than the alternatives. Whichever approach you took, you were practicing economics. You were examining alternatives and making choices. This is what economics is about.

■ 1. Why Study Economics?

1 | Why study economics?

Why are you studying economics? Is it because you are required to, because you have an interest in it, because you are looking for a well-paying job, or because you want to do something to help others? All of these are valid reasons. The college degree is important to your future living standards; economics is a fascinating subject, as you will see; an economics degree can lead to a good job; and understanding economics can help policymakers, charities, and individuals think about better ways to help the unfortunate.

1.a. The Value of a Degree

What is the difference between a high school diploma and a medical degree? About \$3.2 million (U.S.), says the U.S. Census Bureau. Someone whose education does not go beyond high school and who works full-time can expect to earn about \$1.2 million between the ages of 25 and 64. Graduating from college and earning an advanced degree translate into much higher lifetime earnings: an estimated \$4.4 million for doctors, lawyers, and others with professional degrees; \$2.5 million for those with a master's degree; and \$2.1 million for college graduates.

Putting money into a four-year college education turns out to be a better financial investment than putting the same money into the stock market, even before the 2006–2009 stock-market collapse. The rate of return on the money spent to earn a bachelor's degree is 12 percent per year, compared with the long-run average annual return on stocks of 7 percent. Despite the high return on investment, just 30 percent of the American adults have a college degree. In comparison, more than 50 percent of Americans invest in the stock market, according to the American Shareholders Association.

In the 1970s, when the information age was young, kids from poorer, less educated families were catching up to kids fro m more affluent families when it came to earning college degrees. But now the gap between rich and poor is widening. Students in the poorest quarter of the population have an 8.6 percent chance of getting a college degree, whereas students in the top quarter have a 74.9 percent chance. The difference between being college-educated and not extends to more than just income. Divorce rates for college grads are plummeting, but they are not for everyone else. The divorce rate for high school grads is now twice as high as that of college grads. High school grads are twice as likely to smoke as college grads, they are much less likely to exercise, and they are likely to live shorter and less healthy lives.

Once you choose to go to college, how do you choose what to study? A bachelor's degree in economics prepares you for a career in any number of occupations—in business, finance, banking, the nonprofit sector, journalism, international relations, education, or government. Graduates find positions at investment banking companies and public utilities, in real estate and international relations, in government and private organizations. An economics degree is also excellent preparation for graduate study—in law, finance, business, economics, government, public administration, environmental studies, health-care administration, labor relations, urban planning, diplomacy, and other fields.

1.b. What Is Economics?

Economists are concerned with why the world is what it is. In 1990, the Soviet Union collapsed, setting countries free throughout eastern Europe and Asia, because of economics. The nations of Latin America are struggling with progress and development because of economics. It is estimated that somewhere between 11 and 20 million people live in the United States illegally, and they do so because of economics. The campaign for the 2008 U.S. presidency started out largely as a debate over national security but ended up being mostly about economics. Nationally, the unemployment rate soared from about 4 percent in 2005 to nearly 10 percent in 2009. Millions of workers were worried that their jobs and pension plans might disappear. Barack Obama won the presidency because, very possibly, more U.S. voters thought that Obama would be able to handle the economy than thought McCain would. In fact, every issue in the news today concerns economics. It is a broad, fascinating field of study that deals with every aspect of life.

Economics is often counterintuitive. In fact, economics is probably best defined as the study of *unintended consequences*. When you study economics, you learn that there are costs to everything—there is no free lunch. This is the logic of economics that those who have not studied economics may fail to understand.

Your study of economics will be interesting and challenging. It will challenge some beliefs that you now hold. It will also help you build skills that will be of value to you in your life and in whatever occupation you choose.

■ 2. The Definition of Economics

2 | **What is economics?**

What is economics? It is the study of how *scarce* resources are allocated among *unlimited wants*. People have unlimited wants—they always want more goods and services than they have or can purchase with their incomes; they want more time; they want more love or health care, or chocolate cake, or coffee, or time. Whether they are wealthy or poor, what they have is never enough. Since people do not have everything they want, they have to make choices. The choices they make and the manner in which these choices are made explain much of why the real world is what it is.

2.a. Scarcity

scarcity: the shortage that exists when less of something is available than is wanted at a zero price

economic good: any item that is scarce

Scarcity is the reason the study of economics exists—without scarcity, there would be no need to worry about who gets what. Everyone would have everything that he or she wants. **Scarcity** of something means that there is not enough of that item to satisfy everyone who wants it. Any item that costs something is scarce. If it were not scarce, it would be free, and you could have as much as you wanted without paying for it. Anything with a price on it is called an **economic good**. An economic good refers to *goods and services*—where goods are physical products, such as books or food, and services are nonphysical products, such as haircuts or golf lessons.

free good: a good for which there is no scarcity

2.a.1. Free Goods, Economic Bads, and Resources If there is enough of an item to satisfy wants, even at a zero price, the item is said to be a **free good**. It is difficult to think of examples of free goods. At one time people referred to air as free, but with air pollution control devices and other costly activities directed toward the maintenance of air quality standards, *clean* air, at least, is not a free good.

economic bad: any item for which we would pay to have less

An **economic bad** is anything that you would pay to get rid of. It is not so hard to think of examples of bads: pollution, garbage, and disease fit the description.

Some goods are used to produce other goods. For instance, to make chocolate chip cookies, we need flour, sugar, chocolate chips, butter, our own labor, and an oven. To distinguish between the ingredients of a good and the good itself,

resources, factors of production or **inputs:** goods used to produce other goods, i.e., land, labor, and capital

we call the ingredients **resources**. (Resources are also called **factors of production** and **inputs**; the terms are interchangeable.) The ingredients of the cookies are the resources, and the cookies are the goods.

Economists have classified resources into three broad categories: land, labor, and capital.

land: all natural resources, such as minerals, timber, and water, as well as the land itself

1. **Land** includes all natural resources, such as minerals, timber, and water, as well as the land itself.

labor: the physical and intellectual services of people, including the training, education, and abilities of the individuals in a society

2. **Labor** refers to the physical and intellectual services of people, including the training, education, and abilities of the individuals in a society.

capital: products such as machinery and equipment that are used in production

3. **Capital** refers to products such as machinery and equipment that are used in production. You will often hear the term *capital* used to describe the financial backing for some project or the stocks and bonds used to finance some business. This common usage is not incorrect, but it should be distinguished from the physical entity—the machinery and equipment and the buildings, warehouses, and factories. Thus we refer to stocks and bonds as *financial capital* and to the physical entity as capital.

People obtain income by selling their resources or the use of their resources. Owners of land receive *rent*; people who provide labor services are paid *wages*; and owners of capital receive *interest*.

The income that resource owners acquire from selling the use of their resources provides them with the ability to buy goods and services. And producers use the money received from selling their goods to pay for the resource services.

2.b. Choices

Scarcity means that people have to make choices. People don't have everything they want, and they do not have the time or the money to purchase everything they want. When people choose some things, they have to give up, or forgo, other things. *Economics is the study of how people choose to use their scarce resources to attempt to satisfy their unlimited wants.*

2.c. Rational Self-Interest

rational self-interest: the means by which people choose the options that give them the greatest amount of satisfaction

Rational self-interest is the term that economists use to describe how people make choices. It means that people will make the choices that, at the time and with the information they have at their disposal, will give them the greatest amount of satisfaction.

You chose to attend college, although many in your age group chose not to attend. All of you made rational choices based on what you perceived was in your best interest. How could it be in your best interest to do one thing and in another person's best interest to do exactly the opposite? Each person has unique goals and attitudes and faces different costs. Although your weighing of the alternatives came down on the side of attending college, other people weighed similar alternatives and came down on the side of not attending college. Both decisions were rational because in both cases the individual compared alternatives and selected the option that the *individual* thought was in his or her best interest.

It is important to note that rational self-interest depends on the information at hand and the individual's perception of what is in his or her best interest. Even though the probability of death in an accident is nearly 20 percent less if seat belts are worn, many people choose not to use them. Are these people rational? The answer is yes. Perhaps they do not want their clothes wrinkled, or perhaps seat belts are just too inconvenient, or perhaps they think the odds of getting in an accident are just too small to worry about. Whatever the reason, these people are choosing the option that at the time gives them the greatest satisfaction. *This is rational self-interest.* Economists sometimes use the term *bounded rationality* to emphasize the point that people do not have perfect knowledge or perfect insight. In this book we simply use the term *rational* to refer to the comparison of costs and benefits.

Economists think that most of the time most human beings are weighing alternatives, looking at costs and benefits, and making decisions in a way that they believe makes them better off. This is not to say that economists look upon human beings as androids who lack feelings and are only able to carry out complex calculations like a computer. Rather, economists believe that people's feelings and attitudes enter into their comparisons of alternatives and help determine how people decide that something is in their best interest.

Human beings are self-interested, *not selfish.* People do contribute to charitable organizations and help others; people do make individual sacrifices because those sacrifices benefit their families or people that they care about; soldiers do risk their lives to defend their country. All these acts are made in the name of rational self-interest.

RECAP

1. Scarcity exists when people want more of an item than exists at a zero price.

2. Goods are produced with resources (also called factors of production and inputs). Economists have classified resources into three categories: land, labor, and capital.

3. Choices have to be made because of scarcity. People cannot have or do everything that they desire all the time.

4. People make choices in a manner known as rational self-interest; people make the choices that at the time and with the information they have at their disposal will give them the greatest satisfaction.

■ 3. The Economic Approach

3 | **What is the economic way of thinking?**

Economists often refer to the "economic approach" or to "economic thinking." By this, they mean that the principles of scarcity and rational self-interest are used in a specific way to search out answers to questions about the real world.

3.a. Positive and Normative Analysis

In applying the principles of economics to questions about the real world, it is important to avoid imposing your opinions or value judgments on others. Analysis that does not impose the value judgments of one individual on the decisions of others is called **positive analysis**. If you demonstrate that unemployment in the automobile industry in the United States rises when people purchase cars produced in other countries instead of cars produced in the United States, you are undertaking positive analysis.

positive analysis: analysis of what is

normative analysis:
analysis of what ought to be

> Conclusions based on opinion or value judgments do not advance one's understanding of events.

However, if you claim that there ought to be a law to stop people from buying foreign-made cars, you are imposing your value judgments on the decisions and desires of others. That is not positive analysis. It is, instead, **normative analysis**. *Normative means "what ought to be"; positive means "what is."* If you demonstrate that the probability of death in an automobile accident is 20 percent higher if seat belts are not worn, you are using positive analysis. If you argue that there should be a law requiring seat belts to be worn, you are using normative analysis.

3.b. Common Mistakes

Why are so many items sold for $2.99 rather than $3? Most people attribute this practice to ignorance on the part of others: "People look at the first number and round to it—they see $2.99 but think $2." Although this reasoning may be correct, no one admits to such behavior when asked. A common error in the attempt to understand human behavior is to argue that other people do not understand something or are stupid. Instead of relying on rational self-interest to explain human behavior, ignorance or stupidity is called on.

fallacy of composition:
the mistaken assumption that what applies in the case of one applies to the case of many

Another common mistake in economic analysis, called the **fallacy of composition**, is the error of attributing what applies in the case of one to the case of many. If one person in a theater realizes that a fire has broken out and races to the exit, that one person is better off. If we assume that a thousand people in a crowded theater would be better off if they all behaved exactly like the single individual, we would be committing the mistake known as the fallacy of composition. For example, you reach an intersection just as the light switches to yellow. You reason that you can make it into the intersection before the light turns red. However, others reason the same way. Many people enter the intersection with the yellow light; it turns red, and traffic in the intersection is congested. The traffic going the other way can't move. You correctly reasoned that you alone could enter the intersection on the yellow light and then move on through. But it would be a fallacy of composition to assume that many drivers could enter the intersection and pass on through before the intersection is congested.

association of causation:
the mistaken assumption that because two events seem to occur together, one causes the other

The mistaken interpretation of **association as causation** occurs when unrelated or coincidental events that occur at about the same time are believed to have a cause-and-effect relationship. For example, the result of the football Super Bowl game is sometimes said to predict how the stock market will perform. According to this "theory," if the NFC team wins, the stock market will rise in the new year, but if the AFC team wins, the market will fall. This bit of folklore is a clear example of confusion between causation and association. Simply because two events seem to occur together does not mean that one causes the other. Clearly, a football game cannot cause the stock market to rise or fall. For another example, on Gobbler's Knob, Punxsutawney, Pennsylvania, at 7:27 A.M. on February 2, Punxsutawney Phil saw his shadow. Six more weeks of winter followed. However, whether the sun was or was not hidden behind a cloud at 7:27 A.M. on February 2 had nothing to do with causing a shortened or extended winter. Groundhog Day is the celebration of the mistake of attributing association as causation.

3.c. Microeconomics and Macroeconomics

Economics is the study of how people choose to allocate their scarce resources among their unlimited wants and involves the application of certain principles—scarcity, choice, and rational self-interest—in a consistent manner. The study of

microeconomics: the study of economics at the level of the individual

macroeconomics: the study of the economy as a whole

economics is usually separated into two general areas, microeconomics and macroeconomics. **Microeconomics** is the study of economics at the level of the individual economic entity: the individual firm, the individual consumer, and the individual worker. In **macroeconomics**, rather than analyzing the behavior of an individual consumer, we look at the sum of the behaviors of all consumers together, which is called the consumer sector, or household sector. Similarly, instead of examining the behavior of an individual firm, in macroeconomics we examine the sum of the behaviors of all firms, called the business sector.

Topics such as whether President Obama's stimulus plan is working, whether government debt is beneficial or not, whether the Federal Reserve should control interest rates of money supply and whether it has been too loose or too tight, as well as what China's economic slowdown means for the United States are discussed in macroeconomics. How a firm manages during a recession, whether to raise or lower prices, whether to alter the brand or the advertising, whether people will purchase slightly less or significantly less gasoline as gas prices rise, and the effect on firms and employees of increased government regulations are generally microeconomic topics. Remember that the focus in microeconomics is the individual—the individual firm, employee, customer, government official, etc.—while the focus in macroeconomics is on the entire consumer sector, business sector, government sector, and global sector.

RECAP

1. The objective of economics is to understand why the real world is the way it is.

2. Positive analysis refers to what is, while normative analysis refers to what ought to be.

3. Assuming that others are ignorant, the fallacy of composition, and interpreting association as causation are three commonly made errors in economic analysis.

4. The study of economics is typically divided into two parts, macroeconomics and microeconomics.

SUMMARY

1 | Why study economics?

- The study of economics may be the road to a better job and will add skills that have value to you in your life and in your occupation. *§1*

- Economics is interesting; it might be called the study of unintended consequences. *§1.b*

2 | What is economics?

- The resources that go into the production of goods are land, labor, and capital. *§2.a*

- Economics is the study of how people choose to allocate scarce resources to satisfy their unlimited wants. *§2.b*

- Scarcity is universal; it applies to anything people would like more of than is available at a zero price. Because of scarcity, choices must be made, and these choices are made in a way that is in the decision maker's rational self-interest. *§2.a, 2.b, 2.c*

- People make choices that, at the time and with the information at hand, will give them the greatest satisfaction. *§2.c*

3 | What is the economic way of thinking?

- Positive analysis is analysis of what is; normative analysis is analysis of what ought to be. *§3.a*

- Assuming that others are ignorant, the fallacy of composition, and interpreting association as causation are three commonly made errors in economic analysis. *§3.b*

- The study of economics is typically divided into two parts, macroeconomics and microeconomics. *§3.c*

KEY TERMS

scarcity *§2.a*

economic good *§2.a*

free good *§2.a*

economic bad *§2.a*

resources *§2.a*

factors of production *§2.a*

inputs *§2.a*

land *§2.a*

labor *§2.a*

capital *§2.a*

rational self-interest *§2.c*

positive analysis *§3.a*

normative analysis *§3.a*

fallacy of composition *§3.b*

association as causation *§3.b*

microeconomics *§3.c*

macroeconomics *§3.c*

EXERCISES

1. Which of the following are economic goods? Explain why each is or is not an economic good.
   a. Steaks
   b. Houses
   c. Cars
   d. Garbage
   e. T-shirts

2. Many people go to a medical doctor every time they are ill; others never visit a doctor. Explain how human behavior could include such opposite behaviors.

3. Erin has purchased a $35 ticket to a Dave Matthews concert. She is invited to a send off party for a friend who is moving to another part of the country. The party is scheduled for the same day as the concert. If she had known about the party before she bought the concert ticket, she would have chosen to attend the party. Will Erin choose to attend the concert? Explain.

4. It is well documented in scientific research that smoking is harmful to health. Smokers have higher incidences of coronary disease, cancer, and other catastrophic illnesses. Knowing this, about 30 percent of young people begin smoking, and about 20 percent of the U.S. population smokes. Are the people who choose to smoke irrational? What do you think of the argument that we should ban smoking in order to protect these people from themselves?

5. Indicate whether each of the following statements is true or false. If the statement is false, change it to make it true.

   a. Positive analysis imposes the value judgments of one individual on the decisions of others.
   b. Rational self-interest is the same thing as selfishness.
   c. An economic good is scarce if it has a positive price.
   d. An economic bad is an item that has a positive price.
   e. A resource is an ingredient used to make factors of production.

6. Are the following statements normative or positive? If a statement is normative, change it to a positive statement.
   a. The government should provide free tuition to all college students.
   b. An effective way to increase the skills of the work force is to provide free tuition to all college students.
   c. The government must provide job training if we are to compete with other countries.

7. If people behave in ways that they believe are in their best self-interest, how would you explain the following?
   a. Mother Teresa devoted her entire life to living in the worst slums of Asia, providing aid to others.
   b. Bernie Madoff created a scheme whereby people gave him billions of dollars to invest that he simply kept for himself.
   c. Pat Tillman gave up millions of dollars when he chose to enlist in the military following the 9/11 attack on the United States rather than play professional football.

8. Use economics to explain why men's and women's restrooms tend to be located near each other in airports and other public buildings.

9. Use economics to explain why diamonds are more expensive than water, when water is necessary for survival and diamonds are not.

10. Use economics to explain why people leave tips (a) at a restaurant they visit often and (b) at a restaurant they visit only once.

11. Use economics to explain why people contribute to charities.

12. Use economics to explain this statement: "Increasing the speed limit has, to some degree, compromised highway safety on interstate roads but enhanced safety on non-interstate roads."

You can find further practice tests in the Online Quiz at **www.cengage.com/economics/boyes**.

Not Earning as Much as the Guys? Here's Why

The Washington Post **June 3, 2007**

Ah, graduation—that time of optimism, of looking to the future and its possibilities. Of dreaming big. For girls now finishing high school, the future has never looked brighter. Many will go on to college; women comprised 55 percent of college students in 2005. They'll be equal to the men at their schools, paying the same tuition and taking the same classes. They'll be the student equivalents of stem cells, capable of becoming anything. That's certainly what Pace University sophomore Liz Funk believes. The twenty-year-old already has a contract from a major publisher for a book about overachieving girls, and she can't imagine that she'll ever earn less than a future husband will. But unless today's women make some changes, that's exactly what may happen. This goes beyond that conventional salary-disparity culprit, workplace discrimination, that was the subject of a Supreme Court ruling last week. If Funk and her female classmates don't prosper as much as their male colleagues do, it will probably be because they didn't dream rich enough dreams in choosing their major. As they head into the working world, most of this year's female college grads will never be equal to their male colleagues again. Last month, the American Association of University Women reported that in the first year after graduating, women working full-time make 20 percent less on average than their male classmates. That's certainly the fate of one young graduate from Tulane University. Laden with honors and boasting killer GRE scores, she is hoping to get hired as an intern in psychology, at a salary of about $30,000 a year. Her more business-oriented classmates—mostly male, as she recalls—are already making more than twice that.

The conventional wisdom assumes that employers are discriminating against young women, despite the laws against it. And some of the disparity—about 5 percent—does appear to be at least partly discrimination. But most of it isn't. Somewhere during their four years in the college womb, women develop into candidates for the world of work with 15 percent less market value than men. Why does this happen? It's not as though the women are 15 percent dumber. After all, they enter college with better grades and graduate with better grades. Nor is it self-inflicted, driven by women who opt out to care for children or pick up socks. Most of the competing workers are single and childless. In fact, what the AAUW report reveals is that, at almost every step of the way, women could make decisions that would keep them even with their male classmates. But they don't. The biggest decision any student keeping an eye on the bottom line can make is the choice of a major. According to the AAUW report, women who major in education make 60 percent of what female engineers make in their first year of work. But far more women still choose education over engineering. Despite the talk of discrimination, the same disparity holds true for the guys. (A male accounting trainee just out of the University of Albany is making close to six figures, while another young man I know, who has a degree in anthropology and political science from Brandeis, is hoping it won't be too cold in Boston this winter so he can live on his $20,000 internship salary.) But here's a difference: Unlike the female Tulane psych grad, the Brandeis guy is thinking about his long-term income and going to law school. Even within the same major, students can prepare for the jobs that pay better, if they care to. Teaching math (which many women choose) pays less than working for a computer company or going into business. And there is the choice of employer. Even when men and women pick the same majors and go into the same fields, the woman who chooses local government or nonprofit sectors starts out at a lower pay level than the guy sporting the next mortarboard who decides to get into the market economy or take a federal job. Liz Funk, to her credit, has already figured out that she'd be better off working as a staff writer at a magazine, earning benefits, than trying to make it out of college as a freelancer. But she's an exception.

The situation in the first year out of college is bad enough, but the decisions women make in college set in motion a process that will accelerate until, ten years after graduating, they are making only 69 percent of what men make. That's because, if women earn less from the outset, it's an easy choice as to who will bear the responsibility for child care and housekeeping when the time comes to start a family.

Stay-at-home moms often talk about the loving husbands who would gladly take time off to be with the kids, except that they earn the larger salary. But men's making more money is not a fact of nature; it's a result of the choices adults make starting out. And the crucial difference is not gender; it's mindset. I interviewed a young, male classics major just as he was setting out for a summer trip to study Greek philosophy before his junior year. Classics was his "passion," he told me. But his plan after college is to do something in finance. He is not prepared to experience, as he put it, the "culture shock" of poverty after his affluent upbringing.

Similarly, the male accountant from the University of Albany didn't even think about majoring in accounting until he got a scholarship in that subject because his math scores were so high. As a result, "I don't have a lot of debt," he told me proudly. By contrast, the Tulane psych major was surprised to learn what bankers earn ten years out. "I guess I'll end up making a lot less than half," she concluded, laughing nervously. "It's okay. It is what it is."

Certainly someone needs to teach math and to work for nonprofits and local government. And, of course, money isn't everything. The Tulane psych major won a significant award for her community organizing before she even left school. She's frustrated with the "unfairness" of her classmates' earning so much more when she is "helping people." But it's alarming when the altruism is so heavily concentrated in one sex. And colleges offer precious little career counseling to tell women a different story from the one society has always told them.

And in the end, college-educated women often don't make lasting careers of mathematical pedagogy or become the head of the Ford Foundation. They weigh their 69 percent paychecks against the money their business- or computer science-oriented spouses bring in, and they leave their jobs, in whole or in part. Even the high-achieving Liz Funk thinks that writing would be a great job to do from home after the babies come. When I asked her how she planned to continue her

productive ways with infants crying for attention, she responded that she has screaming roommates now.

Maybe, on the whole, women just aren't as interested in worldly success as men are. According to AAUW, 25 percent more men than women go to "highly selective" schools. In that very formative first year in the work world, 10 percent more men are working full-time for one employer rather than holding several part-time or successive full-time jobs, as women are more apt to do. Studies show women are less willing to take the higher risks that often accompany higher-paying jobs. If women just don't want to become engineers or run big firms, well, it's a free country. But the social consequences of these decisions are not positive. Consider that just as AAUW released its report, the big news about women in the media—as reported by Women in Media and the News—was that the reality-TV show "America's Next Top Model" was running an episode featuring the scarily thin competitors posing as victims in a shoot about murder and suicide. Surely this isn't the best we can offer our young women to aspire to.

The poet Wordsworth said the child is father to the man. If the girl is mother to the woman, her child-rearing skills are sorely in need of some sharpening.

© Linda Hirshman

Economics is the study of human behavior, so it ought to be able to explain why people would choose one occupation over another or choose one college major over another.

Economists argue that decisions are the result of comparing costs and benefits. In this article, two major decisions are discussed, going to college and selecting a major. The first decision compares the future income and quality of living that a college degree will offer with the costs of obtaining that college degree. The article notes that "The biggest decision any student keeping an eye on the bottom line can make is the choice of a major." Why would this be an important decision? It is significant because what you major in determines your value to a firm or the skills you have to pursue graduate study or other careers. What is the cost of the degree? It is the expense of college—what many students take out loans to pay. It is also the forgone income—that is, the income that you would have earned had you not gone to college. Someone who takes four or five years to complete college has paid tuition, purchased books and materials, and paid for room and board over those years. Those costs range from a bare minimum of $20,000 to well over $100,000. You may have worked part-time while you were attending college, but if you had not been attending college, you could have worked full-time.

The difference for the years of college would have been about $50,000. Thus, the cost of college could have been $150,000 or more. But the cost of a major also includes the opportunity costs of the time devoted to completing the program. It is more costly to get an engineering degree than an education degree because the engineering program is difficult: The time commitment above and beyond the education major is significant. According to the article, ". . . women who major in education make 60 percent of what female engineers make in their first year of work. But far more women still choose education over engineering." Why would they do this?

Selecting a major involves a comparison of costs and benefits. As we just mentioned, different majors mean different amounts of future income. If the choice of major were only a matter of comparisons of future income, there would be fewer art history majors and elementary-school teachers but more engineers and medical doctors. But income is not the only thing that enters into one's benefit calculations. Interest in the subject, living styles, amount of leisure time, and other aspects of life enter into one's choice of a college major. Every college student tends to select the major that fits with the life style they hope to have—the major that yields the greatest net benefits to each individual.

Working with Graphs

According to the old saying, one picture is worth a thousand words. If that maxim is correct, and, in addition, if producing a thousand words takes more time and effort than producing one picture, it is no wonder that economists rely so extensively on pictures. The pictures that economists use to explain concepts are called *graphs*. The purpose of this appendix is to explain how graphs are constructed and how to interpret them.

■ 1. Reading Graphs

The three kinds of graphs used by economists are shown in Figures 1, 2, and 3. Figure 1 is a *line graph*. It is the most commonly used type of graph in economics. Figure 2 is a *bar graph*. It is probably used more often in popular magazines than any other kind of graph. Figure 3 is a *pie graph,* or *pie chart*. Although it is less popular than bar and line graphs, it appears often enough that you need to be familiar with it.

1.a. Relationships between Variables

Figure 1 is a line graph showing the ratio of the median income of people who have completed four or more years of college to the median income of those who have completed just four years of high school. The line shows the value of a college education in terms of the additional income earned relative to the income earned without a college degree on a year-to-year basis. You can see that the premium for completing college rose from the mid-1970s until 2001 and has declined slightly since.

Figure 2 is a bar graph indicating the unemployment rate by educational attainment. The blue refers to high school dropouts, the red refers to those with four years of high school, and the green refers to those with four or more years of college. One set of bars is presented for males and one set for females. The bars are arranged in order, with the highest incidence of unemployment depicted first, the next highest second, and the lowest third. This arrangement is made only for ease in reading and interpretation. The bars could be arranged in any order. The graph illustrates that unemployment strikes those with less education more than it does those with more education.

Figure 3 is a pie chart showing the percentage of the U.S. population completing various numbers of years of schooling. Unlike line and bar graphs, a pie chart is not actually a picture of a relationship between two variables. Instead, the pie represents the whole, 100 percent of the U.S. population, and the pieces of the pie represent parts of the whole—the percentage of the population completing one to four years of elementary school only, five to seven years of elementary school, and so on, up to four or more years of college.

Because a pie chart does not show the relationship between variables, it is not as useful for explaining economic concepts as line and bar graphs. Line graphs are used more often than bar graphs to explain economic concepts.

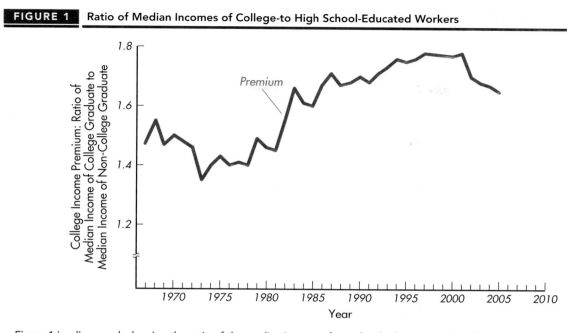

FIGURE 1 Ratio of Median Incomes of College-to High School-Educated Workers

Figure 1 is a line graph showing the ratio of the median income of people who have completed four or more years of college to the median income of those who have completed four years of high school. The line shows the income premium for educational attainment, or the value of a college education in terms of income, from year to year. The rise in the line since about 1979 shows that the premium for completing college has risen.
Source: U.S. Statistical Abstract, 2005. *U.S. Census Bureau:* www.census.gov.

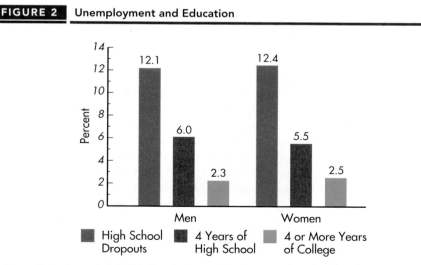

FIGURE 2 Unemployment and Education

Figure 2 is a bar graph indicating the unemployment rate by educational attainment. The blue refers to high school dropouts, the red refers to those with four years of high school, and the green refers to those with four or more years of college. One set of bars is presented for males and one set for females. The bars are arranged in order, with the highest incidence of unemployment shown first, the next highest second, and the lowest third. This arrangement is made only for ease in reading and interpretation. The bars could be arranged in any order.
Source: U.S. Census Bureau: www.census.gov/population.

FIGURE 3 Educational Attainment

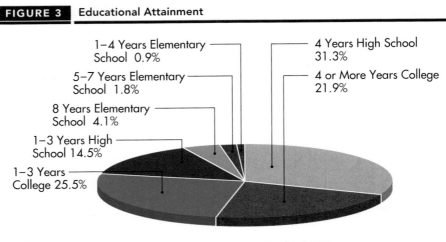

Total = 100%

Figure 3 is a pie chart showing the percentage of the U.S. population completing various years of schooling. Unlike line and bar graphs, a pie chart is not actually a picture of a relationship between two variables. Instead, the pie represents the whole, 100 percent of the U.S. population in this case, and the pieces of the pie represent parts of the whole—the percentage of the population completing one to four years of elementary school only, five to seven years of elementary school, and so on, up to four or more years of college.
Source: U.S. Census Bureau, 2009; www.census.gov/population.

1.b. Independent and Dependent Variables

independent variable: a variable whose value does not depend on the values of other variables

Most line and bar graphs involve just two variables, an **independent variable** and a **dependent variable**. An independent variable is one whose value does not depend on the values of other variables; a dependent variable, on the other hand, is one whose value does depend on the values of other variables. The value of the dependent variable is determined after the value of the independent variable is determined.

dependent variable: a variable whose value depends on the value of the independent variable

In Figure 2, the *independent* variable is the educational status of the man or woman, and the *dependent* variable is the incidence of unemployment (the percentage of the group that is unemployed). The incidence of unemployment depends on the educational attainment of the man or woman.

1.c. Direct and Inverse Relationships

direct, or **positive, relationship:** the relationship that exists when the values of related variables move in the same direction

If the value of the dependent variable increases as the value of the independent variable increases, the relationship between the two types of variables is called a **direct**, or **positive**, **relationship**. If the value of the dependent variable decreases as the value of the independent variable increases, the relationship between the two types of variables is called an **inverse**, or **negative**, **relationship**.

inverse, or **negative, relationship:** the relationship that exists when the values of related variables move in opposite directions

In Figure 2, unemployment and educational attainment are inversely, or negatively, related: As people acquire more education, they become less likely to be unemployed.

■ 2. Constructing a Graph

Let's now construct a graph. We will begin with a consideration of the horizontal and vertical axes, or lines, and then we will put the axes together. We are going to construct a *straight-line curve*. This sounds contradictory, but it is common terminology. Economists often refer to the demand or supply *curve*, and that curve may be a straight line.

2.a. The Axes

It is important to understand how the *axes* (the horizontal and vertical lines) are used and what they measure. Let's begin with the horizontal axis, the line running across the page. Notice in Figure 4(a) that the line is divided into equal segments. Each point on the line represents a quantity, or the value of the variable being measured. For example, each segment could represent one year or 10,000 pounds of diamonds or some other value. Whatever is measured, the value increases from left to right, beginning with negative values, going on to zero, which is called the *origin,* and then moving on to positive numbers.

A number line in the vertical direction can be constructed as well, and this is also shown in Figure 4(a). Zero is the origin, and the numbers increase from bottom to top. Like the horizontal axis, the vertical axis is divided into equal segments; the distance between 0 and 10 is the same as the distance between 0 and –10, the distance between 10 and 20, and so on.

In most cases, the variable measured along the horizontal axis is the independent variable. This isn't always true in economics, however. Economists

---

FIGURE 4   The Axes, the Coordinate System, and the Positive Quadrant

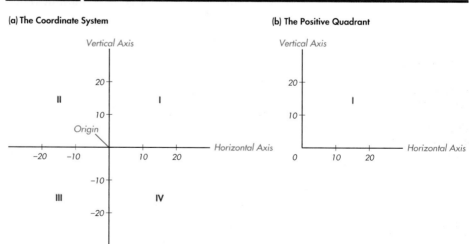

Figure 4(a) shows the vertical and horizontal axes. The horizontal axis has an origin, measured as zero, in the middle. Negative numbers are to the left of zero, and positive numbers are to the right. The vertical axis also has an origin in the middle. Positive numbers are above the origin, and negative numbers are below. The horizontal and vertical axes together show the entire coordinate system. Positive numbers are in quadrant I, negative numbers in quadrant III, and combinations of negative and positive numbers in quadrants II and IV.

Figure 4(b) shows only the positive quadrant. Because most economic data are positive, often only the upper right quadrant, the positive quadrant, of the coordinate system is used.

often measure the independent variable on the vertical axis. Do not assume that the variable on the horizontal axis is independent and the variable on the vertical axis is dependent.

Putting the horizontal and vertical lines together lets us express relationships between two variables graphically. The axes cross, or intersect, at their origins, as shown in Figure 4(a). From the common origin, movements to the right and up, in the area—called a quadrant—marked I, are combinations of positive numbers; movements to the left and down, in quadrant III, are combinations of negative numbers; movements to the right and down, in quadrant IV, are negative values on the vertical axis and positive values on the horizontal axis; and movements to the left and up, in quadrant II, are positive values on the vertical axis and negative values on the horizontal axis.

Economic data are typically positive numbers: the unemployment rate, the inflation rate, the price of something, the quantity of something produced or sold, and so on. Because economic data are usually positive numbers, the only part of the coordinate system that usually comes into play in economics is the upper right portion, quadrant I. That is why economists may simply sketch a vertical line down to the origin and then extend a horizontal line out to the right, as shown in Figure 4(b). Once in a while, economic data are negative—for instance, profit is negative when costs exceed revenues. When data are negative, quadrants II, III, and IV of the coordinate system may be used.

2.b. Constructing a Graph from a Table

Now that you are familiar with the axes—that is, the coordinate system—you are ready to construct a graph using the data in the table in Figure 5. The table lists a series of possible price levels for a T-shirt and the corresponding number of T-shirts that people choose to purchase. The data are only hypothetical; they are not drawn from actual cases.

The information given in the table is graphed in Figure 5. We begin by marking off and labeling the axes. The vertical axis is the list of possible price levels. We begin at zero and move up the axis in equal increments of $10. The horizontal axis is the number of T-shirts sold. We begin at zero and move out the axis in equal increments of 1,000 T-shirts. According to the information presented in the table, if the price is higher than $100, no one buys a T-shirt. The combination of $100 and 0 T-shirts is point *A* on the graph. To plot this point, find the quantity zero on the horizontal axis (it is at the origin), and then move up the vertical axis from zero to a price level of $100. (Note that we have measured the units in the table and on the graph in thousands.) At a price of $90, there are 1,000 T-shirts purchased. To plot the combination of $90 and 1,000 T-shirts, find 1,000 units on the horizontal axis and then measure up from there to a price of $90. This is point *B*. Point *C* represents a price of $80 and 2,000 T-shirts. Point *D* represents a price of $70 and 3,000 T-shirts. Each combination of price and T-shirts purchased listed in the table is plotted in Figure 5.

The final step in constructing a line graph is to connect the points that are plotted. When the points are connected, the straight line slanting downward from left to right in Figure 5 is obtained. It shows the relationship between the price of T-shirts and the number of T-shirts purchased.

2.c. Interpreting Points on a Graph

Let's use Figure 5 to demonstrate how points on a graph may be interpreted. Suppose the current price of a T-shirt is $30. Are you able to tell how many T-shirts are being purchased at this price? By tracing that price level from the vertical axis over to the curve and then down to the horizontal axis, you find

FIGURE 5 Constructing a Line Graph

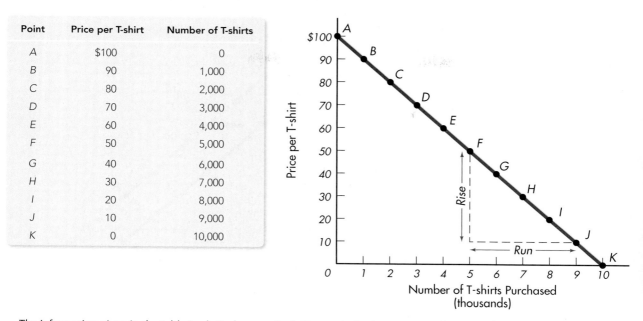

Point	Price per T-shirt	Number of T-shirts
A	$100	0
B	90	1,000
C	80	2,000
D	70	3,000
E	60	4,000
F	50	5,000
G	40	6,000
H	30	7,000
I	20	8,000
J	10	9,000
K	0	10,000

The information given in the table is plotted or graphed. The vertical axis measures price per T-shirt. The horizontal axis measures the number of T-shirts in thousands. We begin at zero in each case and then go up (if the vertical axis) or out (if the horizontal axis) in equal amounts. The vertical axis goes from $0 to $10 to $20 and so on, while the horizontal axis goes from 0 to 1,000 to 2,000 and so on. Each point is plotted. For instance, point A is a price of $100 and a number of T-shirts of 0. This is found by going to 0 on the horizontal axis and then up to $100 on the vertical axis. Point B is a price of $90 and a number of 1,000. Once the points are plotted, a line connecting the points is drawn.

that 7,000 T-shirts are being purchased. You can also find what happens to the number purchased if the price falls from $30 to $10. By tracing from the price of $10 horizontally to the curve and then down to the horizontal axis, you discover that 9,000 T-shirts are purchased. Thus, according to the graph, a decrease in the price from $30 to $10 results in 2,000 more T-shirts being purchased.

2.d. Shifts of Curves

Graphs can be used to illustrate the effects of a change in a variable that is not represented on the graph. For instance, the curve drawn in Figure 5 shows the relationship between the price of T-shirts and the number of T-shirts purchased. When this curve was drawn, the only two variables that were allowed to change were the price and the number of T-shirts. However, it is likely that people's incomes determine their reaction to the price of T-shirts as well. An increase in income would enable people to purchase more T-shirts. Thus, at every price, more T-shirts would be purchased. How would this be represented? As an outward shift of the curve, from points *A, B, C,* and so on to *A', B', C',* and so on, as shown in Figure 6.

Following the shift of the curve, we can see that more T-shirts are purchased at each price than was the case prior to the income increase. For instance, at a price of $20, the increased income allows 10,000 T-shirts to be purchased rather than 8,000. The important point to note is that if some variable that influences the relationship shown in a curve or line graph changes, then *the entire curve or line changes—that is, it shifts.*

FIGURE 6 Shift of Curve

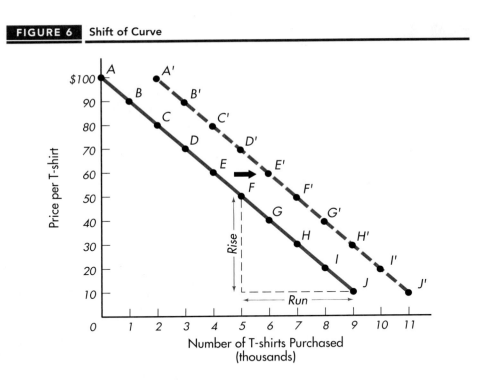

An increase in income allows more people to purchase T-shirts at each price. At a price of $80, for instance, 4,000 T-shirts are purchased instead of 2,000.

■ 3. Slope

A curve may represent an inverse, or negative, relationship or a direct, or positive, relationship. The slope of the curve reveals the kind of relationship that exists between two variables.

3.a. Positive and Negative Slopes

slope: the steepness of a curve, measured as the ratio of the rise to the run

The **slope** of a curve is its steepness, the rate at which the value of a variable measured on the vertical axis changes with respect to a given change in the value of the variable measured on the horizontal axis. If the value of a variable measured on one axis goes up when the value of the variable measured on the other axis goes down, the variables have an inverse (or negative) relationship. If the values of the variables rise or fall together, the variables have a direct (or positive) relationship. Inverse relationships are represented by curves that run downward from left to right; direct relationships, by curves that run upward from left to right.

Slope is calculated by measuring the amount by which the variable on the vertical axis changes and dividing that figure by the amount by which the variable on the horizontal axis changes. The vertical change is called the *rise,* and the horizontal change is called the *run.* Slope is referred to as the *rise over the run:*

$$\text{Slope} = \frac{\text{rise}}{\text{run}}$$

The slope of any inverse relationship is negative. The slope of any direct relationship is positive.

Let's calculate the slope of the curve in Figure 5. Price (P) is measured on the vertical axis, and quantity of T-shirts purchased (Q) is measured on the horizontal axis. The rise is the change in price (ΔP), the change in the value of the variable measured on the vertical axis. The run is the change in quantity of T-shirts purchased (ΔQ), the change in the value of the variable measured on the horizontal axis. (The symbol Δ means "change in"—it is the Greek letter delta—so ΔP means "change in P" and ΔQ means "change in Q.") Remember that slope equals the rise over the run. Thus, the equation for the slope of the straight-line curve running downward from left to right in Figure 5 is

$$\frac{\Delta P}{\Delta Q}$$

As the price (P) declines, the number of T-shirts purchased (Q) increases. The rise is negative, and the run is positive. Thus, the slope is a negative value. The slope is the same anywhere along a straight line. Thus, it does not matter where we calculate the changes along the vertical and horizontal axes. For instance, from 0 to 10,000 on the horizontal axis—a run of 10,000—the vertical change, the rise, is a negative $100 (from $100 down to $0). Thus, the rise over the run is $-100/10,000$, or $-.01$. Similarly, from 5,000 to 9,000 in the horizontal direction,

FIGURE 7   T-Shirts Offered for Sale at Each Price

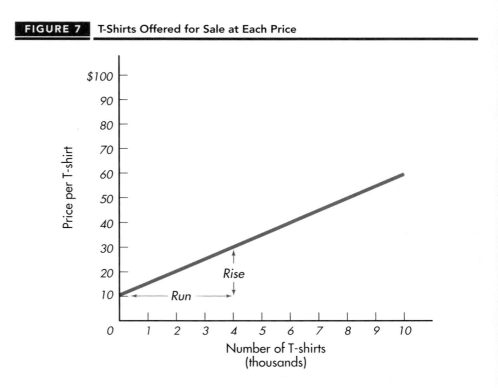

Figure 7 is a graph showing the number of T-shirts offered for sale at various prices. The line shows that as price rises so does the number of T-shirts offered for sale. At a price of $10, no shirts are offered. At a price of $20, 2,000 shirts are offered for sale. At a price of $30, 4,000 shirts are offered for sale, and so on. The rise over the run is 20/4,000 = .005.

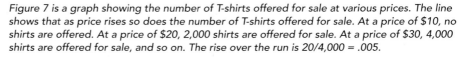

the corresponding rise is $50 to $10, so that the rise over the run is −40/4,000 or −.01.

Remember that direct, or positive, relationships between variables are represented by lines that run upward from left to right. Figure 7 is a graph showing the number of T-shirts that producers offer for sale at various price levels. The curve represents the relationship between the two variables number of T-shirts offered for sale and price. It shows that as price rises, so does the number of T-shirts offered for sale. The slope of the curve is positive. The change in the rise (the vertical direction) that comes with an increase in the run (the horizontal direction) is positive. Because the graph is a straight line, you can measure the rise and run using any two points along the curve and the slope will be the same. We find the slope by calculating the rise that accompanies the run. Moving from 0 to 4,000 T-shirts gives us a run of 4,000. Looking at the curve, we see that the corresponding rise is $20. Thus, the rise over the run is 20/4,000, or .005.

SUMMARY

- There are three commonly used types of graphs: the line graph, the bar graph, and the pie chart. §1.a

- An independent variable is a variable whose value does not depend on the values of other variables. The values of a dependent variable do depend on the values of other variables. §1.b

- A direct, or positive, relationship occurs when the value of the dependent variable increases as the value of the independent variable increases. An indirect, or negative, relationship occurs when the value of the dependent variable decreases as the value of the independent variable increases. §1.c

- Most economic data are positive numbers, and so only the upper right quadrant of the coordinate system is often used in economics. §2.a

- A curve shifts when a variable that affects the dependent variable and is not measured on the axes changes. §2.d

- The slope of a curve is the rise over the run: the change in the variable measured on the vertical axis over the corresponding change in the variable measured on the horizontal axis. §3.a

- The slope of a straight-line curve is the same at all points along the curve. §3.a

KEY TERMS

independent variable §1.b   direct, or positive, relationship §1.c   slope §3.a

dependent variable §1.b   inverse, or negative, relationship §1.c

EXERCISES

1. Listed in the following table are two sets of figures: the total quantity of Mexican pesos (new pesos) in circulation (the total amount of Mexican money available) and the peso price of a dollar (how many pesos are needed to purchase one dollar). Values are given for the years 1990- through 2009 for each variable.

   a. Plot each variable by measuring time (years) on the horizontal axis and, in the first graph, pesos in circulation on the vertical axis and, in the

   second graph, peso price of a dollar on the vertical axis.

   b. Plot the combinations of variables by measuring pesos in circulation on the horizontal axis and peso prices of a dollar on the vertical axis.

   c. In each of the graphs in parts a and b, what are the dependent and independent variables?

   d. In each of the graphs in parts a and b, indicate whether the relationship between the dependent and independent variables is direct or inverse.

Year	Pesos in Circulation *(billions)*	Peso Price of a Dollar
1990	19.6	2.8126
1991	27.0	3.0184
1992	36.2	3.0949
1993	42.0	3.1156
1994	47.2	3.3751
1995	56.9,	6.4194
1996	66.8	7.5994
1997	84.0	8.5850
1998	109.0	9.9680
1999	131.0	9.4270
2000	188.8	9.6420
2001	209.0	9.2850
2002	225.0	9.5270
2003	264.0	10.9000
2004	303.0	11.4000
2005	340.0	10.4750
2006	380.0	10.87
2007	450.0	10.86
2008	495.0	13.53
2009	578.0	13.76

2. Plot the data listed in the table:
   a. Use price as the vertical axis and quantity as the horizontal axis and plot the first two columns.
   b. Show what quantity is sold when the price is $550.
   c. Directly below the graph in part a, plot the data in columns 2 and 3. Use total revenue as the vertical axis and quantity as the horizontal axis.
   d. What is total revenue when the price is $550? Will total revenue increase or decrease when the price is lowered?

Price	Quantity Sold	Total Revenue
$1,000	200	200,000
900	400	360,000
800	600	480,000
700	800	560,000
600	1,000	600,000
500	1,200	600,000
400	1,400	560,000
300	1,600	480,000
200	1,800	360,000
100	2,000	200,000

© lofoto/Drea

Choice, Opportunity Costs, and Specialization

Fundamental Questions

1 | What are opportunity costs? Are they part of the economic way of thinking?

2 | What is a production possibilities curve?

3 | Why does specialization occur?

4 | What are the benefits of trade?

In the previous chapter, we learned that scarcity forces people to make choice. A choice means that you select one thing instead of selecting others. What you don't select is the cost of the choice you make. The old saying that "there is no free lunch" means that every choice requires that something be given up or sacrificed. This chapter explains how costs affect the behavior of individuals, firms, and societies as a whole.

■ 1. Opportunity Costs

A choice is simply a comparison of alternatives: to attend class or not to attend class, to purchase a double latte mocha with whipped cream or to buy four songs from iTunes, to purchase a new car or to keep the old one. When one option is chosen, the benefits of the alternatives are forgone. When you choose to purchase the double latte mocha for $4, you don't have that $4 to spend on anything else. *Economists refer to the forgone opportunities or forgone benefits of the next best alternative as* **opportunity costs**. Opportunity costs are the highest-valued alternative that must be forgone when a choice is made. If you would

1 | **What are opportunity costs? Are they part of the economic way of thinking?**

opportunity costs: the highest-valued alternative that must be forgone when a choice is made

have bought four iTunes if you had not purchased the latte, then we say the opportunity cost of the latte is the benefit you don't enjoy from the iTunes.

The concept of cost is often more than the dollars and cents that you shell out at the cash register. Buying used books saves money but often increases frustration and may affect your grades. The book might be missing pages, unreadable in spots, or out of date. The full cost of the book is the price you paid for the used copy plus the frustration of having an incomplete book. An attorney in Scottsdale, Arizona, is paid $125 an hour to write contracts. The attorney loves Ralph Lauren dress shirts and knows that these can be purchased for $100 at Nordstrom in Scottsdale or, when they are available, for $50 at the outlet mall in Casa Grande. He likes to purchase just one or two shirts at a time and usually buys the shirts at Nordstrom, taking 15 minutes out of his lunch time to go to the store. Is this smart? Well, he figures he could spend two hours driving to Casa Grande and back and save $50 per shirt. But this also means that he is not writing contracts and charging $125 per hour during those two hours. The real cost of the $50 saved on a single shirt in Casa Grande includes the $250 that the attorney would be giving up in income.

When economists refer to costs, it is opportunity costs they are measuring. The cost of anything is what must be given up to get that item. Every human activity responds to costs in one way or another. When the cost of something falls, that something becomes more attractive to us, all else being the same. For instance, when the cost of text messaging phone service dropped, more of us signed up for the service. Conversely, when the cost of something rises, and all else remains unchanged, we tend to use less of it. When photo radar machines were placed on the freeways in Arizona, the cost of speeding went up because the likelihood of getting caught speeding dramatically increased. As a result, the amount of speeding dropped—average speeds went from 78 to 65 virtually overnight.

1.a. Tradeoffs

tradeoff: the giving up of one good or activity in order to obtain some other good or activity

Life is a continuous sequence of decisions, and every single decision involves choosing one thing over another or trading off something for something else. A **tradeoff** means a sacrifice—giving up one good or activity in order to obtain some other good or activity. Each term you must decide whether to register for college or not. You could work full-time and not attend college, attend college and not work, or work part-time and attend college. The time you devote to college will decrease as you devote more time to work. You trade off hours spent at work for hours spent in college; in other words, you compare the benefits you think you will get from going to college this term with the costs of college this term.

2 | **What is a production possibilities curve?**

production possibilities curve (PPC): a graphical representation showing all possible combinations of quantities of goods and services that can be produced using the existing resources fully and efficiently

1.b. The Production Possibilities Curve

Tradeoffs can be illustrated in a graph known as the **production possibilities curve (PPC)**. The production possibilities curve shows all possible combinations of quantities of goods and services that can be produced when the existing resources are used *fully and efficiently*. Figure 1 shows a production possibilities curve (based on information in the table in Figure 1) for the production of defense goods and services and nondefense goods and services by a nation. Defense goods and services include guns, ships, bombs, personnel, and so forth that are used for national defense. Nondefense goods and services

FIGURE 1   **The Production Possibilities Curve**

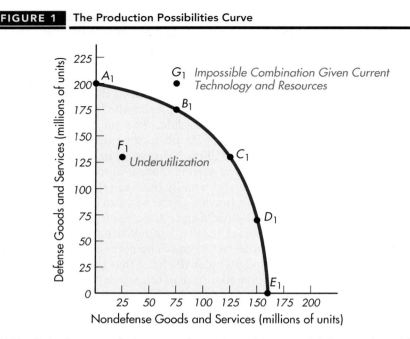

With a limited amount of resources, only certain combinations of defense and nondefense goods and services can be produced. The maximum amounts that can be produced, given various tradeoffs, are represented by points A1 through E1. Point F1 lies inside the curve and represents the underutilization of resources. More of one type of goods could be produced without producing less of the other, or more of both types could be produced. Point G1 represents an impossible combination. There are insufficient resources to produce quantities lying beyond the curve.

include education, housing, health care, and food that are not used for national defense. All societies allocate their scarce resources in order to produce some combination of defense and nondefense goods and services. Because resources are scarce, a nation cannot produce as much of everything as it wants. When it produces more health care, it cannot produce as much education or automobiles; when it devotes more of its resources to the military area, fewer resources are available to devote to health care.

In Figure 1, units of defense goods and services are measured on the vertical axis, and units of nondefense goods and services are measured on the horizontal axis. If all resources are allocated to producing defense goods and services, then 200 million units can be produced, but there will be no production of nondefense goods and services. The combination of 200 million units of defense goods and services and 0 units of nondefense goods and services is point $A1$, a point on the vertical axis. At 175 million units of defense goods and services, 75 million units of nondefense goods and services can be produced (point $B1$). Point $C1$ represents 125 million units of nondefense goods and services and 130 million units of defense goods. Point $D1$ represents 150 million units of nondefense goods and services and 70 million units of defense goods and services. Point $E1$, a point on the horizontal axis, shows the combination of no production of defense goods and services and 160 million units of nondefense goods and services.

1.b.1. Points Inside the Production Possibilities Curve

Suppose a nation produces 130 million units of defense goods and services and 25 million units of nondefense goods and services. That combination, Point F1 in Figure 1, lies inside the production possibilities curve. A point lying inside the production possibilities curve indicates that resources are not being fully or efficiently used. If the existing work force is employed only 20 hours per week, it is not being fully used. If two workers are used when one would be sufficient—say, two people in each Domino's Pizza delivery car—then resources are not being used efficiently. If there are resources available for use, society can move from point F1 to a point on the PPC, such as point C1. The move would gain 100 million units of nondefense goods and services with no loss of defense goods and services.

During recessions, unemployment rises and other resources are not fully and efficiently used. A point inside a nation's PPC could represent recession. This would be represented as a point inside the PPC, such as F1. Should the economy expand, and resources become more fully and efficiently used, this would be represented as a move out from a point such as F1 to a point on the PPC, such as point C1.

1.b.2. Points Outside the Production Possibilities Curve

Point G1 in Figure 1 represents the production of 200 million units of defense goods and services and 75 million units of nondefense goods and services. Point G1, however, represents the use of more resources than are available—it lies outside the production possibilities curve. Unless more resources can be obtained and/or the quality of resources improved (for example, through technological change) so that the nation can produce more with the same quantity of resources, there is no way that the society can currently produce 200 million units of defense goods and 75 million units of nondefense goods.

1.b.3. Shifts of the Production Possibilities Curve

If a nation obtains more resources or if the existing resources become more efficient, then the PPC shifts outward. Suppose a country discovers new sources of oil within its borders and is able to greatly increase its production of oil. Greater oil supplies would enable the country to increase production of all types of goods and services.

Figure 2 shows the production possibilities curve before (*PPC*1) and after (*PPC*2) the discovery of oil. *PPC*1 is based on the data given in the table in Figure 1. *PPC*2 is based on the data given in the table in Figure 2, which shows the increase in production of goods and services that results from the increase in oil supplies. The first combination of goods and services on *PPC*2, point *A*2, is 220 million units of defense goods and 0 units of nondefense goods. The second point, *B*2, is a combination of 200 million units of defense goods and 75 million units of nondefense goods. *C*2 through *F*2 are the combinations shown in the table in Figure 2. Connecting these points yields the bowed-out curve *PPC*2. Because of the availability of new supplies of oil, the nation is able to increase production of all goods, as shown by the *shift* from *PPC*1 to *PPC*2. A comparison of the two curves shows that more goods and services for both defense and nondefense are possible along *PPC*2 than along *PPC*1.

The outward shift of the PPC can be the result of an increase in the quantity of resources, but it also can occur because the quality of resources improves. Economists call an increase in the quality of resources an increase in the productivity of resources. Consider a technological breakthrough that improves the speed with which

FIGURE 2   **A Shift of the Production Possibilities Curve**

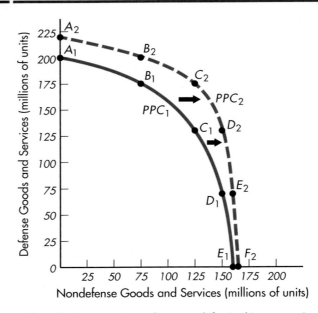

Whenever everything else is not constant, the curve shifts. In this case, an increase in the quantity of a resource enables the society to produce more of both types of goods. The curve shifts out, away from the origin.

data are transmitted. Following this breakthrough, it might require fewer people and machines to do the same amount of work, and it might take less time to produce the same quantity and quality of goods. Each quality improvement in resources is illustrated as an outward shift of the PPC.

RECAP

1. Opportunity costs are the benefits that are forgone as a result of a choice. When you choose one thing, you must give up—forgo—others.

2. The production possibilities curve (PPC) illustrates the concept of opportunity cost. Each point on the PPC means that every other point is a forgone opportunity.

3. The production possibilities curve represents all combinations of goods and services that can be produced using limited resources efficiently to their full capabilities.

4. Points inside the production possibilities curve represent the underutilization, unemployment, or inefficient use of resources—more goods and services could be produced by using the limited resources more fully or efficiently.

5. Points outside the production possibilities curve represent combinations of goods and services that are unattainable given the limitation of resources.

6. If more resources are obtained or a technological change or innovation occurs, the PPC shifts out.

3 | Why does specialization occur?

■ 2. Specialization and Trade

The PPC illustrates the idea of scarcity—there are limits, and combinations outside of the curve are not attainable. The PPC also illustrates the idea of costs—no matter which combination of goods and services a society chooses to produce, other combinations of goods and services are sacrificed. And, the PPC illustrates the idea that choices have to be made—it is not possible to satisfy unlimited wants.

2.a. Marginal Cost

As the production of some types of goods is increased, some other types of goods and services cannot be produced. According to the table and graph in Figure 1, we see that moving from point *A*1 to point *B*1 on the PPC means increasing nondefense production from 0 to 75 million units and decreasing defense production from 200 million to 175 million units. Thus, the marginal cost of 75 million units of nondefense is 25 million units of defense. The incremental amount of defense given up with each increase in the production of nondefense goods is known as the **marginal cost** or **marginal opportunity cost**. *Marginal* means "change" or "incremental," so marginal cost is the incremental amount of one good or service that must be given up to obtain one additional unit of another good or service.

marginal cost or **marginal opportunity cost:** the amount of one good or service that must be given up to obtain one additional unit of another good or service, no matter how many units are being produced

Each move along the PPC means giving up some defense goods to get some more nondefense goods. Each additional nondefense good produced requires giving up an increasing number of defense goods. The marginal cost increases with each successive increase of nondefense production. In other words, all other things being equal, it gets more and more costly to produce nondefense goods the more nondefense goods you have.

The marginal cost increases because of specialization. The first resources transferred from defense to nondefense production are those that are least specialized in the production of defense goods. Switching these resources is less costly (less has to be given up) than switching the specialists. Shifting an accountant who can do accounting in either defense-or nondefense-related industries equally well would not cause a big change in defense production. However, shifting a rocket scientist, who is not very useful in producing nondefense goods, would make a big difference.

4 | What are the benefits of trade?

Individuals, firms, and nations select the option with the lowest opportunity costs.

2.b. Specialize Where Opportunity Costs Are Lowest

If we have a choice, we should devote our time and efforts to those activities that cost the least. In other words, we should specialize in those activities that require us to give up the smallest amount of other things. A plumber does plumbing and leaves teaching to the teachers. The teacher teaches and leaves electrical work to the electrician. A country such as Grenada specializes in spice production and leaves manufacturing to other countries.

2.b.1. Trade If we focus on one thing, how do we get the other things that we want? The answer is that we trade or exchange goods and services. The teacher teaches, earns a salary, and hires a plumber to fix the sinks. This is called voluntary trade or voluntary exchange. The teacher is trading money to the plumber for the plumber's services. The teacher is trading her time to the students and getting money in return.

By specializing in the activities in which opportunity costs are lowest and then trading, everyone will end up with more than if everyone tried to produce everything. This is the **gains from trade**. Consider two students, Josh and Elena, who are taking the same math and economics classes and are considering working together. They are deciding whether to specialize and trade or not.

If Josh and Elena both devote all their time and effort to doing the math homework, each can do 10 math problems. If they spend all their time and effort on economics, Josh is able to complete 5 economics problems, while Elena can do 10 economics problems.

gains from trade: the difference between what can be produced and consumed without specialization and trade and with specialization and trade

	Elena		Josh	
	Math	*Econ*	*Math*	*Econ*
All resources devoted:				
To Economics	0	10	0	5
To Math	10	0	10	0

Since Elena is better at economics and just as good at math, why should she want to work with Josh? The answer depends on relative costs. What does it cost Elena to do 1 math problem? She has to not do 1 economics problem. So, it costs her 1 economics problem to do 1 math problem. Josh can do 2 math problems in the time he can complete just 1 economics problem. So, it costs Josh just 1/2 economics problem to do 1 math problem. Josh is *relatively* better at doing math—he can do it for lower costs than can Elena. Who is relatively better at economics? It costs Josh 2 math problems to do 1 economics problem, and it costs Elena 1 math problem to do 1 economics problem. So Elena is relatively more efficient at doing economics.

If Elena specializes in economics and Josh in math, and then they trade, they will both be better off. To see this, let's begin where there is no trade and Josh and Elena each spend half their time and effort on math and half on economics. By spending half her time on economics problems, Elena can do 5, whereas Josh can only do 2.5 by spending half his time on economics problems. They each can do 5 math problems if they devote half their time to math.

	Elena		Josh	
	Math	*Econ*	*Math*	*Econ*
All resources devoted:				
To Economics	0	10	0	5
To Math	10	0	10	0
No Specialization	5	5	5	2.5

Now, let's assume that they specialize according to comparative advantage and then trade at a rate of 1 math problem for 1 economics problem. Elena produces

10 economics problems. To get 5 math problems, she needs to trade 5 economics problems. She ends up the same as if she did not specialize. Josh, on the other hand, specializes by producing 10 math problems. He can get 5 economics problems for his 5 math problems, and he ends up 2.5 economics problems better than if he had not traded.

	Elena		Josh	
	Math	Econ	Math	Econ
Specialization and trade at ratio of 2:1	5	5	5	5

Notice that there are gains from trade. There are 2.5 more completed economics problems as a result of specialization and trade. In this case, the gains all went to Josh because the trading price, 1 to 1, was the same as Elena's personal opportunity cost ratio. Let's now change the trading price so that Elena gets the gains. Let's assume that they specialize and trade at a ratio of 2 math problems for 1 economics problem, Josh's personal opportunity cost ratio. In this case, Elena trades 2.5 economics problems to get 5 math problems. She is the one who gains this time:

	Elena		Josh	
	Math	Econ	Math	Econ
Specialization and trade at ratio of 2:1	5	7.5	5	2.5

In each of the two examples, just one party gained. This is because the trades took place first at Elena's opportunity cost ratio and then at Josh's opportunity cost ratio. In reality, people won't trade voluntarily unless they gain. Elena and Josh would work out how many economics problems to trade for a math problem so that they both gained something.

Specialization and trade enable individuals, firms, and nations to acquire combinations of goods that lie beyond their own resource capabilities. Voluntary, free trade results in more being created—more income being generated, that is—and higher standards of living are being created because everything is produced at the lowest possible cost.

When you buy something, you are trading—you are exchanging money for some item. Similarly, when you sell something, you are trading—exchanging some item for money. Imagine your world without trade. A good start would be to put yourself in the place of Tom Hanks's character in the movie *Cast Away*. If you've seen the movie, you can remember the scene where he was able to rub two sticks together to create fire. From then on, he had some light at night and some means for cooking food. But until you got the fire going, you would go to bed in the dark and wake up in a small, drafty tent-house that you had built yourself. You would put on clothes made from items that you had found. You might be able to create some tea or coffee from something you had grown and eat something that you had caught or raised, but

Mexico has a comparative advantage in low-skilled, low-wage workers relative to the United States. Free trade means that Mexico should specialize in those activities requiring low-skilled, low-wage workers. However, Mexico's government has intervened in the country's economy to such an extent that resources cannot flow to where their value is highest. As a result, many of the labor resources have to leave Mexico in order to be able to earn a living.

© James Steid/Shutterstock

you would spend all your waking hours just trying to survive. Not living in a world like that illustrates what your gains from trade are.

2.c. Comparative Advantage

comparative advantage:
the ability to produce a good or service at a lower opportunity cost than someone else

We have seen that the choice of which area or activity to specialize in is made on the basis of opportunity costs. Economists refer to the ability of one person or nation to do something with a lower opportunity cost than another as **comparative advantage**. In the example, Elena had a comparative advantage in economics and Josh in math.

Comparative advantage applies to every case of trade or exchange. This sometimes seems counterintuitive. Shouldn't countries that have lots of natural resources and a skilled labor force do everything themselves? The answer is no. Even though the United States has many more natural resources and a much larger and better-educated population than Grenada, Grenada has a comparative advantage in producing spices. The United States could produce more of everything than Grenada, but the opportunity cost of producing spices is higher in the United States than it is in Grenada. Both Grenada and the United States gain by having Grenada specialize in spice production and trade with the United States.

If you go around the world and look at what goods and services are traded, you can usually identify the comparative advantage. Some trade occurs simply because a country has more of something. Saudi Arabia trades oil because it has more than anyone else. But countries don't have to have more of something for there to be gains from trade. They simply have to do something at a lower cost than another country. For instance, most developing nations have a comparative advantage in activities that use unskilled labor. Unskilled labor is much less expensive in Mexico, China, India, Pakistan, Bangladesh, and many other countries than in the United States. So gains from trade occur when these countries do things that use unskilled labor and then trade with the United States for foodstuffs or high-technology goods. The United States is sending many unskilled speaking jobs, such as telephone call agents, to India because Indians speak English and their wages are low.

Trade is not based solely on wage differences. Most trade in the world occurs between industrial or developed nations rather than between a developed and a less-developed nation. Each of the nations has comparative advantages in some goods and services. Germany might have a comparative advantage in engineering automobiles, Denmark in producing Havarti cheese, France in wine, Switzerland in banking, and so on. Each country gains by specializing according to comparative advantage and then trading.

> *Individuals specialize in the activity in which their opportunity costs are lowest.*

2.d. Private Property Rights

Each of us will specialize in some activity, earn income, and then trade our output (or income) for other goods and services that we want. Specialization and trade ensure that we are better off than we would be if we did everything ourselves. *Specialization according to comparative advantage followed by trade allows everyone to acquire more of the goods they want.* But, for trade to occur, we must have confidence that we own what we create, and that what we own cannot be taken away. **Private property rights** are necessary for trade to occur. If I order a pizza to be delivered by Papa John's to my house, but anyone can come over and eat it when it arrives, I won't have an incentive to order any pizzas. If I can live in a house, but I can't own it, I have no incentive to take care of it. Private property rights refer to the right of ownership, and it requires a legal system of laws and courts and police to ensure ownership. If someone steals my car, someone will be penalized, since stealing a car is against the law. And that if someone mugs me, takes my wallet, and leaves me bleeding on the sidewalk, then that is theft of person and property and is also against the law. I have ownership rights to my body, to my assets, and to the things I have bought.

> **Private property rights:** the right of ownership

If no one owns something, no one has the incentive to take care of it. An example is presented in the Land Titling in Argentina box. Consider the fish in the ocean. No one owns the fish, and hence, no one has the incentive to protect them, raise them, and ensure that future generations of fish exist. Someone has to own an item for someone to care for it. Also, it is *private* property rights that count, not *public* property rights. If no one owns something, no one takes care of it. But equally, if everyone owns something, no one has an incentive to take care of it. In the former Soviet Union, the government owned virtually everything. No one had an incentive to take care of anything. As a result, housing was decrepit and dingy, industries were inefficient and run down, chemicals were dumped in the rivers and on the land, the air was polluted, and, in general, standards of living were very low.

RECAP

1. Marginal cost is the incremental amount of one good or service that must be given up to obtain one additional unit of another good or service.

2. The rule of specialization is: specialize where the opportunity cost is lowest.

3. Comparative advantage exists whenever one person (firm, nation) can do something with lower opportunity costs than some other individual (firm, nation) can.

Economic Insight

The Importance of Private Property Rights

There are many real-life cases showing the importance of property rights in the behavior and standards of living of people. In Korea, those who have lived under private property rights and economic freedom (South Korea) have flourished economically relative to those grinding out tough lives under a despotic regime that allows no freedom and no private property (North Korea). Korea was occupied by Japan from 1905 until it was divided into two countries following World War II. North Korea retained a strong version of communism and totalitarianism, while South Korea slowly moved in the direction of private property rights and, eventually, political democracy. The differences in economic growth and changes in standards of living during the past thirty years are astounding. North Korea is mired in poverty, unable to feed its population. The economy is in such shambles that over two million people have starved to death and more than 60 percent of the children are malnourished. South Koreans enjoy a standard of living far higher than that of North Korea.

In Buenos Aires, Argentina, a group of squatters organized by a Catholic chapel took over some vacant land as their residences.[1] Some of the squatters were able to obtain property rights while others were not. After about twenty years, the differences between the lives of those with property rights and those without were substantial. Those with property rights invested in their properties, while those without property rights did not. The result was that there is a significant difference in housing quality between the owned and unowned properties. The owned properties were upgraded, expanded, and improved. The unowned properties were run down, crumbling shanties. The really amazing thing though is that those with ownership behaved so differently than those without ownership: They had fewer children and the children acquired more education and had better health. Why does a title make a difference?

The problem with a lack of property rights or a system in which property rights are not secure and established is that people can not use the property for collateral or cannot expect to get anything back if they invest in the property.

In the 1930s, the Finns and Estonians enjoyed a similar standard of living. The two countries are virtually neighbors. Their languages share a common linguistic root, they are culturally similar, and share many values. In 2000, the average Finn earned two and a half times to more than seven times what the average Estonian earned. Fifty years of Communist rule surely had something to do with the gap in incomes that opened between the two countries. In the past, substantial differences existed between the standard of living in East and West Germany—two countries with essentially the same resources, education, culture, language, religion, history, and geography. Despite its own recent economic miracle, China's real per-capita GDP in 2000 was still just under $4,000. Taiwan's is over $17,000, more than four times China's.[2] In each of these comparisons, culture, language, and traditions are the same. Outcomes are markedly different. The countries with private property rights grew richer; the others faltered or went backwards.

[1] See the study by Sebastian Galiani and Ernesto Schargrodsky, "Property Rights for the Poor: Effects of Land Titling", Coase Institute Working Paper, August 9, 2005, for a complete discussion of this and other issues related to the Argentine case.
[2] Gerald P. O'Driscoll Jr. and Lee Hoskins, "Property Rights: The Key to Economic Development," Policy Analysis No. 482, Cato Institute, August 7, 2003

4. Specialization and trade enable individuals, firms, and nations to get more than they could without specialization and trade. This is called *gains from trade*.

5. Private property rights are necessary for voluntary trade to develop. Private property rights refer to the laws, courts, and police required to enforce the prohibition of theft and murder.

SUMMARY

1 | What are opportunity costs? Are they part of the economic way of thinking?

- Opportunity costs are the forgone opportunities of the next best alternative. Choice means both gaining something and giving up something. When you choose one option, you forgo all others. The benefits of the next best alternative are the opportunity costs of your choice. *§1*

2 | What is a production possibilities curve?

- A production possibilities curve represents the trade-offs involved in the allocation of scarce resources. It shows the maximum quantity of goods and services that can be produced using limited resources to the fullest extent possible. *§1.b*

3 | Why does specialization occur?

- Comparative advantage accounts for specialization. We specialize in the activities in which we have the

lowest opportunity costs, that is, in which we have a comparative advantage. *§2.c*

4 | What are the benefits of trade?

- Voluntary trade enables people to get more than they could get by doing everything themselves. The amount they get by specializing and trading is called gains from trade. *§2.b*
- Specialization and trade enable those involved to acquire more than they could if they did not specialize and engage in trade. *§2.c*
- Private property rights are necessary for voluntary trade to occur. Private property rights refer to the legal system that ensures that people own their persons and their property. Others cannot steal that property or harm that person. *§2.d*

KEY TERMS

opportunity costs §1

tradeoff *§1.a*

production possibilities curve (PPC) *§1.b*

marginal cost *§2.a*

marginal opportunity cost *§2.a*

gains from trade *§2.b*

comparative advantage *§2.c*

private property rights *§2.d*

EXERCISES

1. In most political campaigns, candidates promise more than they can deliver. In the United States, both Democrats and Republicans promise better health care, a better environment, only minor reductions in defense, better education, and an improved system of roads, bridges, sewer systems, water systems, and so on. What economic concept do candidates ignore?

2. Janine is an accountant who makes $30,000 a year. Robert is a college student who makes $8,000 a year. All other things being equal, who is more likely to stand in a long line to get a concert ticket? Explain.

3. In 2009, President Barack Obama and Congress enacted a budget that included increases in spending for the war in Iraq and national defense, as well as huge increases in welfare programs, education, and many other programs. The budget expenditures

exceeded the revenues by over a trillion dollars. The argument was that "we need these things," and therefore there is no limit to what the government should provide. Is there a limit? What concept is ignored by those politicians who claim that there is no limit to what the government should provide?

4. The following numbers measure the tradeoff between grades and income:

Total Hours	Hours Studying	GPA	Hours Working	Income
60	60	4.0	0	$0
60	40	3.0	20	$100
60	30	2.0	30	$150
60	10	1.0	50	$250
60	0	0.0	60	$300

a. Calculate the opportunity cost of an increase in the number of hours spent studying in order to earn a 3.0 grade point average (GPA) rather than a 2.0 GPA.

b. Is the opportunity cost the same for a move from a 0.0 GPA to a 1.0 GPA as it is for a move from a 1.0 GPA to a 2.0 GPA?

c. What is the opportunity cost of an increase in income from $100 to $150?

5. Suppose a second individual has the following tradeoffs between income and grades:

Total Hours	Hours Studying	GPA	Hours Working	Income
60	50	4.0	10	$60
60	40	3.0	20	$120
60	20	2.0	40	$240
60	10	1.0	50	$300
60	0	0.0	60	$360

a. Define comparative advantage.

b. Does either individual (the one in exercise 4 or the one in exercise 5) have a comparative advantage in both activities?

c. Who should specialize in studying and who should specialize in working?

6. A doctor earns $250,000 per year, while a professor earns $40,000. They play tennis against each other each Saturday morning, each giving up a morning of relaxing, reading the paper, and playing with their children. They could each decide to work a few extra hours on Saturday and earn more income. But they choose to play tennis or to relax around the house. Are their opportunity costs of playing tennis different?

7. Plot the PPC of a nation given by the following data.

Combination	Health Care	All Other Goods
A	0	100
B	25	90
C	50	70
D	75	40
E	100	0

a. Calculate the marginal opportunity cost of each combination.

b. What is the opportunity cost of combination C?

c. Suppose a second nation has the following data. Plot the PPC, and then determine which nation has the comparative advantage in which activity. Show whether the two nations can gain from specialization and trade.

Combination	Health Care	All Other Goods
A	0	50
B	20	40
C	40	25
D	60	5
E	65	0

8. A doctor earns $200 per hour, a plumber $40 per hour, and a professor $20 per hour. Everything else the same, which one will devote more hours to negotiating the price of a new car? Explain.

9. Perhaps you've heard of the old saying, "There is no such thing as a free lunch." What does it mean? If someone invites you to a lunch and offers to pay for it, is it free to you?

10. You have waited 30 minutes in a line for the Star Tours ride at Disneyland. You see a sign that says, "From this point on, your wait is 45 minutes." You must decide whether to remain in the line or to move elsewhere. On what basis do you make the decision? Do the 30 minutes you've already stood in line come into play?

11. A university is deciding between two meal plans. One plan charges a fixed fee of $600 per semester and allows students to eat as much as they want. The other plan charges a fee based on the quantity of food consumed. Under which plan will students eat the most?

12. Evaluate this statement: "You are a natural athlete, an attractive person who learns easily and communicates well. Clearly, you can do everything better than your friends and acquaintances. As a result, the term *specialization* has no meaning for you. Specialization would cost you rather than benefit you."

13. During China's Cultural Revolution in the late 1960s and early 1970s, highly educated people were forced to move to farms and work in the fields. Some were common laborers for eight or more years. What does this policy say about specialization and the PPC? Would you predict that the policy would lead to an increase in output?

14. In elementary school and through middle school, most students have the same teacher throughout the day and for the entire school year. Then, beginning in high school, different subjects are taught by different teachers. In college, the same subject is often

taught at different levels—freshman, sophomore, junior-senior, or graduate—by different faculty. Is education taking advantage of specialization only from high school on? Comment on the differences between elementary school and college and the use of specialization.

15. The top officials in the federal government and high-ranking officers of large corporations often have chauffeurs to drive them around the city or from meeting to meeting. Is this simply one of the perquisites of their position, or is the use of chauffeurs justifiable on the basis of comparative advantage?

16. In Botswana, Zimbabwe, and South Africa, individuals can own and farm elephants. In other African countries, the elephants are put on large reserves. Explain why the elephant population in Botswana, Zimbabwe, and South Africa has risen, whereas that in the rest of Africa has fallen.

You can find further practice tests in the Online Quiz at **www.cengage.com/economics/boyes**.

Venezuela's Chavez Urges Cooperation from Ranchers amid Land Reform

Associated Press World Stream **September 23, 2005**

Venezuelan President Hugo Chavez has urged large land owners to cooperate with his government as it pushes ahead with a land reform despite concerns over property rights.

Speaking to government supporters organized into cooperatives, Chavez said: "Whoever doesn't want to cooperate, well, we will apply full weight of the law . . . we are moving forward on the path to socialism."

Business leaders accuse authorities of illegally seizing lands without giving farmers and ranchers an opportunity to prove ownership. Under a 2001 law, the government can seize lands if they are declared idle or if legitimate ownership cannot be proved as far back as 1847.

Land owners have complained that officials of Venezuela's National Lands Institute have unfairly seized their property, but Chavez responded by telling them "to stop squealing."

Authorities have declared at least 21 cattle ranches state property, because they were allegedly "idle" or those who claimed ownership couldn't prove it.

Chavez's administration has helped poor farmers to start to work the lands.

"It's about opening small spaces for socialism," Chavez told supporters inside a packed auditorium. "We are preparing for a period of post-capitalism."

In recent months, government officials accompanied by troops have arrived at dozens of ranches or opened investigations into others across the country.

The president was granting government loans totaling 2.7 billion bolivars (US$1.3 million, €1.06 million) to poor Venezuelans who will be raising cattle and growing crops such as coffee.

Chavez, a close ally of Cuban leader Fidel Castro, says he is leading this oil-rich South American nation toward "21st-century socialism" as part of a "revolution" to help improve living conditions for the poor.

Government opponents claim Chavez is steering Venezuela, the world's fifth largest oil exporter, toward Cuba-style communism.

Business leader Rafael Alfonzo urged Venezuelans who support Chavez's policies "to wake up," and warned that poverty-stricken citizens would remain poor if private property rights are not respected.

Chavez "wants to establish a regime in which the state is the only property owner, and you will be.... eating only what the government wants you to eat," Alfonzo told the local Globovision television channel.

"I'm talking to businessmen, house wives, shop owners and politicians, wake up! If you don't do it now, it will be too late," added Alfonzo.

Chavez fiercely criticized capitalism, saying it only leads to "misery for the majority" and will eventually endanger the survival of the human race.

Chavez, former paratroop commander, has rejected allegations that he is becoming authoritarian. He claims that his political movement is "deeply democratic" and that Venezuelans will keep him in power through elections until 2013.

Christopher Toothaker

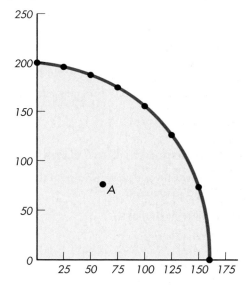

There is a story that goes something like this: Everybody, Somebody, Anybody, and Nobody were faced with an important task. Everybody was sure that Somebody would do it. Anybody could have done it, but Nobody did it. Somebody got angry about that because it was Everybody's job. Everybody thought Anybody could do it. But Nobody realized that Everybody wouldn't do it. The end result was that Everybody blamed Somebody when Nobody did what Anybody could have.

The story points out that if you own something, you have an incentive to take care of it. When no one owns something or when everyone owns something, no one has an incentive to take care of it. That is what private property rights are all about: They ensure individual ownership. When all housing in China's major cities was owned by the government, the houses and apartments were not taken care of. Similarly, in the projects of the large cities in the eastern United States, where apartments are owned by the government, no one has an incentive to ensure that the housing is cared for. But, as soon as China allowed some private ownership of apartments, the improvements were amazing—clean hallways, lighted hallways, and improvements in the buildings. When the projects are sold to private owners, the apartments are improved and cared for.

The PPC shows combinations of two goods, services, or activities that people can devote their resources to producing. Points along the curve are all possible combinations of two goods that can be produced using an individual's resources fully and efficiently. If you can own what you create, you have an incentive to produce somewhere along the PPC. But, if you don't own what you create, why should you worry about whether you are using resources efficiently or fully? You will operate at a point inside the PPC, such as point *A*. You will produce less than you are capable of producing.

Not only will you produce less, but you will not have an incentive to specialize and trade. Since you don't own what you create, you don't care whether what you produce is in accordance with comparative advantage. There is nothing to trade because you own nothing. This is the situation toward which Venezuela is being driven by Hugo Chavez. According to the article, Chavez's administration has helped poor farmers start to work the lands.

"'It's about opening small spaces for socialism,' Chavez told supporters inside a packed auditorium." The problem is not that the poor farmers have no place to work, it is that they own nothing. Over 75 percent of the population in most Latin American nations do not hold title to the property on which their houses rest or the fields in which they labor. Without ownership, the poor farmers have no incentive to improve the property. It is no different for the large rich landowners—when they do not own their property, they have no incentive to take care of it. The direction in which Chavez is taking Venezuela is the direction in which Castro took Cuba, Mao took China, and Lenin, Stalin, and others took Russia. The result is a shrinking PPC and a reduction in standards of living.

Chapter 3

© Olga Chernetskaya & Leonid Yastremsky/

Markets, Demand and Supply, and the Price System

Fundamental Questions

1 | How do we decide who gets the scarce goods and resources?

2 | What is demand?

3 | What is supply?

4 | How is price determined by demand and supply?

5 | What causes price to change?

6 | What happens when price is not allowed to change with market forces?

People (and firms and nations) can get more if they specialize in certain activities and then trade with one another to acquire the goods and services that they desire than they can if they do everything themselves. This is what we described in the previous chapter as gains from trade. But how does everyone get together to trade? Who decides who specializes in what, and who determines who gets what?

In some countries, the government decides who gets what and what is produced. In India until the mid-1990s, in the Soviet Union from 1917 until 1989, and in Cuba, Venezuela, and Cameroon and other African nations today, a few government officials dictate what is produced, by whom it is produced, where it is produced, what price it sells at, and who may buy it.

In most developed or industrial nations, government officials dictate what, how, for whom, and at what price certain things are produced, but for most goods and

A market arises when buyers and sellers exchange a well-defined good or service. In the case of a supermarket like this one, buyers purchase groceries and household items. The market occurs in a building at a specific location.

© Monkey business/Dreamstime LLC

services, private individuals decide. When you walk into your local Starbucks to get a tall coffee, do you wonder who told the people working there to work there or who told the coffee growers to send their coffee beans to this particular Starbucks, or who told the bakery to provide this Starbucks with croissants? Probably not. Most of us take all these things for granted. Yet, it is a remarkable phenomenon—we get what we want, when we want it, and where we want it. How does this work? It is the market process; no one dictates what is produced, how it is produced, the price at which it sells, or who buys it. All this occurs through the self-interested behavior of individuals interacting in a **market**.

market: a place or service that enables buyers and sellers to exchange goods and services

The term "market" refers to the interaction of buyers and sellers. A market may be a specific location, such as the supermarket, or it may be the exchange of particular goods or services at many different locations, such as the foreign exchange market. A market makes possible the exchange of goods and services. It may be a formally organized exchange, such as the New York Stock Exchange, or it may be loosely organized, like the market for used bicycles or automobiles. A market may be confined to one location, as in the case of a supermarket, or it may encompass a city, a state, a country, or the entire world.

In this chapter we discuss the allocation of goods and services—how it is determined what is produced and who gets what.

A market arises when buyers and sellers exchange a well-defined good or service. In this case, shoppers at a market can examine the day's assortment and make their choices. The flower market does not occur at a specific location nor in a fixed building.

© Dennis Albert Richardson/Shutterstock

■ 1. Allocation Systems

1 | How do we decide who gets the scarce goods and resources?

An allocation system is the process of determining who gets the goods and services and who doesn't. There are many different allocation systems that we might use. One is to have someone, say the government, determine who gets what, as in Cuba or Cameroon. Another is to have a first-come, first-served system, where those who arrive first get the goods and services. A third is to have a lottery, with the lucky winners getting the goods and services. A fourth is the market or price system, where those with the incomes are able to buy the goods and services. Which is best? Take the quiz on the next page, and then we'll discuss allocation systems some more.

1.a. Fairness

How did you respond to the four questions in each scenario? If you are like most people, you believe that the price on the bottles of water ought to be raised and that the first patients showing up at the doctor's office ought to get service. Very few believe that the price or the market ought to be used to allocate important items like health care. Most claim that the price system is not fair. Yet none of the allocation approaches is "fair" if fairness means that everyone gets what he or she wants. In every case, someone gets the good or service and someone does not. This is what scarcity is all about—there is not enough to go around. With the market system, it is those without income or wealth who must do without. Is this fair? No. Under the first-come, first-served system, it is those who arrive later who do without. This isn't fair either, since those who are slow, old, disabled, or otherwise not first to arrive won't get the goods and services. Under the government scheme, it is those who are not in favor or those who do not match up with the government's rules who do without. In the former Soviet Union, Cuba, Cameroon, and other government-run countries, it is the government officials who get most of the goods and services, through what we call corruption, graft, and bribes. And, with a random procedure, it is those who do not have the lucky ticket or the correct number who are left out.

None of these allocation systems is fair in the sense that no one gets left out. Scarcity means that someone gets left out. Only if your measure of fair is equal

---

Allocation Quiz

I. At a sightseeing point reachable only after a strenuous hike, a firm has established a stand where bottled water is sold. The water, carried in by the employees of the firm, is sold to thirsty hikers in six-ounce bottles. The price is $1 per bottle. Typically only 100 bottles of the water are sold each day. On a particularly hot day, however, 200 hikers each want to buy at least one bottle of water. Indicate what you think of each of the following means of distributing the water to the hikers by responding to each allocation approach with one of the following five responses:
a. Agree completely
b. Agree with slight reservation
c. Disagree
d. Strongly disagree
e. Totally unacceptable

1. Increasing the price until the quantity of bottles of water that hikers are willing and able to purchase exactly equals the number of bottles available for sale
2. Selling the water for $1 per bottle on a first-come, first-served basis
3. Having the local authority (government) buy the water for $1 per bottle and distribute it according to its own judgment
4. Selling the water for $1 per bottle following a random selection procedure or lottery

II. A physician has been providing medical services at a fee of $100 per patient and typically sees 30 patients per day. One day the flu bug has been so vicious that the number of patients attempting to visit the physician exceeds 60. Indicate what you think of each of the following means of distributing the physician's services to the sick patients by responding with one of the following five answers:
a. Agree completely
b. Agree with slight reservation
c. Disagree
d. Strongly disagree
e. Totally unacceptable

1. Raising the price until the number of patients the doctor sees is exactly equal to the number of patients who are willing and able to pay the doctor's fee
2. Selling the services for $100 per patient on a first-come, first-served basis
3. Having the local authority (government) pay the physician $100 per patient and choose who is to receive the services according to its own judgment
4. Selling the physician's services for $100 per patient following a random selection procedure or lottery

---

opportunity is the lottery system fair. When everything is allocated by lottery, everyone has an equal chance of winning.

1.b. Incentives

Since each allocation mechanism is unfair, how do we decide which to use? One way might be by the incentives that each creates. Do the incentives lead to behavior that will improve things, increase supplies, and raise standards of living?

With the first-come, first-served allocation scheme, the incentive is to be first. You have no reason to improve the quality of your products or to increase the value of your resources. There is no incentive to increase the amounts of goods and services supplied. Why would anyone produce when all everyone wants is to be first? As a result, with a first-come, first-served allocation system, growth will not occur, and standards of living will not rise. A society based solely on first-come, first-served would die a quick death.

A government scheme provides an incentive either to be a member of government and thus help determine the allocation rules or to do exactly what the government orders you to do. There are no incentives to improve production and efficiency or to increase the quantities supplied, and thus there is no reason for the economy to grow. This type of system is a failure, as evidenced by the Soviet Union, Mao Tse-Tung's China, Cuba, and socialist systems in Latin America and Africa and in virtually every poor country in the world.

The random allocation provides no incentives at all—you simply hope that manna from heaven falls on you.

With the market system, the incentive is to acquire purchasing ability—to obtain income and wealth. This means that you must provide goods that have high value to others and provide resources that have high value to producers—to enhance your worth as an employee by acquiring education or training, and to enhance the value of the resources you own.

The market system also provides incentives for quantities of scarce goods to increase. In the case of the water stand in Scenario I, if the price of the water increases and the owner of the water stand is earning significant profits, others may carry or truck water to the top of the hill and sell it to thirsty hikers; the amount of water available thus increases. In the case of the doctor in Scenario II, other doctors may think that opening an office near the first might be a way to earn more; the amount of physician services available increases. Since the market system creates the incentive for the amount supplied to increase, economies grow and expand, and standards of living improve. The market system also ensures that resources are allocated to where they are most highly valued. If the price of an item rises, consumers may switch to another item, or another good or service, that can serve about the same purpose. When consumers switch, production of the alternative good rises, and thus the resources used in its production must increase as well. As a result, resources are reallocated from lower-valued uses to higher-valued uses.

1.c. The Market Process: Arbitrage

When the Mazda Miata was introduced in the United States in 1990, the little sports roadster was an especially desired product in southern California. As shown in Figure 1, the suggested retail price was $13,996, the price at which it was selling in Detroit. In Los Angeles, the purchase price was nearly $25,000. Several entrepreneurs recognized the profit potential in the $10,000 price differential and sent hundreds of students to Detroit to pick up Miatas and drive them back to Los Angeles. Within a reasonably short time, the price differential between Detroit and Los Angeles was reduced. The increased sales in Detroit drove the price there up, while the increased number of Miatas being sold in Los Angeles reduced the price there. The price differential continued to decline until it was less than the cost of shipping the cars from Detroit to Los Angeles. This story of the Mazda Miata illustrates how markets work to allocate scarce goods, services, and resources. A product is purchased where its price is low and sold where its price is high. As a result, resources devoted to that product flow to where they have the highest value. The same type of situation occurred with the introduction of the Mini Cooper

| FIGURE 1 | Production Possibilities Curve |

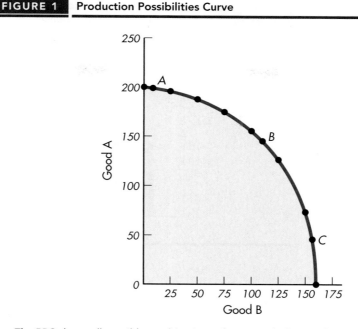

The PPC shows all possible combinations of two goods that can be produced, given that resources are fully and efficiently used. The exact point on the curve where a country produces depends on consumers—what they are willing and able to purchase.

in 2001. The car was selling for much more in California than in New York and Chicago, so people purchased the car in Chicago or New York and had the cars shipped to California.

Suppose an electronics firm is inefficient, its employees are surly, and its products are not displayed well. To attempt to earn a profit, the firm charges more than the efficiently run firm down the street. Where do customers go? Obviously, they seek out the best deal and go to the more efficient firm. The more efficient store has to get more supplies, hire more employees, acquire more space, and so on. The inefficient store lays off employees, sells used equipment, and gets rid of its inventory. The resources thus go from where they were not as highly valued to where they are most highly valued.

Why does the market process work? For a very simple reason: People are looking for the best deal—the highest-quality products at the lowest prices. So when an opportunity for a "best deal" arises, people respond to it by purchasing where the price is low and selling where the price is high.

As long as the market is free to change, it will ensure that resources are allocated to where they have the highest value and people get what they want at the lowest price. But what happens if something interferes with the market process? Each year *The Economist* magazine[1] publishes its Big Mac Index. This index lists the price of a Big Mac in many different countries. Adjusting for different currencies, one year the index looked something like Figure 2.

What do you bright entrepreneurs see? That's right—an arbitrage opportunity: You could load up a Boeing 747 with Big Macs in Phoenix and fly to Tokyo

[1] http://www.economist.com/markets/indicators/displaystory.cfm?story_id=12991434, accessed January 22, 2009.

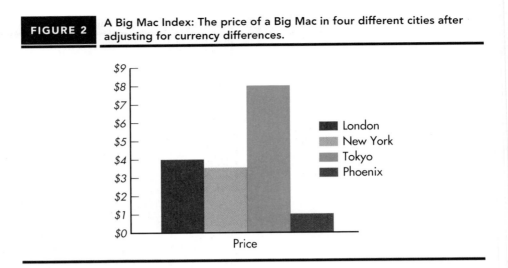

FIGURE 2 A Big Mac Index: The price of a Big Mac in four different cities after adjusting for currency differences.

and sell the Big Macs for a nice profit. The larger supply in Tokyo would reduce the Tokyo price, and the greater demand in Phoenix would raise the price there. Why does that not happen? Part of the reason might be that the food is not portable; it deteriorates in the airplane. Another reason is that regulations would not allow it: Japan would not allow someone to simply land on the tarmac and beginning selling Big Macs out of a cargo hold. Arbitrage in the movement of Big Macs does not take place. So, when something interferes with the market process, resources do not go to where they are most highly valued, and consumers don't get what they want at the lowest prices.

RECAP

1. Scarce goods and resources can be allocated in many different ways. Four common approaches are first-come-first-serve, prices, government, and random.

2. No allocation mechanism is fair in the sense that everyone gets everything they want. This would defy the idea of scarcity. Some people will get the goods and resources and others will not.

3. The incentives each allocation system creates is a fundamental reason that markets are selected to do the allocation. Only a market system creates the incentives that lead to increasing standards of living.

■ 2. Markets and Money

The market process refers to the way that scarce goods and services are allocated through the individual actions of buyers and sellers. The price adjusts to the actions of buyers and sellers so as to ensure that resources are used where they have the highest value—the price of the Miata in L.A. declines as more Miata's end up in L.A. The price measures the opportunity cost—how much has to be given up in order to get something else. If you pay a dollar for a cup of coffee, then the opportunity cost of that coffee is everything else that dollar could have been used to buy. In most cases, when you buy something you exchange money for that something. There are cases where you actually exchange one good for another—you might mow someone's lawn in exchange for them taking care of your house while you are on vacation. Every market exchange is not necessarily a monetary exchange.

2.a. Barter and Money Exchanges

barter: the direct exchange of goods and services without the use of money

The purpose of markets is to facilitate the exchange of goods and services between buyers and sellers. In some cases, money changes hands; in others, only goods and services are exchanged. Recall from the previous chapter that the cost (price) of something is what must be given up to acquire a unit of that something. If the price of a gallon of milk is $2, then the cost of that gallon of milk is whatever would have been purchased with that $2. Suppose that the $2 would have been used to purchase one piece of chocolate cake. Then we could say that the cost of a gallon of milk is one piece of chocolate cake. If we simply exchanged a gallon of milk for the piece of cake, we would be engaging in **barter**. The exchange of goods and services directly, without money, is called barter. Barter occurs when a plumber fixes a leaky pipe for a lawyer in exchange for the lawyer's work on a will or when a Chinese citizen provides fresh vegetables to a U.S. visitor in exchange for a pack of U.S. cigarettes.

double coincidence of wants: the situation that exists when A has what B wants and B has what A wants

Most markets involve money because goods and services can be exchanged more easily with money than without it. When IBM purchases microchips from Yakamoto of Japan, IBM and Yakamoto don't exchange goods directly. Neither firm may have what the other wants. Barter requires a **double coincidence of wants**: IBM must have what Yakamoto wants, and Yakamoto must have what IBM wants. The difficulty of finding a double coincidence of wants for barter transactions is typically very high. Using money makes trading easier. To obtain the microchips, all IBM has to do is provide dollars to Yakamoto. Yakamoto is willing to accept the money, since it can spend that money to obtain the goods that it wants.

RECAP

1. Barter refers to exchanges made without the use of money.

2. Money makes it easier and less expensive to exchange goods and services.

2 | What is demand?

■ 3. Demand

A market is demand and supply—buyers and sellers. To understand how a price level is determined and why a price rises or falls, it is necessary to know how demand and supply function. We begin by considering demand alone, then supply, and then we put the two together. Before we begin, we discuss some economic terminology that is often confusing.

demand: the amount of a product that people are willing and able to purchase at each possible price during a given period of time, everything else held constant

Economists distinguish between the terms **demand** and **quantity demanded**. When they refer to the *quantity demanded,* they are talking about the amount of a product that people are willing and able to purchase at a *specific* price. When they refer to *demand,* they are talking about the amount that people would be willing and able to purchase at *every possible* price. Demand is the quantities demanded at every price. Thus, the statement that "the demand for U.S. white wine rose following an increase in the price of French white wine" means that at each price for U.S. white wine, more people were willing and able to purchase U.S. white wine. And the statement that "the quantity demanded of white wine

quantity demanded: the amount of a product that people are willing and able to purchase at a specific price fell as the price of white wine rose" means that people were willing and able to purchase less white wine because the price of the wine rose.

3.a. The Law of Demand

Consumers and merchants know that if you lower the price of a good or service without altering its quality or quantity, people will beat a path to your doorway. This simple truth is referred to as the **law of demand**.

According to the law of demand, people purchase more of something when the price of that item falls. More formally, the law of demand states that the quantity of some item that people are willing and able to purchase during a particular period of time decreases as the price rises, and vice versa.

The more formal definition of the law of demand can be broken down into five phrases:

1. The quantity of a well-defined good or service that
2. people are willing and able to purchase
3. during a particular period of time
4. decreases as the price of that good or service rises and increases as the price falls,
5. everything else held constant.

law of demand: the quantity of a well-defined good or service that people are willing and able to purchase during a particular period of time decreases as the price of that good or service rises and increases as the price falls, everything else held constant

The first phrase ensures that we are referring to the same item, that we are not mixing different goods. A watch is a commodity that is defined and distinguished from other goods by several characteristics: quality, color, and design of the watch face, to name a few. The law of demand applies to a well-defined good, in this case, a watch. If one of the characteristics should change, the good would no longer be well defined—in fact, it would be a different good. A Rolex watch is different from a Timex watch; Polo brand golf shirts are different goods from generic brand golf shirts; Mercedes-Benz automobiles are different goods from Saturn automobiles.

The second phrase indicates that not only must people *want* to purchase some good, but they must be *able* to purchase that good in order for their wants to be counted as part of demand. For example, Sue would love to buy a membership in the Paradise Valley Country Club, but because the membership costs $35,000, she is not able to purchase the membership. Though she is willing, she is not able. At a price of $5,000, however, she is willing and able to purchase the membership.

The third phrase points out that the demand for any good is defined for a specific period of time. Without reference to a time period, a demand relationship would not make any sense. For instance, the statement that "at a price of $3 per Happy Meal, 13 million Happy Meals are demanded" provides no useful information. Are the 13 million meals sold in one week or one year? Think of demand as a rate of purchase at each possible price over a period of time—2 per month, 1 per day, and so on.

The fourth phrase points out that price and quantity demanded move in opposite directions; that is, as the price rises, the quantity demanded falls, and as the price falls, the quantity demanded rises.

determinants of demand: factors other than the price of the good that influence demand—income, tastes, prices of related goods and services, expectations, and number of buyers

Demand is a measure of the relationship between the price and quantity demanded of a particular good or service when the determinants of demand do not change. The **determinants of demand** are income, tastes, prices of related goods and services, expectations, and the number of buyers. If any one of these items changes, demand changes. The final phrase, everything else held constant, ensures that the determinants of demand do not change.

3.b. The Demand Schedule

A **demand schedule** is a table or list of prices and the corresponding quantities demanded for a particular good or service. Consider the demand for access time to online games. Console games made their debut in the 1970s, but it has been in the first decade of this century in which the growth of online games or interactive console games have really exploded. There are different formats and ways to download games and access networks, but let us deal with a simple setting wherein you can purchase access to a network featuring games such as World of Warcraft on a weekly basis. The table in Figure 3 is a demand schedule for hours of access to the games. It shows the number of hours per week that a consumer named Bob would be willing and able to buy at each price during a month, everything else held constant. As the price of the access time gets higher relative to the prices of other goods, Bob would be willing and able to purchase fewer access hours.

At a price of $5 per hour, Bob indicates that he will purchase only ten hours during the week. At a price of $4, Bob tells us that he will purchase twenty hours during the week. As the price drops from $5 to $4 to $3 to $2 and to $1, Bob is willing and able to purchase more access time. At a price of $1, Bob would purchase fifty hours of access for the week.

3.c. The Demand Curve

A **demand curve** is a graph of the demand schedule. The demand curve shown in Figure 3 is plotted from the information given in the demand schedule. The price per hour of access time (price per unit) is measured on the vertical axis, and the number of hours of access per week (quantity per unit of time) is measured on the horizontal axis. The demand curve slopes downward because of the inverse relationship between the price and the quantity that Bob is willing and able to purchase. Point *A* in Figure 3 corresponds to combination *A* in the table: a price of $5 and ten hours per week demanded. Similarly, points *B, C, D,* and *E* in Figure 3 represent the corresponding combinations in the table. The line connecting these points is Bob's demand curve for hours of access to a network game.

All demand curves slope down because of the law of demand: As price falls, quantity demanded increases. The demand curves for bread, electricity, automobiles, colleges, labor services, health care, and any other good or service you can think of slope down. You might be saying to yourself, "That's not true. When the price of some rock concerts goes up, more people want to attend the concert. As the ticket price goes up, going to the concert becomes more prestigious, and the quantity demanded actually rises." To avoid confusion in such circumstances, we say "everything else held constant." With this statement, we are assuming that tastes don't change and that, therefore, the goods *cannot* become more prestigious as the price changes. Similarly, we do not allow the quality or the brand name of a product to change as we define the demand schedule or demand curve. We concentrate on the one quality or the one brand; so when we say that the price of a good has risen, we are talking about a good that is identical at all prices.

3.d. From Individual Demand Curves to a Market Curve

Bob's demand curve for hours of access to a network game is plotted in Figure 3. Unless Bob is the only person who plays the game, his demand curve is not the total or market demand curve. Market demand is derived by adding up the quantities that everyone is willing and able to purchase at each price—the sum

| FIGURE 3 | Bob's Demand Schedule and Demand Curve for Hours of Access per Week |

Combination	Price per Hour (constant quality units)	Quantity Demanded per Week (constant quality units)
A	$5	10
B	$4	20
C	$3	30
D	$2	40
E	$1	50

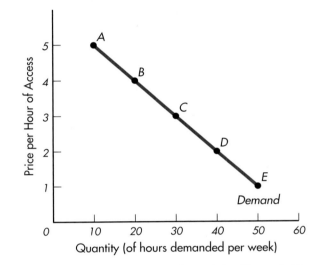

The number of hours of access to online games that Bob is willing and able to buy at each price during the week is listed in the table, or demand schedule. The demand curve is derived from the combinations given in the demand schedule. The price-quantity combination of $5 per hour and 10 hours is point A. The combination of $4 per hour and 20 hours is point B. Each combination is plotted, and the points are connected to form the demand curve.

of all individual demands. The market demand curve is the horizontal sum of all individual demand curves of all consumers in the market. The table in Figure 4 lists the demand schedules of three individuals, Bob, Maria, and Liu. If these three were the only consumers in the market, then the market demand would be the sum of their individual demands, shown as the last column of the table.

Bob's, Maria's, and Liu's demand schedules are plotted as individual demand curves in Figure 4(a). In Figure 4(b), their individual demand curves have been added together to obtain the market demand curve for hours of access per week to a network game. (Notice that we add in a horizontal direction—that is, we add the quantities at each price, not the prices at each quantity.) At a price of $5, we add the quantity that Bob would be willing and able to buy, 10, to the quantity that Maria would be willing and able buy, 5, to the quantity that Liu would be willing and able buy, 15, to get the market quantity demanded of 30. At a price of $4, we add the quantities that each of the consumers is willing and able to buy to get the total quantity demanded of 48. At all prices, then, we add the quantities demanded by each individual consumer to get the total, or market quantity, demanded.

FIGURE 4 The Market Demand Schedule and Demand Curve

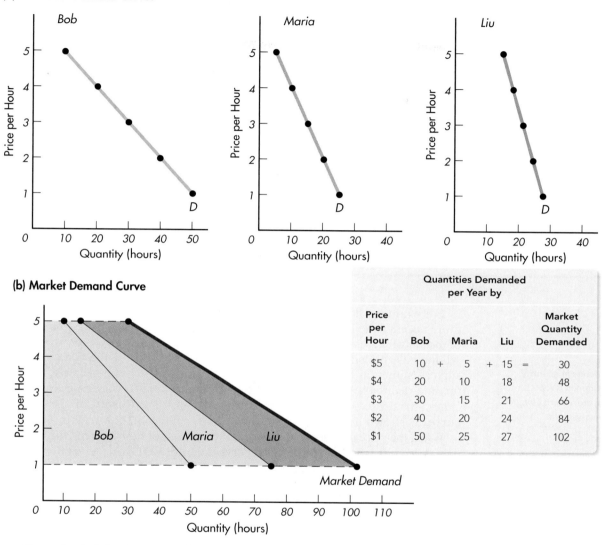

(a) Individual Demand Curves

(b) Market Demand Curve

Price per Hour	Quantities Demanded per Year by			
	Bob	Maria	Liu	Market Quantity Demanded
$5	10 +	5 +	15 =	30
$4	20	10	18	48
$3	30	15	21	66
$2	40	20	24	84
$1	50	25	27	102

The market is defined to consist of three individuals: Bob, Maria, and Liu. Their demand schedules are listed in the table and plotted as the individual demand curves shown in Figure 4(a). By adding the quantities that each demands at every price, we obtain the market demand curve shown in Figure 4(b). At a price of $1, we add Bob's quantity demanded of 50 to Maria's quantity demanded of 25 to Liu's quantity demanded of 27 to obtain the market quantity demanded of 102. At a price of $2, we add Bob's 40 to Maria's 20 to Liu's 24 to obtain the market quantity demanded of 84. To obtain the market demand curve, for every price we sum the quantities demanded by each market participant.

3.e. Changes in Demand and Changes in Quantity Demanded

A change in demand is represented by a shift of the demand curve.

When one of the determinants of demand—income, tastes, prices of related goods, expectations, or number of buyers—is allowed to change, the demand for a good or service changes as well. What does it mean to say that demand changes? Demand is the entire demand schedule, or demand curve. When we say that demand changes, we are referring to a change in the quantities demanded at each and every price.

FIGURE 5   An Increase and a Decrease in Demand

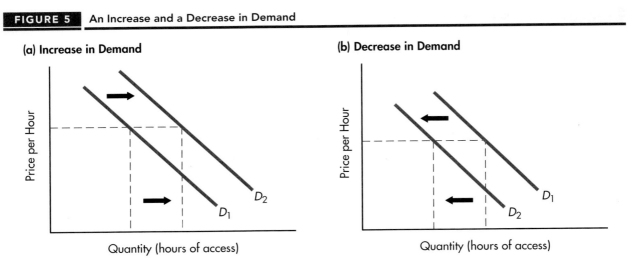

(a) Increase in Demand

(b) Decrease in Demand

In Figure 5(a), an increase in demand occurs due to an increase in income. The consumer is willing and able to purchase more at every price. This change is expressed as a rightward shift of the demand curve from D_1 to D_2. Figure 5(b) shows a decrease in demand due to a decrease in income. The consumer is willing to purchase less at every price. This is illustrated as a leftward shift of demand from D_1 to D_2.

For example, if Bob's income rises, then he is willing and able to purchase more access time for the network game. At each and every price, the number of hours of access time that Bob is willing and able to buy each week rises. An increase in demand is expressed by a rightward shift of the demand curve, such as shown in Figure 5(a) in the move from D_1 to D_2. Conversely, if Bob's income declined, then he would be willing and able to purchase less access time. This decrease in demand is expressed as a leftward shift of the demand curve, as shown in Figure 5(b) in the move from D_1 to D_2.

> A change in quantity demanded is represented by a movement along one demand curve.

When the price of a good or service is the only factor that changes, the quantity demanded changes, but the demand curve does not shift. Instead, as the price of the access time is decreased (increased), everything else held constant, the quantity that people are willing and able to purchase increases (decreases). This change is merely a movement from one point on the demand curve to another point on the same demand curve, not a shift of the demand curve. A *change in the quantity demanded* is the phrase that economists use to describe the change in the quantities of a particular good or service that people are willing and able to purchase as the price of that good or service changes. A change in the quantity demanded, from point A to point B on the demand curve, is shown in Figure 6(b). Compare this to a change in demand illustrated by the shift of the entire curve as shown in Figure 6(a).

The demand curve shifts when income, tastes, prices of related goods, expectations, or the number of buyers changes. Let's consider how each of these determinants of demand affects the demand curve.

3.e.1. Income The demand for any good or service depends on income. For most goods and services, the higher someone's income is, everything else the same, the more that person can purchase at any given price. These are called **normal goods**. The increase in Bob's income causes his demand to increase. This change is shown in Figure 6(a) by the shift to the right from the curve labeled D_1 to the curve labeled D_2. Increased income means a greater ability to purchase goods and services. At every price, more hours of access time are demanded along curve D_2 than along curve D_1; this is an increase in demand.

normal goods: goods for which demand increases as income increases

FIGURE 6 A Change in Demand and a Change in the Quantity Demanded

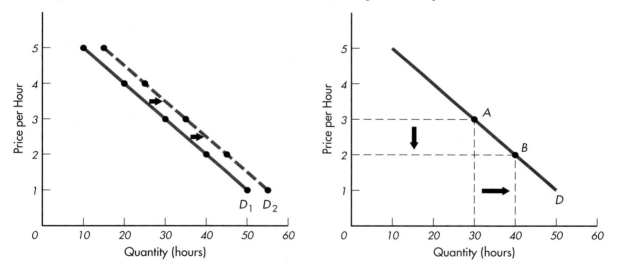

	Quantities Demanded per Week	
Price per Hour	Before	After
$5	10	15
$4	20	25
$3	30	35
$2	40	45
$1	50	55

(a) Change in Demand

(b) Change in Quantity Demanded

According to the table, Bob's demand for access time has increased by 5 hours at each price. In Figure 6(a), this change is shown as a shift of the demand curve from D_1 to D_2. Figure 6(b) shows a change in the quantity demanded. The change in quantity demanded is an increase in the quantity that consumers are willing and able to purchase at a lower price. It is shown as a movement along the demand curve from point A to point B.

For some goods and services, however, the amount demanded declines as income rises, everything else the same. The reason could be that these are goods or services that people use only when their incomes are declining—such as bankruptcy services. In addition, people might not like the good or service as well as they like a more expensive good or service, so when their income rises, they purchase the more expensive items. These types of items are called **inferior goods**.

inferior goods: goods for which demand decreases as income increases

3.e.2. Tastes The demand for any good or service depends on individuals' tastes and preferences. When the iPod came out in 2000, it became an instant success. The Sony Walkman lost market share and essentially disappeared. Tastes changed toward the more mobile iPod and, more important, toward the more powerful iPod. Thousands of songs could be stored on an iPod, while the Walkman was constrained by the size of the CD. The iPhone incorporates the iPod into a mobile phone, and it too has been a huge success. Consumers no longer demand the old fixed-line phones but instead want more capabilities in their mobile phones and MP3 devices; their tastes have changed.

3.e.3. Prices of Related Goods and Services Goods and services may be related in two ways. **Substitute goods** can be used in place of each other, so that as the cost of one rises, everything else the same, people will buy more of the other. Bread and crackers, BMWs and Acuras, movie downloads and theater movies, universities and community colleges, electricity and natural gas, time used to access network games and time used for other activities are, more or less, pairs of substitutes. As the price of entertainment venues rises, everything else held constant, the demand for access time for network games will rise; the demand curve for access time will shift to the right.

substitute goods: goods that can be used in place of each other; as the price of one rises, the demand for the other rises

Complementary goods are goods that are used together, and so as the price of one rises, everything else the same, consumers buy less of it but also buy less of the complementary good. Bread and margarine, beer and peanuts, cameras and film, shoes and socks, CDs and CD players, a computer or game board and access to network games, and iPods and iTunes are examples of pairs of complementary goods. As the price of a machine on which to play network games rises, people purchase less access time to those network games. The demand curve for a complementary good shifts to the left when the price of the related good increases.

complementary goods: goods that are used together; as the price of one rises, the demand for the other falls

3.e.4. Expectations Expectations about future events can have an effect on demand today. People make purchases today because they expect their income level to be a certain amount in the future, or because they expect the price of certain items to be higher in the future. You might buy running shoes today if you expect the price of those shoes to be higher tomorrow. You might buy your airline ticket home now rather than wait until semester break if you expect the price to be higher next month.

3.e.5. Number of Buyers Market demand consists of the sum of the demands of all individuals. The more individuals there are with income to spend, the greater the market demand is likely to be. For example, the populations of Florida and Arizona are much larger during the winter than they are during the summer. The demand for any particular good or service in Arizona and Florida rises (the demand curve shifts to the right) during the winter and falls (the demand curve shifts to the left) during the summer.

RECAP

1. According to the law of demand, as the price of any good or service rises (falls), the quantity demanded of that good or service falls (rises), during a specific period of time, everything else held constant.

2. A demand schedule is a listing of the quantity demanded at each price.

3. The demand curve is a downward-sloping line plotted using the values in the demand schedule.

4. Market demand is the sum of all individual demands.

5. Demand changes when one of the determinants of demand changes. A demand change is illustrated as a shift of the demand curve.

6. The determinants of demand are income, tastes, prices of related goods and services, expectations, and number of buyers.

7. The quantity demanded changes when the price of the good or service changes. This is a change from one point on the demand curve to another point on the same demand curve.

3 | What is supply?

■ 4. Supply

Why do students get discounts at movie theaters? Demand *and* supply. Why do restaurants offer early bird specials? Demand *and* supply. Why is the price of hotel accommodations in Phoenix higher in the winter than in the summer? Demand *and* supply. Why is the price of beef higher in Japan than in the United States? Demand *and* supply. Both demand and supply determine price; neither demand nor supply alone determines price. We now discuss supply.

4.a. The Law of Supply

Just as demand is the relation between the price and the quantity demanded of a good or service, supply is the relation between the price and the quantity supplied. **Supply** is the amount of the good or service that producers are willing and able to offer for sale at each possible price during a period of time, everything else held constant. **Quantity supplied** is the amount of the good or service that producers are willing and able to offer for sale at a *specific* price during a period of time, everything else held constant. According to the **law of supply**, as the price of a good or service rises, the quantity supplied rises, and vice versa.

The formal statement of the law of supply consists of five phrases:

1. The quantity of a well-defined good or service that
2. producers are willing and able to offer for sale
3. during a particular period of time
4. increases as the price of the good or service increases and decreases as the price decreases,
5. everything else held constant.

The first phrase is the same as the first phrase in the law of demand. The second phrase indicates that producers must not only *want* to offer the product for sale but be *able* to offer the product. The third phrase points out that the quantities producers will offer for sale depend on the period of time being considered. The fourth phrase points out that more will be supplied at higher than at lower prices. The final phrase ensures that the **determinants of supply** do not change. The determinants of supply are those factors other than the price of the good or service that influence the willingness and ability of producers to offer their goods and services for sale—the prices of resources used to produce the product, technology and productivity, expectations of producers, the number of producers in the market, and the prices of related goods and services. If any one of these should change, supply changes.

4.b. The Supply Schedule and Supply Curve

A **supply schedule** is a table or list of the prices and the corresponding quantities supplied of a good or service. The table in Figure 7 presents a single firm's supply schedule for access to network games. (We will assume that three firms offer access to the same network games.) The schedule lists the quantities that each firm is willing and able to supply at each price, everything else held constant. As the price increases, the firm is willing and able to offer more access time to the network games.

supply: the amount of a good or service that producers are willing and able to offer for sale at each possible price during a period of time, everything else held constant

quantity supplied: the amount that sellers are willing and able to offer at a given price during a particular period of time, everything else held constant

law of supply: the quantity of a well-defined good or service that producers are willing and able to offer for sale during a particular period of time increases as the price of the good or service increases and decreases as the price decreases, everything else held constant

determinants of supply: factors other than the price of the good that influence supply—prices of resources, technology and productivity, expectations of producers, number of producers, and the prices of related goods and services

supply schedule: a table or list of prices and the corresponding quantities supplied of a particular good or service

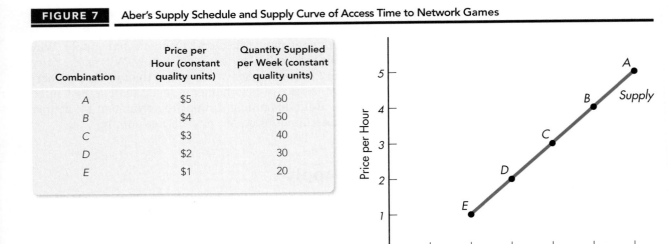

FIGURE 7   Aber's Supply Schedule and Supply Curve of Access Time to Network Games

Combination	Price per Hour (constant quality units)	Quantity Supplied per Week (constant quality units)
A	$5	60
B	$4	50
C	$3	40
D	$2	30
E	$1	20

The quantity that Aber is willing and able to offer for sale at each price is listed in the supply schedule and shown on the supply curve. At point A, the price is $5 per hour and the quantity supplied is 60 hours. The combination of $4 per hour and 50 hours is point B. Each price-quantity combination is plotted, and the points are connected to form the supply curve.

supply curve: a graph of a supply schedule that measures price on the vertical axis and quantity supplied on the horizontal axis

A **supply curve** is a graph of the supply schedule. Figure 7 shows Aber's supply curve of access time to the network games. The price and quantity combinations given in the supply schedule correspond to the points on the curve. For instance, combination *A* in the table corresponds to point *A* on the curve; combination *B* in the table corresponds to point *B* on the curve, and so on for each price-quantity combination.

The supply curve slopes upward. This means that a supplier is willing and able to offer more for sale at higher prices than it is at lower prices. This should make sense—if prices rise, everything else held constant, the supplier will earn more profits. Higher profits create the incentive for the supplier to offer more for sale.

4.c. From Individual Supply Curves to the Market Supply

To derive market supply, the quantities that each producer supplies at each price are added together, just as the quantities demanded by each consumer are added together to get market demand. The table in Figure 8 lists the supply schedules of three firms that sell access to network games: Aber, Broadband, and Courage. The supply schedules are plotted in Figure 8(a). Then in Figure 8(b) the individual supply curves have been added together (in a horizontal direction) to obtain the market supply curve. At a price of $5, the quantity supplied by Aber is 60, the quantity supplied by Broadband is 30, and the quantity supplied by Courage is 12. This means a total quantity supplied in the market of 102. At a price of $4, the quantities supplied are 50, 25, and 9, for a total market quantity supplied of 84. The market supply schedule is the last column in the table. The graph of the price and quantity combinations listed in this column is the market supply curve. The market supply curve slopes up because each of the individual supply curves has a positive slope. The market supply curve tells us that the quantity supplied in the market increases as the price rises.

FIGURE 8	The Market Supply Schedule and Curve of Access Time to Network Games

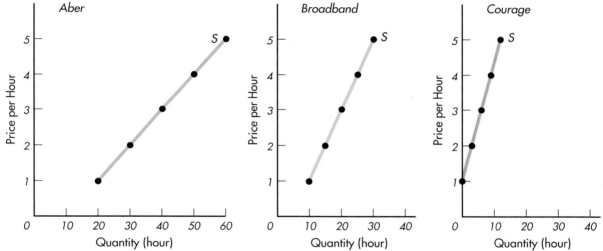

	Quantities Supplied per Year by			
Price per Hour	Aber	Broadband	Courage	Market Quantity Supplied
$5	60 +	30 +	12 =	102
$4	50	25	9	84
$3	40	20	6	66
$2	30	15	3	48
$1	20	10	0	30

(a) Individual Supply Curves

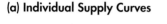

(b) Market Supply Curve

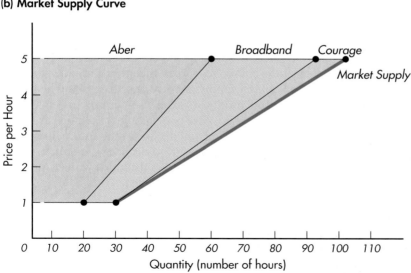

The market supply is derived by summing the quantities that each supplier is willing and able to offer for sale at each price. In this example, there are three producers: The supply schedules of each are listed in the table and plotted as the individual supply curves shown in Figure 8(a). By adding the quantities supplied at each price, we obtain the market supply curve shown in Figure 8(b). For instance, at a price of $5, Aber offers 60 units, Broadband 30 units, and Courage 12 units, for a market supply quantity of 102. The market supply curve reflects the quantities that each producer is able and willing to supply at each price.

4.d. Changes in Supply and Changes in Quantity Supplied

When we draw the supply curve, we allow only the price and quantity supplied of the good or service that we are discussing to change. Everything else that might affect supply is assumed not to change. If any of the determinants of supply—the prices of resources used to produce the product, technology and productivity, expectations of producers, the number of producers in the market, and the prices of related goods and services—changes, the supply schedule changes and the supply curve shifts.

4.d.1. Prices of Resources
If labor costs rise, higher prices will be necessary to induce each store to offer as many hours of access as it did before the cost of the resource rose. The higher cost of resources causes a decrease in supply, meaning a leftward shift of the supply curve, from S_1 to S_2 in Figure 9(a). Compare point B on curve S_2 with point A on curve S_1. Both points correspond to a price of \$3, but along curve S_1, sellers are willing to offer 66 hours of access time, whereas curve S_2 indicates that sellers will offer only 57 hours of access time.

4.d.2. Technology and Productivity
If resources are used more efficiently in the production of a good or service, more of that good or service can be supplied for the same cost, or the original quantity supplied can be produced for a lower cost. As a result, the supply curve shifts to the right, as in Figure 9(b).

The move from horse-drawn plows to tractors or from mainframe computers to personal computers meant that each worker was able to produce more. The increase in output produced by each unit of a resource is called a *productivity increase*. **Productivity** is defined as the quantity of output produced per unit of resource. Improvements in technology cause productivity increases, which lead to an increase in supply.

productivity: the quantity of output produced per unit of resource

4.d.3. Expectations of Suppliers
Sellers may choose to alter the quantity offered for sale today because of a change in expectations regarding the determinants of supply. A supply curve illustrates the quantities that suppliers are willing and able to supply at every possible price. If suppliers expect that something is going to occur to resource supplies or the cost of resources, then they may alter the quantities that they are willing and able to supply at every possible price. The key point is that the supply curve will shift if producers expect something to occur that will alter their anticipated profits at every possible price, not just a change in one price. For instance, the expectation that demand will decline in the future does not lead to a shift of the supply curve; it leads instead to a decline in quantity supplied, because the new demand curve (the expected lower demand) would intersect the supply curve at a lower price and a smaller output level.

4.d.4. Number of Suppliers
When more people decide to supply a good or service, the market supply increases. More is offered for sale at each and every price, causing a rightward shift of the supply curve.

4.d.5. Prices of Related Goods or Services
The opportunity cost of producing and selling any good or service is the forgone opportunity to produce any other good or service. If the price of an alternative good changes, then the opportunity cost of producing a particular good changes. This could cause the supply curve to change. For instance, if McDonald's can offer hamburgers or salads with

FIGURE 9 A Shift of the Supply Curve

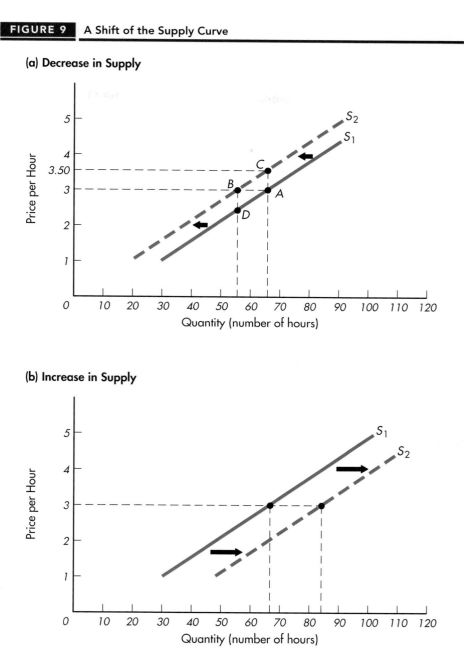

(a) Decrease in Supply

(b) Increase in Supply

Figure 9(a) shows a decrease in supply and the shift of the supply curve to the left, from S_1 to S_2. The decrease is caused by a change in one of the determinants of access time to network games—an increase in the price of labor. Because of the increased price of labor, producers are willing and able to offer fewer access hours at each price than they were before the cost of labor rose. Supply curve S_2 shows that at a price of $3 per hour of access, suppliers will offer 57 hours. That is 9 hours less than the 66 hours at $3 per access hour indicated by supply curve S_1. Conversely, to offer a given quantity, producers must receive a higher price per access hour than they previously were getting: $3.50 per hour for 66 hours (on supply curve S_2) instead of $3 per hour (on supply curve S_1).

Figure 9(b) shows an increase in supply. A technological improvement or an increase in productivity causes the supply curve to shift to the right, from S_1 to S_2. At each price, a higher quantity is offered for sale. At a price of $3, 66 hours were offered, but with the shift of the supply curve, the quantity of hours for sale at $3 apiece increases to 84. Conversely, producers can reduce prices for a given quantity—for example, charging $2 per hour for 66 hours.

FIGURE 10   A Change in Supply and a Change in the Quantity Supplied

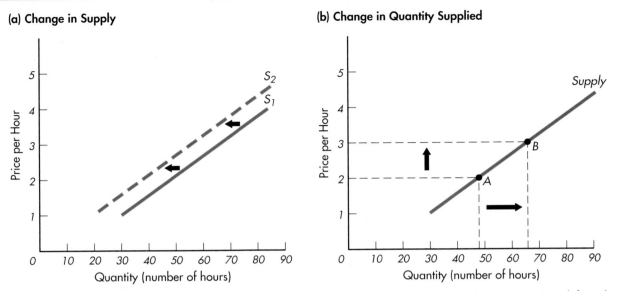

In Figure 10(a), the quantities that producers are willing and able to offer for sale at every price decrease, causing a leftward shift of the supply curve from S₁ to S₂. In Figure 10(b), the quantities that producers are willing and able to offer for sale increase, because of an increase in the price of the good, causing a movement along the supply curve from point A to point B.

equal ease, an increase in the price of salads could lead the manager to offer more salads and fewer hamburgers. The supply curve of salads would shift to the right, and the supply curve of hamburgers would shift to the left.

A *change in supply* occurs when the quantity supplied at each and every price changes or there is a shift in the supply curve—like the shift from S_1 to S_2 in Figure 10(a). A change in one of the determinants of supply brings about a change in supply.

When only the price changes, a greater or smaller quantity is supplied. This is shown as a movement along the supply curve, not as a shift of the curve. A change in price is said to cause a *change in the quantity supplied.* An increase in quantity supplied is shown in the move from point A to point B on the supply curve of Figure 10(b).

RECAP

1. According to the law of supply, the quantity supplied of any good or service is directly related to the price of the good or service during a specific period of time, everything else held constant.

2. Market supply is found by adding together the quantities supplied at each price by every producer in the market.

3. Supply changes if the prices of relevant resources change, if technology or productivity changes, if producers' expectations change, if the number of producers changes, or if the prices of related goods and services change.

4. Changes in supply are reflected in shifts of the supply curve. Changes in the quantity supplied are reflected in movements along the supply curve.

4 | How is price
determined by
demand and supply?

equilibrium: the price and
quantity at which quantity
demanded and quantity
supplied are equal

■ 5. Equilibrium: Putting Demand and Supply Together

The demand curve shows the quantity of a good or service that buyers are willing and able to purchase at each price. The supply curve shows the quantity that producers are willing and able to offer for sale at each price. Only where the two curves intersect is the quantity supplied equal to the quantity demanded. This intersection is the point of **equilibrium**.

5.a. Determination of Equilibrium

Figure 11 brings together the market demand and market supply curves for access hours to network games. The supply and demand schedules are listed

---

FIGURE 11   Equilibrium

Price per Hour	Quantity Demanded per Week	Quantity Supplied per Week)	Status
$5	30	102	Surplus of 72
$4	48	84	Surplus of 36
$3	66	66	Equilibrium
$2	84	48	Shortage of 36
$1	102	30	Shortage of 72

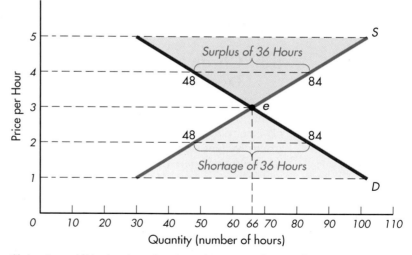

Equilibrium is established at the point where the quantity that suppliers are willing and able to offer for sale is the same as the quantity that buyers are willing and able to purchase. Here, equilibrium occurs at the price of $3 per hour of access to network games and the quantity of 66 hours of access per week. It is shown as point e, at the intersection of the demand and supply curves. At prices above $3, the quantity supplied is greater than the quantity demanded, and the result is a surplus. At prices below $3, the quantity supplied is less than the quantity demanded, and the result is a shortage. The area shaded tan shows all prices at which there is a surplus—where quantity supplied is greater than the quantity demanded. The amount of the surplus is measured in a horizontal direction at each price. The area shaded blue represents all prices at which a shortage exists—where the quantity demanded is greater than the quantity supplied. The amount of the shortage is measured in a horizontal direction at each price.

in the table, and the curves are plotted in the graph in Figure 11. Notice that the curves intersect at only one point, labeled *e,* a price of $3 and a quantity of 66. The intersection point is the equilibrium price, the only price at which the quantity demanded and quantity supplied are the same. You can see that at any other price, the quantity demanded and quantity supplied are not the same. This is called **disequilibrium**.

disequilibrium: prices at which quantity demanded and quantity supplied are not equal at a particular price

surplus: a quantity supplied that is larger than the quantity demanded at a given price; it occurs whenever the price is greater than the equilibrium price

shortage: a quantity supplied that is smaller than the quantity demanded at a given price; it occurs whenever the price is less than the equilibrium price

Whenever the price is greater than the equilibrium price, a **surplus** arises. For example, at $4, the quantity of hours of access demanded is 48, and the quantity supplied is 84. Thus, at $4 per hour, there is a surplus of 36 hours— that is, 36 hours supplied are not purchased. Conversely, whenever the price is below the equilibrium price, the quantity demanded is greater than the quantity supplied and there is a **shortage**. For instance, if the price is $2 per hour of access, consumers will want and be able to pay for more hours of access than are available. As shown in the table in Figure 11, the quantity demanded at a price of $2 is 84, but the quantity supplied is only 48. There is a shortage of 36 hours of access at the price of $2.

Neither a surplus nor a shortage will exist for long if the price of the product is free to change. Suppliers who are stuck with hours of access not being purchased will lower the price and reduce the quantities they are offering for sale in order to eliminate a surplus. Conversely, suppliers who cannot supply enough hours to meet demand and who have consumers on hold or losing connection will raise the price to eliminate a shortage. Surpluses lead to decreases in the price and the quantity supplied and increases in the quantity demanded. Shortages lead to increases in the price and the quantity supplied and decreases in the quantity demanded.

A shortage exists only when the quantity that people are willing and able to purchase at a particular price is more than the quantity supplied *at that price.* Scarcity occurs when more is wanted at a zero price than is available.

> Note that a shortage is not
> the same thing as scarcity.

5 | **What causes price to change?**

5.b. Changes in the Equilibrium Price: Demand Shifts

Equilibrium is the combination of price and quantity at which the quantities demanded and supplied are the same. Once an equilibrium is achieved, there is no incentive for suppliers or consumers to move away from it. An equilibrium price changes only when demand and/or supply changes—that is, when the determinants of demand or the determinants of supply change.

Let's consider a change in demand and what it means for the equilibrium price. Suppose that experiments on rats show that playing network games causes brain damage. As a result, a large segment of the human population decides not to purchase access time to the games. Suppliers experience a decrease in the number of customers willing and able to pay for access, as shown in Figure 12 by a leftward shift of the demand curve, from curve D_1 to curve D_2.

Once the demand curve has shifted, the original equilibrium price of $3 per hour of access per week at point e_1 is no longer equilibrium. At a price of $3, the quantity supplied is still 66, but the quantity demanded has declined to 48 (look at the demand curve D_2 at a price of $3). There is, therefore, a surplus of 18 hours of access time per week at the price of $3.

With a surplus comes downward pressure on the price. This downward pressure occurs because producers acquire fewer hours of access for purchase and reduce the price in an attempt to sell those hours not being used. Suppliers continue reducing the price and the quantity available until consumers purchase all the

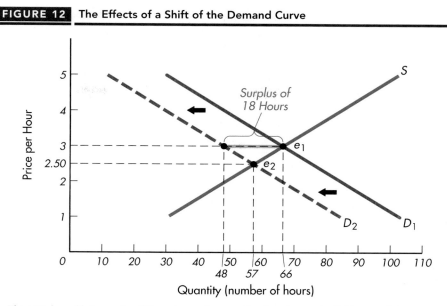

FIGURE 12 The Effects of a Shift of the Demand Curve

The initial equilibrium price ($3 per hour of access time) and quantity (66 hours of access time) are established at point e_1, where the initial demand and supply curves intersect. A change in the tastes for access hours to the network games causes demand to decrease, and the demand curve shifts to the left. At $3 per hour of access, the initial quantity supplied, 66 hours, is now greater than the quantity demanded, 48 hours. The surplus of 18 hours causes suppliers to reduce the amount of hours of access offered and to lower the price. The market reaches a new equilibrium, at point e_2, $2.50 per hour and 57 hours per week.

hours that the sellers have available, or until a new equilibrium is established. That new equilibrium occurs at point e_2 with a price of $2.50 and a quantity of 57.

The decrease in demand is represented by the leftward shift of the demand curve. A decrease in demand results in a lower equilibrium price and a lower equilibrium quantity as long as there is no change in supply. Conversely, an increase in demand would be represented as a rightward shift of the demand curve and would result in a higher equilibrium price and a higher equilibrium quantity as long as there is no change in supply.

5.c. Changes in the Equilibrium Price: Supply Shifts

The equilibrium price and quantity may be altered by a change in supply as well. If the price of relevant resources, technology and productivity, the expectations of suppliers, the number of suppliers, or the prices of related products change, supply changes.

Let's consider an example. Suppose a tax is imposed on all Internet access and that this tax increases the cost for the network game suppliers to provide access time. This is represented by a leftward shift of the supply curve in Figure 12.

The leftward shift of the supply curve, from curve S_1 to curve S_2, leads to a new equilibrium price and quantity. At the original equilibrium price of $3 at point $e1$, 66 hours of access are supplied. After the shift in the supply curve, 48 hours are supplied at a price of $3 per hour, and there is a shortage of 18 hours per week. The shortage puts upward pressure on price. As the price rises, consumers decrease the quantities that they are willing and able to purchase, and suppliers increase the quantities that they are willing and able to supply. Eventually, a new

FIGURE 13   The Effects of a Shift of the Supply Curve

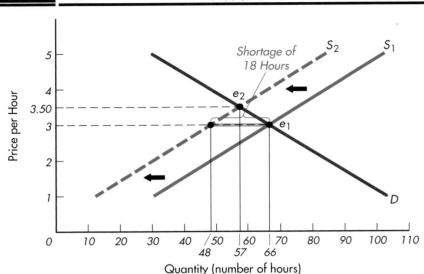

The initial equilibrium price and quantity are $3 and 66 hours, at point e_1. When the Internet tax is imposed, suppliers' costs have risen, and so they are willing and able to offer fewer hours for sale at each price. The result is a leftward (upward) shift of the supply curve, from S_1 to S_2. At the old price of $3, the quantity demanded is still 66, but the quantity supplied falls to 48. The shortage is 18 hours of access time. The shortage leads to a new equilibrium, e_2, the intersection between curves S_2 and D, is $3.50 per hour of access time and 57 hours of access time.

equilibrium price and quantity is established at $3.50 and 57 hours of access each week at point e_2.

The decrease in supply is represented by the leftward shift of the supply curve. A decrease in supply with no change in demand results in a higher price and a lower quantity. Conversely, an increase in supply would be represented as a rightward shift of the supply curve. An increase in supply with no change in demand would result in a lower price and a higher quantity.

5.d. Market Adjustment and Market Interference

We have examined a hypothetical (imaginary) market for access time to network games in order to represent what goes on in real markets. We have established that the price of a good or service is defined by an equilibrium between demand and supply. We noted that an equilibrium could be disturbed by a change in demand, a change in supply, or simultaneous changes in demand and supply. The important point of this discussion is to demonstrate that when they are not in equilibrium, the price and the quantities demanded and/or supplied change until equilibrium is established. The market is always attempting to reach equilibrium.

Looking at last year's sweaters piled up on the sale racks, waiting over an hour for a table at a restaurant, or hearing that 5 or 6 percent of people who are willing and able to work are unemployed may make you wonder whether equilibrium is ever established. In fact, it is not uncommon to observe situations in which quantities demanded and quantities supplied are not equal. But this observation does not cast doubt on the usefulness of the equilibrium concept. Even if not all markets clear, or reach equilibrium, all the time, we can be reasonably assured that market forces

6 What happens when price is not allowed to change with market forces?

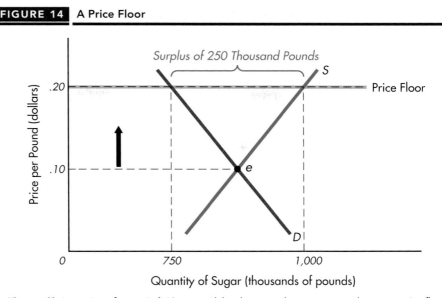

FIGURE 14   A Price Floor

The equilibrium price of sugar is $.10 a pound, but because the government has set a price floor of $.20 a pound, as shown by the solid yellow line, the price is not allowed to move to its equilibrium level. A surplus of 250,000 pounds of sugar results from the price floor. Sugar growers produce 1 million pounds of sugar, and consumers purchase 750,000 pounds of sugar.

are operating so that the market is moving toward an equilibrium. When you see the store having a sale, you know that the market is moving toward equilibrium. When you hear that the price of something is rising because so many people are buying it, you know that the market is moving toward equilibrium. Sometimes the market is not allowed to move toward equilibrium, as discussed in the following section.

price floor: a situation in which the price is not allowed to decrease below a certain level

5.d.1. Market Interference: Price Ceilings and Price Floors A **price floor** is a situation in which the price is not allowed to decrease below a certain level. Consider Figure 14, representing the market for sugar. The equilibrium price of sugar is $.10 a pound, but because the government has set a price floor of $.20 a pound, as shown by the solid yellow line, the price is not allowed to move to its equilibrium level. A surplus of 250,000 pounds of sugar results from the price floor. Sugar growers produce 1 million pounds of sugar, and consumers purchase 750,000 pounds of sugar.

We saw previously that whenever the price is above the equilibrium price, a surplus arises and begins to force the price to decline. The price floor interferes with the functioning of the market; a surplus exists because the government will not allow the price to drop. The sugar surplus builds up as each week, more sugar is produced than is consumed.

What would occur if the government had set the price floor at $.09 a pound? Since at $.09 a pound, a shortage of sugar would result, the price would rise. A price floor keeps the price only from falling, not from rising. So the price rises to its equilibrium level of $.10. Only if the price floor is set above the equilibrium price is it an effective price floor.

price ceiling: a situation in which the price is not allowed to rise above a certain level

A **price ceiling** is the situation in which a price is not allowed to rise to its equilibrium level. Los Angeles, San Francisco, and New York are among over 125 U.S. cities that have some type of *rent controls*. The New York City rent control law places a ceiling on the rents that landlords can charge for apartments. Figure 15 is a demand and supply graph representing the market for apartments in New York. The equilibrium price is $3,000 a month. The government has set a

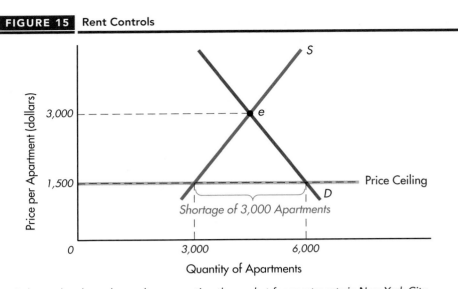

FIGURE 15   Rent Controls

A demand and supply graph representing the market for apartments in New York City is shown. The equilibrium price is $3,000 a month. The government has set a price of $1,500 a month. The government's price ceiling is shown by the solid yellow line. At the government's price, 3,000 apartments are available but consumers want 6,000. There is a shortage of 3,000 apartments.

price of $1,500 a month as the maximum that can be charged. The price ceiling is shown by the solid yellow line. At the rent control price of $1,500 per month, 3,000 apartments are available, but consumers want 6,000 apartments. There is a shortage of 3,000 apartments.

The shortage means that not everyone who is willing and able to rent an apartment will be able to. Since the price is not allowed to ration the apartments, something else will have to. It may be that those who are willing and able to stand in line the longest get the apartments. Perhaps bribing an important official might be the way to get an apartment. Perhaps relatives of officials or important citizens will get the apartments. Whenever a price ceiling exists, a shortage results, and some rationing device other than price will arise.

Had the government set the rent control price at $4,000 per month, the price ceiling would not have had an effect. Since the equilibrium is $3,000 a month, the price would not have risen to $4,000. Only if the price ceiling is below the equilibrium price will it be an effective price ceiling.

Price ceilings are not uncommon in the United States or in other economies. China had a severe housing shortage for 30 years because the price of housing was kept below equilibrium. Faced with unhappy citizens and realizing the cause of the shortage, officials began to lift the restrictions on housing prices in 1985. The shortage has diminished. In the former Soviet Union, prices for all goods and services were defined by the government. For most consumer items, the price was set below equilibrium, and shortages existed. The long lines of people waiting to purchase food or clothing were the result of the price ceilings on all goods and services. In the United States, price ceilings on all goods and services have been imposed at times. During the First and Second World Wars and during the Nixon administration of the early 1970s, wage and price controls were imposed. These were price ceilings on all goods and services. As a result of the ceilings, people were unable to purchase many of the products they desired. The Organization of Petroleum Exporting Countries (OPEC) restricted the quantity of oil in the early 1970s and drove its price up considerably.

The U.S. government responded by placing a price ceiling on gasoline. The result was long lines at gas stations because of shortages of gasoline.

Price floors are quite common in economies as well. The agricultural policies of most of the developed nations are founded on price floors—the government guarantees that the price of an agricultural product will not fall below some level. Price floors result in surpluses, and this has been the case with agricultural products as well. The surpluses in agricultural products in the United States have resulted in cases where dairy farmers dumped milk in the river, where grain was given to other nations at taxpayer expense, and where citrus ranchers picked and then discarded thousands of tons of citrus, all to reduce huge surpluses.

When price ceiling or price floors do not allow a market to reach equilibrium, shortages or surpluses will result. Since the price is not allowed to allocate the goods or services, another allocation mechanism will—first-come-first-served, government, or lottery.

5.e. Market Adjustment: Watch the Price of Eggs

During the 1990s, country after country turned from government-run economies to market economies. In Latin America, in eastern Europe and Russia, in China, and in India, former socialist or dictatorial nations sought to free their stagnant and collapsing economies from government control. In these countries, government price controls were lifted, and people were allowed to buy and sell what they wanted. The leaders of the reforms were often told by their economic advisers, "Watch the price of eggs. If the price rises and more eggs are offered for sale, and then the price falls, it is a sign that markets are working."

So, when the price control was lifted, prices shot upward, frightening both the leaders and the individual people. But, within hours or a few days of the lifting of price controls, markets arose in which eggs, other produce, and some clothing items appeared. Shortages disappeared. Why? What was occurring?

Why did the advisers focus on eggs and not the heavy industries like shipbuilding, oil refining, or power generation? They focused on eggs because the market for eggs would be the quickest to emerge. Once they were free to do so,

FIGURE 16 Ending Price Controls

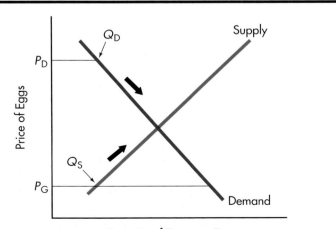

Quantity of Eggs per Day

*The controlled price is at P*G*. When price controls are lifted, price immediately shoots up to P*D *because the quantity supplied does not immediately change. Eventually, the quantity that is supplied rises, and as it rises, the price is driven to the equilibrium level.*

local farmers would bring their eggs to the city to sell. As the price of eggs rose, more eggs would be brought to market. Items such as ships, airplanes, tractors, etc., would not increase in supply nearly as rapidly as would eggs.

The market for eggs is depicted in Figure 16. The government-controlled price is P_G. The price ceiling meant shortages, as the quantity demanded is larger than the quantity supplied. When the price ceiling is lifted, the price immediately shoots up to P_D, but the quantity supplied does not change. Eventually, the high price leads to increasing quantities of eggs being supplied. Quite rapidly, in the case of eggs, the price drops to the equilibrium.

The adjustment process took much more time in the heavy industries. Once the price controls on items like gasoline, electricity, or industrial products were lifted, the price shot up, but the quantities supplied could not increase for quite some time. As a result, prices remained very high for months or years, until suppliers could begin offering more gasoline, electricity, ships, airplanes, and tractors. To the citizens, it seemed as if the markets were not working because the higher price did not bring forth increased quantities supplied.

Years, not days, were necessary for a complete transition from government-run to market-based economies in those countries where heavy industry was a large part of the economy, such as Russia.[2] In countries that were primarily agricultural, such as China, the transition occurred much more rapidly.

RECAP

1. Equilibrium occurs when the quantity demanded and the quantity supplied are equal: It is the price-quantity combination where the demand and supply curves intersect.

2. A price that is above the equilibrium price creates a surplus. Producers are willing and able to offer more for sale than buyers are willing and able to purchase.

3. A price that is below the equilibrium price leads to a shortage, because buyers are willing and able to purchase more than producers are willing and able to offer for sale.

4. When demand changes, price and quantity change in the same direction—both rise as demand increases, and both fall as demand decreases.

5. When supply changes, price and quantity change, but not in the same direction. When supply increases, price falls and quantity rises. When supply decreases, price rises and quantity falls.

6. When both demand and supply change, the direction of the change in price and quantity depends on the relative sizes of the changes of demand and supply.

7. The exchange rate is a determinant of demand when a good is sold in both the United States and other countries. It is also a determinant of supply because it affects the costs of producing goods.

8. A price floor is a situation in which a price is set above the equilibrium price. This creates a surplus.

---

[2] The video *Commanding Heights*, based on the book of the same name by Daniel Yergin and Joseph Stanislaus, provides a vivid portrayal of the transition from government to market economies during the 1990s.

9. A price ceiling is a case in which a price is set below the equilibrium price. This creates a shortage.

10. When a price ceiling is lifted, the market will adjust. The speed of adjustment of the quantity supplied and prices depends on how rapidly resources can be altered, goods and services produced, and supplies brought to market.

SUMMARY

1 | How do we decide who gets the scarce goods and resources?

• An allocation system is a way to determine who gets the scarce goods and resources. Allocation schemes include first-come, first-served, lottery, government, and market. *§1*

• The advantage of a market system over other allocation schemes is the incentives created by the market system. *§1.b*

2 | What is demand?

• Demand is the quantities that buyers are willing and able to buy at alternative prices. *§3*

• The quantity demanded is a specific amount at one price. *§3*

• The law of demand states that as the price of a well-defined commodity rises (falls), the quantity demanded during a given period of time will fall (rise), everything else held constant. *§3.a*

• Demand will change when one of the determinants of demand changes, that is, when income, tastes, prices of related goods and services, expectations, or number of buyers changes. A demand change is illustrated as a shift of the demand curve. *§3.e*

3 | What is supply?

• Supply is the quantities that sellers will offer for sale at alternative prices. *§4.a*

• The quantity supplied is the amount that sellers offer for sale at one price. *§4*

• The law of supply states that as the price of a well-defined commodity rises (falls), the quantity

supplied during a given period of time will rise (fall), everything else held constant. *§4.a*

• Supply changes when one of the determinants of supply changes, that is, when prices of resources, technology and productivity, expectations of producers, the number of producers, or the prices of related goods or services change. A supply change is illustrated as a shift of the supply curve. *§4.d*

4 | How is price determined by demand and supply?

• Together, demand and supply determine the equilibrium price and quantity. *§5*

5 | What causes price to change?

• A price that is above equilibrium creates a surplus, which leads to a lower price. A price that is below equilibrium creates a shortage, which leads to a higher price. *§5.a*

• A change in demand or a change in supply (a shift of either curve) will cause the equilibrium price and quantity to change. *§5.b, 5.c*

6 | What happens when price is not allowed to change with market forces?

• Markets are not always in equilibrium, but when not, surpluses or shortages arise and force the price to move them toward equilibrium. *§5.d*

• A price floor is a situation in which a price is not allowed to decrease below a certain level—it is set above the equilibrium price. This creates a surplus. A price ceiling is a case in which a price is not allowed to rise—it is set below the equilibrium price. This creates a shortage. *§5.d*

KEY TERMS

market *§2.a*	law of demand *§3.a*	inferior goods *§3.e.1*
barter *§2.b*	determinants of demand *§3.a*	substitute goods *§3.e.3*
double coincidence of wants *§2.b*	demand schedule *§3.b*	complementary goods *§3.e.3*
demand *§3*	demand curve *§3.c*	supply *§4.a*
quantity demanded *§3*	normal goods *§3.e.1*	quantity supplied *§4.a*

law of supply §4.a   productivity §4.d.2   shortage §5.a
determinants of supply §4.a   equilibrium §5   price floor §5.d.1
supply schedule §4.b   disequilibrium §5.a   price ceiling §5.d.1
supply curve §4.b   surplus §5.a

EXERCISES

1. Illustrate each of the following events using a demand and supply diagram for bananas.
   a. Reports surface that imported bananas are infected with a deadly virus.
   b. Consumers' incomes drop.
   c. The price of bananas rises.
   d. The price of oranges falls.
   e. Consumers expect the price of bananas to decrease in the future.

2. Answer true or false, and if the statement is false, change it to make it true. Illustrate your answers on a demand and supply graph.
   a. An increase in demand is represented by a movement up the demand curve.
   b. An increase in supply is represented by a movement up the supply curve.
   c. An increase in demand without any changes in supply will cause the price to rise.
   d. An increase in supply without any changes in demand will cause the price to rise.

3. Using the following schedule, define the equilibrium price and quantity. Describe the situation at a price of $10. What will occur? Describe the situation at a price of $2. What will occur?

Price	Quantity Demanded	Quantity Supplied
$1	500	100
$2	400	120
$3	350	150
$4	320	200
$5	300	300
$6	275	410
$7	260	500
$8	230	650
$9	200	800
$10	150	975

4. Suppose the government imposed a minimum price of $7 in the schedule of exercise 3. What would occur? Illustrate.

5. In exercise 3, indicate what the price would have to be to represent an effective price ceiling. Point out the surplus or shortage that results. Illustrate a price floor and provide an example of a price floor.

6. A common feature of skiing is waiting in lift lines. Does the existence of lift lines mean that the price is not working to allocate the scarce resource? If so, what should be done about it?

7. Why don't we observe barter systems as often as we observe the use of currency?

8. A severe drought in California has resulted in a nearly 30 percent reduction in the quantity of citrus grown and produced in California. Explain what effect this event might have on the Florida citrus market.

9. The prices of the Ralph Lauren Polo line of clothing are considerably higher than those of comparable-quality lines. Yet this line sells more than a J. C. Penney brand line of clothing. Does this violate the law of demand?

10. In December, the price of Christmas trees rises and the quantity of trees sold rises. Is this a violation of the law of demand?

11. In recent years, the price of artificial Christmas trees has fallen while the quality has risen. What impact has this event had on the price of cut Christmas trees?

12. Many restaurants don't take reservations. You simply arrive and wait your turn. If you arrive at 7:30 in the evening, you have at least an hour wait. Notwithstanding that fact, a few people arrive, speak quietly with the maitre d', hand him some money, and are promptly seated. At some restaurants that do take reservations, there is a month wait for a Saturday evening, three weeks for a Friday evening, two weeks for Tuesday through Thursday, and virtually no wait for Sunday or Monday evening. How do you explain these events using demand and supply?

13. Evaluate the following statement: "The demand for U.S. oranges has increased because the quantity of U.S. oranges demanded in Japan has risen."

14. In December 1992, the federal government began requiring that all foods display information about fat content and other ingredients on food packages. The displays had to be verified by independent laboratories. The price of an evaluation of a food product could run as much as $20,000. What impact do you think this law had on the market for meat?

15. Draw a PPC. Which combination shown by the PPC will be produced? How is this combination determined? Does the combination that is produced depend on how goods and services are allocated?

You can find further practice tests in the Online Quiz at www.cengage.com/economics/boyes.

The Wrong Answer for High Gas Prices

The Baltimore Sun **September 8, 2005**

Washington—When Rudyard Kipling said it was a great virtue "if you can keep your head when all about you are losing theirs and blaming it on you," he was not thinking of Sen. Maria Cantwell, a Democrat from Washington. This week, as gasoline prices remained above $3 a gallon, she proposed giving the president the power to tell retailers what they can charge at the pump.

A lot of people grew anxious seeing long lines forming the week before last, as motorists rushed to fill their tanks in the aftermath of Hurricane Katrina. But Ms. Cantwell apparently enjoyed the sight well enough that she'd like to make those lines a permanent feature of the landscape. If so, she has the right approach. The government does many things badly, but one thing it knows how to do is create shortages through the vigorous use of price controls.

That's what it did in the oil market in 1979–80, under President Jimmy Carter. He was replaced by Ronald Reagan, who lifted price caps on gas and thus not only banished shortages but brought about an era of low prices.

Ms. Cantwell thinks oil companies have manipulated the energy market to gouge consumers, though she is awaiting evidence to support that theory. "I just don't have the document to prove it," she declared. Her suspicions were roused when she noticed that prices climbed in Seattle—though most of its oil comes from Alaska, which was not hit by a hurricane.

Maybe no one has told Ms. Cantwell that oil trades in an international market, and that when companies and consumers in the South can't get fuel from their usual sources, they will buy it from other ones, even if they have to go as far as Prudhoe Bay.

If prices rose in Dallas and didn't rise in Seattle, oil producers would have a big incentive to ship all their supplies to Texas—leaving Washingtonians to pay nothing for nothing. When a freeze damages Florida's orange juice crop, does Ms. Cantwell think only Floridians feel the pain?

Sen. Byron Dorgan, a Democrat from North Dakota, meanwhile, was outraged by the thought of giant oil companies making money merely for supplying the nation's energy needs. He claimed they will reap $80 billion in "windfall profits" and wants the government to confiscate a large share of that sum through a special federal tax.

But the prospect of occasional "windfall" profits is one reason corporations are willing to risk their money drilling wells that may turn out to be drier than Alan Greenspan's reading list. Take them away, and investors may decide they'd rather speculate in real estate.

It's hard to see why oil companies shouldn't make a lot of money when the commodity they provide is suddenly in short supply. After all, they are vulnerable to weak profits or even losses during times of glut. Back when Americans were enjoying abundant cheap gasoline, the joke was that the surest way to make a small fortune in the oil industry was to start with a large fortune.

Oil companies are also subject to the whims of nature. No one is holding a charity fundraiser for the business people whose rigs and refineries were smashed by Katrina. No one will come to their aid if prices drop by half.

Besides, high prices serve two essential functions: encouraging production and fostering conservation. Spurred by the lure of windfall profits, oil companies will move heaven and earth to get more gasoline to consumers. Shocked by the tab when they fill up a 5,600-pound SUV, motorists will look for opportunities to leave the Suburban at home. They may even commit a sin not covered by the Ten Commandments: Coveting their neighbor's Prius.

Controlling prices, by contrast, would have exactly the opposite effect: telling consumers they should waste fuel to their hearts' content and telling producers to leave the black stuff in the ground. When events in the world conspire to make oil dear, there is nothing to be gained from masking that fact. We can ignore reality, but reality won't ignore us.

Steve Chapman

ictating the retail price that companies can sell gasoline at is nothing more than a price ceiling. In the figure below left, the ceiling price of Pm is less than the equilibrium price P_1. This price ceiling creates a shortage: At the controlled price Pm, the quantity of gasoline demanded is Q_d, while the quantity supplied is only Q_s. The difference, $Q_d - Q_s$, is the quantity of gasoline that consumers would be willing and able to buy but can't because there is none available. What does a shortage in gasoline look like? It is long lines at gas pumps. It is people stranded because they have run out of gas.

How is this shortage resolved? Since price cannot be used to resolve the shortage, something else will. Common replacements for price are first-come, first-served and corruption.

First-come, first-served is what we typically see. Long lines form at gas stations. People "top off" their tanks, driving into a station whenever they see an opening in order to keep their gas tanks full. One result is many more people at pumps than would otherwise be the case. Another is that some gas stations close because they can't obtain supplies.

Crude oil, the main source of gasoline, is traded in a global market. If prices rise in one part of the world but are not allowed to rise in others, the crude oil will be shipped to where its return is highest. As the article notes, "If prices rose in Dallas and didn't rise in Seattle, oil producers would have a big incentive to ship all their supplies to Texas—leaving Washingtonians to pay nothing for nothing. When a freeze damages Florida's orange juice crop, does Ms. Cantwell think only Floridians feel the pain?" If the United States limited gasoline prices to $2 per gallon and other parts of the world allowed the price to rise to $4 per gallon, the oil would be shipped to where it could be refined and a profit made from selling gasoline. In short, price ceilings lead to shortages. Even if the oil was not shipped around the world, why would anyone invest millions of dollars in drilling for oil when they would not make a profit? As the commentary notes, controlling prices tells producers to leave the black stuff in the ground. Refineries would be shut down, and no new spending on oil wells and facilities would occur. Over time, the supply of gasoline would decline even further, shown as the move from S_1 to S_2 in the figure below on the right. This would create larger shortages.

In the Soviet Union, China, Cuba, India, and other nations that imposed price controls on many goods and services for a long period of time, first-come, first-served allocation was replaced with graft and corruption. If you bribed the right official, you could get some bread or milk. If you paid off the manager, you could find other items that you needed. Corruption leads to a collapse of civilization—standards of living decline.

As noted in the chapter, allocation schemes other than price do not create incentives for improvement and increases in standards of living. What incentive does the first-come, first served system create? Just to be first. All you do is stand in lines. Nothing more is produced, and no alternatives to gasoline are ever discovered. In contrast, if price is not controlled, it rises to equilibrium, the quantity supplied rises, and the quantity demanded falls. The higher price brings out entrepreneurs seeking profits. These entrepreneurs will discover more efficient ways to transport people and alternative energy sources to oil and gasoline.

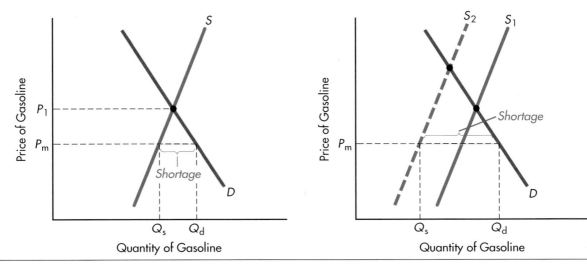

Chapter 4

The Market System and the Private and Public Sectors

? Fundamental Questions

1 | In a market system, who decides what goods and services are produced and how they are produced, and who obtains the goods and services that are produced?

2 | What is a household, and what is household income and spending?

3 | What is a business firm, and what is business spending?

4 | How does the international sector affect the economy?

5 | What is the public sector? What is public sector spending?

6 | How do the private and public sectors interact?

You decide to buy a new Toyota, so you go to a Toyota dealer and exchange money for the car. The Toyota dealer has rented land and buildings and hired workers in order to make cars available to you and other members of the public. The employees earn incomes paid by the Toyota dealer and then use those incomes to buy food from the grocery store. This transaction generates revenue for the grocery store, which hires workers and pays them incomes that they then use to buy groceries and Toyotas. Your expenditure for the Toyota is part of a circular flow. Revenue is received by the Toyota dealer, which pays its employees, who, in turn, buy goods and services.

Of course, the story is complicated by the fact that your Toyota may have been manufactured in Japan and then shipped to the United States before it was sold by the local

Toyota dealer. Your purchase of the Toyota creates revenue for both the local dealer and the manufacturer, which pays autoworkers to assemble the cars. When you buy your Toyota, you pay a sales tax, which the government uses to support its expenditures on police, fire protection, national defense, the legal system, and other services. In short, many people in different areas of the economy are involved in what seems to be a single transaction.

We begin this chapter by examining the interaction of buyers and sellers in a market system. We then look at the main sectors of an economy—households, firms, the international, and the government—to determine how they interact.

■ 1. The Market System

1 | In a market system, who decides what goods and services are produced and how they are produced, and who obtains the goods and services that are produced?

As we learned in Chapter 2, the production possibilities curve represents all possible combinations of goods and services that a society can produce if its resources are used fully and efficiently. Which combination, that is, which point on the PPC, will society choose? In a price or market system, the answer is given by demand and supply. Consumers demonstrate what they are willing and able to pay for by buying different goods and services. If a business is to succeed, it must supply what people want at a price that people can afford.

1.a. Consumer Sovereignty

The technology love affair is occurring all over the world. Laptop computer sales exceed those of desktop PCs, and there has been a massive move from mobile phone to smartphones. Think of a daily task, any daily task, and it's likely that there's a specialized, pocket-sized device designed to help you accomplish it. You can get a machine to make phone calls or one that keeps your calendar and address book, another that entertains you or plays your music, and another that gives directions, one that takes pictures, checks your e-mail, and does other things. Today you don't have to have a separate device for each task. A smartphone can take care of all of your handheld computing and communication needs in a single, small package. And future applications promise to be even more impressive, such as using the phone as a wireless credit card. The first smartphone was called Simon; it was designed by IBM in 1992. Smartphone adoption in the U.S. initially lagged that of other developed areas, such as Japan or Europe, but the North American market expanded considerably beginning in 2008.

In the 1990s, people wanted mobile devices to carry out those daily tasks. The Blackberry, iPod, and other devices served various functions. By emphasizing convenience and flexibility, Nokia, Sharp, Fujitsu, and RIM grabbed a big share of the smartphone market worldwide, and Apple did well in North America. While these and a few manufacturers became successful, the star of the story is not these companies. It is the consumer. In a market system, if consumers are willing and able to pay for more powerful and flexible phones, more such phones appear. If consumers are willing and able to pay for a small phone that takes pictures and entertains you and does other tasks, such a phone will be available.

Consumer sovereignty:
the authority of consumers
to determine what is
produced through their
purchases of goods and
services

Why does the consumer have such power? The name of the game for business is profit, and the only way a business can make a profit is by satisfying consumer wants. Consumers, not politicians or business firms, ultimately determine what is to be produced. A firm that produces something that no consumers want will not remain in business very long. **Consumer sovereignty**—the authority of consumers to determine what is produced through their purchases of goods and services—dictates what goods and services will be produced. Firms and inventors come up with new products, but if consumers are not willing and able to purchase these products, the products will not exist for long.

1.b. Profit and the Allocation of Resources

When a good or service seems to have the potential to generate a profit, some entrepreneur will put together the resources needed to offer that good or service for sale. If the potential profit turns into a loss, the entrepreneur may stop buying resources and turn to some other occupation or project. The resources used in the losing operation will then be available for use in an activity where they are more highly valued.

To illustrate how resources get allocated in the market system, let's look at the market for PDAs and smartphones. The PDA was introduced in the market several years before the smartphone. Figure 1 shows a change in demand for PDAs .The initial demand curve, D_1, and supply curve, S, are shown in Figure 1(a). With these demand and supply curves, the equilibrium price (P_1) is $80, and the equilibrium quantity (Q_1) is 100 thousand units per year. At this price-quantity combination, the number of PDAs demanded equals the number of PDAs offered for sale; equilibrium is reached, so we say that the market clears (there is no shortage or surplus).

The second part of the figure shows what happened when consumer tastes changed; people preferred to have a smartphone rather than just a PDA. This change in tastes caused the demand for PDAs to decline; illustrated by a leftward shift of the demand curve, from D_1 to D_2, in Figure 1(b). The demand curve shifted to the left because fewer PDAs were demanded at each price. Consumer tastes, not the price of PDAs, changed first. (A price change would have led to a change in the quantity demanded and would be represented by a move *along* demand curve D_1.) The change in tastes caused a change in demand and a leftward shift of the demand curve. The shift from D_1 to D_2 created a new equilibrium point. The equilibrium price (P_2) decreased to $60, and the equilibrium quantity (Q_2) decreased to 80 (thousand) units.

While the market for PDAs was changing, so was the market for smartphones. Figure 2(a) shows the original demand for the smartphone and its original price of $500. Figure 2(b) shows a rightward shift of the demand curve, from D_1 to D_2, representing the increased demand for smartphones. This demand change resulted in a higher market-clearing price for smartphones, from $500 to $600.

The changing profit potential of the two markets induced existing firms to switch from PDAs to smartphones and for new firms to offer smartphones from the start. Nokia dominated the smartphone market, but Apple, which at first did not offer smartphones had to play catch up and begin offering its own smartphone. It did so with its iPhone.

As demand fell for the PDA, the market-clearing price of PDAs fell (from $80 to $60 in Figure 1[b]) and the quantity of PDAs sold also declined (from 100 to 80). The decreased demand led to a lower price, which meant that many PDA firms saw declining profits. In the smartphone business, the opposite occurred. As the demand for smartphones rose, the market-clearing price rose (from $500 to $600 in Figure 2[b]); the number of smartphones sold also rose (from 50 to

FIGURE 1 A Demand Change in the Market for PDAs

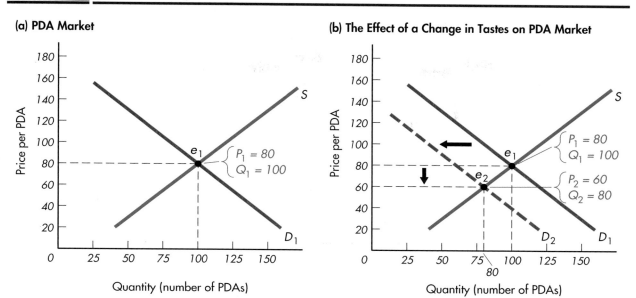

In Figure 1(a), the initial market-clearing price (P_1) and market-clearing quantity (Q_1) are shown. In Figure 1(b), the market-clearing price and quantity change from P_1 and Q_1 to P_2 and Q_2 as the demand curve shifts to the left because of a change in tastes. The result of decreased demand is a lower price and a lower quantity produced.

FIGURE 2 A Demand Change in the Market for Smartphones

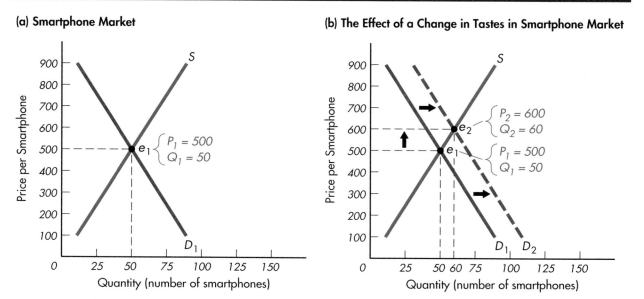

In Figure 2(a), the initial market-clearing price (P_1) and quantity (Q_1) are shown. In Figure 2(b), the demand for smartphones increases, thus driving up the market-clearing price (P_2) and quantity (Q_2) as the demand curve shifts to the right, from D_1 to D_2.

60 thousand). The increased demand, higher price, and resulting higher profit induced firms to increase production.

Why did the production of smartphones increase while the production of PDAs declined? Not because of a government decree. Not because of the desires of the business sector, especially the owners of the smartphone manufacturers. The consumer—*consumer sovereignty*—made all this happen. Businesses that failed to respond to consumer desires and failed to provide the desired good at the lowest price failed to survive.

1.c. Creative Destruction

After demand shifted to smartphones, the resources that had been used in the production of PDAs were available for use elsewhere. A few former employees were able to get jobs in the smartphone industry. Some of the equipment used in manufacturing PDAs was purchased by the smartphone firms; and some of the components that previously would have gone to the PDAs were used in the smartphones. Although a few former employees of the PDA business became employed in the smartphone business, others had to find entirely new positions in totally different businesses. Some of the equipment used to manufacture PDAs was sold as scrap; other equipment was sold to other manufacturers. In other words, the resources moved from an activity where their value was relatively low to an activity where they were more highly valued. No one commanded the resources to move. They moved because they could earn more in some other activity.

This same story applies in case after case after case. The Sony Walkman was replaced by Apple's iPod, and the early iPod is now contained in the iPhone. The process of new products and new firms replacing existing products and firms is called *creative destruction*. This is what the market process is all about—creating new ideas, new products, and new ways of doing things, and replacing the obsolete, costly, and inefficient. Every year *Forbes* magazine publishes a list of the 100 largest companies in terms of sales. In 1987, *Forbes* compared that year's list to the 100 largest firms in 1917. Only 39 of the 1917 group remained in 1987. Of the 39 that remained in business, 18 had managed to stay in the top 100. Of the 18 that stayed in the top 100, only 2 had performed better than the market average—Kodak and GE. Both of these have since fallen, barely surviving. This seems an amazing change, but the pace of change has only quickened since 1987. Fewer than 25 percent of today's major corporations will continue to exist in 25 years.

In 1900, over 60 percent of the U.S. workforce was employed in agriculture. Today, less than 3 percent are employed in agriculture. Yet the U.S. produces far more agriculture today than it did in 1900. The technology used in agriculture so increased the productivity on farms that only 3 percent of the workforce is needed. What happened to the 57 percent of the workforce that were not on the farms today? Since they were no longer needed in agriculture, people received training in high technology or many other fields that had a greater value for them than working on the farm would have. In a sense, jobs on the farm were destroyed, but they were destroyed by the creation of new jobs in technology or services.

Firms produce the goods and services and use the resources that enable them to generate the highest profits. If one firm does this better than others, then that firm earns a greater profit than others. Seeing that success, other firms copy or mimic the first firm. If a firm cannot be as profitable as the others, it will eventually go out of business or move to another line of business where it can be successful. In the process of firms always seeking to lower their costs and make higher profits, society finds that the goods and services that buyers want are produced in the least costly manner. Not only do consumers get the goods and services that they want and will pay for, but they get these products at the lowest possible price.

1.d. The Determination of Income

Consumer demands dictate what is produced, and the search for profit defines how goods and services are produced. For whom are the goods and services produced, that is, who gets the goods and services? As we discussed in Chapter 3, in a price or market system, those who have the ability to pay for the products get the products. Your income determines your ability to pay, but where does income come from? A person's income is obtained by selling the services of the resources that person owns.

In reality, households own all resources. Everyone owns his or her own labor; some households also own land, and many also own firms or portions of firms. When a household owns shares of stock, it owns a portion of the firm whose shares it owns. Many households own shares of stock either as direct investments or as part of their retirement fund. The firm you or your parents work for might provide a 401(k) or some other retirement plan. A portion of these plans typically own shares of stock. All firms, whether private firms or firms traded through stock markets, are owned by households in some way. Thus, if a firm acquires equipment, buildings, land, and natural resources, it is actually households that ultimately own those things. If a firm were taken apart and its parts sold off, households would end up with the money.

Typically we think of our income as what we are paid for our labor services. But you may also receive income from the shares of stock that you own (dividends and appreciation) and the various savings accounts that you own (interest). You may receive rent from being a landlord or from allowing a firm to use the services of your land. You may get profits from a business that you started.

RECAP

1. In a market system, consumers are sovereign and decide by means of their purchases what goods and services will be produced.

2. In a market system, firms decide how to produce the goods and services that consumers want. In order to earn maximum profits, firms use the least-cost combinations of resources.

3. Income and prices determine who gets what in a market system. Income is determined by the ownership of resources.

■ 2. The Private Sector

Buyers and sellers of goods and services and resource owners are linked together in an economy. For every dollar someone spends, someone else receives a dollar as income. In the remainder of this chapter, we learn more about the linkages among the sectors of the economy. We classify the buyers and the resource owners into the household sector; the sellers or business firms are the business sector; households and firms in other countries, who may also be buyers and sellers of this country's goods and services, are the international sector. These three sectors—households, business firms, and the international firms and consumers—constitute the **private sector** of the economy. The **private sector** refers to any of the economy that is not part of government. The **public sector** refers to the government, government spending and taxing, and government sponsored and run entities. The relative sizes of private and public sectors vary from economy to economy. The market economies tend to have smaller public sectors relative to the total economy than do the more socialist or centrally planned economies.

private sector: households, businesses, and the international sector

public sector: the government

2 | What is a household, and what is household income and spending?

household: one or more persons who occupy a unit of housing

consumption: household spending

2.a. Households

A **household** consists of one or more persons who occupy a unit of housing. The unit of housing may be a house, an apartment, or even a single room, as long as it constitutes separate living quarters. A household may consist of related family members, like a father, mother, and children, or it may comprise unrelated individuals, like three college students sharing an apartment. The person in whose name the house or apartment is owned or rented is called the householder.

Household spending is called **consumption**. Householders consume housing, transportation, food, entertainment, and other goods and services. Household spending (also called consumer spending) per year in the United States is shown in Figure 3, along with household income. The pattern is one of steady increase. Spending by the household sector is the largest component of total spending in the economy—rising to over \$12 trillion in 2009.

FIGURE 3   Household Spending and Income

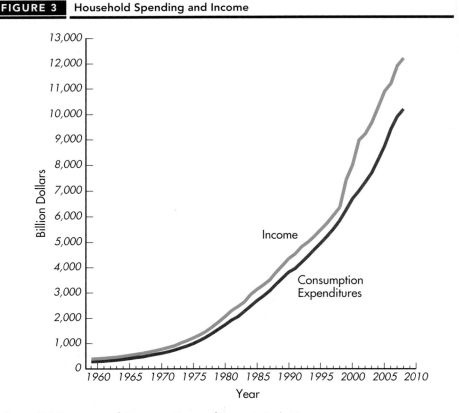

Source: U.S. Department of Commerce, (Bureau of Economic Analysis); www.census.gov.

3 What is a business firm, and what is business spending?

business firm: a business organization controlled by a single management

sole proprietorship: a business owned by one person who receives all the profits and is responsible for all the debts incurred by the business

partnership: a business with two or more owners who share the firm's profits and losses

corporation: a legal entity owned by shareholders whose liability for the firm's losses is limited to the value of the stock they own

multinational business: a firm that owns and operates producing units in foreign countries

investment: spending on capital goods to be used in producing goods and services

4 How does the international sector affect the economy?

2.b. Business Firms

A **business firm** is a business organization controlled by a single management. The firm's business may be conducted at more than one location. The terms *company*, *enterprise*, and *business* are used interchangeably with *firm*.

Firms are organized as sole proprietorships, partnerships, or corporations. A **sole proprietorship** is a business owned by one person. This type of firm may be a one person operation or a large enterprise with many employees. In either case, the owner receives all the profits and is responsible for all the debts incurred by the business.

A **partnership** is a business owned by two or more partners who share both the profits of the business and responsibility for the firm's losses. The partners can be individuals, estates, or other businesses.

A **corporation** is a business whose identity in the eyes of the law is distinct from the identity of its owners. State law allows the formation of corporations. A corporation is an economic entity that, like a person, can own property and borrow money in its own name. The owners of a corporation are shareholders. If a corporation cannot pay its debts, creditors cannot seek payment from the shareholders' personal wealth. The corporation itself is responsible for all its actions. The shareholders' liability is limited to the value of the stock they own.

Many firms are global in their operations, even though they may have been founded and may be owned by residents of a single country. Firms typically first enter the international market by selling products to foreign countries. As revenues from these sales increase, the firms realize advantages by locating subsidiaries in foreign countries. A **multinational business** is a firm that owns and operates producing units in foreign countries. The best-known U.S. corporations are multinational firms. Ford, IBM, PepsiCo, and McDonald's all own operating units in many different countries. Ford Motor Company, for instance, is the parent firm of sales organizations and assembly plants located around the world. As transportation and communication technologies progress, multinational business activity undoubtedly will grow.

Expenditures by business firms for capital goods—machines, tools, and buildings—that will be used to produce goods and services are called **investments**. Notice that the meaning of investment here is different from the everyday meaning, "a financial transaction such as buying bonds or stocks." In economics, the term investment refers to business spending for capital goods.

Investment spending in 2009 was lower than in 2006; businesses had reduced expenditures on capital goods in 2008 and 2009 because their sales had declined and their outlook for future sales was bleak. Investment is equal to roughly one-fourth of consumption, or household spending, but fluctuates a great deal more than consumption. Investment spending between 1959 and 2009 is shown in Figure 4. Compare Figures 3 and 4 and notice how much investment fluctuates relative to consumption.

2.c. The International Sector

Economic conditions in the United States affect conditions throughout the world. Today, foreign buyers and sellers also have a significant effect on economic conditions in the United States.

The nations of the world may be divided into two categories: industrial countries and developing countries. Developing countries greatly outnumber industrial countries (see Figure 5). The World Bank (an international organization that makes loans to developing countries) groups countries according to per capita income (income per person). Low-income economies are those with per capita incomes of less than $1,000. Middle-income economies have per capita annual incomes of $1,000–$10,000. High-income economies—oil exporters and industrial

FIGURE 4   U.S. Investment Spending

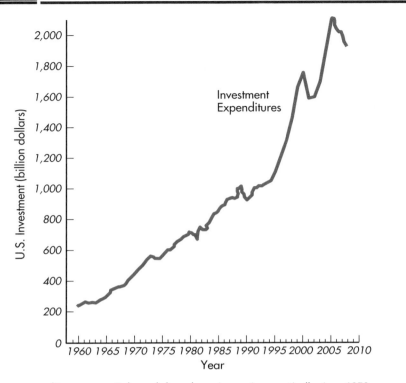

Business expenditures on capital goods have been increasing erratically since 1959.
Source: *Economic Report of the President, 2009.*

"*The best and brightest are leaving.*" Statements like this are heard in many nations throughout the world. The best trained and most innovative people in many countries find their opportunities greater in the United States. As a result, they leave their countries to gain citizenship in the United States. But it is not easy for people to move from one country to another. The flow of goods and services among nations—international trade—occurs more readily than does the flow of workers.

Economic Insight

The Successful Entrepreneur
(Sometimes It's Better to Be Lucky Than Good)

Entrepreneurs do not always develop an abstract idea into reality when starting a new firm. Sometimes people stumble onto a good thing by accident and then are clever enough and willing to take the necessary risk to turn their lucky find into a commercial success.

In 1875, a Philadelphia pharmacist on his honeymoon tasted tea made from an innkeeper's old family recipe. The tea, made from 16 wild roots and berries, was so delicious that the pharmacist asked the innkeeper's wife for the recipe. When he returned to his pharmacy, he created a solid concentrate of the drink that could be sold for home consumption.

The pharmacist was Charles Hires, a devout Quaker, who intended to sell "Hires Herb Tea" to hard-drinking Pennsylvania coal miners as a nonalcoholic alternative to beer and whiskey. A friend of Hires suggested that miners would not drink anything called "tea" and recommended that he call his drink "root beer."

The initial response to Hires Root Beer was so enthusiastic that Hires soon began nationwide distribution. The yellow box of root beer extract became a familiar sight in homes and drugstore fountains across the United States. By 1895, Hires, who started with a $3,000 loan, was operating a business valued at half a million dollars (a lot of money in 1895) and bottling ready-to-drink root beer across the country.

Hires, of course, is not the only entrepreneur who was clever enough to turn a lucky discovery into a business success. In 1894, in Battle Creek, Michigan, a sanitarium handyman named Will Kellogg was helping his older brother prepare wheat meal to serve to patients in the sanitarium's dining room. The two men would boil wheat dough and then run it through rollers to produce thin sheets of meal. One day they left a batch of the dough out overnight. The next day, when the dough was run through the rollers, it broke up into flakes instead of forming a sheet.

By letting the dough stand overnight, the Kelloggs had allowed moisture to be distributed evenly to each individual wheat berry. When the dough went through the rollers, the berries formed separate flakes instead of binding together. The Kelloggs toasted the wheat flakes and served them to the patients. They were an immediate success. In fact, the brothers had to start a mailorder flaked-cereal business because patients wanted flaked cereal for their households.

Kellogg saw the market potential of the discovery and started his own cereal company (his brother refused to join him in the business). He was a great promoter who used innovations like four-color magazine ads and free-sample promotions. In New York City, he offered a free box of corn flakes to every woman who winked at her grocer on a specified day. The promotion was considered risqué, but Kellogg's sales in New York increased from two railroad cars of cereal a month to one car a day.

Will Kellogg, a poorly paid sanitarium worker in his mid-forties, became a daring entrepreneur after his mistake with wheat flour led to the discovery of a way to produce flaked cereal. He became one of the richest men in America because of his entrepreneurial ability.

market economies—are distinguished from the middle-income economies and have per capita incomes of greater than $10,000. Some countries are not members of the World Bank and so are not categorized, and information about a few small countries is so limited that the World Bank is unable to classify them.

It is readily apparent from Figure 5 that low-income economies are heavily concentrated in Africa and Asia. An important question in economics is *Why*? Why are some countries rich and others poor? Why are poor countries concentrated in Africa and Asia with some in Latin America? These are questions discussed in both microeconomics and macroeconomics.

FIGURE 5 World Economic Development

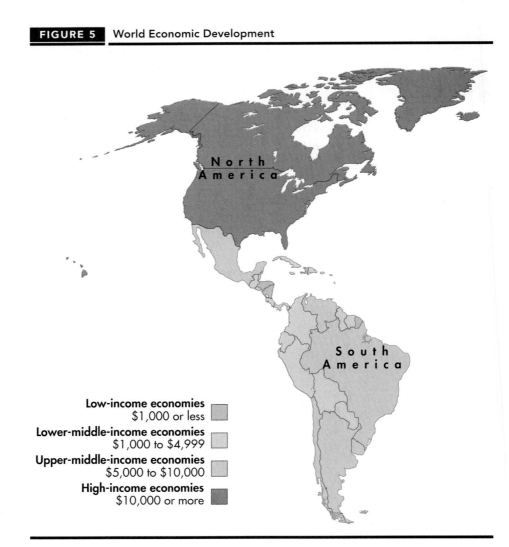

Low-income economies
$1,000 or less

Lower-middle-income economies
$1,000 to $4,999

Upper-middle-income economies
$5,000 to $10,000

High-income economies
$10,000 or more

The World Bank uses per capita income to classify 23 countries as "industrial market economies." They are listed in the bar chart in Figure 6. The 23 countries listed in Figure 6 are among the wealthiest countries in the world. Not appearing on the list are the high-income oil-exporting nations like Libya, Saudi Arabia, Kuwait, and the United Arab Emirates. The World Bank considers those countries to be "still developing."

The economies of the industrial nations are highly interdependent. As conditions change in one country, business firms and individuals may shift large sums of money between countries. As funds flow from one country to another, economic conditions in one country spread to other countries. As a result, the major economic powers like the United States, European Monetary Union, Japan, and China are forced to pay close attention to each other's economic policies.

The United States tends to buy, or *import*, primary products such as agricultural produce and minerals from the developing countries and manufactured products from the industrial nations. Products that a country buys from another country are called **imports**. Products that a country sells to another country are called **exports**. The United States tends to sell, or *export*, manufactured goods to all countries. In addition, the United States is the largest producer and exporter of grains and other agricultural output in the world. The efficiency of U.S. farming

imports: products that a country buys from other countries

exports: products that a country sells to other countries

FIGURE 5   (Continued)

The colors on the map identify low-income, middle-income, and high-income economies. Countries have been placed in each group on the basis of GNP per capita and, in some instances, other distinguishing economic characteristics.
Source: World Bank, http://nebula.worldbank.org/website/GNIwdi/viewer.htm.

trade surplus: the situation that exists when imports are less than exports

trade deficit: the situation that exists when imports exceed exports

net exports: the difference between the value of exports and the value of imports

relative to farming in much of the rest of the world gives the United States a comparative advantage in many agricultural products.

Economic activity of the United States with the rest of the world includes U.S. spending on foreign goods and foreign spending on U.S. goods. Figure 7 shows how U.S. exports and imports are spread over different countries. Notice that the largest trading partners with the US are Canada, Mexico, China, and Western Europe.

When exports exceed imports, a **trade surplus** exists. When imports exceed exports, a **trade deficit** exists. Figure 8 shows that the United States is importing much more than it exports.

The term **net exports** refers to the difference between the value of exports and the value of imports: Net exports equals exports minus imports. Figure 8 traces U.S. net exports over time. Positive net exports represwent trade surpluses; negative net exports represent trade deficits. The trade deficits (indicated by negative net exports) starting in the 1980s were unprecedented. Reasons for this pattern of international trade are discussed in later chapters.

FIGURE 6   The Industrial Market Economies

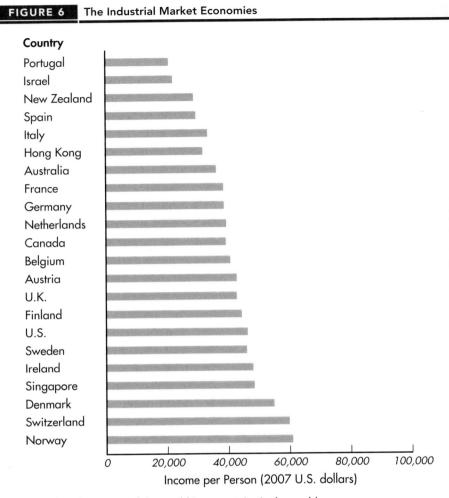

The bar chart lists some of the wealthiest countries in the world.
Source: World Bank, *World Development Report, 2009*; http://siteresources.worldbank.org/
DATASTATISTICS/Resources/GNOPC.pdf.

RECAP

1. A household consists of one or more persons who occupy a unit of housing.

2. Household spending is called consumption.

3. Business firms may be organized as sole proprietorships, partnerships, or corporations.

4. Business investment spending fluctuates widely over time.

5. The majority of U.S. trade is with the industrial market economies.

6. Exports are product s sold to foreign countries; imports are products bought from foreign countries. Exports minus imports equal net exports.

7. Positive net exports signal a trade surplus; negative net exports signal a trade deficit.

FIGURE 7 Direction of U.S. Trade

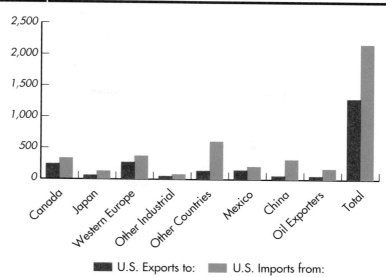

This chart shows that a trade deficit exists for the United States, since U.S. imports greatly exceed U.S. exports. The chart also shows that the largest trading partners with the U.S. are western Europe, Japan, Canada, Mexico, and China.
Source: *Economic Report of the President, 2009*; www.census.gov/foreign-trade/Press-Release/current_press_release/exh14a.xls.

FIGURE 8 U.S. Net Exports

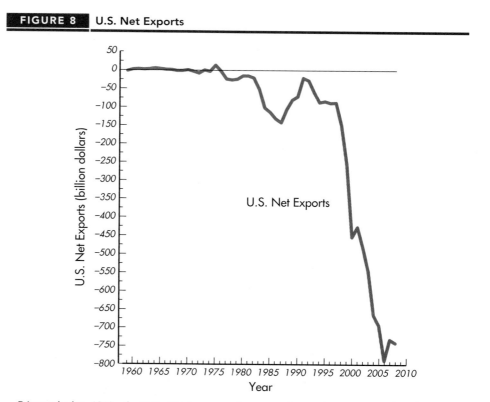

Prior to the late 1960s, the United States generally exported more than it imported and had a trade surplus. Since 1976, net exports have been negative, and the United States has had a trade deficit.
Source: *Economic Report of the President, 2009*; www.gpoaccess.gov/eop/2009/B103.xls.

The United States Capitol is where the Senate and House of Representatives meet. The Capitol represents the public sector—government. Thomas Jefferson insisted the legislative building be called the "Capitol" rather than "Congress House." He thought "Capitol" represented the shining city on a hill. The word capitol comes from Latin, meaning city on a hill.

5 | **What is the public sector? What is public sector spending?**

■ 3. The Public Sector

When we refer to the public sector, it is government that we are talking about, either federal, state, or local government. Government's influence is extensive. From conception to death, individuals are affected by the activities of the government. Many mothers receive prenatal care through government programs. We are born in hospitals that are subsidized or run by the government. We are delivered by doctors who received training in subsidized colleges. Our births are recorded on certificates filed with the government. Ninety percent of students attend public schools as opposed to private schools. Many people live in housing that is directly subsidized by the government or have mortgages that are insured by the government. Most people, at one time or another, put savings into accounts that are insured by the government. Virtually all of us, at some time in our lives, receive money from the government—from student loan programs, unemployment compensation, disability insurance, social security, or Medicare.

3.a. Growth of Government

Government in the United States exists at the federal, state, and local levels. Local government includes county, regional, and municipal units. Economic discussions tend to focus on the federal government because national economic policy is set at that level. Nevertheless, each level affects us through its taxing and spending decisions and its laws regulating behavior.

According to virtually any measure, government in the United States has been a growth industry since 1930. The number of people employed by the local, state, and federal governments combined grew from 3 million in 1930 to over 18 million today; there are now more people employed in government than in manufacturing. Annual expenditures by the federal government rose from $3 billion in 1930 to more than $1 trillion today. In 1929, government spending constituted less than 2.5 percent of total spending in the economy. Today, it is around 30 percent, as shown in Figure 9. The number of rules and regulations created by the government is so large that it is measured by the number of telephone-book–sized

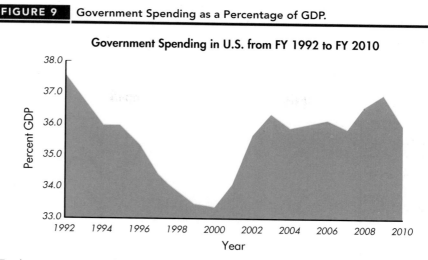

FIGURE 9   Government Spending as a Percentage of GDP.

Total government spending—federal, state, and local divided by gross domestic product—the total spending of all sectors in the economy.
Source: www.usgovernmentspending.com.

6 | How do the private and public sectors interact?

3.b. Government Spending

Federal, state, and local government spending for goods and services is shown in Figure 10. Spending on goods and services by all levels of government combined is larger than investment spending but much smaller than consumption. In 2009, combined government spending was about $5,000 billion, investment spending was about $2.012 billion, and consumption was about $12,163 billion.

FIGURE 10   Federal, State, and Local Government Expenditures for Goods and Services

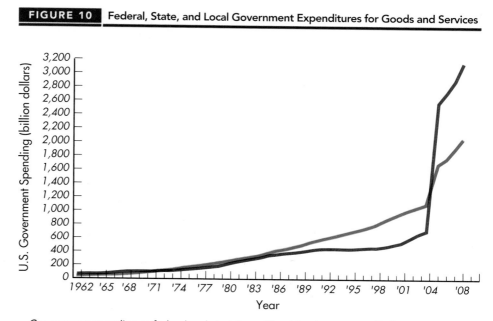

Government spending at federal and at state and local levels rose steadily from the 1960s until about 1980. Then state and local rose more quickly than federal spending until 2003. Since then, federal spending has increased at a very rapid pace. Total government spending approached $7 trillion in 2009, with federal spending reaching nearly $4 trillion, and state and local reaching nearly $3 trillion.
Source: Data are from the *Economic Report of the President, 2009.*

FIGURE 11	U.S. Federal Budget Deficits

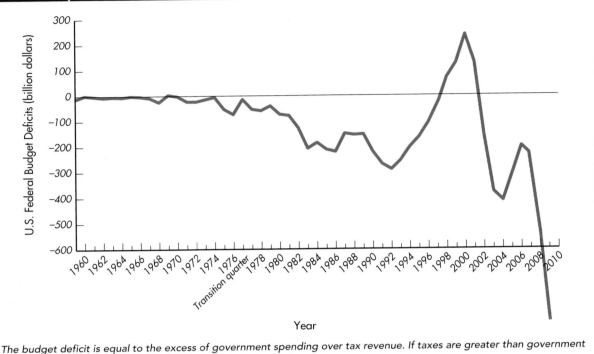

The budget deficit is equal to the excess of government spending over tax revenue. If taxes are greater than government spending, a budget surplus (shown as a positive number) exists.
Source: Data are from the *Economic Report of the President, 2009.*

transfer payments:
income transferred by the government from a citizen who is earning income to another citizen

In addition to purchasing goods and services, government also takes money from some taxpayers and transfers it to others. Such **transfer payments** are a part of total government expenditures, so the total government budget is much larger than just the expenditures for goods and services. In 2008, total expenditures of federal, state, and local government for goods and services were about $4,802 billion. In this same year, transfer payments made by all levels of government were about $1,906 billion.

The magnitude of federal government spending relative to federal government revenue from taxes has become an important issue in recent years. Figure 11 shows that the federal budget was roughly balanced until the early 1970s. The budget is a measure of spending and revenue. A balanced budget occurs when federal spending is approximately equal to federal revenue. This was the case through the 1950s and 1960s.

budget surplus: the excess that results when government spending is less than tax revenue

budget deficit: the shortage that results when government spending is greater than tax revenue

If federal government spending is less than tax revenue, a **budget surplus** exists. By the early 1980s, federal government spending was much larger than revenue, so a large **budget deficit** existed. The federal budget deficit grew very rapidly to about $290 billion by the early 1990s before beginning to drop and turning to surplus by 1998. After four years of surpluses, a deficit was again realized in 2002, and the deficit has grown since then.

RECAP

1. The public sector refers to government.

2. Government spending is larger than investment spending but much smaller than consumption spending.

3. When government spending exceeds tax revenue, a budget deficit exists. When government spending is less than tax revenue, a budget surplus exists.

■ 4. Linking the Sectors

Now that we have an idea of the size and structure of each of the private sectors—households, businesses, international—and the public sector—government—let's see how the sectors are connected. This is illustrated quite simply in what is referred to as the *circular flow diagram,* shown in Figure 12.

circular flow diagram:
a model showing the flow of output and income from one sector of the economy to another

4.a. Households and Businesses and the Circular Flow

Households own all the basic resources, or factors of production, in the economy. Household members own land and provide labor, and they are the entrepreneurs, stockholders, proprietors, and partners who own business firms. Households interact with the other sectors by means of buying and selling. Businesses employ the services of resources in order to produce goods and services. Business firms pay households for their resource services. The flow of resource services from households to businesses is shown by the blue-green line at the bottom of Figure 12. The flow of money payments from firms to households is shown by the gold line at the bottom of Figure 12. Households use the money payments to buy goods and services from firms. These money payments are the firms' revenues. The flow of money payments from households to firms is shown by the gold line at the top of the diagram. The flow of goods and services from firms to households is shown by the blue-green line at the top of Figure 12. Notice that if households and firms were the only two sectors in the economy, income and output would be identical. What occurs when we add the government and international sectors?

Households do not spend all of the money that they receive. They save some. In Figure 12 we see that household saving is deposited in **financial intermediaries** like banks, credit unions, and savings and loan firms. A financial intermediary accepts deposits from savers and makes loans to borrowers. Businesses borrow money to invest to purchase additional capital. The money that is saved by the households thus reenters the economy in the form of investment spending as business firms borrow for expansion of their productive capacity.

financial intermediaries:
institutions that accept deposits from savers and make loans to borrowers

4.b. Government and the Circular Flow

The government sector buys resource services from households and goods and services from firms. This government spending represents income for the households and revenue for the firms. The government uses the resource services and goods and services to provide government services for households and firms. Households and firms pay taxes to the government to finance government expenditures. The yellow line from firms and households to government is taxes paid while the purple line from government to households represents government spending or government services other than payments for resources services and business goods and services. The blue line from households and firms to government are resource services and goods and services purchased by government. The yellow line from government to households and to firms is the payment for the resource services and the goods and service the government buys.

With the introduction of the government in the circular flow, the total value of private production no longer equals the value of household income. Households receive income from government so that the total value of output in the economy is equal to the total income received, but government is both a source of income and a provider of services.

FIGURE 12 The Circular Flow: Households, Firms, Government, and Foreign Countries

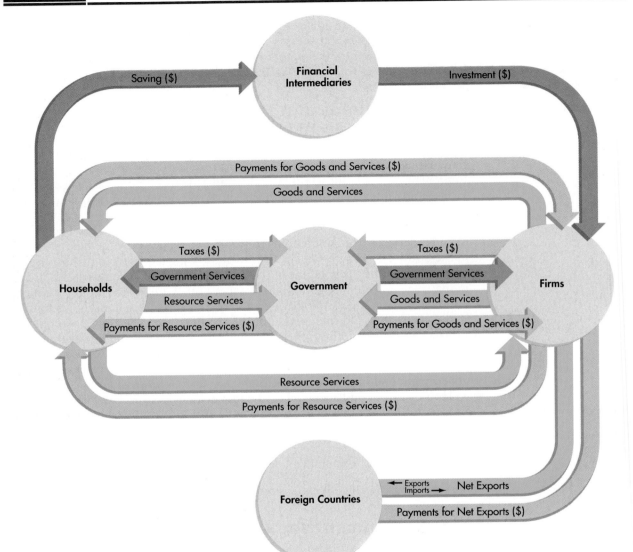

Firms and governments hire resources from households. The payments for these resources represent household income. Households spend their income for goods and services produced by the firms. Household spending represents revenue for firms. Households save some of their income and pay taxes to the government. The amounts saved reenters the circular flow as investment spending. Financial intermediaries like banks take in the saving of households and then lend this money to business firms for investment spending. The diagram assumes that households and government are not directly engaged in international trade. Domestic firms trade with firms in foreign countries. The flow of goods and services between countries is represented by the line labeled "net exports." Neither the net exports line nor the line labeled "payments for net exports" has an arrow indicating the direction of the flow because the flow can go from the home country to foreign countries or vice versa. When the domestic economy has positive net exports (a trade surplus), goods and services flow out of the domestic firms toward foreign countries and money payments flow from the foreign countries to the domestic firms. With negative net exports (a trade deficit), the reverse is true.

The government sector buys resource services from households and goods and services from firms. This government spending represents income for the households and revenue for the firms. The government uses the resource services and goods and services to provide government services for households and firms. Households and firms pay taxes to the government to finance government expenditures.

4.c. The International Sector and the Circular Flow

Foreign countries also affect and are affected by the household, business, and government sectors. But to simplify the circular flow diagram, let's assume that households are not directly engaged in international trade and that only business firms are buying and selling goods and services across international borders. This assumption is not far from the truth for the industrial countries and for many developing countries. We typically buy a foreign-made product from a local business firm rather than directly from the foreign producer. Also, let's ignore the government's participation in foreign exchanges. In Figure 12, a line labeled "net exports" connects firms and foreign countries, as does a line labeled "payments for net exports." Notice that neither line has an arrow indicating the direction of flow as do the other lines in the diagram. The reason is that net exports of the home country may be either positive (a trade surplus) or negative (a trade deficit). When net exports are positive, there is a net flow of goods from the firms of the home country to foreign countries and a net flow of money from foreign countries to the firms of the home country. When net exports are negative, the opposite occurs. A trade deficit involves net flows of goods from foreign countries to the firms of the home country and net money flows from the domestic firms to the foreign countries. If exports and imports are equal, net exports are zero because the value of exports is offset by the value of imports.

RECAP

1. The circular flow diagram illustragtes how the main sectors of an economy fit together.

2. The private sector refers to the household, business, and international sectors.

3. The public sector refers to government.

Summary

1 | **In a market system, who decides what goods and services are produced and how they are produced, and who obtains the goods and services that are produced?**

- In a market system, consumers are sovereign and decide by means of their purchases what goods and services will be produced. §1.a

- In a market system, firms decide how to produce the goods and services that consumers want. In order to earn maximum profits, firms use the least-cost combinations of resources. §1.c

- Income and prices determine who gets what in a market system. Income is determined by the ownership of resources. §1.d

2 | **What is a household, and what is household income and spending?**

- A household consists of one or more persons who occupy a unit of housing. §2.a

- Household spending is called consumption and is the largest component of spending in the economy. §2.a

3 | **What is a business firm, and what is business spending?**

- A business firm is a business organization controlled by a single management. §2.b

- Businesses may be organized as sole proprietorships, partnerships, or corporations. §2.b

- Business investment spending—the expenditure by business firms for capital goods—fluctuates a great deal over time. §2.b

4 | **How does the international sector affect the economy?**

- The international trade of the United States occurs predominantly with the other industrial economies. §2.c

- Exports are products sold to the rest of the world. Imports are products bought from the rest of the world. §2.c

• Exports minus imports equal net exports. Positive net exports mean that exports are greater than imports and a trade surplus exists. Negative net exports mean that imports exceed exports and a trade deficit exists. *§2.c*

5 | What is the public sector? What is public sector spending?

• The public sector refers to government, all levels of government–federal, state, and local.

• When a government spends more than it receives in taxes the government runs a deficit; when it receives more than it spends, it runs a surplus.

6 | How do the private and public sectors interact?

• The circular flow diagram illustrates how the main sectors of the economy fit together.

• Government interacts with both households and firms. Households get government services and pay taxes; they provide resource services and receive income. Firms sell goods and services to government and receive income.

KEY TERMS

consumer sovereignty *§1.a*	partnership *§2.b*	trade deficit *§2.c*
private sector *§2*	corporation *§2.b*	net exports *§2.c*
public sector *§2*	multinational business *§2.b*	budget surplus *§3.b*
household *§2.a*	investment *§2.b*	budget deficit *§3.b*
consumption *§2.a*	imports *§2.c*	transfer payments *§3.b*
business firm *§2.b*	exports *§2.c*	financial intermediaries *§4.a*
sole proprietorship *§2.b*	trade surplus *§2.c*	circular flow diagram *§4*

EXERCISES

1. What is consumer sovereignty? What does it have to do with determining what goods and services are produced? Who determines how goods and services are produced? Who receives the goods and services in a market system?

2. Is a family a household? Is a household a family?

3. Which sector (households, business, or international) spends the most? Which sector spends the least? Which sector has the most volatility of spending?

4. What does it mean if net exports are negative?

5. Total spending in the economy is equal to consumption plus investment plus government spending plus net exports. If households want to save and thus do not use all of their income for consumption, what will happen to total spending? Because total spending in the economy is equal to total income and output, what will happen to the output of goods and services if households want to save more?

6. People sometimes argue that imports should be limited by government policy. Suppose a government quota on the quantity of imports causes net exports to rise. Using the circular flow diagram as a guide, explain why total expenditures and national output may rise after the quota is imposed. Who is likely to benefit from the quota? Who will be hurt?

7. Use the circular flow diagram to explain the effects of a decision by the household sector to increase saving.

8. Suppose there are three countries in the world. Country A exports $11 million worth of goods to country B and $5 million worth of goods to country C; country B exports $3 million worth of goods to country A and $6 million worth of goods to country C; and country C exports $4 million worth of goods to country A and $1 million worth of goods to country B.
   a. What are the net exports of countries A, B, and C?
   b. Which country is running a trade deficit? A trade surplus?

9. Over time, there has been a shift away from outdoor drive-in movie theaters to indoor movie theaters. Use supply and demand curves to illustrate and explain how consumers can bring about such a change when their tastes change.

10. List the four sectors of the economy along with the type of spending associated with each sector. Order the types of spending in terms of magnitude and give an example of each kind of spending.

11. Using the circular flow diagram, illustrate the effects of imposing an increase in taxes on the household sector.

12. Using the circular flow diagram, explain how the government can run budget deficits—that is, spend more than it receives in tax revenue.

Impact of Bailouts

The Globe and Mail (Canada) **January 28, 2009**

GENEVA

Government bailouts of banks and the auto sector could trigger trade disputes over their impact on competition, the head of the World Trade Organization said yesterday. In a report to the WTO's 153 member states, director-general Pascal Lamy said state aid packages meant to stave off financial crises need to be implemented so they do not violate global trade rules or discriminate against foreign companies.

"Nothing can be said, for the time being, about the likely trade impact of these measures, many of which are still lacking publicly announced details," Mr. Lamy said, suggesting the market effects of cash infusions, guarantees and other bailout steps will become clearer with time.

"It must be recognized that some of the measures at least, which, in most cases, constitute some form of state aid or subsidy, may eventually have negative spillover effects on other markets or introduce distortions to competition between financial institutions," he said.

The WTO's dispute settlement body arbitrates disagreements between governments about tariffs, subsidies and other barriers that are seen to create an uneven playing field.

Some of the biggest WTO disputes to date have centered on the European Union's rules on banana imports, state aid for aircraft makers, and European bans on genetically modified foods. and auto industry aid packages in Canada, Germany, France, Australia, Argentina, South Korea, China and elsewhere all could lead to WTO complaints.

Efforts to infuse liquidity and remove toxic assets from big banks in the United States and Europe also could lead to WTO litigation if they disrupt the availability of funds or give domestic banks an unfair advantage, Mr. Lamy's report said.

Several countries have imposed trade-restricting policies since the onset of the financial crisis in September, 2008, the report said.

Laura MacInnis

A government bailout is the government's transfer of money to a particular company or industry. The bailouts of auto and banks means that the government is using tax revenues or running a deficit to provide the money to auto companies and banks either as a loan or a subsidy. Why would the director-general of the World Trade Organization (WTO), Pascal Lamy, state that "the aid packages meant to stave off financial crises need to be implemented so they do not violate global trade rules or discriminate against foreign companies"?

How could bailouts lead to trade restrictions? If an aid package from the U.S. government to the U.S. auto manufacturers—Ford, GM, and Chrysler—did not also provide aid to other auto manufacturers who produce in the United States, such as Toyota, BMW, and Honda, then it would provide an advantage to the U.S. auto makers compared to the foreign auto makers. Since the cost of manufacturing a car by Ford, GM, and Chrysler in the United States. is about 25% more than the cost of manufacturing a car by the foreign auto companies due to pay and benefits provided workers, the foreign auto producers have an advantage. They can offer the same quality car at a lower price than the U.S. companies can.

Now, what occurs if the U.S. government offers billions of dollars in aid to the U.S. auto companies? The aid enables the U.S. companies to offer their products for lower prices than the foreign auto companies. Now the foreign auto companies are at a disadvantage. How can they offset the disadvantage? Their government could provide aid to them or conversely, could penalize the U.S. government by imposing barriers on the sale of U.S. goods into their country. The article noted that India raised tariffs on some imported steel products, Ecuador raised tariffs on 940 products, including cell phones, eyeglasses, building materials, and transport equipment.

Argentina imposed licensing requirements on products such as auto parts and textiles, and the European Commission said it would reintroduce export subsidies for butter, cheese, and whole and skim milk powder. All these actions reduce international trade.

In terms of the circular flow diagram, the trade restrictions would mean the sales by U.S. firms to the international sector would decline. If, in the circular flow, there is no foreign sector, then there are no gains from international trade. The total income of every country will be reduced.

Chapter 5

© Chad Ehlers/Jupiter Images

National Income Accounting

 Fundamental Questions

1. How is the total output of an economy measured?

2. Who produces the nation's goods and services?

3. Who purchases the goods and services produced?

4. Who receives the income from the production of goods and services?

5. What is the difference between nominal and real GDP?

6. What is a price index?

The Korean economy grew at an average rate of 3.8 percent per year from 2000 to 2007. This compares with an average rate of 1.7 percent per year for the United States over the same period. Still, the U.S. economy is much larger than the Korean economy—in fact, it is larger than the economies of the 50 largest developing countries combined. The size of an economy cannot be compared across countries without common standards of measurement. National income accounting provides these standards. Economists use this system to evaluate the economic condition of a country and to compare conditions across time and across countries.

A national economy is a complex arrangement of many different buyers and sellers—households, businesses, and government units—and of their interactions with the rest of the world. To assess the economic health of a country or to compare the performance of an economy from year to year, economists must be able to measure national output and real GDP. Without these data, policymakers cannot evaluate their economic policies. For instance, in the United States, real GDP fell in 1980, 1981, and 1982, and again in 1990–1991, 2001, and 2008. This drop in real GDP was accompanied by widespread job losses and a general decline in the economic health of the country. As this information became known, political and economic debate centered on economic policies, on what should be done to stimulate the economy. Without real GDP statistics, policymakers would not have known that there were problems, let alone how to go about fixing them.

All final goods and services produced in a year are counted in the GDP. For instance, the value of a horseback excursion through the Grand Canyon is part of the national output of the United States. The value of the trip would be equal to the amount that travelers would have to pay the guide company in order to take the trip. This price would reflect the value of the personnel, equipment, and food provided by the guide company.

© Tony Gervis/Jupiter Images

■ 1. Measures of Output and Income

1 | How is the total output of an economy measured?

national income accounting: the framework that summarizes and categorizes productive activity in an economy over a specific period of time, typically a year

In this chapter, we discuss gross domestic product, real GDP, and other measures of national productive activity by making use of the **national income accounting** system used by all countries. National income accounting provides a framework for discussing macroeconomics. Figure 1 reproduces the circular flow diagram you saw in Chapter 4. The lines connecting the various sectors of the economy represent flows of goods and services and of money expenditures (income). National income accounting is the process of counting the value of the flows between sectors and then summing them to find the total value of the economic activity in an economy. National income accounting fills in the dollar values in the circular flow.

National income accounting measures the output of an entire economy as well as the flows between sectors. It summarizes the level of production in an economy over a specific period of time, typically a year. In practice, the process *estimates* the

FIGURE 1 The Circular Flow: Households, Firms, Government, and Foreign Countries

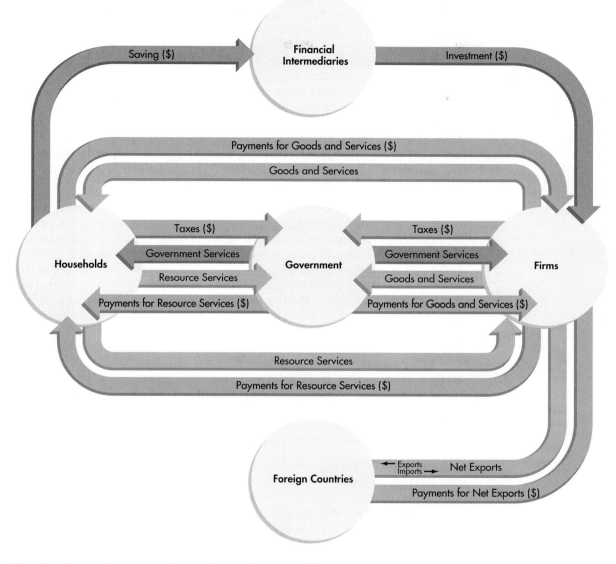

The value of national output equals expenditures plus income. If the domestic economy has positive net exports (a trade surplus), goods and services flow out of the domestic firms toward the foreign countries and money payments flow from the foreign countries to the domestic firms. If the domestic economy has negative net exports (a trade deficit), just the reverse is true.

amount of activity that occurs. It is beyond the capability of government officials to count every transaction that takes place in a modern economy. Still, national income accounting generates useful and fairly accurate measures of economic activity in most countries, especially wealthy industrial countries that have comprehensive accounting systems.

1.a. Gross Domestic Product

Modern economies produce an amazing variety of goods and services. To measure an economy's total production, economists combine the quantities of oranges, golf balls, automobiles, and all the other goods and services produced into a single measure of output. Of course, simply adding up the number of things produced—the number of oranges, golf balls, and automobiles—does not reveal the *value* of what is being produced. If a nation produces 1 million more oranges and 1 million fewer automobiles this year than it did last year, the total number of things produced remains the same. But because automobiles are much more valuable than oranges, the value of the nation's output has dropped substantially. Prices reflect the value of goods and services in the market, so economists use the money value of things to create a measure of total output, a measure that is more meaningful than the sum of the units produced.

The most common measure of a nation's output is gross domestic product. **Gross domestic product (GDP)** is the market value of all final goods and services produced in a year within a country's borders. A closer look at three parts of this definition—*market value, final goods and services,* and *produced in a year*—will make clear what the GDP does and does not include.

gross domestic product (GDP): the market value of all final goods and services produced in a year within a country

Market Value The *market value* of final goods and services is their value at market price. The process of determining market value is straightforward when prices are known and transactions are observable. However, there are cases in which prices are not known and transactions are not observable. For instance, illegal drug transactions are not reported to the government, which means that they are not included in GDP statistics. In fact, almost any activity that is not traded in a market is not included. For example, production that takes place in households, such as homemakers' services, is not counted, nor are unreported barter and cash transactions. For instance, if a lawyer has a sick dog and a veterinarian needs some legal advice, by trading services and not reporting the activity to the tax authorities, each can avoid taxation on the income that would have been reported had they sold their services to each other. If the value of a transaction is not recorded as taxable income, it generally does not appear in the GDP. There are some exceptions, however. Contributions to GDP are estimated for *in-kind wages,* such as nonmonetary compensation like room and board. GDP values also are assigned to the output consumed by a producer—for example, the home consumption of crops by a farmer.

The most common measure of a nation's output is GDP.

Final Goods and Services The second part of the definition of GDP limits the measure to *final goods and services,* the goods and services that are available to the ultimate consumer. This limitation avoids double-counting. Suppose a retail store sells a shirt to a consumer for $20. The value of the shirt in the GDP is $20. But the shirt is made of cotton that has been grown by a farmer, woven at a mill, and cut and sewn by a manufacturer. What would happen if we counted the value of the shirt at each of these stages of the production process? We would overstate the market value of the shirt.

intermediate good: a good that is used as an input in the production of final goods and services

Intermediate goods are goods that are used in the production of a final product. For instance, the ingredients for a meal are intermediate goods to a restaurant. Similarly, the cotton and the cloth are intermediate goods in the production of the shirt. The stages of production of the $20 shirt are shown in Figure 2. The value-of-output axis measures the value of the product at each stage. The cotton produced by the farmer sells for $1. The cloth woven by the textile mill sells for $5. The shirt manufacturer sells the shirt wholesale to the retail store for $12. The retail store sells the shirt—the final good—to the ultimate consumer for $20. Remember that GDP is based on the market value of final goods and services. In our example, the market value of the shirt is $20. That price already includes the value of the intermediate goods that were used to produce the shirt. If we added to it the value of output at every stage of production, we would be counting the value of the intermediate goods twice, and we would be overstating the GDP.

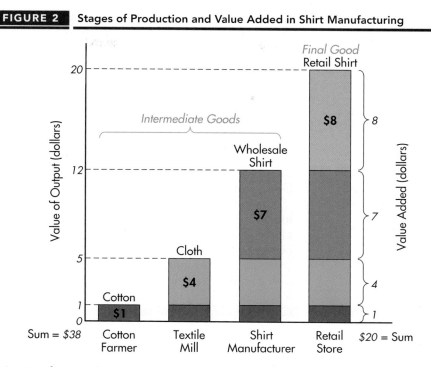

FIGURE 2 Stages of Production and Value Added in Shirt Manufacturing

A cotton farmer sells cotton to a textile mill for $1, adding $1 to the value of the final shirt. The textile mill sells cloth to a shirt manufacturer for $5, adding $4 to the value of the final shirt. The manufacturer sells the shirt wholesale to the retail store for $12, adding $7 to the value of the final shirt. The retail store sells the final shirt to a consumer for $20, adding $8 to the value of the final shirt. The sum of the prices received at each stage of production equals $38, which is greater than the price of the final shirt. The sum of the value added at each stage of production equals $20, which equals the market value of the shirt.

value added:
the difference between the value of output and the value of the intermediate goods used in the production of that output

It is possible to compute GDP by computing the **value added** at each stage of production. Value added is the difference between the value of output and the value of the intermediate goods used in the production of that output. In Figure 2, the value added by each stage of production is listed at the right. The farmer adds $1 to the value of the shirt. The mill takes the cotton worth $1 and produces cloth worth $5, adding $4 to the value of the shirt. The manufacturer uses $5 worth of cloth to produce a shirt that it sells for $12, so the manufacturer adds $7 to the shirt's value. Finally, the retail store adds $8 to the value of the shirt: It pays the manufacturer $12 for the shirt and sells it to the consumer for $20. The sum of the value added at each stage of production is $20. The total value added, then, is equal to the market value of the final product.

Economists can thus compute GDP using two methods. The final goods and services method uses the market value of the final good or service; the value-added method uses the value added at each stage of production. Both methods count the value of intermediate goods only once. This is an important distinction: GDP is not based on the market value of *all* goods and services, but on the market value of all *final* goods and services.

Produced in a Year GDP measures the value of the output *produced in a year.* The value of goods produced last year is counted in last year's GDP; the value of goods produced this year is counted in this year's GDP. The year of production, not the year of sale, determines the allocation to GDP. Although the value of last year's goods is not counted in this year's GDP, the value of services involved in the sale is. This year's GDP does not include the value of a house built last year, but it does include the value of the real estate broker's fee; it does not include the value of a used car, but it does include the income earned by the used-car dealer in the sale of that car.

inventory: the stock of unsold goods held by a firm

To determine the value of goods produced in a year but not sold in that year, economists calculate changes in inventory. **Inventory** is a firm's stock of unsold goods. If a shirt that is produced this year remains on the retail store's shelf at the end of the year, it increases the value of the store's inventory. A $20 shirt increases that value by $20. Changes in inventory allow economists to count goods in the year in which they are produced, whether or not they are sold.

Changes in inventory can be planned or unplanned. A store may want a cushion above expected sales (*planned inventory changes*), or it may not be able to sell all the goods that it expected to sell when it placed the order (*unplanned inventory changes*). For instance, suppose Jeremy owns a surfboard shop, and he always wants to keep 10 more surfboards than he expects to sell. He does this so that in case business is surprisingly good, he does not have to turn away customers and lose those sales to his competitors. At the beginning of the year, Jeremy has 10 surfboards, and he then builds as many new boards during the year as he expects to sell. He *plans* on having an inventory at the end of the year of 10 surfboards. Suppose Jeremy expects to sell 100 surfboards during the year, so he builds 100 new boards. If business is surprisingly poor and he sells only 80 surfboards, how do we count the 20 new boards that he made but did not sell? We count the change in his inventory. He started the year with 10 surfboards and ends the year with 20 more unsold boards, for a year-end inventory of 30. The change in inventory of 20 (equal to the ending inventory of 30 minus the starting inventory of 10) represents output that is counted in GDP. In Jeremy's case, the inventory change is unplanned, since he expected to sell the 20 extra surfboards that he has in his shop at the end of the year. But whether the inventory change is planned or unplanned, changes in inventory will count output that is produced but not sold in a given year.

1.a.1 GDP as Output The GDP is a measure of the market value of a nation's total output in a year. Remember that economists divide the economy into four sectors: households, businesses, government, and the international sector. Figure 1 shows how the total value of economic activity equals the sum of the output produced in each sector. Figure 3 indicates where the U.S. GDP

2 | Who produces the nation's goods and services?

FIGURE 3   U.S. Gross Domestic Product by Sector (billion dollars)

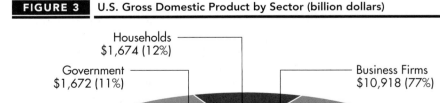

Households
$1,674 (12%)

Government
$1,672 (11%)

Business Firms
$10,918 (77%)

Business firms produce 77 percent of the U.S. GDP. Government produces 11 percent; households, 12 percent.
Source: Bureau of Economic Analysis; www.bea.gov.

is actually produced.[1] Since GDP counts the output produced in the United States, U.S. GDP is produced in business firms, households, and government located within the boundaries of the United States.

Not unexpectedly in a capitalist country, privately owned businesses account for the largest percentage of output: In the United States, 77 percent of the GDP is produced by private firms. Government produces 11 percent of the GDP, and households produce 12 percent. Figure 3 defines GDP in terms of output: GDP is the value of final goods and services produced by domestic households, businesses, and government units. Even if some of the firms producing in the United States are foreign owned, the output that they produce in the United State is counted in the U.S. GDP.

> **GDP is the value of final goods and services produced by domestic households, businesses, and government.**

1.a.2 GDP as Expenditures The circular flow diagram in Figure 1 shows not only the output of goods and services from each sector, but also the payments for goods and services. Here we look at GDP in terms of what each sector pays for the goods and services that it purchases.

The dollar value of total expenditures—the sum of the amount that each sector spends on final goods and services—equals the dollar value of output. In Chapter 4, you learned that household spending is called *consumption.* Households spend their income on goods and services to be consumed. Business spending is called *investment.* Investment is spending on capital goods that will be used to produce other goods and services. The other two components of total spending are *government spending* and *net exports.* Net exports are the value of *exports* (goods and services sold to the rest of the world) minus the value of *imports* (goods and services bought from the rest of the world).

> ### 3 | Who purchases the goods and services produced?

$$\text{GDP} = \text{consumption} + \text{investment} + \text{government spending} + \text{net exports}$$

Or, in the shorter form commonly used by economists,

$$\text{GDP} = C + I + G + X$$

> **GDP = C = I + G + X**

where X is net exports.

Figure 4 shows the U.S. GDP in terms of total expenditures. Consumption, or household spending, accounts for 71 percent of national expenditures. Government spending represents 20 percent of expenditures, and business investment represents 14 percent. Net exports are negative (−5 percent), which means that imports exceeded exports. To determine total national expenditures on domestic output, the value of imports, or spending on foreign output, is subtracted from total expenditures.

1.a.3 GDP as Income The total value of output can be calculated by adding up the expenditures of each sector. And because one sector's expenditures are another's income, the total value of output can also be computed by adding up the income of all sectors.

> ### 4 | Who receives the income from the production of goods and services?

Business firms use factors of production to produce goods and services. Remember that the income earned by factors of production is classified as wages, interest, rent, and profits. *Wages* are payments to labor, including fringe benefits, social security contributions, and retirement payments. *Interest* is the net interest paid by businesses to households plus the net interest received from foreigners (the interest that they pay us minus the interest that we pay them). *Rent* is income earned from selling the use of real property (houses, shops, and farms). Finally,

---

[1] Due to rounding, percentages and dollar amounts in the next three figures will not add exactly to the totals given.

FIGURE 4   U.S. Gross Domestic Product as Expenditures (billion dollars)

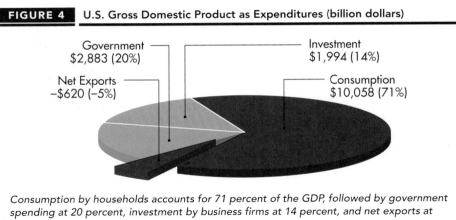

Consumption by households accounts for 71 percent of the GDP, followed by government spending at 20 percent, investment by business firms at 14 percent, and net exports at −5 percent.
Source: U.S. Bureau of Economic Analysis; www.bea.gov.

---

profits are the sum of corporate profits plus proprietors' income (income from sole proprietorships and partnerships).

Figure 5 shows the U.S. GDP in terms of income. Notice that wages account for 56 percent of the GDP. Interest and profits account for 5 and 10 percent of the GDP, respectively. Proprietors' income accounts for 7 percent. Rent (0.5 percent) is very small in comparison. *Net factor income from abroad* is income received from U.S.- owned resources located in other countries minus income paid to foreign-owned resources located in the United States. Since U.S. GDP refers only to income earned within U.S. borders, we must add income payments from the rest of the world and subtract income payments to the rest of the world to arrive at GDP (1 percent).

FIGURE 5   U.S. Gross Domestic Product as Income Received (billion dollars)

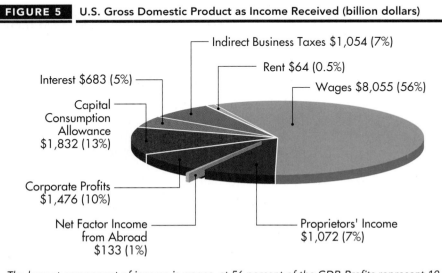

The largest component of income is wages, at 56 percent of the GDP. Profits represent 10 percent; interest, 5 percent; proprietors' income, 7 percent; and rent, 0.5 percent. Capital consumption allowance (13 percent) and indirect business taxes (7 percent) are not income received but still must be added; net factor income from abroad must be added (1 percent). (Note: Percentages do not always equal 100 percent.)
Source: Data from Bureau of Economic Analysis.

capital consumption allowance: the estimated value of depreciation plus the value of accidental damage to capital stock

depreciation: a reduction in the value of capital goods over time as a result of their use in production

Figure 5 also includes two income categories that we have not discussed: capital consumption allowance and indirect business taxes. **Capital consumption allowance** is not a money payment to a factor of production; it is the estimated value of capital goods used up or worn out in production plus the value of accidental damage to capital goods. The value of accidental damage is relatively small, so it is common to hear economists refer to capital consumption allowance as **depreciation.** Machines and other capital goods wear out over time. The reduction in the value of the capital stock as a result of its being used up or worn out over time is called depreciation. A depreciating capital good loses value each year of its useful life until its value is zero.

Even though capital consumption allowance does not represent income received by a factor of production, it must be accounted for in GDP as income. If it were not, the value of GDP measured as output would be higher than the value of GDP measured as income. Depreciation is a kind of resource payment, part of the total payment to the owners of capital. All of the income categories—wages, interest, rent, profits, and capital consumption allowance—are expenses incurred in the production of output.

indirect business tax: a tax that is collected by businesses for a government agency

The last item in Figure 5 is indirect business taxes. **Indirect business taxes,** like capital consumption allowance, are not payments to a factor of production. They are taxes collected by businesses that then are turned over to the government. Both excise taxes and sales taxes are forms of indirect business taxes.

For example, suppose a motel room in Florida costs $80 a night, but a consumer would be charged $90. The motel receives $80 of that $90 as the value of the service sold; the other $10 is an excise tax. The motel cannot keep the $10; it must turn it over to the state government. (In effect, the motel is acting as the government's tax collector.) The consumer spends $90; the motel earns $80. To balance expenditures and income, we have to allocate the $10 difference to indirect business taxes.

The GDP as income is equal to the sum of wages, interest, rent, and profits, less net factor income from abroad, plus capital consumption allowance and indirect business taxes.

To summarize, GDP measured as income includes the four payments to the factors of production: wages, interest, rent, and profits. These income items represent expenses incurred in the production of GDP. From these we must subtract net factor income from abroad and then add two nonincome items—capital consumption allowance and indirect business taxes—to find real GDP.

$$GDP = \text{wages} + \text{interest} + \text{rent} + \text{profits} - \text{net factor income from abroad} + \text{capital consumption allowance} + \text{indirect business taxes}$$

The GDP is the total value of output produced in a year, the total value of expenditures made to purchase that output, and the total value of income received by the factors of production. Because all three are measures of the same thing—GDP—all must be equal.

1.b. Other Measures of Output and Income

GDP is the most commonly used measure of a nation's output, but it is not the only measure. Economists rely on a number of other measures as well in analyzing the performance of components of an economy.

gross national product (GNP): gross domestic product plus receipts of factor income from the rest of the world minus payments of factor income to the rest of the world

1.b.1 Gross National Product
Gross national product (GNP) equals GDP plus receipts of factor income from the rest of the world minus payments of factor income to the rest of the world. If we add to GDP the value of income earned by U.S. residents from factors of production located outside the United States and subtract the value of income earned by foreign residents from factors

of production located inside the United States, we have a measure of the value of output produced by U.S.-owned resources—GNP.

Figure 6 shows the national income accounts in the United States. The figure begins with the GDP and then shows the calculations necessary to obtain the GNP and other measures of national output. In 2008, the U.S. GNP was $14,397.8 billion.

net national product (NNP): gross national product minus capital consumption allowance

1.b.2 Net National Product **Net national product (NNP)** equals GNP minus capital consumption allowance. The NNP measures the value of goods and services produced in a year less the value of capital goods that became obsolete or were used up during the year. Because NNP includes only net additions to a nation's capital, it is a better measure of the expansion or contraction of current output than is GNP. Remember how we defined GDP in terms of expenditures in section 1.a.2:

GDP = consumption + investment + government spending + net exports

gross investment: total investment, including investment expenditures required to replace capital goods consumed in current production

The investment measure in GDP (and GNP) is called **gross investment.** Gross investment is total investment, which includes investment expenditures required

---

FIGURE 6   U.S. National Income Accounts, 2008 (billion dollars)

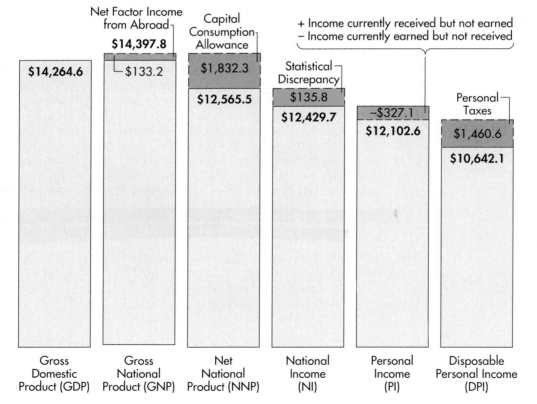

Gross domestic product plus receipts of factor income from the rest of the world minus payments of factor income to the rest of the world equals gross national product. Gross national product minus capital consumption allowance equals net national product. Net national product minus statistical discrepancy equals national income. National income plus income currently received but not earned (transfer payments, personal interest, dividend income) minus income currently earned but not received (retained corporate profits, net interest, social security taxes) equals personal income. Personal income minus personal taxes equals disposable personal income.
Source: Data from Bureau of Economic Analysis.

to replace capital goods consumed in current production. The NNP does not include investment expenditures required to replace worn-out capital goods; it includes only net investment. **Net investment** is equal to gross investment minus capital consumption allowance. Net investment measures business spending over and above that required to replace worn-out capital goods.

net investment: gross investment minus capital consumption allowance

Figure 6 shows that in 2008, the U.S. NNP was $12,565.5 billion. This means that the U.S. economy produced over $12 trillion worth of goods and services above those required to replace capital stock that had depreciated. Over $1 trillion in capital was "worn out" in 2008.

national income (NI): net national product plus or minus statistical discrepancy

1.b.3 National Income
National income (NI) equals the NNP plus or minus a small adjustment called "statistical discrepancy." The NI captures the costs of the factors of production used in producing output. Remember that GDP includes a nonincome expense item: capital consumption allowance (section 1.a.3). Subtracting this plus the statistical discrepancy from the GDP leaves the income payments that actually go to resources.

Because the NNP equals the GNP minus capital consumption allowance, we can subtract the statistical discrepancy from the NNP to find NI, as shown in Figure 6. This measure helps economists analyze how the costs of (or payments received by) resources change.

personal income (PI): national income plus income currently received but not earned, minus income currently earned but not received

1.b.4 Personal Income
Personal income (PI) is national income adjusted for income that is received but not earned in the current year and income that is earned but not received in the current year. Social security and welfare benefits are examples of income that is received but not earned in the current year. As you learned in Chapter 4, these are called **transfer payments.** Transfer payments represent income transferred from one citizen who is earning income to another citizen, who may not be. The government transfers income by taxing one group of citizens and using the tax payments to fund the income for another group. An example of income that is currently earned but not received is profits that are retained by a corporation to finance current needs rather than paid out to stockholders. Another is social security (FICA) taxes, which are deducted from workers' paychecks.

transfer payment: income transferred by the government from a citizen who is earning income to another citizen

disposable personal income (DPI): personal income minus personal taxes

1.b.5 Disposable Personal Income
Disposable personal income (DPI) equals personal income minus personal taxes—income taxes, excise and real estate taxes on personal property, and other personal taxes. DPI is the income that individuals have at their disposal for spending or saving. The sum of consumption spending plus saving must equal disposable personal income.

 RECAP

1. Gross domestic product (GDP) is the market value of all final goods and services produced in an economy in a year.

2. The GDP can be calculated by summing the market value of all final goods and services produced in a year, by summing the value added at each stage of production, by adding total expenditures on goods and services (GDP = consumption + investment + government spending + net exports), and by using the total income earned in the production of goods and services (GDP = wages + interest + rent + profits), subtracting net factor income from abroad, and adding depreciation and indirect business taxes.

3. Other measures of output and income include gross national product (GNP), net national product (NNP), national income (NI), personal income (PI), and disposable personal income (DPI).

National Income Accounts

$$GDP = consumption + investment + government\ spending + net\ exports$$

$$GNP = GDP + receipts\ of\ factor\ income\ from\ the\ rest\ of\ the\ world$$
$$- payments\ of\ factor\ income\ to\ the\ rest\ of\ the\ world$$

$$NNP = GNP - capital\ consumption\ allowance$$

$$NI = NNP - statistical\ discrepancy$$

$$PI = NI - income\ earned\ but\ not\ received + income\ received\ but$$
$$not\ earned$$
$$DPI = PI - personal\ taxes$$

■ 2. Nominal and Real Measures

5 | **What is the difference between nominal and real GDP?**

The GDP is the market value of all final goods and services produced within a country in a year. Value is measured in money terms, so the U.S. GDP is reported in dollars, the German GDP in euro, the Mexican GDP in pesos, and so on. Market value is the product of two elements: the money price and the quantity produced.

2.a. Nominal and Real GDP

nominal GDP: a measure of national output based on the current prices of goods and services

real GDP: a measure of the quantity of final goods and services produced, obtained by eliminating the influence of price changes from the nominal GDP statistics

Nominal GDP measures output in terms of its current dollar value. **Real GDP** is adjusted for changing price levels. In 1980, the U.S. GDP was $2,790 billion; in 2008, it was $14,265 billion—an increase of 411 percent. Does this mean that the United States produced 411 percent more goods and services in 2008 than it did in 1980? If the numbers reported are for nominal GDP, we cannot be sure. Nominal GDP cannot tell us whether the economy produced more goods and services, because nominal GDP changes both when prices change *and* when quantity changes.

Real GDP measures output in constant prices. This allows economists to identify the changes in the actual production of final goods and services: Real GDP measures the quantity of goods and services produced after eliminating the influence of price changes contained in nominal GDP. In 1980, real GDP in the United States was $5,161.7 billion; in 2008, it was $11,652 billion, an increase of just 126 percent. A large part of the 411 percent increase in nominal GDP reflects increased prices, not increased output.

Because we prefer more goods and services to higher prices, it is better to have nominal GDP rise because of higher output than because of higher prices. We want nominal GDP to increase as a result of an increase in real GDP.

Consider a simple example that illustrates the difference between nominal GDP and real GDP. Suppose a hypothetical economy produces just three goods: oranges, coconuts, and pizzas. The dollar value of output in three different years is listed in Figure 7.

As shown in Figure 7, in year 1, 100 oranges were produced at $.50 per orange, 300 coconuts at $1 per coconut, and 2,000 pizzas at $8 per pizza. The total dollar value of output in year 1 is $16,350. In year 2, prices remain constant at the year 1 values, but the quantity of each good has increased by 10 percent. The dollar value of output in year 2 is $17,985, 10 percent higher than the value of output in year 1. In year 3, the quantity of each good is back at the year 1 level, but prices have increased by 10 percent. Oranges now cost $.55, coconuts $1.10, and pizzas $8.80. The dollar value of output in year 3 is $17,985.

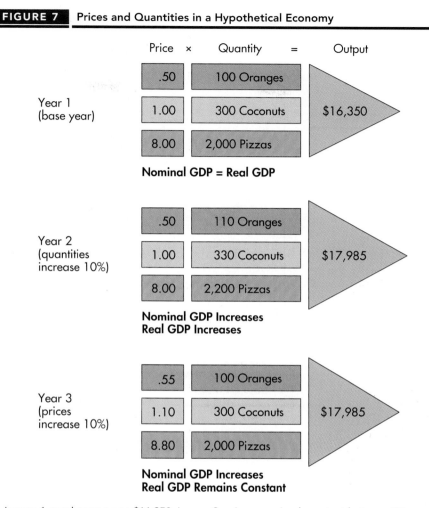

FIGURE 7 Prices and Quantities in a Hypothetical Economy

In year 1, total output was $16,350. In year 2, prices remained constant but quantities produced increased by 10 percent, resulting in a higher output of $17,985. With prices constant, we can say that both nominal GDP and real GDP increased from year 1 to year 2. In year 3, quantities produced returned to the year 1 level but prices increased by 10 percent, resulting in the same increased output as in year 2, $17,985. Production has not changed from year 1 to year 3, however, so although nominal GDP has increased, real GDP has remained constant.

Notice that the dollar value of output ($17,985) in years 2 and 3 is 10 percent higher than the dollar value in year 1. But there is a difference here. In year 2, the increase in output is due entirely to an increase in the production of the three goods. In year 3, the increase is due entirely to an increase in the prices of the goods.

Because prices did not change between years 1 and 2, the increase in nominal GDP is entirely accounted for by an increase in real output, or real GDP. In years 1 and 3, the actual quantities produced did not change, which means that real GDP was constant; only nominal GDP was higher, a product only of higher prices.

Figure 8 plots the growth rate of real GDP for several of the industrial countries. One can see in the figure that the countries show somewhat different patterns of real GDP growth over time. For instance, over the period beginning in the mid-1990s, real GDP grew at a slower pace in Japan than in the other countries. Most of the countries had fairly fast rates of GDP growth in the late 1990s, only

| FIGURE 8 | Real GDP Growth in Some Industrial Countries |

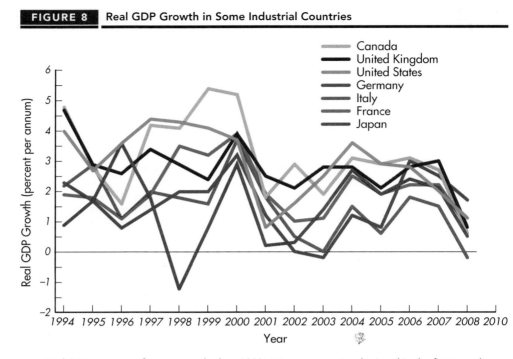

Real GDP grew at a fast pace in the late 1990s in most countries depicted in the figure, only to fall dramatically in 2001 and 2002. Japan has experienced slower growth of real GDP over this period than the other countries.

to experience a falling growth rate in the early 2000s followed by a pickup in growth, and then the most recent downturn associated with the global recession.

2.b. Price Indexes

6 | What is a price index?

The total dollar value of output or income is equal to price multiplied by the quantity of goods and services produced:

$$\text{Dollar value of output} = \text{price} \times \text{quantity}$$

By dividing the dollar value of output by price, you can determine the quantity of goods and services produced:

$$\text{Quantity} = \frac{\text{dollar value of output}}{\text{price}}$$

price index: a measure of the average price level in an economy

In macroeconomics, a **price index** is a measure of the average level of prices in an economy; it shows how prices, on average, have changed. Prices of individual goods can rise and fall relative to one another, but a price index shows the general trend in prices across the economy.

base year: the year against which other years are measured

2.b.1 Base Year The example in Figure 7 provides a simple introduction to price indexes. The first step is to pick a **base year**, the year against which other years are measured. Any year can serve as the base year. Suppose we pick year 1 in Figure 7. The value of the price index in year 1, the base year, is defined to be 100. This simply means that prices in year 1 are 100 percent of prices in year 1 (100 percent of 1 is 1). In the example, year 2 prices are equal to year 1 prices, so the price index

Economic Insight

The Consumer Price Index

The CPI is calculated by the Department of Labor using price surveys taken in 87 U.S. cities. Although the CPI often is called a *cost-of-living index*, it is not. The CPI represents the cost of a fixed market basket of goods purchased by a hypothetical household, not a real one.

In fact, no household consumes the exact market basket used to estimate the CPI. As relative prices change, households alter their spending patterns. But the CPI market basket changes only every two years. This is due in part to the high cost of surveying the public to determine spending patterns. Then, too, individual households have different tastes and spend different portions of their budgets on the various components of

household spending (housing, food, clothing, transportation, medical care, and so on). Only a household that spends exactly the same portion of its income on each item counted in the CPI would find the CPI representative of its cost of living.

The Department of Labor surveys spending in eight major areas. The figure shows these areas and the percentage of the typical household budget devoted to each area. If you kept track of your spending over the course of several months, you probably would find that you spend much more than the typical household on some items and much less on others. In other words, the CPI is not a very good measure of *your* cost of living.

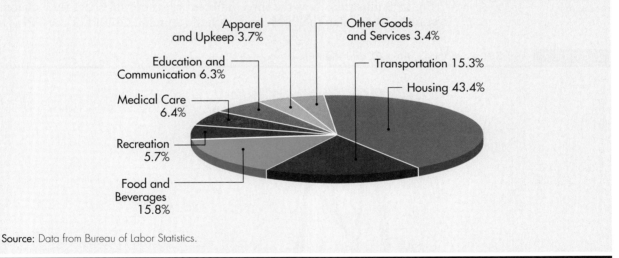

Source: Data from Bureau of Labor Statistics.

> *The value of the price index in any particular year indicates how prices have changed relative to the base year.*

is equal to 100 in year 2 as well. In year 3, every price has risen 10 percent relative to the base-year (year 1) prices, so the price index is 10 percent higher in year 3, or 110. The value of the price index in any particular year indicates how prices have changed relative to the base year. A value of 110 indicates that prices are 110 percent of base-year prices, or that the average price level has increased 10 percent.

$$\text{Price index in any year} = 100 \pm \text{percentage change in prices from the base year}$$

2.b.2 Types of Price Indexes The price of a single good is easy to determine. But how do economists determine a single measure of the prices of the millions of goods and services produced in an economy? They have constructed price indexes to measure the price level; there are several different price indexes used to measure the

GDP price index (GDPPI):
a broad measure of the prices of goods and services included in the gross domestic product

consumer price index (CPI): a measure of the average price of goods and services purchased by the typical household

cost-of-living adjustment (COLA): an increase in wages that is designed to match increases in the prices of items purchased by the typical household

producer price index (PPI): a measure of average prices received by producers

price level in any economy. Not all prices rise or fall at the same time or by the same amount. This is why there are several measures of the price level in an economy.

The price index that is used to estimate constant-dollar real GDP is the **GDP price index (GDPPI),** a measure of prices across the economy that reflects all of the categories of goods and services included in GDP. The GDP price index is a very broad measure. Economists use other price indexes to analyze how prices in more specific categories of goods and services change.

Probably the best-known price index is the **consumer price index (CPI).** The CPI measures the average price of consumer goods and services that a typical household purchases. (See the Economic Insight "The Consumer Price Index.") The CPI is a narrower measure than the GDPPI because it includes fewer items. However, because of the relevance of consumer prices to the standard of living, news reports on price changes in the economy typically focus on consumer price changes. In addition, labor contracts sometimes include provisions that raise wages as the CPI goes up. Social security payments also are tied to increases in the CPI. These increases are called **cost-of-living adjustments (COLAs)** because they are supposed to keep nominal income rising along with the cost of items purchased by the typical household.

The **producer price index (PPI)** measures average prices received by producers. At one time this price index was known as the *wholesale price index (WPI).* Because the PPI measures price changes at an earlier stage of production than the CPI, it can indicate a coming change in the CPI. If producer input costs are rising, we can expect the price of goods produced to go up as well.

Figure 9 illustrates how the three different measures of prices have changed over time. Notice that the PPI is more volatile than the GDPPI or the CPI. This

---

FIGURE 9   The GDP Price Index, the CPI, and the PPI

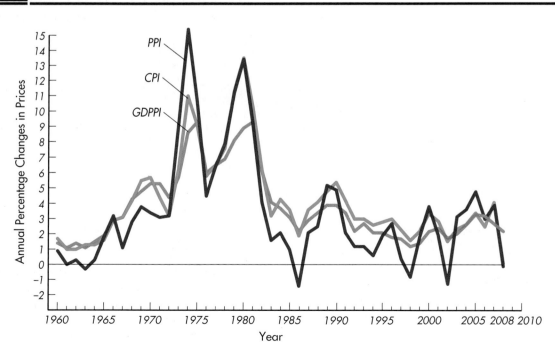

The graph plots the annual percentage change in the GDP price index (GDPPI), the consumer price index (CPI), and the producer price index (PPI). The GDPPI is used to construct constant-dollar real GDP. The CPI measures the average price of consumer goods and services that a typical household purchases. The PPI measures the average price received by producers; it is the most variable of the three because fluctuations in equilibrium prices of intermediate goods are much greater than those for final goods.
Source: www.bls.gov and www.bea.gov.

is because there are smaller fluctuations in the equilibrium prices of final goods than in those of intermediate goods.

RECAP

1. Nominal GDP is measured using current dollars.

2. Real GDP measures output with price effects removed.

3. The GDP price index, the consumer price index, and the producer price index are all measures of the level of prices in an economy.

◼ 3. Flows of Income and Expenditures

GDP is both a measure of total expenditures on final goods and services and a measure of the total income earned in the production of those goods and services. The idea that total expenditures equal total income is clearly illustrated in Figure 1.

The figure links the four sectors of the economy: households, firms, government, and foreign countries. The arrows between the sectors indicate the direction of the flows. Gold arrows with dollar signs represent money flows; blue green arrows without dollar signs represent flows of real goods and services. The money flows are both income and expenditures. For instance, household expenditures for goods and services from business firms are represented by the gold arrow at the top of the diagram. Household income from firms is represented by the gold arrow flowing from firms to households at the bottom of the diagram. Because one sector's expenditures are another sector's income, the total expenditures on goods and services must be the same as the total income from selling goods and services, and those must both be equal to the total value of the goods and services produced.

RECAP

1. Total spending on final goods and services equals the total income received from producing those goods and services.

2. The circular flow model shows that one sector's expenditures become the income of other sectors.

SUMMARY

1 │ How is the total output of an economy measured?

• National income accounting is the system that economists use to measure both the output of an economy and the flows between sectors of that economy. *§1*

• Gross domestic product (GDP) is the market value of all final goods and services produced in a year in a country. *§1.a*

• GDP also equals the value added at each stage of production. *§1.a*

2 │ Who produces the nation's goods and services?

• GDP as output equals the sum of the output of households, business firms, and government within

the country. Business firms produce 77 percent of the U.S. GDP. *§1.a.1*

3 │ Who purchases the goods and services produced?

• The GDP as expenditures equals the sum of consumption plus investment plus government spending plus net exports. In the United States, consumption accounts for roughly two-thirds of total expenditures. *§1.a.2*

4 │ Who receives the income from the production of goods and services?

• The GDP as income equals the sum of wages, interest, rent, profits, proprietors' income, capital consumption allowance, and indirect business taxes less net factor income from abroad. Wages account for about 60 percent of the total. *§1.a.3*

- Capital consumption allowance is the estimated value of depreciation plus the value of accidental damage to capital stock. *§1.a.3*

- Other measures of national output include gross national product (GNP), net national product (NNP), national income (NI), personal income (PI), and disposable personal income (DPI). *§1.b*

5 | What is the difference between nominal and real GDP?

- Nominal GDP measures output in terms of its current dollar value, including the effects of price changes; real GDP measures output after eliminating the effects of price changes. *§2.a*

6 | What is a price index?

- A price index is a measure of the average level of prices across an economy. *§2.b*

- The GDP price index is a measure of the prices of all the goods and services included in the GDP. *§2.b.2*

- The consumer price index (CPI) measures the average price of goods and services consumed by the typical household. *§2.b.2*

- The producer price index (PPI) measures average prices received by producers (wholesale prices). *§2.b.2*

- Total expenditures on final goods and services equal total income. *§3*

KEY TERMS

national income accounting *§1*	gross national product (GNP) *§1.b.1*	nominal GDP *§2.a*
gross domestic product (GDP) *§1.a*	net national product (NNP) *§1.b.2*	real GDP *§2.a*
intermediate good *§1.a*	gross investment *§1.b.2*	price index *§2.b*
value added *§1.a*	net investment *§1.b.2*	base year *§2.b.1*
inventory *§1.a*	national income (NI) *§1.b.3*	GDP price index *§2.b.2*
capital consumption allowance *§1.a.3*	personal income (PI) *§1.b.4*	consumer price index (CPI) *§2.b.2*
depreciation *§1.a.3*	transfer payment *§1.b.4*	cost-of-living adjustment (COLA) *§2.b.2*
indirect business tax *§1.a.3*	disposable personal income (DPI) *§1.b.5*	producer price index (PPI) *§2.b.2*

EXERCISES

1. The following table lists the stages in the production of a personal computer. What is the value of the computer in GDP?

Stage	Value Added
Components manufacture	$50
Assembly	$250
Wholesaler	$500
Retailer	$1,500

2. What is the difference between GDP and each of the following?
   a. Gross national product
   b. Net national product
   c. National income
   d. Personal income
   e. Disposable personal incom

3.

	Year 1		Year 2	
	Quantity	Price	Quantity	Price
Oranges	100	$3	150	$3
Pears	100	$3	75	$4

   a. What is the growth rate of constant-dollar real GDP using year 1 as the base year?
   b. What is the growth rate of constant-dollar real GDP using year 2 as the base year?

4. Why do total expenditures on final goods and services equal total income in the economy?

5. Why don't we measure national output by simply counting the total number of goods and services produced each year?

6. Why isn't the CPI a useful measure of *your* cost of living?

Use the following national income accounting information to answer exercises 7–11:

Consumption	$400
Imports	$10
Net investment	$20
Government purchases	$100
Exports	$20
Capital consumption allowance	$20
Statistical discrepancy	$5
Receipts of factor income from the rest of the world	$12
Payments of factor income to the rest of the world	$10

7. What is the GDP for this economy?

8. What is the GNP for this economy?

9. What is the NNP for this economy?

10. What is the national income for this economy?

11. What is the gross investment in this economy?

12. Indirect business taxes and capital consumption allowance are not income, yet they are included in the calculation of GDP as income received. Why do we add these two nonincome components to the other components of income (like wages, rent, interest, profits, and net factor income from abroad) to find GDP?

13. Why has nominal GDP increased faster than real GDP in the United States over time? What would it mean if an economy had real GDP increasing faster than nominal GDP?

14. We usually discuss GDP in terms of what is included in the definition. What is *not* included in GDP? Why are these things excluded?

15. If a surfboard is produced this year but not sold until next year, how is it counted in this year's GDP and not next year's?

You can find further practice tests in the Online Quiz at www.cengage.com/economics/boyes.

Hiding in the Shadows: The Growth of the Underground Economy

International Monetary Fund March 2002

A factory worker has a second job driving an unlicensed taxi at night; a plumber fixes a broken water pipe for a client, gets paid in cash, but doesn't declare his earnings to the tax collector; a drug dealer brokers a sale with a prospective customer on a street corner. These are all examples of the underground or shadow economy—activities, both legal and illegal, that add up to trillions of dollars a year that take place "off the books," out of the gaze of taxmen and government statisticians.

Although crime and shadow economic activities have long been a fact of life—and are now increasing around the world—almost all societies try to control their growth, because a prospering shadow economy makes official statistics (on unemployment, official labor force, income, consumption) unreliable. Policies and programs that are framed on the basis of unreliable statistics may be inappropriate and self-defeating. . . .

Also called the underground, informal, or parallel economy, the shadow economy includes not only illegal activities but also unreported income from the production of legal goods and services, either from monetary or barter transactions. Hence, the shadow economy comprises all economic activities that would generally be taxable were they reported to the tax authorities.

TABLE 1 Shadow Economy as Percent of Official GDP, 1988–2000

Country Group	Percent of GDP
Developing	35–44
Transition	21–30
OECD	14–16

The ranges reflect the different estimation methods used by different sources.

Estimating the size of the shadow economy is difficult. After all, people engaged in underground activities do their best to avoid detection. But policymakers and government administrators need information about how many people are active in the shadow economy, how often underground activities occur, and the size of these activities, so that they can make appropriate decisions on resource allocation.

Table 1 shows average estimates for the three main country groups—developing countries, transition economies, and 21 advanced economies, the last all members of the Organization for Economic Cooperation and Development (OECD). The comparisons among countries remain somewhat crude because they are based on different estimation methods.

Countries with relatively low tax rates, fewer laws and regulations, and a well-established rule of law tend to have smaller shadow economies.

Macroeconomic and microeconomic modeling studies based on data for several countries suggest that the major driving forces behind the size and growth of the shadow economy are an increasing burden of tax and social security payments, combined with rising restrictions in the official labor market. Wage rates in the official economy also play a role. . . .

Shadow economies tend to be smaller in countries where government institutions are strong and efficient. Indeed, some studies have found that it is not higher taxes per se that increase the size of the shadow economy, but ineffectual and discretionary application of the tax system and regulations by governments.

Source: Friedrich Schneider with Dominik Enste, *Hiding in the Shadows: The Growth of the Underground Economy, Economic Issues,* No. 30, International Monetary Fund, March 2002.

In this chapter, we learned about different measures of macroeconomic performance. It is important to have accurate measures in order to formulate appropriate policy. Bad data on economic performance could result in policymakers attempting to fix problems that don't really exist or failing to address problems that have not been identified. However, it is not easy to measure the performance of an economy. This article indicates a particular type of problem that exists in every economy: the underground economy.

The presence of a large and active underground economy means that the official GDP figure is missing much of the economic activity that occurs. As indicated in the article, this is more than just illegal activity, like dealing in illicit drugs. Perfectly legal activities that are conducted "off the books" are also missed in the official GDP accounting. So if a carpenter performs work for someone, is paid in cash, and never reports the transaction as income to be taxed, this activity is part of the underground economy. Although the carpenter was engaged in productive activity, it will not be counted, and so the official GDP measure will underestimate the true amount of production undertaken in a year.

This article serves as a reminder that, although government officials may do the best job they can of counting economic activity, they will never be able to count everything. As shown in Table 1 of the article, the problems are worse for developing countries and those countries that are in transition from socialism than for the industrial countries (referred to as OECD countries in the table). Yet even in the industrial countries, it is estimated that between 14 and 16 percent of GDP takes place in the underground economy.

An Introduction to the Foreign Exchange Market and the Balance of Payments

 Fundamental Questions

1 | How do individuals of one nation trade money with individuals of another nation?

2 | How do changes in exchange rates affect international trade?

3 | How do nations record their transactions with the rest of the world?

In Chapter 5, you learned that gross domestic product equals the sum of consumption, investment, government spending, and net exports (GDP = $C + I + G + X$). Net exports (X) are one key measure of a nation's transactions with other countries, a principal link between a nation's GDP and developments in the rest of the world. In this chapter, we extend the macroeconomic accounting framework to include more detail on a nation's international transactions. This extension is known as balance of payments accounting.

International transactions have grown rapidly in recent years as the economies of the world have become increasingly interrelated. Improvements in transportation and communication, and global markets for goods and services, have created a community of world economies. Products made in one country are sold in the world market, where they compete against products from other nations. Europeans purchase stocks listed on the New York Stock Exchange; Americans purchase bonds issued in Japan.

Different countries use different monies. When goods and services are exchanged across international borders, national monies also are traded. To make buying and selling decisions in the global marketplace, people must be able to compare prices across countries, to compare prices quoted in Japanese yen with those quoted in Mexican pesos. This chapter begins with a look at how national monies are priced and traded in the foreign exchange market.

Because different countries use different currencies, international business requires the exchange of monies in the foreign exchange market.

© Voloh/Shutterstock

■ 1. The Foreign Exchange Market

1 How do individuals of one nation trade money with individuals of another nation?

foreign exchange:
currency and bank deposits that are denominated in foreign money

foreign exchange market:
a global market in which people trade one currency for another

Foreign exchange is foreign money, including paper money and bank deposits like checking accounts, that are denominated in foreign currency. When someone with U.S. dollars wants to trade those dollars for Japanese yen, the trade takes place in the **foreign exchange market**, a global market in which people trade one currency for another. Many financial markets are located in a specific geographic location. For instance, the New York Stock Exchange is a specific location in New York City where stocks are bought and sold. The Commodity Exchange is a specific location in New York City where contracts to deliver agricultural and metal commodities are bought and sold. The foreign exchange market is not in a single geographic location, however. Trading occurs all over the world, electronically and by telephone. Most of the activity involves large banks in New York, London, and other financial centers. A foreign exchange trader at Citigroup in New York can buy or sell currencies with a trader at Barclays Bank in London by calling the other trader on the telephone or exchanging computer messages.

Only tourism and a few other transactions in the foreign exchange market involve an actual movement of currency. The great majority of transactions involve the buying and selling of bank deposits denominated in foreign currency. A bank deposit can be a checking account that a firm or individual writes checks against to make payments to others, or it can be an interest-earning savings account with no check-writing privileges. Currency notes, like dollar bills, are used in a relatively small fraction of transactions. When a large corporation or a government buys foreign currency, it buys a bank deposit denominated in the foreign currency. Still, all exchanges in the market require that monies have a price.

1.a. Exchange Rates

exchange rate: the price of one country's money in terms of another country's money

An **exchange rate** is the price of one country's money in terms of another country's money. Exchange rates are needed to compare prices quoted in two different currencies. Suppose a shirt that has been manufactured in Canada sells for 20 U.S. dollars in Seattle, Washington, and for 25 Canadian dollars in Vancouver, British Columbia. Where would you get the better buy? Unless you know the exchange rate between U.S. and Canadian dollars, you can't tell. The exchange rate allows you to convert the foreign currency price into its domestic currency equivalent, which then can be compared to the domestic price.

Table 1 lists exchange rates for February 25, 2009. The rates are quoted in U.S. dollars per unit of foreign currency in the second column, and in units of foreign currency per U.S. dollar in the last column. For instance, the Canadian dollar was selling for $.8011, or about 80 U.S. cents. The same day, the U.S. dollar was selling for 1.2490 Canadian dollars (1 U.S. dollar would buy 1.2490 Canadian dollars).

If you know the price of a currency in U.S. dollars, you can find the price of the U.S. dollar in that currency by taking the reciprocal. To find the reciprocal of a number, write it as a fraction and then turn the fraction upside down. Let's say that 1 British pound sells for 2 U.S. dollars. In fraction form, 2 is 2/1. The

TABLE 1   Exchange Rates, February 25, 2009

Country	U.S.$ per Currency	Currency per U.S.$
Argentina (peso)	.2825	3.5475
Australia (dollar)	.6453	1.5503
Britain (pound)	1.4502	.6898
Canada (dollar)	.8011	1.2490
China (renminbi)	.1464	6.8485
Israel (shekel)	.2403	4.1704
Japan (yen)	.00105	95.55
Mexico (peso)	.0671	14.9249
New Zealand (dollar)	.5107	1.9599
Russia (ruble)	.0279	36.0698
Singapore (dollar)	.6543	1.5286
Switzerland (franc)	.8589	1.1645
EU (euro)	1.2750	.7843

Note: The second column lists U.S. dollars per unit of foreign currency, or how much one unit of foreign currency is worth in U.S. dollars. On this day, you could get about 80 U.S. cents for 1 Canadian dollar. The third column lists units of foreign currency per U.S. dollar, or how much 1 U.S. dollar is worth in foreign currency. On the same day, you could get about 1.25 Canadian dollars for 1 U.S. dollar.

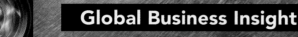

Global Business Insight

Active Trading Around the World

It is often said that the foreign exchange market never closes, since trading can take place in different parts of the world as time passes. However, people in each region tend to work certain normal business hours, and so each major foreign exchange trading location has fairly regular hours during which active trading occurs. The figure below shows the normal hours of active trading in each major trading region. The times are in *Greenwich Mean Time*, or *GMT*, which is the time in London. For instance, we see that active trading in London opens at 0800. This is 8 A.M. in London. Active trading stops in London at 1600, which is 4 P.M. in London. (In many parts of the world, a 24-hour clock registers time from 0000 to 1200 in the morning, where 1200 is noon. Then in the afternoon, time starts to count up from 1200. So 1 P.M. is 1300, 2 P.M. is 1400, and so on.)

The figure shows trading in New York as opening at 1200, or noon in London. Eastern time in the United States is 5 hours behind London time (as seen by the −5 for that region of the world at the bottom of the figure), so that when it is noon in London, it is 5 hours earlier, or 7 A.M., in New York. Note that active trading in London closes at 1600 and active trading in New York opens at 1200, so London and New York trading overlap for 4 hours each day. Similarly, the figure shows that trading in New York also overlaps with trading in Frankfurt, Germany. However, there is no overlap of trading in North America with trading in Asia, as Asian trading centers open after trading has ended in North America and close before trading begins in North America. There is a short overlap of Asian trading with European trading. This figure reminds us that the world of foreign exchange trading, and that of business in general, tends to be conducted during regular business hours in each region.

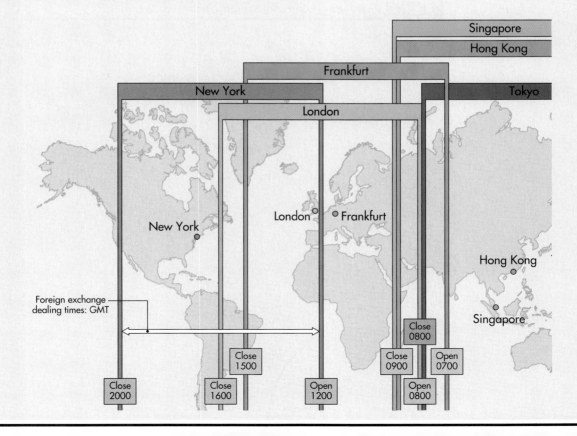

reciprocal of 2/1 is 1/2, or .5. So 1 U.S. dollar sells for .5 British pound. The table shows that the actual dollar price of the pound was 1.7705. The *reciprocal exchange rate*—the number of pounds per dollar—is .5648 (1/1.7705), which was the pound price of 1 dollar that day.

Let's go back to comparing the price of the Canadian shirt in Seattle and in Vancouver. The International Standards Organization (ISO) symbol for the U.S. dollar is USD. The symbol for the Canadian dollar is CAD. (Table 2 lists the symbols for a number of currencies.) The shirt sells for USD20 in Seattle and CAD25 in Vancouver. Suppose the exchange rate between the U.S. dollar and the Canadian dollar is .8. This means that CAD1 costs .8 U.S. dollar, or 80 U.S. cents. To find the domestic currency value of a foreign currency price, multiply the foreign currency price by the exchange rate:

Domestic currency value = foreign currency price × exchange rate

In our example, the U.S. dollar is the domestic currency:

U.S. dollar value = CAD25 × .8 = USD20

If we multiply the price of the shirt in Canadian dollars (CAD25) by the exchange rate (.8), we find the U.S. dollar value ($20). After adjusting for the exchange rate, then, we can see that the shirt sells for the same price in both countries when the price is measured in a single currency.

The euro is the common currency of the following western European countries: Austria, Belgium, Finland, France, Germany, Greece, Ireland, Italy, Luxembourg, Malta, Netherlands, Portugal, Slovakia, Slovenia, and Spain. The Global Business Insight "The Euro" provides more discussion.

Find the reciprocal of a number by writing it as a fraction and then turning the fraction upside down. In other words, make the numerator the denominator and the denominator the numerator.

TABLE 2   International Currency Symbols, Selected Countries

Country	Currency	ISO Symbol
Australia	Dollar	AUD
Canada	Dollar	CAD
China	Yuan	CNY
Denmark	Krone	DKK
India	Rupee	INR
Iran	Rial	IRR
Japan	Yen	JPY
Kuwait	Dinar	KWD
Mexico	Peso	MXN
Norway	Krone	NOK
Russia	Ruble	RUB
Saudi Arabia	Riyal	SAR
Singapore	Dollar	SGD
South Africa	Rand	ZAR
Sweden	Krona	SEK
Switzerland	Franc	CHF
United Kingdom	Pound	GBP
United States	Dollar	USD
Venezuela	Bolivar	VEB
European Union	Euro	EUR

Global Business Insight

The Euro

The euro began trading in January 1999 and for more than three years circulated jointly with the national currencies of the original 12 countries that adopted the euro. The former currencies of these countries are the Austrian schilling, Belgian franc, Finnish markka, French franc, German mark, Greek drachma, Irish pound, Italian lira, Luxembourg franc, Netherlands guilder, Portuguese escudo, and Spanish peseta. Prior to the beginning of the euro, the value of each of the "legacy currencies" of the euro area was fixed in terms of the euro. For instance, 1 euro was equal to 40.3399 Belgian francs or 1.95583 German marks. In February 2002, the former monies of each of the euro-area countries were withdrawn from circulation, and now only the euro is used in the 12-country area.

Euro coins are available in the following denominations: 1, 2, 5, 10, 20, and 50 cents and 1 and 2 euro. One side

of each coin has an image that is common in all euroland countries. The other side has a design that is individualized for each country. For instance, a 2-euro coin has a common side with a big number 2 placed over a map of Europe. But the reverse side differs across countries. In Germany, the 2-euro coin has an eagle surrounded by a ring of stars, while in Spain, the 2-euro coin has a portrait of the Spanish king, Carlos I. However, even though each country can issue its own coins, the coins are all usable in any euroland country. You could receive French coins in Paris and then spend them in Rome. Euro currency or banknotes are available in the following denominations: 5, 10, 20, 50, 100, 200, and 500 euro. The paper money is identical in all countries.

2 | How do changes in exchange rates affect international trade?

1.b. Exchange Rate Changes and International Trade

Because exchange rates determine the domestic currency value of foreign goods, changes in those rates affect the demand for and supply of goods traded internationally. Suppose the price of the shirt in Seattle and in Vancouver remains the same, but the exchange rate changes from .8 to .9 U.S. dollar per Canadian dollar. What happens? The U.S. dollar price of the shirt in Vancouver increases. At the new rate, the shirt that sells for CAD25 in Vancouver costs a U.S. buyer USD22.50 (CAD25 × .9).

A rise in the value of a currency is called *appreciation.* In our example, as the exchange rate moves from USD.8 = CAD1 to USD.9 = CAD1, the Canadian dollar appreciates against the U.S. dollar. As a country's currency appreciates, international demand for its products falls, other things equal.

A currency appreciates in value when its value rises in relation to another currency.

Suppose the exchange rate in our example moves from USD.8 = CAD1 to USD.7 = CAD1. Now the shirt that sells for CAD25 in Vancouver costs a U.S. buyer USD17.50 (CAD25 × .7). In this case, the Canadian dollar has *depreciated* in value relative to the U.S. dollar. As a country's currency depreciates, its goods sell for lower prices in other countries and the demand for its products increases, other things equal.

A currency depreciates in value when its value falls in relation to another currency.

When the Canadian dollar is appreciating against the U.S. dollar, the U.S. dollar must be depreciating against the Canadian dollar. For instance, when the exchange rate between the U.S. dollar and the Canadian dollar moves from USD.8 = CAD1 to USD.9 = CAD1, the reciprocal exchange rate—the rate between the Canadian dollar and the U.S. dollar—moves from CAD1.25 = USD1 (1/.8 = 1.25) to CAD1.11 = USD1 (1/.9 = 1.11). At the same time that Canadian goods are becoming more expensive to U.S. buyers, U.S. goods are becoming cheaper to Canadian buyers.

In later chapters we look more closely at how changes in exchange rates affect international trade and at how governments use exchange rates to change their net exports.

RECAP

1. The foreign exchange market is a global market in which foreign money, largely bank deposits, is bought and sold.

2. An exchange rate is the price of one money in terms of another.

3. Foreign demand for domestic goods decreases as the domestic currency appreciates and increases as the domestic currency depreciates.

■ 2. The Balance of Payments

1 | **How do nations record their transactions with the rest of the world?**

The U.S. economy does not operate in a vacuum. It affects and is affected by the economies of other nations. This point is brought home to Americans when newspaper headlines announce a large trade deficit and politicians denounce foreign countries for running trade surpluses against the United States. In such times, it seems as if everywhere there is talk of the balance of payments.

balance of payments: a record of a country's trade in goods, services, and financial assets with the rest of the world

The **balance of payments** is a record of a country's trade in goods, services, and financial assets with the rest of the world. This record is divided into categories, or accounts, that summarize the nation's international economic transactions. For example, one category measures transactions in merchandise; another measures transactions involving financial assets (bank deposits, bonds, stocks, loans). Balance of payments data are reported quarterly for most developed countries.

Once we understand the various definitions of the balance of payments, there remains the issue of why we should care. One important reason is that balance of payments issues are often hot political topics. One cannot make sense of the political debate without an understanding of balance of payments basics. For instance, the United States is said to have a large deficit in its merchandise trade with the rest of the world. Is this bad? Some politicians will argue that a large trade deficit calls for government action, as it is harmful for a nation to buy more from than it sells to the rest of the world. The economics of the balance of payments allows us to judge the value of such arguments. Some policymakers, labor leaders, and business people will argue that it is bad if a country has a trade deficit with another single country. For instance, if the United States has a trade deficit with Japan, it is common to hear calls for policy aimed at eliminating this *bilateral* trade deficit. Once again, an understanding of the economics of the trade deficit allows a proper evaluation of calls for policies aimed at eliminating bilateral trade imbalances. We will encounter references to policy issues related to the balance of payments in later chapters.

2.a. Accounting for International Transactions

double-entry bookkeeping: a system of accounting in which every transaction is recorded in at least two accounts

The balance of payments is an accounting statement known as a balance sheet. A balance sheet is based on **double-entry bookkeeping,** a system in which every transaction is recorded in at least two accounts. We do not need to know the details of accounting rules to understand the balance of payments. We can simply think of transactions bringing money into a country as being positive numbers that are recorded as *credits* and transactions taking money out of a country as being negative numbers that are recorded as *debits*. Double-entry bookkeeping requires that the debit and credit entries for any transaction must balance. Suppose a U.S. tractor manufacturer sells a $50,000 tractor to a resident of France. This transaction would have a positive effect on the U.S. balance of trade in merchandise. If a U.S. resident bought a $500 bicycle from a Japanese firm, this would have a negative effect on the U.S. balance of trade in merchandise. Of course, people buy and sell things other than merchandise. The classification of international transactions into major accounts is now considered.

2.b. Balance of Payments Accounts

The balance of payments uses several different accounts to classify transactions (see Table 3). The **current account** is the sum of the balances in the merchandise, services, income, and unilateral transfers accounts.

Merchandise This account records all transactions involving goods. The exports of goods by the United States are merchandise credits, bringing money into the United States; its imports of foreign goods are merchandise debits, taking money out of the United States. When exports (or credits) exceed imports (or debits), the merchandise account shows a **surplus.** When imports exceed exports, the account shows a **deficit.** The balance in the merchandise account is frequently referred to as the **balance of trade.**

In the third quarter of 2008, the merchandise account in the U.S. balance of payments showed a deficit of $214,710 million. This means that the merchandise credits created by U.S. exports were $214,710 million less than the merchandise debits created by U.S. imports. In other words, the United States bought more goods from other nations than it sold to them.

Services This account measures trade involving services. It includes travel and tourism, royalties, transportation costs, and insurance premiums. In Table 3, the balance on the services account was a $38,175 million surplus.

Income Both investment income and employee compensation are included here. The income earned from investments in foreign countries is a credit; the income paid on foreign-owned investments in the United States is a debit. Investment income is the return on a special kind of service: It is the value of services provided by capital in foreign countries. Compensation earned by U.S. workers abroad is a credit. Compensation earned by foreign workers in the United States is a debit. In Table 3, there is a surplus of $38,175 million in the income account.

Unilateral Transfers In a unilateral transfer, one party gives something but gets nothing in return. Gifts and retirement pensions are forms of unilateral transfers.

current account: the sum of the merchandise, services, income, and unilateral transfers accounts in the balance of payments

surplus: in a balance of payments account, the amount by which credits exceed debits

deficit: in a balance of payments account, the amount by which debits exceed credits

balance of trade: the balance in the merchandise account in a nation's balance of payments

TABLE 3 Simplified U.S. Balance of Payments, 2008 Third Quarter (million dollars)

Account	Net Balance
Merchandise	−$214,710
Services	$38,175
Income	$30,835
Unilateral transfers	−$28,390
Current account	−$174,091
Financial account	$116,187
Statistical discrepancy	−$39,487

Source: Data from Bureau of Economic Analysis.

financial account: the record in the balance of payments of the flow of financial assets into and out of a country

For instance, if a farmworker in El Centro, California, sends money to his family in Guaymas, Mexico, this is a unilateral transfer from the United States to Mexico. In Table 3, the unilateral transfers balance is a deficit of $28,390 million.

The current account is a useful measure of international transactions because it contains all of the activities involving goods and services. The **financial account** is where trade involving financial assets and international investment is recorded. In the third quarter of 2008, the current account showed a deficit of $174,091 million. This means that U.S. imports of merchandise, services, investment income, and unilateral transfers were $174,091 million greater than exports of these items.

If we draw a line in the balance of payments under the current account, then all entries below the line relate to financing the movement of merchandise, services, investment income, and unilateral transfers into and out of the country. Credits to the financial account reflect foreign purchases of U.S. financial assets or real property like land and buildings, and debits reflect U.S. purchases of foreign financial assets and real property. In Table 3, the U.S. financial account showed a surplus of $116,187 million.

The *statistical discrepancy* account, the last account listed in Table 3, could be called *omissions and errors*. The government cannot accurately measure all transactions that take place. Some international shipments of goods and services go uncounted or are miscounted, as do some international flows of financial assets. The statistical discrepancy account is used to correct for these omissions and errors. In Table 3, measured credits were less than measured debits, so the statistical discrepancy was $39,487 million.

Over all of the balance of payments accounts, the sum of credits must equal the sum of debits. The bottom line—the *net balance*—must be zero. It cannot show a surplus or a deficit. When people talk about a surplus or a deficit in the balance of payments, they are actually talking about a surplus or a deficit in one of the balance of payments accounts. The balance of payments itself, by definition, is always in balance, a function of double-entry bookkeeping.

2.c. The Current Account and the Financial Account

The current account reflects the movement of goods and services into and out of a country. The financial account reflects the flow of financial assets into and out of a country. In Table 3, the current account shows a deficit balance of $174,091 million. Remember that the balance of payments must *balance*. If there is a deficit in the current account, there must be a surplus in the financial account that exactly offsets that deficit.

What is important here is not the bookkeeping process, the concept that the balance of payments must balance, but rather the meaning of deficits and surpluses in the current and financial accounts. These deficits and surpluses tell us whether a country is a net borrower from or lender to the rest of the world. A deficit in the current account means that a country is running a net surplus in its financial account. And it signals that a country is a net borrower from the rest of the world. A country that is running a current account deficit must borrow from abroad an amount sufficient to finance that deficit. A financial account surplus is achieved by selling more bonds and other debts of the domestic country to the rest of the world than the country buys from the rest of the world.

In Chapter 5, we learned that the value of a nation's output, GDP, is equal to the sum of consumption, investment, government spending, and net exports, or $GDP = C + I + G + X$. We could rewrite this equation in terms of X as $X = GDP - C - I - G$. The X in total spending is net exports involving trade

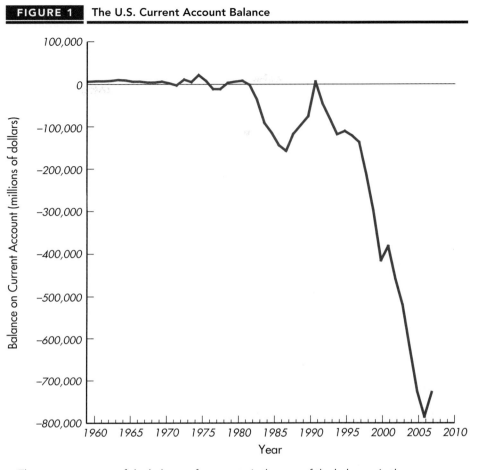

FIGURE 1 The U.S. Current Account Balance

The current account of the balance of payments is the sum of the balances in the merchandise, services, income, and unilateral transfers accounts. The United States experienced very large current account deficits in the 1980s and again more recently.
Source: Bureau of Economic Analysis.

in goods and services. As can be seen in Table 3, this is the largest component of the current account. Thus, a country that is running a current account deficit will have a negative X. Since $X = \text{GDP} - C - I - G$, one can see that negative net exports or a current account deficit is consistent with domestic spending being in excess of domestic production. A country that is running a current account deficit is spending more than it produces. Such a country must borrow to cover this difference between production and spending.

Figure 1 shows the annual current account balance in the United States. The United States experienced large current account deficits in the 1980s and then again from the mid-1990s to the present. These deficits indicate that the United States consumed more than it produced. This means that the United States sold financial assets to and borrowed large amounts of money from foreign residents to finance its current account deficits. This large amount of foreign borrowing made the United States the largest debtor in the world. A *net debtor* owes more to the rest of the world than it is owed; a *net creditor* is owed more than it owes. The United States was an international net creditor from the end of World War I until the mid-1980s. The country financed its large current account deficits in the 1980s by borrowing from the rest of the world. As a result of this accumulated borrowing, in 1985 the United States became an international net debtor for the first time in almost 70 years. Since that time, the net debtor status of the United States has grown steadily.

RECAP

1. The balance of payments is a record of a nation's international transactions.

2. Double-entry bookkeeping requires that every transaction be entered in at least two accounts, so that credits and debits are balanced.

3. In the balance of payments, credits record activities that represent payments into the country, and debits record activities that represent payments out of the country.

4. The current account is the sum of the balances in the merchandise, services, income, and unilateral transfers accounts.

5. A surplus exists when credits exceed debits; a deficit exists when credits are less than debits.

6. The financial account is where the transactions necessary to finance the movement of merchandise, services, income, and unilateral transfers into and out of the country are recorded.

7. The net balance in the balance of payments must be zero.

SUMMARY

1 | How do individuals of one nation trade money with individuals of another nation?

- Foreign exchange is currency and bank deposits that are denominated in foreign currency. *§1*
- The foreign exchange market is a global market in which people trade one currency for another. *§1*
- Exchange rates, the price of one country's money in terms of another country's money, are necessary to compare prices quoted in different currencies. *§1.a*
- The value of a good in a domestic currency equals the foreign currency price times the exchange rate. *§1.a*

2 | How do changes in exchange rates affect international trade?

- When a domestic currency appreciates, domestic goods become more expensive to foreigners, and foreign goods become cheaper to domestic residents. *§1.b*
- When a domestic currency depreciates, domestic goods become cheaper to foreigners, and foreign goods become more expensive to domestic residents. *§1.b*

3 | How do nations record their transactions with the rest of the world?

- The balance of payments is a record of a nation's transactions with the rest of the world. *§2*

- The balance of payments is based on double-entry bookkeeping. *§2.a*
- Credits record activities that bring payments into a country; debits record activities that take payments out of a country. *§2.a*
- The current account is the sum of the balances in the merchandise, services, income, and unilateral transfers accounts. *§2.b*
- In a balance of payments account, a surplus is the amount by which credits exceed debits, and a deficit is the amount by which debits exceed credits. *§2.b*
- The financial account reflects the transactions necessary to finance the movement of merchandise, services, income, and unilateral transfers into and out of the country. *§2.b*
- The net balance in the balance of payments must be zero. *§2.b*
- A deficit in the current account must be offset by a surplus in the financial account. *§2.c*
- A country that shows a deficit in its current account (or a surplus in its financial account) is a net borrower. *§2.c*

KEY TERMS

foreign exchange §1

foreign exchange market §1

exchange rate §1.a

balance of payments §2

double-entry bookkeeping §2.a

current account §2.b

surplus §2.b

deficit §2.b

balance of trade §2.b

financial account §2.b

EXERCISES

1. What is the price of 1 U.S. dollar in terms of each of the following currencies, given the following exchange rates?
   a. 1 euro = $.90
   b. 1 Chinese yuan = $.12
   c. 1 Israeli shekel = $.30
   d. 1 Kuwaiti dinar = $3.20

2. A bicycle manufactured in the United States costs $100. Using the exchange rates listed in Table 1, what would the bicycle cost in each of the following countries?
   a. Argentina
   b. Britain
   c. Canada

3. The U.S. dollar price of a Swedish krona changes from $.1572 to $.1730.
   a. Has the dollar depreciated or appreciated against the krona?
   b. Has the krona appreciated or depreciated against the dollar?

Use the information in the following table on Mexico's 2007 international transactions to answer exercises 4–6 (the amounts are the U.S. dollar values in millions):

Merchandise exports	$271,594
Merchandise imports	$281,649
Services exports	$17,512
Services imports	$23,784
Income receipts	$7,972
Income payments	$26,036
Unilateral transfers	$24,197

4. What is the balance of trade?

5. What is the current account?

6. Did Mexico become a larger international net debtor during 2007?

7. How reasonable is it for every country to follow policies aimed at increasing net exports?

8. How did the United States become the world's largest debtor nation in the 1980s?

9. If the U.S. dollar appreciated against the Japanese yen, what would you expect to happen to U.S. net exports to Japan?

10. Suppose the U.S. dollar price of a British pound is $1.50; the dollar price of a euro is $1; a hotel room in London, England, costs 120 British pounds; and a comparable hotel room in Hanover, Germany, costs 200 euro.
    a. Which hotel room is cheaper for a U.S. tourist?
    b. What is the exchange rate between the euro and the British pound?

11. Many residents of the United States send money to relatives living in other countries. For instance, a Salvadoran farmworker who is temporarily working in San Diego, California, sends money back to his family in El Salvador. How are such transactions recorded in the balance of payments? Are they debits or credits?

12. Suppose the U.S. dollar price of the Canadian dollar is $.75. How many Canadian dollars will it take to buy a set of dishes selling for $60 in Detroit, Michigan?

13. Why is it true that if the dollar depreciates against the yen, the yen must appreciate against the dollar?

14. Why does the balance of payments contain an account called "statistical discrepancy"?

15. Use the national income identity $GDP = C + I + G + X$ to explain what a current account deficit (negative net exports) means in terms of domestic spending, production, and borrowing.

You can find further practice tests in the Online Quiz at **www.cengage.com/economics/boyes**.

French Cross Channel to Buy Chanel in London

London Evening Standard **March 23, 2009**

Channel-hopping shoppers are taking advantage of the weak pound and flocking to London to snap up famous French brands, retailers said today.

Chanel, Chloe and Louis Vuitton goods are proving most popular with the French shoppers, according to Selfridges.

The department store, which has a flagship shop in Oxford Street, said trade from France soared by 70 per cent in January and February compared with the same months last year. The trend held for shoppers from other countries using the euro, with trade growing by more than 40 per cent.

The pound's weakness means European customers can make big savings on purchases such as designers handbags, with a Chanel quilted leather bag costing the equivalent of £1,780 in Paris available at Selfridges for £1,525.

Euro shoppers are also snapping up British brands, with sales of Vivienne Westwood handbags up more than 50 per cent this year.

Selfridges' buying director, Anne Pitcher, said: "European customers have clearly resolved not to give up on life's uplifting luxuries and are coming to London to get them at the best possible price."

Mark Blunden

Source: From www.thisisLondon.co.uk/standard, March 23, 2009.

Why were French shoppers traveling to London to shop? The article says that it has to do with a weak British pound. There are two elements involved in determining the price of an internationally traded good: the price in terms of the home currency of the country in which the good is produced and the exchange rate. With constant pound prices of goods in London, if the British pound depreciates in value against the euro, British goods will become cheaper to French buyers, as emphasized in the article.

If one examines how the euro value of a pound has changed in recent times, it is easy to see how the price of goods in London has changed for French residents.

In early 2007, 1 pound was worth about 1.50 euros. But by early 2009, a pound was only worth about 1.05 euros. So if the prices of goods and services in London did not change at all, the prices of London goods to French shoppers fell by about a third. A luxury purse that sells for 1,000 pounds in London would have cost a French shopper about 1,500 euros in 2007 but fell in price to about 1,050 euros by 2009.

This brief article reminds us of how interdependent countries are. The story of the increase in French shoppers in London in 2009 is a good example of how the exchange rate between currencies is one of the key variables linking countries together.

Chapter 7

© Sharon Day/S

Unemployment and Inflation

? Fundamental Questions

1 | What is a business cycle?

2 | How is the unemployment rate defined and measured?

3 | What is the cost of unemployed resources?

4 | What is inflation?

5 | Why is inflation a problem?

If you were graduating from college today, what would your job prospects be? In 1932, they would have been bleak. A large number of people were out of work (about one in four workers), and a large number of firms had laid off workers or gone out of business. At any given time, job opportunities depend not only on the individual's ability and experience, but also on the current state of the economy.

Economies follow cycles of activity: Periods of expansion, in which output and employment increase, are followed by periods of contraction, in which output and employment decrease. For instance, during the expansionary period of the 1990s and 2000, only 4 percent of U.S. workers had no job by 2000. But during the period of contraction of 1981–1982, 9.5 percent of U.S. workers had no job. When the economy is growing, the demand for goods and services tends to increase. To produce those goods and services, firms hire more workers. Economic expansion also has an impact on inflation: As the demand for goods and services goes up, the prices of those goods and services also tend to rise. By 2000, following several years of economic growth, consumer prices in the United States were rising by about 3 percent a year. During periods of contraction, when more people are out of work, demand for goods and services tends to fall, and there is less pressure for rising prices.

During the period of the Great Depression in the 1930s in the United States, consumer prices fell by more than 5 percent in 1933. Both price increases and the fraction of workers without jobs are affected by business cycles in fairly regular ways. But their effects on individual standards of living, income, and purchasing power are much less predictable.

Why do certain events move in tandem? What are the links between unemployment and inflation? What causes the business cycle to behave as it does? What effect does government activity have on the business cycle—and on unemployment and inflation? Who is harmed by rising unemployment and inflation? Who benefits? Macroeconomics attempts to answer all of these questions.

As real income falls, living standards go down. This 1937 photo of a Depression-era breadline indicates the paradox of the world's richest nation, as emphasized on the billboard in the background, having to offer public support to feed able-bodied workers who were out of work due to the severity of the business-cycle downturn.

© Margaret Bourke-White/Time Life Pictures/Getty Images

■ 1. Business Cycles

In this chapter, we describe the business cycle and examine measures of unemployment and inflation. We talk about the ways in which the business cycle, unemployment, and inflation are related. And we describe their effects on the participants in the economy.

The most widely used measure of a nation's output is gross domestic product. When we examine the value of real GDP over time, we find periods in which it rises and other periods in which it falls.

1.a. Definitions

This pattern—real GDP rising, then falling—is called a **business cycle.** The pattern occurs over and over again, but as Figure 1 shows, the pattern over time is anything but regular. Historically, the duration of business cycles and the rate at which real GDP rises or falls (indicated by the steepness of the line in Figure 1) vary considerably.

1 | **What is a business cycle?**

business cycle:
fluctuations in the economy between growth (expressed in rising real GDP) and stagnation (expressed in falling real GDP)

FIGURE 1   U.S. Real GDP

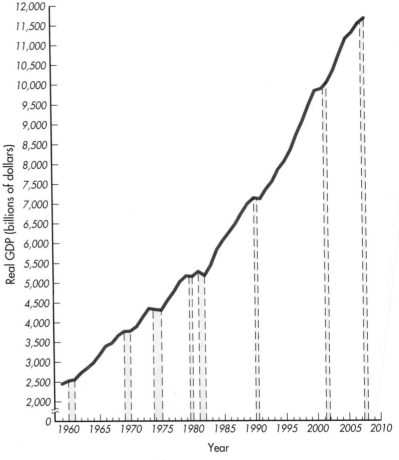

Peaks	Troughs
April 1960	February 1961
December 1969	November 1970
November 1973	March 1975
January 1980	July 1980
July 1981	November 1982
July 1990	March 1991
March 2001	November 2001
December 2007	

The shaded areas represent periods of economic contraction (recession). The table lists the dates of business-cycle peaks and troughs. The peak dates indicate when contractions began; the trough dates, when expansions began.
Source: Data from Bureau of Economic Analysis; (www.bea.gov/bea/an/nipaguid.pdf).

recession: a period in which real GDP falls

Looking at Figure 1, it is clear that the U.S. economy has experienced up-and-down swings in the years since 1959. Still, real GDP has grown at an average rate of approximately 3 percent per year over the long run. While it is important to recognize that periods of economic growth, or prosperity, are followed by periods of contraction, or **recession,** it is also important to recognize the presence of long-term economic growth despite the presence of periodic recessions. In the long run, the economy produces more goods and services. The long-run growth in the economy depends on the growth in productive resources, like land, labor, and capital, along with technological advance. Technological change increases the productivity of resources so that output increases even with a fixed amount of inputs.

Figure 2 shows how real GDP behaves over a hypothetical business cycle and identifies the stages of the cycle. The vertical axis on the graph measures the level of real GDP; the horizontal axis measures time in years. In year 1, real GDP is growing; the economy is in the *expansion* phase, or *boom* period, of the business cycle. Growth continues until the *peak* is reached, in year 2. Real GDP begins to fall during the *contraction* phase of the cycle, which continues until year 4. The *trough* marks the

| FIGURE 2 | The Business Cycle |

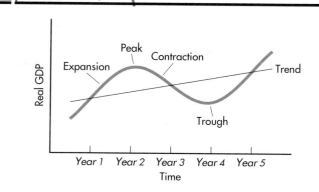

The business cycle contains four phases: the expansion (boom), when real GDP is increasing; the peak, which marks the end of an expansion and the beginning of a contraction; the contraction (recession), when real GDP is falling; and the trough, which marks the end of a contraction and the beginning of an expansion.

end of the contraction and the start of a new expansion. Even though the economy is subject to periodic ups and downs, real GDP, the measure of a nation's output, has risen over the long term, as illustrated by the upward-sloping line labeled *Trend*.

If an economy is growing over time, why do economists worry about business cycles? Economists try to understand the causes of business cycles so that they can learn how to moderate or avoid recessions and their harmful effects on standards of living.

1.b. Historical Record

The official dating of recessions in the United States is the responsibility of the National Bureau of Economic Research (NBER), an independent research organization. The NBER has identified the shaded areas in the graph in Figure 1 as recessions and the unshaded areas as expansions. Recessions are periods between cyclical peaks and the troughs that follow them. Expansions are periods between cyclical troughs and the peaks that follow them. There have been 14 recessions since 1929. The most severe was the period between 1929 and 1933, called the Great Depression. During this period, national output fell by 25 percent. A **depression** is a prolonged period of severe economic contraction. The fact that people speak of "the Depression" when they talk about the recession that began in 1929 indicates the severity of that contraction relative to others in recent experience. There was widespread suffering during the Depression. Many people were jobless and homeless, and many firms went bankrupt.

The NBER defines a recession as "a period of significant decline in total output, income, employment, and trade, usually lasting from six months to a year, and marked by widespread contractions in many sectors of the economy." People sometimes say that a recession is defined by two consecutive quarters of declining real GDP. This informal idea of what constitutes a recession seems to be consistent with the past recessions experienced by the United States, as every recession through the 1990s has had at least two quarters of falling real GDP. However, this is not the official definition of a recession. The business cycle dating committee of the NBER generally focuses on monthly data. Close attention is paid to the following monthly data series: employment, real personal income less transfer payments, the volume of sales of the manufacturing and wholesale–retail sectors adjusted for price changes, and industrial production. The focus is not on real GDP, because it is measured only quarterly and does not permit the identification of the month in which business-cycle turning points occur.

depression: a severe, prolonged economic contraction

On November 28, 2008, the NBER Business Cycle Dating Committee met and determined that December 2007 was the most recent business-cycle peak. It always takes some time for the committee that dates business cycles to have enough evidence to be convinced that the data have identified the turning point in the business cycle. For instance, in determining the end of the previous recession, it wasn't until July 17, 2003, that the NBER announced the recession had ended in November 2001. It took more than 1.5 years to identify the trough that marked the end of the prior recent recession. At the time this edition of the text went to press, the U.S. was still in recession, but of course, we will not find out the date of the end of the recession until well after the fact.

1.c. Indicators

We have been talking about the business cycle in terms of real GDP. There are a number of other variables that move in a fairly regular manner over the business cycle. These variables are classified into three categories—leading indicators, coincident indicators, and lagging indicators—depending on whether they move up or down before, at the same time as, or following a change in real GDP (see Table 1).

leading indicator: a variable that changes before real output changes

Leading indicators generally change before real GDP changes. As a result, economists use them to forecast changes in output. Looking at Table 1, it is easy to see how some of these leading indicators could be used to forecast future output. For instance, new building permits signal new construction. If the number of new permits issued goes up, economists can expect the amount of new construction to increase. Similarly, if manufacturers receive more new orders, economists can expect more goods to be produced.

Leading indicators are not infallible, however. The link between them and future output can be tenuous. For example, leading indicators may fall one month and then rise the next, although real output rises steadily. Economists want to see several consecutive months of a new direction in the leading indicators before forecasting a change in output. Short-run movements in the indicators can be very misleading.

coincident indicator: a variable that changes at the same time as real output changes

Coincident indicators are economic variables that tend to change at the same time as real output changes. For example, as real output increases, economists expect to see employment and sales rise. The coincident indicators listed in Table 1 have demonstrated a strong tendency over time to change along with changes in real GDP.

TABLE 1	Indicators of the Business Cycle

Leading Indicators	
Average workweek	New building permits
Unemployment claims	Delivery times of goods
Manufacturers' new orders	Interest rate spread
Stock prices	Money supply
New plant and equipment orders	Consumer expectations

Coincident Indicators	Lagging Indicators
Payroll employment	Labor cost per unit of output
Industrial production	Inventories to sales ratio
Personal income	Unemployment duration
Manufacturing and trade sales	Consumer credit to personal income ratio
	Outstanding commercial loans
	Prime interest rate
	Inflation rate for services

lagging indicator: a variable that changes after real output changes

The final group of variables listed in Table 1, **lagging indicators,** do not change in value until after the value of real GDP has changed. For instance, as output increases, jobs are created and more workers are hired. It makes sense, then, to expect the duration of unemployment (the average length of time that workers are unemployed) to fall. The duration of unemployment is a lagging indicator. Similarly, the inflation rate for services (which measures how prices for things like dry cleaners, veterinarians, and other services change) tends to change after real GDP changes. Lagging indicators are used along with leading and coincident indicators to identify the peaks and troughs in business cycles.

RECAP

1. The business cycle is a recurring pattern of rising and falling real GDP.

2. Although all economies move through periods of expansion and contraction, the duration of the periods of expansion and recession varies.

3. Real GDP is not the only variable affected by business cycles; leading, lagging, and coincident indicators also show the effects of economic expansion and contraction.

2 | **How is the unemployment rate defined and measured?**

■ 2. Unemployment

Recurring periods of prosperity and recession are reflected in the nation's labor markets. In fact, this is what makes understanding the business cycle so important. If business cycles signified only a little more or a little less profit for businesses, governments would not be so anxious to forecast or to control their swings. It is the human costs of lost jobs and incomes—the inability to maintain standards of living—that make an understanding of business cycles and of the factors that affect unemployment so important.

2.a. Definition and Measurement

unemployment rate: the percentage of the labor force that is not working

The **unemployment rate** is the percentage of the labor force that is not working. The rate is calculated by dividing the number of people who are unemployed by the number of people in the labor force:

$$\text{Unemployment rate} = \frac{\text{number unemployed}}{\text{number in labor force}}$$

This ratio seems simple enough, but there are several subtle issues at work here. First, the unemployment rate does not measure the percentage of the total population that is not working; it measures the percentage of the *labor force* that is not working. Who is in the labor force? Obviously, everybody who is employed is part of the labor force. But only some of those who are not currently employed are counted in the labor force.

You are in the labor force if you are working or actively seeking work.

The Bureau of Labor Statistics of the Department of Labor compiles labor data each month based on an extensive survey of U.S. households. All U.S. residents are potential members of the labor force. The Labor Department arrives at the size of the actual labor force by using this formula:

Labor force = all U.S. residents
minus residents under 16 years of age
minus institutionalized adults
minus adults not looking for work

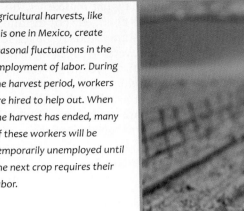

Agricultural harvests, like this one in Mexico, create seasonal fluctuations in the employment of labor. During the harvest period, workers are hired to help out. When the harvest has ended, many of these workers will be temporarily unemployed until the next crop requires their labor.

© Richard Thornton/Shutterstock

So the labor force includes those adults (an adult being someone 16 or older) who are currently employed or actively seeking work. It is relatively simple to see to it that children and institutionalized adults (for instance, those in prison or in long-term care facilities) are not counted in the labor force. It is more difficult to identify and accurately measure adults who are not actively looking for work.

A person is actively seeking work if he or she is available to work, has looked for work in the past 4 weeks, is waiting for a recall after being laid off, or is starting a job within 30 days. Those who are not working and who meet these criteria are considered unemployed.

2.b. Interpreting the Unemployment Rate

Is the unemployment rate an accurate measure? The fact that the rate does not include those who are not actively looking for work is not necessarily a failing. Many people who are not actively looking for work—homemakers, older citizens, and students, for example—have made a decision not to work—to do housework, to retire, or to stay in school. These people rightly are not counted among the unemployed.

But there are people missing from the unemployment statistics who are not working and are not looking for work yet would take a job if one were offered. **Discouraged workers** have looked for work in the past year but have given up looking for work because they believe that no one will hire them. These individuals are ignored by the official unemployment rate, even though they are able to work and may have spent a long time looking for work. Estimates of the number of discouraged workers indicate that in January 2006, 1.6 million people were not counted in the labor force yet claimed that they were available for work. Of this group, 25 percent, or 396,000 people, were considered to be discouraged workers. It is clear that the reported unemployment rate underestimates the true burden of unemployment in the economy because it ignores discouraged workers.

Discouraged workers are one source of hidden unemployment; underemployment is another. **Underemployment** is the underutilization of workers, employing them in tasks that do not fully utilize their productive potential; this

discouraged workers: workers who have stopped looking for work because they believe that no one will offer them a job

underemployment: the employment of workers in jobs that do not utilize their productive potential

includes part-time workers who would prefer full-time employment. Even if every worker has a job, substantial underemployment leaves the economy producing less than its potential GDP.

The effect of discouraged workers and underemployment is to produce an unemployment rate that *understates* actual unemployment. In contrast, the effect of the *underground economy* is to produce a rate that *overstates* actual unemployment. A sizable number of the officially unemployed are actually working. The unemployed construction worker who plays in a band at night may not report that activity because he or she wants to avoid paying taxes on his or her earnings as a musician. This person is officially unemployed but has a source of income. Many officially unemployed individuals have an alternative source of income. This means that official statistics overstate the true magnitude of unemployment. The larger the underground economy, the greater this overstatement.

> *Activity in the underground economy is not included in official statistics.*

We have identified two factors, discouraged workers and underemployment, that cause the official unemployment rate to underestimate true unemployment. Another factor, the underground economy, causes the official rate to overestimate the true rate of unemployment. There is no reason to expect these factors to cancel one another out, and there is no way to know for sure which is most important. The point is to remember what the official data on unemployment do and do not measure.

2.c. Types of Unemployment

Economists have identified four basic types of unemployment:

Seasonal unemployment A product of regular, recurring changes in the hiring needs of certain industries on a monthly or seasonal basis

Frictional unemployment A product of the short-term movement of workers between jobs and of first-time job seekers

Structural unemployment A product of technological change and other changes in the structure of the economy

Cyclical unemployment A product of business-cycle fluctuations

> *Frictional and structural unemployment are always present in a dynamic economy.*

In certain industries, labor needs fluctuate throughout the year. When local crops are harvested, farms need lots of workers; the rest of the year, they do not. (Migrant farmworkers move from one region to another, following the harvests, to avoid seasonal unemployment.) Ski resort towns like Park City, Utah, are booming during the ski season, when employment peaks, but need fewer workers during the rest of the year. In the nation as a whole, the Christmas season is a time of peak employment and low unemployment rates. To avoid confusing seasonal fluctuations in unemployment with other sources of unemployment, unemployment data are seasonally adjusted.

Frictional and structural unemployment exist in any dynamic economy. For individual workers, frictional unemployment is short term in nature. Workers quit one job and soon find another; students graduate and soon find a job. This kind of unemployment cannot be eliminated in a free society. In fact, it is a sign of efficiency in an economy when workers try to increase their income or improve their working conditions by leaving one job for another. Frictional unemployment is often called *search unemployment* because workers take time to search for a job after quitting a job or leaving school.

Frictional unemployment is short term; structural unemployment, on the other hand, can be long term. Workers who are displaced by technological change (assembly line workers who have been replaced by machines, for example) or by a permanent reduction in the demand for an industry's output (cigar makers who have been laid off because of a decrease in demand for tobacco) may not have the necessary skills to maintain their level of income in another industry. Rather than accept a much lower salary, these workers tend to prolong their job search. Eventually they either adjust their expectations to the realities of the job market or enter the pool of discouraged workers.

Structural unemployment is very difficult for those who are unemployed. But for society as a whole, the technological advances that cause structural unemployment raise living standards by giving consumers a greater variety of goods at lower cost.

Cyclical unemployment is a result of the business cycle. When a recession occurs, cyclical unemployment increases, and when growth occurs, cyclical unemployment decreases. It is also a primary focus of macroeconomic policy. Economists believe that a greater understanding of business cycles and their causes may enable them to find ways to smooth out those cycles and swings in unemployment. Much of the analysis in future chapters is related to macroeconomic policy aimed at minimizing business-cycle fluctuations. In addition to macroeconomic policy aimed at moderating cyclical unemployment, other policy measures—for example, job training and counseling—are being used to reduce frictional and structural unemployment.

2.d. Costs of Unemployment

The cost of unemployment is more than the obvious loss of income and status suffered by the individual who is not working. In a broader sense, society as a whole loses when resources are unemployed. Unemployed workers produce no output. So an economy with unemployment will operate inside its production possibilities curve rather than on the curve. Economists measure this lost output in terms of the *GDP gap*:

$$\text{GDP gap} = \text{potential real GDP} - \text{actual real GDP}$$

Potential real GDP is the level of output produced when nonlabor resources are fully utilized and unemployment is at its natural rate. The **natural rate of unemployment** is the unemployment rate that would exist in the absence of cyclical unemployment, so it includes seasonal, frictional, and structural unemployment. The natural rate of unemployment is not fixed; it can change over time. For instance, some economists believe that the natural rate of unemployment has risen in recent decades, a product of the influx of baby boomers and women into the labor force. As more workers move into the labor force (begin looking for jobs), frictional unemployment increases, raising the natural rate of unemployment. The natural rate of unemployment is sometimes called the "nonaccelerating inflation rate of unemployment," or NAIRU. The idea is that there would be upward pressure on wages and prices in a tight labor market in which the unemployment rate fell below the NAIRU. We will see macroeconomic models of this phenomenon in later chapters.

Potential real GDP measures what we are capable of producing at the natural rate of unemployment. If we compute potential real GDP and then subtract actual real GDP, we have a measure of the output lost as a result of unemployment, or the cost of unemployment.

The GDP gap in the United States from 1960 to 2008 is shown in Figure 3. The gap widens during recessions and narrows during expansions. As the gap widens (as the output that is not produced increases), there are fewer goods and services available, and living standards are lower than they would be at the natural rate of unemployment. Figure 3(b) is a graph of the gap between potential and real GDP, taken from Figure 3(a). During the strong expansion of the late 1990s and more recently, the gap went to zero.

Until recently, economists used the term *full employment* instead of *natural rate of unemployment*. Today the term *full employment* is rarely used because it may be interpreted as implying a zero unemployment rate. If frictional and structural unemployment are always present, zero unemployment is impossible; there must always be unemployed resources in an economy. *Natural rate of unemployment*

Sidebar notes:

Cyclical unemployment is a product of recession.

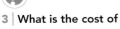

3 | **What is the cost of unemployed resources?**

potential real GDP: the output produced at the natural rate of unemployment

natural rate of unemployment: the unemployment rate that would exist in the absence of cyclical unemployment

Because frictional and structural unemployment are always present, the term full employment is misleading. Today economists use the term natural rate of unemployment instead.

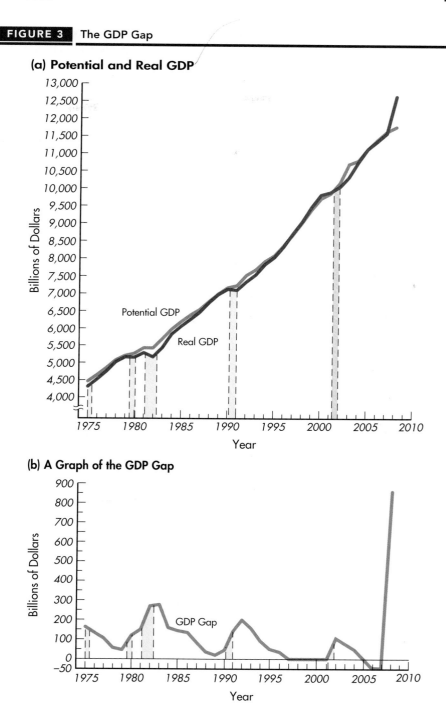

FIGURE 3 The GDP Gap

(a) Potential and Real GDP

Billions of Dollars (y-axis)

Potential GDP

Real GDP

Year (x-axis)

(b) A Graph of the GDP Gap

Billions of Dollars (y-axis)

GDP Gap

Year (x-axis)

The GDP gap is the difference between what the economy can produce at the natural rate of unemployment (potential GDP) and actual output (actual GDP). When the unemployment rate is higher than the natural rate, actual GDP is less than potential GDP. The gap between potential and actual real GDP is a cost associated with unemployment. Recession years are shaded to highlight how the gap widens around recessions.

describes the labor market when the economy is producing what it realistically can produce in the absence of cyclical unemployment.

What is the natural rate of unemployment in the United States? In the 1950s and 1960s, economists generally agreed on 4 percent. By the 1970s, the agreed-upon rate had gone up to 5 percent. In the early 1980s, many economists placed the natural rate of unemployment in the United States at 6 to 7 percent. By the late 1980s, some had revised their thinking, placing the rate back at 5 percent. In the late 1990s, one could have said that 4 percent was correct. In fact, economists do not know exactly what the natural rate of unemployment is. It varies over time within a range from around 4 percent to around 7 percent. It will also vary across countries, as labor markets and macroeconomic policies differ.

2.e. The Record of Unemployment

Unemployment rates in the United States from 1960 to 2008 are listed in Table 2. Over this period, the unemployment rate for all workers reached a low of 3.5 percent

---

TABLE 2　　Unemployment Rates in the United States

| | Unemployment Rate, Civilian Workers[1] | | | | | | | |
| | By Gender | | | | By Race | | | |
Year	All Civilian Workers	Males	Females	Both Sexes 16–19 Years	White	Black or African American	Asian (NSA)	Hispanic or Latino
1960	5.5	5.4	5.9	14.7	5.0	—	—	—
1961	6.7	6.4	7.2	16.8	6.0	—	—	—
1962	5.5	5.2	6.2	14.7	4.9	—	—	—
1963	5.7	5.2	6.5	17.2	5.0	—	—	—
1964	5.2	4.6	6.2	16.2	4.6	—	—	—
1965	4.5	4.0	5.5	14.8	4.1	—	—	—
1966	3.8	3.2	4.8	12.8	3.4	—	—	—
1967	3.8	3.1	5.2	12.9	3.4	—	—	—
1968	3.6	2.9	4.8	12.7	3.2	—	—	—
1969	3.5	2.8	4.7	12.2	3.1	—	—	—
1970	4.9	4.4	5.9	15.3	4.5	—	—	—
1971	5.9	5.3	6.9	16.9	5.4	—	—	—
1972	5.6	5.0	6.6	16.2	5.1	10.4	—	—
1973	4.9	4.2	6.0	14.5	4.3	9.4	—	7.5
1974	5.6	4.9	6.7	16.0	5.0	10.5	—	8.1
1975	8.5	7.9	9.3	19.9	7.8	14.8	—	12.2
1976	7.7	7.1	8.6	19.0	7.0	14.0	—	11.5
1977	7.1	6.3	8.2	17.8	6.2	14.0	—	10.1
1978	6.1	5.3	7.2	16.4	5.2	12.8	—	9.1
1979	5.8	5.1	6.8	16.1	5.1	12.3	—	8.3
1980	7.1	6.9	7.4	17.8	6.3	14.3	—	10.1
1981	7.6	7.4	7.9	19.6	6.7	15.6	—	10.4

(Continuted)

TABLE 2 Unemployment Rates in the United States *(Continued)*

1982	9.7	9.9	9.4	23.2	8.6	18.9	—	13.8
1983	9.6	9.9	9.2	22.4	8.4	19.5	—	13.7
1984	7.5	7.4	7.6	18.9	6.5	15.9	—	10.7
1985	7.2	7.0	7.4	18.6	6.2	15.1	—	10.5
1986	7.0	6.9	7.1	18.3	6.0	14.5	—	10.6
1987	6.2	6.2	6.2	16.9	5.3	13.0	—	8.8
1988	5.5	5.5	5.6	15.3	4.7	11.7	—	8.2
1989	5.3	5.2	5.4	15.0	4.5	11.4	—	8.0
1990	5.6	5.7	5.5	15.5	4.8	11.4	—	8.2
1991	6.8	7.2	6.4	18.7	6.1	12.5	—	10.0
1992	7.5	7.9	7.0	20.1	6.6	14.2	—	11.6
1993	6.9	7.2	6.6	19.0	6.1	13.0	—	10.8
1994	6.1	6.2	6.0	17.6	5.3	11.5	—	9.9
1995	5.6	5.6	5.6	17.3	4.9	10.4	—	9.3
1996	5.4	5.4	5.4	16.7	4.7	10.5	—	8.9
1997	4.9	4.9	5.0	16.0	4.2	10.0	—	7.7
1998	4.5	4.4	4.6	14.6	3.9	8.9	—	7.2
1999	4.2	4.1	4.3	13.9	3.7	8.0	—	6.4
2000	4.0	3.9	4.1	13.1	3.5	7.6	3.6	5.7
2001	4.7	4.8	4.7	14.7	4.2	8.6	4.5	6.6
2002	5.8	5.9	5.6	16.5	5.1	10.2	5.9	7.5
2003	6.0	6.3	5.7	17.5	5.2	10.8	6.0	7.7
2004	5.5	5.6	5.4	17.0	4.8	10.4	4.4	7.0
2005	5.1	5.1	5.1	16.6	4.4	10.0	4.0	6.0
2006	4.6	4.6	4.6	15.4	4.0	8.9	3.0	5.2
2007	4.6	4.7	4.5	15.7	4.1	8.3	3.2	5.6
2008	5.8	6.1	5.4	—	5.5	11.4	4.1	7.6

[1] Unemployed as a percentage of the civilian labor force in the group specified.
Source: Bureau of Labor Statistics; http://data.bls.gov/.

in 1969 and a high of 9.7 percent in 1982. The table shows some general trends in the incidence of unemployment across different demographic groups:

Teenagers have the highest unemployment rates in the economy. This makes sense because teenagers are the least-skilled segment of the labor force.

Whites have lower unemployment rates than nonwhites. Discrimination plays a role here. To the extent that discrimination extends beyond hiring practices and job opportunities for minority workers to the education that is necessary to prepare students to enter the work force, minority workers will have fewer opportunities for employment. The quality of education provided in many schools with large minority populations may not be as good as that provided in schools with large white populations. Equal opportunity programs and legislation are aimed at rectifying this inequality.

Although exact comparisons across countries are difficult to make because different countries measure unemployment in different ways, it is interesting to look at the reported unemployment rates of different countries. Table 3 lists unemployment rates for seven major industrial nations. The rates have been adjusted to match the U.S. definition of unemployment as closely as possible.

Knowing their limitations, we can still identify some important trends from the data in Table 3. In the early 1980s, both U.S. and European unemployment rates increased substantially. But in the mid-1980s, when U.S. unemployment began to fall, European unemployment remained high. The issue of high unemployment rates in Europe has become a major topic of discussion at international summit meetings and is addressed in the Global Business Insight "High Unemployment in Europe."

TABLE 3   Unemployment Rates in Major Industrial Countries

Civilian Unemployment Rate (percent)							
Year	United States	Canada	Japan	France	Germany	Italy	United Kingdom
1980	7.1	7.3	2.0	6.5	2.8	4.4	6.9
1981	7.6	7.3	2.2	7.6	4.0	4.9	9.7
1982	9.7	10.7	2.4	8.3	5.6	5.4	10.8
1983	9.6	11.6	2.7	8.6	6.9	5.9	11.5
1984	7.5	10.9	2.8	10.0	7.1	5.9	11.8
1985	7.2	10.2	2.7	10.5	7.2	6.0	11.4
1986	7.0	9.3	2.8	10.6	6.6	7.5	11.4
1987	6.2	8.4	2.9	10.8	6.3	7.9	10.5
1988	5.5	7.4	2.5	10.3	6.3	7.9	8.6
1989	5.3	7.1	2.3	9.6	5.7	7.8	7.3
1990	5.6	7.7	2.1	8.6	5.0	7.0	7.1
1991	6.8	9.8	2.1	9.1	5.6	6.9	9.5
1992	7.5	10.6	2.2	10.0	6.7	7.3	10.2
1993	6.9	10.8	2.5	11.3	8.0	9.8	10.4
1994	6.1	9.6	2.9	11.9	8.5	10.7	9.5
1995	5.6	8.6	3.2	11.3	8.2	11.3	8.7
1996	5.4	8.8	3.4	11.8	9.0	11.3	8.1
1997	4.9	8.4	3.4	11.7	9.9	11.4	7.0
1998	4.5	7.7	4.1	11.2	9.3	11.5	6.3
1999	4.2	7.0	4.7	10.5	8.5	11.0	6.0
2000	4.0	6.1	4.8	9.1	7.8	10.2	5.5
2001	4.7	6.5	5.1	8.4	7.9	9.2	5.1
2002	5.8	7.0	5.4	8.8	8.6	8.7	5.2
2003	6.0	6.9	5.3	9.2	9.3	8.5	5.0
2004	5.5	6.4	4.8	9.6	10.3	8.1	4.8
2005	5.1	6.0	4.5	9.6	11.2	7.8	4.9
2006	4.6	5.5	4.2	9.5	10.4	6.9	5.5
2007	4.6	5.3	3.9	8.6	8.7	6.2	5.4

Source: *Economic Report of the President, 2009.*

Global Business Insight

High Unemployment in Europe

The data in Table 3 indicate that European countries tend to have higher unemployment rates than other industrial countries. This is not true for all European countries, but it is certainly true for the biggest: France, Germany, Italy, and Spain. One factor that contributes to the higher unemployment rates in these countries is government policy with regard to the labor market. Countries that have policies that encourage unemployment should be expected to have more unemployed workers. In a recent speech, a British scholar gave his analysis of why Europe has such high unemployment. One story he told illustrates how government policy aimed at protecting citizens against unemployment can create the very unemployment that is the focus of its concern. In Italy, laws require parents to support their adult children who do not work, even if the children are entirely capable of working. The story goes as follows:

> The Italian Court of Cessation ruled that a professor at Naples University, separated from his family, must continue to pay his 30-year-old son €775 per month until he can find himself suitable employment. This despite the fact that the son owns a house and possesses an investment trust fund worth €450,000. The judges said that an adult son who refused work that did not reflect his training, abilities and personal interests could not be held to blame. In particular the judges said, "You cannot blame a young person, particularly from a well-off family, who refuses a job that does not fit his aspirations." By contrast, under UK law, a separated father would only have to support his children until they completed full-time education. (Nickell, 2002.)

The government requirement that parents support unemployed adult children encourages those children to remain unemployed.

Among men of prime working age (age 25–54), there are more who are inactive and not participating in the labor force than there are who are unemployed.

The majority of these men are receiving benefits from the government, claiming disability or illness. In the 1970s, there were many fewer disabled or ill workers as a fraction of the population. But as social benefits were increased and the eligibility rules were relaxed, the number of people claiming to suffer from such problems increased also. The unfortunate truth of human nature is that when you provide better support for those who truly need help, there will be more and more who do not truly need it, yet claim a need. The experience of Denmark is instructive in this regard. Denmark has generous unemployment benefits. But in the 1990s, Danish eligibility requirements were tightened, creating greater incentives for the unemployed to look for work. Danish unemployment rates fell dramatically as a result.

Yet another factor contributing to higher unemployment rates in some countries is restrictions on the ability of firms to terminate workers and the requirement that firms pay high separation costs to workers whom they do fire. The more difficult it is for firms to adjust their labor force in the face of economic fluctuations, the less likely firms are to hire new workers. If you own a business and your sales increase, you are likely to hire extra employees to meet the increased demand for your product. However, you cannot be sure that your sales will be permanently higher, so you would be very conservative about hiring new workers if you would have to pay terminated workers a large amount of money if your sales fell and you needed to lay off some of your employees. Such labor market rigidities, aimed at protecting workers from losing their jobs, create incentives against hiring, so that those who would like to work cannot get hired.

The lesson from large European countries is that government policies aimed at protecting workers from unemployment may create a bigger unemployment problem. Thus, the costs imposed on the economy in the form of taxes and reduced labor market flexibility may exceed the benefits to those who keep their jobs or receive unemployment compensation because of the programs.

Sources: Stephen Nickell, "A Picture of European Unemployment: Success and Failure," speech given to CESifo Conference in Munich, December 2002, and Lars Ljungqvist and Thomas Sargent, "The European Unemployment Dilemma," *Journal of Political Economy,* 1998.

The inflexibility of labor markets in Europe is a factor that makes the European economies more prone to slow growth. Japanese unemployment rates, like those in Europe, were much lower than U.S. and Canadian rates in the 1980s. However, by the late 1990s, Japanese rates began to approach those of the United States.

RECAP

1. The unemployment rate is the number of people unemployed as a percentage of the labor force.

2. To be in the labor force, one must either have or be looking for a job.

3. Through its failure to include discouraged workers and the output lost because of underemployment, the unemployment rate understates real unemployment in the United States.

4. Through its failure to include activity in the underground economy, the U.S. unemployment rate overstates actual unemployment.

5. Unemployment data are adjusted to eliminate seasonal fluctuations.

6. Frictional and structural unemployment are always present in a dynamic economy.

7. Cyclical unemployment is a product of recession; it can be moderated by controlling the period of contraction in the business cycle.

8. Economists measure the cost of unemployment in terms of lost output.

9. Unemployment data show that women generally have higher unemployment rates than men, that teenagers have the highest unemployment rates in the economy, and that blacks and other minority groups have higher unemployment rates than whites.

■ 3. Inflation

4 | What is inflation?

inflation: a sustained rise in the average level of prices

Inflation is a sustained rise in the average level of prices. Notice the word *sustained.* Inflation does not mean a short-term increase in prices; it means that prices are rising over a prolonged period of time. Inflation is measured by the percentage change in price level. The inflation rate in the United States was 0.1 percent in 2008. This means that, on average, the level of prices was almost unchanged over the year. Such low inflation is what one typically expects during a recession when spending falls.

3.a. Absolute versus Relative Price Changes

5 | Why is inflation a problem?

In the modern economy, over any given period, some prices rise faster than others. To evaluate the rate of inflation in a country, then, economists must know what is happening to prices on average. Here it is important to distinguish between *absolute* and *relative* price changes.

Let's look at an example using the prices of fish and beef:

	Year 1	Year 2
1 pound of fish	$1	$2
1 pound of beef	$2	$4

In year 1, beef is twice as expensive as fish. This is the price of beef *relative* to the price of fish. In year 2, beef is still twice as expensive as fish. The relative prices have not changed between years 1 and 2. What has changed? The prices of both beef and fish have doubled. The *absolute* levels of all prices have gone up, but because they have increased by the same percentage, the relative prices are unchanged.

Inflation measures changes in absolute prices. In our example, all prices doubled, so the inflation rate is 100 percent. There was a 100 percent increase in the prices of beef and fish. In reality, inflation does not take place evenly throughout the economy. Prices of some goods rise faster than others, which means that relative prices are changing at the same time that absolute prices are rising. The measured inflation rate records the *average* change in absolute prices.

3.b. Effects of Inflation

The purchasing power of a dollar is the amount of goods and services it can buy.

To understand the effects of inflation, you have to understand what happens to the value of money in an inflationary period. The real value of money is what it can buy, its *purchasing power:*

$$\text{Real value of \$1} = \frac{\$1}{\text{price level}}$$

The higher the price level, the lower the real value (or *purchasing power*) of the dollar. For instance, suppose an economy had only one good—milk. If a glass of milk sold for \$.50, then \$1 would buy two glasses of milk. If the price of milk rose to \$1, then a dollar would buy only one glass of milk. The purchasing power, or real value, of money falls as prices rise.

Table 4 lists the real value of the dollar in selected years from 1946 to 2008. The price level in each year is measured relative to the average level of prices over the 1982–1984 period. For instance, the 1946 value, .195, means that prices in 1946 were, on average, only 19.5 percent of prices in the 1982–1984 period. Notice that as prices go up, the purchasing power of the dollar falls. In 1946, a dollar bought five times as much as it bought in the early 1980s. The value 5.13 means that one could buy 5.13 times as many goods and services with a dollar in 1946 as one could buy in 1982–1984.

Prices have risen steadily in recent decades. By 2008, they had risen to more than 100 percent above the average level of prices in the 1982–1984 period. Consequently, the purchasing power of a 2008 dollar was lower. In 2008, \$1 bought just 49 percent of the goods and services that one could buy with a dollar in 1982–1984.

If prices and nominal income rise by the same percentage, it might seem that inflation is not a problem. It doesn't matter if it takes twice as many dollars to buy fish and beef now than it did before if we have twice as many dollars of income available to buy the products. Obviously, inflation is very much a problem when a household's nominal income rises at a slower rate than prices. Inflation hurts those households whose income does not keep up with the prices of the goods they buy.

In the 1970s, the rate of inflation in the United States rose to near-record levels. Many workers believed that their incomes were lagging behind the rate of inflation, so they negotiated cost-of-living raises in their wage contracts. The typical cost-of living raise ties salary to changes in the consumer price index. If the CPI rises 8 percent during a year, workers receive an 8 percent raise plus compensation for experience or productivity increases. As the U.S. rate of inflation fell during the 1980s, concern about cost-of-living raises subsided as well.

It is important to distinguish between expected and unexpected inflation. *Unexpectedly high inflation* redistributes income away from those who receive fixed incomes (like creditors who receive debt repayments of a fixed amount

Unexpectedly high inflation redistributes income away from those who receive fixed incomes and toward those who make fixed expenditures.

TABLE 4	The Real Value of a Dollar	
Year	Average Price Level	Purchasing Power Power of a Dollar
1946	0.195	5.13
1950	0.241	4.15
1954	0.269	3.72
1958	0.289	3.46
1962	0.302	3.31
1966	0.324	3.09
1970	0.388	2.58
1974	0.493	2.03
1978	0.652	1.53
1982	0.965	1.04
1986	1.096	0.91
1990	1.307	0.77
1994	1.482	0.67
1998	1.63	0.61
2002	1.809	0.55
2006	2.016	0.50
2008	2.153	0.46

¹ Measured by the consumer price index as given at http://data.bls.gov/cgi-bin/surveymost.
² Found by taking the reciprocal of the consumer price index (1/CPI).

of dollars per month) and toward those who make fixed expenditures (like debtors who make fixed debt repayments per month). For example, consider a simple loan agreement:

> *Maria borrows $100 from Ali, promising to repay the loan in one year at 10 percent interest. One year from now, Maria will pay Ali $110—principal of $100 plus interest of $10 (10 percent of $100, or $10).*

When Maria and Ali agree to the terms of the loan, they do so with some expected rate of inflation in mind. Suppose they both expect 5 percent inflation over the year. In other words, they expect that one year from now, it will take 5 percent more money to buy goods than it does now. Ali will need $105 to buy what $100 buys today. Because Ali will receive $110 for the principal and interest on the loan, he will gain purchasing power. However, if the inflation rate over the year turns out to be surprisingly high—say, 15 percent—then Ali will need $115 to buy what $100 buys today. He will lose purchasing power if he makes a loan at a 10 percent rate of interest.

nominal interest rate: the observed interest rate in the market

real interest rate: the nominal interest rate minus the rate of inflation

Economists distinguish between nominal and real interest rates when analyzing economic behavior. The **nominal interest rate** is the observed interest rate in the market and includes the effect of inflation. The **real interest rate** is the nominal interest rate minus the rate of inflation:

> *Real interest rates are lower than expected when inflation is higher than expected.*

Real interest rate = nominal interest rate − rate of inflation

If Ali charges Maria a 10 percent nominal interest rate and the inflation rate is 5 percent, the real interest rate is 5 percent (10% − 5% = 5%). This means that Ali will earn a positive real return from the loan. However, if the inflation rate is 10 percent, the real return from a nominal interest rate of 10 percent is zero (10% − 10% = 0). The interest that Ali will receive from the loan will just compensate him for the rise in prices; he will not realize an increase in purchasing power. If the inflation rate is higher than the nominal interest rate, then the real interest rate is negative—the lender will lose purchasing power by making the loan.

Now you can see how unexpected inflation redistributes income. Borrowers and creditors agree to loan terms based on what they *expect* the rate of inflation to be over the period of the loan. If the *actual* rate of inflation turns out to be different from what was expected, then the real interest rate paid by the borrower and received by the lender will be different from what was expected. If Ali and Maria both expect a 5 percent inflation rate and agree to a 10 percent nominal interest rate for the loan, then they both expect a real interest rate of 5 percent (10% − 5% = 5%) to be paid on the loan. If the actual inflation rate turns out to be greater than 5 percent, then the real interest rate will be less than expected. Maria will get to borrow Ali's money at a lower real cost than she expected, and Ali will earn a lower real return than he expected. Unexpectedly high inflation hurts creditors and benefits borrowers because it lowers real interest rates.

Figure 4 shows the real interest rates on U.S. Treasury bills from 1970 through 2008. You can see a pronounced pattern in the graph. In the late 1970s, there was a period of negative real interest rates, followed by high positive real rates in the 1980s. The evidence suggests that nominal interest rates did not rise fast enough in the 1970s to offset high inflation. This was a time of severe strain for

FIGURE 4 The Real Interest Rate on U.S. Treasury Bills

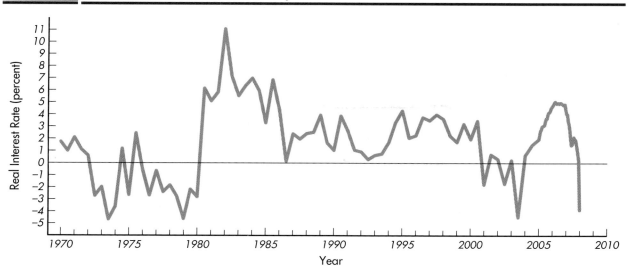

The real interest rate is the difference between the nominal interest rate (the interest rate actually observed) and the rate of inflation over the life of the bond. The figure shows the real interest rate in June and December for each year. For instance, in the first observation, for June 1970, a six-month Treasury bill paid the holder 6.91 percent interest. This is the nominal rate of interest. To find the real rate of interest on the bond, we subtract the rate of inflation that existed over the six months of the bond's life (June to December 1970), which was 5.17 percent. The difference between the nominal interest rate (6.91 percent) and the rate of inflation (5.17 percent) is the real interest rate, 1.74 percent. Notice that real interest rates were negative during most of the 1970s and then turned highly positive (by historical standards) in the early 1980s.

many creditors, including savings and loan associations and banks. These firms had lent funds at fixed nominal rates of interest. When those rates of interest turned out to be lower than the rate of inflation, the financial institutions suffered significant losses. In the early 1980s, the inflation rate dropped sharply. Because nominal interest rates did not drop nearly as fast as the rate of inflation, real interest rates were high. In this period, many debtors were hurt by the high costs of borrowing to finance business or household expenditures.

Unexpected inflation affects more than the two parties to a loan. Any contract calling for fixed payments over some long-term period changes in value as the rate of inflation changes. For instance, a long-term contract that provides union members with 5 percent raises each year for five years gives the workers more purchasing power if inflation is low than if it is high. Similarly, a contract to sell a product at a fixed price over a long-term period will change in value as inflation changes. Suppose a lumber company promises to supply a builder with lumber at a fixed price for a two-year period. If the rate of inflation in one year turns out to be higher than expected, the lumber company will end up selling the lumber for less profit than it had planned. Inflation raises the lumber company's costs. Usually the company would raise its prices to compensate for the higher costs. Because the company contracted to sell its goods to the builder at a fixed price, however, the builder benefits at the lumber company's expense. Again, unexpectedly high inflation redistributes real income or purchasing power away from those receiving fixed payments to those making fixed payments.

One response to the effects of unexpected inflation is to allow prices, wages, or interest rates to vary with the rate of inflation. Labor unions sometimes negotiate cost-of-living adjustments as part of new wage contracts. Financial institutions offer variable interest rates on home mortgages to reflect current market conditions. Any contract can be written to adjust dollar amounts over time as the rate of inflation changes.

3.c. Types of Inflation

Economists often classify inflation according to the source of the inflationary pressure. The most straightforward method defines inflation in terms of pressure from the demand side of the market or the supply side of the market:

> *Demand-pull inflation* Increases in total spending that are not offset by increases in the supply of goods and services and so cause the average level of prices to rise

> *Cost-push inflation* Increases in production costs that cause firms to raise prices to avoid losses

Sometimes inflation is blamed on "too many dollars chasing too few goods." This is a roundabout way of saying that the inflation stems from demand pressures. Because demand-pull inflation is a product of increased spending, it is more likely to occur in an economy that is producing at maximum capacity. If resources are fully employed, it may not be possible in the short run to increase output to meet increased demand. The result: Existing goods and services are rationed by rising prices.

Some economists claim that the rising prices in the late 1960s were a product of demand-pull inflation. They believe that increased government spending for the Vietnam War caused the level of U.S. prices to rise.

Cost-push inflation can occur in any economy, whatever its output. If prices go up because the costs of resources are rising, the rate of inflation can go up regardless of demand. For example, some economists argue that the inflation in the United States in the 1970s was largely the result of rising oil prices. This means that decreases in the oil supply (a shift to the left in the supply curve) brought about higher oil prices. Because oil is so important in the production of many goods, higher oil prices led to increases in prices throughout the economy. Cost-push inflation stems from changes in the supply side of the market.

Cost-push inflation is sometimes attributed to profit-push or wage-push pressures. *Profit-push pressures* are created by suppliers who want to increase their profit margins by raising prices faster than their costs increase. *Wage-push pressures* are created by labor unions and workers who are able to increase their wages faster than their productivity. There have been times when "greedy" businesses and unions have been blamed for periods of inflation in the United States. The problem with these "theories" is that people have always wanted to improve their economic status and always will. In this sense, people have always been greedy. But inflation has not always been a problem. Were people less greedy in the early 1980s, when inflation was low, than they were in the late 1970s, when inflation was high? Obviously, we have to look for other reasons to explain inflation. We discuss some of those reasons in later chapters.

3.d. The Inflationary Record

Many of our students, having always lived with inflation, are surprised to learn that it is a relatively new problem for the United States. From 1789, when the U.S. Constitution was ratified, until 1940, there was no particular trend in the general price level. At times prices rose, and at times they fell. The average level of prices in 1940 was approximately the same as it was in the late eighteenth century.

Since 1940, prices in the United States have gone up markedly. The price level today is eight times what it was in 1940. But the rate of growth has varied.

Annual rates of inflation for several industrial and developing nations in 2007 are shown in Table 5. Look at the diversity across countries: Rates range from deflations of −0.6 percent in Japan to 27.9 percent inflation in high-inflation nations like Tajikistan.

hyperinflation: an extremely high rate of inflation

Hyperinflation is an extremely high rate of inflation. In most cases, hyperinflation eventually makes a country's currency worthless and leads to the introduction of a new money. Argentina experienced hyperinflation in the 1980s. People had to carry large stacks of currency for small purchases. Cash registers and calculators ran out of digits as prices reached ridiculously high levels. After years of high inflation, Argentina replaced the old peso with the peso Argentino in June 1983. The government set the value of 1 peso Argentino equal to 10,000 old pesos (striking four zeros from all prices). A product that had sold for 10,000 old pesos before the reform sold for 1 new peso after. But Argentina did not follow up its monetary reform with a noninflationary change in economic policy. In 1984 and 1985, the inflation rate exceeded 600 percent each year. As a result, in June 1985, the government again introduced a new currency, the austral, setting its value at 1,000 pesos Argentino. However, the economic policy associated with the introduction of the austral lowered the inflation rate only temporarily. By 1988, the inflation rate was over 300 percent, and in 1989 the inflation rate was over 3,000 percent. The rapid rise in prices associated with the austral resulted in the introduction of yet another currency, again named the peso Argentino, in January 1992, with a value equal to 10,000 australes. This new peso was fixed at a value of 1 peso per 1 U.S. dollar, and this exchange rate lasted for about 10 years because of reasonably stable inflation in Argentina. In late 2001, Argentina experienced another financial crisis brought on by large government budget deficits; the fixed

TABLE 5	Rates of Inflation for Selected Countries, 2007

Country	Inflation Rate (percent)
Selected Industrial	
Canada	2.2
Germany	1.8
Italy	2.8
Japan	−0.6
United Kingdom	2.6
United States	2.7
Selected Developing	
Botswana	8.4
Brazil	4.5
Egypt	10.5
Hong Kong, China	2.7
India	4.3
Israel	−0.2
Mexico	3.2
Philippines	2.7
Poland	3
South Africa	8.1
Tajikistan	27.9
Zambia	9.4

Note: Data are average annual percentage changes in the GDP price index as reported by the World Bank; http://web.worldbank.org/WBSITE/EXTERNAL/DATASTATISTICS/.

rate of exchange between the peso and the dollar ended, but the peso remained the currency of Argentina.

The most dramatic hyperinflation in recent years, and one of the most dramatic ever, occurred in Zimbabwe in 2007–2008. Although the government was not forthcoming about inflation data, research[1] indicates that the price index rose from a value of 1.00 in January 2007 to 853,000,000,000,000,000,000,000 by mid-November 2008, when the price level was doubling every 24 hours. As prices rose, the government issued larger and larger units of paper money as people had to carry huge stacks of old currency to buy anything. A 100 trillion Zimbabwe dollar bill was issued in January 2009. Then in the same month, the government sanctioned the use of U.S. dollars as a substitute currency in Zimbabwe as the local currency had become essentially worthless.

Table 6 provides data on the other recent cases of hyperinflation. The Zimbabwe episode lasted 26 months until the U.S. dollar was sanctioned as a substitute currency. The hyperinflation episodes in Table 6 range in duration from only 3 months in Turkmenistan, when prices rose by 291 percent, to 58 months in

---

[1] Steve H. Hanke, "R.I.P. Zimbabwe Dollar," www.cato.org/zimbabwe.

TABLE 6	Recent Hyperinflations		
Country	Dates	Months Duration	Cumulative Inflation (percent)
Angola	Dec. 94–Jun. 96	19	62,445
Argentina	May 89–Mar. 90	11	15,167
Armenia	Oct. 93–Dec. 94	15	34,158
Azerbaijan	Dec. 92–Dec. 94	25	41,742
Bolivia	Apr. 84–Sep. 85	18	97,282
Brazil	Dec. 89–Mar. 90	4	693
Congo, Dem. Rep.	Nov. 93–Sep. 94	11	69,502
Georgia	Sep. 93–Sep. 94	13	76,219
Nicaragua	Jun. 86–Mar. 91	58	11,895,866,143
Serbia	Feb. 93–Jan. 94	12	156,312,790
Tajikistan	Aug. 93–Dec. 93	9	3,636
Turkmenistan	Nov. 95–Jan. 96	3	291
Ukraine	Apr. 91–Nov. 94	44	1, 864,715

Source: Stanley Fischer, Ratna Sahay, and Carlos A. Vegh, "Modern Hyper- and High Inflations," *Journal of Economic Literature*, September 2002, pp. 837–880.

Nicaragua, when prices rose an astounding 11,895,866,143 percent. Hyperinflation is often associated with crises that lead to new governments, new economic policies, and new monies that replace the essentially worthless old money.

In later chapters, we will see how high rates of inflation generally are caused by rapid growth of the money supply. When a central government wants to spend more than it is capable of funding through taxation or borrowing, it simply issues money to finance its budget deficit. As the money supply increases faster than the demand to hold it, spending increases and prices go up.

RECAP

1. Inflation is a sustained rise in the average level of prices.

2. The higher the price level, the lower the real value (purchasing power) of money.

3. Unexpectedly high inflation redistributes income away from those who receive fixed-dollar payments (like creditors) and toward those who make fixed-dollar payments (like debtors).

4. The real interest rate is the nominal interest rate minus the rate of inflation.

5. Demand-pull inflation is a product of increased spending; cost-push inflation reflects increased production costs.

6. Hyperinflation is a very high rate of inflation that often results in the introduction of a new currency.

SUMMARY

1 | What is a business cycle?

- Business cycles are recurring changes in real GDP, in which expansion is followed by contraction. *§1.a*

- The four stages of the business cycle are expansion (boom), peak, contraction (recession), and trough. *§1.a*

- Leading, coincident, and lagging indicators are variables that change in relation to changes in output. *§1.c*

2 | How is the unemployment rate defined and measured?

- The unemployment rate is the percentage of the labor force that is not working. *§2.a*

- To be in the U.S. labor force, an individual must be working or actively seeking work. *§2.a*

- Unemployment can be classified as seasonal, frictional, structural, or cyclical. *§2.c*

- Frictional and structural unemployment are always present in a dynamic economy; cyclical unemployment is a product of recession. *§2.c*

3 | What is the cost of unemployed resources?

- The GDP gap measures the output lost because of unemployment. *§2.d*

4 | What is inflation?

- Inflation is a sustained rise in the average level of prices. *§3*

- The higher the level of prices, the lower the purchasing power of money. *§3.b*

5 | Why is inflation a problem?

- Inflation becomes a problem when income rises at a slower rate than prices. *§3.b*

- Unexpectedly high inflation hurts those who receive fixed-dollar payments (like creditors) and benefits those who make fixed-dollar payments (like debtors). *§3.b*

- Inflation can stem from demand-pull or cost-push pressures. *§3.c*

- Hyperinflation—an extremely high rate of inflation—can force a country to introduce a new currency. *§3.d*

KEY TERMS

business cycle *§1.a*

recession *§1.a*

depression *§1.b*

leading indicator *§1.c*

coincident indicator *§1.c*

lagging indicator *§1.c*

unemployment rate *§2.a*

discouraged workers *§2.b*

underemployment *§2.b*

potential real GDP *§2.d*

natural rate of unemployment *§2.d*

inflation *§3*

nominal interest rate *§3.b*

real interest rate *§3.b*

hyperinflation *§3.d*

EXERCISES

1. What is the labor force? Do you believe that the U.S. government's definition of the labor force is a good one—that it includes all the people it should include? Explain your answer.

2. List the reasons why the official unemployment rate may not reflect the true social burden of unemployment. Explain whether the official numbers overstate or understate *true* unemployment in light of each reason you discuss.

3. Suppose you are able-bodied and intelligent, but lazy. You'd rather sit home and watch television than work, even though you know you could find an acceptable job if you looked.
   a. Are you officially unemployed?
   b. Are you a discouraged worker?

4. Can government do anything to reduce the number of people in the following categories? If so, what?
   a. Frictionally unemployed
   b. Structurally unemployed
   c. Cyclically unemployed

5. Does the GDP gap measure all of the costs of unemployment? Why or why not?

6. Why do teenagers have the highest unemployment rate in the economy?

7. Suppose you are currently earning $10 an hour. If the inflation rate over the current year is 10 percent and your firm provides a cost-of-living raise based on the rate of inflation, what would you expect to earn after your raise? If the cost-of-living raise is always granted

on the basis of the past year's inflation, is your nominal income really keeping up with the cost of living?

8. Write an equation that defines the real interest rate. Use the equation to explain why unexpectedly high inflation redistributes income from creditors to debtors.

9. Many home mortgages in recent years have been made with variable interest rates. Typically, the interest rate is adjusted once a year on the basis of current interest rates on government bonds. How do variable interest rate loans protect creditors from the effects of unexpected inflation?

10. The word *cycle* suggests a regular, recurring pattern of activity. Is there a regular pattern to the business cycle? Support your answer by examining the duration (number of months) of each expansion and contraction in Figure 1.

11. Using the list of leading indicators in Table 1, write a brief paragraph explaining why each variable changes before real output changes. In other words, provide an economic reason why each indicator is expected to lead the business cycle.

12. Suppose 500 people were surveyed, and of those 500, 450 were working full time. Of the 50 not working, 10 were full-time college students, 20 were retired, 5 were under 16 years of age, 5 had stopped looking for work because they believed there were no jobs for them, and 10 were actively looking for work.
    a. How many of the 500 surveyed are in the labor force?
    b. What is the unemployment rate among the 500 surveyed people?

13. Consider the following price information:

	Year 1	Year 2
Cup of coffee	$ .50	$1.00
Glass of milk	$1.00	$2.00

    a. Based on the information given, what was the inflation rate between year 1 and year 2?
    b. What happened to the price of coffee relative to that of milk between year 1 and year 2?

14. Use a supply and demand diagram to illustrate:
    a. Cost-push inflation caused by a labor union successfully negotiating for a higher wage
    b. Demand-pull inflation caused by an increase in demand for domestic products from foreign buyers.

15. During the Bolivian hyperinflation in the 1980s, Bolivians used U.S. dollars as a substitute for the domestic currency (the peso) for many transactions. Explain how the value of money is affected by hyperinflation and the incentives to use a low-inflation currency like the dollar as a substitute for a high-inflation currency like the Bolivian peso.

16. Suppose the government raises the benefits available to unemployed workers and then discovers that the number of unemployed workers has increased substantially, although there has been no other change in the economy. How can government policies aimed at helping the unemployed actually create more unemployment?

You can find further practice tests in the Online Quiz at www.cengage.com/economics/boyes.

Older Workers and the Recession

San Diego Union-Tribune **December 8, 2008**

Last week's triple dose of grim employment news stirred memories of the early 1980s. Made official on Monday, the current recession has already outlasted any downturn since 1982. . . . Friday's sock to the solar plexus? The economy lost 533,000 jobs last month, the largest monthly decline since 1974.

It gets worse. For older workers, this recession is unprecedented. Last month, 298,000 Americans ages 65 and older were unemployed, 50 percent more than when the recession began a year ago.

During previous downturns, relatively few older Americans were counted as unemployed. Although many lost their jobs, they generally retired instead of looking for work. During the severe 1981–82 recession, seniors' unemployment rate grew by just 0.8 percentage points—only about one-fourth the increase for prime-age workers (25 to 54).

Today, however, seniors are nearly as likely as their juniors to join unemployment lines, because pink-slipped seniors can no longer afford to put their feet up. Shrinking Social Security benefits, traditional pension plans, and 401(k) balances combine with soaring health care costs to force them to keep pounding the pavement.

Rising medical expenses, which consume 15 percent of older people's budgets, can also jinx retirement. And only one in three large private employers offers retiree health benefits to supplement Medicare, compared with two in three in the 1980s. Meanwhile, Medicare's new drug benefit has barely dented seniors' out-of-pocket spending.

Whipsawed by these trends, it's no surprise that three in 10 Americans ages 65 to 69 were working or job-hunting in 2007, up from two in 10 in 1982. Paychecks provided nearly one-fifth of this group's income in 2006.

The stock market shed about half its value over the past 14 months, destroying $2.8 trillion in 401(k) and individual retirement accounts and intensifying pressure on seniors to work. Older Americans have been hit hardest because those 50 and older hold nearly three-quarters of these assets. (During the 1981–82 recession, the S&P 500 index fell by only 6 percent.)

California should do more to help. Other states already train career center staff on the special challenges older workers face, certify employers friendly to mature workers, develop the entrepreneurial skills of older dislocated workers, and create Web sites for older job-seekers.

It's also time for a federal stimulus package committing billions of dollars to rebuilding our crumbling infrastructure. That's a sure way to create jobs, some of them for seniors.

Budgets are tight. But investing in getting willing-and-able seniors back to work would boost the nation's output, spur spending, get the economy back on track and ease the recession's toll on our oldest workers, most of whom have done their bit for their families and the economy for decades.

Richard W. Johnson, The Urban Institute

The article says that the recession in 2008 had created many more unemployed older workers than in prior recessions. Partly, this is because people retired at earlier ages in past decades but now, due to longer life expectancy as well as delayed and smaller retirement benefits, older workers remain in the labor force seeking jobs. Should we expect older workers to have an easier or tougher time finding a job than younger workers? What does economics have to say about why older workers might find it harder to find new jobs than younger workers? The answer lies in the type of knowledge that workers possess that may make them attractive to certain employers.

Many newly unemployed workers have worked for many years and have earned higher salaries than they can expect to earn in other jobs. This, of course, is the problem. If they could simply find another job that offered them comparable pay, they would not be so devastated by the prospect of losing their jobs. This raises an interesting question: If someone is highly valued at one firm and paid accordingly, why isn't that person as valuable to other companies who could now hire her or him? In fact, laid-off workers with successful job histories at one firm are often unable to meet entry-level requirements at other jobs.

We can better understand the causes of the plight of many laid-off industrial workers if we consider the determinants of people's wages. Economic theory suggests that people's wages are tied to the amount they contribute to their firm, which implies that people's wages increase with their skills. We can think of two broad categories of skills: general skills that make people valuable to any firm, and more specialized skills that make people valuable to certain firms. Examples of general skills include welding, bookkeeping, and an ability to manage people. Skills that are useful to only one firm are those that are specifically tied to the product or structure of that firm. Specific knowledge of this second type is not transferable to other firms.

People who work in a particular firm for an extended period learn both general skills that make them valuable to any similar company and specific skills that make them valuable to their company only. Experienced workers who are seeking new jobs must possess or else learn general skills that make them attractive in an economy with rapid technological change.

The distinction between general and firm-specific skills suggests why the workers who are least likely to benefit from retraining are those within a few years of retirement. Older workers who must undergo on-the-job training will not be able to use their new firm-specific skills for as many years as younger workers will. It is not worthwhile for firms to hire and train workers who are near retirement.

Structural change is an integral part of a dynamic, growing economy. Dislocations are probably inevitable when large-scale structural change occurs, and these dislocations benefit some people while hurting others. Although retraining helps mitigate some of the effects of the upheaval that accompanies structural change, unfortunately it cannot solve all the problems that arise. For the economy as a whole, such change is necessary. Unfortunately, some people are always harmed when the economy undergoes structural change.

Chapter 8

© Yui/S

Macroeconomic Equilibrium: Aggregate Demand and Supply

Fundamental Questions

1 | What factors affect aggregate demand?

2 | What causes the aggregate demand curve to shift?

3 | What factors affect aggregate supply?

4 | Why does the short-run aggregate supply curve become steeper as real GDP increases?

5 | Why is the long-run aggregate supply curve vertical?

6 | What causes the aggregate supply curve to shift?

7 | What determines the equilibrium price level and real GDP?

Total output and income in the United States have grown over time. Each generation has experienced a higher standard of living than the previous generation. Yet, as we learned in the chapter titled "Unemployment and Inflation," economic growth has not been steady. Economies go through periods of expansion followed by periods of contraction or recession, and such business cycles have major impacts on people's lives, incomes, and living standards.

Economic stagnation and recession throw many, often those who are already relatively poor, out of their jobs and into real poverty. Economic growth increases the number of jobs and draws people out of poverty and into the mainstream of economic progress. To understand why economies grow and why they go through cycles, we must discover why firms decide to produce more or less and why buyers decide to buy more or less. The approach we take is similar to the approach we followed in the first five chapters of the text, using demand and supply curves. In the chapter titled "Markets, Demand and

Supply, and the Price System" and the chapter titled "The Market System and the Private and Public Sectors," we derived demand and supply curves and used them to examine questions involving the equilibrium price and quantities demanded and supplied of a single good or service. This simple yet powerful microeconomic technique of analysis has a macroeconomic counterpart: aggregate demand and aggregate supply, which are used to determine an equilibrium price level and quantity of goods and services produced for the *entire economy*. In this chapter we shall use aggregate demand and supply curves to illustrate the causes of business cycles and economic growth.

Technology advance shifts the aggregate supply curve outward and increases output. An example of a technological advance that has increased efficiency in the airline industry is the self check-in kiosk. This allows the airlines to lower costs, as customers do not require an airline employee for assistance.

© Jacqueline Abromeit/Shutterstock

■ 1. Aggregate Demand, Aggregate Supply, and Business Cycles

What causes economic growth and business cycles? We can provide some answers to this important question using aggregate demand (AD) and aggregate supply (AS) curves. Suppose we represent the economy with a simple demand and supply diagram, as shown in Figure 1. Aggregate demand represents the total spending in the economy at alternative price levels. Aggregate supply represents the total output of the economy at alternative price levels. To understand the causes of business cycles and inflation, we must understand how aggregate demand and aggregate supply cause the equilibrium price level and real GDP, the nation's output of goods and services, to change. The intersection between the AD and AS curves defines the equilibrium level of real GDP and level of prices. The equilibrium price level is P_e, and the equilibrium level of real GDP is Y_e. This price and output level represents the level of prices and output for some particular period of time, say 2010. Once that equilibrium is established, there is no tendency for prices and output to change until changes occur in either the aggregate demand curve or the aggregate supply curve. Let's first consider a change in aggregate demand and then look at a change in aggregate supply.

FIGURE 1 Aggregate Demand and Aggregate Supply Equilibrium

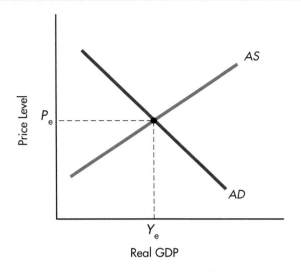

The equilibrium price level and real GDP are determined by the intersection of the AD and AS curves.

1.a. Aggregate Demand and Business Cycles

An increase in aggregate demand is illustrated by a shift of the *AD* curve to the right, like the shift from AD_1 to AD_2 in Figure 2. This represents a situation in which buyers are buying more at every price level. The shift causes the equilibrium level of real GDP to rise from Y_{e1} to Y_{e2}, illustrating the expansionary phase of the

FIGURE 2 Effects of a Change in Aggregate Demand

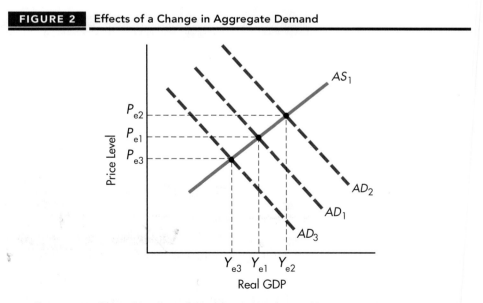

If aggregate demand increases from AD_1 to AD_2, the equilibrium price level increases to P_{e2} and the equilibrium level of real GDP rises to Y_{e2}. If aggregate demand decreases from AD_1 to AD_3, the equilibrium price level falls to P_{e3} and the equilibrium level of real GDP drops to Y_{e3}.

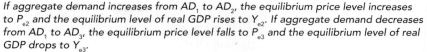

business cycle. As output rises, unemployment decreases. The increase in aggregate demand also leads to a higher price level, as shown by the change in the price level from P_{e1} to P_{e2}. The increase in the price level represents an example of **demand-pull inflation,** which is inflation caused by increasing demand for output.

demand-pull inflation:
inflation caused by increasing demand for output

If aggregate demand falls, like the shift from AD_1 to AD_3, then there is a lower equilibrium level of real GDP, Y_{e3}. In this case, buyers are buying *less* at every price level. The drop in real GDP caused by lower demand would represent an economic slowdown or a recession when output falls and unemployment rises.

1.b. Aggregate Supply and Business Cycles

Changes in aggregate supply can also cause business cycles. Figure 3 illustrates what happens when aggregate supply changes. An increase in aggregate supply is illustrated by the shift from AS_1 to AS_2, leading to an increase in the equilibrium level of real GDP from Y_{e1} to Y_{e2}. An increase in aggregate supply comes about when firms produce more at every price level. Such an increase could result from an improvement in technology or a decrease in the costs of production.

If aggregate supply decreases, as in the shift from AS_1 to AS_3, then the equilibrium level of real GDP would fall to Y_{e3} and the equilibrium price level would increase from P_{e1} to P_{e3}. A decrease in aggregate supply could be caused by higher production costs that lead producers to raise their prices. This is an example of **cost-push inflation**—where the price level rises as a result of increased costs of production and the associated decrease in aggregate supply.

cost-push inflation:
inflation caused by rising costs of production

1.c. A Look Ahead

Business cycles result from changes in aggregate demand, from changes in aggregate supply, and from changes in both *AD* and *AS*. The degree to which real GDP declines during a recession or increases during an expansion depends on the amount by which

---

FIGURE 3   Effects of a Change in Aggregate Supply

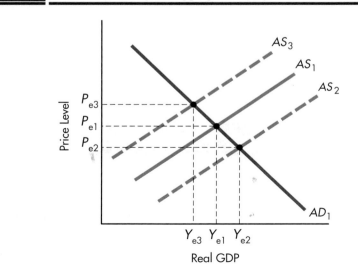

If aggregate supply increases from AS_1 to AS_2, the equilibrium price level falls from P_{e1} to P_{e2} and the equilibrium level of real GDP rises to Y_{e2}. If aggregate supply decreases from AS_1 to AS_3, the equilibrium price level rises to P_{e3} and the equilibrium level of real GDP falls to Y_{e3}.

the *AD* and/or *AS* curves shift. The degree to which an expansion produces output growth or increased inflation depends on the shapes of the *AD* and *AS* curves. We need to consider why the curves have the shapes they do, and what causes them to shift.

The comparison we made earlier, between aggregate demand, aggregate supply, and their microeconomic counterparts, the supply and demand curves, is only superficial. As we examine the aggregate demand and supply curves, you will see that the reasons underlying the shapes and movements of *AD* and *AS* are in fact quite different from those explaining the shapes and movements of the supply and demand curves.

RECAP

1. Aggregate demand (*AD*) represents the total spending in the economy at alternative price levels.

2. Aggregate supply (*AS*) represents the total output of the economy at alternative price levels.

3. The intersection between the *AD* and *AS* curves defines the equilibrium level of real GDP and the level of prices.

4. Business cycles result from changes in *AD* and/or *AS*.

1 | What factors affect aggregate demand?

■ 2. Factors That Influence Aggregate Demand

Aggregate demand is the relation between aggregate expenditures, or total spending, and the price level. Aggregate expenditures are the sum of the expenditures of each sector of the economy: households (consumption), business firms (investment), government, and the rest of the world (net exports). Each sector of the economy has different reasons for spending; for instance, household spending depends heavily on household income, whereas business spending depends on the profits that businesses expect to earn. Because each sector of the economy has a different reason for the amount of spending it undertakes, aggregate spending depends on all of these reasons. To understand aggregate demand, therefore, requires that we look at the factors that influence the expenditures of each sector of the economy.

2.a. Consumption

How much households spend depends on their income, their wealth, expectations about future prices and incomes, demographics like the age distribution of the population, and taxes.

- Income: If current income rises, households purchase more goods and services.

- Wealth: Wealth is different from income. It is the value of the assets owned by a household, including homes, cars, bank deposits, stocks, and bonds. An increase in household wealth will increase consumption.

- Expectations: Expectations regarding future changes in income or wealth can affect consumption today. If households expect a recession and worry about job loss, consumption tends to fall. On the other hand, if households become more optimistic regarding future increases in income and wealth, consumption rises today.

- Demographics: Demographic change can affect consumption in several different ways. Population growth is generally associated with higher consumption for an economy. Younger households and older households generally consume more and save less than middle-aged households. Therefore, as the age distribution of a nation changes, so will consumption.

- Taxes: Higher taxes will lower the disposable income of households and decrease consumption, while lower taxes will raise disposable income and increase consumption. Government policy may change taxes and thereby bring about a change in consumption.

2.b. Investment

Investment is business spending on capital goods and inventories. In general, investment depends on the expected profitability of such spending, so any factor that could affect profitability will be a determinant of investment. Factors affecting the expected profitability of business projects include the interest rate, technology, the cost of capital goods, and capacity utilization.

- Interest rate: Investment is negatively related to the interest rate. The interest rate is the cost of borrowed funds. The greater the cost of borrowing, other things being equal, the fewer the investment projects that offer sufficient profit to be undertaken. As the interest rate falls, investment is stimulated, as the cost of financing the investment is lowered.

- Technology: New production technology stimulates investment spending, as firms are forced to adopt new production methods to stay competitive.

- Cost of capital goods: If machines and equipment purchased by firms rise in price, then the higher costs associated with investment will lower profitability, and investment will fall.

- Capacity utilization: The more excess capacity (unused capital goods) there is available, the more firms can expand production without purchasing new capital goods, and the lower investment will be. As firms approach full capacity, more investment spending will be required to expand output further.

2.c. Government Spending

Government spending may be set by government authorities independent of current income or other determinants of aggregate expenditures.

2.d. Net Exports

Net exports are equal to exports minus imports. We assume that exports are determined by conditions in the rest of the world, such as foreign income, tastes, prices, exchange rates, and government policy. Imports are determined by similar domestic factors.

- Income: As domestic income rises and consumption rises, some of this consumption includes goods produced in other countries. Therefore, as domestic income rises, imports rise and net exports fall. Similarly, as foreign income rises, foreign residents buy more domestic goods, and net exports rise.

- Prices: Other things being equal, higher (lower) foreign prices make domestic goods relatively cheaper (more expensive) and increase (decrease) net exports. Higher (lower) domestic prices make domestic goods relatively more expensive (cheaper) and decrease (increase) net exports.

- Exchange rates: Other things being equal, a depreciation of the domestic currency on the foreign exchange market will make domestic goods cheaper to foreign buyers and make foreign goods more expensive to domestic buyers, so that net exports will rise. An appreciation of the domestic currency will have just the opposite effects.

- Government policy: Net exports may fall if foreign governments restrict the entry of domestic goods into their countries, reducing domestic exports. If the domestic government restricts imports into the domestic economy, net exports may rise.

2.e. Aggregate Expenditures

You can see how aggregate expenditures, the sum of all spending on U.S. goods and services, must depend on prices, income, and all of the other determinants discussed in the previous sections. As with the demand curve for a specific good or service, we want to classify the factors that influence spending into the price and the nonprice determinants for the aggregate demand curves. The components of aggregate expenditures that change as the price level changes will lead to movements along the aggregate demand curve—changes in quantity demanded—whereas changes in aggregate expenditures caused by nonprice effects will cause shifts of the aggregate demand curve—changes in aggregate demand. In the following section, we look first at the price effects, or movements along an aggregate demand curve. Following that discussion, we focus on the nonprice determinants of aggregate demand.

RECAP

1. Aggregate expenditures are the sum of consumption, investment, government spending, and net exports.

2. Consumption depends on household income, wealth, expectations, demographics, and taxation.

3. Investment depends on the interest rate, technology, the cost of capital goods, and capacity utilization.

4. Government spending is determined independent of current income.

5. Net exports depend on foreign and domestic incomes, prices, government policies, and exchange rates.

■ 3. The Aggregate Demand Curve

When we examined the demand curves in Chapter 3, we divided our study into two parts: the movement along the curve—changes in quantity demanded—and the shifts of the curve—changes in demand. We take the same approach here in examining aggregate demand. We first look at the movements along the aggregate demand curve caused by changes in the price level. We then turn to the nonprice determinants of aggregate demand that cause shifts in the curve.

3.a. Why the Aggregate Demand Curve Slopes Downward

Aggregate demand curves are downward sloping just like the demand curves for individual goods that were shown in Chapter 3, although for different reasons.

Along the demand curve for an individual good, the price of that good changes while the prices of all other goods remain constant. This means that the good in question becomes relatively more or less expensive compared to all other goods in the economy. Consumers tend to substitute a less expensive good for a more expensive good. The effect of this substitution is an inverse relationship between price and quantity demanded. As the price of a good rises, the quantity demanded falls. For the economy as a whole, however, it is not a substitution of a less expensive good for a more expensive good that causes the demand curve to slope down. Instead, the aggregate quantity demanded, or total spending, will change as the price level changes as a result of the wealth effect, the interest rate effect, and the international trade effect of a price-level change on aggregate expenditures. We will discuss each of these effects in turn.

3.a.1. The Wealth Effect Individuals and businesses own money, stocks, bonds, and other financial assets. The purchasing power of these assets is the quantity of goods and services for which the assets can be exchanged. When the level of prices falls, the purchasing power of these assets increases, allowing households and businesses to purchase more. When prices go up, the purchasing power of financial assets falls, causing households and businesses to spend less. This is the **wealth effect** (sometimes called the *real-balance effect*) of a price change: a change in the real value of wealth that causes spending to change when the level of prices changes. *Real values* are values that have been adjusted for price-level changes. Here *real value* means "purchasing power." When the price level changes, the purchasing power of financial assets also changes. When prices rise, the real value of assets and wealth falls, and aggregate expenditures tend to fall. When prices fall, the real value of assets and wealth rises, and aggregate expenditures tend to rise.

wealth effect: a change in the real value of wealth that causes spending to change when the level of prices changes

3.a.2. The Interest Rate Effect When the price level rises, the purchasing power of each dollar falls, which means that more money is required to buy any particular quantity of goods and services (see Figure 4). Suppose that a family of three needs $100 each week to buy food. If the price level doubles, the same quantity of food costs $200. The household must have twice as much money to buy the same amount of food. Conversely, when prices fall, the family needs less money to buy food because the purchasing power of each dollar is greater.

When prices go up, people need more money. So they sell their other financial assets, such as bonds, to get that money. The increase in the supply of bonds lowers bond prices and raises interest rates. Since bonds typically pay fixed-dollar interest payments each year, as the price of a bond varies, the interest rate (or yield) will change. For instance, suppose you pay $1,000 for a bond that pays $100 a year in interest. The interest rate on this bond is found by dividing the annual interest payment by the bond price, or $100/$1,000 = 10 percent. If the price of the bond falls to $900, then the interest rate is equal to the annual interest payment (which remains fixed at $100 for the life of the bond) divided by the new price of $900: $100/$900 = 11 percent. When bond prices fall, interest rates rise, and when bond prices rise, interest rates fall.

> When the price level changes, the purchasing power of financial assets changes.

If people want more money and they sell some of their bond holdings to raise the money, bond prices will fall and interest rates will rise. The rise in interest rates is necessary to sell the larger quantity of bonds, but it causes investment expenditures to fall, which causes aggregate expenditures to fall.

When prices fall, people need less money to purchase the same quantity of goods. So they use their money holdings to buy bonds and other financial assets. The increased demand for bonds increases bond prices and causes interest rates to fall. Lower interest rates increase investment expenditures, thereby pushing aggregate expenditures up.

FIGURE 4   The Interest Rate Effect of Price-Level Changes on Aggregate Expenditures

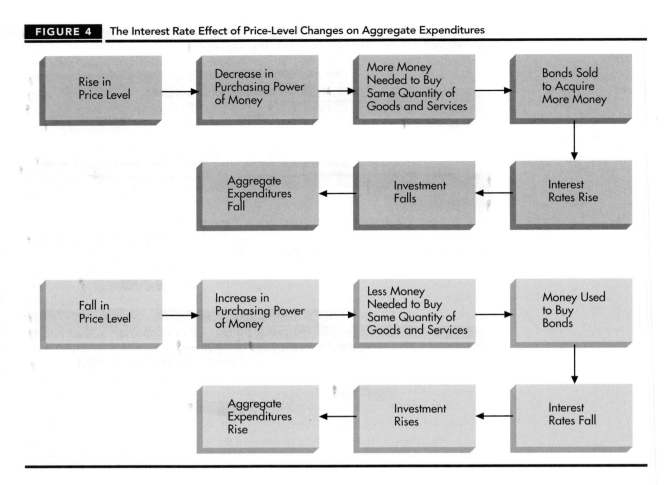

interest rate effect: a change in interest rates that causes investment and therefore aggregate expenditures to change as the level of prices changes

Figure 4 shows the **interest rate effect,** the relationship among the price level, interest rates, and aggregate expenditures. As the price level rises, interest rates rise and aggregate expenditures fall. As the price level falls, interest rates fall and aggregate expenditures rise.

3.a.3. The International Trade Effect

The third channel through which a price-level change affects the quantity of goods and services demanded is called the **international trade effect.** A change in the level of domestic prices can cause net exports to change. If domestic prices rise while foreign prices and the foreign exchange rate remain constant, domestic goods become more expensive in relation to foreign goods.

international trade effect: a change in aggregate expenditures resulting from a change in the domestic price level that changes the price of domestic goods relative to that of foreign goods

Suppose the United States sells oranges to Japan. If the oranges sell for $1 per pound and the yen-dollar exchange rate is 100 yen = $1, a pound of U.S. oranges costs a Japanese buyer 100 yen. What happens if the level of prices in the United States goes up 10 percent? All prices, including the price of oranges, increase 10 percent. Oranges in the United States sell for $1.10 a pound after the price increase. If the exchange rate is still 100 yen = $1, a pound of oranges now costs the Japanese buyer 110 yen (100 × 1.10). If the prices of oranges from other countries do not change, some Japanese buyers may buy oranges from those countries instead of from the United States. The increase in the level of U.S. prices makes U.S. goods more expensive relative to foreign goods and causes U.S. net exports to fall; a decrease in the level of U.S. prices makes U.S. goods cheaper in relation to foreign goods, which increases U.S. net exports.

When the price of domestic goods increases in relation to the price of foreign goods, net exports fall, causing aggregate expenditures to fall. When the price of domestic goods falls in relation to the price of foreign goods, net exports rise, causing aggregate expenditures to rise. The international trade effect of a change in the level of domestic prices causes aggregate expenditures to change in the opposite direction.

aggregate demand curve: a curve that shows the different equilibrium levels of expenditures on domestic output at different levels of prices

3.a.4. The Sum of the Price-Level Effects
The **aggregate demand curve** (*AD*) shows how the equilibrium level of expenditures for the economy's output changes as the price level changes. In other words, the curve shows the amount that people spend at different price levels.

Figure 5 displays the typical shape of the *AD* curve. The price level is plotted on the vertical axis, and real GDP is plotted on the horizontal axis. Suppose that initially the economy is at point *A*, with prices at P_0. At this point, spending equals $500. If prices fall to P_1, expenditures equal $700 and the economy is at point *C*. If prices rise from P_0 to P_2, expenditures equal $300 at point *B*.

Because aggregate expenditures increase when the price level decreases and decrease when the price level increases, the aggregate demand curve slopes down. The aggregate demand curve is drawn with the price level for the *entire economy* on the vertical axis. A price-level change here means that, on average, *all prices in the economy change*; there is no relative price change among domestic goods. The negative slope of the aggregate demand curve is a product of the wealth effect, the interest rate effect, and the international trade effect.

A lower domestic price level increases consumption (the wealth effect), investment (the interest rate effect), and net exports (the international trade effect). As the price level drops, aggregate expenditures rise.

A higher domestic price level reduces consumption (the wealth effect), investment (the interest rate effect), and net exports (the international trade effect). As prices rise, aggregate expenditures fall. These price effects are summarized in Figure 6.

FIGURE 5 The Aggregate Demand Curve

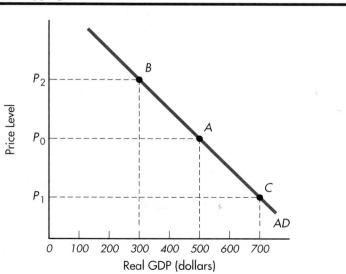

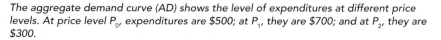

The aggregate demand curve (AD) shows the level of expenditures at different price levels. At price level P_0, expenditures are $500; at P_1, they are $700; and at P_2, they are $300.

FIGURE 6   Why the Aggregate Demand Curve Slopes Downward

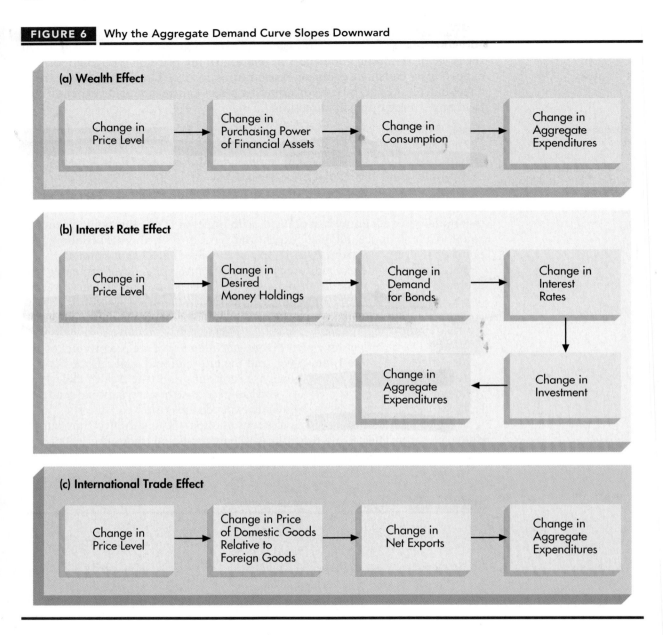

(a) Wealth Effect

(b) Interest Rate Effect

(c) International Trade Effect

2 | What causes the aggregate demand curve to shift?

3.b. Changes in Aggregate Demand: Nonprice Determinants

The aggregate demand curve shows the level of aggregate expenditures at alternative price levels. We draw the curve by varying the price level and finding out what the resulting total expenditures are, holding all other things constant. As those "other things"—the nonprice determinants of aggregate demand—change, the aggregate demand curve shifts. The nonprice determinants of aggregate demand include all of the factors covered in the discussion of the components of expenditures—income, wealth, demographics, expectations, taxes, the interest rate (interest rates can change for reasons other than price-level changes), the cost of capital goods, capacity utilization, foreign income and price levels, exchange rates, and government policy. A change in any one of these can cause the

FIGURE 7 Nonprice Determinants: Changes in Aggregate Demand

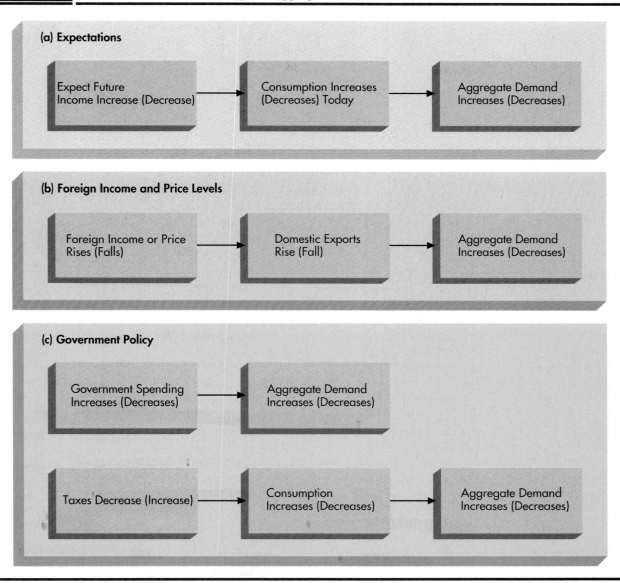

AD curve to shift. In the discussions that follow, we will focus particularly on the effects of expectations, foreign income, and price levels; we will also mention government policy, which will be examined in detail in the chapter titled "Fiscal Policy." Figure 7 summarizes these effects, which are discussed next.

3.b.1. Expectations Consumption and business spending are affected by expectations. Consumption is sensitive to people's expectations of future income, prices, and wealth. For example, when people expect the economy to do well in the future, they increase their consumption today at every price level. This is reflected in a shift of the aggregate demand curve to the right, from AD_0 to AD_1, as shown in Figure 8. When aggregate demand increases, aggregate expenditures increase at every price level.

On the other hand, if people expect a recession in the near future, they tend to reduce their consumption and increase their saving in order to protect

FIGURE 8 Shifting the Aggregate Demand Curve

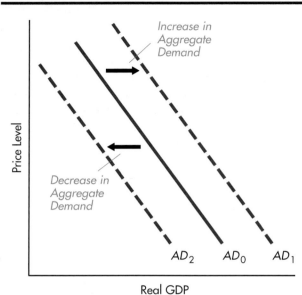

As aggregate demand increases, the AD curve shifts to the right, like the shift from AD_0 to AD_1. At every price level, the quantity of output demanded increases. As aggregate demand falls, the AD curve shifts to the left, like the shift from AD_0 to AD_2. At every price level, the quantity of output demanded falls.

themselves against a greater likelihood of losing a job or a forced cutback in hours worked. As consumption drops, aggregate demand decreases. The *AD* curve shifts to the left, from AD_0 to AD_2. At every price level along AD_2, planned expenditures are less than they are along AD_0.

Expectations also play an important role in investment decisions. Before undertaking a particular project, businesses forecast the likely revenues and costs associated with that project. When the profit outlook is good—say, a tax cut is on the horizon—investment and therefore aggregate demand increase. When profits are expected to fall, investment and aggregate demand decrease.

3.b.2. Foreign Income and Price Levels When foreign income increases, so does foreign spending. Some of this increased spending is for goods produced in the domestic economy. As domestic exports increase, aggregate demand rises. Lower foreign income has just the opposite effect. As foreign income falls, foreign spending falls, including foreign spending on the exports of the domestic economy. Lower foreign income, then, causes domestic net exports and domestic aggregate demand to fall.

If foreign prices rise in relation to domestic prices, domestic goods become less expensive relative to foreign goods, and domestic net exports increase. This means that aggregate demand rises, or the aggregate demand curve shifts right, as the level of foreign prices rises. Conversely, when the level of foreign prices falls, domestic goods become more expensive relative to foreign goods, causing domestic net exports and aggregate demand to fall.

Let's go back to the market for oranges. Suppose U.S. growers compete with Brazilian growers for the Japanese orange market. If the level of prices in Brazil rises while the level of prices in the United States remains stable, the price of Brazilian oranges to the Japanese buyer rises in relation to the price of U.S.

Higher foreign income increases net exports and aggregate demand; lower foreign income reduces net exports and aggregate demand.

Changes in the level of foreign prices change domestic net exports and aggregate demand in the same direction.

oranges. What happens? Exports of U.S. oranges to Japan should rise, while exports of Brazilian oranges to Japan should fall.[1]

3.b.3. Government Policy One of the goals of macroeconomic policy is to achieve economic growth without inflation. For GDP to increase, either *AD* or *AS* would have to change. Government economic policy can cause the aggregate demand curve to shift. An increase in government spending or a decrease in taxes will increase aggregate demand; a decrease in government spending or an increase in taxes will decrease aggregate demand. We devote an entire chapter to fiscal policy, an examination of the effect of taxes and government spending on aggregate demand. In another chapter, on monetary policy, we describe how changes in the money supply can cause the aggregate demand curve to shift.

RECAP

1. The aggregate demand curve shows the level of aggregate expenditures at different price levels.

2. Aggregate expenditures are the sum of consumption, investment, government spending, and net exports.

3. The wealth effect, the interest rate effect, and the international trade effect are three reasons why the aggregate demand curve slopes down. These effects explain movements along a given *AD* curve.

4. The aggregate demand curve shifts with changes in the nonprice determinants of aggregate demand: expectations, foreign income and price levels, and government policy.

■ 4. Aggregate Supply

3 | **What factors affect aggregate supply?**

aggregate supply curve: a curve that shows the amount of real GDP produced at different price levels

The **aggregate supply curve** shows the quantity of real GDP produced at different price levels. The aggregate supply curve (*AS*) looks like the supply curve for an individual good, but, as with aggregate demand and the microeconomic demand curve, different factors are at work. The positive relationship between price and quantity supplied of an individual good is based on the change in the price of that good relative to the prices of all other goods. As the price of a single good rises relative to the prices of other goods, sellers are willing to offer more of the good for sale. With aggregate supply, on the other hand, we are analyzing how the amount of all goods and services produced changes as the level of prices changes. The direct relationship between prices and national output is explained by the effect of changing prices on profits, not by relative price changes.

4.a. Why the Aggregate Supply Curve Slopes Upward

Along the aggregate supply curve, everything is held fixed except the price level and the output. The price level is the price of output. The prices of resources— that is, the costs of production (wages, rent, and interest)—are assumed to be constant, at least for a short time following a change in the price level.

---

[1] This assumes no change in exchange rates. If the Brazilian currency were to depreciate in value as Brazilian prices rose, then the cheaper exchange rate would at least partially offset the higher price and reduce the impact of the price change on exports.

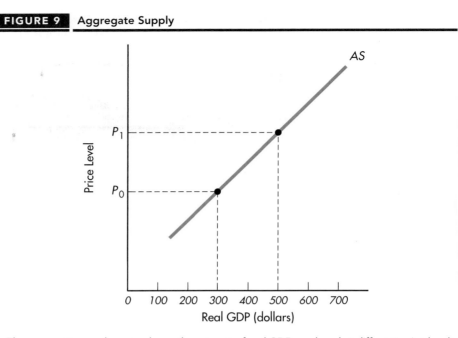

| FIGURE 9 | Aggregate Supply |

The aggregate supply curve shows the amount of real GDP produced at different price levels. The AS curve slopes up, indicating that the higher the price level, the greater the quantity of output produced.

If the price level rises while the costs of production remain fixed, business profits go up. As profits rise, firms are willing to produce more output. As the price level rises, then, the quantity of output that firms are willing to supply increases. The result is the positively sloped aggregate supply curve shown in Figure 9.

As the price level rises from P_0 to P_1 in Figure 9, real GDP increases from $300 to $500. The higher the price level, the higher are profits, everything else held constant, and the greater is the quantity of output produced in the economy. Conversely, as the price level falls, the quantity of output produced falls.

4.b. Short-Run versus Long-Run Aggregate Supply

The curve in Figure 9 is a *short-run* aggregate supply curve because the costs of production are held constant. Although production costs may not rise immediately when the price level rises, eventually they will. Labor will demand higher wages to compensate for the higher cost of living; suppliers will charge more for materials. The positive slope of the *AS* curve, then, is a short-run phenomenon. How short is the short run? It is the period of time over which production costs remain constant. (In the long run, all costs change or are variable.) For the economy as a whole, the short run can be months or, at most, a few years.

4.b.1. Short-Run Aggregate Supply Curve Figure 9 represents the general shape of the short-run aggregate supply curve. In Figure 10, you see a more realistic version of the same curve—its steepness varies. The steepness of the aggregate supply curve depends on the ability and willingness of producers to respond to price-level changes in the short run. Figure 10 shows the typical shape of the short-run aggregate supply curve.

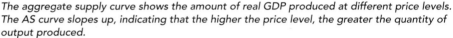

4 | Why does the short-run aggregate supply curve become steeper as real GDP increases?

FIGURE 10   The Shape of the Short-Run Aggregate Supply Curve

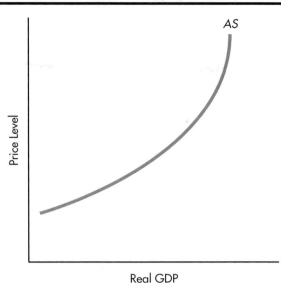

The upward-sloping aggregate supply curve occurs when the price level must rise to induce further increases in output. The curve gets steeper as real GDP increases, since the closer the economy comes to the capacity level of output, the less output will rise in response to higher prices as more and more firms reach their maximum level of output in the short run.

Notice that as the level of real GDP increases in Figure 10, the *AS* curve becomes steeper. This is because each increase in output requires firms to hire more and more resources, until eventually full capacity is reached in some areas of the economy, resources are fully employed, and some firms reach maximum output. At this point, increases in the price level bring about smaller and smaller increases in output from firms as a whole. The short-run aggregate supply curve becomes increasingly steep as the economy approaches maximum output.

4.b.2. Long-Run Aggregate Supply Curve Aggregate supply in the short run is different from aggregate supply in the long run (see Figure 11). That difference stems from the fact that in the long run, quantities and costs of resources are not fixed. Over time, contracts expire, and wages and other resource costs adjust to current conditions. The increased flexibility of resource costs in the long run has costs rising and falling with the price level and changes the shape of the aggregate supply curve. Lack of information about economic conditions in the short run also contributes to the inflexibility of resource prices as compared to the long run. The Economic Insight "How Lack of Information in the Short Run Affects Wages in the Long Run" shows why this is true for labor, as well as for other resources.

The **long-run aggregate supply curve (*LRAS*)** is viewed by most economists as being a vertical line at the potential level of real GDP or output (Y_p), as shown in Figure 11. Remember that the potential level of real GDP is the income level that is produced in the absence of any cyclical unemployment, or when the natural rate of unemployment exists. In the long run, wages and other resource costs fully adjust to price changes. The short-run *AS* curve slopes upward because we assume that the costs of production, particularly wages, do not change to offset changing prices. In the short run, then, higher prices increase producers' profits

5 | Why is the long-run aggregate supply curve vertical?

long-run aggregate supply curve (*LRAS*): a vertical line at the potential level of real GDP

Economic Insight

How Lack of Information in the Short Run Affects Wages in the Long Run

Workers do not have perfect information. In other words, they do not know everything that occurs. This lack of information includes information about the price level. If workers form incorrect expectations regarding the price level in the short run, they may be willing to work for a different wage in the short run than in the long run. For example, if workers thought that the inflation rate would be 3 percent over the next year, they would want a smaller wage raise than if they believed that the inflation rate would be 6 percent. If, in fact, they base their wage negotiations on 3 percent inflation and accept a wage based on that inflation rate, but it turns out that the price level has increased by 6 percent, workers will then seek higher wages. In the long run, wages will reflect price-level changes.

If it cost nothing to obtain information, everyone who was interested would always know the current economic conditions. However, since there are costs of obtaining and understanding information about the economy, people will make mistakes in the short run. Both managers and employees make mistakes as a result of lack of information. Such mistakes are not caused by stupidity but by ignorance—ignorance of future as well as current economic conditions. In the long run, mistakes about the price level are recognized, and wages adjust to the known price level.

We now have two reasons why wages will be more flexible in the long run than in the short run: long-term contracts and lack of information in the short run. The same arguments could be made for other resources as well. For these two reasons, the short-run aggregate supply curve is generally upward sloping because resource prices are relatively fixed in the short run.

FIGURE 11   The Shape of the Long-Run Aggregate Supply Curve

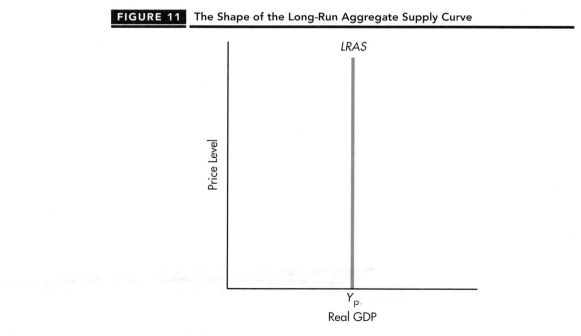

In the long run, the AS curve is a vertical line at the potential level of real GDP, which indicates that there is no relationship between price-level changes and the quantity of output produced.

and stimulate production. In the long run, however, because the costs of production adjust completely to the change in prices, neither profits nor production increases. What we find here are higher wages and other costs of production to match the higher level of prices.

4.c. Changes in Aggregate Supply: Nonprice Determinants

6 | What causes the aggregate supply curve to shift?

The aggregate supply curve is drawn with everything but the price level and real GDP held constant. There are several things that can change and cause the aggregate supply curve to shift. The shift from AS_0 to AS_1 in Figure 12 represents an increase in aggregate supply. The AS_1 curve lies to the right of AS_0, which means that at every price level, production is higher on AS_1 than on AS_0. The shift from AS_0 to AS_2 represents a decrease in aggregate supply. The AS_2 curve lies to the left of AS_0, which means that at every price level, production along AS_2 is less than that along AS_0. The nonprice determinants of aggregate supply are resource prices, technology, and expectations. Figure 13 summarizes the nonprice determinants of aggregate supply, discussed in detail next.

4.c.1. Resource Prices When the price of output changes, the costs of production do not change immediately. At first, then, a change in profits induces a change in production. Costs eventually change in response to the change in prices and production, and when they do, the aggregate supply curve shifts. When the cost of resources —labor, capital goods, and materials—falls, the aggregate supply curve shifts to the right, from AS_0 to AS_1 in Figure 12. This means that firms

FIGURE 12 | Changes in Aggregate Supply

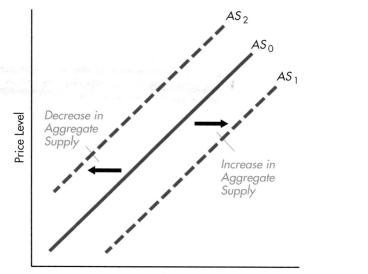

The aggregate supply curve shifts with changes in resource prices, technology, and expectations. When aggregate supply increases, the curve shifts to the right, like the shift from AS_0 to AS_1, so that at every price level more is being produced. When aggregate supply falls, the curve shifts to the left, like the shift from AS_0 to AS_2, so that at every price level less is being produced.

FIGURE 13   Determinants of Aggregate Supply Shift the *AS* Curve

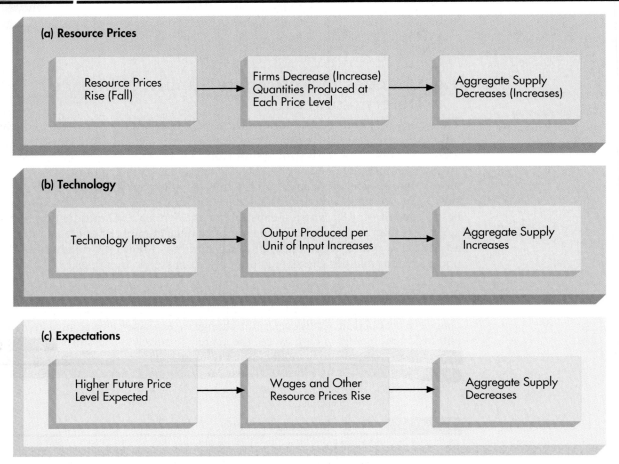

are willing to produce more output at any given price level. When the cost of resources goes up, profits fall and the aggregate supply curve shifts to the left, from AS_0 to AS_2. Here, at any given level of price, firms produce less output.

Remember that the vertical axis of the aggregate supply graph represents the price level for all goods and services produced in the economy. Only those changes in resource prices that raise the costs of production across the economy have an impact on the aggregate supply curve. For example, oil is an important raw material. If a new source of oil is discovered, the price of oil falls and aggregate supply increases. However, if oil-exporting countries restrict oil supplies and the price of oil increases substantially, aggregate supply decreases, a situation that occurred in the 1970s when OPEC reduced the supply of oil (see the Global Business Insight "Oil and Aggregate Supply"). If the price of only one minor resource were to change, then aggregate supply would be unlikely to change. For instance, if the price of land in Las Cruces, New Mexico, increased, we would not expect the U.S. aggregate supply curve to be affected.

4.c.2. Technology   Technological innovations allow businesses to increase the productivity of their existing resources. As new technology is adopted, the amount of output that can be produced by each unit of input increases, moving the aggregate supply curve to the right. For example, personal computers and word-processing

Global Business Insight

Oil and Aggregate Supply

It seems that every few years there are big fluctuations in oil prices that lead to much talk about high oil prices leading to a fall in GDP for oil-importing countries. What is the link between oil prices and real GDP? A look back to recent history helps develop our understanding of this link.

In 1973 and 1974, and again in 1979 and 1980, the Organization of Petroleum Exporting Countries (OPEC) reduced the supply of oil, driving the price of oil up dramatically. For example, the price of Saudi Arabian crude oil more than tripled between 1973 and 1974, and more than doubled between 1979 and 1980. Researchers estimate that the rapid jump in oil prices reduced output by 17 percent in Japan, by 7 percent in the United States, and by 1.9 percent in Germany.*

Oil is an important resource in many industries. When the price of oil increases as a result of restricted oil output, aggregate supply falls. You can see this in the graph shown at the right. When the price of oil goes up, the aggregate supply curve falls from AS_1 to AS_2. When aggregate supply falls, the equilibrium level of real GDP (the intersection of the AS curve and the AD curve) falls from Y_1 to Y_2.

Higher oil prices caused by restricted oil output would decrease not only short-run aggregate supply and current equilibrium real GDP, as shown in the graph, but also potential equilibrium income at the natural rate of unemployment. Unless other factors change to contribute to economic growth, the higher resource (oil) price reduces the productive capacity of the economy.

There is evidence that fluctuations in oil prices have less effect on the economy today than they did in the past.[†] The amount of energy that goes into producing a dollar of GDP has declined over time so that oil plays a less important role in determining aggregate supply today than in the 1970s and earlier. This means that any

given change in oil prices today will be associated with smaller shifts in the AS curve than in earlier decades.

While we have focused on the AS curve and oil prices, more recently, the AD curve has entered the discussion. Unlike earlier episodes, where oil price rises were the result of restricting the supply of oil, in the mid-2000s, the price of oil was being driven higher by rising demand—in particularly from China and the United States.[‡] The recession of 2008 showed that oil prices can drop just as dramatically due to demand shifts as in the earlier supply-driven episodes once supply increased. As spending fell during the recession, oil prices fell sharply from over $140 per barrel in July 2008, to $90 by September, and then to less than $40 by December.

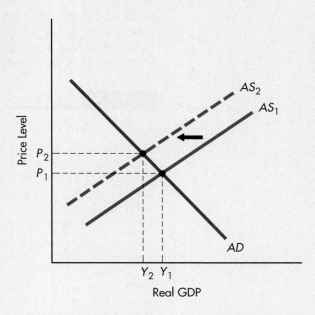

* These estimates were taken from Robert H. Rasche and John A. Tatom, "Energy Price Shocks, Aggregate Supply, and Monetary Policy: The Theory and the International Evidence," *Carnegie-Rochester Conference Series on Public Policy*, Vol. 14, eds. Karl Brunner and Allan H. Meltzer (North-Holland, 1981), pp. 9–93.

† See Stephen P. A. Brown and Mine K. Yücel, "Oil Prices and the Economy," Federal Reserve Bank of Dallas, *Southwest Economy*, July–August 2000.

‡ See Christopher J. Neely, "Will Oil Prices Choke Growth," Federal Reserve Bank of St. Louis, *International Economic Trends*, July 2004.

software have allowed secretaries to produce much more output in a day than type-writers allowed.

4.c.3. Expectations

To understand how expectations can affect aggregate supply, consider the case of labor contracts. Manufacturing workers typically contract for a nominal wage based on what they and their employers expect the future level of prices to be. Because wages typically are set for at least a year, any unexpected increase in the price level during the year lowers real wages. Firms receive higher prices for their output, but the cost of labor stays the same. So profits and production go up.

If wages rise in anticipation of higher prices but prices do not go up, the cost of labor rises. Higher real wages caused by expectations of higher prices reduce current profits and production, moving the aggregate supply curve to the left. Other things being equal, anticipated higher prices cause aggregate supply to decrease; conversely, anticipated lower prices cause aggregate supply to increase. In this sense, expectations of price-level changes that shift aggregate supply actually bring about price-level changes.

4.c.4. Economic Growth: Long-Run Aggregate Supply Shifts

The vertical long-run aggregate supply curve, as shown in Figure 11, does not mean that the economy is forever fixed at the current level of potential real gross domestic product. Over time, as new technologies are developed and the quantity and quality of resources increase, potential output also increases, shifting both the short- and the long-run aggregate supply curves to the right. Figure 14 shows long-run economic growth by the shift in the aggregate supply curve from $LRAS$ to $LRAS_1$. The movement of the long-run aggregate supply curve to the right reflects the increase in potential real GDP from Y_p to Y_{p1}. Even though the price level has no effect on the level of output in the long run, changes in the determinants of the supply of real output in the economy do.

| FIGURE 14 | Shifting the Long-Run Aggregate Supply Curve |

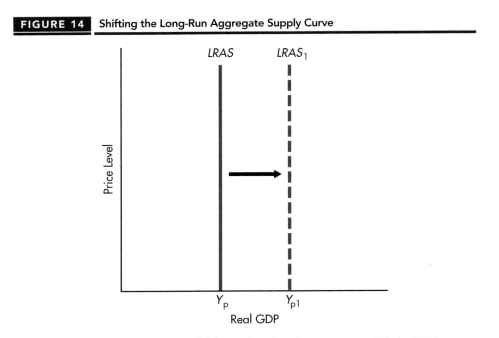

Changes in technology and the availability and quality of resources can shift the LRAS curve. For instance, a new technology that increases productivity would move the curve to the right, from LRAS to LRAS₁.

1. The aggregate supply curve shows the quantity of output (real GDP) produced at different price levels.

2. The aggregate supply curve slopes up because, everything else held constant, higher prices increase producers' profits, creating an incentive to increase output.

3. The aggregate supply curve shifts with changes in resource prices, technology, and expectations. These are nonprice determinants of aggregate supply.

4. The short-run aggregate supply curve is upward sloping, showing that increases in production are accompanied by higher prices.

5. The long-run aggregate supply curve is vertical at potential real GDP because, eventually, wages and the costs of other resources adjust fully to price-level changes.

7 | **What determines the equilibrium price level and real GDP?**

■ 5. Aggregate Demand and Supply Equilibrium

Now that we have defined the aggregate demand and aggregate supply curves separately, we can put them together to determine the equilibrium price level and real GDP.

5.a. Short-Run Equilibrium

Figure 15 shows the level of equilibrium in a hypothetical economy. Initially, the economy is in equilibrium at point 1, where AD_1 and AS_1 intersect. At this point, the equilibrium price level is P_1, and the equilibrium real GDP is \$500. At price level P_1, the amount of output demanded is equal to the amount supplied. Suppose aggregate demand increases from AD_1 to AD_2. In the short run, aggregate supply does not change, so the new equilibrium is at the intersection of the new aggregate demand curve, AD_2, and the same aggregate supply curve, AS_1, at point 2. The new equilibrium price level is P_2, and the new equilibrium real GDP is \$600. Note that in the short run, the equilibrium point on the short-run aggregate supply curve can lie to the right of the long-run aggregate supply curve (*LRAS*). This is because the *LRAS* represents the potential level of real GDP, not the capacity level. It is possible to produce more than the potential level of real GDP in the short run if the unemployment rate falls below the natural rate of unemployment.

5.b. Long-Run Equilibrium

An increase in aggregate demand increases real GDP only temporarily.

Point 2 is not a permanent equilibrium because aggregate supply decreases to AS_2 once the costs of production rise in response to higher prices. Final equilibrium is at point 3, where the price level is P_3 and real GDP is \$500. Notice that equilibrium real GDP here is the same as the initial equilibrium at point 1. Points 1 and 3 both lie along the long-run aggregate supply curve (*LRAS*). The initial shock to or change in the economy was an increase in aggregate demand. The change in aggregate expenditures initially led to higher output and higher prices.

FIGURE 15   Aggregate Demand and Supply Equilibrium

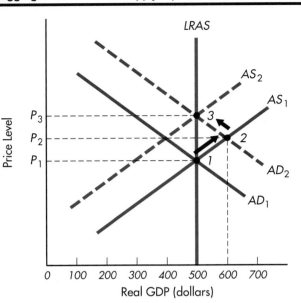

The equilibrium price level and real GDP is at the intersection of the AD and AS curves. Initially, equilibrium occurs at point 1, where the AD_1 and AS_1 curves intersect. Here the price level is P_1 and real GDP is $500. If aggregate demand increases, moving from AD_1 to AD_2, in the short run there is a new equilibrium at point 2, where AD_2 intersects AS_1. The price level rises to P_2, and the equilibrium level of real GDP increases to $600. Over time, as wages and the costs of other resources rise in response to higher prices, aggregate supply falls, moving AS_1 to AS_2. Final equilibrium occurs at point 3, where the AS_2 curve intersects the AD_2 curve. The price level rises to P_3, but the equilibrium level of real GDP returns to its initial level, $500. In the long run, there is no relationship between prices and the equilibrium level of real GDP because the costs of resources adjust to changes in the level of prices.

Over time, however, as resource costs rise and profit falls, output falls back to its original value.

We are not saying that the level of output never changes. The long-run aggregate supply curve shifts as technology changes and new supplies of resources are obtained. But the output change that results from a change in aggregate demand is a temporary, or short-run, phenomenon. The price level eventually adjusts, and output eventually returns to the potential level.

RECAP

1. The equilibrium price level and real GDP are at the point where the aggregate demand and aggregate supply curves intersect.

2. In the short run, a shift in aggregate demand establishes a temporary equilibrium along the short-run aggregate supply curve.

3. In the long run, the short-run aggregate supply curve shifts so that changes in aggregate demand affect only the price level, not the equilibrium level of output or real GDP.

SUMMARY

1 | **What factors affect aggregate demand?**

- Aggregate demand is the relation between aggregate expenditures and the price level. *§2*

- Aggregate demand is the sum of consumption, investment, government spending, and net exports at alternative price levels. *§2.a, 2.b, 2.c, 2.d*

- Aggregate expenditures change with changes in the price level because of the wealth effect, the interest rate effect, and the international trade effect. These cause a movement along the AD curve. *§3.a.1, 3.a.2, 3.a.3*

2 | **What causes the aggregate demand curve to shift?**

- The aggregate demand (*AD*) curve shows the level of expenditures for real GDP at different price levels. *§3.a.4*

- Because expenditures and prices move in opposite directions, the *AD* curve is negatively sloped. *§3.a.4*

- The nonprice determinants of aggregate demand include expectations, foreign income and price levels, and government policy. *§3.b.1, 3.b.2, 3.b.3*

3 | **What factors affect aggregate supply?**

- The aggregate supply curve shows the quantity of real GDP produced at different price levels. *§4*

- Movements along the *AS* curve are caused by changes in price. Shifts in the curve are caused by the determinants of AS. *§4.c*

4 | **Why does the short-run aggregate supply curve become steeper as real GDP increases?**

- As real GDP rises and the economy pushes closer to capacity output, the level of prices must rise to induce increased production. *§4.b.1*

5 | **Why is the long-run aggregate supply curve vertical?**

- The long-run aggregate supply curve is a vertical line at the potential level of real GDP. The shape of the curve indicates that higher prices have no effect on output when an economy is producing at potential real GDP. *§4.b.2*

6 | **What causes the aggregate supply curve to shift?**

- The nonprice determinants of aggregate supply are resource prices, technology, and expectations. *§4.c.1, 4.c.2, 4.c.3*

7 | **What determines the equilibrium price level and real GDP?**

- The equilibrium price level and real GDP are at the intersection of the aggregate demand and aggregate supply curves. *§5.a*

- In the short run, a shift in aggregate demand establishes a new, but temporary, equilibrium along the short-run aggregate supply curve. *§5.a*

- In the long run, the short-run aggregate supply curve shifts so that changes in aggregate demand determine the price level, but not the equilibrium level of output or real GDP. *§5.b*

KEY TERMS

demand-pull inflation *§1.a*

cost-push inflation *§1.b*

wealth effect *§3.a.1*

interest rate effect *§3.a.2*

international trade effect *§3.a.3*

aggregate demand curve *§3.a.4*

aggregate supply curve *§4*

long-run aggregate supply curve (LRAS) *§4.b.2*

EXERCISES

1. How is the aggregate demand curve different from the demand curve for a single good, like hamburgers?

2. Why does the aggregate demand curve slope downward? Give real-world examples of the three effects that explain the slope of the curve.

3. How does an increase in foreign income affect domestic aggregate expenditures and demand? Draw a diagram to illustrate your answer.

4. How does a decrease in foreign price levels affect domestic aggregate expenditures and demand? Draw a diagram to illustrate your answer.

5. How is the aggregate supply curve different from the supply curve for a single good, like pizza?

6. There are several determinants of aggregate supply that can cause the aggregate supply curve to shift.

a. Describe those determinants and give an example of a change in each.

b. Draw and label an aggregate supply diagram that illustrates the effect of the change in each determinant.

7. Draw a short-run aggregate supply curve that gets steeper as real GDP rises.

a. Explain why the curve has this shape.

b. Now draw a long-run aggregate supply curve that intersects a short-run AS curve. What is the relationship between short-run AS and long-run AS?

8. Draw and carefully label an aggregate demand and supply diagram with initial equilibrium at P_0 and Y_0.

a. Using the diagram, explain what happens when aggregate demand falls.

b. How is the short run different from the long run?

9. Draw an aggregate demand and supply diagram for Japan. In the diagram, show how each of the following affects aggregate demand and supply.

a. The U.S. gross domestic product falls.

b. The level of prices in Korea falls.

c. Labor receives a large wage increase.

d. Economists predict higher prices next year.

10. If the long-run aggregate supply curve gives the level of potential real GDP, how can the short-run aggregate supply curve ever lie to the right of the long-run aggregate supply curve?

11. What will happen to the equilibrium price level and real GDP if:

a. Aggregate demand and aggregate supply both increase?

b. Aggregate demand increases and aggregate supply decreases?

c. Aggregate demand and aggregate supply both decrease?

d. Aggregate demand decreases and aggregate supply increases?

12. During the Great Depression, the U.S. economy experienced a falling price level and declining real GDP. Using an aggregate demand and aggregate supply diagram, illustrate and explain how this could occur.

13. Suppose aggregate demand increases, causing an increase in real GDP but no change in the price level. Using an aggregate demand and aggregate supply diagram, illustrate and explain how this could occur.

14. Suppose aggregate demand increases, causing an increase in the price level but no change in real GDP. Using an aggregate demand and aggregate supply diagram, illustrate and explain how this could occur.

15. Use an aggregate demand and aggregate supply diagram to illustrate and explain how each of the following will affect the equilibrium price level and real GDP:

a. Consumers expect a recession.

b. Foreign income rises.

c. Foreign price levels fall.

d. Government spending increases.

e. Workers expect higher future inflation and negotiate higher wages now.

f. Technological improvements increase productivity.

16. In the boom years of the late 1990s, it was often said that rapidly increasing stock prices were responsible for much of the rapid growth of real GDP. Explain how this could be true, using aggregate demand and aggregate supply analysis.

17. Suppose you read in the newspaper that rising oil prices would contribute to a global recession. Use aggregate demand and supply analysis to explain how high oil prices could reduce real GDP.

You can find further practice tests in the Online Quiz at **www.cengage.com/economics/boyes**.

The Conference Board Consumer Confidence Index Plummets Further in February

The Conference Board **February 24, 2009**

The Conference Board Consumer Confidence Index, which had decreased moderately in January, declined in February, reaching yet another all-time low. The Index now stands at 25.0 (1985 = 100), down from 37.4 in January. The Present Situation Index declined to 21.2 from 29.7 last month. The Expectations Index decreased to 27.5 from 42.5 in January.

The Consumer Confidence Survey is based on a representative sample of 5,000 U.S. households. . . .

Says Lynn Franco, Director of The Conference Board Consumer Research Center: "The Consumer Confidence Index, which was relatively flat in January, reached yet another all-time low in February (Index began in 1967). The decline in the Present Situation Index, driven by worsening business conditions and a rapidly deteriorating job market, suggests that overall economic conditions have weakened even further this quarter. Looking ahead, increasing concerns about business conditions, employment and earnings have further sapped confidence and driven expectations to their lowest level ever. In addition, inflation expectations, which had been easing over the past several months, have moderately picked up. All in all, not only do consumers feel overall economic conditions have grown more dire, but just as disconcerting, they anticipate no improvement in conditions over the next six months."

Consumers' appraisal of overall current conditions, which was already bleak, worsened further. Those claiming business conditions are "bad" rose to 51.1 percent from 47.9 percent, while those saying business conditions are "good" edged up to 6.8 percent from 6.5 percent last month. Consumers' assessment of the labor market turned considerably more pessimistic in February. Those saying jobs are "hard to get" increased to 47.8 percent from 41.1 percent in January, while those stating jobs are "plentiful" fell to 4.4 percent from 7.1 percent.

Consumers' short-term outlook turned significantly more negative this month. Consumers anticipating business conditions will worsen over the next six months increased to 40.5 percent from 31.1 percent, while those expecting conditions to improve declined to 8.7 percent from 12.8 percent in January.

The employment outlook was also much grimmer. The percentage of consumers expecting fewer jobs in the months ahead increased to 47.3 percent from 36.9 percent, while those expecting more jobs declined to 7.1 percent from 9.1 percent. The proportion of consumers expecting an increase in their incomes declined to 7.6 percent from 10.3 percent.

Source: *February 2009 Consumer Confidence Survey™ The Conference Board.*

Commentary

Why would a business firm want to receive reports regarding consumer confidence in the U.S. economy? The answer lies in the role of expectations as a determinant of consumption spending and therefore aggregate demand. If households are confident that incomes will rise and prosperous times are ahead, they are much more likely to spend more than if they expect a recession. By monitoring consumer confidence in the economy, we can better understand consumer spending. Since consumption accounts for about two-thirds of GDP, changes in household spending can play a big role in business-cycle fluctuations.

In terms of aggregate demand and supply analysis, if households are more optimistic about the economy's performance, then the aggregate demand curve should shift to the right, like the shift from AD_0 to AD_1 in the accompanying figure. This would increase the equilibrium level of real GDP from Y_0 to Y_1. If households are less optimistic about the economy's performance, then the aggregate demand curve should shift to the left, like the shift from AD_0 to AD_2. This would decrease the equilibrium level of real GDP from Y_0 to Y_2.

Because of the implications of shifts in consumer confidence for business-cycle fluctuations, government officials, along with businesspeople, watch the consumer confidence measures to maintain a sense of what is happening in the typical household. The two best-known surveys, the University of Michigan and Conference Board surveys, ask questions like: "Six months from now,

do you think business conditions will be better, the same, or worse?" "Would you say that you are better off or worse off financially than you were a year ago?" The answers to these questions and others are used as inputs in constructing an index of consumer confidence so that the press typically reports only how the overall index changes rather than the responses to any particular question.

Although the popular consumer confidence indexes fluctuate up and down every month, researchers have found that the monthly fluctuations are not very useful in predicting consumption or GDP. However, major shifts in the indexes or several months of rising or falling indexes may provide an early signal of forthcoming changes in consumption and GDP.

Chapter 9

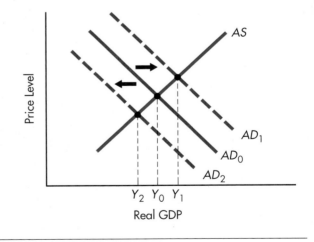

© Dmitrijs Dmitrijevs/Shutterstock

Aggregate Expenditures

 Fundamental Questions

1 | How are consumption and saving related?

2 | What are the determinants of consumption?

3 | What are the determinants of investment?

4 | What are the determinants of government spending?

5 | What are the determinants of net exports?

6 | What is the aggregate expenditures function?

To understand why real GDP, unemployment, and inflation rise and fall over time, we must know what causes the aggregate demand and aggregate supply curves to shift. We cannot understand why the U.S. economy has experienced 11 recessions since 1945 or why in the 1990s and 2000s, we witnessed the longest peacetime business-cycle expansion in modern times unless we understand why the *AD* and *AS* curves shift. In this chapter, we examine in more detail the demand side of the economy.

In the chapter titled "Macroeconomic Equilibrium: Aggregate Demand and Supply," we discussed how the price level affects aggregate expenditures through the interest rate, international trade, and wealth effects. This chapter examines the nonprice determinants of spending and shifts in aggregate demand in greater detail and assumes that the price level is fixed. This assumption means that the aggregate supply curve is a horizontal line at the fixed-price level. This approach was used by John Maynard Keynes, who analyzed the macro economy during the Great Depression.

FIGURE 1　The Fixed-Price Keynesian Model

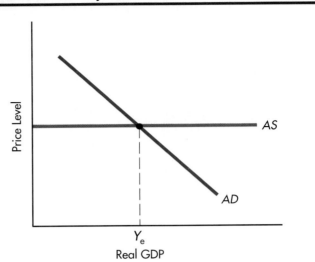

The Keynesian assumption that the price level is fixed requires a horizontal aggregate supply curve. In this case, aggregate demand will determine the equilibrium level of real GDP.

A fixed-price level, as shown in Figure 1, suggests a situation in which unemployment and excess capacity exist. Firms can hire from this pool of unemployed labor and increase their output at no extra cost and without any pressure on the price level. It is not surprising that Keynes would rely on such a model at a time when he was surrounded by mass unemployment. He was more interested in the determination of income and output than in the problem of inflation.

With a horizontal *AS* curve, as shown in Figure 1, the location of the *AD* curve will determine the equilibrium level of real GDP, Y_e. If we understand what determines aggregate demand—consumption, investment, government spending, and net exports—we will understand what determines real GDP.

We begin our detailed examination of aggregate expenditures by discussing consumption, which accounts for approximately 70 percent of total expenditures in the U.S. economy. We then look at investment (16 percent of total expenditures), government spending (19 percent of total expenditures), and net exports (−5 percent of total expenditures).

■ 1. Consumption and Saving

1 | How are consumption and saving related?

Households can do three things with their income: They can spend it for the consumption of goods and services, they can save it, or they can pay taxes with it. Disposable income is what is left after taxes have been paid. It is the sum of consumption and saving:

$$\text{Disposable income} = \text{consumption} + \text{saving}$$

or

$$Yd = C + S$$

Disposable income is the income that households actually have available for spending after taxes. Whatever disposable income is not spent is saved.

Consumption spending is the largest component of aggregate expenditures. Households in Chichicastenango, Guatemala, come to the produce market shown here to purchase food. Their expenditures on food will be counted in the consumption and the GDP of Guatemala. If the households decide to save less and spend more, then, other things being equal, the higher consumption will raise the GDP of Guatemala.

Why are we talking about saving, which is not a component of total spending, in a chapter that sets out to discuss the components of total spending? Saving is simply "not consuming"; it is impossible to separate the incentives to save from the incentives to consume.

1.a. Saving and Savings

> **Saving occurs over a unit of time; it is a flow concept.**

Before we go on, it is necessary to understand the difference between *saving* and *savings*. *Saving* occurs over a unit of time—a week, a month, a year. For instance, you might save $10 a week or $40 a month. Saving is a *flow* concept. *Savings* are an amount accumulated at a particular point in time—today, December 31, or your 65th birthday. For example, you might have savings of $2,500 on December 31. Savings are a *stock* concept.

> **Savings are an amount accumulated at a point in time; they are a stock concept.**

Like saving, GDP and its components are flow concepts. They are measured by the year or quarter of the year. Consumption, investment, government spending, and net exports are also flows. Each of them is an amount spent over a period of time.

1.b. The Consumption and Saving Functions

consumption function:
the relationship between disposable income and consumption

The primary determinant of the level of consumption over any given period is the level of disposable income. The higher the disposable income, the more households are willing and able to spend. This relationship between disposable income and consumption is called the **consumption function**. Figure 2 contains the consumption function for the United States over the long-run period from 1990 to 2005. For each year in this period, the values of disposable income and consumption are plotted in the figure. Note that Figure 2 also contains a 45-degree line. (A 45-degree line makes a graph easier to read because every point on the line represents the same value on both axes.) This line splits the area of the figure in half and shows all points at which the value of disposable income and the value of consumption are equal. Since the actual consumption function lies below the 45-degree line, it can be seen that consumption is less than disposable income—but not much less.

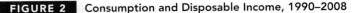

| **FIGURE 2** | Consumption and Disposable Income, 1990–2008 |

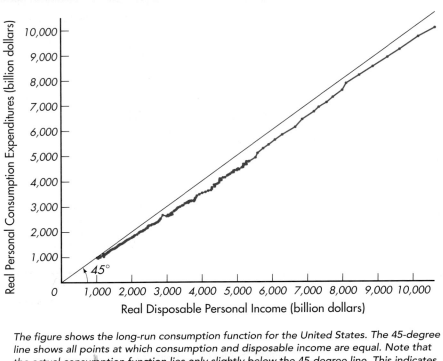

The figure shows the long-run consumption function for the United States. The 45-degree line shows all points at which consumption and disposable income are equal. Note that the actual consumption function lies only slightly below the 45-degree line. This indicates that consumption is less than disposable income but not much less.

Source: www.bea.gov.

The consumption function in Figure 2 is a long-run consumption function. In the short run, like this year, the relationship between consumption and disposable income may be much flatter than that shown in Figure 2. We now turn to a deeper analysis of the consumption function to better understand this important relationship.

To focus on the relationship between income and consumption, we draw a new graph, Figure 3, with income on the horizontal axis and consumption on the vertical axis. Figure 3(a) shows a hypothetical consumption function. In this economy, when disposable income is zero, consumption is $30. As disposable income rises, consumption rises. For instance, when disposable income is $100, consumption is $100.

We use C to represent consumption and Yd to represent disposable income. The line labeled C in Figure 3(a) is the consumption function: It represents the relationship between disposable income and consumption. The other line in the figure creates a 45-degree angle with either axis. In Figure 3(a), as in Figure 2, the 45-degree line shows all the points where consumption equals disposable income.

The level of disposable income at which all disposable income is being spent occurs at the point where the consumption function (line C) crosses the 45-degree line. In the graph, C equals Yd when disposable income is $100. Consumers save a fraction of any disposable income above $100. You can see this in the graph. Saving occurs at any level of disposable income at which the consumption function lies below the 45-degree line (at which consumption is less than disposable income). The amount of saving is measured by the vertical distance between the 45-degree line and the consumption function. If disposable income is $600, consumption is $450 and saving is $150.

FIGURE 3 **Disposable Income Consumption and Saving in a Hypothetical Economy**

Disposable Income (Yd)	Consumption (C)	Saving (S)
$0	$30	– $30
$100	$100	$0
$200	$170	$30
$300	$240	$60
$400	$310	$90
$500	$380	$120
$600	$450	$150
$700	$570	$180

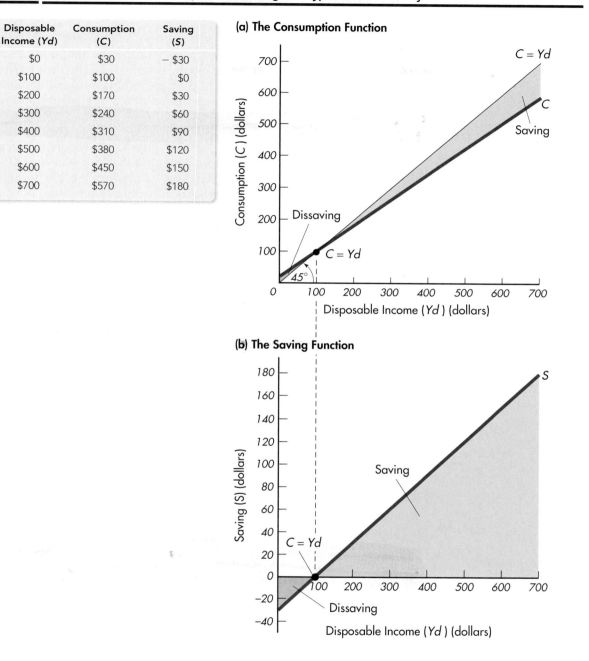

(a) The Consumption Function

(b) The Saving Function

Figure 3(a) shows that consumption is a positive function of disposable income: It goes up as disposable income rises. The line labeled C = Yd forms a 45-degree angle at the origin. It shows all points where consumption equals disposable income. The point at which the consumption function (line C) crosses the 45-degree line—where disposable income measures $100—is the point at which consumption equals disposable income. At lower levels of disposable income, consumption is greater than disposable income; at higher levels, consumption is less than disposable income. Figure 3(b) shows the saving function. Saving equals disposable income minus consumption. When consumption equals disposable income, saving is 0. At higher levels of disposable income, we find positive saving; at lower levels, we find negative saving, or dissaving.

saving function: the relationship between disposable income and saving

The **saving function** is the relationship between disposable income and saving. Figure 3(b) plots the saving function (*S*). When the level of disposable income is at $100, consumption equals disposable income, so saving is zero. As disposable income increases beyond $100, saving goes up. In Figure 3(a), saving is the vertical distance between the 45-degree line and the consumption function. In Figure 3(b), we can read the level of saving directly from the saving function.

Notice that at relatively low levels of disposable income, consumption exceeds disposable income. How can consumption be greater than disposable income? When a household spends more than it earns in income, the household must finance the spending above income by borrowing or using savings. This is called **dissaving.** In Figure 3(a), dissaving occurs at levels of disposable income between 0 and $100, where the consumption function lies above the 45-degree line. Dissaving, like saving, is measured by the vertical distance between the 45-degree line and the consumption function, but dissaving occurs when the consumption function lies *above* the 45-degree line. In Figure 3(b), dissaving occurs when the saving function (line *S*) lies below the disposable income axis, at disposable income levels between zero and $100. For example, when disposable income is $0, dissaving (negative saving) is −$30.

dissaving: spending financed by borrowing or using savings

Both the consumption function and the saving function have positive slopes: As disposable income rises, consumption and saving increase. Consumption and saving, then, are positive functions of disposable income. Notice that when disposable income equals zero, consumption is still positive.

autonomous consumption: consumption that is independent of income

There is a level of consumption, called **autonomous consumption,** that does not depend on income. (*Autonomous* here means "independent of income.") In Figure 3(a), consumption equals $30 when disposable income equals zero. This $30 is autonomous consumption; it does not depend on income but will vary with the nonincome determinants of consumption that will soon be introduced. The intercept of the consumption function (the value of *C* when *Yd* equals zero) measures the amount of autonomous consumption. The intercept in Figure 3(a) is $30, which means that autonomous consumption in this example is $30.

1.c. Marginal Propensity to Consume and Save

Total consumption equals autonomous consumption plus the spending that depends on income. As disposable income rises, consumption rises. This relationship between *change* in disposable income and *change* in consumption is the **marginal propensity to consume (*MPC*).** The *MPC* measures change in consumption as a proportion of the change in disposable income.

marginal propensity to consume (*MPC*): the change in consumption as a proportion of the change in disposable income

$$MPC = \frac{\text{change in consumption}}{\text{change in disposable income}}$$

In Table 1, columns 1 and 2 list the consumption function data used in Figure 3. The marginal propensity to consume is shown in column 4. In our example, each time that disposable income changes by $100, consumption changes by $70. This means that consumers spend 70 percent of any extra income that they receive.

$$MPC = \frac{\$70}{\$100}$$

$$= .70$$

marginal propensity to save (*MPS*): the change in saving as a proportion of the change in disposable income

The *MPC* tells us what fractional change in income is used for consumption. The **marginal propensity to save (*MPS*)** defines the relationship between change

TABLE 1 Marginal Propensity to Consume and to Save

Disposable Income (Yd)	Consumption (C)	Saving (S)	Marginal Propensity to Consume (MPC)	Marginal Propensity to Save (MPS)
$0	$30	−$30	—	—
$100	$100	$0	.70	.30
$200	$170	$30	.70	.30
$300	$240	$60	.70	.30
$400	$310	$90	.70	.30
$500	$380	$120	.70	.30
$600	$450	$150	.70	.30
$700	$520	$180	.70	.30

in saving and change in disposable income. It is the change in saving divided by the change in disposable income:

$$MPC = \frac{\text{change in consumption}}{\text{change in disposable income}}$$

The *MPS* in Table 1 is a constant 30 percent at all levels of income. Each time that disposable income changes by $100, saving changes by $30:

$$MPC = \frac{\$70}{\$100}$$

$$= .30$$

The *MPC* and the *MPS* will always be constant at all levels of disposable income in our examples.

Because disposable income will be either consumed or saved, the marginal propensity to consume plus the marginal propensity to save must total 1:

$$MPC + MPS = 1$$

The percentage of additional income that is not consumed must be saved. If consumers spend 70 percent of any extra income, they save 30 percent of that income. The *MPC* and the *MPS* determine the rate of consumption and saving as disposable income changes. The *MPC* is the slope of the consumption function; the *MPS* is the slope of the saving function. Remember that the slope of a line measures the change along the vertical axis that corresponds to a change along the horizontal axis, the rise over the run (see the Appendix to Chapter 1). In the case of the consumption function, the slope is the change in consumption (the change on the vertical axis) divided by the change in disposable income (the change on the horizontal axis):

The slope of the consumption function is the same as the MPC; the slope of the saving function is the same as the MPS.

$$\text{Slope of consumption function} = \frac{\text{change in consumption}}{\text{change in disposable income}}$$

$$= MPC$$

The higher the *MPC*, the greater the fraction of any additional disposable income that consumers will spend. At an *MPC* of .70, consumers spend 70 percent of any change in disposable income; at an MPC of .85, consumers want to spend 85 percent of any change in disposable income. The size of the MPC shows up graphically as the steepness of the consumption function. The consumption function with an MPC of .85 is a steeper line than the one drawn in Figure 3(a). In general, the steeper the consumption function, the larger the MPC. If the MPC is less than .70, the consumption function will be flatter than the one in the figure.

The slope of the saving function is the MPS:

$$\text{Slope of saving function} = \frac{\text{change in saving}}{\text{change indisposable income}}$$

$$= MPS$$

In general, the steeper the saving function, the greater the slope and the greater the MPS.

Figure 4(a) shows three consumption functions. Since all three consumption functions have the same intercept, autonomous consumption is the same for all. But each consumption function in Figure 4(a) has a different slope. Line C_1 has an MPC of .70. A larger MPC, .80, produces a steeper consumption function (line C_2). A smaller MPC, .60, produces a flatter consumption function (line C_3). The saving functions that correspond to these consumption functions are shown in Figure 4(b). Function S_1, with an MPS of .30, corresponds to consumption function C_1, with an MPC of .70 (remember: $MPS = 1 - MPC$). Function S_2 corresponds to C_2, and S_3 corresponds to C_3. The higher the MPC (the steeper the consumption function), the lower the MPS (the flatter the saving function). If people spend a greater fraction of extra income, they save a smaller fraction.

1.d. Average Propensity to Consume and Save

Suppose our interest is not in the proportion of change in disposable income that is consumed or saved, but in the proportion of disposable income that is consumed or saved. For this, we must know the average propensity to consume and the average propensity to save.

average propensity to consume (APC): the proportion of disposable income spent for consumption

The **average propensity to consume (APC)** is the proportion of disposable income that is spent for consumption:

$$APC = \text{consumption/disposable income}$$

or

$$APS = \frac{C}{Yd}$$

average propensity to save (APS): the proportion of disposable income saved

The **average propensity to save (APS)** is the proportion of disposable income that is saved:

$$APC = \frac{\text{saving}}{\text{disposable income}}$$

or

$$APS = \frac{S}{Yd}$$

Table 2 uses the consumption and saving data plotted in Figure 3. The APC and APS are shown in columns 4 and 5. When disposable income is $100, consumption is also $100, so the ratio of consumption to disposable income (C/Yd) equals 1 ($100/$100). At this point, saving equals 0, so the ratio of saving to disposable income (S/Yd) also equals $0 ($0/$100). We really do not have to compute the APS

| FIGURE 4 | Marginal Propensity to Consume and Save |

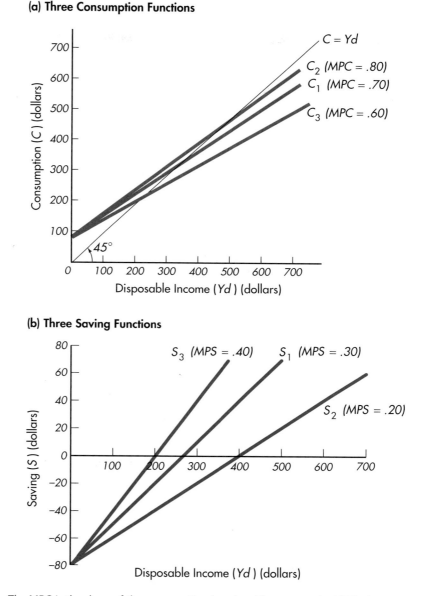

(a) Three Consumption Functions

(b) Three Saving Functions

The MPC is the slope of the consumption function. The greater the MPC, the steeper the consumption function. The MPS is the slope of the saving function. The greater the MPS, the steeper the saving function. Because the sum of the MPC and the MPS is 1, the greater the MPC, the smaller the MPS. The steeper the consumption function, then, the flatter the saving function.

because we already know the *APC*. There are only two things that can be done with disposable income: spend it or save it. The percentage of income spent plus the percentage saved must add up to 100 percent of disposable income. This means that

$$APC + APS = 1$$

If the *APC* equals 1, then the *APS* must equal 0.

TABLE 2   Average Propensity to Consume and to Save

Disposable Income (Yd)	Consumption (C)	Saving (S)	Average Propensity to Consume (APC)	Average Propensity to Save (APS)
$0	$30	$30	—	—
$100	$100	$0	1	0
$200	$170	$30	0.85	0.15
$300	$240	$60	0.80	0.20
$400	$310	$90	0.78	0.22
$500	$380	$120	0.76	0.24
$600	$450	$150	0.75	0.25
$700	$520	$180	0.74	0.26

When disposable income equals $600, consumption equals $450, so the *APC* equals .75 ($450/$600) and the *APS* equals .25 ($150/$600). As always, the *APC* plus the *APS* equals 1. If households are spending 75 percent of their disposable income, they must be saving 25 percent.

Notice in Table 2 that the *APC* falls as disposable income rises. This is because households spend only part of any change in income. In Figure 3(a), the consumption function rises more slowly than the 45-degree line. (Remember that consumption equals disposable income along the 45-degree line.) The consumption function tells us, then, that consumption rises as disposable income rises, but not by as much as disposable income rises. Because households spend a smaller fraction of disposable income as that income rises, they must be saving a larger fraction. You can see this in Table 2, where the *APS* rises as disposable income rises. At low levels of income, the *APS* is negative, a product of dissaving (we are dividing negative saving by disposable income). As disposable income rises, saving rises as a percentage of disposable income; this means that the *APS* is increasing.

1.e. Determinants of Consumption

Disposable income is an important determinant of household spending. But disposable income is not the only factor that influences consumption. Wealth, expectations, demographics, and taxation (taxation effects will be considered in the chapter titled "Fiscal Policy") are other determinants of consumption.

1.e.1. Disposable Income Household income is the primary determinant of consumption, which is why the consumption function is drawn with disposable income on the horizontal axis. Household income is usually measured as current disposable income. By *current* we mean income that is received in the current period—the current period could be today, this month, this year, or whatever period we are discussing. Past income and future income certainly can affect household spending, but they do so through household wealth or expectations, not through income. Disposable income is after-tax income.

The two-dimensional graphs we have been using relate consumption only to current disposable income. A change in consumption caused by a change in disposable income is shown by *movement along* the consumption function. The effects of other variables are shown by *shifting* the intercept of the consumption function up and down as the values of these other variables change. All variables *except* disposable income change *autonomous* consumption.

2 | What are the determinants of consumption?

Changes in taxes will affect disposable income. *If we assume that there are no taxes, then* Yd *equals* Y, *and consumption (and other expenditures) may be drawn as a function of real GDP rather than disposable income.* The chapter titled "Fiscal Policy" is devoted to an analysis of government fiscal policy, including taxation. As a result, we put off our discussion of tax effects until then; this allows us to simplify our analysis of aggregate expenditures. The discussion of the components of aggregate expenditures in the remainder of this chapter and in later chapters will be related graphically to pretax real GDP rather than to disposable income.

wealth: the value of all assets owned by a household

1.e.2. Wealth **Wealth** is the value of all the assets owned by a household. Wealth is a stock variable; it includes homes, cars, checking and savings accounts, and stocks and bonds, as well as the value of income expected in the future. As household wealth increases, households have more resources available for spending, so consumption increases at every level of real GDP. You can see this in Figure 5(a) as a shift of the consumption function from C to C_1. The autonomous increase in consumption shifts the intercept of the consumption function from $60 to $100, so consumption increases by $40 at every level of real GDP. If households spend more of their current income as their wealth increases, they save less. You can see this as the downward shift of the saving function in Figure 5(b), from S to S_1. The higher level of wealth has households more willing to dissave at each income level than before. Dissaving now occurs at any level of income below $500. During the long expansionary period of the 1990s, stock price increases made many households much wealthier and stimulated consumption.

A decrease in wealth has just the opposite effect. For instance, during the 2008 recession, property values in most areas of the United States declined. Household wealth declined as the value of real estate fell, and spending fell as a result. Here you would see an autonomous drop in consumption, like the shift from C to C_2, and an autonomous increase in saving, like the shift from S to S_2. Now at every level of real GDP, households spend $40 less than before and save $40 more. The intercept of the consumption function is $20, not $60, and the intercept of the saving function is −$20, not −$60. The new consumption function parallels the old one; the curves are the same vertical distance apart at every level of income. So consumption is $40 lower at every level of income. Similarly, the saving functions are parallel because saving is $40 greater at every level of real GDP along S_2 compared to S.

1.e.3. Expectations Another important determinant of consumption is consumer expectations about future income, prices, and wealth. When consumers expect a recession, when they are worried about losing their jobs or facing cutbacks in hours worked, they tend to spend less and save more. This means an autonomous decrease in consumption and increase in saving, like the shift from C to C_2 and from S to S_2 in Figure 5. Conversely, when consumers are optimistic, we find an autonomous increase in consumption and decrease in saving, like the shift from C to C_1 and from S to S_1 in Figure 5.

Expectations are subjective opinions; they are difficult to observe and measure. This creates problems for economists trying to analyze the effect of expectations on consumption. The Conference Board surveys households to construct its *Consumer Confidence Index*, a measure of consumer opinion regarding the outlook for the economy. Economists follow the index in order to predict how consumer spending will change. Since consumption is the largest component of GDP, changes in consumption have important implications for business cycles.

Clearly the Consumer Confidence Index is not always a reliable indicator of expansion or recession. Still, economists' increasing use of this and other measures to better understand fluctuations in consumption underscores the importance of consumer expectations in the economy (see the Economic Insight "Permanent Income, Life Cycles, and Consumption").

| FIGURE 5 | Autonomous Shifts in Consumption and in Saving |

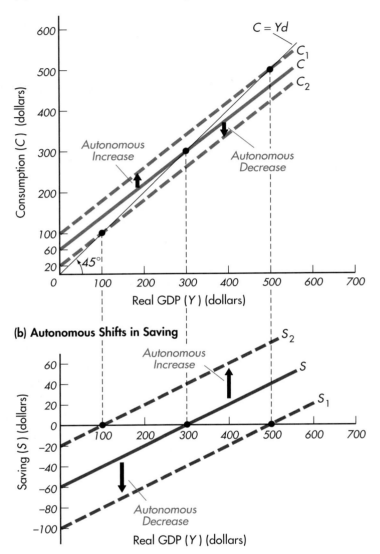

Autonomous consumption is the amount of consumption that exists when real GDP is 0. It is the intercept of the consumption function. The shift from C to C_1 is an autonomous increase in consumption of $40; it moves the intercept of the consumption function from $60 to $100. The shift from C to C_2 is an autonomous decrease in consumption of $40; it moves the intercept of the consumption function from $60 to $20. Autonomous saving is the amount of saving that exists when real GDP is 0. This is the intercept of the saving function. The shift from S to S_1 is an autonomous decrease in saving of $40; it moves the intercept of the saving function from −$60 to −$100. The shift from S to S_2 is an autonomous increase in saving of $40; it moves the intercept of the saving function from −$60 to −$20. Because disposable income minus consumption equals saving, an autonomous increase in consumption is associated with an autonomous decrease in saving, and an autonomous decrease in consumption is associated with an autonomous increase in saving.

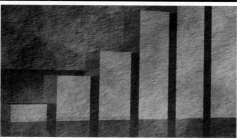

Economic Insight

Permanent Income, Life Cycles, and Consumption

Studies of the consumption function over a long period of time find a function like the one labeled C_L in the graph, as we saw earlier in Figure 2. This function has a marginal propensity to consume of .90 and an intercept of 0. Consumption functions studied over a shorter period of time have lower *MPC*s and positive intercepts, like the function C_S in the graph, with an *MPC* of .60. How do we reconcile these two functions?

Economists offer two related explanations for the difference between long-run and short-run consumption behavior: the permanent income hypothesis and the life-cycle hypothesis. The fundamental idea is that people consume on the basis of their idea of what their long-run or permanent level of income is. A substantial increase in income this month does not affect consumption much in the short run unless it is perceived as a permanent increase.

Let's use point 1 on the graph as our starting point. Here disposable income is $50,000 and consumption is $45,000. Now suppose household income rises to $60,000. Initially consumption increases by 60 percent, the short-run *MPC*. The household moves from point 1 to point 2 along the short-run consumption function (C_s). The short-run consumption function has a lower *MPC* than the long-run consumption function because households do not completely adjust their spending and saving habits with short-run fluctuations in income.

Once the household is convinced that $60,000 is a permanent level of income, it moves from point 2 to point 3 along the long-run consumption function. At point 3, consumption has increased by 90 percent, the long-run *MPC*. In the long run, households adjust fully to changes in income; in the short run, a fluctuation in income does not cause as large a fluctuation in consumption.

When income falls below the permanent income level, the household is willing to dissave or borrow to support its normal level of consumption. When income rises above the permanent income level, the household saves at a higher rate than the long-run *MPS*. The lower *MPC* in the short run works to smooth out consumption in the long run. The household does not adjust current consumption with every up and down movement in household income.

To maintain a steady rate of consumption over time, households follow a pattern of saving over the life cycle. Saving is low when current income is low relative to permanent income (during school years, periods of unemployment, or retirement). Saving is high when current income is high relative to the lifetime average, typically during middle age.

In the long run, households adjust fully to changes in income. In the short run, in order to smooth consumption over time, they do not. This explains both the difference between the long-run and short-run consumption functions and the stability of consumption over time.

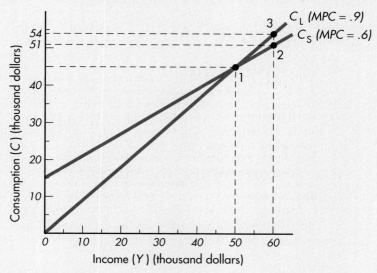

1.e.4. Demographics Other things being equal, economists expect the level of consumption to rise with increases in population. The focus here is on both the number of people in the economy and the composition of that population. The size of the population affects the position of the consumption function; the age of the population affects the slope of the consumption function. The greater the size of the population, other things equal, the higher the intercept of the consumption function. With regard to the effect of age composition on the economy, young households typically are accumulating durable consumer goods (refrigerators, washing machines, automobiles); they have higher *MPC*s than older households.

RECAP

1. It is impossible to separate incentives to save from incentives to consume.

2. Saving is a flow variable; savings is a stock variable.

3. Dissaving is spending financed by borrowing or using savings.

4. The marginal propensity to consume measures change in consumption as a proportion of change in disposable income.

5. The marginal propensity to save measures change in saving as a proportion of change in disposable income.

6. The *MPC* plus the *MPS* must equal 1.

7. Change in the *MPC* changes the slope of the consumption function; change in the *MPS* changes the slope of the saving function.

8. The average propensity to consume measures that portion of disposable income spent for consumption.

9. The average propensity to save measures that portion of disposable income saved.

10. The sum of the *APC* and the *APS* must equal 1.

11. The determinants of consumption include income, wealth, expectations, demographics, and taxation.

12. A change in consumption caused by a change in disposable income is shown by movement along the consumption function.

13. Changes in wealth, expectations, or population change autonomous consumption, which is shown as a shift of the consumption function.

■ 2. Investment

Investment is business spending on capital goods and inventories. It is the most variable component of total spending. In this section of the chapter, we take a look at the determinants of investment and see why investment changes so much over the business cycle.

2.a. Autonomous Investment

In order to simplify our analysis of real GDP in the next chapter, we assume that investment is autonomous, that it is independent of current real GDP. This does not mean that we assume that investment is fixed at a constant amount. There are several factors that cause investment to change, but we assume that current real GDP is not one of them.

As a function of real GDP, autonomous investment is drawn as a horizontal line. This means that investment remains constant as real GDP changes.

FIGURE 6 Investment as a Function of Income

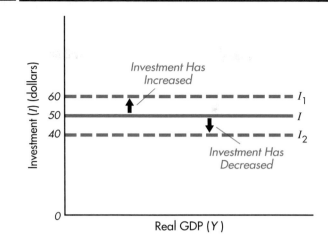

Investment is assumed to be autonomous. Because it is independent of current real GDP, it is drawn as a horizontal line. An autonomous increase in investment shifts the function upward, from I to I_1. An increase could be the product of lower interest rates, optimism in business about future sales and revenues, technological change, an investment tax credit that lowers the cost of capital goods, or a need to expand capacity because of a lack of available productive resources. An autonomous decrease in investment moves the function down, from I to I_2. The same factors that cause investment to rise can also cause it to fall when they move in the opposite direction.

In Figure 6, the investment function (the horizontal line labeled I) indicates that investment equals $50 at every level of real GDP. As the determinants of investment change, the investment function shifts autonomously. As investment increases, the function shifts upward (for example, from I to I_1); as investment decreases, the function shifts downward (from I to I_2).

2.b. Determinants of Investment

Investment is business spending on capital goods and inventories. Capital goods are the buildings and equipment that businesses need to produce their products. Inventories are final goods that have not been sold. Inventories can be planned or unplanned. For example, in the fall, a retail department store wants to have enough sizes and styles of the new clothing lines to attract customers. Without a good-sized inventory, sales will suffer. The goods it buys are *planned* inventory, based on expected sales. But come February, the store wants to have as few fall clothes left unsold as possible. Goods that have not been sold at this stage are *unplanned* inventory. They are a sign that sales were not as good as expected and that too much was purchased last year.

Both types of inventories—planned and unplanned—are called investment. But only planned investment—capital purchases plus planned inventories—is combined with planned consumer, government, and foreign-sector spending to determine the equilibrium level of aggregate expenditures, as we will see in the next chapter. Unplanned investment and unwanted inventories do not affect the equilibrium. They are simply the leftovers of what has recently gone on in the economy. What economists are interested in are the determinants of planned investment.

2.b.1. The Interest Rate Business investment is made in the hopes of earning profits. The greater the expected profit, the greater the investment. A primary determinant of whether an investment opportunity will be profitable is the rate of interest. The interest rate is the cost of borrowed funds. Much of business

3 | What are the determinants of investment?

spending is financed by borrowing. As the rate of interest goes up, fewer investment projects offer enough profit to warrant undertaking them. In other words, the higher the interest rate, the lower the rate of investment. As the interest rate falls, opportunities for greater profits increase and investment rises.

Let's look at a simple example. A firm can acquire a machine for $100 that will yield $120 in output. Whether the firm is willing to undertake the investment depends on whether it will earn a sufficient return on its investment. The return on an investment is the profit from the investment divided by its cost.

If the firm has to borrow $100 to make the investment, it will have to pay interest to the lender. Suppose the lender charges 10 percent interest. The firm will have to pay 10 percent of $100, or $10, interest. This raises the cost of the investment to $110, the $100 cost of the machine plus the $10 interest. The firm's return on the investment is 9 percent:

$$\text{Return on investment} = (\$120 - \$110)/\$110$$

$$= .09$$

As the interest rate rises, the firm's cost of borrowing also rises, and the return on investment falls. When the interest rate is 20 percent, the firm must pay $20 in interest, so the total cost of the investment is $120. Here the return is 0 ([$120 − $120]/$120). The higher interest rate reduces the return on the investment and discourages investment spending.

As the interest rate falls, the firm's cost of borrowing falls and the return on the investment rises. If the interest rate is 5 percent, the firm must pay $5 in interest. The total cost of the investment is $105, and the return is 14 percent ([$120 − $105]/$105). The lower interest rate increases the return on the investment and encourages investment spending.

2.b.2. Profit Expectations

Firms undertake investment in the expectation of earning a profit. Obviously, they cannot know exactly how much profit they will earn. So they use forecasts of revenues and costs to decide on an appropriate level of investment. It is their *expected* rate of return that actually determines their level of investment.

Many factors affect expectations of profit and, therefore, change the level of investment. Among them are new firms entering the market; political change; new laws, taxes, or subsidies from government; and the overall economic health of the country or the world as measured by gross domestic product.

2.b.3. Other Determinants of Investment

Everything that might affect a firm's expected rate of return determines its level of investment. But three factors—technological change, the cost of capital goods, and capacity utilization—warrant special attention.

Technological Change Technological change is often a driving force behind new investment. New products or processes can be crucial to remaining competitive in an industry. The computer industry, for example, is driven by technological change. As faster and larger-capacity memory chips are developed, computer manufacturers must utilize them in order to stay competitive.

The impact of technology on investment spending is not new. For example, the invention of the cotton gin stimulated investment spending in the early 1800s, and the introduction of the gasoline-powered tractor in 1905 created an agricultural investment boom in the early 1900s. More recently, the development of integrated circuits stimulated investment spending in the electronics industry.

One measure of the importance of technology is the commitment to research and development. Data on spending for research and development across countries are listed in Table 3. The data indicate that rich countries tend to spend a

| TABLE 3 | Research and Development Expenditures as a Percentage of GDP, 2008 |

	% of GDP	% Government Financed	Researchers per 1,000 Workers
Australia	1.8	44.4	8.4
Canada	2.0	34.5	7.8
Finland	3.5	25.7	16.6
France	2.1	38.4	8.2
Germany	2.5	31.1	7.2
Italy	1.1	50.8	3.4
Japan	3.3	17.7	11.0
Mexico	0.5	59.1	1.2
Poland	0.6	62.7	4.5
Turkey	0.8	50.6	1.9
United Kingdom	1.8	31.3	5.9
United States	2.6	31.2	9.7

Source: Data from *OECD Factbook*, OECD, 2008.

greater percentage of GDP on research and development, rely less on government financing of research and development, and have a greater fraction of the workforce employed in research positions.

A commitment to research and development is a sign of the technological progress that marks the industrial nations. The industrial nations are the countries in which new technology generally originates. New technology developed in any country tends to stimulate investment spending across all nations, as firms in similar industries are forced to adopt new production methods to keep up with their competition.

Cost of Capital Goods The cost of capital goods also affects investment spending. As capital goods become more expensive, the rate of return on investment in them drops and the amount of investment falls. One factor that can cause the cost of capital goods to change sharply is government tax policy. The U.S. government has enacted and then removed investment tax credits several times in the past. These credits allow firms to deduct part of the cost of investment from their tax bill. When the cost of investment drops, investment increases. When the cost of investment increases, the level of investment falls.

Capacity Utilization If its existing capital stock is being used heavily, a firm has an incentive to buy more. But if much of its capital stock is standing idle, the firm has little incentive to increase that stock. Economists sometimes refer to the productive capacity of the economy as the amount of output that can be produced by businesses. In fact, the Federal Reserve constructs a measure of capacity utilization that indicates how close the economy is to capacity output.

Figure 7 plots the rate of capacity utilization in the U.S. economy. Between 1975 and 2009, U.S. industry operated at a high rate of 85 percent of capacity in 1979 and at a low rate of 73.9 percent of capacity in the recession year of 1982. We never expect to see 100 percent of capacity utilized for the same reasons that we never expect to see zero unemployment. There are always capital goods that are temporarily unused, just as there is frictional unemployment of labor,

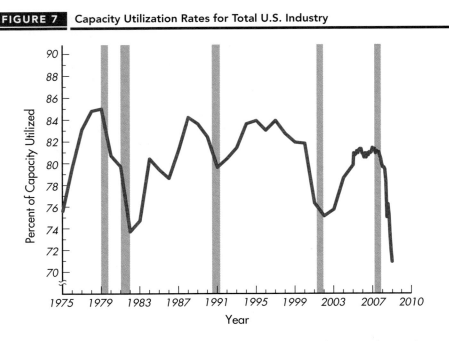

| FIGURE 7 | Capacity Utilization Rates for Total U.S. Industry |

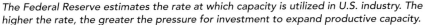

The Federal Reserve estimates the rate at which capacity is utilized in U.S. industry. The higher the rate, the greater the pressure for investment to expand productive capacity.

and there are always capital goods that are obsolete because of technological change, similar to the case of structural unemployment of labor.

When the economy is utilizing its capacity at a high rate, there is pressure to increase the production of capital goods and expand productive capacity. When capacity utilization is low—when factories and machines are sitting idle—investment tends to fall.

2.c. Volatility

We said that investment is the most variable component of total spending. What role do the determinants of investment play in that volatility?

Interest rates fluctuate widely. They are much more variable than income. Interest rates are a very important determinant of investment. Clearly the fact that they are so variable contributes to the variability of investment.

Expectations are subjective judgments about the future. Expectations can and often do change suddenly with new information. A rumor of a technological breakthrough, a speech by the president or a powerful member of Congress, even a revised weather forecast can cause firms to reexamine their thinking about the expected profitability of an investment. In developing economies, the protection of private property rights can have a large impact on investment spending. If a business expects a change in government policy to increase the likelihood of the government's expropriating its property, obviously it is not going to undertake new investments. Conversely, if a firm believes that the government will protect private property and encourage the accumulation of wealth, it will increase its investment spending. The fact that expectations are subject to large and frequent swings contributes to the volatility of investment.

Technological change proceeds very unevenly, making it difficult to forecast. Historically we find large increases in investment when a new technology is first developed and decreases in investment once the new technology is in place. This causes investment to move up and down unevenly through time.

Changes in tax policy occur infrequently, but they can create large incentives to invest or not to invest. Tax laws in the United States have swung back and forth on whether to offer an investment tax credit. A credit was first introduced in 1962. It was repealed in 1969, then readopted in 1971, and later revised in 1975, 1976, and 1981. In 1986, the investment tax credit was repealed again. Each of these changes had an impact on the cost of capital goods and contributed to the volatility of investment.

Finally, investment generally rises and falls with the rate of capacity utilization over the business cycle. As capacity utilization rises, some firms must add more factories and machines in order to continue increasing their output and avoid reaching their maximum output level. As capacity utilization fluctuates, so will investment.

RECAP

1. As a function of real GDP, autonomous investment is drawn as a horizontal line.

2. The primary determinants of investment are the interest rate and profit expectations. Technological change, the cost of capital goods, and the rate of capacity utilization have an enormous impact on those expectations.

3. Investment fluctuates widely over the business cycle because the determinants of investment are so variable.

---

4 | What are the determinants of government spending?

■ 3. Government Spending

Government spending on goods and services is the second largest component of aggregate expenditures in the United States. In later chapters, we examine the behavior of government in detail. Here we focus on how the government sector fits into the aggregate expenditures–income relationship. We assume that government spending is set by government authorities at whatever level they choose, independent of current income. In other words, we assume that government spending, like investment, is autonomous.

Figure 8 depicts government expenditures as a function of real GDP. The function, labeled G, is a horizontal line. If government officials increase government expenditures, the function shifts upward, parallel to the original curve, by an amount equal to the increase in expenditures (for example, from G to G_1). If government expenditures are reduced, the function shifts downward by an amount equal to the drop in expenditures (for example, from G to G_2).

5 | What are the determinants of net exports?

■ 4. Net Exports

The last component of aggregate expenditures is net exports, or spending by the international sector. Net exports equal a country's exports of goods and services (what it sells to the rest of the world) minus its imports of goods and services (what it buys from the rest of the world). When net exports are positive, there is a surplus in the merchandise and services accounts. When net exports are negative, there is a deficit. The United States has had a net exports deficit

FIGURE 8   Government Expenditures as a Function of Real GDP

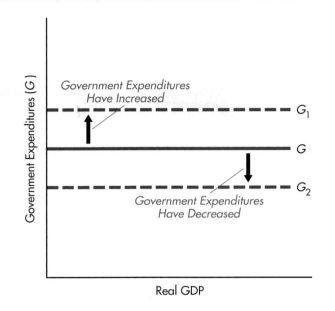

Government spending is assumed to be autonomous and set by government policy. The government spending function is the horizontal line labeled G. Autonomous increases in government spending move the function upward (for example, from G to G₁); decreases move the function downward (for example, from G to G₂).

since 1975. This is a relatively new phenomenon; the country had run surpluses throughout the post–World War II era until that time.

4.a. Exports

We assume that exports are autonomous. There are many factors that determine the actual value of exports, among them foreign income, tastes, prices, government trade restrictions, and exchange rates. But we assume that exports are not affected by current domestic income. You see this in the second column of Table 4, where exports are $50 at each level of real GDP.

TABLE 4   Hypothetical Export and Import Schedule

Real GDP	Exports	Imports	Net Exports
$0	$50	$0	$50
$100	$50	$10	$40
$200	$50	$20	$30
$300	$50	$30	$20
$400	$50	$40	$10
$500	$50	$50	$0
$600	$50	$60	−$10
$700	$50	$70	−$20

As foreign income increases, foreign consumption rises—including consumption of goods produced in other countries—so domestic exports increase at every level of domestic real GDP. Decreases in foreign income lower domestic exports at every level of domestic real GDP. Similarly, changes in tastes or government restrictions on international trade or exchange rates can cause the level of exports to shift autonomously. When tastes favor domestic goods, exports go up. When tastes change, exports go down. When foreign governments impose restrictions on international trade, domestic exports fall. When restrictions are lowered, exports rise. Finally, as discussed in the chapter titled "An Introduction to the Foreign Exchange Market and the Balance of Payments," when the domestic currency depreciates on the foreign exchange market, making domestic goods cheaper in foreign countries, exports rise. When the domestic currency appreciates on the foreign exchange market, making domestic goods more expensive in foreign countries, exports fall.

4.b. Imports

Domestic purchases from the rest of the world (imports) are also determined by tastes, trade restrictions, and exchange rates. Here domestic income plays a role, too. The greater domestic real GDP, the greater domestic imports. The import data in Table 4 show imports increasing with real GDP. When real GDP is 0, autonomous imports equal $0. As real GDP increases, imports increase.

We measure the sensitivity of changes in imports to changes in real GDP by the marginal propensity to import. The **marginal propensity to import (*MPI*)** is the proportion of any extra income spent on imports:

marginal propensity to import (*MPI*): the change in imports as a proportion of the change in income

$$MPI = \frac{\text{change in import}}{\text{change in income}}$$

In Table 4, the *MPI* is .10, or 10 percent. Every time income changes by $100, imports change by $10.

How do other factors—tastes, government trade restrictions, and exchange rates—affect imports? When domestic tastes favor foreign goods, imports rise. When they do not, imports fall. When the domestic government tightens restrictions on international trade, imports fall. When those restrictions are loosened, imports rise. Finally, when the domestic currency depreciates on the foreign exchange market, making foreign goods more expensive to domestic residents, imports fall. And when the domestic currency appreciates on the foreign exchange market, lowering the price of foreign goods, imports rise.

4.c. The Net Export Function

The higher domestic income is, the lower net exports are.

In our hypothetical economy in Table 4, net exports are listed in the last column. They are the difference between exports and imports. Because imports rise with domestic income, the higher that income is, the lower net exports are.

The net exports function, labeled *X*, is shown in Figure 9. The downward slope of the function (given by the *MPI*) indicates that net exports fall as real GDP increases. Net exports are the only component of aggregate expenditures that can take on a negative value (saving can be negative, but it is not part of spending). Negative net exports mean that the domestic economy is importing more than it exports. The net exports function shifts with changes in foreign income, prices, tastes, government trade restrictions, and exchange rates. For example, as foreign income increases, domestic exports increase and the net exports function shifts upward.

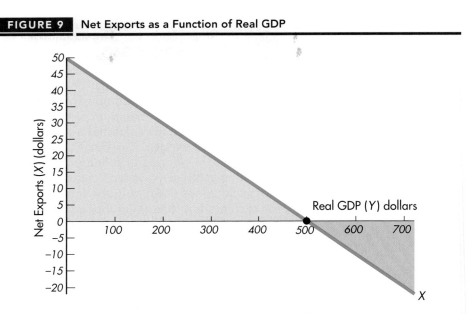

FIGURE 9   Net Exports as a Function of Real GDP

The net exports function is the downward-sloping line labeled X. Because exports are autonomous and imports increase with income, net exports fall as domestic real GDP rises. Notice that net exports can be positive or negative.

RECAP

1. Net exports equal a country's exports minus its imports.

2. Exports are determined by foreign income, tastes, government trade restrictions, and exchange rates; they are independent of domestic real GDP.

3. Imports are a positive function of domestic real GDP; they also depend on tastes, domestic government trade restrictions, and exchange rates.

4. The marginal propensity to import measures the change in imports as a proportion of the change in domestic income.

5. Net exports fall as domestic real GDP rises.

■ 5. The Aggregate Expenditures Function

The aggregate, or total, expenditures function is the sum of the individual functions for each component of planned spending. Aggregate expenditures (AE) equal consumption (C), plus investment (I), plus government spending (G), plus net exports (X):

$$AE = C + I + G + X$$

5.a. Aggregate Expenditures Table and Function

6 | What is the aggregate expenditures function?

The table in Figure 10 lists aggregate expenditures data for a hypothetical economy. Real GDP is in the first column; the individual components of aggregate

FIGURE 10	The Aggregate Expenditures Function

(1) Y	(2) C	(3) I	(4) G	(5) X	(6) AE
$0	$30	$50	$70	$50	$200
$100	$100	$50	$70	$40	$260
$200	$170	$50	$70	$30	$320
$300	$240	$50	$70	$20	$380
$400	$310	$50	$70	$10	$440
$500	$380	$50	$70	$0	$500
$600	$450	$50	$70	−$10	$560
$700	$520	$50	$70	−$20	$620

To find the aggregate expenditures function, we begin with the consumption function (labeled C) and add the investment function (I), to create the C + I function. We then add the government spending function (G) to find the C + I + G function. Notice that the C, C + I, and C + I + G functions are all parallel. They have the same slope because investment and government spending are assumed to be autonomous. Because I and G do not change with income, the slope of the C + I and C + I + G functions is equal to the slope of the consumption function (the MPC). Net exports are added to the C + I + G function to find the aggregate expenditures function, C + I + G + X. The aggregate expenditures function has a smaller slope than the other functions because the slope of the net exports function is negative.

expenditures are in columns 2 through 5. Aggregate expenditures, listed in column 6, are the sum of the components at each level of income.

The aggregate expenditures function (AE) can be derived graphically by summing the individual expenditure functions (Figure 10) in a vertical direction. We begin with the consumption function (C) and then add autonomous investment,

$50, to the consumption function at every level of income to arrive at the $C + I$ function. To this we add constant government spending, $70, at every level of income to find the $C + I + G$ function. Finally, we add the net exports function to find $C + I + G + X$, or the AE function.

Notice that the C, $C + I$, and $C + I + G$ functions are all parallel. They all have the same slope, which is determined by the MPC. This is because I and G are autonomous. The AE function has a smaller slope than the other functions because the slope of the net exports function is negative. By adding the X function to the $C + I + G$ function, we are decreasing the slope of the AE function; the $C + I + G + X$ function has a smaller, flatter slope than the $C + I + G$ function.

The X function increases spending for levels of real GDP below $500 and decreases spending for levels of real GDP above $500. At $500, net exports equal 0 (see column 5). Because domestic imports increase as domestic income increases, net exports fall as income rises. At incomes above $500, net exports are negative, so aggregate expenditures are less than $C + I + G$.

5.b. The Next Step

Though we have also been using *aggregate demand* to refer to total spending, you can see from Figure 10 that the aggregate expenditures line slopes up, whereas the aggregate demand curve you saw in Figure 1 slopes down. In the next chapter we will explore the formal relationship between these two related concepts, when we go about determining the equilibrium level of real GDP using the AE function.

The concept of macroeconomic equilibrium points out the key role that aggregate expenditures play in determining output and income. As you will see, the equilibrium level of real GDP is that level toward which the economy automatically tends to move. Once that equilibrium is established, there is no tendency for real GDP to change unless a change in autonomous expenditures occurs. If aggregate expenditures rise, then the equilibrium level of real GDP rises. If aggregate expenditures fall, then the equilibrium level of real GDP falls. Such shifts in the AE function are associated with shifts in C, I, G, or X.

RECAP

1. Aggregate expenditures are the sum of planned consumption, planned investment, planned government spending, and planned net exports at every level of real GDP.

2. Assuming that I and G are autonomous, the C, $C + I$, and $C + I + G$ functions are parallel lines.

3. Net exports increase aggregate expenditures at relatively low levels of domestic real GDP and decrease aggregate expenditures at relatively high levels of domestic real GDP.

SUMMARY

1 | How are consumption and saving related?

• Consumption and saving are the components of disposable income; they are determined by the same variables. §1

• Dissaving occurs when consumption exceeds income. §1.b

• The marginal propensity to consume (MPC) is change in consumption divided by change in disposable income; the marginal propensity to save (MPS) is change in saving divided by change in disposable income. §1.c

- The average propensity to consume (APC) is consumption divided by disposable income; the average propensity to save (APS) is saving divided by disposable income. *§1.d*

2 **What are the determinants of consumption?**

- The determinants of consumption are income, wealth, expectations, demographics, and taxation. *§1.e.1, 1.e.2, 1.e.3, 1.e.4*

3 **What are the determinants of investment?**

- Investment is assumed to be autonomous, independent of current income. *§2.a*
- The determinants of investment are the interest rate, profit expectations, technological change, the cost of capital goods, and the rate at which capacity is utilized. *§2.b.1, 2.b.2, 2.b.3*
- Firms use the expected return on investment to determine the expected profitability of an investment project. *§2.b.1*
- Investment is highly variable over the business cycle because the determinants of investment are themselves so variable. *§2.c*

4 **What are the determinants of government spending?**

- Government spending is set by government authorities at whatever level they choose. *§3*

5 **What are the determinants of net exports?**

- Net exports are the difference between what a country exports and what it imports; both exports and imports are a product of foreign or domestic income, tastes, foreign and domestic government trade restrictions, and exchange rates. *§4.a, 4.b*
- Because imports rise with domestic income, the higher that income is, the lower net exports are. *§4.c*

6 **What is the aggregate expenditures function?**

- The aggregate expenditures function is the sum of the individual functions for each component of spending. *§5*
- The slope of the aggregate expenditures function is flatter than that of the consumption function because it includes the net exports function, which has a negative slope. *§5.a*

KEY TERMS

consumption function *§1.b*

saving function *§1.b*

dissaving *§1.b*

autonomous consumption *§1.b*

marginal propensity to consume (MPC) *§1.c*

marginal propensity to save (MPS) *§1.c*

average propensity to consume (APC) *§1.d*

average propensity to save (APS) *§1.d*

wealth *§1.e.2*

marginal propensity to import (MPI) *§4.b*

EXERCISES

1. Why do we study the consumption and saving functions together?

2. Explain the difference between a flow variable and a stock variable. Classify each of the following as a stock or a flow: income, wealth, saving, savings, consumption, investment, government expenditures, net exports, GDP.

3. Fill in the blanks in the following table:

Income	Consumption	Saving	MPC	MPS	APC	APS
$1,000	$400					.60
$2,000	$900	$1,100				
$3,000	$1,400			.50		
$4,000		$2,100				

4. Why is consumption so much more stable over the business cycle than investment? In formulating your answer, discuss household behavior as well as business behavior.

5. Assuming investment is autonomous, draw an investment function with income on the horizontal axis. Show how the function shifts if:
   a. The interest rate falls.
   b. An investment tax credit is repealed by Congress.
   c. A new president is expected to be a strong advocate of probusiness policies.
   d. There is a great deal of excess capacity in the economy.

6. Use the following table to answer these questions:

Y	C	I	G	X
$500	$500	$10	$20	$60
$600	$590	$10	$20	$40
$700	$680	$10	$20	$20
$800	$770	$10	$20	$0
$900	$860	$10	$20	−$20
$1,000	$950	$10	$20	−$40

   a. What is the MPC?
   b. What is the MPS?
   c. What is the MPI?
   d. What is the level of aggregate expenditures at each level of income?
   e. Graph the aggregate expenditures function.

7. Based on the table in exercise 6, what is the linear equation for each of the following functions?
   a. Consumption
   b. Investment
   c. Net exports
   d. Aggregate expenditures

8. Is the AE function the same thing as a demand curve? Why or why not?

9. What is the level of saving if:
   a. Disposable income is $500 and consumption is $450?
   b. Disposable income is $1,200 and the APS is .9?
   c. The MPC equals .9, disposable income rises from $800 to $900, and saving is originally $120 when income equals $800?

10. What is the marginal propensity to consume if:
    a. Consumption increases by $75 when disposable income rises by $100?
    b. Consumption falls by $50 when disposable income falls by $100?
    c. Saving equals $20 when disposable income equals $100 and saving equals $40 when disposable income equals $300?

11. How can the APC fall as income rises if the MPC is constant?

12. Why would economies with older populations tend to have consumption functions with greater slopes?

13. Draw a diagram and illustrate the effects of the following on the net exports function for the United States:
    a. The French government imposes restrictions on French imports of U.S. goods.
    b. The U.S. national income rises.
    c. Foreign income falls.
    d. The dollar depreciates on the foreign exchange market.

14. Why is the slope of the $C + I + G$ function different from the slope of the $C + I + G + X$ function?

15. Suppose the consumption function is $C = \$200 + 0.8\,Y$.
    a. What is the amount of autonomous consumption?
    b. What is the marginal propensity to consume?
    c. What would consumption equal when real GDP equals $1,000?

16. Explain why the consumption function is flatter in the short run than in the long run. Draw a diagram to illustrate your answer.

You can find further practice tests in the Online Quiz at **www.cengage.com/economics/boyes**.

2008 Trade Gap Is $681.1 Billion

Bureau of Economic Analysis **March 13, 2009**

The U.S. goods and services deficit decreased in 2008, according to the U.S. Bureau of Economic Analysis and the U.S. Census Bureau. The deficit decreased from $700.3 billion in 2007 to $681.1 billion in 2008, as exports increased more than imports. As a percentage of U.S. gross domestic product, the goods and services deficit was 4.8 percent in 2008, down from 5.1 percent in 2007.

Exports

Exports of goods and services increased $190.1 billion in 2008 to $1,835.8 billion. Goods exports increased $142.9 billion, and services exports increased $47.2 billion.

- The largest increases in goods exports were in *industrial supplies and materials* ($14.9 billion), which includes items such as business, professional, and technical services, insurance and financial services, and *travel* ($13.8 billion).

Imports

Imports of goods and services increased $170.9 billion in 2008 to $2,516.9 billion. Goods imports increased $144.3 billion, and services imports increased $26.6 billion.

- The largest increase in goods imports was in *industrial supplies and materials* ($140.7 billion). A decrease in *automotive vehicles, parts, and engines* ($25.4 billion) was partly offsetting.

- The largest increases in services imports were in *other private services* ($8.7 billion) and *other transportation* ($4.8 billion), which includes freight and port services.

Goods by Geographic Area

- The goods deficit with Canada increased from $68.2 billion in 2007 to $74.2 billion in 2008. Exports increased $12.5 billion to $261.4 billion, while imports increased $18.5 billion to $335.6 billion.

- The goods deficit with China increased from $256.2 billion in 2007 to $266.3 billion in 2008. Exports increased $6.2 billion to $72.5 billion, while imports increased $16.3 billion to $337.8 billion.

- The goods deficit with the European Union decreased from $107.2 billion in 2007 to $93.4 billion in 2008. Exports increased $27.3 billion to $274.5 billion, while imports increased $13.5 billion to $367.9 billion.

Source: U.S. Department of Commerce.

Commentary

In this chapter, we saw how net exports contribute to aggregate expenditures. Merchandise exports bring money from the rest of the world, and higher net exports mean greater aggregate expenditures. Merchandise imports involve outflows of money to foreign countries, and lower net exports mean lower aggregate expenditures.

We saw in the chapter that higher domestic real GDP leads to higher imports and lower net exports. This article points out that the U.S. net export deficit fell in 2008, a year of recession. As U.S. incomes fell, U.S. demand for foreign goods fell and the deficit with the rest of the world shrank. However, in a time of falling incomes, international trade deficits become more politically sensitive than in good times. Because of the effect of net exports on aggregate expenditures, we often hear arguments for policies aimed at increasing exports and decreasing imports. Domestic residents are often resentful of foreign producers and blame foreign competitors for job losses in the home country. However, we must consider the circumstances and then ask if a policy aimed at increasing the national trade surplus (or decreasing the deficit) is really desirable.

Since one country's export is another's import, it is impossible for everyone to have a surplus—on a worldwide basis, the total value of exports equals the total value of imports. If someone must always have a trade deficit when others have trade surpluses, is it necessarily true that surpluses are good and deficits bad so that one country is benefiting at another's expense? In a sense, imports should be preferred to exports, since exports represent goods that are no longer available for domestic consumption and will be consumed by foreign importers. In later chapters you will learn that the benefits of free international trade include more efficient production and increased consumption. Furthermore, if trade among nations is voluntary, it is difficult to argue that deficit countries are harmed while surplus countries benefit from trade.

In general, it is not obvious whether a country is better or worse off running merchandise surpluses rather than deficits. Consider the following simple example of a world with two countries, R and P. Country R is a rich creditor country that is growing rapidly and has a net exports deficit. Country P is a poor debtor country that is growing slowly and has positive net exports. Should we prefer living conditions in P to living conditions in R based solely on the knowledge that P has a net exports surplus and R has a net exports deficit? Although this is indeed a simplistic example, there are real-world analogues of rich creditor countries with international trade deficits and poor debtor nations with international trade surpluses. The point is that you cannot analyze the balance of payments apart from other economic considerations. Deficits are not inherently bad, nor are surpluses necessarily good.

An Algebraic Model of Aggregate Expenditures

Aggregate expenditures (AE) equal consumption (C) plus investment (I) plus government spending (G) plus net exports (X). If we can develop an equation for each component of spending, we can put them together in a single model.

Consumption The consumption function can be written in general form as

$$C = C^a + cYd$$

where C^a is autonomous consumption and c is the MPC. The consumption function for the data in the chapter titled "Aggregate Expenditures" is

$$C = \$30 + .70\,Yd$$

as shown in Figure 1.

Saving The corresponding saving function is

$$S = -\$30 + .30\,Yd$$

as illustrated in Figure 2.

Investment Investment is autonomous at I^a, which is equal to $50.

Government Spending Government spending is autonomous at G^a, which is equal to $70.

Net Exports Exports are autonomous at EX^a and are equal to $50. Imports are given by the function

$$IM = IM^a = im\,Y$$

FIGURE 1   The Consumption Function

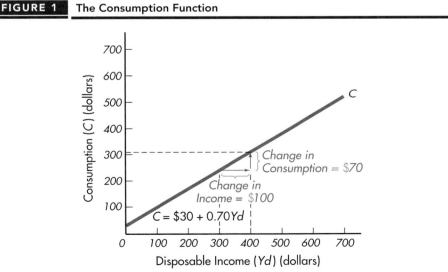

Change in Consumption = $70

Change in Income = $100

$C = \$30 + 0.70Yd$

Consumption (C) (dollars)

Disposable Income (Yd) (dollars)

FIGURE 2   The Saving Function

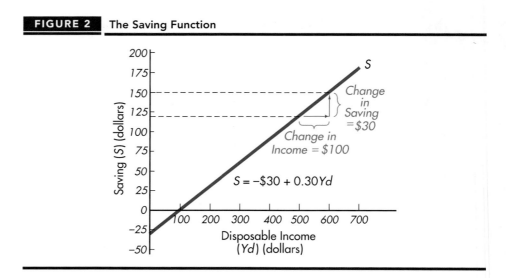

where *im* is the *MPI.* Here, then,

$$IM = \$0 + .10Y$$

Net exports equal exports minus imports, or

$$X = \$50 - \$0 - .10Y$$
$$= \$50 - .10Y$$

as shown in Figure 3.

Aggregate Expenditures Summing the functions for the four components (and ignoring taxes, so that *Yd* equals *Y*) gives

$$AE = C^a + cY + I^a + G^a + EX^a - IM^a - imY$$
$$= \$30 + .70Y + \$50 + \$70 + \$50 - \$0 - .10Y$$
$$= \$200 + .60Y$$

as shown in Figure 4.

FIGURE 3   The Net Exports Function

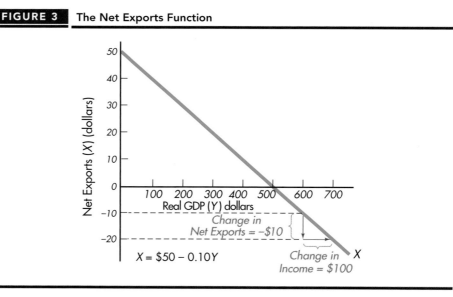

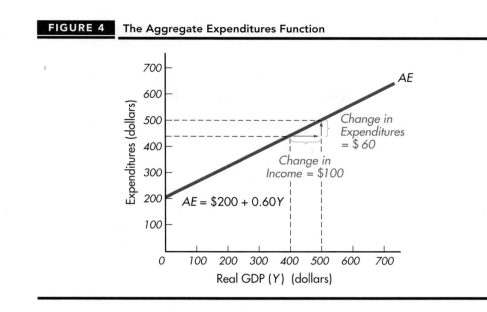

FIGURE 4 The Aggregate Expenditures Function

In the Appendix to Chapter 10, we use the algebraic model of aggregate expenditures presented here to solve for the equilibrium level of real GDP.

Chapter 10

Income and Expenditures Equilibrium

 Fundamental Questions

1 | What does equilibrium mean in macroeconomics?

2 | How do aggregate expenditures affect income, or real GDP?

3 | What are the leakages from and injectins into spending?

4 | Why does equilibrium real GDP change by a multiple of a change in autonomous expenditures?

5 | What is the spending multiplier?

6 | What is the relationship between the GDP gap and the recessionary gap?

7 | How does international trade affect the size of the multiplier?

8 | Why does the aggregate expenditures curve shift with changes in the price level?

What determines the level of income and expenditures, or real GDP? In the chapter titled "Macroeconomic Equilibrium: Aggregate Demand and Supply," we used aggregate demand and aggregate supply to answer this question. Then, in the chapter titled "Aggregate Expenditures," we developed the components of aggregate expenditures in more detail to provide the foundation for an additional approach to answering the question "What determines the level of real GDP?" If you know the answer to this question, you are well on your way to understanding business cycles. Sometimes real GDP is growing and jobs are relatively easy to find; at other times real GDP is falling and large numbers of people are out of work. Macroeconomists use several models to analyze the causes of business cycles. Underlying all of these models is the concept of macroeconomic equilibrium.

Equilibrium here means what it did when we talked about supply and demand: a point of balance, a point from which there is no tendency to move. In macroeconomics, equilibrium is the level of income and expenditures that the economy tends to move toward and remain at until autonomous spending changes.

Economists have not always agreed on how an economy reaches equilibrium or on the forces that move an economy from one equilibrium to another. This last issue formed the basis of economic debate during the Great Depression of the 1930s. Before the 1930s, economists generally believed that the economy was always at or moving toward an equilibrium consistent with a high level of employed resources. The British economist John Maynard Keynes did not agree. He believed that an economy can come to rest at a level of real GDP that is too low to provide employment for all those who desire it. He also believed that certain actions are necessary to ensure that the economy rises to a level of real GDP consistent with a high level of employment. In particular, Keynes argued that government must intervene in the economy in a big way (see the Economic Insight "John Maynard Keynes").

To understand the debate that began during the 1930s and continues on various fronts today, it is necessary to understand the Keynesian view of how equilibrium real GDP is determined. This is our focus here. We have seen in the chapter titled "Macroeconomic Equilibrium: Aggregate Demand and Supply" that the aggregate demand and supply model of macroeconomic equilibrium allows the price level to fluctuate as the equilibrium level of real GDP changed. The Keynesian income-expenditures model assumes that the price level is fixed. It emphasizes aggregate expenditures without explicitly considering the supply side of the economy. This is why we considered the components of spending in detail in the chapter titled "Aggregate Expenditures"—to provide a foundation for the analysis in this chapter. The Keynesian model may be viewed as a special fixed-price case of the aggregate demand and aggregate supply model. In later chapters, we examine the relationship between equilibrium and the level of employed resources and the effect of government policy on both of these elements.

Net exports equal exports minus imports. These papayas being washed in Tapapulcha, Mexico, will be shipped to the United States. Once sold to a U.S. importer, the papayas represent Mexican exports and contribute to increased GDP in Mexico by means of higher net exports.

Economic Insight

John Maynard Keynes

John Maynard Keynes (pronounced "canes") is con-sidered by many to be the greatest economist of the twentieth century. His major work, *The General Theory of Employment, Interest, and Money,* had a profound impact on macroeconomics, both thought and policy. Keynes was born in Cambridge, England, on June 5, 1883. He studied economics at Cambridge University, where he became a lecturer in economics in 1908. During World War I, Keynes worked for the British treasury. At the end of the war, he was the treasury's representative at the Versailles Peace Conference. He resigned from the British delegation at the conference to protest the harsh terms being imposed on the de-feated countries. His resignation and the publication of *Economic Consequences of the Peace* (1919) made him an international celebrity.

In 1936, Keynes published *The General Theory.* It was a time of world recession (it has been estimated that around one-quarter of the U.S. labor force was unemployed at the height of the Depression), and policymakers were searching for ways to explain the persistent unemploy-ment. In the book, Keynes suggested that an economy could be at equilibrium at less than potential GDP. More important, he argued that government policy could be altered to end recession. His analysis emphasized aggre-gate expenditures. If private expenditures were not suf-ficient to create equilibrium at potential GDP, government expenditures could be increased to stimulate income and output. This was a startling concept. Most economists of the time believed that government should not take an ac-tive role in the economy. With his *General Theory,* Keynes started a "revolution" in macroeconomics.

1 | What does equilibrium mean in macroeconomics?

■ 1. Equilibrium Income and Expenditures

Equilibrium is a point from which there is no tendency to move. People do not change their behavior when everything is consistent with what they expect. However, when plans and reality do not match, people adjust their behavior to make them match. Determining a nation's equilibrium level of income and expenditures is the process of defining the level of income and expenditures at which plans and reality are the same.

2 | How do aggregate expenditures affect income, or real GDP?

1.a. Expenditures and Income

We use the aggregate expenditures function described at the end of the chapter titled "Aggregate Expenditures" to demonstrate how equilibrium is determined. Keep in mind that the aggregate expenditures function represents *planned* ex-penditures at different levels of income, or real GDP. We focus on planned expenditures because they represent the amount that households, firms, govern-ment, and the foreign sector expect to spend.

Actual expenditures always equal income and output because they reflect changes in inventories. That is, inventories automatically raise or lower invest-ment expenditures so that actual spending equals income, which equals output, which equals real GDP. However, aggregate expenditures (which are planned spending) may not equal real GDP. What happens when planned spending and real GDP are not equal?

When planned spending on goods and services *exceeds* the current value of output, the production of goods and services increases. Because output equals income, the level of real GDP also increases. This is the situation for all income levels below $500 in Figure 1. At these levels, total spending is greater than real GDP, which means that more goods and services are being purchased than are being produced. The only way this can happen is for goods produced in the past to be sold. When planned spending is greater than real GDP, business inventories fall. This change in inventories offsets the excess of planned expenditures over real GDP, so that actual expenditures (including the unplanned change in inventories) equal real GDP. You can see this in column 7 of the table in Figure 1, where the change in inventories offsets the excess of aggregate expenditures over real GDP (the difference between columns 6 and 1).

FIGURE 1	The Equilibrium Level of Real GDP

(1) Real GDP (Y)	(2) Consumption (C)	(3) Investment (I)	(4) Government Spending (G)	(5) Net Exports (X)	(6) Aggregate Expenditures (AE)	(7) Unplanned Change in Inventories	(8) Change in Real GDP
$0	$30	$50	$70	$50	$200	−$200	Increase
$100	$100	$50	$70	$40	$260	−$160	Increase
$200	$170	$50	$70	$30	$320	−$120	Increase
$300	$240	$50	$70	$20	$380	−$80	Increase
$400	$310	$50	$70	$10	$440	−$40	Increase
$500	$380	$50	$70	$0	$500	$0	No change
$600	$450	$50	$70	−$10	$560	$40	Decrease
$700	$520	$50	$70	−$20	$620	$80	Decrease

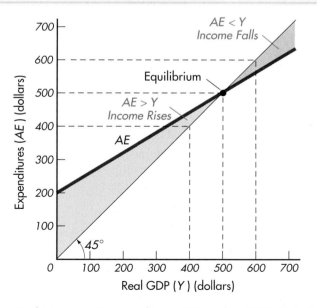

Macroeconomic equilibrium occurs where aggregate expenditures (AE) equal real GDP (Y). In the graph it is the point where the AE line crosses the 45-degree line, where expenditures and real GDP both equal $500. When aggregate expenditures exceed real GDP (as they do at a real GDP level of $400, for example), real GDP rises to the equilibrium level. When aggregate expenditures are less than real GDP (as they are at a real GDP level of $600, for example), real GDP falls back to the equilibrium level.

When aggregate expenditures exceed real GDP, real GDP rises.

What happens when inventories fall? As inventories fall, manufacturers increase production to meet the demand for products. The increased production raises the level of real GDP. *When aggregate expenditures exceed real GDP, real GDP rises.*

At real GDP levels above $500 in the table, aggregate expenditures are less than income. As a result, inventories are accumulating above planned levels—more goods and services are being produced than are being purchased. As inventories rise, businesses begin to reduce the quantity of output they produce. The unplanned increase in inventories is counted as a form of investment spending so that actual expenditures equal real GDP. For example, when real GDP is $600, aggregate expenditures are only $560. The $40 of goods that are produced but not sold are measured as inventory investment. The $560 of aggregate expenditures plus the $40 of unplanned inventories equal $600, the level of real GDP. As inventories increase, firms cut production; this causes real GDP to fall. *When aggregate expenditures are less than real GDP, real GDP falls.*

When aggregate expenditures are less than real GDP, real GDP falls.

There is only one level of real GDP in the table in Figure 1 at which real GDP does not change. When real GDP is $500, aggregate expenditures equal $500. The equilibrium level of real GDP (or output) is that point at which aggregate expenditures equal real GDP (or output).

The equilibrium level of real GDP is where aggregate expenditures equal real GDP.

When aggregate expenditures equal real GDP, planned spending equals the output produced and the income generated from producing that output. As long as planned spending is consistent with real GDP, real GDP does not change. But if planned spending is higher or lower than real GDP, real GDP does change. Equilibrium is that point at which planned spending and real GDP are equal.

The graph in Figure 1 illustrates equilibrium. The 45-degree line shows all possible points where aggregate expenditures (measured on the vertical axis) equal real GDP (measured on the horizontal axis). The equilibrium level of real GDP, then, is simply the point where the aggregate expenditures line (*AE*) crosses the 45-degree line. In the figure, equilibrium occurs where real GDP and expenditures are $500.

When the *AE* curve lies above the 45-degree line—for example, at a real GDP level of $400—aggregate expenditures are greater than real GDP. What happens? Real GDP rises to the equilibrium level, where it tends to stay. When the *AE* curve lies below the 45-degree line—at a real GDP level of $600, for example—aggregate expenditures are less than real GDP; this pushes real GDP down. Once real GDP falls to the equilibrium level ($500 in our example), it tends to stay there.

1.b. Leakages and Injections

3 | What are the leakages from and injections into spending?

Equilibrium can be determined by using aggregate expenditures and real GDP, which represents income. Another way to determine equilibrium involves leakages from and injections into the income stream, the circular flow of income and expenditures.

Leakages reduce autonomous aggregate expenditures. There are three leakages in the stream from domestic income to spending: saving, taxes, and imports.

Saving, taxes, and imports are leakages that reduce autonomous aggregate expenditures.

- The more households save, the less they spend. An increase in autonomous saving means a decrease in autonomous consumption, which could cause the equilibrium level of real GDP to fall (see the Economic Insight "The Paradox of Thrift").

- Taxes are an involuntary reduction in consumption. The government transfers income away from households. Higher taxes lower autonomous consumption, in the process lowering autonomous aggregate expenditures and the equilibrium level of real GDP.

Economic Insight

The Paradox of Thrift

People generally believe that saving is good and more saving is better. However, if every family increased its saving, the result could be less income for the economy as a whole. In fact, increased saving could actually lower savings for all households.

An increase in saving may provide an example of the *paradox of thrift*. A *paradox* is a true proposition that seems to contradict common beliefs. We believe that we will be better off if we increase our saving, but in the aggregate, increased saving could cause the economy to be worse off. The paradox of thrift is a *fallacy of composition:* the assumption that what is true of a part is true of the whole. It often is unsafe to generalize from what true at the micro level to what is true at the macro level.

The graph illustrates the effect of higher saving. Initial equilibrium occurs where the $S_1 + T + IM$ curve intersects the $I + G + EX$ curve, at an income of $500.

Suppose saving increases by $20 at every level of income. The $S_1 + T + IM$ curve shifts up to the $S_2 + T + IM$ curve. A new equilibrium is established at an income level of $400. The higher rate of saving causes equilibrium income to fall by $100.

Notice that the graph is drawn with a constant $I + G + EX$ line. If investment increases along with saving, equilibrium income will not necessarily fall. In fact, because saving is necessary before there can be any investment, we would expect a greater demand for investment funds to induce higher saving. If increased saving is used to fund investment expenditures, the economy should grow over time to higher and higher levels of income. Only if the increased saving is not injected back into the economy is there a paradox of thrift. The fact that governments do not discourage saving suggests that the paradox of thrift generally is not a real-world problem.

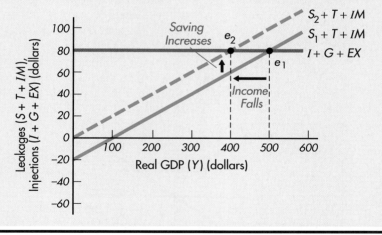

Imports are expenditures for foreign goods and services. They reduce expenditures on domestic goods and services. An autonomous increase in imports reduces net exports, causing autonomous aggregate expenditures and the equilibrium level of real GDP to fall.

For equilibrium to occur, these leakages must be offset by corresponding *injections* of spending into the domestic economy through investment, government spending, and exports.

> **Investment, government spending, and exports are injections that increase autonomous aggregate expenditures.**

Household saving generates funds that businesses can borrow and spend for investment purposes.

• The taxes collected by government are used to finance government purchases of goods and services.

• Exports bring foreign expenditures into the domestic economy.

> The equilibrium level of real GDP occurs where leakages equal injections.

There is no reason to expect that each injection will match its corresponding leakage—that investment will equal saving, that government spending will equal taxes, or that exports will equal imports. But for equilibrium to occur, total injections must equal total leakages.

Figure 2 shows how leakages and injections determine the equilibrium level of real GDP. Column 5 of the table lists the total leakages from aggregate expenditures: saving (S) plus taxes (T) plus imports (IM). Saving and imports both increase when real GDP increases. We assume that there are no taxes, so the total amount of leakages ($S + T + IM$) increases as real GDP increases.

Column 9 lists the injections at alternative income levels. Because investment (I), government spending (G), and exports (EX) are all autonomous, total injections ($I + G + EX$) are constant at all levels of real GDP.

FIGURE 2   Leakages, Injections, and Equilibrium Income

(1) Real GDP (Y)	(2) Saving (S)	(3) Taxes (T)	(4) Imports (IM)	(5) Leakages (S + T + IM)	(6) Investment (I)	(7) Government Spending (G)	(8) Exports (EX)	(9) Injections (I + G + EX)	(10) Change in Real GDP
$0	$30	$0	$0	−$30	$50	$70	$50	$170	Increase
$100	$0	$0	$10	$10	$50	$70	$50	$170	Increase
$200	$30	$0	$20	$50	$50	$70	$50	$170	Increase
$300	$60	$0	$30	$90	$50	$70	$50	$170	Increase
$400	$90	$0	$40	$130	$50	$70	$50	$170	Increase
$500	$120	$0	$50	$170	$50	$70	$50	$170	No change
$600	$150	$0	$60	$210	$50	$70	$50	$170	Decrease
$700	$180	$0	$70	$250	$50	$70	$50	$170	Decrease

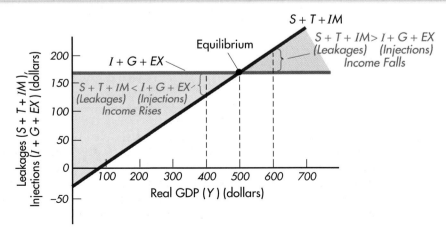

Leakages equal saving (S), taxes (T), and imports (IM). Injections equal investment (I), government spending (G), and exports (EX). Equilibrium is that point where leakages equal injections. In the graph, equilibrium is the point at which the S + T + IM curve intersects the I + G + EX curve, where real GDP (Y) equals $500. At lower levels of income, injections exceed leakages, so Y rises. At higher levels of income, leakages exceed injections, so Y falls.

To determine the equilibrium level of real GDP, we compare leakages with injections. When injections exceed leakages, planned spending is greater than current income or output, so real GDP rises. In the table in Figure 2, this occurs for levels of real GDP under $500, so real GDP increases if it is under $500 (see the last column). When leakages exceed injections, planned spending is less than current real GDP, so real GDP falls. In Figure 2, at all levels of real GDP above $500, real GDP falls. Only when leakages equal injections is the equilibrium level of real GDP established. When real GDP equals $500, both leakages and injections equal $170, so there is no pressure for real GDP to change. The equilibrium level of real GDP occurs where leakages ($S + T + IM$) equal injections ($I + G + EX$).

Figure 2 shows the interaction of leakages and injections graphically. The equilibrium point is where the $S + T + IM$ and $I + G + EX$ curves intersect, at a real GDP level of $500. At higher levels of real GDP, leakages are greater than injections (the $S + T + IM$ curve lies above the $I + G + EX$ curve). When leakages are greater than injections, real GDP falls to the equilibrium point. At lower levels of income, injections are greater than leakages (the $I + G + EX$ curve lies above the $S + T + IM$ curve). Here real GDP rises until it reaches $500. Only at $500 is there no pressure for real GDP to change.

If you compare Figures 1 and 2, you can see that it does not matter whether we use aggregate expenditures or leakages and injections—the equilibrium level of real GDP is the same.

RECAP

1. Equilibrium is a point from which there is no tendency to move.

2. When aggregate expenditures exceed real GDP, real GDP rises.

3. When aggregate expenditures are less than real GDP, real GDP falls.

4. Saving, taxes, and imports are leakages of planned spending from domestic aggregate expenditures.

5. Investment, government spending, and exports are injections of planned spending into domestic aggregate expenditures.

6. Equilibrium occurs at the level of real GDP at which aggregate expenditures equal real GDP, and leakages equal injections.

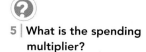

4 | Why does equilibrium real GDP change by a multiple of a change in autonomous expenditures?

■ 2. Changes in Equilibrium Income and Expenditures

Equilibrium is a point from which there is no tendency to move. But in fact, the equilibrium level of real GDP does move. In the last section, we described how aggregate expenditures push real GDP, representing the economy's income and output, up or down toward their level of equilibrium. Here we examine how changes in autonomous expenditures affect equilibrium. This becomes very important in understanding macroeconomic policy, the kinds of things that government can do to control the business cycle.

2.a. The Spending Multiplier

5 | What is the spending multiplier?

Remember that equilibrium is that point where aggregate expenditures equal real GDP. If we increase autonomous expenditures, then we raise the equilibrium level of real GDP. But by how much? It seems logical to expect a one-to-one

Any change in autonomous
expenditures is multiplied
into a larger change in
equilibrium real GDP.

ratio: If autonomous spending increases by a dollar, equilibrium real GDP should increase by a dollar. Actually, equilibrium real GDP increases by *more* than a dollar. The change in autonomous expenditures is *multiplied* into a larger change in the equilibrium level of real GDP.

In the chapter titled "National Income Accounting," we used a circular flow diagram to show the relationship of expenditures to income. In that diagram, we saw how one sector's expenditures become another sector's income. This concept helps explain the effect of a change in autonomous expenditures on the equilibrium level of income or real GDP. If A's autonomous spending increases, then B's income rises. Then B spends part of that income in the domestic economy (the rest is saved or used to buy foreign goods), generating new income for C. In turn, C spends part of that income in the domestic economy, generating new income for D. And the rounds of increased spending and income continue. All of this is the product of A's initial autonomous increase in spending. And each round of increased spending and income affects the equilibrium level of income, or real GDP

Let's look at an example, using Table 1. Suppose government spending goes up $20 to improve public parks. What happens to the equilibrium level of income? The autonomous increase in government spending increases the income of park employees by $20. As the income of the park employees increases, so does their consumption. For example, let's say they spend more money on hamburgers. In the process, they are increasing the income of the hamburger producers, who in turn increase their consumption.

TABLE 1	The Spending Multiplier Effect			
	(1) Change in Income	(2) Change in Domestic Expenditures	(3) Change in Saving	(4) Change in Imports
Round 1	$20.00	$12.00	$6.00	$2.00
Round 2	12.00	7.20	3.60	1.20
Round 3	7.20	4.32	2.16	0.72
Round 4	4.32	2.59	1.30	0.43
	⋮	⋮	⋮	⋮
Totals	$50.00	$30.00	$15.00	$5.00

Column 2 = column 1 × (MPC − MPI)

Column 3 = column 1 × MPS

Column 4 = column 1 × MPI

$$\text{Multiplier} = \frac{1}{MPS + MPI}$$

$$= \frac{1}{(.30 + .10)}$$

$$= \frac{1}{.40}$$

$$= 2.50$$

Table 1 shows how a single change in spending generates further changes. Round 1 is the initial increase in government spending to improve public parks. That $20 expenditure increases the income of park employees by $20 (column 1). As income increases, those components of aggregate expenditures that depend on current income—consumption and net exports—also increase by some fraction of the $20.

Consumption changes by the marginal propensity to consume multiplied by the change in income; imports change by the marginal propensity to import multiplied by the change in income. To find the total effect of the initial change in spending, we must know the fraction of any change in income that is spent in the domestic economy. In the hypothetical economy we have been using, the *MPC* is .70 and the *MPI* is .10. This means that for each $1 of new income, consumption rises by $.70 and imports rise by $.10. Spending on *domestic* goods and services, then, rises by $.60. Because consumption is spending on domestic goods and services, and imports are spending on foreign goods and services, the percentage of a change in income that is spent domestically is the difference between the *MPC* and the *MPI*. If the *MPC* equals .70 and the *MPI* equals .10, then 60 percent of any change in domestic income (*MPC* − *MPI* = .60) is spent on domestic goods and services.

> *The percentage of a change in income that is spent domestically is the difference between the MPC and the MPI.*

In round 1 of Table 1, the initial increase in income of $20 induces an increase in spending on domestic goods and services of $12 (.60 × $20). Out of the $20, $6 is saved, because the marginal propensity to save is .30 (1 − *MPC*). The other $2 is spent on imports (*MPI* = .10). The park employees receive $20 more income. They spend $12 on hamburgers at a local restaurant, they save $6, and they spend $2 on imported coffee.

Only $12 of the workers' new income is spent on goods produced in the domestic economy, hamburgers. That $12 becomes income to the restaurant's employees and owner. When their income increases by $12, they spend 60 percent of that income ($7.20) on domestic goods (round 2, column 2). The rest of the income is saved or spent on imports.

Each time income increases, expenditures increase. But the increase is smaller and smaller in each new round of spending. Why? Because 30 percent of each change in income is saved and another 10 percent is spent on imports. These are leakages out of the income stream. This means that just 60 percent of the change in income is spent and passed on to others in the domestic economy as income in the next round.

To find the total effect of the initial change in spending of $20, we could keep on computing the change in income and spending round after round, and then sum the total of all rounds. The change in income and spending never reaches zero, but it becomes infinitely small.

Fortunately, we do not have to compute the increases in spending round by round to find the total increase. If we know the percentage of additional income that "leaks" from domestic consumption at each round, we can determine the total change in income, or real GDP, by finding its reciprocal. This measure is called the **spending multiplier.** The leakages are that portion of the change in income that is saved (the *MPS*) and that proportion of the change in income that is spent on imports (the *MPI*).

spending multiplier: a measure of the change in equilibrium income or real GDP produced by a change in autonomous expenditures

$$\text{Multiplier} = \frac{1}{\text{leakages}}$$

$$= \frac{1}{MPS + MPI}$$

When the *MPS* is .30 and the *MPI* is .10, the multiplier equals 2.5 (1/.4). An initial change in expenditures of $20 results in a total change in real GDP of $50, 2.5 times the original change in expenditures. The greater the leakages, the smaller the multiplier. When the *MPS* equals .35 and the *MPI* equals .15, the multiplier equals 2 (1/.50). The multiplier is smaller here because less new income is being spent in the domestic economy. The more people save, the smaller the expansionary effect on income of a change in spending. And the more people spend on imports, the smaller the expansionary effect on income of a change in spending. Notice that the multiplier would be larger in a *closed economy*, an economy that does not trade with the rest of the world. In that economy, because the *MPI* equals zero, the spending multiplier is simply equal to the reciprocal of the *MPS*.

2.b. The Spending Multiplier and Equilibrium

6 | **What is the relationship between the GDP gap and the recessionary gap?**

The spending multiplier is an extremely useful concept. It allows us to calculate how a change in autonomous expenditures affects real GDP. To better understand how changes in spending can bring about changes in equilibrium income, or real GDP, let's modify the example we used in Figure 1. In the table in Figure 3, we have increased government spending to $110. The autonomous increase in government spending raises aggregate expenditures by $40 at every level of income. Aggregate expenditures now equal real GDP at $600. The increase in government spending of $40 yields an increase in equilibrium real GDP of $100.

The graph in Figure 3 illustrates the multiplier effect and shows the change in equilibrium income when spending increases by $40. The original aggregate expenditures curve, AE_1, intersects the 45-degree line at a real GDP level of $500. A spending increase of $40 at every level of real GDP creates a new aggregate expenditures curve, AE_2, which lies $40 above the original curve. The curve AE_2 is parallel to AE_1 because the increase is in autonomous spending. The new curve, AE_2, intersects the 45-degree line at an income of $600.

In the chapter titled "Unemployment and Inflation," we introduced the concept of the natural rate of unemployment—the unemployment rate that exists in the absence of cyclical unemployment. When the economy operates at the natural rate of unemployment, the corresponding level of output (and income) is called potential real GDP. However, equilibrium does not necessarily occur at potential real GDP. Equilibrium occurs at any level of real GDP at which planned expenditures equal real GDP. Suppose that equilibrium real GDP is not at the level of potential real GDP and that government policymakers make the achievement of potential real GDP an important goal. In this case, government policy is addressed toward closing the *GDP gap*, the difference between potential real GDP and actual real GDP. The nature of that policy depends on the value of the multiplier.

If we know the size of the GDP gap and we know the size of the spending multiplier, we can determine by how much spending needs to change in order to yield equilibrium at potential real GDP. Remember that the GDP gap equals potential real GDP minus actual real GDP:

$$\text{GDP gap} = \text{potential real GDP} - \text{actual real GDP}$$

When real GDP is less than potential real GDP, the GDP gap is the amount by which GDP must rise to reach its potential. Suppose potential real GDP is $500, but the economy is in equilibrium at $300. The GDP must rise by $200 to reach potential real GDP. How much must spending rise? If we know the size of the spending multiplier, we simply divide the spending multiplier into the GDP

FIGURE 3	A Change in Equilibrium Expenditures and Income

(1) Real GDP (Y)	(2) Consumption (C)	(3) Investment (I)	(4) Government Spending (G)	(5) Net Exports (X)	(6) Aggregate Expenditures (AE)	(7) Unplanned Change in Inventories	(8) Change in Real GDP
$0	$30	$50	$110	$50	$240	−$240	Increase
$100	$100	$50	$110	$40	$300	−$200	Increase
$200	$170	$50	$110	$30	$360	−$160	Increase
$300	$240	$50	$110	$20	$440	−$120	Increase
$400	$310	$50	$110	$10	$480	−$80	Increase
$500	$380	$50	$110	$0	$540	−$40	Increase
$600	$450	$50	$110	−$10	$600	$0	No Change
$700	$520	$50	$110	−$20	$660	$40	Decrease

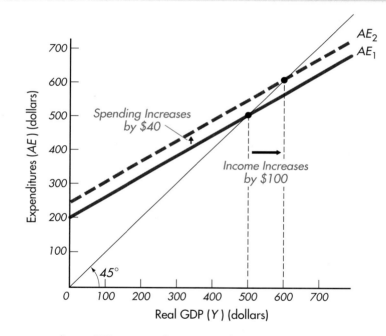

A change in aggregate expenditures (AE) causes a change in equilibrium real GDP (Y). Initially equilibrium is $500, the point at which the AE_1 curve intersects the 45-degree line. If autonomous expenditures increase by $40, the aggregate expenditures curve shifts up to AE_2. The new curve intersects the 45-degree line at a new equilibrium level of real GDP, $600. An increase in autonomous expenditures of $40, then, causes equilibrium real GDP to increase by $100.

recessionary gap: the increase in expenditures required to reach potential GDP

gap to determine how much spending must rise to achieve equilibrium at potential real GDP. This required change in spending is called the **recessionary gap:**

$$\text{Recessionary gap} = \frac{\text{GDP gap}}{\text{spending multiplier}}$$

Figure 4 shows an economy in which equilibrium real GDP (Y_e) is less than potential real GDP (Y_p). The difference between the two—the GDP gap—is $200. It is the *horizontal* distance between equilibrium real GDP and potential real GDP. The amount by which spending must rise in order for real GDP to

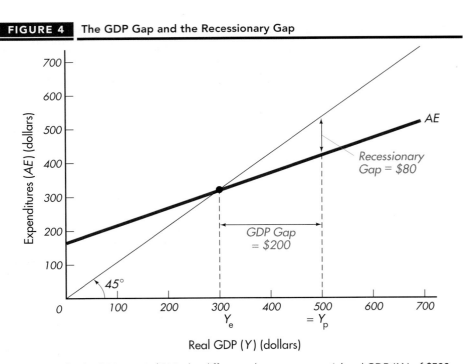

FIGURE 4　The GDP Gap and the Recessionary Gap

In the graph, the GDP gap is $200, the difference between potential real GDP (Y_p) of $500 and equilibrium real GDP (Y_e) of $300. The GDP gap tells us that equilibrium real GDP must rise by $200 to reach equilibrium at the potential level of real GDP. The recessionary gap indicates the amount that autonomous expenditures must rise to close the GDP gap. The recessionary gap is the vertical distance between the 45-degree line and the AE curve at the potential level of real GDP, or $80. If autonomous expenditures are increased by $80, the AE curve will move up, intersecting with the 45-degree line at $500.

reach a new equilibrium level of $500 is measured by the recessionary gap. The recessionary gap is the *vertical* distance between the aggregate expenditures curve and the 45-degree line at the potential real GDP level.

The recessionary gap in Figure 4 is $80:

$$\text{Recessionary gap} = \frac{\$200}{2.5}$$
$$= \$80$$

With a spending multiplier of 2.5, if aggregate expenditures rise by $80, equilibrium income rises by the $200 necessary to close the GDP gap. Government policy may be addressed to closing the gap, as an increase in government expenditures of $80 would move the economy to the potential level of real GDP in this example.

2.c. Real-World Complications

7 | How does international trade affect the size of the multiplier?

Our definition of the spending multiplier,

$$\frac{1}{MPS + MPI}$$

is a simplification of reality. Often other factors besides the *MPS* and *MPI* determine the actual multiplier in an economy. If prices rise when spending increases, the spending multiplier will not be as large as shown here. Also, taxes (which are ignored until the chapter titled "Fiscal Policy") will reduce the size of the multiplier. Another factor is the treatment of imports. We have assumed that whatever is spent on imports is permanently lost to the domestic economy. For a country whose imports are a small fraction of the exports of its trading partners, this is a realistic assumption. But for a country whose imports are very important in determining the volume of exports of the rest of the world, this simple spending multiplier understates the true multiplier effect. To see why, let's examine how U.S. imports affect income in the rest of the world.

2.c.1. Foreign Repercussions of Domestic Imports

When a resident of the United States buys goods from another country, that purchase becomes income to foreign residents. If Mike in Miami buys coral jewelry from Victor in the Dominican Republic, Mike's purchase increases Victor's income. So the import of jewelry into the United States increases income in the Dominican Republic.

Imports purchased by one country can have a large effect on the level of income in other countries. For instance, Canada and Mexico are very dependent on sales to the United States, since about 80 percent of their exports go to the United States. South Africa, on the other hand, sells about 5 percent of its total exports to U.S. buyers. If U.S. imports from South Africa doubled, the effect on total South African exports and income would be small. But if imports from Canada or Mexico doubled, the effect on those countries' exports and income would be substantial.

Imports into the United States play a key role in determining the real GDP of the major U.S. trading partners. This is important because foreign income is a determinant of U.S. exports. As that income rises, U.S. exports rise (see the chapter titled "Aggregate Expenditures"). That is, foreign imports increase with foreign income, and some of those imports come from the United States. And, of course, when foreign spending on U.S. goods increases, national income in the United States rises.

The simple spending multiplier understates the true multiplier effects of increases in autonomous expenditures because of the foreign repercussions of domestic spending. Some spending on imports comes back to the domestic economy in the form of exports. This means that the chain of spending can be different from that assumed in the simple spending multiplier. Figure 5 illustrates the difference.

Figure 5(a) shows the sequence of spending when there are no foreign repercussions from domestic imports. In this case, domestic spending rises, which causes domestic income, or real GDP, to rise. Higher domestic real GDP leads to increased spending on imports as well as further increases in domestic spending, which induce further increases in real GDP, and so on, as the multiplier process works itself out. Notice, however, that the imports are simply a leakage from the spending stream.

In Figure 5(b), the sequence of expenditures includes the foreign repercussions of domestic imports. As before, increases in domestic spending cause domestic income, or real GDP, to rise; this, in turn, leads to more domestic spending as well as greater domestic imports. Now, however, the greater imports increase foreign income, or real GDP, which increases foreign imports of goods produced in the domestic economy. As domestic exports rise, domestic real GDP rises. This is a more realistic view of how spending and income interact to create interdependencies among nations.

The diagrams in Figure 5 show why the multiplier effect is higher with foreign repercussions than without. Rather than complicate the multiplier definition, we continue to use the simple spending multiplier. But remember that (holding prices constant and ignoring taxes) our definition underestimates the true magnitude of the multiplier's effects in open economies. In fact, the foreign repercussions of domestic imports help explain the similarity in business cycles across countries. When the United States is booming, the economies of other countries that depend on exports to the U.S. market also boom. When the United States is in recession, income in these other countries tends to fall.

FIGURE 5   The Sequence of Expenditures

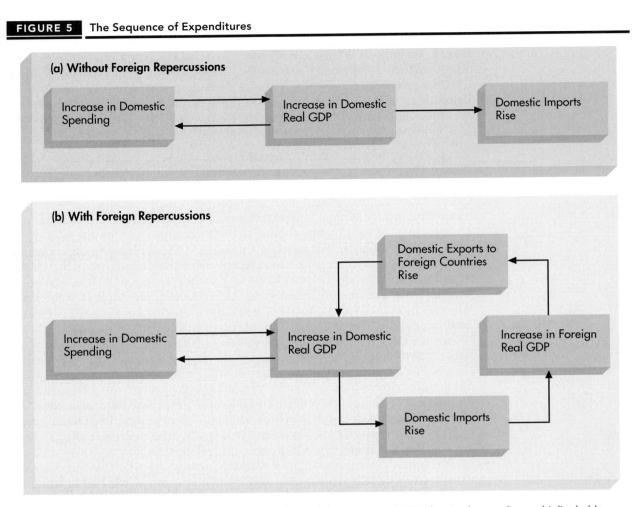

If there are no foreign repercussions from changes in domestic income or real GDP, the simple spending multiplier holds. Increases in domestic spending increase domestic income or real GDP, which causes domestic spending—including spending on foreign goods—to rise further. Here higher expenditures on domestic imports do not have any effect on domestic exports to foreign countries.

If there are foreign repercussions from changes in domestic real GDP, the simple spending multiplier underestimates the actual effect of a change in autonomous expenditures on the equilibrium level of real GDP. As Figure 5(b) shows, increases in domestic spending increase domestic income, or real GDP, which causes domestic spending—including spending on foreign goods—to rise further. Here higher spending on foreign goods causes foreign real GDP to rise, and with it, spending on domestic exports. Higher domestic exports stimulate domestic real GDP further. The actual multiplier effect of an increase in domestic spending, then, is larger than it is when domestic imports have no effect on domestic exports.

2.c.2. Multiplier Estimates Many private and public organizations have developed models that are used to analyze current economic developments and to forecast future ones. A large number of these models include foreign repercussions. From these models, we get a sense of just how much the simple multiplier can vary from the true multiplier.

An increase in U.S. autonomous expenditures has a multiplier of about 0.8. This means that if autonomous government expenditures increased by $25, U.S. equilibrium GDP would be $20 higher after one year. A multiplier less than 1 suggests important "leakages" in the operation of the economy. One such leakage stems from the openness of the U.S. economy. Thus, when there is an expansionary fiscal policy in the United States, the GDP of other countries is increased because some of that spending is on U.S. imports from the rest of the world. Estimates of spending multipliers indicate that the equilibrium level of GDP for the industrial countries taken as a whole increases by 0.4 times the change in U.S. expenditures. For developing countries, the multiplier effect is smaller, at 0.1. So increases in U.S. government spending have a bigger impact on the GDP of other industrial countries than on the GDP of developing countries. Because trade between industrial countries is much larger than the trade between industrial countries and developing countries, it is not surprising that increases in spending in one industrial country, like the United States, have a bigger impact on other industrial countries than on developing countries.

The multiplier examples we use in this chapter show autonomous government spending changing. It is important to realize that the multiplier effects apply to any change in autonomous expenditures in any sector of the economy.

RECAP

1. Any change in autonomous expenditures is multiplied into a larger change in the equilibrium level of real GDP.

2. The multiplier measures the change in equilibrium real GDP produced by a change in autonomous spending.

3. The multiplier equals

$$\frac{1}{\text{Leakages}} = \frac{1}{MPS + MPI}$$

4. The recessionary gap is the amount by which spending must increase in order to achieve equilibrium at potential real GDP. Graphically, it is measured by the vertical distance between the 45-degree line and the aggregate expenditures curve at potential real GDP.

5. The true spending multiplier may differ from the simple spending multiplier [$1/(MPS + MPI)$] because of the foreign repercussions of domestic spending. Price changes and taxes cause the simple spending multiplier to overestimate the true multiplier.

■ 3. Aggregate Expenditures and Aggregate Demand

The approach to macroeconomic equilibrium presented in this chapter focuses on aggregate expenditures and income. It is called the *Keynesian model*. This model of the economy can be very useful in explaining some real-world events, but it suffers from a serious drawback: It assumes that the supply of goods and services in the economy always adjusts to aggregate expenditures, that there is no need for price changes. The Keynesian model is a *fixed-price model*.

In the real world, we find that shortages of goods and services are often met by rising prices, not just increased production. We also find that when supply increases in the face of relatively constant demand, prices may fall. In other words, prices as well as production adjust to differences between demand and supply. We introduced price as a component of macroeconomic equilibrium in Chapter 8 in the aggregate demand and supply model. You may recall that aggregate expenditures represent demand when the price level is constant. This can be demonstrated by using the income and expenditures approach developed in this chapter to derive the aggregate demand curve that was introduced in Chapter 8.

3.a. Aggregate Expenditures and Changing Price Levels

8 | Why does the aggregate expenditures curve shift with changes in the price level?

As discussed in Chapter 8, the *AE* curve will shift with changes in the price level because of the wealth effect, the interest rate effect, and the international trade effect. Wealth is one of the nonincome determinants of consumption. Households hold part of their wealth in financial assets like money and bonds. As the price level falls, the purchasing power of money rises and aggregate expenditures increase. As the price level rises, the purchasing power of money falls and aggregate expenditures fall.

The interest rate is a determinant of investment spending. As the price level changes, interest rates may change as households and business firms change their demand for money. The change in interest rates will then affect investment spending. For instance, when the price level rises, more money is needed to buy any given quantity of goods and services. To acquire more money, households and firms sell their nonmonetary financial assets, like bonds. The increased supply of bonds will tend to raise interest rates to attract buyers. The higher interest rates will tend to lower investment spending and aggregate expenditures. Conversely, a lower price level will tend to be associated with lower interest rates, greater investment spending, and greater aggregate expenditures.

Net exports may change, causing aggregate expenditures to change, when the domestic price level changes. If domestic prices rise while foreign prices and the exchange rate are constant, then domestic goods become more expensive relative to foreign goods, and net exports and aggregate expenditures tend to fall. If domestic prices fall while foreign prices and the exchange rate are constant, then domestic goods become cheaper relative to foreign goods, and net exports and aggregate expenditures tend to rise.

3.b. Deriving the Aggregate Demand Curve

The aggregate demand curve (*AD*) shows how the equilibrium level of expenditures changes as the price level changes. In other words, the curve shows the amount that people spend at different price levels. Let's use the example of Figure 6 to show how aggregate demand is derived from the shifting aggregate expenditures curve (*AE*).

The aggregate demand curve is derived from the *AE* curve. Figure 6(a) shows three *AE* curves, each drawn for a different price level. Suppose that the initial equilibrium occurs at point *A* on curve AE_0 with prices at P_0. At this point, equilibrium real GDP and expenditures are $500. If prices fall to P_1, the *AE* curve shifts up to AE_1. Here equilibrium is at point *C*, where real GDP equals $700. If prices rise from P_0 to P_2, the *AE* curve falls to AE_2. Here equilibrium is at point *B*, where real GDP equals $300.

In Figure 6(b), price level is plotted on the vertical axis and real GDP is plotted on the horizontal axis. A price-level change here means that, on average, all prices in the economy change. The negative slope of the aggregate demand curve results from the effect of changing prices on wealth, interest rates, and international trade. If you move vertically down from points *A*, *B*, and *C* in Figure 6(a), you find corresponding points along the aggregate demand curve in Figure 6(b). The *AD* curve shows all of the combinations of price levels and corresponding equilibrium levels of real GDP and aggregate expenditures.

3.c. A Fixed-Price AD–AS Model

The Keynesian model of fixed-price equilibrium may be considered a special case of the aggregate demand and aggregate supply equilibrium. We can define

| FIGURE 6 | Aggregate Expenditures and Aggregate Demand |

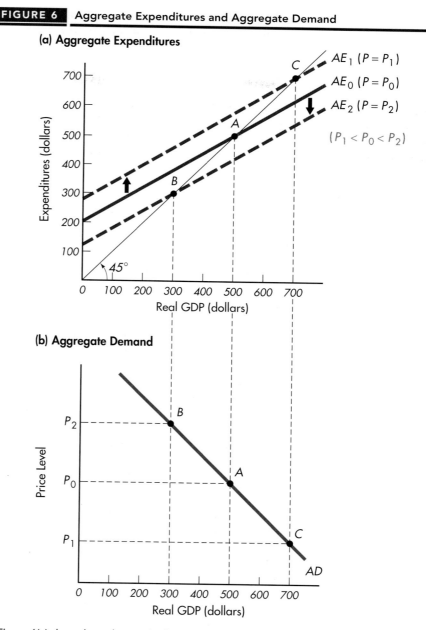

Figure 6(a) shows how changes in the price level cause the AE curve to shift. The initial curve, AE_0, is drawn at the initial level of prices, P_0. On this curve, the equilibrium level of aggregate expenditures (where expenditures equal real GDP) is $500. If the price level falls to P_1, autonomous expenditures increase, shifting the curve up to AE_1, and moving the equilibrium level of aggregate expenditures to $700. If the price level rises to P_2, autonomous expenditures fall, shifting the curve down to AE_2 and moving the equilibrium level of aggregate expenditures to $300.

The aggregate demand curve (AD) in Figure 6(b) is derived from the aggregate expenditures curves. The AD curve shows the equilibrium level of aggregate expenditures at different price levels. At price level P_0, equilibrium aggregate expenditures are $500; at P_1, they are $700; and at P_2, they are $300.

FIGURE 7　A Fixed-Price AD–AS Model

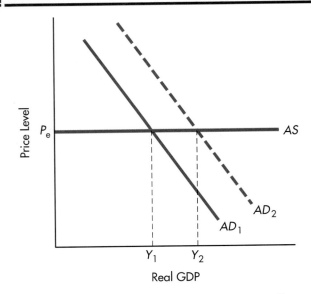

If the AS curve is horizontal, then shifts in the AD curve will have no effect on the equilibrium level of prices but will change the equilibrium level of real GDP.

---

a horizontal segment of the aggregate supply curve as the Keynesian region of the curve. This represents an economy with substantial unemployment and excess capacity, so that real GDP and output may be increased without pressure on the price level. Figure 7 illustrates this case.

> *The Keynesian model is a fixed-price model.*

In Figure 7, the aggregate supply curve is horizontal at price level P_e. Throughout the range of the AS curve, the price level is fixed. Suppose aggregate expenditures increase for some reason other than a price-level change. For instance, consumers could expect their future incomes to rise, so they increase consumption now; or business firms could expect sales to rise in the future, so they increase investment spending now; or government spending rises to improve the national highway system; or foreign prices rise, and so net exports increase. If aggregate expenditures rise as a result of something other than a domestic price-level change, then the aggregate demand curve shifts to the right, like the shift from AD_1 to AD_2 in Figure 7. This increase in AD causes real GDP to rise to Y_2, yet the price level remains fixed at P_e.

Because the fixed-price model of macroeconomic equilibrium requires a horizontal AS curve, many economists believe that this model is too restrictive and not representative of the modern economy. As a result, we will generally see the AD–AS model using upward-sloping AS curves so that price as well as real GDP fluctuates with shifts in aggregate demand.

RECAP

1. As the price level rises (falls), aggregate expenditures fall (rise).

2. Aggregate demand is the equilibrium level of aggregate expenditures at alternative price levels.

3. The Keynesian fixed-price model is represented by a horizontal aggregate supply curve.

SUMMARY

1 │ What does equilibrium mean in macroeconomics?

- Macroeconomic equilibrium is the point at which aggregate expenditures equal real GDP. *§1.a*

2 │ How do aggregate expenditures affect income, or real GDP?

- When aggregate expenditures exceed income, or real GDP, real GDP rises; when they are less than real GDP, real GDP falls. *§1.a*

3 │ What are the leakages from and injections into spending?

- Leakages are saving, taxes, and imports; injections are investment, government spending, and exports. *§1.b*

- Equilibrium real GDP occurs where leakages equal injections. *§1.b*

4 │ Why does equilibrium real GDP change by a multiple of a change in autonomous expenditures?

- The effect of a change in autonomous spending is multiplied by a spiral of increased spending and income. *§2.a*

5 │ What is the spending multiplier?

- The spending multiplier equals the reciprocal of the sum of the *MPS* and the *MPI*. *§2.a*

6 │ What is the relationship between the GDP gap and the recessionary gap?

- The recessionary gap is the amount by which autonomous expenditures must change to eliminate the GDP gap and reach potential GDP. *§2.b*

7 │ How does international trade affect the size of the spending multiplier?

- The actual spending multiplier may be larger than the reciprocal of the sum of the *MPS* and the *MPI* because of the foreign repercussions of changes in domestic spending. *§2.c.1*

8 │ Why does the aggregate expenditures curve shift with changes in the price level?

- The *AE* curve shifts with changes in the price level because of the wealth effect, the interest rate effect, and the international trade effect. *§3.a*

- The Keynesian model of fixed-price equilibrium is a special case of the *AD* and *AS* equilibrium. *§3.c*

KEY TERMS

spending multiplier *§2.a*   recessionary gap *§2.b*

EXERCISES

1. Explain the role of inventories in keeping actual expenditures equal to real GDP.

2. Rework Figure 1 assuming a closed economy (net exports equal zero at all levels of income). What is the equilibrium level of real GDP? What is the spending multiplier?

3. Draw a graph representing a hypothetical economy. Carefully label the two axes, the $S + T + IM$ curve, the $I + G + EX$ curve, and the equilibrium level of real GDP. Illustrate the effect of an increase in the level of autonomous saving.

4. Given the following information, what is the spending multiplier in each case?

   a. $MPC = .90$, $MPI = .10$
   b. $MPC = .90$, $MPI = .30$
   c. $MPC = .80$, $MPI = .30$
   d. $MPC = .90$, $MPI = 0$

5. Draw a graph representing a hypothetical economy in a recession. Carefully label the two axes, the 45-degree line, the *AE* curve, and the equilibrium level of real GDP. Indicate and label the GDP gap and the recessionary gap.

6. Explain the effect of foreign repercussions on the value of the spending multiplier.

7. Suppose the *MPC* is .80, the *MPI* is .10, and the income tax rate is 10 percent. What is the multiplier in this economy?

Use the information in the following table to do exercises 8–15:

Y	C	I	G	X
$100	$120	$20	$30	−$10
$300	$300	$20	$30	−$10
$500	$480	$20	$30	−$30
$700	$660	$20	$30	−$50

8. What is the *MPC*?

9. What is the *MPI*?

10. What is the *MPS*?

11. What is the multiplier?

12. What is the equilibrium level of real GDP?

13. What is the value of autonomous consumption?

14. If government spending increases by $20, what is the new equilibrium level of real GDP?

15. What are the equations for the consumption, net exports, and aggregate expenditures functions?

16. Derive the aggregate demand curve from an aggregate expenditures diagram. Explain how aggregate demand relates to aggregate expenditures.

17. In the chapter titled "Macroeconomic Equilibrium: Aggregate Demand and Supply," the aggregate supply (*AS*) curve was upward sloping. Now, in this chapter, we have a flat *AS* curve. What are the implications for equilibrium real GDP if *AD* shifts by some amount and the *AS* curve is perfectly flat in one economy and upward sloping in another?

18. Why should the business cycles of Canada and Mexico be much like the U.S. business cycle, while those of South Africa and Turkey may differ from the U.S. pattern of economic expansion and contraction?

You can find further practice tests in the Online Quiz at **www.cengage.com/economics/boyes.**

Results: North Americans Are Better Off after 14 Years of NAFTA

The North American Free Trade Agreement (NAFTA) revolutionized trade and investment in North America, helping to unlock our region's economic potential. . . . NAFTA has helped to stimulate economic growth and create higher-paying jobs across North America. It has also paved the way for greater market competition and enhanced choice and purchasing power for North American consumers, families, farmers, and businesses.

Furthermore, NAFTA has provided North American businesses with better access to materials, technologies, investment capital, and talent available across North America.

This has helped make our businesses more competitive, both within North America and around the world. With rapidly growing economies in Asia and South America challenging North America's competitiveness, NAFTA remains key to sustained growth and prosperity in the region.

NAFTA has proven that trade liberalization plays an important role in promoting transparency, economic growth, and legal certainty. In the face of increased global competition, Canada, the United States, and Mexico will work to strengthen the competitiveness of the North American region by continuing to pursue trade within the NAFTA region. . . .

Did you know?

- Since NAFTA came into effect, trade among the NAFTA partners has more than tripled, reaching US$894.3 billion in 2007. Over that period, Canada–U.S. trade has more than doubled, while trade between Mexico and the U.S. has quadrupled. (C$ figure = $961 billion).

- Today, the NAFTA partners exchange about US$2.5 billion in goods on a daily basis with each other. That's about US$10.2 million per hour. (C$ figures = $2.6 billion and $11 million).

Source: *http:/www.naftanow.org.*

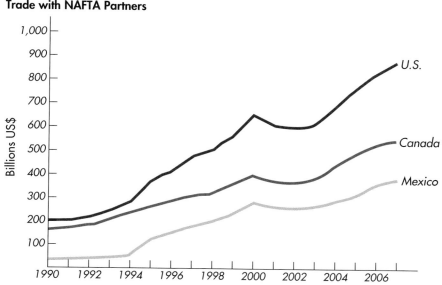

Trade with NAFTA Partners

Chart showing climbing trade in US$ 1993–2007; Canada–U.S., Canada–Mexico, U.S.–Mexico.

Sources: U.S.: Department of Commerce (Bureau of Census); Canada: Statistics Canada; Mexico: Secretary of Economy.

Commentary

This article reemphasizes a main point made in this chapter: Countries are linked internationally, and so aggregate expenditure shifts in one country will have an impact on other nations. When other countries, like Mexico, sell goods to the United States, those exports increase Mexican GDP, since net exports is one of the components of GDP. Remembering that net exports increase with a country's GDP, we should expect net exports to vary over the business cycle. Since U.S. imports vary with U.S. GDP, slower growth in the United States tends to reduce U.S. imports, leading to lower GDP in the countries that export to the United States. Conversely, when the U.S. economy is booming, U.S. imports from Mexico will rise and stimulate GDP growth in Mexico.

The article discusses how the economies of the United States and Mexico have become more highly synchronized. As the U.S. experiences business-cycle fluctuations, these fluctuations tend to be matched in Mexico.

The United States had a recession in 2008. Did the economies of the major trading partners of the United States have recessions around this time? There was a recession in Canada that roughly coincided with the U.S. recession. However, in Europe, real GDP continued to grow for a while following the onset of the U.S. recession. This reflects the fact that the Canadian economy is much more integrated with that of the United States than European economies.

We should also expect Mexico to be greatly affected by U.S. business cycles, since about 85 percent of Mexican exports go to the United States. Australia, South Africa, Sweden, and Turkey are likely to have business cycles that are more independent of U.S. influences, since their exports to the United States as a share of their total exports are less than 10 percent.

The international links between countries should grow over time as restrictions on international trade are removed and transportation and communication costs continue to fall. The future may be one in which national business cycles are increasingly interdependent, and such interdependencies will have to be given greater emphasis in national policymaking.

An Algebraic Model of Income and Expenditures Equilibrium

Continuing the example we began in the Appendix to Chapter 9, if we know the equation for each component of aggregate expenditures (AE), we can solve for the equilibrium level of real GDP (Y) for the economy represented in Figure 1 of the chapter:

$$C = \$30 + .70\,Y$$
$$I = \$50$$
$$G = \$70$$
$$X = \$50 - .10\,Y$$

Summing these components, we can find the aggregate expenditures function:

$$AE = \$30 + .70\,Y + \$50 + \$70 + \$50 - .10\,Y$$
$$= \$200 + .60\,Y$$

Given the AE function, we can solve for the equilibrium level of Y, where

$$Y = AE$$
$$= \$200 + .60\,Y$$
$$Y - .60\,Y = \$200$$
$$.40\,Y = \$200$$
$$.40\,Y/.40 = \$200/.40$$
$$Y = \$500$$

The Spending Multiplier It is also possible to solve for the spending multiplier algebraically. We start by writing the general equations for each function, where C^a, I^a, G^a, EX^a, and IM^a represent autonomous consumption, investment, government spending, exports, and imports, respectively, and where c represents the MPC and im represents the MPI:

$$C = C^a + cY$$
$$I = I^a$$
$$G = G^a$$
$$X = EX^a - IM^a - im\,Y$$

Now we sum the individual equations for the components of aggregate expenditures to get the aggregate expenditures function:

$$AE = C + I + G + X$$
$$= C^a + cY + I^a + G^a + EX^a + IM^a + im\,Y$$
$$= (C^a + I^a + EX^a + IM^a) + cY + im\,Y$$

We know that aggregate expenditures equal income. So

$$Y = (C^a + I^a + G^a + EX^a + IM^a) + cY + im Y$$

Solving for Y, we first gather all of the terms involving Y on the left side of the equation:

$$Y[1 - (c - im)] + C^a + I^a + G^a + EX^a - IM^a$$

Next we divide each side of the equation by $[1 - (c - im)]$ to get an equation for Y:

$$Y = \frac{1}{1 - (c - im)} C^a + I^a + G^a + EX^a - IM^a$$

. A change in autonomous expenditures causes Y to change by

$$\frac{1}{1 - (c - im)}$$

times the change in expenditures. Because c is the *MPC* and im is the *MPI*, the multiplier can be written

$$\frac{1}{1 - (MPC - MPI)}$$

or, since $1 - MPC + MPS$, then $1 - (MPC + MPI) = MPS + MPI$, and the spending multiplier equals

$$\frac{1}{MPC - MPI}$$

Fiscal Policy

? Fundamental Questions

1 | How can fiscal policy eliminate a GDP gap?

2 | How has U.S. fiscal policy changed over time?

3 | What are the effects of budget deficits?

4 | How does fiscal policy differ across countries?

Macroeconomics plays a key role in national politics. When Jimmy Carter ran for the presidency against Gerald Ford in 1976, he created a "misery index" to measure the state of the economy. The index was the sum of the inflation rate and the unemployment rate, and Carter showed that it had risen during Ford's term in office. When Ronald Reagan challenged Carter in 1980, he used the misery index to show that inflation and unemployment had gone up during the Carter years as well. The implication is that presidents are responsible for the condition of the economy. If the inflation rate or the unemployment rate is relatively high coming into an election year, an incumbent president is open to criticism by opponents. For instance, many people believe that George Bush was defeated by Bill Clinton in 1992 because of the recession that began in 1990—a recession that was not announced as having ended in March 1991 until after the election. Clinton's 1992 campaign made economic growth a focus of its attacks on Bush, and his 1996 campaign emphasized the strength of the economy.

In 1996, a healthy economy helped Clinton defeat Bob Dole. And in the election of 2004, Bush supporters made economic growth a major focal point of their campaign against Kerry. More recently, Barack Obama's successful campaign for president had economic issues as a leading concern with the U.S. recession beginning in 2008. This was

Fiscal policy includes government spending on the provision of goods and services as well as infrastructure. In this photo, workers create mud bricks in the desert. The bricks will be used in infrastructure construction projects. Such activities are often provided by government and funded by taxpayers.

more than just campaign rhetoric, however. By law the government *is* responsible for the macroeconomic health of the nation. The Employment Act of 1946 states:

> It is the continuing policy and responsibility of the Federal Government to use all practical means consistent with its needs and obligations and other essential considerations of national policy to coordinate and utilize all its plans, functions, and resources for the purpose of creating and maintaining, in a manner calculated to foster and promote free competitive enterprise and the general welfare conditions under which there will be afforded useful employment opportunities, including self-employment for those able, willing, and seeking to work, and to promote maximum employment, production, and purchasing power.

Fiscal policy is one tool that government uses to guide the economy along an expansionary path. In this chapter, we examine the role of fiscal policy—government spending and taxation—in determining the equilibrium level of income. Then we review the budget process and the history of fiscal policy in the United States. Finally, we describe the difference in fiscal policy between industrial and developing countries.

1 | How can fiscal policy eliminate a GDP gap?

■ 1. Fiscal Policy and Aggregate Demand

The GDP gap is the difference between potential real GDP and the equilibrium level of real GDP. If the government wants to close the GDP gap so that the equilibrium level of real GDP reaches its potential, it must use fiscal policy to alter aggregate expenditures and cause the aggregate demand curve to shift.

Fiscal policy is the government's policy with respect to spending and taxation. Since aggregate demand includes consumption, investment, net exports, and government spending, government spending on goods and services has a direct effect on the level of aggregate demand. Taxes affect aggregate demand indirectly by changing the disposable income of households, which alters consumption.

1.a. Shifting the Aggregate Demand Curve

By varying the level of government spending, policymakers can affect the level of real GDP.

Changes in government spending and taxes shift the aggregate demand curve. Remember that the aggregate demand curve represents combinations of equilibrium aggregate expenditures and alternative price levels. An increase in government spending or a decrease in taxes raises the level of expenditures at every level of prices and moves the aggregate demand curve to the right.

Figure 1 shows the increase in aggregate demand that would result from an increase in government spending or a decrease in taxes. Only if the aggregate

---

FIGURE 1   Eliminating the Recessionary Gap: Higher Prices Mean Greater Spending

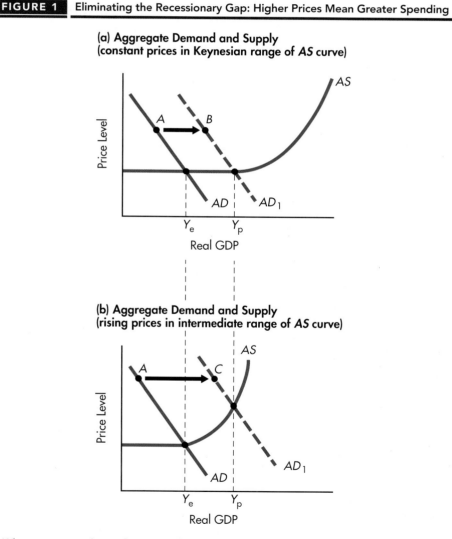

When aggregate demand increases from AD to AD₁ in Figure 1(a), equilibrium real GDP increases by the full amount of the shift in demand. This is because the aggregate supply curve is horizontal over the area of the shift in aggregate demand. In Figure 1(b), in order for equilibrium real GDP to rise from Y_e to Y_p, aggregate demand must shift by more than it does in Figure 1(a). In reality, the aggregate supply curve begins to slope up before potential real GDP (Y_p) is reached, as shown in Figure 1(b) of the figure.

supply curve is horizontal do prices remain fixed as aggregate demand increases. In Figure 1(a), equilibrium occurs along the horizontal segment (the Keynesian region) of the AS curve. If government spending increases and the price level remains constant, aggregate demand shifts from AD to AD_1; it increases by the horizontal distance from point A to point B. Once aggregate demand shifts, the AD_1 and AS curves intersect at potential real GDP, Y_p.

But Figure 1(a) is not realistic. The AS curve is not likely to be horizontal all the way to the level of potential real GDP; it should begin sloping up well before Y_p. And once the economy reaches the capacity level of output, the AS curve should become a vertical line, as shown in Figure 1(b).

If the AS curve slopes up before reaching the potential real GDP level, as it does in Figure 1(b), expenditures have to go up by more than the amount suggested in Figure 1(a) for the economy to reach Y_p. Why? Because when prices rise, the effect of spending on real GDP is reduced. This effect is shown in Figure 1(b). To increase the equilibrium level of real GDP from Y_e to Y_p, aggregate demand must shift by the amount from point A to point C, a larger increase than that shown in Figure 1(a), where the price level is fixed.

1.b. Multiplier Effects

Changes in government spending may have an effect on real GDP that is a multiple of the original change in government spending; a $1 change in government spending may increase real GDP by more than $1. This is because the original $1 of expenditure is spent over and over again in the economy as it passes from person to person. The government spending multiplier measures the multiple by which an increase in government spending increases real GDP. Similarly, a change in taxes may have an effect on real GDP that is a multiple of the original change in taxes. (The appendix to this chapter provides an algebraic analysis of the government spending and tax multipliers.)

If the price level rises as real GDP increases, the multiplier effects of any given change in aggregate expenditures are smaller than they would be if the price level remained constant.

If the price level rises as real GDP increases, the multiplier effects of any given change in aggregate demand are smaller than they would be if the price level remained constant. In addition to changes in the price level modifying the effect of government spending and taxes on real GDP, there are other factors that affect how much real GDP will change following a change in government spending. One such factor is how the government pays for, or finances, its spending.

Government spending must be financed by some combination of taxing, borrowing, and creating money:

Government spending = taxes + change in government debt + change in government-issued money

In the chapter titled "Monetary Policy," we discuss the effect of financing government spending by creating money. As you will see, this source of government financing is relied on heavily in some developing countries. Here we talk about the financing problem that is relevant for industrial countries: how taxes and government debt can modify the expansionary effect of government spending on national income.

1.c. Government Spending Financed by Tax Increases

Suppose that government spending rises by $100 billion and that this expenditure is financed by a tax increase of $100 billion. Such a "balanced-budget" change in fiscal policy will cause equilibrium real GDP to rise. This is because government

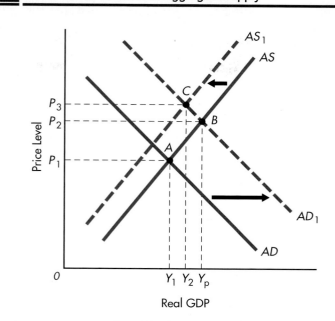

FIGURE 2 The Effect of Taxation on Aggregate Supply

An increase in government spending shifts the aggregate demand curve from AD to AD_1, moving equilibrium from point A to point B, and equilibrium real GDP from Y_1 to Y_p. If higher taxes reduce the incentive to work, aggregate supply could fall from AS to AS_1, moving equilibrium to point C and equilibrium real GDP to Y_2, a level below potential real GDP.

spending increases aggregate expenditures directly, but higher taxes lower aggregate expenditures indirectly through consumption spending. For instance, if taxes increase by $100, consumers will not cut their spending by $100, but will cut it by some fraction, say 9/10, of the increase. If consumers spend 90 percent of a change in their disposable income, then a tax increase of $100 would lower consumption by $90. So the net effect of raising government spending and taxes by the same amount is an increase in aggregate demand, illustrated in Figure 2 as the shift from AD to AD_1. However, it may be incorrect to assume that the only thing that changes is aggregate demand. An increase in taxes may also affect aggregate supply.

Aggregate supply measures the output that producers offer for sale at different levels of prices. When taxes go up, workers have less incentive to work because their after-tax income is lower. The cost of taking a day off or extending a vacation for a few extra days is less than it is when taxes are lower and after-tax income is higher. When taxes go up, then, output can fall, causing the aggregate supply curve to shift to the left. Such supply-side effects of taxes have been emphasized by the so-called supply-side economists, as discussed in the Economic Insight "Supply-Side Economics and the Laffer Curve."

Figure 2 shows the possible effects of an increase in government spending financed by taxes. The economy is initially in equilibrium at point A, with prices at P_1 and real GDP at Y_1. The increase in government spending shifts the aggregate demand curve from AD to AD_1. If this were the only change, the economy would be in equilibrium at point B. But if the increase in taxes reduces output, the aggregate supply curve moves back from AS to AS_1, and output does not expand all the way to Y_p. The decrease in aggregate supply creates a new equilibrium at point C. Here real GDP is at Y_2 (less than Y_p), and the price level is P_3 (higher than P_2).

Economic Insight

Supply-Side Economics and the Laffer Curve

The large budget deficits incurred by the U.S. government in the 1980s were in part a product of lower tax rates engineered by the Reagan administration. President Reagan's economic team took office in January 1981 hoping that lower taxes would stimulate the supply of goods and services to a level that would raise tax revenues, even though tax rates as a percentage of income had been cut. These arguments were repeated in 1995 by members of Congress pushing for tax-rate cuts. This emphasis on greater incentives to produce created by lower taxes has come to be known as *supply-side economics.*

The most widely publicized element of supply-side economics was the *Laffer curve.* The curve is drawn with the tax rate on the vertical axis and tax revenue on the horizontal axis. When the rate of taxation is zero, there is no tax revenue. As the tax rate increases, tax revenue increases up to a point. The assumption here is that there is some rate of taxation that is so high that it discourages productive activity. Once this rate is reached, tax revenue begins to fall as the rate of taxation goes up. In the graph, tax revenue is maximized at R_{max} with a tax rate of t percent. Any increase in the rate of taxation above t percent produces lower tax revenues. In the extreme case—a 100 percent tax rate—no one is willing to work because the government taxes away all income.

Critics of the supply-side tax cuts proposed by the Reagan administration argued that lower taxes would increase the budget deficit. Supply-side advocates

insisted that if the United States were in the backward-bending region of the Laffer curve (above t percent in the graph), tax cuts would actually raise, not lower, tax revenue. The evidence following the tax cuts indicates that the tax cuts did, however, contribute to a larger budget deficit, implying that the United States was not on the backward-bending portion of the Laffer curve.

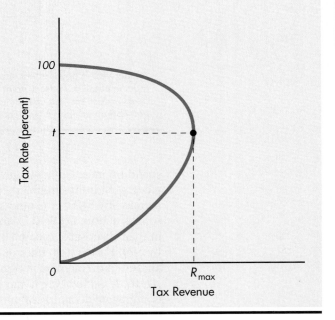

The standard analysis of government spending and taxation assumes that aggregate supply is not affected by the change in fiscal policy, leading us to expect a greater change in real GDP than may actually occur. If tax changes do affect aggregate supply, the expansionary effects of government spending financed by tax increases are moderated. The actual magnitude of this effect is the subject of debate among economists. Most argue that the evidence in the United States indicates that tax increases have a fairly small effect on aggregate supply.

1.d. Government Spending Financed by Borrowing

The standard multiplier analysis of government spending does not differentiate among the different methods of financing that spending. Yet you just saw how taxation can offset at least part of the expansionary effect of higher government spending. Borrowing to finance government spending can also limit the increase in aggregate demand.

A government borrows funds by selling bonds to the public. These bonds represent debt that must be repaid at a future date. Debt is, in a way, a kind of substitute for current taxes. Instead of increasing current taxes to finance higher spending, the government borrows the savings of households and businesses. Of course, the debt will mature and have to be repaid. This means that taxes will have to be higher in the future in order to provide the government with the funds to pay off the debt.

Current government borrowing, then, implies higher future taxes. This can limit the expansionary effect of increased government spending. If households and businesses take higher future taxes into account, they tend to save more today so that they will be able to pay those taxes in the future. And as saving today increases, consumption today falls.

> *Ricardian equivalence holds if taxation and government borrowing both have the same effect on spending in the private sector.*

The idea that current government borrowing can reduce current nongovernment expenditures was suggested originally by the early-nineteenth-century English economist David Ricardo. Ricardo recognized that government borrowing could function like increased current taxes, reducing current household and business expenditures. *Ricardian equivalence* is the principle that government spending activities financed by taxation and those financed by borrowing have the same effect on the economy. If Ricardian equivalence holds, it doesn't matter whether the government raises taxes or borrows more to finance increased spending. The effect is the same: Private-sector spending falls by the same amount today, and this drop in private spending will at least partially offset the expansionary effect of government spending on real GDP. Just how much private spending drops (and how far to the left the aggregate demand curve shifts) depends on the degree to which current saving increases in response to expected higher taxes. The less that people respond to the future tax liabilities arising from current government debt, the smaller the reduction in private spending.

There is substantial disagreement among economists over the extent to which current government borrowing acts like an increase in taxes. Some argue that it makes no difference whether the government raises current taxes or borrows. Others insist that the public does not base current spending on future tax liabilities. If the first group is correct, we would expect government spending financed by borrowing to have a smaller effect than if the second group is correct. Research on this issue continues, with most economists questioning the relevance of Ricardian equivalence and a small but influential group arguing its importance.

1.e. Crowding Out

crowding out: a drop in consumption or investment spending caused by government spending

Expansionary fiscal policy can crowd out private-sector spending; that is, an increase in government spending can reduce consumption and investment. **Crowding out** is usually discussed in the context of government spending financed by borrowing rather than by taxes. We have just seen how future taxes can cause consumption to fall today, but investment can also be affected. Increases in government borrowing drive up interest rates. As interest rates go up, investment falls. This sort of indirect crowding out works through the bond market. The U.S government borrows by selling Treasury bonds or bills. Because the government is not a profit-making institution, it does not have to earn a profitable return on the money it raises by selling bonds. A corporation does, however. When interest rates rise, fewer corporations offer new bonds to raise investment funds because the cost of repaying the bond debt may exceed the rate of return on the investment.

Crowding out, like Ricardian equivalence, is important in principle, but economists have never demonstrated conclusively that its effects can substantially alter spending in the private sector. Still, you should be aware of the possibility in order to understand the potential shortcomings of changes in government spending and taxation.

RECAP

1. Fiscal policy refers to government spending and taxation.

2. By increasing spending or cutting taxes, a government can close the GDP gap.

3. If government spending and taxes increase by the same amount, equilibrium real GDP rises.

4. If a tax increase affects aggregate supply, then a balanced-budget change in fiscal policy will have a smaller expansionary effect on equilibrium real GDP than otherwise.

5. Current government borrowing reduces current spending in the private sector if people increase current saving in order to pay future tax liabilities.

6. Ricardian equivalence holds when taxation and government borrowing have the same effect on current spending in the private sector.

7. Increased government borrowing can crowd private borrowers out of the bond market so that investment falls.

■ 2. Fiscal Policy in the United States

2 | **How has U.S. fiscal policy changed over time?**

Our discussion of fiscal policy assumes that this policy is made at the federal level. In the modern economy, this is a reasonable assumption. This was not the case before the 1930s, however. Before the Depression, the federal government limited its activities largely to national defense and foreign policy and left other areas of government policy to the individual states. With the growth in the importance of the federal government in fiscal policy has come a growth in the role of the federal budget process.

When one is talking about the federal budget, the monetary amounts of the various categories of expenditures are so huge that they are often difficult to comprehend. But if you were to divide up the annual budget by the number of individual taxpayers, you'd come up with an average individual statement that might make more sense, as shown in the Economic Insight "The Taxpayer's Federal Government Credit Card Statement."

The federal budget is determined as much by politics as by economics. Politicians respond to different groups of voters by supporting different government programs, regardless of the needed fiscal policy. It is the political response to constituents that tends to drive up federal budget deficits (the difference between government expenditures and tax revenues), not the need for expansionary fiscal policy. As a result, deficits have become commonplace.

2.a. The Historical Record

The U.S. government has grown dramatically since the early part of the century. Figure 3 shows federal revenues and expenditures over time. Note that expenditures

Economic Insight

The Taxpayer's Federal Government Credit Card Statement

Suppose the U.S. government's expenditures and revenues were accounted for annually to each individual income taxpayer like a credit card statement. For 2008, the statement would look like the accompanying table.

Statement for 2008 Budget Year	
Previous balance	$32,695.45
New purchases	
Defense	$3,983.11
Social Security	$3,974.02
Medicare	$2,957.14
Medicaid	$1,472.07
Other	$6,983.11
Total Spending	$19,369.48
Payments received	
Individual income and social security taxes	$7,439.61
Corporate income taxes	$1,975.97
Other	$6,975.97
Total payments	$16,391.56
Finance charge	$1,616.23
New balance due	$37,679.87

were lower than revenues in the 1998–2001 period. Figure 4 places the growth of government in perspective by plotting U.S. government spending as a percentage of gross domestic product over time. Before the Great Depression, federal spending was approximately 3 percent of the GDP; by the end of the Depression, it had risen to about 10 percent. The ratio of spending to GDP reached its peak during World War II, when federal spending hit 44 percent of the GDP. After the war, the ratio fell dramatically and then slowly increased to a peak of about 24 percent in 1983. In recent years, the ratio has been around 20 percent.

Fiscal policy has two components: discretionary fiscal policy and automatic stabilizers. **Discretionary fiscal policy** refers to changes in government spending and taxation that are aimed at achieving a policy goal. **Automatic stabilizers** are elements of fiscal policy that automatically change in value as national income changes. Figures 3 and 4 suggest that government spending is dominated by growth over time. But there is no indication here of discretionary changes in fiscal policy, changes in government spending and taxation that are aimed at meeting specific policy goals. Perhaps a better way to evaluate the fiscal policy record is in terms of the budget deficit. Government expenditures can rise, but the effect on aggregate demand could be offset by a simultaneous increase in taxes so that there is no expansionary effect on the equilibrium level of national income. By looking at

discretionary fiscal policy: chages in goverment spending and taxation that are aimed at achieving a policy goal

automatic stabilizer: an element of fiscal policy that changes automatically as income changes

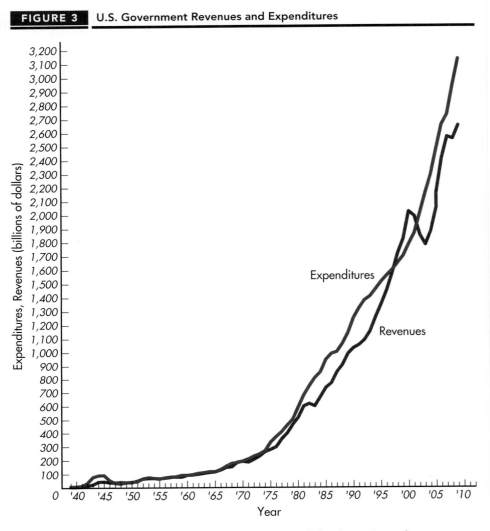

FIGURE 3   U.S. Government Revenues and Expenditures

Revenues are total revenues of the U.S. government in each fiscal year. Expenditures are total spending of the U.S. government in each fiscal year. The difference between the two curves equals the U.S. budget deficit (when expenditures exceed revenues) or surplus (when revenues exceed expenditures).

Source: Data are drawn from *Economic Report of the President*, 2009.

the deficit, we see the combined spending and tax policy results, which are missing if only government expenditures are considered.

Figure 5 illustrates the pattern of the U.S. federal deficit and the deficit as a percentage of GDP over time. Figure 5(a) shows that the United States ran close to a balanced budget for much of the 1950s and 1960s. There were large deficits associated with financing World War II, and then large deficits resulting from fiscal policy decisions in recent decades. However, from 1998 to 2001, the first surpluses since 1969 were recorded. Figure 5(b) shows that the deficit as a percentage of GDP was much larger during World War II than it was in the 1980s and 1990s.

Historically, aside from wartime, budget deficits increase the most during recessions. When real GDP falls, tax revenues go down, and government spending on unemployment and welfare benefits goes up. These are examples of automatic stabilizers in action. As income falls, taxes fall and personal benefit payments

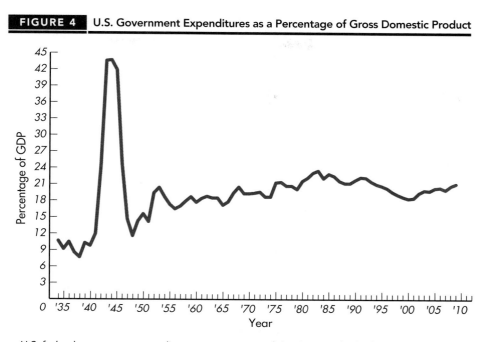

U.S. federal government spending as a percentage of the GDP reached a high of 44 percent in 1943 and 1944. Discounting wartime spending and cutbacks after the war, you can see the upward trend in U.S. government spending, which constituted a larger and larger share of the GDP until the early 1980s.

FIGURE 5 The U.S. Deficit

(a) Federal Surplus (+) or Deficit (−)

(b) Federal Deficit as a Percent of GDP (absolute value of deficit)

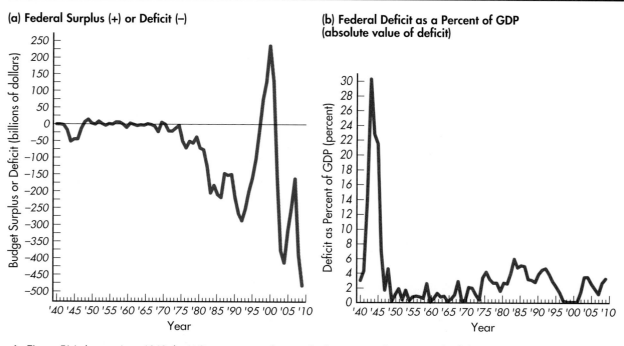

As Figure 5(a) shows, since 1940 the U.S. government has rarely shown a surplus. For much of the 1950s and 1960s, the United States was close to a balanced budget. Figure 5(b) shows the federal deficit as a percentage of GDP. The deficits during the 1950s and 1960s generally were small. The early 1980s were a time of rapid growth in the federal budget deficit, and this is reflected in the growth of the deficit as a percentage of GDP.

rise to partially offset the effect of the drop in income. The rapid growth of the deficit in the 1980s involved more than the recessions in 1980 and 1982, however. The economy grew rapidly after the 1982 recession ended, but so did the fiscal deficit. The increase in the deficit was the product of a rapid increase in government spending to fund new programs and enlarge existing programs while taxes were held constant. In the late 1990s, the deficit decreased. This was the result of surprisingly large tax revenue gains, generated by strong economic growth, combined with only moderate government spending increases. The deficit is unlikely to fall significantly in the next few years, however, as government spending for defense and homeland security rises.

2.b. Deficits and the National Debt

The large federal deficits of the 1980s and 1990s led many observers to question whether a deficit can harm the economy. Figure 5 shows how the fiscal deficit has changed over time. One major implication of a large deficit is the resulting increase in the national debt, the total stock of government bonds outstanding. Table 1 lists data on the debt of the United States. Notice that the total debt doubled between 1981 ($994.8 billion) and 1986 ($2,120.6 billion), and then doubled again between

TABLE 1 Debt of the U.S. Government (Dollar Amounts in Billions)

(1) Year	(2) Total Debt	(3) Debt/GDP (percent)	(4) Net Interest	(5) Interest/ Government Spending (percent)
1958	$279.7	63	$5.6	6.8
1960	$290.5	57	$6.9	7.5
1962	$302.9	55	$6.9	6.5
1964	$316.1	50	$8.2	6.9
1966	$328.5	44	$9.4	7.0
1968	$368.7	43	$11.1	6.2
1970	$380.9	39	$14.4	7.4
1972	$435.9	38	$15.5	6.7
1974	$483.9	34	$21.4	8.0
1976	$629.0	37	$26.7	7.3
1978	$776.6	36	$35.4	7.9
1980	$909.1	34	$52.5	9.1
1981	$994.8	34	$68.8	10.5
1982	$1,137.3	36	$85.0	11.6
1983	$1,371.7	41	$89.8	11.2
1984	$1,564.7	42	$111.1	13.2
1985	$1,817.5	46	$129.5	13.6
1986	$2,120.6	50	$136.0	13.7
1987	$2,396.1	53	$138.7	13.8
1988	$2,601.3	54	$151.8	14.3
1989	$2,868.0	55	$169.3	14.8
1990	$3,206.6	56	$184.2	14.7

(Continued)

3 | What are the effects of budget deficits?

TABLE 1	Debt of the U.S. Government (Dollar Amounts in Billions) *(Continued)*			
1991	$3,598.5	61	$194.5	14.7
1992	$4,002.1	65	$199.4	14.4
1993	$4,351.4	67	$198.8	14.1
1994	$4,643.7	66	$203.0	13.9
1995	$4,921.0	66	$232.2	15.3
1996	$5,181.9	66	$241.1	15.5
1997	$5,369.7	65	$244.0	15.2
1998	$5,478.7	63	$241.2	14.6
1999	$5,606.1	57	$229.7	13.5
2000	$5,628.7	57	$222.9	12.5
2001	$5,769.9	57	$206.2	11.1
2002	$6,198.4	59	$171.0	8.5
2003	$6,760.0	63	$153.1	7.1
2004	$7,354.7	64	$160.2	7.0
2005	$7,905.3	64	$184.0	7.4
2006	$8,451.4	64	$226.6	8.5
2007	$8,950.7	65	$237.1	8.7
2008	$9,623.4	67	$248.9	8.4
2009	$10,438.4	70	$228.0	7.3

1986 and 1993. Column 3 shows debt as a percentage of GDP. In the late 1990s, the debt was falling as a percentage of GDP. During World War II, the debt was greater than the GDP for five years. Despite the talk of "unprecedented" federal deficits in the 1980s and 1990s, clearly the ratio of the debt to GDP was by no means unprecedented.

We have not yet answered the question of whether deficits are bad. To do so, we have to consider their potential effects.

2.b.1. Deficits, Interest Rates, and Investment Because government deficits mean government borrowing and debt, many economists argue that deficits raise interest rates as lenders require a higher interest rate to induce them to hold more government debt. Increased government borrowing raises interest rates; this, in turn, can depress investment. (Remember that as interest rates rise, the rate of return on investment drops, along with the incentive to invest.) What happens when government borrowing crowds out private investment? Lower investment means fewer capital goods in the future. So deficits lower the level of output in the economy, both today and in the future. In this sense, deficits are potentially bad.

Through their effects on investment, deficits can lower the level of output in the economy.

2.b.2. Deficits and International Trade If government deficits raise real interest rates (the nominal interest rate minus the expected inflation rate), they also may have an effect on international trade. A higher real return on U.S. securities makes those securities more attractive to foreign investors. As the foreign demand for U.S. securities increases, so does the demand for U.S. dollars in exchange for Japanese yen, British pounds, and other foreign currencies. As the demand for dollars increases, the dollar *appreciates* in value on the foreign exchange market. This means that the dollar becomes more expensive to foreigners, while foreign currency becomes cheaper to U.S. residents. This kind of change in the exchange rate encourages U.S. residents to buy more foreign goods and encourages foreign residents to buy fewer U.S. goods. Ultimately, then, as deficits and government debt increase, U.S. net exports tend to fall. Such foreign trade effects are another potentially bad effect of deficits.

2.b.3. Interest Payments on the National Debt The national debt is the stock of government bonds outstanding. It is the product of past and current budget deficits. As the size of the debt increases, the amount of interest that must be paid on the debt tends to rise. Column 4 of Table 1 lists the amount of interest paid on the debt; column 5 lists the interest as a percentage of government expenditures. The numbers in both columns have risen steadily over time and only recently started to drop.

The increase in the interest cost of the national debt is an aspect of fiscal deficits that worries some people. However, to the extent that U.S. citizens hold government bonds, we owe the debt to ourselves. The tax liability of funding the interest payments is offset by the interest income that bondholders earn. In this case there is no net change in national wealth when the national debt changes.

Of course, we do not owe the national debt just to ourselves. The United States is the world's largest national financial market, and many U.S. securities, including government bonds, are held by foreign residents. Today, foreign holdings of the U.S. national debt amount to about 28 percent of the outstanding debt. Because the tax liability for paying the interest on the debt falls on U.S. taxpayers, the greater the payments made to foreigners, the lower the wealth of U.S. residents, other things being equal.

Other things are not equal, however. To understand the real impact of foreign holdings on the economy, we have to evaluate what the economy would have been like if the debt had not been sold to foreign investors. If the foreign savings placed in U.S. bonds allowed the United States to increase investment and its productive capacity beyond what would have been possible in the absence of foreign lending, then the country could very well be better off for having sold government bonds to foreigners. The presence of foreign funds may keep interest rates lower than they would otherwise be, preventing the substantial crowding out associated with an increase in the national debt.

So while deficits are potentially bad as a result of the crowding out of investment, larger trade deficits with the rest of the world, and greater interest costs of the debt, we cannot generally say that all deficits are bad. It depends on what benefit the deficit provides. If the deficit spending allowed for greater productivity than would have occurred otherwise, the benefits may outweigh the costs. The financial crisis of 2008 provides a great example: Fiscal policy around the world involved governments increasing spending dramatically so that budget deficits increased substantially. However, the thinking was that the cost of not having government stimulate the economy would have been a much worse recession with many more people unemployed and incomes falling even more, so that the benefits of the deficits were widely thought to outweigh the costs.

2.c. Automatic Stabilizers

We have largely been talking about discretionary fiscal policy, the changes in government spending and taxing that policymakers make consciously. *Automatic stabilizers* are the elements of fiscal policy that change automatically as income changes. Automatic stabilizers partially offset changes in income: As income falls, automatic stabilizers increase spending; as income rises, automatic stabilizers decrease spending. Any program that responds to fluctuations in the business cycle in a way that moderates the effect of those fluctuations is an automatic stabilizer. Examples are progressive income taxes and transfer payments.

In our examples of tax changes, we have been using *lump-sum taxes*—taxes that are a flat dollar amount regardless of income. However, income taxes are determined as a percentage of income. In the United States, the federal income tax is a **progressive tax:**

progressive tax: a tax whose rate rises as income rises

As income rises, so does the rate of taxation. A person with a very low income pays no income tax, while a person with a high income can pay more than a third of that income in taxes. Countries use different rates of taxation on income. Taxes can be regressive (the tax rate falls as income rises) or proportional (the tax rate is constant as income rises) as well as progressive. But most countries, including the United States, use a progressive tax, with the percentage of income paid as taxes rising as taxable income rises.

Progressive income taxes act as an automatic stabilizer. As income falls, so does the average tax rate. Suppose a household earning $60,000 must pay 30 percent of its income ($18,000) in taxes, leaving 70 percent of its income ($42,000) for spending. If that household's income drops to $40,000 and the tax rate falls to 25 percent, the household has 75 percent of its income ($30,000) available for spending. But if the tax rate is 30 percent at all levels of income, the household earning $40,000 would have only 70 percent of its income ($28,000) to spend. By allowing a greater percentage of earned income to be spent, progressive taxes help offset the effect of lower income on spending.

All industrial countries have progressive federal income tax systems. For instance, the tax rate in Japan starts at 5 percent for low-income households and rises to a maximum of 40 percent for high-income households. In the United States, individual income tax rates start at 10 percent and rise to a maximum of 35 percent. In the U.K. tax system, rates rise from 10 percent to 50 percent, while tax rates in Germany rise from 15 to 45 percent and those in France, from 5.5 to 40 percent.

transfer payment:
a payment to one person that is funded by taxing others

A **transfer payment** is a payment to one person that is funded by taxing others. Food stamps, welfare benefits, and unemployment benefits are all government transfer payments: Current taxpayers provide the funds to pay those who qualify for the programs. Transfer payments that use income to establish eligibility act as automatic stabilizers. In a recession, as income falls, more people qualify for food stamps or welfare benefits, raising the level of transfer payments.

Unemployment insurance is also an automatic stabilizer. As unemployment rises, more workers receive unemployment benefits. Unemployment benefits tend to rise in a recession and fall during an expansion. This countercyclical pattern of benefit payments offsets the effect of business-cycle fluctuations on consumption.

RECAP

1. Fiscal policy in the United States is a product of the budget process.

2. Federal spending in the United States has grown rapidly over time, from just 3 percent of GDP before the Great Depression to about 20 percent of GDP today.

3. Government budget deficits can hurt the economy through their effect on interest rates and private investment, net exports, and the tax burden on current and future taxpayers.

4. Automatic stabilizers are government programs that are already in place and that respond automatically to fluctuations in the business cycle, moderating the effect of those fluctuations.

---

4 | How does fiscal policy differ across countries?

■ 3. Fiscal Policy in Different Countries

A country's fiscal policy reflects its philosophy toward government spending and taxation. In this section we present comparative data that demonstrate the variety of fiscal policies in the world.

TABLE 2	Share of Government Spending in GNP in Selected Industrial Countries, 1880, 1929, and 2004 (Percent)

Year	France	Germany	Sweden	United Kingdom	United States
1880	15	10*	6	10	8
1929	19	31	8	24	10
2008	23	18	26	21	16

*1881.
Source: Data are drawn from World Bank, *World Development Report 1996* and *2006* and OECD. StatExtracts.

3.a. Government Spending

Our discussion up to this point has centered on U.S. fiscal policy. But fiscal policy and the role of government in the economy can be very different across countries. Government has played an increasingly larger role in the major industrial countries over time. Table 2 shows how government spending has gone up as a percentage of output in five industrial nations. In every case, government spending accounted for a larger percentage of output in 2008 than it did 100 years earlier. For instance, in 1880, government spending was only 6 percent of the GNP in Sweden. By 1929 it had risen to 8 percent, and by 2008, to 26 percent.

Historically, in industrial countries, the growth of government spending has been matched by growth in revenues. But in the 1960s, government spending began to grow faster than revenues, creating increasingly larger debtor nations.

Developing countries have not shown the uniform growth in government spending found in industrial countries. In fact, in some developing countries (for instance, Chile, the Dominican Republic, and Peru), government spending is a smaller percentage of GDP today than it was 20 years ago. And we find a greater variation in the role of government in developing countries.

One important difference between the typical developed country and the typical developing country is that government plays a larger role in investment spending in the developing country. One reason for this difference is that state-owned enterprises account for a larger percentage of economic activity in developing countries than they do in developed countries. Also, developing countries usually rely more on government rather than the private sector to build their infrastructure—schools, roads, hospitals—than do developed countries.

How a government spends its money is a function of its income. Here we find differences not only between industrial and developing countries, but also among developing countries. Figure 6 reports central government spending for the United States, an industrial country, and a large developing country: China.

This figure clearly illustrates the relative importance of social welfare spending in industrial and developing countries. Although standards of living are lowest in the poorest countries, these countries do not have the resources to spend on social services (education, health, housing, social security, welfare). The United States spends 43 percent of its budget on social security, health, and education programs. China spends 31 percent of its budget on these programs, and that is substantially more than most developing countries.

> Government spending has grown over time as a fraction of GNP in all industrial countries.

3.b. Taxation

There are two different types of taxes: *direct taxes* (on individuals and firms) and *indirect taxes* (on goods and services). Figure 7 compares the importance

FIGURE 6	Central Government Spending by Functional Category

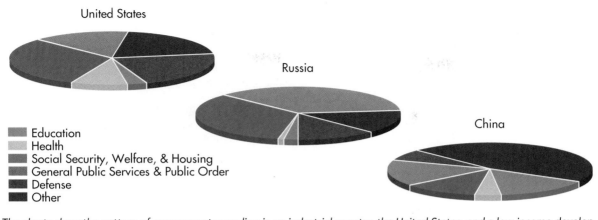

The charts show the pattern of government spending in an industrial country, the United States, and a low-income developing country, China. Social programs (education, health, and social security) account for 43 percent of federal government expenditures in the United States, but only 31 percent in China.

Source: Data are drawn from International Monetary Fund, *Government Finance Statistics Yearbook*, 2008.

of different sources of central government tax revenue for an industrial country, the United States, and a developing country, China. The most obvious difference is that personal income taxes are much more important in industrial countries than in developing countries. Why? Because personal taxes are hard to collect in agricultural nations, where a large percentage of household production is for personal consumption. Taxes on businesses are easier to collect and thus are more important in developing countries.

That industrial countries are better able to afford social programs is reflected in the great disparity in social security taxes between industrial countries and developing countries. With so many workers living near the subsistence level in the poorest countries, their governments simply cannot tax workers for retirement and health security programs.

Figure 7 also shows that taxes on international trade are very important in developing countries. Because goods arriving or leaving a country must pass through customs inspection, export and import taxes are relatively easy to collect compared to income taxes. In general, developing countries depend more heavily on indirect taxes on goods and services than do developed countries.

value-added tax (VAT): a general sales tax collected at each stage of production

Figure 7 lists "Goods and Services" taxes. Of these, 65 percent are **value-added taxes (VATs)** for industrial countries, while 61 percent of developing country commodity taxes come from value-added taxes. A value-added tax is an indirect tax imposed on each sale at each stage of production. Each seller from the first stage of production on collects the VAT from the buyer, then deducts any VATs it has paid in buying its inputs. The difference is remitted to the government. From time to time, Congress has debated the merits of a VAT in the United States, but it has never approved this kind of tax. The Global Business Insight "Value-Added Tax" provides further discussion.

RECAP

1. Over time, government spending has become more important in industrial countries.

2. Governments in developing countries typically play a larger role in investment spending in their economies than do the governments of developed countries.

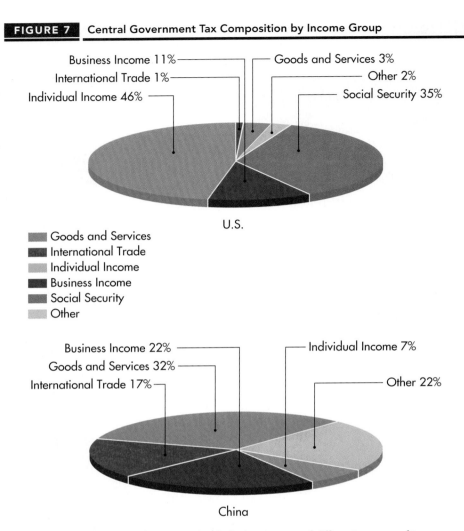

FIGURE 7   Central Government Tax Composition by Income Group

When we group countries by income level, the importance of different sources of tax revenue is obvious. Domestic income taxes account for 46 percent of government revenue in the United States and just 7 percent in China. Business income taxes are more important in developing countries like China. Social security taxes are a major source of government revenue in industrial countries; they are less important in developing countries, which cannot afford social programs. International trade taxes represent just 1 percent of tax revenues in industrial countries like the United States; in China, 17 percent of tax revenue comes from international trade taxes and developing countries rely heavily on these taxes.
(Note: Percentages do not total 100 because of rounding.)
Source: Data are drawn from *Government Finance Statistics*, 2008.

3.   Developing countries depend more on indirect taxes on goods and services as a source of revenue than on direct taxes on individuals and businesses.

4.   Value-added taxes are general sales taxes that are collected at every stage of production.

Global Business Insight

Value-Added Tax

A value-added tax (VAT) is a tax levied on all sales of goods and services at each stage of production. As implied by the name, the tax applies only to the value added at each stage, and so a firm that pays value-added taxes will pay tax only on the value that it added to the good or service that it sells. If a firm sells melons at a fruit stand, the VAT it pays is based on the difference between the cost the firm paid for the melons and the sales price it charges to its customers who buy the fruit. Of course, the customers bear the cost of the VAT, as it is built into the price they must pay.

As the accompanying map indicates, VATs are very popular around the world. Many countries adopted VATs in the 1990s. It is clear that more countries use VATs than do not. Such a tax has its advantages. One important consideration is that a VAT is a tax on consumption.

Anyone who buys goods and services will contribute to the government's VAT revenue. Thus, VATs are very powerful revenue generators. Those individuals who evade income taxes and pay less than their legal obligation will not escape the VAT. For instance, a criminal who earns income illegally and pays no tax on that income will be taxed on all legal goods and services that he or she purchases. In this sense, there is a certain attractiveness to taxing consumption rather than income. But a VAT also acts as a regressive tax in that a poor person would tend to pay a higher fraction of income as VAT than a rich person. It is important to realize that no country relies strictly on a VAT for government revenue. VATs are part of an overall government tax policy that attempts to incorporate fairness along with a need to raise sufficient revenue to finance public expenditures.

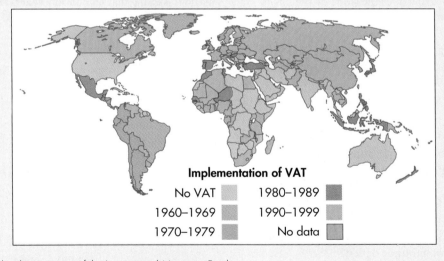

Implementation of VAT

No VAT	1980–1989
1960–1969	1990–1999
1970–1979	No data

Source: Reprinted with permission of the International Monetary Fund.

SUMMARY

1 | How can fiscal policy eliminate a GDP gap?

- A GDP gap can be closed by increasing government spending or by cutting taxes. *§1*

- Government spending affects aggregate expenditures directly; taxes affect aggregate expenditures indirectly through their effect on consumption. *§1*

- Aggregate expenditures must rise to bring equilibrium real GDP up to potential real GDP to eliminate the GDP gap. *§1*

- An increase in government spending that is matched by an increase in taxes raises equilibrium spending and real GDP. *§1.c*

- If the public expects to pay higher taxes as a result of government borrowing, then the expansionary effects of government deficits may be reduced. *§1.d*
- Government borrowing can crowd out private spending by raising interest rates and reducing investments. *§1.e*

2 | How has U.S. fiscal policy changed over time?

- Federal government spending in the United States has increased from just 3 percent of the GDP before the Great Depression to around 20 percent of the GDP today. *§2.a*
- Fiscal policy has two components: discretionary fiscal policy and automatic stabilizers. *§2.b*

3 | What are the effects of budget deficits?

- Budget deficits, through their effects on interest rates, international trade, and the national debt, can reduce investment, output, net exports, and national wealth. *§2.b.1, 2.b.2, 2.b.3*
- Progressive taxes and transfer payments are automatic stabilizers, elements of fiscal policy that change automatically as national income changes. *§2.c*

4 | How does fiscal policy differ across countries?

- Industrial countries spend a much larger percentage of their government budget for social programs than developing countries do. *§3.a*
- Industrial countries depend more on direct taxes and less on indirect taxes than developing countries do. *§3.b*

KEY TERMS

crowding out *§1.e*
discretionary fiscal policy *§2.b*

automatic stabilizer *§2.b*
progressive tax *§2.d*

transfer payment *§2.d*
value-added tax (VAT) *§3.b*

EXERCISES

1. What is the role of aggregate demand in eliminating the GDP gap? How does the slope of the AS curve affect the fiscal policy actions necessary to eliminate the GDP gap?

2. What is the "government budget constraint"? In other words, what are the sources of financing government spending?

3. In what ways are government deficits harmful to the economy?

4. Define and give three examples of automatic stabilizers.

5. Briefly describe the major differences between fiscal policy in industrial countries and that in developing countries.

6. Why will real GDP tend to rise when government spending and taxes rise by the same amount?

7. How can a larger government fiscal deficit cause a larger international trade deficit?

8. Why do government budget deficits grow during recessions?

9. Taxes can be progressive, regressive, or proportional. Define each, and briefly offer an argument for why income taxes are usually progressive.

10. What is a value-added tax (VAT), and what is an advantage of such a tax relative to an income tax?

The following exercises are based on the appendix to this chapter.

Answer exercises 11–14 on the basis of the following information. Assume that equilibrium real GDP is $800 billion, potential real GDP is $900 billion, the *MPC* is .80, and the *MPI* is .40.

11. What is the size of the GDP gap?

12. How much must government spending increase to eliminate the GDP gap?

13. How much must taxes fall to eliminate the GDP gap?

14. If government spending and taxes both change by the same amount, how much must they change to eliminate the recessionary gap?

15. Suppose the *MPC* is .90 and the *MPI* is .10. If government expenditures go up $100 billion while taxes fall $10 billion, what happens to the equilibrium level of real GDP?

Use the following equations for exercises 16–18.

$$C = \$100 + .8\,Y$$
$$I = \$200$$
$$G = \$250$$
$$X = \$100 - .2\,Y$$

16. What is the equilibrium level of real GDP?

17. What is the new equilibrium level of real GDP if government spending increases by $100?

18. What is the new equilibrium level of real GDP if government spending and taxes both increase by $100?

Commission Assesses Stability Programmes of France, Greece, Ireland, Netherlands, Portugal and Spain

European Union *February 22, 2006*

Having examined their updated stability programmes, the European Commission finds that overall Spain and Ireland have sound budgetary strategies and can be considered as providing good examples of fiscal policies in compliance with the Stability and Growth Pact. The Netherlands is also expected to respect its medium-term budgetary objective throughout the programme period after having made major adjustments in the past two years, which should be built on to maintain a strong budgetary position also in 2006 and thereafter, particularly in view of the better-than-expected budgetary results for 2005 and stronger growth in 2006. Greece, France and Portugal, which are subject to the excessive deficit procedure, present strategies that, if successful, would enable them to put their finances on a sound footing in the medium term although, in the case of France and Portugal, further efforts seem needed, and Greece is still struggling with statistical revisions, which might somewhat affect the otherwise significant reduction of its deficit.

"All six countries have set themselves medium-term objectives for their public finances that are in line with the revised Stability and Growth Pact. Spain and Ireland continue to present a winning combination of strong growth and fiscal discipline. The Netherlands show that determined action can ensure a rapid and lasting correction of fiscal imbalances. These examples should encourage other countries, such as Greece, France and Portugal, to pursue their efforts to bring their public finances in order," said Economic and Monetary Affairs Commissioner Joaquín Almunia.

Source: © European Communities, 1995–2006.

Commentary

Government budget deficits are a global concern. While we usually think in terms of internal political and economic pressures on a nation to keep its government budget from generating large and unsustainable deficits, the article discusses the case of the European Union (EU), where member countries face multinational pressure to comply with the EU *stability pact.* When the euro was in the planning stage, it was decided that every country that wanted to use the euro as its currency would have to have a stable, sustainable fiscal policy. The EU created the stability pact to explicitly state the limits on national governments' flexibility with regard to debt and deficits. The stability pact requires all euroland countries to maintain budget deficits of less than 3 percent of GDP and government debt of less than 60 percent of GDP. At the time this article was written, Greece, France, and Portugal exceeded the 3 percent deficit limit and were under pressure from the EU to reform their fiscal policies.

For the countries that share the same currency, the euro, it makes sense that they maintain similar fiscal policies in order to maintain a stable value for the euro against external currencies like the dollar. However, should other countries that have their own national money, like the United States or Japan, worry about maintaining a small deficit?

You may have heard arguments concerning the effects of a budget deficit that proceed by means of an analogy between the government's budget and a family's budget. Just as a family cannot spend more than it earns, so the argument goes, the government cannot follow this practice without bringing itself to ruin. The problem with this analogy is that the government has the ability to raise money through taxes and bond sales, options that are not open to a family.

A more appropriate analogy is to compare the government's budget to that of a large corporation. Large corporations run persistent deficits that are never paid back. Instead, when corporate debt comes due, the corporations "roll over" their debt by selling new debt. They are able to do this because they use their debt to finance investment that enables them to increase their worth. To the extent that the government is investing in projects like road repairs and building the nation's infrastructure, it is increasing the productive capacity of the economy, which widens the tax base and increases potential future tax receipts.

There are, of course, legitimate problems associated with a budget deficit. The government has two options if it cannot pay for its expenditures with tax receipts. One method of financing the budget deficit is by creating money. This is an unattractive option because it leads to inflation. Another method is to borrow funds by selling government bonds. A problem with this option is that the government must compete with private investment for scarce loanable funds. Unless saving increases at the same time, interest rates rise and government borrowing crowds out private investment. This results in a lower capital stock and diminished prospects for future economic growth.

So while the euroland countries face pressure, and potential fines, from the European Union if they exceed the limits of the stability pact, there are pressures from financial markets on all countries. The financial markets punish those countries that have excessive budget deficits. A country with big budget deficits will find its interest rates rising as investors buying the bonds sold by a country that borrows ever larger amounts of money will demand a higher and higher return. Those countries that resort to printing money to finance a budget deficit end up with higher and higher inflation rates. Such a policy has brought down more than one government in the past. Good government, as measured by careful management of the budget, is rewarded with good economic conditions (other things equal) and political survival.

An Algebraic Examination of the Balanced-Budget Change in Fiscal Policy

What would happen if government spending and taxes went up by the same amount?

We can analyze such a change by expanding the analysis begun in the appendix to Chapter 10.

The spending multiplier is the simple multiplier defined in Chapter 10:

$$\text{Spending muliplier} = \frac{1}{MPS + MPI}$$

In the Chapter 10 example, because the MPS equals .30 and the MPI equals .10, the spending multiplier equals 2.5:

$$\text{Spending muliplier} = \frac{1}{MPS + MPI} = \frac{1}{.30 + .10}$$
$$= \frac{1}{.40} = 2.5$$

When government spending increases by \$20, the equilibrium level of real GDP increases by 2.5 times \$20, or \$50.

We also can define a tax multiplier, a measure of the effect of a change in taxes on equilibrium real GDP. Because a percentage of any change in income is saved and spent on imports, we know that a tax cut increases expenditures by less than the amount of the cut. The percentage of the tax cut that actually is spent is the marginal propensity to consume ($MPC - MPI$). If consumers save 30 percent of any extra income, they spend 70 percent, the MPC. But the domestic economy does not realize 70 percent of the extra income because 10 percent of the extra income is spent on imports. The percentage of any extra income that actually is spent at home is the MPC minus the MPI. In our example, 60 percent (.70 − .10) of any extra income is spent in the domestic economy.

With this information, we can define the tax multiplier like this:

$$\text{Tax multiplier} = -(MPC - MPI)\frac{1}{MPS + MPI}$$

In our example, the tax multiplier is -1.5:

$$\text{Tax multiplier} = -(.70 - .10) \, \frac{1}{.30 + .10}$$

$$= -(.60)(2.5) = -1.5$$

A tax cut increases equilibrium real GDP by 1.5 times the amount of the cut. Notice that the tax multiplier is always a *negative* number because a change in taxes moves income and expenditures in the opposite direction. Higher taxes lower income and expenditures; lower taxes raise income and expenditures.

Now that we have reviewed the spending and tax multipliers, we can examine the effect of a balanced-budget change in fiscal policy, where government spending and taxes change by the same amount. To simplify the analysis, we assume that taxes are lump-sum taxes (taxpayers must pay a certain amount of dollars as tax) rather than income taxes (where the tax rises with income). We can use the algebraic model presented in the appendix to Chapter 10 to illustrate the effect of a balanced-budget change in government spending. Here are the model equations.

$$C = \$30 + .70\,Y$$

$$I = \$50$$

$$G = \$70$$

$$X = \$50 - .10\,Y$$

Solving for the equilibrium level of Y (as we did in the appendix to Chapter 10), Y equals \$500, where Y equals aggregate expenditures.

Now suppose that G increases by \$10 and that this increase is funded by taxes of \$10. The increase in G changes autonomous government spending to \$80. The increase in taxes affects the levels of C and X. The new model equations are

$$C = \$30 + .70(Y - \$10) = \$23 + .70\,Y$$

$$X = \$50 - .10(Y - \$10) = \$51 - .10\,Y$$

Using the new G, C, and X functions, we can find the new equilibrium level of real GDP by setting Y equal to $AE\,(C + I + G + X)$:

$$Y = C + I + G + X$$

$$Y = \$23 + .70\,Y + \$50 + \$80 + \$51 - .10\,Y$$

$$Y = \$204 + .60\,Y$$

$$Y - .60\,Y = \$204$$

$$.40\,Y = \$204$$

$$Y = \$510$$

Increasing government spending and taxes by \$10 each raises the equilibrium level of real GDP by \$10. A balanced-budget increase in G increases Y by the change in G. If government spending and taxes both fall by the same amount, then real GDP will also fall by an amount equal to the change in government spending and taxes.

Chapter 12

© Jundangoy/Dreamstime LLC

Money and Banking

 Fundamental Questions

1 | What is money?

2 | How is the U.S. money supply defined?

3 | How do countries pay for international transactions?

4 | Why are banks considered intermediaries?

5 | How does international banking differ from domestic banking?

6 | How do banks create money?

Up to this point, we have been talking about aggregate expenditures, aggregate demand and supply, and fiscal policy without explicitly discussing money. Yet money is used by every sector of the economy in all nations and plays a crucial role in every economy. In this chapter, we discuss what money is, how the quantity of money is determined, and the role of banks in determining this quantity. In the next chapter, we examine the role of money in the aggregate demand and supply model.

As you will see in the next two chapters, the quantity of money has a major impact on interest rates, inflation, and the amount of spending in the economy. Thus, money is important for macroeconomic policymaking, and government officials use both monetary and fiscal policy to influence the equilibrium level of real GDP and prices.

Banks and the banking system also play key roles, both at home and abroad, in the determination of the amount of money in circulation and the movement of money between nations. After we define money and its functions, we look at the banking system. We begin with banking in the United States, and then discuss international banking. Someone once joked that banks follow the rule of 3-6-3: They borrow at 3 percent interest, lend at 6 percent interest, and close at 3 P.M. If those days ever existed, clearly they no longer do today. The banking industry in the United States and the rest of the world has undergone tremendous change in recent years. New technology and government deregulation are allowing banks to respond to changing economic conditions in ways that were unthinkable only a few years ago, and these changes have had dramatic effects on the economy.

money: anything that is generally acceptable to sellers in exchange for goods and services

liquid asset: an asset that can easily be exchanged for goods and services

■ 1.What Is Money?

Money is anything that is generally acceptable to sellers in exchange for goods and services. The cash in your wallet can be used to buy groceries or a movie ticket. You simply present your cash to the cashier, who readily accepts it. If you wanted to use your car to buy groceries or a movie ticket, the exchange would be more complicated. You would probably have to sell the car before you could use it to buy other goods and services. Cars are seldom exchanged directly for goods and services (except for other cars). Because cars are not a generally acceptable means of paying for other goods and services, we don't consider them to be money. Money is the most liquid asset. A **liquid asset** is an asset that can easily be exchanged for goods and services. Cash is a liquid asset; a car is not. How liquid must an asset be before we consider it money? To answer this question, we must first consider the functions of money.

1.a. Functions of Money

Money serves four basic functions: It is a *medium of exchange,* a *unit of account,* a *store of value,* and a *standard of deferred payment.* Not all monies serve all of these functions equally well, as will be apparent in the following discussion. But to be money, an item must perform enough of these functions to induce people to use it.

1.a.1. Medium of Exchange Money is a medium of exchange; it is given in exchange for goods and services. Sellers willingly accept money as payment for the products and services that they produce. Without money, we would have to resort to *barter,* the direct exchange of goods and services for other goods and services.

For a barter system to work, there must be a *double coincidence of wants.* Suppose Bill is a carpenter and Jane is a plumber. In a monetary economy, when Bill needs plumbing repairs in his home, he simply pays Jane for the repairs, using money. Because everyone wants money, money is an acceptable means of payment. In a barter economy, Bill must offer his services as a carpenter in exchange for Jane's work. If Jane does not want any carpentry work done, Bill and Jane cannot enter into a mutually beneficial transaction. Bill has to find a person who can do what he wants and who also wants what he can do—there must be a double coincidence of wants.

The use of money as a medium of exchange lowers transaction costs.

The example of Bill and Jane illustrates the fact that barter is a lot less efficient than using money. This means that the cost of a transaction in a barter economy is higher than the cost of a transaction in a monetary economy.

The people of Yap Island highly value, and thus accept as their medium of exchange, giant stones. In most cultures, however, money must be *portable* in order to be an effective medium of exchange—a property that the stone money of Yap Island clearly lacks. Another important property of money is *divisibility.* Money must be measurable in both small units (for low-value goods and services) and large units (for high-value goods and services). Yap stone money is not divisible, so it is not a good medium of exchange for the majority of goods that are bought and sold.

1.a.2. Unit of Account Money is a unit of account: We price goods and services in terms of money. This common unit of measurement allows us to compare relative values easily. If whole-wheat bread sells for a dollar a loaf and white bread sells for 50 cents, we know that whole-wheat bread is twice as expensive as white bread.

Using money as a unit of account is efficient. It reduces the costs of gathering information on what things are worth. The use of money as a unit of account lowers information costs relative to barter. In a barter economy, people constantly have to evaluate the worth of the goods and services being offered. When money prices are placed on goods and services, their relative value is obvious.

> *The use of money as a unit of account lowers information costs.*

1.a.3. Store of Value Money functions as a store of value or purchasing power. If you are paid today, you do not have to hurry out to spend your money. It will still have value next week or next month. Some monies retain their value better than others. In colonial New England, both fish and furs served as money. But because fish does not store as well as furs, its usefulness as a store of value was limited. An important property of a money is its *durability,* its ability to retain its value over time.

Inflation plays a major role in determining the effectiveness of a money as a store of value. The higher the rate of inflation, the faster the purchasing power of money falls. In high-inflation countries, workers spend their pay as fast as possible because the purchasing power of their money is falling rapidly. It makes no sense to hold on to a money that is quickly losing value. In countries where the domestic money does not serve as a good store of value, it ceases to fulfill this function of money, and people begin to use something else as money, like the currency of another nation. For instance, U.S. dollars have long been a favorite store of value in Latin American countries that have experienced high inflation. This phenomenon—**currency substitution**—has been documented in Argentina, Bolivia, Mexico, and other countries during times of high inflation.

currency substitution:
the use of foreign money as a substitute for domestic money when the domestic economy has a high rate of inflation

2 | **How is the U.S. money supply defined?**

1.a.4. Standard of Deferred Payment Finally, money is a standard of deferred payment. Debt obligations are written in terms of money values. If you have a credit card bill that is due in 30 days, the value you owe is stated in monetary units—for example, dollars in the United States and yen in Japan. We use money values to state amounts of debt, and we use money to pay our debts.

We should make a distinction here between money and credit. Money is what we use to pay for goods and services. **Credit** is available savings that are lent to borrowers to spend. If you use your Visa or MasterCard to buy a shirt, you are not buying the shirt with your money. You are taking out a loan from the bank that issued the credit card in order to buy the shirt. Credit and money are different. Money is an asset, something you own. Credit is *debt,* something you owe.

credit: available savings that are lent to borrowers to spend

1.b. The U.S. Money Supply

The quantity of money that is available for spending is an important determinant of many key macroeconomic variables, since changes in the money supply affect interest rates, inflation, and other indicators of economic health. When economists measure the money supply, they measure spendable assets. Identifying those assets, however, can be difficult. Although it would seem that *all* bank deposits are money, some bank deposits are held for spending, while others are held for saving. In defining the money supply, then, economists must differentiate among assets on the basis of their liquidity and the likelihood of their being used for spending.

The problem of distinguishing among assets has produced more than one definition of the money supply. Today in the United States, the Federal Reserve uses M1 and M2.[1] Economists and policymakers use both definitions to evaluate

---

[1] Until March 2006, the Federal Reserve also published a broader measure of the money supply known as M3.

the availability of funds for spending. Although economists have tried to identify a single measure that best influences the business cycle and changes in interest rates and inflation, research indicates that different definitions work better to explain changes in macroeconomic variables at different times.

1.b.1. M1 Money Supply The narrowest and most liquid measure of the money supply is the **M1 money supply,** or financial assets that are immediately available for spending. This definition emphasizes the use of money as a medium of exchange. The M1 money supply consists of currency held by the nonbank public, traveler's checks, demand deposits, and other checkable deposits. Demand deposits and other checkable deposits are **transactions accounts;** they can be used to make direct payments to a third party.

Surveys find that families use their checking account for about 30 percent of purchases. Cash transactions account for about 44 percent of purchases.

The components of the M1 money supply are used for about 74 percent of family purchases. This is one reason why the M1 money supply may be a useful variable in formulating macroeconomic policy.

- *Currency* includes coins and paper money in circulation (in the hands of the public). In 2009, currency represented 54 percent of the M1 money supply. A common misconception about currency today is that it is backed by gold or silver. This is not true. There is nothing backing the U.S. dollar except the confidence of the public. This kind of monetary system is called a *fiduciary monetary system. Fiduciary* comes from the Latin *fiducia,* which means "trust." Our monetary system is based on trust. As long as we believe that our money is an acceptable form of payment for goods and services, the system works. It is not necessary for money to be backed by any precious object. As long as people believe that a money has value, it will serve as money.

The United States has not always operated under a fiduciary monetary system. At one time, the U.S. government issued gold and silver coins and paper money that could be exchanged for silver. In 1967, Congress authorized the U.S. Treasury to stop redeeming "silver certificate" paper money for silver. Coins with an intrinsic value are known as *commodity money;* they have value as a commodity in addition to their face value. The problem with commodity money is that as the value of the commodity increases, the money stops being circulated. People hoard coins when their commodity value exceeds their face value. For example, no one would take an old $20 gold piece to the grocery store to buy $20 worth of groceries because the gold is worth much more than $20 today.

The tendency to hoard money when its commodity value increases is called *Gresham's Law.* Thomas Gresham was a successful businessman and financial adviser to Queen Elizabeth I. He insisted that if two coins have the same face value but different intrinsic values—perhaps one coin is silver and the other brass—the cheaper coin will be used in exchange, while the more expensive coin will be hoarded. People sometimes state Gresham's Law as "bad money drives out good money," meaning that the money with the low commodity value will be used in exchange, while the money with the high commodity value will be driven out of hand-to-hand use and be hoarded.[2]

- *Traveler's checks.* Outstanding U.S. dollar–denominated traveler's checks issued by nonbank institutions are counted as part of the M1 money supply.

M1 money supply: the financial assets that are the most liquid

transactions account: a checking account at a bank or other financial institution that can be drawn on to make payments

According to Gresham's Law, bad money drives out good money.

---

[2]Actually, Gresham was not the first to recognize that bad money drives out good money. A fourteenth-century French theologian, Nicholas Oresme, made the same argument in his book *A Treatise on the Origin, Nature, Law, and Alterations of Money,* written almost 200 years before Gresham was born.

There are several nonbank issuers, among them American Express and Cook's. (Traveler's checks issued by banks are included in demand deposits. When a bank issues its own traveler's checks, it deposits the amount paid by the purchaser in a special account that is used to redeem the checks. Because this amount is counted as part of demand deposits, it is not counted again as part of outstanding traveler's checks.) Traveler's checks account for less than 1 percent of the M1 money supply.

• *Demand deposits.* Demand deposits are checking account deposits at a commercial bank. These deposits pay no interest. They are called *demand deposits* because the bank must pay the amount of the check immediately upon the demand of the depositor. Demand deposits accounted for 25 percent of the M1 money supply in 2009.

• *Other checkable deposits.* Until the 1980s, demand deposits were the only kind of checking account. Today there are many different kinds of checking accounts, known as *other checkable deposits (OCDs)*. These OCDs are accounts at financial institutions that pay interest and also give the depositor check-writing privileges. Among the OCDs included in the M1 money supply are the following: .

• *Negotiable orders of withdrawal (NOW) accounts* are interest-bearing checking accounts offered by savings and loan institutions.

• *Automatic transfer system (ATS) accounts* are accounts at commercial banks that combine an interest-bearing savings account with a noninterest-bearing checking account. The depositor keeps a small balance in the checking account; any time the checking account balance is overdrawn, funds are automatically transferred from the savings account.

• *Credit union share draft accounts* are interest-bearing checking accounts that credit unions offer their members.

• *Demand deposits at mutual savings banks* are checking account deposits at nonprofit savings and loan organizations. Any profits after operating expenses have been paid may be distributed to depositors.

1.b.2. M2 Money Supply The components of the M1 money supply are the most liquid assets, the assets that are most likely to be used for transactions. The **M2 money supply** is a broader definition of the money supply that includes assets in somewhat less liquid forms. The M2 money supply includes the M1 money supply plus savings deposits, small-denomination time deposits, and balances in retail money market mutual funds.

M2 money supply: M1 plus less liquid assets

• *Savings deposits* are accounts at banks and savings and loan associations that earn interest but offer no check-writing privileges.

• *Small-denomination time deposits* are often called *certificates of deposit.* Funds in these accounts must be deposited for a specified period of time. (Small means less than $100,000.)

• *Retail money market mutual fund balances* combine the *deposits of many* individuals and invest them in government Treasury bills and other short-term securities. Many money market mutual funds grant check-writing privileges but limit the size and number of checks.

Figure 1 summarizes the two definitions of the money supply.

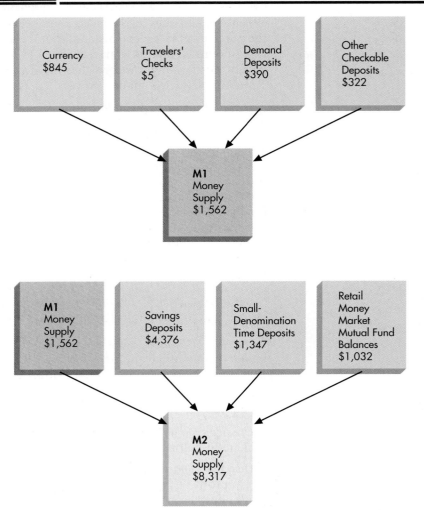

FIGURE 1   The U.S. Money Supply: M1 and M2 (billions of dollars)

1.c. Global Money

So far we have discussed the money supply in a domestic context. Just as the United States uses dollars as its domestic money, every nation has its own monetary unit of account. Japan has the yen, Mexico the peso, Canada the Canadian dollar, and so on. Since each nation uses a different money, how do countries pay for transactions that involve residents of other countries? As you saw in the chapter titled "An Introduction to the Foreign Exchange Market and the Balance of Payments," the foreign exchange market links national monies together so that transactions can be made across national borders. If Sears in the United States buys a home entertainment system from Sony in Japan, Sears can exchange dollars for yen in order to pay Sony in yen. The exchange rate between the dollar and the yen determines how many dollars are needed to purchase the required number of yen. For instance, if Sony wants 1,000,000 yen for the system and the exchange rate is ¥100 = $1, Sears needs $10,000 (1,000,000/100) to buy the yen.

Sales contracts between developed countries usually are written (invoiced) in the national currency of the exporter. To complete the transaction, the importer buys

3 | How do countries pay for international transactions?

the exporter's currency on the foreign exchange market. Trade between developing and developed nations typically is invoiced in the currency of the developed country, whether the developed country is the exporter or the importer, because the currency of the developed country is usually more stable and more widely traded on the foreign exchange market than the currency of the developing country. As a result, the currencies of the major developed countries tend to dominate the international medium-of-exchange and unit-of-account functions of money.

> *The currencies of the major developed countries tend to dominate the international medium-of-exchange and unit-of-account functions of money.*

1.c.1. International Reserve Currencies Governments hold monies as a temporary store of value until money is needed to settle international debts. At one time, gold was the primary **international reserve asset,** an asset used to settle debts between governments. Although gold still serves as an international reserve asset, its role is unimportant relative to that of currencies. Today national currencies function as international reserves. The currencies that are held for this purpose are called **international reserve currencies.**

international reserve asset: an asset used to settle debts between governments

international reserve currency: a currency held by a government to settle international debts

Table 1 shows the importance of the major international reserve currencies over time. In the mid-1970s, the U.S. dollar made up almost 80 percent of international reserve holdings. By 1990, its share had fallen to less than 50 percent, but that share has risen again recently.

Prior to the euro, there was an artificial currency in Europe, the **European currency unit (ECU).** The industrial nations of western Europe used ECUs to settle debts between them. The ECU was a **composite currency;** its value was an average of the values of several different national currencies: the Austrian schilling, the Belgian franc, the Danish krone, the Finnish markkaa, the French franc, the German mark, the Greek drachma, the Irish pound, the Italian lira, the Luxembourg franc, the Netherlands guilder, the Spanish peseta, and the Portuguese escudo (the U.K. pound was withdrawn from the system in September 1992).

European currency unit (ECU): a unit of account formerly used by western European nations as their official reserve asset

composite currency: an artificial unit of account that is an average of the values of several national currencies

The ECU was not an actual money but an accounting entry that was transferred between two parties. It was a step along the way to a new actual money, the *euro,* which replaced the ECU and circulates throughout the member countries as a real European money.

Another composite currency used in international financial transactions is the **special drawing right (SDR).** The value of the SDR is an average of the values of the currencies of the major industrial countries: the U.S. dollar, the euro, the Japanese yen, and the U.K. pound. This currency was created in 1970 by the International Monetary Fund, an international organization that oversees the monetary relationships among countries. The SDRs are an international reserve asset; they are

special drawing right (SDR): a composite currency whose value is the average of the values of the U.S. dollar, the euro, the Japanese yen, and the U.K. pound

TABLE 1	International Reserve Currencies (Percentage Shares of National Currencies in Total Official Holdings of Foreign Exchange)

Year	U.S. Dollar	Pound Sterling	Deutsche Mark	French Franc	Japanese Yen	Swiss Franc	Netherlands Guilder	Euro	ECU	Unspecified Currencies
1976	78.8	1.0	8.7	1.5	1.9	2.1	0.8	—	—	5.2
1980	56.6	2.5	12.8	1.5	3.7	2.8	1.1	—	16.4	2.7
1990	47.8	2.8	16.5	2.2	7.7	1.2	1.0	—	9.7	11.1
2000	70.5	2.8	—	—	6.3	0.3	—	18.8	—	1.4
2004	65.9	3.3	—	—	3.9	0.2	—	24.9	—	1.9
2008	64.0	4.0	—	—	3.3	0.1	—	26.5	—	2.0

Source: Data are drawn from International Monetary Fund, *Annual Report,* various issues.

used to settle international debts by transferring governments' accounts held at the International Monetary Fund. We discuss the role of the International Monetary Fund in later chapters.

Prior to the actual introduction of the euro, there was much discussion about its potential popularity as a reserve currency. In fact, some analysts were asserting that we should expect the euro to replace the U.S. dollar as the world's dominant currency. As Table 1 shows, the euro is now the second most popular reserve currency, but it has a much lower share of reserve currency use than the dollar does. The dominant world currency evolves over time as business firms and individuals find one currency more useful than another. Prior to the dominance of the dollar, the British pound was the world's most important reserve currency. As the U.S. economy grew in importance and U.S. financial markets developed to the huge size they now have, the growing use of the dollar emerged naturally as a result of the large volume of financial transactions involving the United States. Perhaps over time, the euro will someday replace the dollar as the world's dominant money.

RECAP

1. Money is the most liquid asset.

2. Money serves as a medium of exchange, a unit of account, a store of value, and a standard of deferred payment.

3. The use of money lowers transaction and information costs relative to barter.

4. To be used as money, an asset should be portable, divisible, and durable.

5. The M1 money supply is the most liquid definition of money and equals the sum of currency, travelers' checks, demand deposits, and other checkable deposits.

6. The M2 money supply equals the sum of the M1 money supply, savings deposits, small-denomination time deposits, and retail money market mutual fund balances.

7. International reserve currencies are held by governments to settle international debts.

8. Composite currencies have their value determined as an average of the values of several national currencies.

■ 2. Banking

Commercial banks are financial institutions that offer deposits on which checks can be written. In the United States and most other countries, commercial banks are privately owned. *Thrift institutions* are financial institutions that historically offered just savings accounts, not checking accounts. Savings and loan associations, credit unions, and mutual savings banks are all thrift institutions. Prior to 1980, the differences between commercial banks and thrift institutions were much greater than they are today. For example, only commercial banks could offer checking accounts, and those accounts earned no interest. The law also regulated maximum interest rates. In 1980, Congress passed the Depository Institutions Deregulation and Monetary Control Act, in part to stimulate competition among financial institutions. Now thrift institutions and even brokerage houses offer many of the same services as commercial banks. In

1999, Congress passed the Gramm-Leach-Bliley Act, which allowed commercial banks to expand their business into other areas of finance, including insurance and selling securities. This permitted greater integration of financial products under one umbrella known as a financial holding company. During the financial crisis of 2008, some of these large banks suffered dramatically as a result of aggressive risk-taking in financial products that turned out to be unsuccessful.

2.a. Financial Intermediaries

4 | Why are banks considered intermediaries?

Both commercial banks and thrift institutions are *financial intermediaries,* middlemen between savers and borrowers. Banks accept deposits from individuals and firms, then use those deposits to make loans to individuals and firms. The borrowers are likely to be different individuals or firms from the depositors, although it is not uncommon for a household or business to be both a depositor and a borrower at the same institution. Of course, depositors and borrowers have very different interests. For instance, depositors typically prefer short-term deposits; they don't want to tie up their money for a long time. Borrowers, on the other hand, usually want more time for repayment. Banks typically package short-term deposits into longer-term loans. To function as intermediaries, banks must serve the interests of both depositors and borrowers.

A bank is willing to serve as an intermediary because it hopes to earn a profit from this activity. It pays a lower interest rate on deposits than it charges on loans; the difference is a source of profit for the bank. Islamic banks are prohibited by holy law from charging interest on loans; thus, they use a different system for making a profit (see the Global Business Insight "Islamic Banking").

2.b. U.S. Banking

2.b.1. Current Structure
If you add together all the pieces of the bar graph in Figure 2, you see that there were 99,161 depository institution offices operating in the United States in 2008. Roughly 85 percent of these offices were operated by banks and 15 percent by savings institutions.

Historically, U.S. banks were allowed to operate in just one state. In some states, banks could operate in only one location. This is known as *unit banking.* Today there are still many unit banks, but these are typically small community banks.

Over time, legal barriers have been reduced so that today almost all states permit entry to banks located out of state. In the future, banking is likely to be done on a national rather than a local scale. The growth of automated teller machines (ATMs) is a big step in this direction. The ATM networks give bank customers access to services over a much wider geographic area than any single bank's branches cover. These international networks allow a bank customer from Dallas to withdraw cash in Seattle, Zurich, or almost anywhere in the world. Today more than one-fourth of ATM transactions occur at banks that are not the customer's own bank.

2.b.2. Bank Failures
Banking in the United States has had a colorful history of booms and panics. Banking is like any other business. Banks that are poorly managed can fail; banks that are properly managed tend to prosper. Regional economic conditions are also very important. In the mid-1980s, hundreds of banks in states with large oil industries, like Texas and Oklahoma, and in farming states, like Kansas and Nebraska, could not collect many of their loans as a result of falling oil and agricultural prices. Those states that were heavily dependent on the oil industry and on farming had significantly more banks fail than did other states. The problem was not so much bad management as it was a matter of unexpectedly bad business conditions. The lesson here is simple: Commercial banks, like other profit-making enterprises, are not exempt from failure.

Global Business Insight

Islamic Banking

According to the Muslim holy book, the Koran, Islamic law prohibits interest charges on loans. Banks that operate under Islamic law still act as intermediaries between borrowers and lenders. However, they do not charge interest on loans or pay interest on deposits. Instead, they take a predetermined percentage of the borrowing firm's profits until the loan is repaid, then share those profits with depositors.

Since the mid-1970s, over a hundred Islamic banks have opened, most of them in Arab nations. Deposits in these banks have grown rapidly. In fact, in some banks, deposits have grown faster than good loan opportunities, forcing the banks to refuse new deposits until their loan portfolio could grow to match the available deposits. One bank in Bahrain claimed that over 60 percent of deposits during its first two years in operation were made by people who had never made a bank deposit before. In addition to profit-sharing deposits, Islamic banks typically offer checking accounts, traveler's checks, and trade-related services on a fee basis.

Because the growth of deposits has usually exceeded the growth of local investment opportunities, Islamic banks have been lending money to traditional banks to fund investments that satisfy the moral and commercial needs of both, such as lending to private firms. These funds cannot be used to invest in interest-bearing securities or in firms that deal in alcohol, pork, gambling, or arms. The growth of mutually profitable investment opportunities suggests that Islamic banks are meeting both the dictates of Muslim depositors and the profitability requirements of modern banking.

The potential for expansion and profitability of Islamic financial services has led major banks to create units dedicated to providing Islamic banking services. In addition, there are stock mutual funds that screen firms for compliance with Islamic law before buying their stock. For instance, since most financial institutions earn and pay large amounts of interest, such firms would tend to be excluded from an Islamic mutual fund.

The most popular instrument for financing Islamic investments is *murabaha*. This is essentially cost-plus financing, where the financial institution purchases goods or services for a client and then, over time, is repaid an amount that equals the original cost plus an additional amount of profit. Such an arrangement is even used for financing mortgages on property in the United States. A financial institution will buy a property and then charge a client rent until the rent payments equal the purchase price plus some profit. After the full payment is received, the title to the property is passed to the client.

Sources: Peter Koh, "The Shari'ah Alternative," *Euromoney* (October 2002). A good source of additional information is found on the website www.failaka.com/.

At one time, a bank panic could close a bank. A bank panic occurs when depositors, fearing that a bank will close, rush to withdraw their funds. Banks keep only a fraction of their deposits on reserve, so bank panics often resulted in bank closings as depositors tried to withdraw more money than the banks had on hand on a given day. In the United States today, this is no longer true. The **Federal Deposit Insurance Corporation (FDIC)** was created in 1933. The FDIC is a federal agency that insures bank deposits in commercial banks so that depositors do not lose their deposits if a bank fails. FDIC insurance covers depositors against losses up to $250,000 in a bank account. Figure 3 shows the number of failed banks and the number without deposit insurance. In the 1930s, many of the banks that failed were not insured by the FDIC. In this environment, it made sense for depositors to worry about losing their money. In the 1980s, the number of bank failures increased dramatically, but none of the failed banks were uninsured. Deposits in those banks were

Federal Deposit Insurance Corporation (FDIC): a federal agency that insures deposits in commercial banks

| FIGURE 2 | U.S. Depository Institutions |

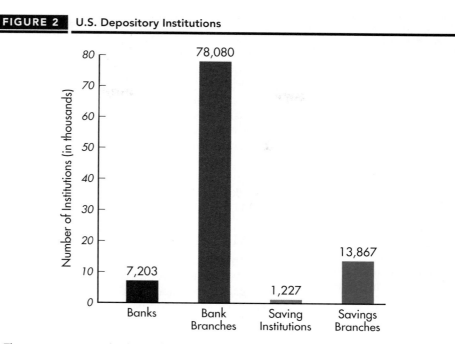

There are many more banks and bank branches than there are savings institutions and savings branches.

Source: Data are drawn from Federal Deposit Insurance Corporation, Statistics on Banking, www.fdic.gov.

| FIGURE 3 | Number of Failed and Uninsured Banks |

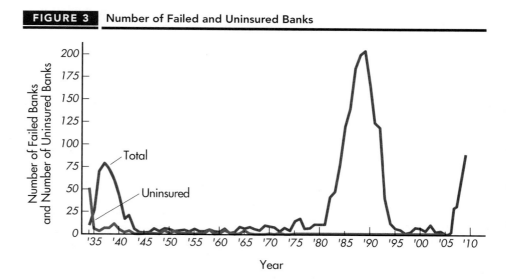

The number of banks that went out of business in the 1980s was the highest it had been since the Depression. Unlike the banks that failed in the 1930s, however, the banks that closed in the 1980s were covered by deposit insurance, so depositors did not lose their money.

Source: Data are from Federal Deposit Insurance Corporation, Statistics on Banking, www.fdic.gov/.

> *A bank panic occurs when depositors become frightened and rush to withdraw their funds.*

protected by the federal government. Even though large banks have failed in recent times, the depositors have not lost their deposits.

Figure 3 shows a rise in the number of bank failures associated with the financial crisis of 2008 (which actually began in 2007). We see that from 0 bank failures in 2006, there were 3 in 2007, 30 in 2008, and 90 by September of 2009. The financial crisis resulted in many banks experiencing large losses on loans due to businesses and households who were unable to repay their debts.

Deposit insurance exists today in most of the world's countries. Africa is the only continent where deposit insurance is not found widely. Looking at the countries that are neighbors of the United States, Canada insures deposits up to 100,000 Canadian dollars (worth about 85,000 U.S. dollars at the time this text was revised), while Mexico insures deposits up to 1,308,000 pesos (worth about 100,000 U.S. dollars at the time this text was revised).

2.c. International Banking

5 | **How does international banking differ from domestic banking?**

Large banks today are truly transnational enterprises. International banks, like domestic banks, act as financial intermediaries, but they operate in a different legal environment. The laws regulating domestic banking in each nation are typically very restrictive, yet many nations allow international banking to operate largely unregulated. Because they are not hampered by regulations, international banks typically can offer depositors and borrowers better terms than could be negotiated at a domestic bank.

Eurocurrency market or offshore banking: the market for deposits and loans generally denominated in a currency other than the currency of the country in which the transaction occurs

2.c.1. Eurocurrency Market Because of the competitive interest rates offered on loans and deposits, there is a large market for deposits and loans at international banks. For instance, a bank in London, Tokyo, or the Bahamas may accept deposits and make loans denominated in U.S. dollars. The international deposit and loan market often is called the **Eurocurrency market,** or **offshore banking.** In the Eurocurrency market, the currency used in a banking transaction generally is not the domestic currency of the country in which the bank is located. (The prefix "Euro-" is misleading here. Although the market originated in Europe, today it is global and operates with different foreign currencies; it is in no way limited to European currencies or European banks.) There are deposits and loans in Eurodollars, Euroyen, Euroeuro, and any other major currency.

In those countries that allow offshore banking, we find two sets of banking rules: restrictive regulations for banking in the domestic market, and little or no regulation for offshore banking activities. Domestic banks are required to hold reserves against deposits and to carry deposit insurance, and they often face government-mandated credit or interest rate restrictions. The Eurocurrency market operates with few or no costly restrictions, and international banks generally pay lower taxes than domestic banks. Because offshore banks operate with lower costs, they are able to offer their customers better terms than domestic banks can.

Offshore banks are able to offer a higher rate on dollar deposits and a lower rate on dollar loans than their domestic competitors. Without these differences, the Eurodollar market probably would not exist because Eurodollar transactions are riskier than domestic transactions in the United States as a result of the lack of government regulation and deposit insurance.

There are always risks involved in international banking. Funds are subject to control by both the country in which the bank is located and the country in whose currency the deposit or loan is denominated. Suppose a Canadian firm wants to withdraw funds from a U.S. dollar–denominated bank deposit in Hong Kong. This transaction is subject to control in Hong Kong. For example, the government may not allow foreign exchange to leave the country freely. It is also subject to U.S. control. If the United States reduces its outflow of dollars, for instance, the Hong Kong bank may have difficulty paying the Canadian firm with U.S. dollars.

The Eurocurrency market exists for all of the major international currencies, but the value of activity in Eurodollars dwarfs the rest. Eurodollars account for about 60 percent of deposit and loan activity in the Eurocurrency market. This emphasizes the important role that the U.S. dollar plays in global finance. Even deposits and loans that do not involve a U.S. lender or borrower often are denominated in U.S. dollars.

2.c.2. International Banking Facilities The term *offshore banking* is somewhat misleading in the United States today. Prior to December 1981, U.S. banks were forced to process international deposits and loans through their offshore branches. Many of the branches in places like the Cayman Islands and the Bahamas were little more than "shells," small offices with a telephone. Yet these branches allowed U.S. banks to avoid the reserve requirements and interest rate regulations that restricted domestic banking activities.

international banking facility (IBF): a division of a U.S. bank that is allowed to receive deposits from and make loans to nonresidents of the United States without the restrictions that apply to domestic U.S. banks

In December 1981, the Federal Reserve Board legalized **international banking facilities (IBFs),** allowing domestic banks to take part in international banking on U.S. soil. The IBFs are not physical entities; they are bookkeeping systems set up in existing bank offices to record international banking transactions. The IBFs can receive deposits from and make loans to nonresidents of the United States and other IBFs. These deposits and loans must be kept separate from other transactions because IBFs are not subject to the reserve requirements, interest rate regulations, or FDIC deposit insurance premiums that apply to domestic U.S. banking. The goal of permitting IBFs was to allow banking offices in the United States to compete with offshore banks without having to use offshore banking offices.

2.d. Informal Financial Markets in Developing Countries

In many developing countries, a sizable portion of the population has no access to formal financial institutions like banks. In these cases, it is common for informal financial markets to develop. Such markets may take many different forms. Sometimes they take the form of an individual making small loans to local residents. Sometimes groups of individuals form a self-help group where they pool their resources to provide loans to each other. To give some idea of the nature of these sorts of arrangements, a few common types are reviewed here.

ROSCA: a rotating savings and credit association popular in developing countries

A common form of informal financial arrangement is rotating savings and credit associations, or **ROSCAs.** These tend to go by different names in different countries, such as *tandas* in Mexico, *susu* in Ghana, *hui* in China, and *chits* in India. ROSCAs are like savings clubs; members contribute money every week or month into a common fund, and then each month one member of the group receives the full amount contributed by everyone. This usually operates for a cycle of as many months as there are members in the group. For instance, if there are 12 members in the group contributing $10 a month, then a cycle would last 12 months, and each month a different member of the group would receive the $120 available. Thus the ROSCA is a vehicle for saving in which only the last member of the group to receive the funds has saved over the full 12-month period before having the use of $120. The determination of who receives the funds in which month is typically made by a random drawing at the beginning of the cycle. So a ROSCA is a means of saving that allows all but one member in each cycle to receive funds faster than the members could save on their own.

The informal market in many countries is dominated by individual lenders, who tend to specialize in a local area and make loans primarily for the acquisition of seeds, fertilizer, or mechanical equipment needed by farmers. Surveys in China indicate that about two-thirds of farm loans to poor rural households are made by informal lenders. Such informal lenders are distinct from friends and relatives, who can also be important in lending to poor households. The interest rate charged by informal lenders is typically significantly higher than that charged by banks or government lending institutions. The higher interest rates may reflect the higher risk associated with the borrower, who may have no collateral (goods or possessions that can be transferred to the lender if the borrower does not repay).

Informal loans among friends or relatives are typically one-time loans for purposes like financing weddings or home construction. If your cousin lends you money today in your time of need, then you are expected to lend to him at some later time if he has a need. Repeat loans, like those to a farmer in advance of the harvest each year, tend to be made by individuals who are unrelated to the borrower and are in the business of providing such financing.

hawala: an international informal financial market used by Muslims

A form of informal financial market that gained much publicity after the September 11, 2001, terrorist attacks on New York City's World Trade Center is the **hawala** network. In much of the developing world with heavy Muslim populations, people can send money all over the world using the hawala network. Let's say that a Pakistani immigrant who is working as a taxi driver in New York wants to send money to a relative in a remote village of Pakistan. He can go to a hawala agent and give the money to the agent, who writes down the destination location and the amount of money to be sent. The agent then gives the taxi driver a code number and the location of an agent in Pakistan, which the driver passes along to his relative. The agent in the United States then calls a counterpart agent in Pakistan and informs that person of the amount of money and the code number. The Pakistani agent will pay the money to whoever walks in his door with the right code number. Since no records of the name or address of either the source of the money or the recipient are kept, it is easy to see how such a network can be an effective source of financing for terrorist activities. For this reason, the hawala network was a source of much investigation following the 2001 terrorist attacks in the United States. Of course, such a network serves many more than just terrorists, and it is an important part of the informal financial market operating in many countries. For poor people without bank accounts, such informal markets allow some access to financial services.

RECAP

1. The Depository Institutions Deregulation and Monetary Control Act (1980) eliminated many of the differences between commercial banks and thrift institutions.

2. Banks are financial intermediaries.

3. The deregulation act also eliminated many of the differences between national and state banks.

4. Since the FDIC insures bank deposits in commercial banks, bank panics are no longer a threat to the banking system.

5. The international deposit and loan market is called the Eurocurrency market or offshore banking.

6. With the legalization of international banking facilities in 1981, the Federal Reserve allowed international banking activities on U.S. soil.

7. Informal financial markets play an important role in developing countries.

6 | **How do banks create money?**

fractional reserve banking system: a system in which banks keep less than 100 percent of their deposits available for withdrawal

■ 3. Banks and the Money Supply

Banks create money by lending money. They take deposits, then lend a portion of those deposits in order to earn interest income. The portion of their deposits that banks keep on hand is a *reserve* to meet the demand for withdrawals. In a **fractional reserve banking system,** banks keep less than 100 percent of their deposits as reserves. If all banks hold 10 percent of their deposits as a reserve, for example, then 90 percent of their deposits are available for loans. When they loan these deposits, money is created.

3.a. Deposits and Loans

Figure 4 shows a simple balance sheet for First National Bank. A *balance sheet* is a financial statement that records a firm's assets (what the firm owns) and liabilities (what the firm owes). The bank has cash assets ($100,000) and loan assets ($900,000). The deposits placed in the bank ($1,000,000) are a liability (they are an asset of the depositors).[3] Total assets always equal total liabilities on a balance sheet.

Banks keep a percentage of their deposits on reserve. In the United States, the reserve requirement is set by the Federal Reserve Board (which will be discussed in detail in the next chapter). Banks can keep more than the minimum reserve if they choose. Let's assume that the reserve requirement is set at 10 percent and that banks always hold actual reserves equal to 10 percent of deposits. With deposits of $1,000,000, the bank must keep $100,000 (.10 × $1,000,000) in cash reserves held in its vault. This $100,000 is the bank's **required reserves,** as the Federal Reserve requires the banks to keep 10 percent of deposits on reserve. This is exactly what First National Bank has on hand in Figure 4. Any cash held in excess of $100,000

required reserves: the cash reserves (a percentage of deposits) that a bank must keep on hand or on deposit with the Federal Reserve

---

| FIGURE 4 | First National Bank Balance Sheet, Initial Position |

First National Bank

Assets		Liabilities	
Cash	$100,000	Deposits	$1,000,000
Loans	900,000		
Total	$1,000,000	Total	$1,000,000

Total reserves = $100,000

Required reserves = 0.1($1,000,000) = $100,000

Excess reserves = 0

The bank has cash totaling $100,000 and loans totaling $900,000, for total assets of $1,000,000. Deposits of $1,000,000 make up its total liabilities. With a reserve requirement of 10 percent, the bank must hold required reserves of 10 percent of its deposits, or $100,000. Because the bank is holding cash of $100,000, its total reserves equal its required reserves. Because it has no excess reserves, the bank cannot make new loans.

---

[3]In our simplified balance sheet, we assume that there is no net worth, or owner's equity. Net worth is the value of the owner's claim on the firm (the owner's equity) and is found as the difference between the value of assets and the value of nonequity liabilities.

FIGURE 5   First National Bank Balance Sheet after $100,000 Deposit

---

First National Bank

Assets		Liabilities	
Cash	$200,000	Deposits	$1,100,000
Loans	900,000		
Total	$1,1000,000	Total	$1,100,000

Total reserves = $200,000

Required reserves = 0.1($1,000,000) = $110,000

Excess reserves = $90,000

A $100,000 deposit increases the bank's cash reserves to $200,000 and its deposits to $1,100,000. The bank must hold 10 percent of deposits, or $110,000, on reserve. The difference between total reserves ($200,000) and required reserves ($110,000) is excess reserves ($90,000). The bank now has $90,000 available for lending.

---

excess reserves: the cash reserves beyond those required, which can be loaned

would represent **excess reserves.** Excess reserves can be loaned by the bank. A bank is *loaned up* when it has zero excess reserves. Because its total reserves equal its required reserves, First National Bank has no excess reserves and is loaned up. The bank cannot make any new loans.

What happens if the bank receives a new deposit of $100,000? Figure 5 shows the bank's balance sheet right after the deposit is made. Its cash reserves are now $200,000, and its deposits are now $1,100,000. With the additional deposit, the bank's total reserves equal $200,000. Its required reserves are $110,000 (.10 × $1,100,000). So its excess reserves are $90,000 ($200,000 − $110,000). Since a bank can lend its excess reserves, First National Bank can loan an additional $90,000.

Suppose the bank lends someone $90,000 by depositing $90,000 in the borrower's First National account. At the time the loan is made, the money supply increases by the amount of the loan, $90,000. By making the loan, the bank has increased the money supply. But this is not the end of the story. The borrower spends the $90,000, and it winds up being deposited in the Second National Bank.

Figure 6 shows the balance sheets of both banks after the loan has been made and the money has been spent and deposited at Second National Bank. First National Bank now has loans of $990,000 and no excess reserves (the required reserves of $110,000 equal total reserves). So First National Bank can make no more loans until a new deposit is made. However, Second National Bank has a new deposit of $90,000 (to simplify the analysis, we assume that this is the first transaction at Second National Bank). Its required reserves are 10 percent of $90,000, or $9,000. With total reserves of $90,000, Second National Bank has excess reserves of $81,000. It can make loans up to $81,000.

Notice what has happened to the banks' deposits as a result of the initial $100,000 deposit in First National Bank. Deposits at First National Bank have increased by $100,000. Second National Bank has a new deposit of $90,000, and the loans it makes will increase the money supply even more. Table 2 shows how the initial deposit of $100,000 is multiplied through the banking system. Each time a new loan is made, the money is spent and redeposited in the banking system. But each bank keeps 10 percent of the deposit on reserve, lending only 90 percent. So the amount of money loaned decreases by 10 percent each time it goes through another bank. If we carried the calculations out, you would

| FIGURE 6 | Balance Sheets after a $90,000 Loan Made by First National Bank Is Spent and Deposited at Second National Bank |

First National Bank

Assets		Liabilities	
Cash	$110,000	Deposits	$1,100,000
Loans	990,000		
Total	$1,100,000	Total	$1,100,000

Total reserves = $110,000

Required reserves = 0.1($1,100,000) = $110,000

Excess reserves = 0

Second National Bank

Assets		Liabilities	
Cash	$90,000	Deposits	$90,000
Total	$90,000	Total	$90,000

Total reserves = $90,000

Required reserves = 0.1($90,000) = $9,000

Excess reserves = $81,000

Once First National Bank makes the $90,000 loan, its cash reserves fall to $110,000 and its loans increase to $990,000. At this point, the bank's total reserves ($110,000) equal its required reserves (10 percent of deposits). Because it has no excess reserves, the bank cannot make new loans.

Second National Bank receives a deposit of $90,000. It must hold 10 percent, or $9,000, on reserve. Its excess reserves equal total reserves ($90,000) minus required reserves ($9,000), or $81,000. Second National Bank can make a maximum loan of $81,000.

see that the total increase in deposits associated with the initial $100,000 deposit is $1,000,000. Required reserves would increase by $100,000, and new loans would increase by $900,000.

3.b. Deposit Expansion Multiplier

Rather than calculate the excess reserves at each bank, as we did in Table 2, we can use a simple formula to find the maximum increase in deposits given a new deposit. The **deposit expansion multiplier** equals the reciprocal of the reserve requirement:

deposit expansion multiplier: the reciprocal of the reserve requirement

$$\text{Deposite expansion multiplier} = \frac{1}{\text{reserve requirement}}$$

In our example, the reserve requirement is 10 percent, or .10. So the deposit expansion multiplier equals 1/.10, or 10. An initial increase in deposits of $100,000 expands deposits in the banking system by 10 times $100,000, or $1,000,000. This is because the new $100,000 deposit creates $90,000 in excess reserves and 10 × $90,000 = $900,000, which when added to the initial deposit of $100,000

TABLE 2   The Effect on Bank Deposits of an Initial Bank Deposit of $100,000

Bank	New Deposit	Required Reserves	Excess Reserves (new loans)
First National	$100,000	$10,000	$90,000
Second National	90,000	9,000	81,000
Third National	81,000	8,100	72,900
Fourth National	72,900	7,290	65,610
Fifth National	65,610	6,561	59,049
Sixth National	59,049	5,905	53,144
...	...	...	...
Total	$1,000,000	$100,000	$900,000

equals $1,000,000. The maximum increase in deposits is found by multiplying the deposit expansion multiplier by the amount of the new deposit.

With no new deposits, the banking system can increase the money supply only by the multiplier times excess reserves:

$$\text{Deposit expansion multiplier} \times \text{excess reserves}$$
$$= \text{maximum increase in deposits}$$

The deposit expansion multiplier indicates the *maximum* possible change in total deposits when a new deposit is made. For the effect to be that large, all excess reserves must be loaned out, and all of the money that is deposited must stay in the banking system.

If banks hold more reserves than the minimum required, they lend a smaller fraction of any new deposits, and this reduces the effect of the deposit expansion multiplier. For instance, if the reserve requirement is 10 percent, we know that the deposit expansion multiplier is 10. If a bank chooses to hold 20 percent of its deposits on reserve, the deposit expansion multiplier is only 5 (1/.20).

If money (currency and coin) is withdrawn from the banking system and kept as cash, deposits and bank reserves are smaller, and there is less money to loan out. This *currency drain*—removal of money—reduces the deposit expansion multiplier. The greater the currency drain, the smaller the multiplier. There is always some currency drain, as people carry currency to pay for day-to-day transactions. However, during historical periods of bank panic, where people lost confidence in banks, large currency withdrawals contributed to declines in the money supply.

Remember that the deposit expansion multiplier measures the *maximum* expansion of the money supply by the banking system. Any single bank can lend only its excess reserves, but the whole banking system can expand the money supply by a multiple of the initial excess reserves. Thus, the banking system as a whole can increase the money supply by the deposit expansion multiplier times the excess reserves of the system. The initial bank is limited to its initial loan; the banking system generates loan after loan based on that initial loan. A new deposit can increase the money supply by the deposit expansion multiplier times the new deposit.

In the next chapter, we discuss how changes in the reserve requirement affect the money supply and the economy. This area of policymaking is controlled by the Federal Reserve.

> *A single bank increases the money supply by lending its excess reserves; the banking system increases the money supply by the deposit expansion multiplier times the excess reserves of the system.*

RECAP

1. The fractional reserve banking system allows banks to expand the money supply by making loans.

2. Banks must keep a fraction of their deposits on reserve; their excess reserves are available for lending.

3. The deposit expansion multiplier measures the maximum increase in the money supply given a new deposit; it is the reciprocal of the reserve requirement.

4. A single bank increases the money supply by lending its excess reserves.

5. The banking system can increase the money supply by the deposit expansion multiplier times the excess reserves in the banking system.

SUMMARY

1 | What is money?

- Money is anything that is generally acceptable to sellers in exchange for goods and services. *§1*

- Money serves as a medium of exchange, a unit of account, a store of value, and a standard of deferred payment. *§1.a*

- Money, because it is more efficient than barter, lowers transaction costs. *§1.a.1*

- Money should be portable, divisible, and durable. *§1.a.1, 1.a.3*

2 | How is the U.S. money supply defined?

- There are two definitions of money based on its liquidity. *§1.b*

- The M1 money supply equals the sum of currency plus traveler's checks plus demand deposits plus other checkable deposits. *§1.b.1*

- The M2 money supply equals the M1 money supply plus savings deposits, small-denomination time deposits, and retail money market mutual fund balances. *§1.b.2*

3 | How do countries pay for international transactions?

- Using the foreign exchange market, governments (along with individuals and firms) are able to convert national currencies to pay for trade. *§1.c*

- The U.S. dollar is the world's major international reserve currency. *§1.c.1*

- The European currency unit (ECU) was a composite currency whose value was an average of the values of several western European currencies. *§1.c.1*

4 | Why are banks considered intermediaries?

- Banks serve as middlemen between savers and borrowers. *§2.a*

5 | How does international banking differ from domestic banking?

- Domestic banking in most nations is strictly regulated; international banking is not. *§2.c*

- The Eurocurrency market is the international deposit and loan market. *§2.c.*

- International banking facilities (IBFs) allow U.S. domestic banks to carry on international banking activities on U.S. soil. *§2.c.2*

- Informal financial markets are important in developing countries. *§2.d*

6 | How do banks create money?

- Banks can make loans up to the amount of their excess reserves, their total reserves minus their required reserves. *§3.a*

- The deposit expansion multiplier is the reciprocal of the reserve requirement. *§3.b*

- A single bank expands the money supply by lending its excess reserves. *§3.b*

- The banking system can increase the money supply by the deposit expansion multiplier times the excess reserves in the system. *§3.b.*

KEY TERMS

money §1

liquid asset §1

currency substitution §1.a.3

credit §1.a.4

M1 money supply §1.b.1

M2 money supply §1.b.1

transactions account §1.b.1

international reserve asset §1.c.1

international reserve currency §1.c.1

European currency unit (ECU) §1.c.1

composite currency §1.c.1

special drawing right (SDR) §1.c.1

Federal Deposit Insurance Corporation (FDIC) §2.b.2

Eurocurrency market or offshore banking §2.c.1

international banking facility (IBF) §2.c.2

ROSCA §2.d

hawala §2.d

fractional reserve banking system §3

required reserves §3.a

excess reserves §3.a

deposit expansion multiplier §3.b

EXERCISES

1. Describe the four functions of money, using the U.S. dollar to provide an example of how dollars serve each function.

2. During World War II, cigarettes were used as money in prisoner of war camps. Considering the attributes that a good money should possess, why would cigarettes emerge as money among prisoners?

3. What is a financial intermediary? Give an example of how your bank or credit union serves as a financial intermediary between you and the rest of the economy.

4. What is the Eurocurrency market, and how is banking in the Eurocurrency market different from domestic banking?

5. What are IBFs? Why do you think they were legalized?

6. First Bank has cash reserves of $200,000, loans of $800,000, and deposits of $1,000,000.
   a. Prepare a balance sheet for the bank.
   b. If the bank maintains a reserve requirement of 12 percent, what is the largest loan it can make?
   c. What is the maximum amount by which the money supply can be increased as a result of First Bank's new loan?

7. Yesterday bank A had no excess reserves. Today it received a new deposit of $5,000.
   a. If the bank maintains a reserve requirement of 2 percent, what is the maximum loan that bank A can make?
   b. What is the maximum amount by which the money supply can be increased as a result of bank A's new loan?

8. "M2 is a better definition of the money supply than M1." Agree or disagree with this statement. In your argument, clearly state the criteria on which you are basing your decision.

9. The deposit expansion multiplier measures the maximum possible expansion of the money supply in the banking system. What factors could cause the actual expansion of the money supply to differ from that given by the deposit expansion multiplier?

10. What is liquidity? Rank the following assets in order of their liquidity: $10 bill, personal check for $20, savings account with $400 in it, stereo, car, house, traveler's check.

Use the following table on the components of money in a hypothetical economy to do exercises 11–12.

Money Component	Amount
Traveler's checks	$100
Currency	$2,000
Small-denomination time deposits	$3,500
Savings deposits	$6,000
Demand deposits	$5,000
Other checkable deposits	$9,000
Retail money market mutual funds	$7,500

11. What is the value of M1 in the above table?

12. What is the value of M2 in the above table?

13. The deposit expansion multiplier has been defined as the reciprocal of the reserve requirement. Suppose that banks must hold 10 percent of their deposits in reserve. However, banks also lose 10 percent of their deposits through cash drains out of the banking system.
   a. What would the deposit expansion multiplier be if there were no cash drain?
   b. With the cash drain, what is the value of the deposit expansion multiplier?

International Demand for the Dollar

Because of its relative stability and near-universal recognition and acceptance, USD function as both a store of value and a medium of exchange when other stable or convenient assets (for example, national currencies) are not available. Thus, during times of economic or political crisis, a stable and familiar currency, such as USD, often is sought as a portable and liquid hedge against possible devaluation. Similarly, USD are a popular medium of exchange in regional or cross-border trade when credit markets are undeveloped or banks are underdeveloped or unreliable.

U.S. currency in the form of banknotes (paper currency) in circulation outside the U.S. Treasury and the Federal Reserve System was about $759 billion by the end of 2005. Current estimates indicate that the proportion of U.S. currency held abroad is as much as 60 percent of the amount in circulation, or roughly $450 billion. The accompanying table shows the total amount of U.S. banknotes in circulation as well as the share attributed to the $100 denomination. In value terms, the share of USD held as $100s has increased from around 21 percent at the end of 1965 to nearly 72 percent at the end of 2005. In addition, the share of $100 notes estimated to be held outside the United States has also increased. As shown in the right-hand column of the table, the

share of $100 notes held outside the United States rose sharply over the period from 1975 to 1995 and then remained relatively stable at around two-thirds of all $100 notes since 1999.

The international circulation of U.S. currency in Europe expanded after World War I in the wake of the hyperinflation induced by the obligations arising from the Treaty of Versailles. At that time, U.S. currency was viewed favorably because the United States was still on the gold standard, while Great Britain, whose currency was the leading alternative to U.S. currency, remained off the gold standard until May 1925. Other countries, such as Panama, adopted U.S. currency as their official currency. In the past two decades, the international usage of U.S. banknotes expanded largely because of two events: the breakup of the Soviet Union and episodes of high and volatile inflation in Latin America.

During a period of instability, the magnitude of the inflows of U.S. banknotes depends on a country's experience with U.S. currency in the past and its economic circumstances. In particular, demand for USD appears to depend on two factors. The first factor is the ability of people to purchase U.S. banknotes, and the second factor is their confidence in the domestic banking system. The less confidence people have that the

value of their bank holdings will be protected, the more likely they are to want to hold U.S. banknotes. Similarly, the more developed the banking system, the more likely it is that people will have a wide variety of options for saving and for making transactions.

Because many holders of U.S. currency view it as a form of insurance against future instability, they are reluctant to alter their usage patterns for USD during periods of economic stability by either shifting out of U.S. banknotes or by switching to another currency, such as the euro. Since the introduction of euro banknotes in the beginning of 2002, it appeared that demand for USD waned somewhat in countries in and near the eurozone. However, responses to International Currency Awareness Program ICAP team inquiries indicated that USD holders have moved to holding euros in addition to, rather than instead of, USD. It is likely that underlying patterns of U.S. currency usage will change slowly in countries that already use USD. In countries that do not now use USD to a significant degree, it is difficult to predict if and when a crisis prompting demand for a second currency might develop.

Source: U.S. Treasury Dept., The Use and Counterfeiting of U.S. Currency Abroad, Part 3, Section 1.3, 2006. http://www.federalreserve.gov/boarddocs/rptcongress/counterfeit/counterfeit2006.pdf.

U.S. Banknotes in Circulation, $100s in Circulation, and $100s Held Abroad (Billions of Dollars, Except as Noted, at Year-Ends)

Year	Total (1)	$100s (2)	Share of $100s in Total (percent) (3)	Estimates of $100s Held Abroad, Wholesale (4)	Estimates of Share of $100s Held Abroad Wholesale (percent) (5)
1965	38.0	8.1	21.4	3.9	48.3
1970	50.8	12.1	23.8	5.7	47.5
1975	77.6	23.1	29.8	10.0	43.2
1980	124.8	49.3	39.5	23.8	48.4
1985	182.0	81.2	44.6	45.8	56.4
1990	268.2	140.2	52.3	85.7	61.1
1995	401.5	241.5	60.2	169.2	70.1
1999	601.2	386.2	64.2	254.6	65.9
2000	563.9	377.7	67.0	256.0	67.7
2001	611.7	421.0	68.8	279.8	66.4
2002	654.8	458.7	70.1	301.3	65.7
2003	690.2	487.8	70.7	317.9	65.2
2004	719.9	516.7	71.8	332.7	64.4
2005	758.8	545.0	71.8	352.0	64.6

Sources: Columns 1 and 2: *Treasury Bulletin*, various issues, Table USCC-2. Figures include vault cash but exclude coin. Column 4: Federal Reserve Board Flow of Funds Accounts (Z.1. Statistical Release, Table L. 204, line 22).

There is considerable evidence that U.S. dollars are held in large amounts in many developing countries. Residents of these countries hold dollars because their domestic inflation rate is (or has been) very high, and by holding dollars, they can avoid the rapid erosion of purchasing power that is associated with holding the domestic currency. This "dollarization" of a country begins with people's holding dollars rather than domestic currency as savings (the store-of-value function of money). But if high inflation continues, dollars, rather than domestic currency, come to be used in day-to-day transactions as the medium of exchange. In the late 1980s, as the Polish economy became heavily dollarized, a common joke in Poland was: "What do America and Poland have in common? In America, you can buy everything for dollars and nothing for zlotys [the Polish currency]. In Poland, it is exactly the same." In 2009, one could have made the same comment about Zimbabwe, where the economy was officially dollarized after hyperinflation that eventually led to the issue of a 100 trillion Zimbabwe dollar bill. These were soon selling on eBay for less than 1 U.S. dollar each.

One implication of the demand for dollars in developing countries is that dollar currency leaves the United States. This currency drain will affect the size of the deposit expansion multiplier. In the chapter, the deposit expansion multiplier was defined as

$$\text{Deposit expansion multiplier} = \frac{1}{\text{reserve requirement}}$$

This definition was based on the assumption that when a bank receives a deposit, all of the deposit will be loaned except for the fraction that the bank is required to keep as the legal reserve requirement set by the Federal Reserve.

With a currency drain, some of the deposit is withdrawn from the banking system as cash. As a result, the deposit expansion multiplier is now

Deposit expansion multiplier

$$= \frac{1}{(\text{reserve requirement} + \text{currency drain})}$$

For instance, if the reserve requirement equals 10 percent, our original definition of the deposit expansion multiplier would provide a multiplier equal to $1/.10 = 10$. But if people withdraw 10 percent of their deposits as cash, then the 10 percent currency drain is added to the 10 percent reserve requirement to yield a deposit expansion multiplier of $1/.20 = 5$. So the larger the currency drain, the smaller the money-creating potential of the banking system.

An additional interesting aspect of the foreign demand for dollars is the *seigniorage,* or revenue earned by the government from creating money. If it costs about 7 cents to print a dollar bill, but the exchange value is a dollar's worth of goods and services, then the government earns about 93 cents for each dollar put into circulation. If foreigners hold U.S. currency, then the government earns a profit from providing a stable-valued dollar that people want to hold. However, we should not overestimate the value of this in terms of the U.S. government budget. Even if all the new currency issued by the U.S. government flowed out to the rest of the world, the seigniorage earned by the United States over the past decade would have averaged less than 1.7 percent of federal government revenue. Given the relatively insignificant revenue earned from seigniorage, it is not surprising that U.S. policy with regard to the dollarization of developing countries has largely been one of disinterest.

Monetary Policy

❓ Fundamental Questions

1 | What does the Federal Reserve do?

2 | How is monetary policy set?

3 | What are the tools of monetary policy?

4 | What role do central banks play in the foreign exchange market?

5 | What are the determinants of the demand for money?

6 | How does monetary policy affect the equilibrium level of real GDP?

In the previous chapter, we saw how banks "create" money by making loans. However, that money must get into the system to begin with. Most of us never think about how money enters the economy. All we worry about is having money available when we need it. But there is a government body that controls the U.S. money supply, and in this chapter we will learn about this agency—the Federal Reserve System and the Board of Governors that oversees monetary policy.

The amount of money that is available for spending by individuals or businesses affects prices, interest rates, foreign exchange rates, and the level of income in the economy. Thus, having control of the money supply gives the Federal Reserve powerful influence over these important economic variables. As we learned in the chapter titled "Fiscal Policy," the control of government spending and taxes is one of two ways by which government can change the equilibrium level of real GDP. Monetary policy as carried out by the Federal Reserve is the other mechanism through which attempts are made to manage the economy. In this chapter we will also explore the tools of monetary policy and see how changes in the money supply affect the equilibrium level of real GDP.

1 | **What does the Federal Reserve do?**

■ 1. The Federal Reserve System

The Federal Reserve is the central bank of the United States. A *central bank* performs several functions: accepting deposits from and making loans to commercial banks, acting as a banker for the federal government, and controlling the money supply. We discuss these functions in greater detail later on, but first we look at the structure of the Federal Reserve System, or the Fed.

1.a. Structure of the Fed

Congress created the Federal Reserve System in 1913, through the Federal Reserve Act. Bank panics and failures had convinced lawmakers that the United States needed an agency that could control the money supply and make loans to commercial banks when those banks found themselves without sufficient reserves. Because Americans tended to distrust large banking interests, Congress called for a decentralized central bank. The Federal Reserve System divides the nation into 12 districts, each with its own Federal Reserve Bank (Figure 1).

1.a.1. Board of Governors

Although Congress created a decentralized system so that each district bank would represent the special interests of its own region, in practice the Fed is much more centralized than its creators intended. Monetary policy is largely set by the Board

---

FIGURE 1 The Federal Reserve System

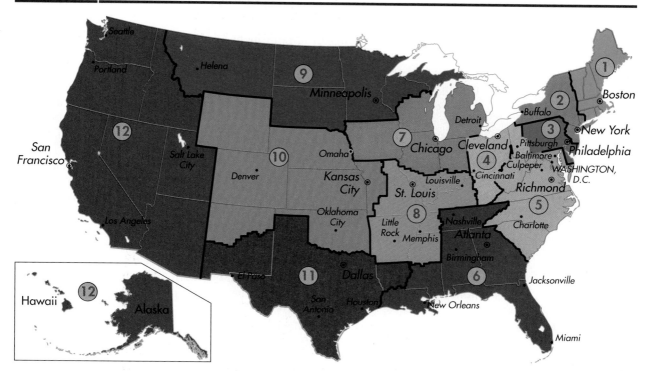

The Federal Reserve System divides the country into 12 districts. Each district has its own Federal Reserve bank, headquarters for Fed operations in that district. For example, the first district bank is in Boston; the twelfth is in San Francisco. There are also branch banks in Los Angeles, Miami, and other cities.
Source: *Federal Reserve Bulletin.*

| TABLE 1 | Recent Chairmen of the Federal Reserve Board |

Name	Age at Appointment	Term Began	Term Ended	Years of Tenure
William McChesney Martin	44	4/2/51	1/31/70	18.8
Arthur Burns	65	1/31/70	2/1/78	8.0
G. William Miller	52	3/8/78	8/6/79	1.4
Paul Volcker	51	8/6/79	8/5/87	8.0
Alan Greenspan	61	8/11/87	1/31/06	18.4
Ben Bernanke	52	2/1/06		

of Governors in Washington, D.C. This board is made up of seven members, who are appointed by the president and confirmed by the Senate.

The most visible and powerful member of the board is the chairman. In fact, the chairman of the Board of Governors has been called *the second most powerful person in the United States.* This individual serves as a leader and spokesperson for the board and typically exercises more authority in determining the course of monetary policy than do the other governors.

The chairman is appointed by the president to a four-year term. In recent years, most chairmen have been reappointed to one or more additional terms (Table 1). The governors serve 14-year terms, with the terms staggered so that a new position comes up for appointment every two years. This system allows continuity in the policymaking process and is intended to place the board above politics. Congress created the Fed as an independent agency: Monetary policy is supposed to be formulated independent of Congress and the president. Of course, this is impossible in practice because the president appoints and the Senate approves the members of the board. But because the governors serve 14-year terms, they outlast the president who appointed them.

1.a.2. District Banks Each of the Fed's 12 district banks is formally directed by a nine-person board of directors. Three directors represent commercial banks in the district, and three represent nonbanking business interests. These six individuals are elected by the Federal Reserve System member banks in the district. The three remaining directors are appointed by the Fed's Board of Governors. District bank directors are not involved in the day-to-day operations of the district banks, but they meet regularly to oversee bank operations. They also choose the president of the bank. The president, who is in charge of operations, participates in monetary policymaking with the Board of Governors in Washington, D.C.

Federal Open Market Committee (FOMC): the official policymaking body of the Federal Reserve System

1.a.3. The Federal Open Market Committee The **Federal Open Market Committee (FOMC)** is the official policymaking body of the Federal Reserve System. The committee is made up of the seven members of the Board of Governors plus five of the 12 district bank presidents. All of the district bank presidents except the president of the Federal Reserve Bank of New York take turns serving on the FOMC. Because the New York Fed actually carries out monetary policy, that bank's president is always on the committee. In section 2 we talk more about the FOMC's role and the tactics it uses.

The chairman of the Federal Reserve Board of Governors is sometimes referred to as the second most powerful person in the United States. At the time this book was written, Ben Bernanke was the Fed chairman. His leadership of the Fed has important implications for money and credit conditions in the United States.

© AP Photo/Kevin Wolf

1.b. Functions of the Fed

The Federal Reserve System offers banking services to the banking community and the U.S. Treasury and supervises the nation's banking system. The Fed also regulates the U.S. money supply.

1.b.1. Banking Services and Supervision The Fed provides several basic services to the banking community: It supplies currency to banks, holds their reserves, and clears checks. The Fed supplies U.S. currency (Federal Reserve notes) to the banking community through its 12 district banks. (See the Economic Insight "What's on a 20-Dollar Bill?")

Commercial banks in each district also hold reserves in the form of deposits at their district bank. In addition, the Fed makes loans to banks. In this sense, the Fed is a *banker's bank.* And the Fed clears checks, transferring funds to the banks where checks are deposited from the banks on which the checks are drawn.

The Fed also supervises the nation's banks, ensuring that they operate in a sound and prudent manner. And it acts as the banker for the U.S. government, selling U.S. government securities for the U.S. Treasury.

1.b.2. Controlling the Money Supply All of the functions that the Federal Reserve carries out are important, but none is more important than managing the nation's money supply. Before 1913, when the Fed was created, the money supply did not change to meet fluctuations in the demand for money. These fluctuations can stem from changes in income or from seasonal patterns of demand. For example, every year during the Christmas season, the demand for currency rises because people carry more money to buy gifts. During the holiday season, the Fed increases the supply of currency to meet the demand for cash withdrawals from banks. After the holiday season, the demand for currency drops and the public deposits currency in banks, which then return the currency to the Fed.

Economic Insight

What's on a 20-Dollar Bill?

The figure shows both sides of a 20-dollar bill. We've numbered several elements for identification.

1. Watermark
A watermark, created during the paper-making process, depicts the same historical figure as the portrait. It is visible from both sides when the bills held up to a light.

2. Security thread
An embedded polymer strip, positioned in a unique spot for each denomination, guards against counterfeiting. The thread itself, which is visible when the bill is held up to a bright light, contains microprinting—the letters USA, the denomination of the bill, and a flag. When viewed under ultraviolet light, the thread glows a distinctive color for each denomination.

3. Color-shifting ink
The ink used in the numeral in the lower right-hand corner on the front of the bill looks green when viewed straight on but copper when viewed at an angle.

4. Serial number
No two notes of the same kind, denomination, and series have the same serial number. This fact can be important in detecting counterfeit notes, as many counterfeiters make large batches of a particular note with the same number.

Notes are numbered in lots of 100 million. Each lot has a different suffix letter, beginning with A and following in alphabetical order through Z, omitting O because of its similarity to the numerical zero.

Serial numbers consist of two prefix letters, eight numerals, and a one-letter suffix. The first letter of the prefix designates the series. The second letter of the prefix designates the Federal Reserve Bank to which the note was issued, with A designating the first district, or the Boston Fed, and L, the twelfth letter in the alphabet, designating the twelfth district, or the San Francisco Fed.

5. "In God We Trust"
Secretary of the Treasury Salmon P . Chase first authorized the use of "In God We Trust" on U.S. money on the 2-cent coin in 1864. In 1955, Congress mandated the use of this phrase on all currency and coins.

Sources: Federal Reserve Bank of Atlanta and Bureau of Engraving and Printing.

The Fed controls the money supply to achieve the policy goals set by the FOMC. It does this largely through its ability to influence bank reserves and the money creating power of commercial banks that we talked about in the chapter titled "Money and Banking."

RECAP

1. As the central bank of the United States, the Federal Reserve accepts deposits from and makes loans to commercial banks, acts as a banker for the federal government, and controls the money supply.

2. The Federal Reserve System is made up of the Board of Governors in Washington, D.C., and 12 district banks.

3. The most visible and powerful member of the Board of Governors is the chairman.

4. The governors are appointed by the president and confirmed by the Senate to serve 14-year terms.

5. Monetary policy is made by the Federal Open Market Committee, whose members include the seven governors and five of the 12 district bank presidents.

6. The Fed provides currency, holds reserves, clears checks, and supervises commercial banks.

7. The most important function that the Fed performs is controlling the U.S. money supply.

■ 2. Implementing Monetary Policy

2 | How is monetary policy set?

Changes in the amount of money in an economy affect the inflation rate, the interest rate, and the equilibrium level of national income. Throughout history, incorrect monetary policy has made currencies worthless and toppled governments. This is why controlling the money supply is so important.

2.a. Policy Goals

The objective of monetary policy is economic growth with stable prices.

The ultimate goal of monetary policy is much like that of fiscal policy: economic growth with stable prices. *Economic growth* means greater output; *stable prices* mean a low, steady rate of inflation.

2.a.1. Intermediate Targets The Fed does not control gross domestic product or the price level directly. Instead, it controls the money supply, which in turn affects GDP and the level of prices. The money supply, or the growth of the money supply, is an **intermediate target,** an objective that helps the Fed achieve its ultimate policy objective—economic growth with stable prices.

intermediate target: an objective used to achieve some ultimate policy goal

Using the growth of the money supply as an intermediate target assumes that there is a fairly stable relationship between changes in the money supply and changes in income and prices. The bases for this assumption are the equation of exchange

equation of exchange:
an equation that relates
the quantity of money to
nominal GDP

and the quantity theory of money. The **equation of exchange** is a definition that relates the quantity of money to nominal GDP:

$$MV = PQ$$

where M = quantity of money

V = velocity of money

P = price level

Q = the quantity of output, like real income or real GDP

This equation is true by definition: Money times the velocity of money will always be equal to nominal GDP.

In the chapter titled "Money and Banking," we said that there are two definitions of the money supply: M1 and M2. The **velocity of money** is the average number of times each dollar is spent on final goods and services in a year. If P is the price level and Q is real GDP (the quantity of goods and services produced in the economy), then PQ equals nominal GDP. If

velocity of money: the
average number of times
each dollar is spent on final
goods and services in a year

$$MV = PQ$$

then

$$V = \frac{PQ}{M}$$

Suppose the price level is 2 and real GDP is $500; PQ, or nominal GDP, is $1,000. If the money supply is $200, then velocity is 5 ($1,000/$200). A velocity of 5 means that each dollar must be spent an average of 5 times during the year if a money supply of $200 is going to support the purchase of $1,000 worth of new goods and services.

**quantity theory of
money:** the theory that with
constant velocity, changes
in the quantity of money
change nominal GDP

The **quantity theory of money** uses the equation of exchange to relate changes in the money supply to changes in prices and output. If the money supply (M) increases and velocity (V) is constant, then nominal GDP (PQ) must increase. If the economy is operating at maximum capacity (producing at the maximum level of Q), an increase in M causes an increase in P. And if there is substantial unemployment, so that Q can increase, the increase in M may mean a higher price level (P) as well as higher real GDP (Q).

The Fed attempts to set money growth targets that are consistent with rising output and low inflation. In terms of the quantity theory of money, the Fed wants to increase M at a rate that supports steadily rising Q with slow and steady increases in P. The assumption that there is a reasonably stable relationship among M, P, and Q is what motivates the Fed to use money supply growth rates as an intermediate target to achieve its ultimate goal—higher Q with slow increases in P.

Of course, other central banks may have different goals. An example of a central bank that pursues inflation targeting is given in the Global Business Insight "The European Central Bank."

The FOMC used to set explicit ranges for money growth targets; however, in 2000 it stopped doing so. Although it no longer publicly announces a range for money growth, the FOMC still monitors the money supply growth rates. This shift away from announced targets reflects the belief that in recent years, money growth has become an unreliable indicator of monetary conditions as a result of unpredictable changes in velocity.

From the late 1950s to the mid-1970s, the velocity of the M1 money supply grew at a steady pace, from 3.5 in 1959 to 5.5 in 1975. Knowing that V was growing at a steady pace, the Fed was able to set a target growth rate for the M1 money supply

Global Business Insight

The European Central Bank

The European Central Bank (ECB) began operations on June 1, 1998, in Frankfurt, Germany, and now conducts monetary policy for the euro-area countries. The national central banks like the Bank of Italy and the German Bundesbank are still operating and perform many of the functions that they had prior to the ECB, such as bank regulation and supervision and facilitating payments systems in each nation. In some sense, they are like the regional banks of the Federal Reserve System in the United States. Monetary policy for the euro area is conducted by the ECB in Frankfurt, just as monetary policy for the United States is conducted by the Federal Reserve in Washington, D.C. Yet the national central banks of the euro area play an important role in their respective countries. The entire network of national central banks and the ECB is called the *European System of Central Banks*. Monetary policy for the euro area is determined by the

Governing Council of the ECB. This council is composed of the heads of the national central banks of the euro-area countries plus the members of the ECB *Executive Board*. The board is made up of the ECB president and vice president and four others chosen by the heads of the governments of the euro-area nations.

The ECB pursues a primary goal of price stability, defined as an inflation rate of less than 2 percent per year. Subject to the achievement of this primary goal, additional issues, such as economic growth, may be addressed. A benefit of a stated policy goal is that people can more easily form expectations of future ECB policy. This builds public confidence in the central bank and allows for greater stability than if the public were always trying to guess what the central bank really cares about and how policy will be changed as market conditions change.

and be confident that this would produce a fairly predictable growth in nominal GDP. But when velocity is not constant, there can be problems with using money growth rates as an intermediate target. This is exactly what happened starting in the late 1970s. Figure 2 plots the velocity of the M1 and M2 money supplies from 1959. Although the M2 velocity continued to indicate a stable pattern of growth, M1 velocity behaved erratically. With the breakdown of the relationship between the M1 money supply and GDP, the Fed shifted its emphasis from the M1 money supply, concentrating instead on achieving targeted growth in the M2 money supply. More recently, the velocity of M2 has also become less predictable.

Economists are still debating the reason for the fluctuations in velocity. Some argue that new deposits and innovations in banking have led to fluctuations in the money held as traditional demand deposits, with bank customers switching to different types of financial assets. These unpredictable changes in financial asset holdings affect the various money supplies and their velocities.

In addition to its interest in money growth, the Fed monitors other key variables that are used to indicate the future course of the economy. These include commodity prices, interest rates, and foreign exchange rates. The Fed may not set formal targets for all of them, but it considers them in setting policy. At the time of this edition, the FOMC had an explicit target for the *federal funds rate* of interest—the interest rate that banks pay for borrowing overnight from other banks. We will discuss this interest rate in more detail in the next section.

2.a.2. Inflation Targeting Some countries have moved away from pursuing intermediate targets like money growth rates and have instead focused on an ultimate goal: a low inflation rate. In part, these countries realize that using monetary policy

| **FIGURE 2** | Velocity of the M1 and M2 Money Supplies |

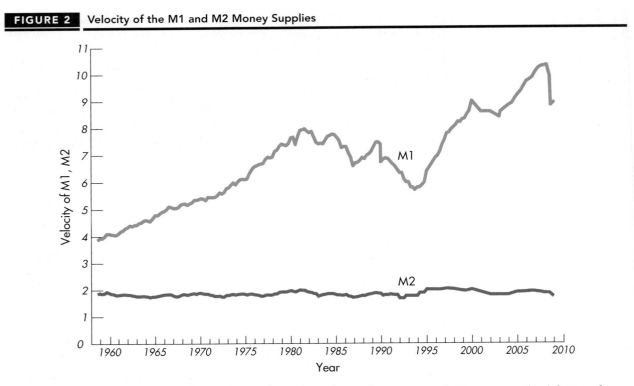

The velocity of money is the ratio of nominal gross domestic product to the money supply. The narrower the definition of money, the higher its velocity. So M1, the narrowest definition, has a higher velocity than M2. In recent years, the velocity of M1 has been much less stable than the velocity of the broader money definitions.

to support economic growth, low unemployment, and also low inflation has often resulted in an inflationary bias. The public generally likes to see policies supporting faster economic growth, like lower interest rates, whereas fighting inflation may mean unpopular higher interest rates and slower growth. Thus, a central bank may find it politically attractive to stimulate the economy, meaning that inflation takes a secondary position. In addition, if the central bank always considers multiple goals like low unemployment and low inflation, the public may not be able to understand the central bank's decision-making process easily, with the result that there is great uncertainty regarding monetary policy, and business firms and households have more difficulty making economic plans for the future. Commitment to a target inflation rate greatly reduces that uncertainty.

Inflation targeting has been adopted in several countries, including New Zealand, Canada, the U.K., Australia, Switzerland, Chile, Korea, South Africa, and Europe (by the European Central Bank). It is important to realize that in order to use inflation targeting, a central bank must be independent from fiscal policy. It is not enough to announce a target for the inflation rate. The central bank must not be in the position of having to help finance government spending. Only with this independence can a central bank truly have a credible inflation target.

2.b. Operating Procedures

The FOMC sets federal funds rate targets and then implements them through the Federal Reserve Bank of New York. The mechanism for translating policy

FOMC directive:
instructions issued by the FOMC to the Federal Reserve Bank of New York to implement monetary policy

federal funds rate: the interest rate that a bank charges when it lends excess reserves to another bank

into action is an **FOMC directive.** At the conclusion of each FOMC meeting, a policy statement is issued to the public that indicates the contents of the directive. The statement and associated directive outline the conduct of monetary policy over the six-week period until the FOMC meets again to reconsider its targets and specify policy tools.

Figure 3 contains the statement issued by the FOMC meeting of April 29, 2009. The FOMC directed the bond traders at the Federal Reserve Bank of New York to buy or sell government bonds as needed to keep the **federal funds rate,** or the interest rate that one bank charges another for overnight lending, between 0 and

---

FIGURE 3   FOMC Directive and Policy Statement

FEDERAL RESERVE press release

Release Date: April 29, 2009

For immediate release

Information received since the Federal Open Market Committee met in March indicates that the economy has continued to contract, though the pace of contraction appears to be somewhat slower. Household spending has shown signs of stabilizing but remains constrained by ongoing job losses, lower housing wealth, and tight credit. Weak sales prospects and difficulties in obtaining credit have led businesses to cut back on inventories, fixed investment, and staffing. Although the economic outlook has improved modestly since the March meeting, partly reflecting some easing of financial market conditions, economic activity is likely to remain weak for a time. Nonetheless, the Committee continues to anticipate that policy actions to stabilize financial markets and institutions, fiscal and monetary stimulus, and market forces will contribute to a gradual resumption of sustainable economic growth in a context of price stability.

In light of increasing economic slack here and abroad, the Committee expects that inflation will remain subdued. Moreover, the Committee sees some risk that inflation could persist for a time below rates that best foster economic growth and price stability in the longer term.

In these circumstances, the Federal Reserve will employ all available tools to promote economic recovery and to preserve price stability. The Committee will maintain the target range for the federal funds rate at 0 to $\frac{1}{4}$ percent and anticipates that economic conditions are likely to warrant exceptionally low levels of the federal funds rate for an extended period. As previously announced, to provide support to mortgage lending and housing markets and to improve overall conditions in private credit markets, the Federal Reserve will purchase a total of up to $1.25 trillion of agency mortgage-backed securities and up to $200 billion of agency debt by the end of the year. In addition, the Federal Reserve will buy up to $300 billion of Treasury securities by autumn. The Committee will continue to evaluate the timing and overall amounts of its purchases of securities in light of the evolving economic outlook and conditions in financial markets. The Federal Reserve is facilitating the extension of credit to households and businesses and supporting the functioning of financial markets through a range of liquidity programs. The Committee will continue to carefully monitor the size and composition of the Federal Reserve's balance sheet in light of financial and economic developments.

Voting for the FOMC monetary policy action were: Ben S. Bernanke, Chairman; William C. Dudley, Vice Chairman; Elizabeth A. Duke; Charles L. Evans; Donald L. Kohn; Jeffrey M. Lacker; Dennis P. Lockhart; Daniel K. Tarullo; Kevin M. Warsh; and Janet L. Yellen.

The FOMC always issues a directive to guide the conduct of monetary policy between meetings. In addition, a press statement at the conclusion of the meeting indicates the committee's view regarding the likely course of policy in the near future and offers guidance as to the contents of the directive. At the meeting that took place on April 29, 2009, the policy statement shown here was issued.

0.25 percent. If the rate starts to rise above 0.25 percent, then the New York Fed will buy bonds from bond dealers. The dealers are paid with funds drawn on the Federal Reserve, which are then deposited in the dealers' accounts in commercial banks. This will inject money into the banking system. It will increase bank excess reserves, giving the banks more money to lend; as a result, the cost of these funds, the federal funds rate, will fall. Due to the financial crisis, the lower bound on interest rates was set at zero. The FOMC was intent on stimulating the economy to help end the recession. In normal times, the lower bound is set at some positive interest rate. If the rate drops below that rate, then the New York Fed will sell bonds to bond dealers. The dealers pay for the bonds with funds drawn on commercial banks. This drains money from the banking system. Bank excess reserves will fall, and since banks will have less money to lend, the cost of these funds, the federal funds rate, will rise. So the actual federal funds rate fluctuates around the target rate set by the FOMC directive.

In Figure 3, the policy statement issued at the conclusion of the meeting held on April 29, 2009, is given. The key part of this statement is the phrase: "Information received since the Federal Open Market Committee met in March indicates that the economy has continued to contract." This phrase indicates that the Fed was concerned about the recession and falling output and incomes. The goals are stable prices and economic growth. If the view was balanced, this would indicate that the FOMC did not clearly see either mounting inflation pressures or recession pressures. However, the concern over a weak economy in the wake of the financial crisis led the FOMC to maintain the historically low interest rate target for federal funds between 0 and 0.25 percent. Given signs of recovery well under way, we would expect the FOMC to raise the target interest rate, to ensure that spending does not rise too quickly and contribute to inflation.

2.b.1. Tools of Monetary Policy The Fed controls the money supply and interest rates by changing bank reserves. There are three tools that the Fed can use to change reserves: the *reserve requirement,* the *discount rate,* and *open market operations.* In the last chapter, you saw that banks can expand the money supply by a multiple of their excess reserves—the deposit expansion multiplier, the reciprocal of the reserve requirement.

Reserve Requirement The Fed requires banks to hold a fraction of their transaction deposits as reserves. This fraction is the reserve requirement. *Transaction deposits* are checking accounts and other deposits that can be used to pay third parties. Large banks hold a greater percentage of deposits in reserve than small banks do (the reserve requirement increases from 0 for the first $10.3 million of deposits to 3 percent for deposits from $10.3 to $44.4 million, and then to 10 percent for deposits in excess of $44.4 million).

Remember from the chapter titled "Money and Banking" that required reserves are the dollar amount of reserves that a bank must hold to meet its reserve requirement. There are two ways in which required reserves may be held: vault cash at the bank or a deposit in the Fed. The sum of a bank's *vault cash* (coin and currency in the bank's vault) and its deposit in the Fed is called its **legal reserves.** When legal reserves equal required reserves, the bank has no excess reserves and can make no new loans. When legal reserves exceed required reserves, the bank has excess reserves available for lending.

As bank excess reserves change, the lending and money-creating potential of the banking system changes. One way in which the Fed can alter excess reserves is by changing the reserve requirement. If it lowers the reserve requirement, a portion of what was previously required reserves becomes excess reserves, which can

---

3 | What are the tools of monetary policy?

legal reserves: the cash a bank holds in its vault plus its deposit in the Fed

be used to make loans and expand the money supply. A lower reserve requirement also increases the deposit expansion multiplier. By raising the reserve requirement, the Fed reduces the money-creating potential of the banking system
and tends to reduce the money supply. A higher reserve requirement also lowers
the deposit expansion multiplier.

Consider the example in Table 2. If First National Bank's balance sheet shows
vault cash of $100,000 and a deposit in the Fed of $200,000, the bank has legal
reserves of $300,000. The amount of money that the bank can lend is determined

---

TABLE 2   The Effect of a Change in the Reserve Requirement

Balance Sheet of First National Bank

Assets		Liabilities	
Vault cash	$100,000	Deposits	$1,000,000
Deposits in Fed	200,000		
Loans	700,000		
Total	$1,000,000	Total	$1,000,000

Legal reserves (LR) equal vault cash plus the deposit in the Fed, or $300,000:

$$LR = \$100,000 + \$200,000$$
$$= \$300,000$$

Excess reserves (ER) equal legal reserves minus required reserves (RR):

$$ER = LR - RR$$

Required reserves equal the reserve requirement (r) times deposits (D):

$$RR = rD$$

If the reserve requirement is 10 percent:

$$RR = (.10)\,(\$1,000,000)$$
$$= \$100,000$$
$$ER = \$300,000 = \$100,000$$
$$= \$200,000$$

First National Bank can make a maximum loan of $200,000.

The banking system can expand the money supply by the deposit expansion multiplier ($1/r$)
times the excess reserves of the bank, or $2,000,000:

$$(1/.10)(\$200,000) = 10(\$200,000)$$
$$= \$2,000,000$$

If the reserve requirement is 20 percent:

$$RR = (.20)(\$1,000,000)$$
$$= \$200,000$$
$$ER = \$300,000 - \$200,000$$
$$= \$100,000$$

First National Bank can make a maximum loan of $100,000.

The banking system can expand the money supply by the deposit expansion multiplier ($1/r$)
times the excess reserves of the bank, or $500,000:

$$(1/.20)(\$100,000) = 5(\$100,000)$$
$$= \$500,000$$

by its excess reserves. Excess reserves (ER) equal legal reserves (LR) minus required reserves (RR):

$$ER = LR - RR$$

If the reserve requirement (r) is 10 percent (.10), the bank must keep 10 percent of its deposits (D) as required reserves:

$$RR = rD$$
$$= .10(\$1,000,000)$$
$$= \$100,000$$

In this case, the bank has excess reserves of $200,000 ($300,000 − $100,000). The bank can make a maximum loan of $200,000. The banking system can expand the money supply by the deposit expansion multiplier ($1/r$) times the excess reserves of the bank, or $2,000,000 ($1/.10 \times$ $200,000).

If the reserve requirement goes up to 20 percent (.20), required reserves are now 20 percent of $1,000,000, or $200,000. Excess reserves are now $100,000, which is the maximum loan that the bank can make. The banking system can expand the money supply by $500,000:

$$\frac{1}{.20}(\$100,000) = 5(\$100,00)$$

$$= \$500,000$$

By raising the reserve requirement, the Fed can reduce the money-creating potential of the banking system and the money supply. And by lowering the reserve requirement, the Fed can increase the money-creating potential of the banking system and the money supply.

Discount Rate If a bank needs more reserves in order to make new loans, it typically borrows from other banks in the federal funds market. The market is called the *federal funds market* because the funds are being loaned from one commercial bank's excess reserves on deposit with the Federal Reserve to another commercial bank's deposit account at the Fed. For instance, if First National Bank has excess reserves of $1 million, it can lend the excess to Second National Bank. When a bank borrows in the federal funds market, it pays a rate of interest called the federal funds rate.

At times, however, banks borrow directly from the Fed. The **discount rate** is the rate of interest that the Fed charges banks. (In other countries, the rate of interest the central bank charges commercial banks is often called the *bank rate.*) Another way in which the Fed controls the level of bank reserves and the money supply is by changing the discount rate.

When the Fed raises the discount rate, it raises the cost of borrowing reserves, reducing the amount of reserves borrowed. Lower levels of reserves limit bank lending and the expansion of the money supply. When the Fed lowers the discount rate, it lowers the cost of borrowing reserves, increasing the amount of borrowing. As bank reserves increase, so do loans and the money supply.

There are actually two different discount rates, both set above the federal funds target rate. The rate on *primary credit* is for loans made to banks that are in good financial condition. At the time this edition was revised, the interest rate on primary credit was set at 0.5 percent. In addition to the discount rate for primary credit loans, there is another discount rate for *secondary credit.* This rate is for banks that are having financial difficulties. At the time of this edition, the secondary credit rate was set at 1 percent. Loans made at these discount rates are for very short terms, typically overnight.

Open Market Operations The major tool of monetary policy is the Fed's **open market operations,** the buying and selling of U.S. government and federal agency

discount rate: the interest rate that the Fed charges commercial banks when they borrow from it

open market operations: the buying and selling of government and federal agency bonds by the Fed to control bank reserves, the federal funds rate, and the money supply

bonds. Suppose the FOMC wants to increase bank reserves to lower the federal funds rate. The committee issues a directive to the bond-trading desk at the Federal Reserve Bank of New York to change the federal funds rate to a lower level. In order to accomplish this, the Fed buys bonds, with the results described earlier. If the higher reserves that result lead to increased bank lending to the public, then the new loans in turn expand the money supply through the deposit expansion multiplier process.

If the Fed wants to increase the federal funds rate, it sells bonds. As a result, the money supply decreases through the deposit expansion multiplier process.

Its open market operations allow the Fed to control the federal funds rate and the money supply. To lower the federal funds rate and increase the money supply, the Fed buys U.S. government bonds. To raise the federal funds rate and decrease the money supply, it sells U.S. government bonds. The effect of selling these bonds, however, varies, depending on whether there are excess reserves in the banking system. If there are excess reserves, the money supply does not necessarily decrease when the Fed sells bonds. The open market sale may simply reduce the level of excess reserves, reducing the rate at which the money supply increases.

Table 3 shows how open market operations change bank reserves and illustrates the money-creating power of the banking system. First National Bank's initial balance sheet shows excess reserves of $100,000 with a 20 percent reserve requirement.

> *To lower the federal funds rate and increase the money supply, the Fed buys U.S. government bonds. To increase the federal funds rate and decrease the money supply, it sells U.S. government bonds.*

TABLE 3	The Effect of an Open Market Operation

Balance Sheet of First National Bank

Assets		Liabilities	
Vault cash	$100,000	Deposits	$1,000,000
Deposits in Fed	200,000		
Loans	700,000		
Total	$1,000,000	Total	$1,000,000

Initially, legal reserves (LR) equal vault cash plus the deposit in the Fed, or $300,000:

$$LR = \$100,000 + \$200,000$$
$$= \$300,000$$

If the reserve requirement (r) is 20 percent (.20), required reserves (RR) equal $200,000:

$$.20(\$1,000,000) = \$200,000$$

Excess reserves (ER), then, equal $100,000 ($300,000 − $200,000). The bank can make a maximum loan of $100,000. The banking system can expand the money supply by the deposit expansion multiplier (1/r) times the excess reserves of the bank, or $500,000:

$$(1/.20)(\$100,000) = 5(\$100,000)$$
$$= \$500,000$$

Open market purchase:

The Fed purchases $100,000 worth of bonds from a dealer, who deposits the $100,000 in an account at First National. At this point the bank has legal reserves of $400,000, required reserves of $220,000, and excess reserves of $180,000. It can make a maximum loan of $180,000, which can expand the money supply by $900,000 [(1/.20)($180,000)].

Open market sale:

The Fed sells $100,000 worth of bonds to a dealer, who pays with a check drawn on an account at First National. At this point, the bank has legal reserves of $200,000, required reserves of $180,000 (its deposits now equal $900,000), and excess reserves of $20,000. It can make a maximum loan of $20,000, which can expand the money supply by $100,000 [(1/.20)($20,000)].

Therefore, the bank can make a maximum loan of $100,000. On the basis of the bank's reserve position, the banking system can increase the money supply by a maximum of $500,000.

If the Fed purchases $100,000 worth of bonds from a private dealer, who deposits the $100,000 in an account at First National Bank, the excess reserves of First National Bank increase to $180,000. These reserves can generate a maximum increase in the money supply of $900,000. The open market purchase increases the excess reserves of the banking system, stimulating the growth of money and, eventually, nominal GDP.

What happens when an open market sale takes place? If the Fed sells $100,000 worth of bonds to a private bond dealer, the dealer pays for the bonds using a check drawn on First National Bank. First National's deposits drop from $1,000,000 to $900,000, and its legal reserves drop from $300,000 to $200,000. With excess reserves of $20,000, the banking system can increase the money supply by only $100,000. The open market sale reduces the money-creating potential of the banking system from $500,000 initially to $100,000.

quantitative easing:
buying financial assets to stimulate the economy when the central bank target interest rate is near or at zero and the interest rate cannot be lowered further

Quantitative Easing   What if a central bank has moved its target interest rate near to zero so that interest rates cannot fall further? If the central bank wants additional stimulus for the economy it can employ a policy known as **quantitative easing.** Quantitative easing is a policy of buying financial assets in order to ease credit conditions and make loans more readily available to the public. These financial assets can be government bonds, private corporate bonds, or any other financial asset the central bank chooses. The idea is to flood the economy with money to try to stimulate spending and provide a boost to GDP growth.

The Bank of Japan employed quantitative easing from March 2001 to March 2006 as the policy interest rate was set at zero, yet the economy was in recession with deflation. During the financial crisis of 2008, several central banks, including the Federal Reserve and the Bank of England, employed quantitative easing by cutting interest rates almost to zero, and still the recession continued. Once the economy starts to recover, the additional purchases of assets ends, and the central bank raises interest rates to avoid inflation creation by overstimulating the economy.

2.b.2. FOMC Directives   When it sets monetary policy, the FOMC begins with its *ultimate goal:* economic growth at stable prices. It defines that goal in terms of GDP and inflation. Then it works backwards to identify its *intermediate target,* the rate at which the money supply must grow to achieve the wanted growth in GDP. Then it must decide how to achieve its intermediate target. In Figure 4, as is usually

---

FIGURE 4   **Monetary Policy: Tools, Targets, and Goals**

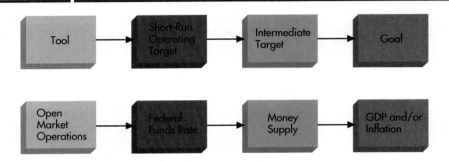

The Fed primarily uses open market operations to implement monetary policy. The decision to buy or sell bonds is based on a short-run operating target, like the federal funds rate. The short-run operating target is set to achieve an intermediate target, a certain level of money supply. The intermediate target is set to achieve the ultimate goal, a certain level of gross domestic product and/or inflation.

the case in real life, the Fed uses open market operations. But to know whether it should buy or sell bonds, the FOMC must have some indication of whether the money supply is growing too fast or too slowly. The committee relies on a *short-run operating target* for this information. The short-run target indicates how the money supply should change. Both the quantity of excess reserves in the banking system and the federal funds rate can serve as short-run operating targets.

The FOMC carries out its policies through directives to the bond-trading desk at the Federal Reserve Bank of New York. The directives specify a short-run operating target that the trading desk must use in its day-to-day operations. In recent years, the target has been the federal funds rate.

2.c. Foreign Exchange Market Intervention

4 | What role do central banks play in the foreign exchange market?

In the mid-1980s, conditions in the foreign exchange market took on a high priority in FOMC directives. There was concern that the value of the dollar in relation to other currencies was contributing to a large U.S. international trade deficit. Furthermore, the governments of the major industrial countries had decided to work together to maintain more stable exchange rates. This meant that the Federal Reserve and the central banks of the other developed countries had to devote more attention to maintaining exchange rates within a certain target band of values. Although more recently exchange rates have had less of a role in FOMC meetings, it is still important to understand how central banks may intervene to change exchange rates. Other central banks have made exchange rates a focus of their policy. For example, in 2009 the Swiss National Bank announced that the Swiss franc had appreciated in value too much and that this was "an inappropriate tightening of monetary conditions." As a result, the Bank sold Swiss francs in the foreign exchange market and stated that they stood ready to do this to ensure that the currency would not appreciate further.

foreign exchange market intervention: the buying and selling of currencies by a central bank to achieve a specified exchange rate

2.c.1. Mechanics of Intervention **Foreign exchange market intervention** is the buying and selling of foreign exchange by a central bank in order to move exchange rates up or down. We can use a simple supply and demand diagram to illustrate the role of intervention. Figure 5 shows the U.S. dollar–Japanese yen exchange market. The demand curve is the demand for dollars produced by the demand for U.S. goods and financial assets. The supply curve is the supply of dollars generated by U.S. residents' demand for the products and financial assets of other countries. Here, the supply of dollars to the dollar–yen market comes from the U.S. demand to buy Japanese products.

The initial equilibrium exchange rate is at point *A,* where the demand curve (D_1) and the supply curve (S_1) intersect. At point *A,* the exchange rate is ¥100 = $1, and Q_1 dollars are exchanged for yen. Suppose that over time, U.S. residents buy more from Japan than Japanese residents buy from the United States. As the supply of dollars increases in relation to the demand for dollars, equilibrium shifts to point *B.* At point *B,* Q_2 dollars are exchanged at a rate of ¥90 = $1. The dollar has *depreciated* against the yen, or, conversely, the yen has *appreciated* against the dollar.

When the dollar depreciates, U.S. goods are cheaper to Japanese buyers (it takes fewer yen to buy each dollar). The depreciated dollar stimulates U.S. exports to Japan. It also raises the price of Japanese goods to U.S. buyers, reducing U.S. imports from Japan. Rather than allowing exchange rates to change, with the subsequent changes in trade, central banks often seek to maintain fixed exchange rates because of international agreements or desired trade in goods or financial assets.

Suppose the Fed sets a target range for the dollar at a minimum exchange rate of ¥100 = $1. If the exchange rate falls below the minimum, the Fed must intervene in the foreign exchange market to increase the value of the dollar. In Figure 5, you

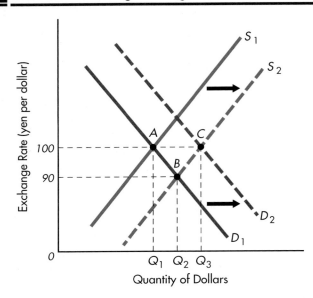

FIGURE 5   The Dollar–Yen Foreign Exchange Market

The demand is the demand for dollars arising out of the Japanese demand for U.S. goods and services. The supply is the supply of dollars arising out of the U.S. demand for Japanese goods and services. Initially, the equilibrium exchange rate is at the intersection of the demand curve (D_1) and the supply curve (S_1), where the exchange rate is ¥100 = $1. An increase in the U.S. demand for Japanese goods increases S_1 to S_2 and pushes the equilibrium exchange rate down to point B, where ¥90 = $1. If the Fed's target exchange rate is ¥100 = $1, the Fed must intervene and buy dollars in the foreign exchange market. This increases demand to D_2 and raises the equilibrium exchange rate to point C, where ¥100 = $1.

Coordinated intervention *involves more than one central bank in attempts to shift the equilibrium exchange rate.*

can see that the only way to increase the dollar's value is to increase the demand for dollars. The Fed intervenes in the foreign exchange market by buying dollars in exchange for yen. It uses its holdings of Japanese yen to purchase $Q_3 - Q_1$ dollars, shifting the demand curve to D_2. Now equilibrium is at point C, where Q_3 dollars are exchanged at the rate of ¥100 = $1.

The kind of intervention shown in Figure 5 is only temporary because the Fed has a limited supply of yen. Under another intervention plan, the Bank of Japan would support the ¥100 = $1 exchange rate by using yen to buy dollars. The Bank of Japan could carry on this kind of policy indefinitely because it has the power to create yen. A third alternative is *coordinated intervention,* in which both the Fed and the Bank of Japan sell yen in exchange for dollars to support the minimum yen–dollar exchange rate.

2.c.2. Effects of Intervention Intervention can be used to shift the demand and supply for currency and thereby change the exchange rate. Foreign exchange market intervention also has effects on the money supply. If the Federal Reserve wanted to increase the dollar price of the euro, it would create dollars to purchase euro. Thus, when foreign exchange market intervention involves the use of domestic currency to buy foreign currency, it increases the domestic money supply. The expansionary effect of this intervention can be offset by a domestic open market operation, in a process called **sterilization**. If the Fed creates dollars to buy euro, for example, it increases the money supply, as we have just seen. To reduce the money supply, the Fed can direct an open market bond sale. The bond sale sterilizes the effect of the intervention on the domestic money supply.

sterilization: the use of domestic open market operations to offset the effects of a foreign exchange market intervention on the domestic money supply

RECAP

1. The ultimate goal of monetary policy is economic growth with stable prices.

2. The Fed controls GDP indirectly, through its control of the money supply.

3. The equation of exchange ($MV = PQ$) relates the quantity of money to nominal GDP.

4. The quantity theory of money states that with constant velocity, changes in the quantity of money change nominal GDP.

5. Every six weeks, the Federal Open Market Committee issues a directive to the Federal Reserve Bank of New York that defines the FOMC's monetary targets and policy tools.

6. The Fed controls the nation's money supply by changing bank excess reserves.

7. The tools of monetary policy are reserve requirements, the discount rate, and open market operations.

8. The money supply tends to increase (decrease) as the reserve requirement falls (rises), the discount rate falls (rises), and the Fed buys (sells) bonds.

9. If the policy interest rate is lowered near zero, quantitative easing can be used to further stimulate the economy.

10. Each FOMC directive defines its short-run operating target in terms of the federal funds rate.

11. Foreign exchange market intervention is the buying and selling of foreign exchange by a central bank to achieve a targeted exchange rate.

12. Sterilization is the use of domestic open market operations to offset the money supply effects of foreign exchange market intervention.

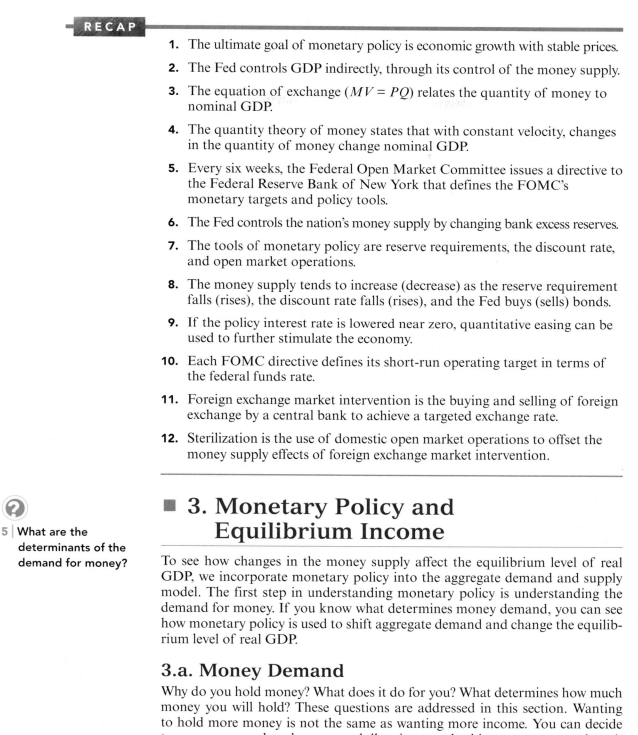

5 | What are the determinants of the demand for money?

■ 3. Monetary Policy and Equilibrium Income

To see how changes in the money supply affect the equilibrium level of real GDP, we incorporate monetary policy into the aggregate demand and supply model. The first step in understanding monetary policy is understanding the demand for money. If you know what determines money demand, you can see how monetary policy is used to shift aggregate demand and change the equilibrium level of real GDP.

3.a. Money Demand

Why do you hold money? What does it do for you? What determines how much money you will hold? These questions are addressed in this section. Wanting to hold more money is not the same as wanting more income. You can decide to carry more cash or keep more dollars in your checking account even though your income has not changed. The quantity of dollars that you want to hold is your demand for money. By summing the quantity of money demanded by each individual, we can find the money demand for the entire economy. Once we understand what determines money demand, we can put that demand together with the money supply and examine how money influences the interest rate and the equilibrium level of income.

transactions demand for money: the demand to hold money to buy goods and services

In the chapter titled "Money and Banking," we discussed the functions of money—that is, what money is used for. People use money as a unit of account, a medium of exchange, a store of value, and a standard of deferred payment. These last functions help explain the demand for money.

People use money for transactions, to buy goods and services. The **transactions demand for money** is a demand to hold money in order to spend it on goods and services. Holding money in your pocket or checking account is a demand for money. Spending money is not demanding it; by spending it, you are getting rid of it.

If your boss paid you the same instant that you wanted to buy something, the timing of your receipts and expenditures would match perfectly. You would not have to hold money for transactions. But because receipts typically occur much less often than expenditures, money is necessary to cover transactions between paychecks.

precautionary demand for money: the demand for money to cover unplanned transactions or emergencies

People also hold money to take care of emergencies. The **precautionary demand for money** exists because emergencies happen. People never know when an unexpected expense will crop up or when actual expenditures will exceed planned expenditures. So they hold money as a precaution.

speculative demand for money: the demand for money created by uncertainty about the value of other assets

Finally, there is a **speculative demand for money,** a demand created by uncertainty about the value of other assets. This demand exists because money is the most liquid store of value. If you want to buy a stock, but you believe the price is going to fall in the next few days, you hold the money until you are ready to buy the stock.

The speculative demand for money is not necessarily tied to a particular use of funds. People hold money because they expect the price of any asset to fall. Holding money is less risky than buying the asset today if the price of the asset seems likely to fall. For example, suppose you buy and sell fine art. The price of art fluctuates over time. You try to buy when prices are low and sell when prices are high. If you expect prices to fall in the short term, you hold money rather than art until the prices do fall. Then you use money to buy art for resale when the prices go up again.

3.a.1. The Money Demand Function If you understand why people hold money, you can understand what changes the amount of money that they hold. As you've just seen, people hold money in order to (1) carry out transactions (transactions demand), (2) be prepared for emergencies (precautionary demand), and (3) speculate on purchases of various assets (speculative demand). The interest rate and nominal income (income measured in current dollars) influence how much money people hold in order to carry out these three activities.

> *The interest rate is the opportunity cost of holding money.*

The Interest Rate There is an inverse relationship between the interest rate and the quantity of money demanded (see Figure 6). The interest rate is the *opportunity cost* of holding money. If you bury one thousand dollar bills in your backyard, that currency is earning no interest—you are forgoing the interest. At a low interest rate, the cost of the forgone interest is small. At a higher interest rate, however, the cost of holding wealth in the form of money means giving up more interest. The higher the rate of interest, the greater the interest forgone by holding money, so the less money held. The costs of holding money limit the amount of money held.

Some components of the money supply pay interest to the depositor. Here the opportunity cost of holding money is the difference between the interest rate on a bond or some other nonmonetary asset and the interest rate on money. If a bond pays 9 percent interest a year and a bank deposit pays 5 percent, the opportunity cost of holding the deposit is 4 percent.

Figure 6 shows a money demand function, where the demand for money depends on the interest rate. The downward slope of the money demand curve (*Md*) shows the inverse relation between the interest rate and the quantity of money demanded. For instance, at an interest rate of 12 percent, the quantity of money demanded is

FIGURE 6 The Money Demand Function

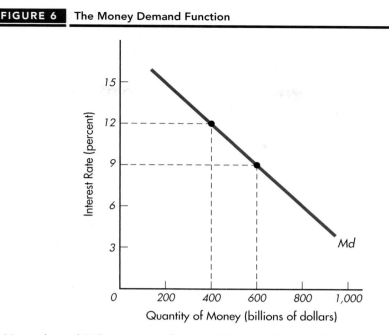

Money demand (Md) is a negative function of the rate of interest. The interest rate is the opportunity cost of holding money. The higher the interest rate, the lower the quantity of money demanded. At an interest rate of 9 percent, the quantity of money demanded is $600 billion. At an interest rate of 12 percent, the quantity of money demanded falls to $400 billion.

$400 billion. If the interest rate falls to 9 percent, the quantity of money demanded increases to $600 billion.

Nominal Income The demand for money also depends on nominal income. Money demand varies directly with nominal income because as income increases, more transactions are carried out and more money is required for those transactions.

> The transactions demand for money rises with nominal income.

The greater nominal income is, the greater the demand for money. This is true whether the increase in nominal income is a product of a higher price level or an increase in real income. Both generate a greater dollar volume of transactions. If the prices of all goods increase, then more money must be used to purchase goods and services. And as real income increases, more goods and services are being produced and sold and living standards rise; this means that more money is being demanded to execute the higher level of transactions.

A change in nominal income changes the demand for money at any given interest rate. Figure 7 shows the effect of changes in nominal income on the money demand curve. If income rises from Y_0 to Y_1, money demand increases from Md to Md_1. If income falls from Y_0 to Y_2, money demand falls from Md to Md_2. When the money demand function shifts from Md to Md_1, the quantity of money demanded at an interest rate of 9 percent increases from $600 billion to $800 billion. When the money demand function shifts from Md to Md_2, the quantity of money demanded at 9 percent interest falls from $600 billion to $400 billion.

3.a.2. The Money Supply Function The Federal Reserve is responsible for setting the money supply. The fact that the Fed can choose the money supply means that the money supply function is independent of the current interest rate and income. Figure 8 illustrates the money supply function (Ms). In the figure, the money

FIGURE 7   The Effect of a Change in Income on Money Demand

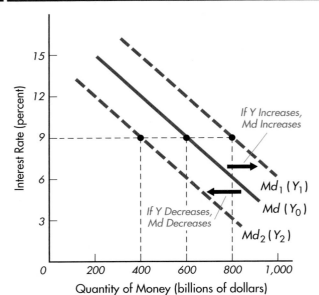

A change in real GDP, whatever the interest rate, shifts the money demand curve. Initially real GDP is Y_0; the money demand curve at that level of income is Md. At an interest rate of 9 percent, the quantity of money demanded is $600 billion. If income increases to Y_1, the money demand shifts to Md_1. Here $800 billion is demanded at 9 percent. If income falls to Y_2, the money demand curve falls to Md_2, where $400 billion is demanded at 9 percent.

FIGURE 8   The Money Supply Function

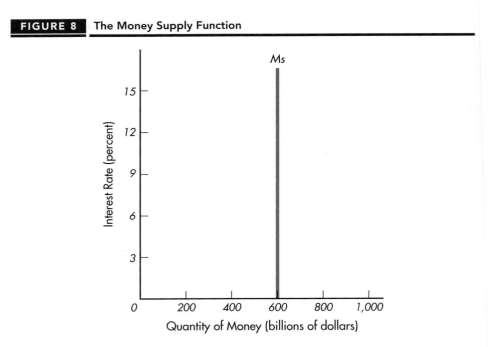

The money supply function (Ms) is a vertical line. This indicates that the Fed can choose any money supply it wants, independent of the interest rate (and real GDP). In the figure, the money supply is set at $600 billion at all interest rates. The Fed can increase or decrease the money supply, shifting the curve to the right or left, but the curve remains vertical.

supply is $600 billion at all interest rate levels. If the Fed increases the money supply, the vertical money supply function shifts to the right. If the Fed decreases the money supply, the function shifts to the left.

3.a.3. Equilibrium in the Money Market

To find the equilibrium interest rate and quantity of money, we have to combine the money demand and money supply functions in one diagram. Figure 9 graphs equilibrium in the money market. Equilibrium, point *e*, is at the intersection of the money demand and money supply functions. In the figure, the equilibrium interest rate is 9 percent, and the quantity of money is $600 billion.

What forces work to ensure that the economy tends toward the equilibrium rate of interest? Let's look at Figure 9 again to understand what happens if the interest rate is not at equilibrium. If the interest rate falls below 9 percent, there will be an excess demand for money. People will want more money than the Fed is supplying. But because the supply of money does not change, the demand for more money just forces the interest rate to rise. How? Suppose people try to increase their money holdings by converting bonds and other nonmonetary assets into money. As bonds and other nonmonetary assets are sold for money, the interest rate goes up.

To understand the connection between the rate of interest and buying and selling bonds, you must realize that the current interest rate (yield) on a bond is determined by the bond price:

$$\text{Current interest rate} = \frac{\text{annual interest payment}}{\text{bond price}}$$

FIGURE 9 Equilibrium in the Money Market

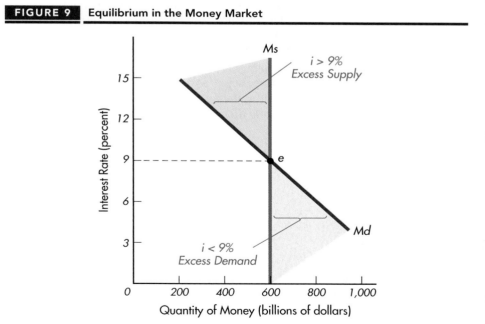

Equilibrium is at point e, where the money demand and money supply curves intersect. At equilibrium, the interest rate is 9 percent and the money supply is $600 billion. An interest rate above 9 percent would create an excess supply of money because the quantity of money demanded falls as the interest rate rises. An interest rate below 9 percent would create an excess demand for money because the quantity of money demanded rises as the interest rate falls.

The numerator, the annual interest payment, is fixed for the life of the bond. The denominator, the bond price, fluctuates with supply and demand. As the bond price changes, the interest rate changes.

Suppose a bond pays $100 a year in interest and sells for $1,000. The interest rate is 10 percent ($100/$1,000). If the supply of bonds increases because people want to convert bonds to money, the price of bonds falls. Suppose the price drops to $800. At that price, the interest rate equals 12.5 percent ($100/$800). This is the mechanism by which an excess demand for money changes the interest rate. As the interest rate goes up, the excess demand for money disappears.

Just the opposite occurs at interest rates above equilibrium. In Figure 9, any rate of interest above 9 percent creates an excess supply of money. Now people are holding more of their wealth in the form of money than they would like. What happens? They want to convert some of their money balances into nonmonetary assets, like bonds. As the demand for bonds rises, bond prices increase. And as bond prices go up, interest rates fall. This drop in interest rates restores equilibrium in the money market.

3.b. Money and Equilibrium Income

6 | How does monetary policy affect the equilibrium level of real GDP?

Now we are ready to relate monetary policy to the equilibrium level of real GDP. We use Figure 10 to show how a change in the money supply affects real GDP. In Figure 10(a), as the money supply increases from Ms_1 to Ms_2, the equilibrium rate of interest falls from i_1 to i_2.

Remember that investment (business spending on capital goods) declines as the rate of interest increases. The interest rate is the cost of borrowed funds. As the interest rate rises, the return on investment falls, and with it the level of investment. As the interest rate falls, the return on investment rises, and with it the level of investment. In Figure 10(a), the interest rate falls. In Figure 10(b), you can see the effect of the lower interest rate on investment spending. As the interest rate falls from i_1 to i_2, investment increases from I_1 to I_2. Figure 10(c) is the aggregate demand and supply equilibrium diagram. When investment spending increases, aggregate expenditures are higher at every price level, so the aggregate demand curve shifts to the right, from AD_1 to AD_2. The increase in aggregate demand increases equilibrium income from Y_1 to Y_2.

FIGURE 10   Monetary Policy and Equilibrium Income

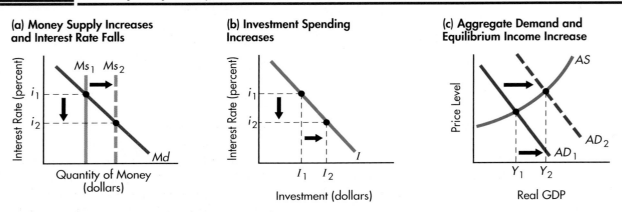

The three diagrams show the sequence of events by which a change in the money supply affects the equilibrium level of real GDP. In Figure 10(a), the money supply increases, lowering the equilibrium interest rate. In Figure 10(b), the lower interest rate pushes the level of investment up. In Figure 10(c), the increase in investment increases aggregate demand and equilibrium real GDP.

An excess supply of (demand for) money can increase (decrease) consumption as well as investment.

How does monetary policy affect equilibrium income? As the money supply increases, the equilibrium interest rate falls. As the interest rate falls, the equilibrium level of investment rises. Increased investment increases aggregate demand and equilibrium income. A decrease in the money supply works in reverse: As the interest rate rises, investment falls; as investment falls, aggregate demand and equilibrium income go down.

The mechanism we have just described is an oversimplification because the only element of aggregate expenditures that changes in this model is investment. But an excess demand for or supply of money involves more than simply selling or buying bonds. An excess supply of money probably would be reflected in increased consumption as well. If households are holding more money than they want to hold, they buy not only bonds but also goods and services, so that consumption increases. If they are holding less money than they want to hold, they will both sell bonds and consume less. So the effect of monetary policy on aggregate demand is a product of a change in both investment and consumption. We discuss this in the chapter titled "Macroeconomic Policy: Tradeoffs, Expectations, Credibility, and Sources of Business Cycles," where we also examine the important role that expected policy changes can play.

RECAP

1. The transactions demand for money is a demand to hold money to buy goods and services.

2. The precautionary demand for money exists because not all expenditures can be planned.

3. The speculative demand for money is created by uncertainty about the value of other assets.

4. There is an inverse relationship between the interest rate and the quantity of money demanded.

5. The greater the nominal income, the greater the demand for money.

6. Because the Federal Reserve sets the money supply, the money supply function is independent of the interest rate and nominal income.

7. The current yield on a bond equals the annual interest payment divided by the price of the bond.

8. An increase in the money supply lowers the interest rate; this raises the level of investment, and this in turn increases aggregate demand and equilibrium income. A decrease in the money supply works in reverse.

SUMMARY

1 | What does the Federal Reserve do?

- The Federal Reserve is the central bank of the United States. *§1*

- The Federal Reserve System is operated by 12 district banks and a Board of Governors in Washington, D.C. *§1.a*

- The Fed services and supervises the banking system, acts as the banker for the U.S. Treasury, and controls the money supply. *§1.b*

2 | How is monetary policy set?

- The Fed controls nominal GDP indirectly by controlling the quantity of money in the nation's economy. *§2.a.1*

- The Fed uses the growth of the money supply as an intermediate target to help it achieve its ultimate goal—economic growth with stable prices. *§2.a.1*

- Some countries have adopted inflation targeting to guide their monetary policy. *§2.a.2*

3 | What are the tools of monetary policy?

- The three tools of monetary policy are the reserve requirement, the discount rate, and open market operations. *§2.b.1*

- The Fed buys bonds to increase the money supply and sells bonds to decrease the money supply. *§2.b.1*

- If the policy interest rate is near zero, a central bank may use quantitative easing to further stimulate the economy and buy financial assets to flood the market with money. *§2.b.1*

- The Federal Open Market Committee (FOMC) issues directives to the Federal Reserve Bank of New York outlining the conduct of monetary policy. *§2.b.2*

4 | What role do central banks play in the foreign exchange market?

- Central banks intervene in the foreign exchange market when it is necessary to maintain a targeted exchange rate. *§2.c*

5 | What are the determinants of the demand for money?

- The demand for money stems from the need to buy goods and services, to prepare for emergencies, and to retain a store of value. *§3.a*

- There is an inverse relationship between the quantity of money demanded and the interest rate. *§3.a.1*

- The greater the nominal income, the greater the demand for money. *§3.a.1*

- Because the Fed sets the money supply, the money supply function is independent of the interest rate and real GDP. *§3.a.2*

6 | How does monetary policy affect the equilibrium level of real GDP?

- By altering the money supply, the Fed changes the interest rate and the level of investment, shifting aggregate demand and the equilibrium level of real GDP. *§3.b*

KEY TERMS

Federal Open Market Committee (FOMC) *§1.a.3*

intermediate target *§2.a.1*

equation of exchange *§2.a.1*

velocity of money *§2.a.1*

quantity theory of money *§2.a.1*

FOMC directive *§2.b*

federal funds rate *§2.b*

legal reserves *§2.b.1*

discount rate *§2.b.1*

open market operations *§2.b.1*

quantitative easing *§2.b.1*

foreign exchange market intervention *§2.c.1*

sterilization *§2.c.2*

transactions demand for money *§3.a*

precautionary demand for money *§3.a*

speculative demand for money *§3.a*

EXERCISES

1. The Federal Reserve System divides the nation into 12 districts.
   a. List the 12 cities in which the district banks are located.
   b. Which Federal Reserve district do you live in?

2. Briefly describe the functions that the Fed performs for the banking community. In what sense is the Fed a banker's bank?

3. Draw a graph showing equilibrium in the money market. Carefully label all curves and axes, and explain why the curves have the slopes that they do.

4. Using the graph you prepared for exercise 3, illustrate and explain what happens when the Fed decreases the money supply.

5. When the Fed decreases the money supply, the equilibrium level of income changes. Illustrate and explain how.

6. Describe the quantity theory of money, defining each variable. Explain how changes in the money supply can affect real GDP and the price level. Under what circumstances could an increase in the money supply have *no* effect on nominal GDP?

7. There are several tools that the Fed uses to implement monetary policy.
   a. Briefly describe these tools.
   b. Explain how the Fed would use each tool in order to increase the money supply.
   c. Suppose the federal funds rate equals zero. Does that mean the Fed can do nothing more to stimulate the economy? Explain your answer.

8. First Bank has total deposits of $2,000,000 and legal reserves of $220,000.

a. If the reserve requirement is 10 percent, what is the maximum loan that First Bank can make, and what is the maximum increase in the money supply based on First Bank's reserve position?

b. If the reserve requirement is changed to 5 percent, how much can First Bank lend, and by how much can the money supply be expanded?

9. Suppose you are a member of the FOMC and the U.S. economy is entering a recession. Write a directive to the New York Fed about the conduct of monetary policy over the next two months. Your directive should address a target for the rate of growth of the M2 money supply, the federal funds rate, the rate of inflation, and the foreign exchange value of the dollar versus the Japanese yen and euro. You may refer to the Board of Governors website, www.federalreserve.gov/monetarypolicy, for examples, since this site posts FOMC directives.

10. Suppose the Fed has a target range for the yen–dollar exchange rate. How would it keep the exchange rate within the target range if free market forces push the exchange rate out of the range? Use a graph to help explain your answer.

11. Why do you demand money? What determines how much money you keep in your pocket, purse, or bank accounts?

12. What is the current yield on a bond? Why do interest rates change when bond prices change?

13. If the Fed increases the money supply, what will happen to each of the following (other things being equal)?
a. Interest rates
b. Money demand
c. Investment spending
d. Aggregate demand
e. The equilibrium level of national income

14. It is sometimes said that the Federal Reserve System is a nonpolitical agency. In what sense is this true? Why might you doubt that politics have no effect on Fed decisions?

15. Suppose the banking system has vault cash of $1,000, deposits at the Fed of $2,000, and demand deposits of $10,000.
a. If the reserve requirement is 20 percent, what is the maximum potential increase in the money supply, given the banks' reserve position?
b. If the Fed now purchases $500 worth of government bonds from private bond dealers, what are the excess reserves of the banking system? (Assume that the bond dealers deposit the $500 in demand deposits.) How much can the banking system increase the money supply, given the new reserve position?

16. What does ECB stand for? Where is the ECB located? In what way is central banking in the euro-area countries similar to the Federal Reserve System?

You can find further practice tests in the Online Quiz at www.cengage.com/economics/boyes.

Bank of England Maintains Bank Rate at 0.5 Percent and Increases Size of Asset Purchase Program by £50 Billion to £125 Billion

May 7, 2009

The Bank of England's Monetary Policy Committee today voted to maintain the official Bank Rate paid on commercial bank reserves at 0.5%. The Committee also voted to continue with its programme of asset purchases financed by the issuance of central bank reserves and to increase its size by £50 billion to a total of £125 billion.

The world economy remains in deep recession. Output has continued to contract and international trade has fallen precipitously. The global banking and financial system remains fragile despite further significant intervention by the authorities. In the United Kingdom, GDP fell sharply in the first quarter of 2009. But surveys at home and abroad show promising signs that the pace of decline has begun to moderate. . . .

The Committee noted that the outlook for economic activity was dominated by two countervailing forces. The process of adjustment in train in the U.K. economy, as private saving rises and banks restructure their balance sheets, combined with weak global demand, will continue to act as a significant drag on economic activity. But pushing in the opposite direction, there is considerable economic stimulus stemming from the easing in monetary and fiscal policy, at home and abroad, the substantial depreciation in sterling, past falls in commodity prices, and actions by authorities internationally to improve the availability of credit. That stimulus should in due course lead to a recovery in economic growth, bringing inflation back towards the 2% target. But the timing and strength of that recovery is highly uncertain.

In the light of that outlook and in order to keep CPI inflation on track to meet the 2% inflation target over the medium term, the Committee judged that maintaining Bank Rate at 0.5% was appropriate. The Committee also agreed to continue with its programme of purchases of government and corporate debt financed by the issuance of central bank reserves and to increase its size by £50 billion to a total of £125 billion. The Committee expected that it would take another three months to complete that programme, and it will keep the scale of the programme under review.

Source: News Release, The Bank of England.

http://www.bankofengland.co.uk/publications/news/2009/037.htm

Like the Board of Governors of the Federal Reserve System sets U.S. monetary policy, the Monetary Policy Committee (MPC) of the Bank of England sets U.K. monetary policy. If a monetary policymaker believes that economic growth is too slow and inflation is not likely to increase, then it tries to increase aggregate demand by increasing money growth. As we learned in this chapter, when the Fed increases the money supply, interest rates fall, aggregate demand rises, and real GDP growth increases. The same holds for other central banks.

The article says that the MPC left its bank rate at 0.5 percent at the meeting of May 7, 2009. The U.K. Bank Rate is the equivalent of the federal funds rate in the United States. It is the key target for monetary policy. The article goes on to describe the uncertainty facing the MPC in May 2009. The financial crisis had resulted in a global recession where GDP was falling along with inflation. The MPC recognized this but also mentioned that "the pace of decline had begun to moderate" and policy was very expansionary so that one should expect economic conditions to improve going forward. However, the MPC statement also says that "the timing and strength of that recovery is highly uncertain."

It is important to realize that policymakers do not have very much information at the time when they must make policy decisions. For instance, the consumer price index is available only with a one-month lag, so our knowledge of inflation is always running a month behind the actual economy. The GDP is even worse. The GDP data are available only quarterly, and we do not find out about GDP until well after a quarter ends, and even then substantial revisions to the numbers often occur many months after the quarter. The point is simply that the Federal Reserve, the MPC, and other policymaking institutions must formulate policy today on the basis of less than complete knowledge of the *current* situation, and the policy must be addressed to a best guess of the *future* situation. It is like trying to drive a car looking only in the rearview mirror. You can see where you have been, but you must make decisions about where you will go next without knowing exactly where you are currently.

For these reasons, policymakers often find themselves the target of critics who dispute their current and future outlook on inflation and other key economic variables. Central banks want to act in advance of rising inflation or slowing GDP growth to avoid a bad economic outcome. However, even central banks cannot always clearly determine the state of the economy and, consequently, the best course of action.

© Dbvirago/Dre

Macroeconomic Policy: Tradeoffs, Expectations, Credibility, and Sources of Business Cycles

? Fundamental Questions

1 | Is there a tradeoff between inflation and the unemployment rate?

2 | How does the tradeoff between inflation and the unemployment rate vary from the short to the long run?

3 | What is the relationship between unexpected inflation and the unemployment rate?

4 | How are macroeconomic expectations formed?

5 | What makes government policies credible?

6 | Are business cycles related to political elections?

7 | How do real shocks to the economy affect business cycles?

8 | How is inflationary monetary policy related to government fiscal policy?

Macroeconomics is a dynamic discipline. Monetary and fiscal policies change over time. And so does our understanding of those policies. Economists debate the nature of business cycles—what causes them and what, if anything, government can do about them. Some economists argue that policies that lower the unemployment rate tend to raise the rate of inflation. Others insist that only unexpected inflation can influence real GDP and employment. If the latter economists are right, does government always have to surprise the public in order to improve economic conditions?

Some economists claim that politicians manipulate the business cycle to increase their chances of reelection. If they are right, we should expect economic growth just before national elections. But what happens after the elections? What are the long-term effects of political business cycles? Because of these issues, the material in this chapter should be considered somewhat controversial. In the chapter titled "Macroeconomic Viewpoints: New Keynesian, Monetarist, and New Classical," we will examine the controversies in more detail, and it will be more apparent where the sources of controversy lie.

Those who were around in the 1970s can remember the long lines and shortages at gas stations and the rapid increase in the price of oil that resulted from the oil embargo imposed by the Organization of Petroleum Exporting Countries. There was another effect of the oil price shock—the aggregate supply curve in the United States and other oil-importing nations shifted to the left, lowering the equilibrium level of real GDP while raising the price level. Such real sources of business cycles can explain why national output can rise or fall in the absence of any discretionary government macroeconomic policy.

© David Falconer/National Archives

■ 1. The Phillips Curve

In 1958, a New Zealand economist, A. W. Phillips, published a study of the relationship between the unemployment rate and the rate of change in wages in England. He found that over the period from 1826 to 1957, there had been an inverse relationship between the unemployment rate and the rate of change in wages: The unemployment rate fell in years when there were relatively large increases in wages and rose in years when wages increased relatively little. Phillips's study started other economists searching for similar relationships in other countries. In those subsequent studies, it became common to substitute the rate of inflation for the rate of change in wages.

Early studies in the United States found an inverse relationship between inflation and the unemployment rate. The graph that illustrates this relationship is called a **Phillips curve.** Figure 1 shows a Phillips curve for the United States in the 1960s. Over this period, lower inflation rates were associated with higher unemployment rates, as shown by the downward-sloping curve.

Phillips curve: a graph that illustrates the relationship between inflation and the unemployment rate

The slope of the curve in Figure 1 depicts an inverse relationship between the rate of inflation and the unemployment rate: As the inflation rate falls, the unemployment rate rises. In 1969, the inflation rate was relatively high, at 5.5 percent, while the unemployment rate was relatively low, at 3.5 percent. In 1967, an inflation rate of 3.1 percent was consistent with an unemployment rate of 3.8 percent; and in 1961, 1 percent inflation occurred with 6.7 percent unemployment.

| **FIGURE 1** | A Phillips Curve, United States, 1961–1969 |

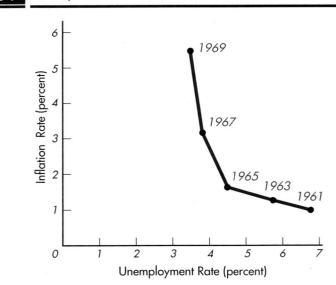

In the 1960s, as the rate of inflation rose, the unemployment rate fell. This inverse relationship suggests a tradeoff between the rate of inflation and the unemployment rate.

The downward-sloping Phillips curve seems to indicate that there is a tradeoff between unemployment and inflation. A country can have a lower unemployment rate by accepting higher inflation, or a lower rate of inflation by accepting higher unemployment. Certainly this was the case in the United States in the 1960s. But is the curve depicted in Figure 1 representative of the tradeoff over long periods of time?

1.a. An Inflation–Unemployment Tradeoff?

Figure 2 shows unemployment and inflation rates in the United States for several years from 1955 to 2009. The points in the figure do not lie along a downward-sloping curve like the one shown in Figure 1. For example, in 1955, the unemployment rate was 4.4 percent and the inflation rate was −0.4 percent. In 1960, the unemployment rate was 5.5 percent and the inflation rate was 1.7 percent. Both the unemployment rate and the inflation rate had increased since 1955. Moving through time, you can see that the inflation rate tended to increase along with the unemployment rate through the 1960s and 1970s. By 1980, the unemployment rate was 7.1 percent and the inflation rate was 13.5 percent.

The scattered points in Figure 2 show no evidence of a tradeoff between unemployment and inflation. A downward-sloping Phillips curve does not seem to exist over the long term.

1.b. Short-Run versus Long-Run Tradeoffs

Most economists believe that the downward-sloping Phillips curve and the tradeoff between inflation and unemployment that it implies are short-term phenomena. Think of a series of Phillips curves, one for each of the points in Figure 2. From 1955 to 1980, the curves shifted out to the right. In the early 1980s, they shifted in to the left.

Figure 3 shows a series of Phillips curves that could account for the data in Figure 2. At any point in time, a downward-sloping Phillips curve indicates a tradeoff between inflation and unemployment. Many economists believe that this kind of tradeoff is

1 | Is there a tradeoff between inflation and the unemployment rate?

2 | How does the tradeoff between inflation and the unemployment rate vary from the short to the long run?

| FIGURE 2 | Unemployment and Inflation in the United States, 1955–2009 |

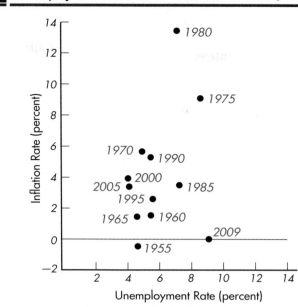

The data on inflation and unemployment rates in the United States between 1955 and 2009 show no particular relationship between inflation and unemployment over the long run. There is no evidence here of a downward-sloping Phillips curve.

| FIGURE 3 | The Shifting Phillips Curve |

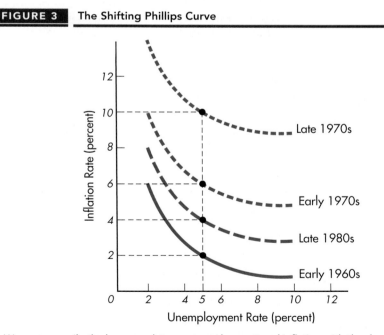

We can reconcile the long-run data on unemployment and inflation with the downward-sloping Phillips curve by using a series of Phillips curves. (In effect, we treat the long run as a series of short-run curves.) The Phillips curve for the early 1960s shows 5 percent unemployment and 2 percent inflation. Over time, the short-run curve shifted out to the right. The early 1970s curve shows 5 percent unemployment and 6 percent inflation. And the short-run curve for the late 1970s shows 5 percent unemployment and 10 percent inflation. In the early 1980s, the short-run Phillips curve began to shift down toward the origin. By the late 1980s, 5 percent unemployment was consistent with 4 percent inflation.

just a short-term phenomenon. Over time, the Phillips curve shifts so that the short-run tradeoff between inflation and unemployment disappears in the long run.

On the early 1960s curve in Figure 3, 5 percent unemployment is consistent with 2 percent inflation. By the early 1970s, the curve had shifted up. Here 5 percent unemployment is associated with 6 percent inflation. On the late 1970s curve, 5 percent unemployment is consistent with 10 percent inflation. For more than two decades, the tradeoff between inflation and unemployment worsened as the Phillips curves shifted up, so that higher and higher inflation rates were associated with any given level of unemployment. Then in the 1980s, the tradeoff seemed to improve as the Phillips curve shifted down. On the late 1980s curve, 5 percent unemployment is consistent with 4 percent inflation.

> The data indicate that the Phillips curve may have shifted out in the 1960s and 1970s and shifted in during the 1980s.

The Phillips curves in Figure 3 represent changes that took place over time in the United States. We cannot be sure of the actual shape of a Phillips curve at any time, but an outward shift of the curve in the 1960s and 1970s and an inward shift during the 1980s are consistent with the data. Later in this chapter, we describe how changing government policy and the public's expectations about that policy may have shifted aggregate demand and aggregate supply and produced these shifts in the Phillips curves.

1.b.1. In the Short Run Figure 4 uses the aggregate demand and supply analysis we developed in the chapter titled "Macroeconomic Equilibrium: Aggregate Demand and Supply" to explain the Phillips curve. Initially the economy is operating at point 1 in both diagrams. In Figure 4(a), the aggregate demand curve (AD_1) and the aggregate supply curve (AS_1) intersect at price level P_1 and real GDP level Y_p, the level of potential real GDP. Remember that potential real GDP is the level of income and output generated at the natural rate of unemployment, the unemployment rate that exists in the absence of cyclical unemployment. In Figure 4(b), point 1 lies on Phillips curve I, where the inflation rate is 3 percent and the unemployment rate is 5 percent. We assume that the 5 percent unemployment rate at the level of potential real GDP is the natural rate of unemployment (U_n). A discussion of the natural rate of unemployment and its determinants is given in the Economic Insight "The Natural Rate of Unemployment."

What happens when aggregate demand goes up from AD_1 to AD_2? A new equilibrium is established along the short-run aggregate supply curve (AS_1) at point 2. Here the price level (P_2) is higher, as is the level of real GDP (Y_2). In part (b), the increase in price and income is reflected in the movement along Phillips curve I to point 2. At point 2, the inflation rate is 6 percent and the unemployment rate is 3 percent. The increase in expenditures raises the inflation rate and lowers the unemployment rate (because national output has surpassed potential output).

Notice that there appears to be a tradeoff between inflation and unemployment on Phillips curve I. The increase in spending increases output and stimulates employment, so that the unemployment rate falls. And the higher spending pushes the rate of inflation up. But this tradeoff is only temporary. Point 2 in both diagrams is only a short-run equilibrium.

1.b.2. In the Long Run As we discussed in the chapter titled "Macroeconomic Equilibrium: Aggregate Demand and Supply," the short-run aggregate supply curve shifts over time as production costs rise in response to higher prices. Once the aggregate supply curve shifts to AS_2, long-run equilibrium occurs at point 3, where AS_2 intersects AD_2. Here, the price level is P_3 and real GDP returns to its potential level, Y_p.

The shift in aggregate supply lowers real GDP. As income falls, the unemployment rate goes up. The decrease in aggregate supply is reflected in the movement from point 2 on Phillips curve I to point 3 on Phillips curve II. As real GDP returns to its potential level (Y_p), unemployment returns to the natural rate (U_n), 5 percent. In the long run, as the economy adjusts to an increase in aggregate demand and expectations adjust to the new inflation rate, there is a period in which real GDP falls and the price level rises.

FIGURE 4 **FIGURE 4**   Aggregate Demand and Supply and the Phillips Curve

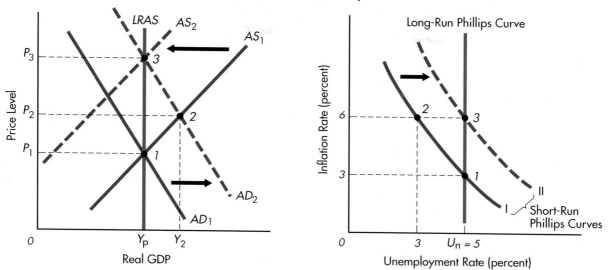

The movement from point 1 to point 2 to point 3 traces the adjustment of the economy to an increase in aggregate demand. Point 1 is initial equilibrium in both diagrams. At this point, potential real GDP is Y_p and the price level is P_1 in the aggregate demand and supply diagram, and the inflation rate is 3 percent with an unemployment rate of 5 percent (the natural rate) along short-run curve 1 in the Phillips curve diagram.

If the aggregate demand curve shifts from AD_1 to AD_2, equilibrium real GDP goes up to Y_2 and the price level rises to P_2 in the aggregate demand and supply diagram. The increase in aggregate demand pushes the inflation rate up to 6 percent and the unemployment rate down to 3 percent along Phillips curve I. The movement from point 1 to point 2 along the curve indicates a tradeoff between inflation and the unemployment rate.

Over time, the AS curve shifts in response to rising production costs at the higher rate of inflation. Along AS_2, equilibrium is at point 3, where real GDP falls back to Y_p and the price level rises to P_3. As we move from point 2 to point 3 in Figure 4(b), we shift to short-run Phillips curve II. Here the inflation rate remains high (at 6 percent), while the unemployment rate goes back up to 5 percent, the rate consistent with production at Y_p. In the long run, then, there is no tradeoff between inflation and unemployment. The vertical long-run aggregate supply curve at the potential level of real GDP is associated with the vertical long-run Phillips curve at the natural rate of unemployment.

The long-run Phillips curve is a vertical line at the natural rate of unemployment.

Over time, there is no relationship between the price level and the level of real GDP. You can see this in the aggregate demand and supply diagram. Points 1 and 3 both lie along the long-run aggregate supply curve (*LRAS*) at potential real GDP. The *LRAS* curve has its analogue in the long-run Phillips curve, a vertical line at the natural rate of unemployment. Points 1 and 3 both lie along this curve.

RECAP

1. The Phillips curve shows an inverse relationship between inflation and unemployment.

2. The downward slope of the Phillips curve indicates a tradeoff between inflation and unemployment.

3. Over the long run, that tradeoff disappears.

4. The long-run Phillips curve is a vertical line at the natural rate of unemployment, analogous to the long-run aggregate supply curve at potential real GDP.

Economic Insight

The Natural Rate of Unemployment

The natural rate of unemployment is defined as the unemployment rate that exists in the absence of cyclical unemployment. As we discussed in the chapter titled "Unemployment and Inflation," the natural rate of unemployment reflects the normal amount of frictional unemployment (people who are temporarily between jobs), structural unemployment (people who have lost jobs because of technological change), and seasonal unemployment (people who have lost jobs because the jobs are available only at certain times of the year). What factors determine the normal amount of frictional and structural unemployment?

One of the most important factors is demographic change. As the age, gender, and racial makeup of the labor force changes, the natural rate of unemployment also changes. For instance, when the baby boom generation entered the labor force, the natural rate of unemployment increased because new workers typically have the highest unemployment rates. Between 1956 and 1979, the proportion of young adults (ages 16 to 24) in the labor force increased, increasing the natural rate of unemployment. Since 1980, the average age of U.S. workers has been rising. As workers age, employers can more easily evaluate a worker's ability based upon that worker's job history. In addition, younger workers are more likely to have difficulty finding a good job match for their skills and so are likely to have higher frictional unemployment, whereas older workers are more likely to have a long-term job with a single employer. As the labor force ages, therefore, we should expect the natural rate of unemployment to fall.

In addition to the composition of the labor force, several other factors affect the natural rate of unemployment:

- In the early 1990s, structural changes in the economy, such as the shift from manufacturing to service

jobs and the downsizing and restructuring of firms throughout the economy, contributed to a higher natural rate of unemployment. Related to these structural changes is a decline in the demand for low-skilled workers, so that rising unemployment is overwhelmingly concentrated among workers with limited education and skills.
- Increases in the legal minimum wage tend to raise the natural rate of unemployment. When the government mandates that employers pay some workers a higher wage than a freely competitive labor market would pay, fewer workers are employed.
- The more generous the unemployment benefits, the higher the natural rate of unemployment. Increased benefits reduce the cost of being out of work and allow unemployed workers to take their time finding a new job. For these reasons, we observe higher natural rates of unemployment in European countries, where unemployed workers receive higher benefits.
- Income taxes can also affect the natural rate of unemployment. Higher taxes mean that workers keep less of their earned income and so have less incentive to work.

The effect of these factors on the unemployment rate is complex, so it is difficult to state exactly what the natural rate of unemployment is. But as these factors change over time, the natural rate of unemployment also changes.

One last thing: It is not clear that minimizing the natural rate of unemployment is a universal goal. Minimum wages, unemployment benefits, and taxes have other important implications besides their effect on the natural rate of unemployment. We cannot expect these variables to be set solely in terms of their effect on unemployment.

■ 2. The Role of Expectations

The data and analysis in the previous section indicate that there is no long-run tradeoff between inflation and unemployment. But they do not explain the movement of the Phillips curve in the 1960s, 1970s, and 1980s. To understand why the short-run curve shifts, you must understand the role that unexpected inflation plays in the economy.

3 | What is the relationship between unexpected inflation and the unemployment rate?

2.a. Expected versus Unexpected Inflation

Figure 5 shows two short-run Phillips curves like those in Figure 4. Each curve is drawn for a particular expected rate of inflation. Curve I shows the tradeoff between inflation and unemployment when the inflation rate is expected to be 3 percent. If the actual rate of inflation (measured along the vertical axis) is 3 percent, the economy is operating at point 1, with an unemployment rate of 5 percent (the natural rate). If the inflation rate unexpectedly increases to 6 percent, the economy moves from point 1 to point 2 along Phillips curve I. Obviously, unexpected inflation can affect the unemployment rate. There are three factors at work here: wage expectations, inventory fluctuations, and wage contracts.

2.a.1. Wage Expectations and Unemployment

reservation wage: the minimum wage that a worker is willing to accept

Unemployed workers who are looking for a job choose a **reservation wage,** the minimum wage that they are willing to accept. They continue to look for work until they receive an offer that equals or exceeds their reservation wage.

Wages are not the only factor that workers take into consideration before accepting a job offer. A firm that offers good working conditions and fringe benefits can pay a lower wage than a firm that does not offer these advantages. But other things being equal, workers choose higher wages over lower wages. We simplify our analysis here by assuming that the only variable that affects the unemployed worker who is looking for a job is the reservation wage.

The link between unexpected inflation and the unemployment rate stems from the fact that wage offers are surprisingly high when the rate of inflation is surprisingly high. An unexpected increase in inflation means that prices are higher than anticipated, as are nominal income and wages. If aggregate demand increases unexpectedly, then prices, output, employment, and wages go up. Unemployed workers with a constant reservation wage find it easier to obtain a satisfactory wage offer

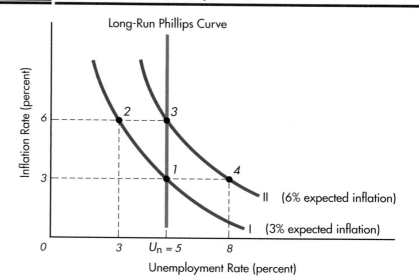

FIGURE 5   **Expectations and the Phillips Curve**

Short-run Phillips curve I shows the tradeoff between inflation and the unemployment rate as long as people expect 3 percent inflation. When the actual rate of inflation is 3 percent, the rate of unemployment (U_n) is 5 percent (point 1). Short-run Phillips curve II shows the tradeoff as long as people expect 6 percent inflation. When the actual rate of inflation is 6 percent, the unemployment rate is 5 percent (point 3).

FIGURE 6 Inflation, Unemployment, and Wage Expectations

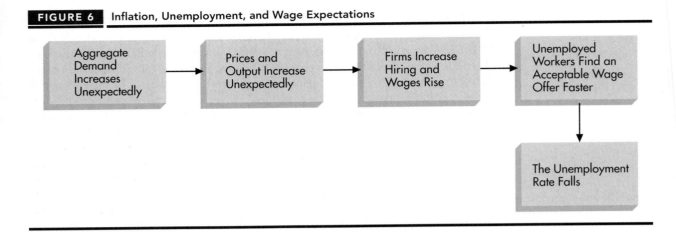

during a period when wages are rising faster than the workers expected. This means that more unemployed workers find jobs, and they find those jobs more quickly than they do in a period when the rate of inflation is expected. So the unemployment rate falls during a period of unexpectedly high inflation (Figure 6).

Consider an example. Suppose an accountant named Jason determines that he must find a job that pays at least $105 a day. Jason's reservation wage is $105. Furthermore, Jason expects prices and wages to be fairly stable across the economy; he expects no inflation. Jason looks for a job and finds that the jobs he qualifies for are offering wages of only $100 a day. Because his job offers are all paying less than his reservation wage, he keeps on looking. Let's say that aggregate demand rises unexpectedly. Firms increase production and raise prices. To hire more workers, they increase the wages they offer. Suppose wages go up 5 percent. Now the jobs that Jason qualifies for are offering 5 percent higher wages, $105 a day instead of $100 a day. At this higher wage rate, Jason quickly accepts a job and starts working. This example explains why the move from point 1 to point 2 in Figure 5 occurs.

The short-run Phillips curve assumes a constant *expected* rate of inflation. It also assumes that every unemployed worker who is looking for a job has a constant reservation wage. When inflation rises unexpectedly, then, wages rise faster than expected and the unemployment rate falls. The element of surprise is critical here. If the increase in inflation is *expected*, unemployed workers who are looking for a job will revise their reservation wage to match the expected change in the level of prices. If reservation wages go up with the rate of inflation, there is no tradeoff between inflation and the unemployment rate. Higher inflation is associated with the original unemployment rate.

> If the reservation wage goes up with the rate of inflation, there is no tradeoff between inflation and the unemployment rate.

Let's go back to Jason, the accountant who wants a job that pays $105 a day. Previously we said that if wages increased to $105 because of an unexpected increase in aggregate demand, he would quickly find an acceptable job. However, if Jason knows that the price level is going to go up 5 percent, then he knows that a wage increase from $100 to $105 is not a real wage increase because he will need $105 in order to buy what $100 would buy before. The *nominal wage* is the number of dollars earned; the *real wage* is the purchasing power of those dollars. If the nominal wage increases 5 percent at the same time that prices have gone up 5 percent, it takes 5 percent more money to buy the same goods and services. The real wage has not changed. What happens? Jason revises his reservation wage to account for the higher price level. If he wants a 5 percent higher real wage, his reservation wage goes up to $110.25 (5 percent more than $105). Now if employers offer him $105, he refuses and keeps searching.

In Figure 5, an expected increase in inflation moves us from point 1 on curve I to point 3 on curve II. When increased inflation is expected, the reservation wage reflects the higher rate of inflation, and there is no tradeoff between inflation and the unemployment rate. Instead, the economy moves along the long-run Phillips curve, with unemployment at its natural rate. The clockwise movement from point 1 to point 2 to point 3 is the pattern that follows an unexpected increase in aggregate demand.

What if the inflation rate is lower than expected? Here we find a reservation wage that reflects higher expected inflation. This means that those people who are looking for jobs are going to have a difficult time finding acceptable wage offers, the number of unemployed workers is going to increase, and the unemployment rate is going to rise. This sequence is shown in Figure 5 as the economy moves from point 3 to point 4. When the actual inflation rate is 6 percent and the expected inflation rate is also 6 percent, the economy is operating at the natural rate of unemployment. When the inflation rate falls to 3 percent but workers still expect 6 percent inflation, the unemployment rate rises (at point 4 along curve II). Eventually, if the inflation rate remains at 3 percent, workers adjust their expectations to the lower rate and the economy moves to point 1 on curve I. The short-run effect of unexpected *disinflation* is rising unemployment. Over time, the short-run increase in the unemployment rate is eliminated.

> *As long as the actual rate of inflation equals the expected rate, the economy operates at the natural rate of unemployment*

As long as the actual rate of inflation equals the expected rate, the economy remains at the natural rate of unemployment. The tradeoff between inflation and the unemployment rate comes from unexpected inflation.

2.a.2. Inventory Fluctuations and Unemployment Businesses hold inventories based on what they expect their sales to be. When aggregate demand is greater than expected, inventories fall below the targeted levels. To restore inventories to the levels wanted, production is increased. Increased production leads to increased employment. If aggregate demand is lower than expected, inventories rise above the targeted levels. To reduce inventories, production is cut back and workers are laid off from their jobs until sales have lowered the unwanted inventories. Once production increases, employment rises again.

> *When aggregate demand is higher than expected, inventories are lower than expected and prices are higher than expected, so the unemployment rate falls. When aggregate demand is lower than expected, inventories are higher than expected and prices are lower than expected, so the unemployment rate rises.*

Inventory, production, and employment all play a part in the Phillips curve analysis (Figure 7). Expected sales and inventory levels are based on an expected level of aggregate demand. If aggregate demand is greater than expected, inventories fall and prices of the remaining goods in stock rise. With the unexpected increase in inflation, the unemployment rate falls as businesses hire more workers to increase output to offset falling inventories. This sequence represents movement along a short-run Phillips curve because there is a tradeoff between inflation and the unemployment rate. We find the same tradeoff if aggregate demand is lower than expected. Here inventories increase and prices are lower than anticipated. With the unexpected decrease in inflation, the unemployment rate goes up as workers are laid off to reduce output until inventory levels fall.

2.a.3. Wage Contracts and Unemployment Another factor that explains the short-run tradeoff between inflation and unemployment is labor contracts that fix wages for an extended period of time. When an existing contract expires, management must renegotiate with labor. A firm that is facing lower demand for its products may negotiate lower wages in order to keep as many workers employed as

FIGURE 7 Inflation, Unemployment, and Inventories

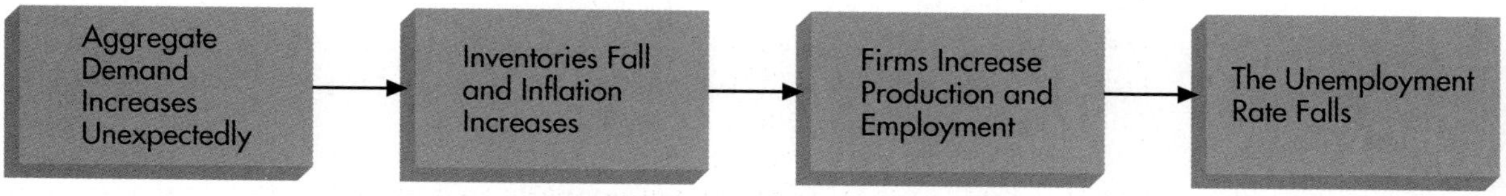

Aggregate Demand Increases Unexpectedly → Inventories Fall and Inflation Increases → Firms Increase Production and Employment → The Unemployment Rate Falls

before. If the demand for a firm's products falls while a wage contract is in force, the firm must maintain wages; this means that it is going to have to lay off workers.

For example, a pizza restaurant with $1,000 a day in revenues employs 4 workers at $40 a day each. The firm's total labor costs are $160 a day. Suppose revenues fall to $500 a day. If the firm wants to cut its labor costs in half, to $80, it has two choices: It can maintain wages at $40 a day and lay off 2 workers, or it can lower wages to $20 a day and keep all 4 workers. If the restaurant has a contract with the employees that sets wages at $40 a day, it must lay off 2 workers.

If demand increases while a wage contract is in force, a business hires more workers at the fixed wage. Once the contract expires, the firm's workers will negotiate higher wages, to reflect the increased demand. For instance, suppose prices in the economy, including the price of pizzas, go up 10 percent. If the pizza restaurant can raise its prices 10 percent and sell as many pizzas as before (because the price of every other food also has gone up 10 percent), its daily revenues increase from $1,000 to $1,100. If the restaurant has a labor contract that fixes wages at $40 a day, its profits are going to go up, reflecting the higher price of pizzas. With its increased profits, the restaurant may be willing to hire more workers. Once the labor contract expires, the workers ask for a 10 percent wage increase to match the price level increase. If wages go up to $44 a day (10 percent higher than $40), the firm cannot hire more workers because wages have gone up in proportion to the increase in prices. If the costs of doing business rise at the same rate as prices, both profits and employment remain the same.

In the national economy, wage contracts are staggered; they expire at different times. Only 30 to 40 percent of all contracts expire each year across the entire economy. As economic conditions change, firms with expiring wage contracts can adjust *wages* to those conditions, whereas firms with existing contracts must adjust *employment* to those conditions.

How do long-term wage contracts tie in with the Phillips curve analysis? The expected rate of inflation is based on expected aggregate demand and is reflected in the wage that is agreed on in the contract. When the actual rate of inflation equals the expected rate, businesses retain the same number of workers that they had planned on when they signed the contract. For the economy overall, when actual and expected inflation rates are the same, the economy is operating at the natural rate of unemployment. That is, businesses are not hiring new workers because of an unexpected increase in aggregate demand, and they are not laying off workers because of an unexpected decrease in aggregate demand.

When aggregate demand is higher than expected, those firms with unexpired wage contracts hire more workers at the fixed wage, reducing unemployment (Figure 8). Those firms with expiring contracts have to offer higher wages in order to maintain the existing level of employment at the new demand condition. When aggregate demand is lower than expected, those firms with unexpired contracts have to lay off workers because they cannot lower the wage, while those firms with expiring contracts negotiate lower wages in order to keep their workers.

If wages were always flexible, unexpected changes in aggregate demand might be reflected largely in *wage* rather than *employment* adjustments. Wage contracts

Wage contracts force businesses to adjust employment rather than wages in response to an unexpected change in aggregate demand.

FIGURE 8   Inflation, Unemployment, and Wage Contracts

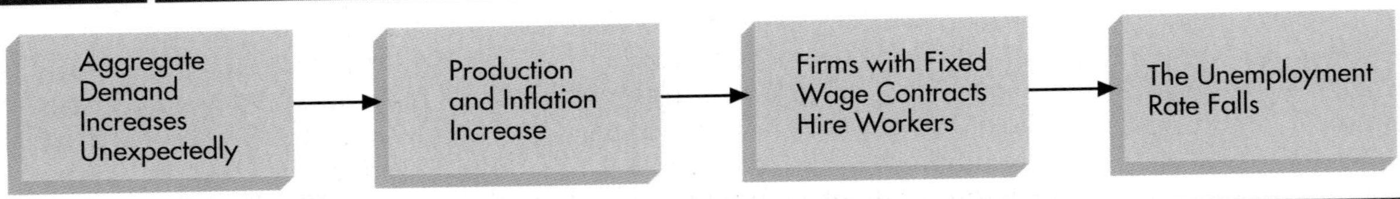

Economic Insight

Why Wages Don't Fall During Recessions

A look at macroeconomic data across countries reveals that when economies experience recessions, unemployment rates rise, but wages fall very little, if at all. If we think of a supply and demand diagram for labor, we would think that as demand for labor falls in a recession, both the equilibrium quantity of labor and the equilibrium price, the wage rate, would fall. We do see the quantity effect, as workers lose their jobs and the unemployment rate rises. Why don't we see wages falling also?

The text discusses long-term labor contracts as one reason why wages may be relatively inflexible over time. Beyond the presence of contracts, recent research points to human behavior as a contributing factor. Surveys of firms and workers indicate that worker morale is a major reason why wages are not reduced during recessions. Workers would view a wage cut as

an indication that the firm does not value their work as much, and they might, therefore, suffer lower morale, with the result being lower effort. When some workers are laid off, those workers suffer from the job loss, but they are no longer at the firm and thus cannot harm morale and work effort. Only in cases where the very survival of the firm is clearly at stake do wage cuts appear to be acceptable to workers.

So wages are "sticky downwards" because this promotes good worker effort and ensures that workers and firms share the same goals of efficient production and profit maximization. Rather than keep all workers when demand falls by paying lower wages to all, it may be better for the firm to lay off some workers and keep paying the remaining employees the same wage as before.

Sources: Truman F. Bewley, *Why Wages Don't Fall During a Recession* (Cambridge: Harvard University Press, 1999), and Peter Howitt, "Looking Inside the Labor Market: A Review Article," *Journal of Economic Literature*, March 2002.

---

force businesses to adjust employment when aggregate demand changes unexpectedly. The Economic Insight "Why Wages Don't Fall During Recessions" addresses this issue further.

2.b. Forming Expectations

Expectations play a key role in explaining the short-run Phillips curve, the tradeoff between inflation and the unemployment rate. How are these expectations formed?

2.b.1. Adaptive Expectations Expectations can be formed solely on the basis of experience. **Adaptive expectations** are expectations that are determined by what has happened in the recent past.

People learn from their experiences. For example, suppose the inflation rate has been 3 percent for the past few years. Based on past experience, then, people expect the inflation rate in the future to remain at 3 percent. If the Federal Reserve increases the growth of the money supply to a rate that produces 6 percent inflation, the public will be surprised by the higher rate of inflation. This unexpected inflation creates a short-run tradeoff between inflation and the unemployment rate along a short-run Phillips curve. Over time, if the inflation rate remains at 6 percent, the public will learn that the 3 percent rate is too low and will adapt its expectations to the actual, higher inflation rate. Once public expectations have adapted to the new rate of inflation, the economy returns to the natural rate of unemployment along the long-run Phillips curve.

4 | How are macroeconomic expectations formed?

adaptive expectation: an expectation formed on the basis of information collected in the past

rational expectation: an expectation that is formed using all available relevant information

2.b.2. Rational Expectations Many economists believe that adaptive expectations are too narrow. If people look only at past information, they are ignoring what could be important information in the current period. **Rational expectations** are based on all available relevant information.

We are not saying that people have to know everything in order to form expectations. Rational expectations require only that people consider all the information that they believe to be relevant. This information includes their past experience, but also what is currently happening and what they expect to happen in the future. For instance, in forming expectations about inflation, people consider rates in the recent past, current policy, and anticipated shifts in aggregate demand and supply that could affect the future rate of inflation.

If the inflation rate has been 3 percent over the past few years, adaptive expectations suggest that the future inflation rate will be 3 percent. No other information is considered. Rational expectations are based on more than the historical rate. Suppose the Fed announces a new policy that everyone believes will increase inflation in the future. With rational expectations, the effect of this announcement will be considered. Thus, when the actual rate of inflation turns out to be more than 3 percent, there is no short-run tradeoff between inflation and the unemployment rate. The economy moves directly along the long-run Phillips curve to the higher inflation rate, while unemployment remains at the natural rate.

RECAP

1. Wage expectations, inventory fluctuations, and wage contracts help explain the short-run tradeoff between inflation and the unemployment rate.

2. The reservation wage is the minimum wage that a worker is willing to accept.

3. Because wage expectations reflect expected inflation, when the inflation rate is surprisingly high, unemployed workers find jobs faster and the unemployment rate falls.

4. Unexpected increases in aggregate demand lower inventories and raise prices. To increase output (to replenish shrinking inventories), businesses hire more workers, which reduces the unemployment rate.

5. When aggregate demand is higher than expected, those businesses with wage contracts hire more workers at the fixed wage, lowering unemployment.

6. If wages were always flexible, unexpected changes in aggregate demand would be reflected in wage adjustments rather than employment adjustments.

7. Adaptive expectations are formed on the basis of information about the past.

8. Rational expectations are formed using all available relevant information.

■ 3. Credibility and Time Inconsistency

The rate of inflation is a product of growth in the money supply. That growth is controlled by the country's central bank. If the Federal Reserve follows a policy of rapidly increasing the money supply, one consequence is rapid inflation. If it follows a policy of slow growth, it keeps inflation down.

To help the public predict the future course of monetary policy, Congress passed the Federal Reserve Reform Act (1977) and the Full Employment and Balanced Growth Act (1978). The Full Employment Act requires that the chairman of the

time inconsistent: a characteristic of a policy or plan that changes over time in response to changing conditions

Board of Governors of the Federal Reserve System testify before Congress semi-annually about the Fed's targets for money growth, along with other policy plans.

Of course, the Fed's plans are only plans. There is no requirement that the central bank actually follow the plans it announces to Congress. During the course of the year, the Fed may decide that a new policy is necessary in light of economic developments. Changing conditions mean that plans can be **time inconsistent.** A plan is time inconsistent when it is changed over time in response to changed conditions.

3.a. The Policymaker's Problem

Time inconsistency gives the Fed a credibility problem and the public the problem of guessing where monetary policy and the inflation rate are actually heading. Figure 9 shows an example of how announced monetary policy can turn out to be time inconsistent. The Fed, like all central banks, always announces that it plans to follow a low-money-growth policy to promote a low rate of inflation. (It is unlikely that a central bank would ever state that it intends to follow an inflationary monetary policy.) Yet we know that the world is often characterized by higher rates of inflation. Because the actual inflation rate often ends up being higher than the intended inflation rate, low-inflation plans often are time inconsistent.

In Figure 9, labor contracts are signed following the central bank's announcement. The contracts call for either low wage increases or high wage increases. If everyone believes that the money supply is going to grow at the announced low rate, then the low-wage contracts are signed. However, if there is reason to believe that the announced policy is time inconsistent, the high-wage contracts are signed.

Over time, the central bank either follows the announced low-money-growth policy or implements a high-money-growth policy. If the low-wage contract is in force and the central bank follows the low-money-growth policy, the actual inflation rate will match the low rate that people expected, and the unemployment rate will equal the natural rate. If the central bank follows a high-money-growth policy, the rate of inflation will be higher than expected, and the unemployment rate will fall below the natural rate.

If the high-wage contract is in force and the low-money-growth policy is followed, the inflation rate will be lower than expected, and the unemployment rate will exceed the natural rate. If the high-money-growth policy is followed, the inflation rate will be as expected, and the unemployment rate will be at the natural rate.

Look at what happens to unemployment. Regardless of which labor contract is signed, if the central bank wants to keep unemployment as low as possible, it must deviate from its announced plan. The plan turns out to be time inconsistent. Because the public knows that unemployment, like the rate of inflation, is a factor in the Fed's policymaking, the central bank's announced plan is not credible.

3.b. Credibility

5 | **What makes government policies credible?**

If the public does not believe the low-money-growth plans of the central bank, high-wage contracts will always be signed, and the central bank will always have to follow a high-money-growth policy to maintain the natural rate of unemployment. This cycle creates an economy in which high inflation persists year after year. If the central bank always followed its announced plan of low money growth and low inflation, the public would believe the plan, low-wage contracts would always be signed, and the natural rate of unemployment would exist at the low rate of inflation. In either case, high or low inflation, if the inflation rate is at the expected level, the unemployment rate does not change. If the central bank eliminates the goal of reducing unemployment below the natural rate, the problem of inflation disappears. However, the public must be convinced that the central bank intends to pursue low money growth in the long run, avoiding the temptation to reduce the unemployment rate in the short run.

| FIGURE 9 | Time Inconsistency: An Example |

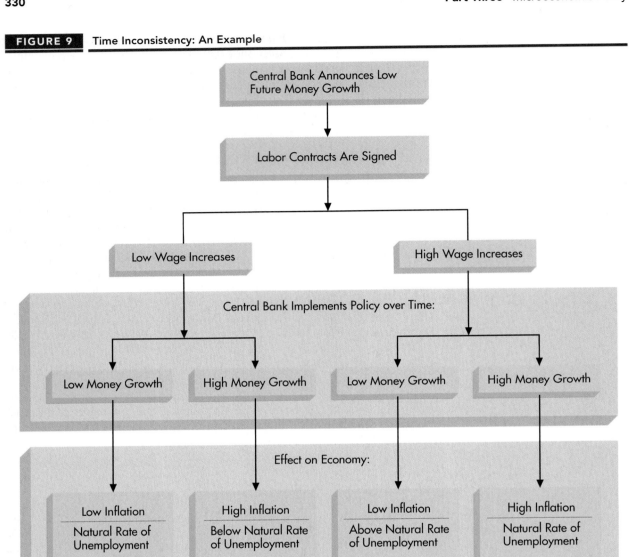

Regardless of which labor contract is signed, the central bank achieves the lowest unemployment rate by following the high-money-growth policy—the opposite of its announced policy.

How does the central bank achieve credibility? One way is to fix the growth rate of the money supply by law. Congress could pass a law requiring that the Fed maintain a growth rate of, say, 3 to 5 percent a year. There would be problems in defining the money supply, but this kind of law would give the Fed's policies credibility.

In the past decade, central banks around the world have increasingly turned to inflation targeting as a manner of achieving credibility. By establishing a publicly announced target for inflation, the public can anticipate what policy will be by knowing whether the inflation rate is above or below the target. For instance, some banks target a particular inflation rate—for example, the Bank of England targets a rate of 2 percent. Other banks target a range for inflation—for example, the European Central Bank's target of near or below 2 percent, as well as the Bank of Canada's 1–3 percent. The Federal Reserve does not announce an official inflation target, but it is believed by many that an inflation rate in the range of 1–2 percent is implicit in Fed policy.

A key for establishing credibility is to create incentives for monetary authorities to take a long-term view of monetary policy. In the long run, the economy is better off if policymakers do not try to exploit the short-run tradeoff between inflation and the unemployment rate. The central bank can achieve a lower rate of inflation at the natural rate of unemployment by avoiding unexpected increases in the rate at which money and inflation grow.

Reputation is a key factor here. If the central bank considers the effects of its actual policy on public expectations, it will find it easier to achieve low inflation by establishing a reputation for low-inflation policies. A central bank with a reputation for time-consistent plans will find that labor contracts will call for low wage increases because people believe that the bank is going to follow its announced plans and generate a low rate of inflation. In other words, by maintaining a reputation for following through on its announced policy, the Fed can earn the public confidence necessary to produce a low rate of inflation in the long run.

RECAP

1. A plan is time inconsistent when it changes over time in response to changing conditions.

2. If the public believes that an announced policy is time inconsistent, policymakers have a credibility problem that can limit the success of their plans.

3. Credibility can be achieved by fixing the growth rate of the money supply by law or by creating incentives for policymakers to follow through on their announced plans.

■ 4. Sources of Business Cycles

In the chapter titled "Fiscal Policy," we examined the effect of fiscal policy on the equilibrium level of real GDP. Changes in government spending and taxes can expand or contract the economy. In the chapter titled "Monetary Policy," we described how monetary policy affects the equilibrium level of real GDP. Changes in the money supply can also produce booms and recessions. In addition to the policy-induced sources of business cycles covered in earlier chapters, there are other sources of economic fluctuations that economists have studied. One is the election campaign of incumbent politicians; when a business cycle results from this action, it is called a *political business cycle*. Macroeconomic policy may be used to promote the reelection of incumbent politicians. We also examine another source of business cycles that is not related to discretionary policy actions, the *real business cycle*.

4.a. The Political Business Cycle

6 | Are business cycles related to political elections?

If a short-run tradeoff exists between inflation and unemployment, an incumbent administration could stimulate the economy just before an election to lower the unemployment rate, making voters happy and increasing the probability of reelection. Of course, after the election, the long-run adjustment to the expansionary policy would lead to higher inflation and move unemployment back to the natural rate.

Figure 10 illustrates the pattern. Before the election, the economy is initially at point 1 in Figure 10(a) and Figure 10(b). The incumbent administration stimulates the economy by increasing government spending or increasing the growth of the money supply. Aggregate demand shifts from AD_1 to AD_2 in Figure 10(a). In the

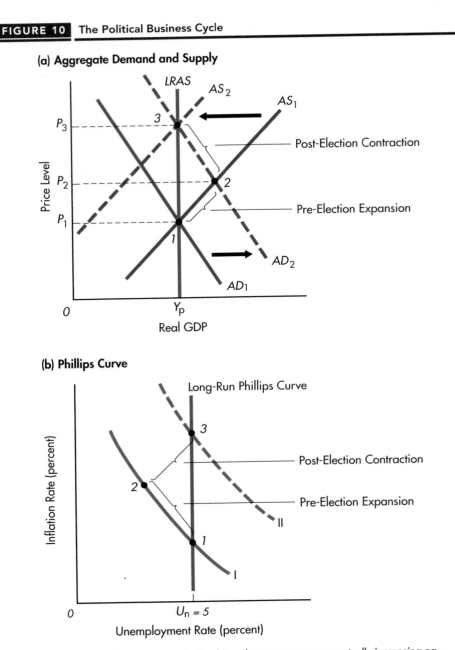

FIGURE 10 The Political Business Cycle

(a) Aggregate Demand and Supply

(b) Phillips Curve

Before the election, the government stimulates the economy, unexpectedly increasing aggregate demand. The economy moves from point 1 to point 2, pushing equilibrium real GDP above Y_p (Figure 10[a]) and the unemployment rate below U_n (Figure 10[b]). The incumbent politicians hope that rising incomes and lower unemployment will translate into votes. After the election comes adjustment to the higher aggregate demand, as the economy moves from point 2 to point 3. The aggregate supply curve shifts to the left, and equilibrium real GDP falls back to Y_p. Unemployment goes back up to U_n, and the rate of inflation rises.

short run, the increase in aggregate demand is unexpected, so the economy moves along the initial aggregate supply curve (AS_1) to point 2. This movement is reflected in Figure 10(b) of the figure, in the movement from point 1 to point 2 along short-run Phillips curve I. The pre-election expansionary policy increases real GDP and lowers the unemployment rate. Once the public adjusts its expectations to the higher inflation rate, the economy experiences a recession. Real GDP falls back to its potential level (Y_p), and the unemployment rate goes back up to the natural rate (U_n), as shown by the movement from point 2 to point 3 in both parts of the figure.

An unexpected increase in government spending or money growth temporarily stimulates the economy. If an election comes during the period of expansion, higher incomes and lower unemployment may increase support for the incumbent administration. The long-run adjustment back to potential real GDP and the natural rate of unemployment comes after the election.

Economists do not agree on whether a political business cycle exists in the United States. But they do agree that an effort to exploit the short-run tradeoff between inflation and the unemployment rate would shift the short-run Phillips curve out, as shown in Figure 10(b).

The evidence for a political business cycle is not clear. If government macroeconomic policy is designed to stimulate the economy before elections and to bear the costs of rising unemployment and inflation after elections, we should see recessions regularly following national elections. Table 1 lists the presidential elections since 1948 along with the recessions that followed them. In six cases, a recession occurred the year after an election. A recession began before President Kennedy's election, and there was no recession during the Johnson, second Reagan, and Clinton administrations. Of course, just because recessions do not follow every election does not guarantee that some business cycles have not stemmed from political manipulation. If a short-run Phillips curve exists, the potential for a political business cycle exists as long as the public does not expect the government to stimulate the economy before elections.

7 | How do real shocks to the economy affect business cycles?

shock: an unexpected change in a variable

4.b. Real Business Cycles

In recent years, economists have paid increasing attention to real **shocks**— unexpected changes—to the economy as a source of business cycles. Many

TABLE 1 Presidential Elections and U.S. Recessions, 1948–2008

Presidential Election (Winner)	Next Recession
November 1948 (Truman)	November 1948–October 1949
November 1952 (Eisenhower)	June 1953–May 1954
November 1956 (Eisenhower)	June 1957–April 1958
November 1960 (Kennedy)	April 1960–February 1961
November 1964 (Johnson)	
November 1968 (Nixon)	October 1969–November 1970
November 1972 (Nixon)	December 1973–March 1975
November 1976 (Carter)	January 1980–July 1980
November 1980 (Reagan)	May 1981–November 1982
November 1984 (Reagan)	
November 1988 (G. H. W. Bush)	July 1990–March 1991
November 1992 (Clinton)	
November 1996 (Clinton)	
November 2000 (G. W. Bush)	March 2001–November 2001
November 2004 (G. W. Bush)	December 2007–
November 2008 (Obama)	

believe that it is not only fiscal or monetary policy that triggers expansion or contraction in the economy, but also technological change, change in tastes, labor strikes, weather, war, terrorism, or other real changes. A real business cycle is one that is generated by a change in one of those real variables.

Interest in the real business cycle was stimulated by the oil price shocks in the early 1970s and the important role they played in triggering the recession of 1973–1975. At that time, many economists were focusing on the role of unexpected changes in monetary policy in generating business cycles. They argued that these kinds of policy changes (changes in a nominal variable, the money supply) were responsible for the shifts in aggregate demand that led to expansions and contractions. When OPEC raised oil prices, it caused major shifts in aggregate supply. Higher oil prices in 1973 and 1974, and in 1979 and 1980, reduced aggregate supply, pushing the equilibrium level of real GDP down. Lower oil prices in 1986 raised aggregate supply and equilibrium real GDP.

An economy-wide real shock, like a substantial change in the price of oil, can affect output and employment across all sectors of the economy. Even an industry-specific shock can generate a recession or expansion in the entire economy if the industry produces a product used by a substantial number of other industries. For example, a labor strike in the steel industry would have major recessionary implications for the economy as a whole. If the output of steel fell, the price of steel would be bid up by all the industries that use steel as an input. This would shift the short-run aggregate supply curve to the left, as shown in Figure 11(a), and would move equilibrium real GDP from Y_1 down to Y_2.

> *A business cycle can be the product of discretionary government policy or of real shocks that occur independent of government actions.*

Real shocks can also have expansionary effects on the economy. Suppose that the weather is particularly good one year, so that harvests are surprisingly large. What happens? The price of food, cotton, and other agricultural output tends to fall, and the short-run aggregate supply curve shifts to the right, as shown in Figure 11(b), raising equilibrium real GDP from Y_1 to Y_2.

Real business cycles explain why national output can expand or contract in the absence of a discretionary macroeconomic policy that would shift aggregate

Extreme weather can be a source of real business-cycle fluctuations. Hurricane Katrina destroyed some of the capital stock of the nation along the Gulf Coast and was associated with a temporary reduction in output.

FIGURE 11 **FIGURE 11** The Impact of Real Shocks on Equilibrium Real GDP

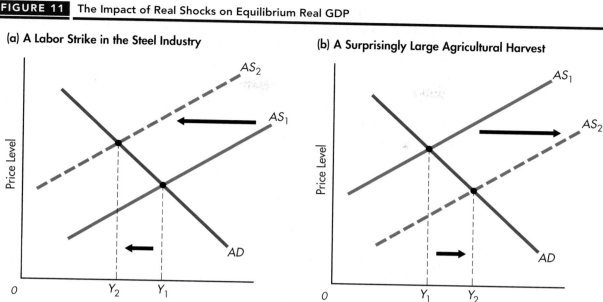

(a) A Labor Strike in the Steel Industry

(b) A Surprisingly Large Agricultural Harvest

A labor strike in a key industry can shift the aggregate supply curve to the left, like the shift from AS_1 to AS_2. This pushes equilibrium real GDP down from Y_1 to Y_2.

If good weather leads to a banner harvest, the aggregate supply curve shifts to the right, like the shift from AS_1 to AS_2, raising equilibrium real GDP from Y_1 to Y_2.

demand. To fully understand business cycles, we must consider both policy-induced changes in real GDP, as covered in the chapters titled "Fiscal Policy" and "Monetary Policy," and real shocks that occur independent of government actions.

4.c. Output Volatility

Since the mid-1980s, U.S. output growth had become noticeably less volatile prior to the financial crisis and the associated global recession that began in 2007. Some economists have referred to this period of relatively low variability of real GDP growth as the "Great Moderation." The global recession beginning in 2007 ended this "moderation" in the volatility of real GDP. Why was output growth so stable prior to this most recent recession, and what should determine how volatile real GDP is? Several factors, which are also important determinants of output volatility, may have contributed to the moderation of real GDP prior to 2007.

4.c.1. Better Inventory Management Research suggests that at least part of the dampening of real GDP growth fluctuatons is due to advances in inventory management techniques, made possible by improvements in information technology and communications. Inventories do not fluctuate as much as they used to, because firms are now able to order what they want to hold in inventory with relatively short lags for delivery. This means that they can hold less inventory and respond to changes in sales as needed. In the past, inventory management was aimed at managing with longer delivery times, and so firms tended to hold larger inventories than they expected to need in order to avoid being caught short if sales were greater than expected. In this earlier environment, if sales were lower than expected, then orders for new goods, and consequently production, dropped dramatically in order to allow inventories to be reduced over time to match the lower level of sales. If sales were much higher than expected, inventories dropped to very low levels until firms could restock to catch up with sales. Today, firms are able to receive shipments of new inventory with a much shorter delay; "just in time" inventory management allows firms to adjust inventories to changing business conditions quickly. This has helped level out both inventories and overall production of goods and has contributed to lower real output volatility.

4.c.2. Changes in Financial Markets
Prior to the early 1980s, the maximum rate of interest that U.S. banks could pay on deposits was limited by a Federal Reserve regulation known as *Regulation Q*. Thus, when interest rates rose above what banks could pay, people would withdraw money from banks and seek higher interest rates elsewhere. This forced banks to reduce their lending on things like home mortgages. As a result, investment in residential housing was much more volatile during the era prior to the removal of the ceiling on interest rates. In addition to changes in financial market regulations, which contribute to less output volatility, more and better financial products have become available to help people smooth their consumption across fluctuations in income. The greater availability of financial products for saving and borrowing has resulted in less variability in consumer spending over time, which in turn contributes to less variability in real output.

The financial crisis beginning in 2007 revealed that some financial products and lending practices, which had been developed during the good times in the earlier part of the decade, created excessive borrowing and risk taking. This tendency was sharply reversed during the financial crisis: Banks dramatically reduced credit availability, cut lending, and tightened credit policies in an attempt to improve the quality of their loans. Financial innovation can help business firms and households smooth consumption against income fluctuations and reduce volatility. However, prudent regulation of financial institutions and adequate controls on lending practices are necessary to avoid financial crises that lead to greater volatility.

4.c.3. Improved Macroeconomic Policy
The belief in a tradeoff between inflation and unemployment, as suggested by the Phillips curve of the 1960s in Figure 1, led policymakers to try to exploit this tradeoff. Their attempts to stimulate the economy resulted in higher inflation, and when they tightened policy to restrain inflation, real output contracted. In the 1980s, it was generally acknowledged that such a tradeoff was probably not easily exploitable, if it was exploitable at all. This realization led to more stable macroeconomic policy, which contributed to less variability in real output.

4.c.4. Good Luck
The real-business-cycle approach emphasizes real shocks to the economy as an important catalyst of business-cycle fluctuations. From the mid-1980s, real economic shocks tended to be less severe than in earlier times. For instance, the oil price shocks of the 1970s were much more destabilizing than more recent oil price shocks. In addition, shifts in productivity were much more pronounced in earlier decades than during the last 20 years. If good luck with regard to the size and impact of real shocks was important in explaining the Great Moderation, such luck does not continue forever: It is not surprising that, eventually, the variability of real output growth increased in 2007–2009.

It is important to realize that there is disagreement among economists as to the causes of the reduction in the variability of real output growth that occurred prior to the financial crisis. It is also possible that all the explanations offered are not independent, and that each has been partly affected by the others. For instance, if monetary policy has become better over time and has contributed to low and stable inflation, then even major real economic shocks should not lead to big changes in inflation, which means that the effects of the shocks could be more moderate than in earlier times. Only time will tell whether the reduction in the growth of real output volatility is a permanent or a temporary economic phenomenon.

1. The political business cycle is a short-term expansion stimulated by an administration before an election to earn votes. After the election comes the long-term adjustment (rising unemployment and inflation).

2. A real business cycle is an expansion and contraction caused by a change in tastes or technology, strikes, weather, or other real factors.

3. Prior to the recent financial crisis, the growth rate of real output was much less volatile in the 1980s and 1990s than in earlier decades. Reasons given include better inventory management, development of financial markets, better macroeconomic policy, and smaller real shocks.

■ 5. The Link Between Monetary and Fiscal Policies

In earlier chapters, we described how monetary and fiscal policies determine the equilibrium level of prices and national income. In our discussions, we have talked about monetary policy and fiscal policy individually. Here we consider the relationship between them.

In some countries, monetary and fiscal policies are carried out by a single central authority. Even in the United States, where the Federal Reserve was created as an independent agency, monetary policy and fiscal policy are always related. The actions of the central bank have an impact on the proper role of fiscal policy, and the actions of fiscal policymakers have an impact on the proper role of monetary policy.

For example, suppose the central bank follows a monetary policy that raises interest rates. That policy raises the interest cost of new government debt, in the process increasing government expenditures. On the other hand, a fiscal policy that generates large fiscal deficits could contribute to higher interest rates. If the central bank has targeted an interest rate that lies below the current rate, the central bank could be drawn into an expansionary monetary policy. This interdependence of monetary and fiscal policy is important to policymakers, and also to businesspeople and others who seek to understand current economic developments.

5.a. The Government Budget Constraint

8 | How is inflationary monetary policy related to government fiscal policy?

The *government budget constraint* clarifies the relationship between monetary and fiscal policies:

$$G = T + B + \Delta M$$

where

$$G = \text{government spending}$$

$$T = \text{tax revenue}$$

$$B = \text{government borrowing}$$

$$\Delta M = \text{change in the money supply}[1]$$

---

[1]The M in the government budget constraint is government-issued money (usually called base money or high-powered money). It is easiest to think of this kind of money as currency, although in practice base money includes more than currency.

The government budget constraint always holds because there are only three ways for the government to finance its spending: by taxing, by borrowing, and by creating money.

We can rewrite the government budget constraint with the change in M on the left-hand side of the equation:

$$\Delta M = (G - T) - B$$

In this form, you can see that the change in government-issued money equals the government fiscal deficit $(G - T)$ minus borrowing. This equation is always true. A government that has the ability to borrow at reasonable costs will not have the incentive to create rapid money growth and the consequent inflation that results in order to finance its budget deficit.

5.b. Monetary Reforms

In the United States and other industrial nations, monetary and fiscal policies are conducted by separate, independent agencies. Fiscal authorities (Congress and the president in the United States) cannot impose monetary policy on the central bank. But in some developing countries, monetary and fiscal policies are controlled by a central political authority. Here monetary policy is often an extension of fiscal policy. Fiscal policy can impose an inflationary burden on monetary policy. If a country is running a large fiscal deficit and much of this deficit cannot be financed by government borrowing, monetary authorities must create money to finance the deficit.

Creating money to finance fiscal deficits has produced very rapid rates of inflation in several countries. As prices reach astronomical levels, currency with very large face values must be issued. For instance, when Bolivia faced a sharp drop in the availability of willing lenders in the mid-1980s, the government began to create money to finance its fiscal deficit. As the money supply increased in relation to the output of goods and services, prices rose. In 1985, the government was creating money so fast that the rate of inflation reached 8,170 percent. Lunch in a La Paz hotel could cost 10 million Bolivian pesos. You can imagine the problem of counting money and recording money values with cash registers and calculators. As the rate of inflation increased, Bolivians had to carry stacks of currency to pay for goods and services. Eventually the government issued a 1 million peso note, then 5 million and 10 million peso notes.

This extremely high inflation, or hyperinflation, ended when a new government introduced its economic program in August 1985. The program reduced government spending dramatically, which slowed the growth of the fiscal deficit. At the same time, a monetary reform was introduced. A **monetary reform** is a new monetary policy that includes the introduction of a new monetary unit. The central bank of Bolivia announced that it would restrict money creation and introduced a new currency, the boliviano, in January 1987. It set 1 boliviano equal to 1 million Bolivian pesos.

monetary reform: a new monetary policy that includes the introduction of a new monetary unit

The new monetary unit, the boliviano, did not lower prices; it lowered the units in which prices were quoted. Lunch now cost 10 bolivianos instead of 10 million pesos. More important, the rate of inflation dropped abruptly.

Did the new unit of currency end the hyperinflation? No. The rate of inflation dropped because the new fiscal policy controls introduced by the government relieved the pressure on the central bank to create money in order to finance government spending. Remember the government budget constraint: The only way to reduce the amount of money being created is to reduce the fiscal deficit $(G - T)$ minus borrowing (B). Once fiscal policy is under control, monetary reform is possible. If a government introduces a new monetary unit without changing its fiscal policy, the new monetary unit by itself has no lasting effect on the rate of inflation.

The introduction of a new monetary unit without a change in fiscal policy has no lasting effect on the rate of inflation.

Table 2 lists monetary reforms enacted in recent years. Argentina had a monetary reform in June 1983. Yet by June 1985, another reform was needed. The inflationary problems that Argentina faced could not be solved just by issuing a new unit of currency. Fiscal reform also was needed, and none was made. In any circumstances involving inflationary monetary policy, monetary reform by itself is not enough. It must be coupled with a reduction in the fiscal deficit or an increase in government borrowing to produce a permanent change in the rate of inflation.

Monetary policy is tied to fiscal policy through the government budget constraint. Although money creation is not an important source of deficit financing in developed countries, it has been and still is a significant source of revenue for developing countries, where taxes are difficult to collect and borrowing is limited.

TABLE 2 | **Recent Monetary Reforms**

Country	Old Currency	New Currency	Date of Change	Change
Angola	Readjusted kwanza	Kwanza	December 1999	1 kwanza = 1,000,000 readjusted kwanza
Argentina	Peso	Peso argentino	June 1983	1 peso argentine = 10,000 pesos
	Peso argentino	Austral	June 1985	1 austra = 1,000 pesos argentino
	Austral	Peso argentino	January 1992	1 peso argentino = 10,000 australes
Bolivia	Peso	Boliviano	January 1987	1 boliviano = 1,000,000 pesos
Brazil	Cruzeiro	Cruzado	February 1986	1 cruzado = 1,000 cruzeiros
	Cruzado	New cruzado	January 1989	1 new cruzado = 1,000,000 cruzados
	New cruzado	Cruzeiro	March 1990	1 cruzeiro = 1 new cruzado
	Cruzeiro	Real	July 1994	1 real = 2,700 cruzeiros
Chile	Peso	Escudo	January 1969	1 escudo = 1,000 pesos
	Escudo	Peso	September 1975	1 peso = 1,000 escudos
Congo, D.R.	New Zaire	Congolese franc	June 1998	1 Congolese franc = 100,000 new Zaire
Georgia	Kuponi	Lari	September 1995	1 lari = 1,000,000 kuponi
Israel	Pound	Shekel	February 1980	1 shekel = 10 pounds
	Old shekel	New shekel	September 1985	1 new shekel = 1,000 old shekels
Mexico	Peso	New peso	January 1993	1 new peso = 1,000 pesos
Peru	Sol	Inti	February 1985	1 inti = 1,000 soles
	Inti	New Sol	July 1991	1 new sol = 1,000,000 intis

(Continued)

TABLE 2	Recent Monetary Reforms (*Continued*)			
Poland	Zloty	New zloty	January 1995	1 new zloty = 10,000 zlotys
Russia	Ruble	New ruble	January 1998	1 new ruble = 1,000 rubles
Turkey	Lira	New Lira	January 2005	1 new lira = 1,000,000 lira
Ukraine	Karbovanets	Hryvnia	September 1996	1 hryvnia = 100,000 karbovanets
Uruguay	Old peso	New peso	July 1975	1 new peso = 1,000 old pesos
Yugoslavia	Dinar	New dinar	January 1994	1 new dinar = 13,000,000 dinars

RECAP

1. The government budget constraint ($G = T + B + \Delta M$) defines the relationship between fiscal and monetary policies.

2. The implications of fiscal policy for the growth of the money supply can be seen by rewriting the government budget constraint this way:

$$\Delta M = (G - T) - B$$

3. A monetary reform is a new monetary policy that includes the introduction of a new unit of currency.

4. A government can end an inflationary monetary policy only with a fiscal reform that lowers the fiscal deficit ($G - T$) minus borrowing (B).

SUMMARY

1 | Is there a tradeoff between inflation and the unemployment rate?

- The Phillips curve shows the relationship between inflation and the unemployment rate. *§1*

2 | How does the tradeoff between inflation and the unemployment rate vary from the short to the long run?

- In the long run, there is no tradeoff between inflation and the unemployment rate. *§1.b*
- The long-run Phillips curve is a vertical line at the natural rate of unemployment. *§1.b.2*

3 | What is the relationship between unexpected inflation and the unemployment rate?

- Unexpected inflation can affect the unemployment rate through wage expectations, inventory fluctuations, and wage contracts. *§2.a, 2.a.1, 2.a.2, 2.a.3*

4 | How are macroeconomic expectations formed?

- Adaptive expectations are formed on the basis of past experience; rational expectations are formed on the basis of all available relevant information. *§2.b.1, 2.b.2*

5 | What makes government policies credible?

- A policy is credible only if it is time consistent. *§3.b*

6 | Are business cycles related to political elections?

- A political business cycle is created by politicians who want to improve their chances of reelection by stimulating the economy just before an election. *§4.a*

7 | How do real shocks to the economy affect business cycles?

- Real business cycles are the product of an unexpected change in technology, weather, or some other real variable. *§4.b*

8 | How is inflationary monetary policy related to government fiscal policy?

- The government budget constraint defines the relationship between monetary and fiscal policies. *§5.a*
- When government-issued money is used to finance fiscal deficits, inflationary monetary policy can be a product of fiscal policy. *§5.b*

KEY TERMS

Phillips curve §1

reservation wage §2.a.1

adaptive expectation §2.b.1

rational expectation §2.b.2

time inconsistent §3

shock §4.b

monetary reform §5.b

EXERCISES

1. What is the difference between the short-run Phillips curve and the long-run Phillips curve? Use an aggregate supply and demand diagram to explain why there is a difference between them.

2. Give two reasons why there may be a short-run tradeoff between unexpected inflation and the unemployment rate.

3. "Unexpected increases in the money supply cause clockwise movements in the Phillips curve diagram; unexpected decreases in the money supply cause counterclockwise movements in the Phillips curve diagram." Evaluate this statement, using a graph to illustrate your answer.

4. Economists have identified two kinds of macroeconomic expectations.
   a. Define them
   b. What are the implications for macroeconomic policy of these two forms of expectations?

5. Write down the government budget constraint and explain how it can be used to understand the relationship between fiscal and monetary policies.

6. Using the government budget constraint, explain:
   a. Why some countries experience hyperinflation
   b. How fiscal policy must change in order to implement a noninflationary monetary policy

7. Parents, like governments, establish credibility by seeing to it that their "policies" (the rules that they outline for their children) are time consistent. Analyze the potential for time consistency of these rules:
   a. If you don't eat the squash, you'll go to bed 30 minutes early tonight!
   b. If you get any grades below a C, you won't be allowed to watch television on school nights!
   c. If you don't go to my alma mater, I won't pay for your college education!
   d. If you marry that disgusting person, I'll disinherit you!

8. Suppose an economy has witnessed an 8 percent rate of growth in its money supply and prices over the last few years. How do you think the public will respond to an announced plan to increase the money supply by 4 percent over the next year if:

   a. The central bank has a reputation for always meeting its announced policy goals.
   b. The central bank rarely does what it says it will do.

9. What are the implications for the timing of business cycle fluctuations over the years if all business cycles are
   a. Manipulated by incumbent administrations.
   b. A product of real shocks to the economy.

10. Suppose the Federal Reserve System were abolished and the Congress assumed responsibility for monetary policy along with fiscal policy. What potential harm to the economy could result from such a change?

11. Suppose tax revenues equal $100 billion, government spending equals $130 billion, and the government borrows $25 billion. How much do you expect the money supply to increase, given the government budget constraint?

12. If the government budget deficit equals $220 billion and the money supply increases by $100 billion, how much must the government borrow?

13. Discuss how each of the following sources of real business cycles would affect the economy.
    a. Farmers go on strike for six months.
    b. Oil prices fall substantially.
    c. Particularly favorable weather increases agricultural output nationwide.

14. Using an aggregate demand and aggregate supply diagram, illustrate and explain how a political business cycle is created.

15. Use a Phillips curve diagram to illustrate and explain how a political business cycle is created.

16. What is the natural rate of unemployment? What can cause it to change over time?

17. Many developing countries have experienced high money growth rates and, consequently, high inflation. Use the government budget constraint to explain how a poor country that wants to increase government spending can get into an inflationary situation.

18. What factors should affect the variability of the growth rate of real output? Which do you think could provide for more stability going forward and which are likely to be less important?

You can find further practice tests in the Online Quiz at **www.cengage.com/economics/boyes**.

Testimony of Chairman Ben S. Bernanke Before the Joint Economic Committee, U.S. Congress, Washington, D.C.

The Economic Outlook **May 5, 2009**

Chair Maloney, Vice Chairman Schumer, Ranking Members Brownback and Brady, and other members of the Committee, I am pleased to be here today to offer my views on recent economic developments, the outlook for the economy, and current conditions in financial markets.

Recent Economic Developments

The U.S. economy has contracted sharply since last autumn, with real gross domestic product (GDP) having dropped at an annual rate of more than 6 percent in the fourth quarter of 2008 and the first quarter of this year. Among the enormous costs of the downturn is the loss of some 5 million payroll jobs over the past 15 months. The most recent information on the labor market— the number of new and continuing claims for unemployment insurance through late April—suggests that we are likely to see further sizable job losses and increased unemployment in coming months.

However, the recent data also suggest that the pace of contraction may be slowing, and they include some tentative signs that final demand, especially demand by households, may be stabilizing. Consumer spending, which dropped sharply in the second half of last year, grew in the first quarter. In coming months, households'

spending power will be boosted by the fiscal stimulus program, and we have seen some improvement in consumer sentiment. Nonetheless, a number of factors are likely to continue to weigh on consumer spending, among them the weak labor market and the declines in equity and housing wealth that households have experienced over the past two years. In addition, credit conditions for consumers remain tight. . . .

As economic activity weakened during the second half of 2008 and prices of energy and other commodities began to fall rapidly, inflationary pressures diminished appreciably. Weakness in demand and reduced cost pressures have continued to keep inflation low so far this year. . . . Core PCE inflation (prices excluding food and energy) dropped below an annual rate of 1 percent in the final quarter of 2008, when retailers and auto dealers marked down their prices significantly. In the first quarter of this year, core consumer price inflation moved back up, but to a still-low annual rate of 1.5 percent.

The Economic Outlook

We continue to expect economic activity to bottom out, then to turn up later this year. Key elements of this forecast are our assessments that the housing market is beginning to stabilize and that the sharp inventory liquidation that has been in progress

will slow over the next few quarters. Final demand should also be supported by fiscal and monetary stimulus. An important caveat is that our forecast assumes continuing gradual repair of the financial system; a relapse in financial conditions would be a significant drag on economic activity and could cause the incipient recovery to stall. . . . Even after a recovery gets under way, the rate of growth of real economic activity is likely to remain below its longer-run potential for a while, implying that the current slack in resource utilization will increase further. We expect that the recovery will only gradually gain momentum and that economic slack will diminish slowly. In particular, businesses are likely to be cautious about hiring, implying that the unemployment rate could remain high for a time, even after economic growth resumes.

In this environment, we anticipate that inflation will remain low. Indeed, given the sizable margin of slack in resource utilization and diminished cost pressures from oil and other commodities, inflation is likely to move down some over the next year relative to its pace in 2008. However, inflation expectations, as measured by various household and business surveys, appear to have remained relatively stable, which should limit further declines in inflation. . . .

Macroeconomic policy in the United States is determined by Congress, the presidential administration, and the Federal Reserve. Twice a year, the chairman of the Federal Reserve Board must testify before Congress on Fed monetary policy. The article reports a recent appearance by Federal Reserve Chairman Ben Bernanke, which highlights some of the issues raised in this chapter.

The U.S. economy was in the deepest recession since the 1930s at the time of Bernanke's testimony. Unemployment was rising and inflation was low due to weak demand for goods and services. The issue of government credibility was highlighted by Bernanke's statement, "Inflation expectations, as measured by various household and business surveys, appear to have remained relatively stable, which should limit further declines in inflation." In other words, the Fed predicted that the United States would not experience a serious deflation from the recession because the public believed that inflation would remain low but positive due to Fed policies.

Bernanke highlighted the source of business cycles, saying, "Credit conditions for consumers remain tight." This condition is consistent with a recession associated with a financial crisis and a sharp reduction in borrowing by business firms and households. In addition, the "improvement in consumer sentiment" was expected to lead to increased spending by households and stimulate the economy. However, the wealth destruction associated with a large drop in housing prices would need to be overcome to see a return to normalcy. The most valuable asset for most households is the home. When home values dropped dramatically, household wealth dropped dramatically as well. Much of the government's policy during the crisis was aimed at stimulating the housing market and making home mortgage lending more affordable.

Of course, there is no guarantee that government policy aimed at minimizing business-cycle fluctuations will be successful. Since the policy is taken today, yet is aimed at bettering economic conditions in the future, there is always the possibility that an activist policy will aggravate business-cycle fluctuations rather than moderate them. For instance, suppose the Fed lowers the federal funds rate today because of a belief that the economy needs to be stimulated in order to increase spending. If the economy is already starting to improve without the Fed's intervention (perhaps because of some earlier Fed action), the new stimulus may cause spending to grow too much and generate inflation that otherwise would not have occurred. Economic policymaking is always done with some degree of uncertainty. Although policymakers such as Ben Bernanke may support policy changes aimed at growing the economy with low inflation, there is always a chance that their policies will have unintended consequences.

Chapter 15

Macroeconomic Viewpoints: New Keynesian, Monetarist, and New Classical

Fundamental Questions

1 | What do Keynesian economists believe about macroeconomic policy?

2 | What role do monetarists believe the government should play in the economy?

3 | What is new classical economics?

4 | How do theories of economics change over time?

Economists do not all agree on macroeconomic policy. Sometimes disagreements are due to normative differences, or differences in personal values, regarding what the truly pressing needs are that should be addressed. Other disagreements are based on different views of how the economy operates and what determines the equilibrium level of real GDP.

It would be very easy to classify economists, to call them liberals or conservatives, for example. But an economist who believes that the government should not intervene in social decisions (abortion, censorship) may favor an active role for government in economic decisions (trade protection, unemployment insurance, welfare benefits). Another economist may support an active role for government in regulating the social behavior of individuals, yet believe that government should allow free markets to operate without interference.

In this chapter, an overview of important differences among schools of macroeconomic thought is presented. Most economists probably do not align themselves solely with any one theory of macroeconomics, choosing instead to incorporate pieces of various schools of thought. But the three approaches we discuss in this chapter—Keynesian, monetarist, and new classical—have had enormous impact on macroeconomic thinking and policy. Economic thinking has evolved over time as economists develop new economic theories to fit the realities of a changing world.

1 | What do Keynesian economists believe about macroeconomic policy?

■ 1. Keynesian Economics

Keynesian macroeconomics (named after the English economist John Maynard Keynes) dominated the economics profession from the 1940s through the 1960s. Some economists today refer to themselves as "new Keynesians." The common thread that pervades Keynesian economics is an emphasis on the inflexibility of wages and prices. This leads many Keynesians to recommend an activist government macroeconomic policy aimed at achieving a satisfactory rate of economic growth.

1.a. The Keynesian Model

Keynesian economics grew out of the Great Depression, when inflation was no problem but output was falling. As a result, the Keynesian model of macroeconomic equilibrium assumes that prices are constant and that changes in aggregate expenditures determine equilibrium real GDP. In an aggregate demand and supply analysis, the simple Keynesian model looks like the graph in Figure 1. The aggregate supply curve is a horizontal line at a fixed level of prices, P_1. Changes in aggregate demand, such as from AD_1 to AD_2, cause changes in real GDP with no change in the price level.

Figure 1 reflects the traditional Keynesian emphasis on aggregate demand as a determinant of equilibrium real GDP. But no economist today would

FIGURE 1   The Fixed-Price Keynesian Model

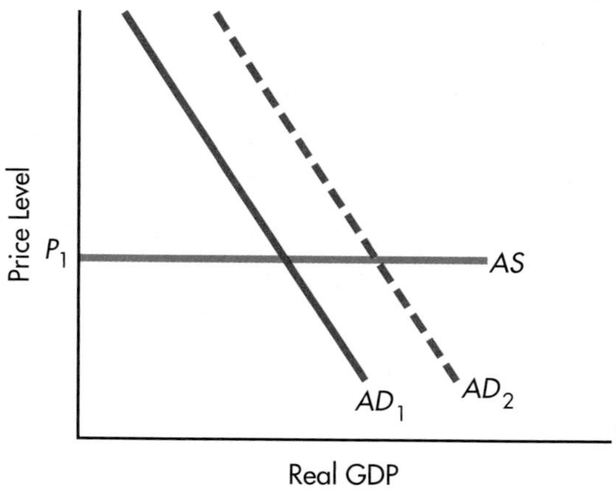

In the simple Keynesian model, prices are fixed at P_1 by the horizontal aggregate supply curve, so that changes in aggregate demand determine equilibrium real GDP.

FIGURE 2   The Modern Keynesian Model

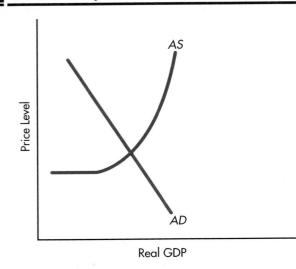

Modern Keynesians typically believe that the aggregate supply curve is horizontal only at relatively low levels of real GDP. As real GDP increases, more and more industries reach their capacity level of output, and the aggregate supply curve becomes positively sloped.

argue that the aggregate supply curve is always horizontal at every level of real GDP. More representative of Keynesian economics today is the aggregate supply curve shown in Figure 2. At low levels of real GDP, the curve is flat. In this region (the Keynesian region), increases in aggregate demand are associated with increases in output, but not with increases in prices. This flat region of the aggregate supply curve reflects the Keynesian belief that inflation is not a problem when unemployment is high. As the level of real GDP increases, and more and more industries reach their capacity level of output, the aggregate supply curve becomes positively sloped.

The economic theories that John Maynard Keynes proposed in the 1930s have given way to new theories. Today **Keynesian economics** focuses on the role the government plays in stabilizing the economy by managing aggregate demand. *New Keynesians* believe that wages and prices are not flexible in the short run. They use their analysis of business behavior to explain the Keynesian region on the aggregate supply curve of Figure 2. They believe that the economy is not always in equilibrium. For instance, if the demand for labor falls, we would expect the equilibrium price of labor (the wage) to fall and, because fewer people want to work at a lower wage, the number of people employed to fall. New Keynesians argue that wages do not tend to fall, because firms choose to lay off workers rather than decrease wages. Businesses retain high wages for their remaining employees in order to maintain morale and productivity. As a result, wages are quite rigid. This wage rigidity is reflected in price rigidity in goods markets, according to new Keynesian economics.

Keynesian economics: a school of thought that emphasizes the role government plays in stabilizing the economy by managing aggregate demand

New Keynesian macroeconomists argue that wages and prices are not flexible in the short run.

1.b. The Policymakers' Role

Keynesians believe that the government must take an active role in the economy to restore equilibrium. Traditional Keynesians identified the private sector as an important source of shifts in aggregate demand. For example, they argued that investment is susceptible to sudden changes. If business spending falls, the argument continued, monetary and fiscal policies should be used to stimulate spending and offset the drop in business spending. Government intervention is necessary to offset private-sector shifts in aggregate demand and avoid recession. And if private spending increases, creating inflationary pressure, then monetary and fiscal policies should restrain spending, again to offset private-sector shifts in aggregate demand.

New Keynesian macroeconomics does not focus on fluctuations in aggregate demand as the primary source of the problems facing policymakers. Keynesian economists realize that aggregate supply shocks can be substantial. But whatever the source of the instability—aggregate demand or aggregate supply—they emphasize active government policy to return the economy to equilibrium.

RECAP

1. Keynesian economists today reject the simple fixed-price model in favor of a model in which the aggregate supply curve is relatively flat at low levels of real GDP and slopes upward as real GDP approaches its potential level.

2. Keynesians believe that the tendency for the economy to experience disequilibrium in labor and goods markets forces the government to intervene in the economy.

■ 2. Monetarist Economics

monetarist economics: a school of thought that emphasizes the role changes in the money supply play in determining equilibrium real GDP and price level

The Keynesian view dominated macroeconomics in the 1940s, the 1950s, and most of the 1960s. In the late 1960s and the 1970s, Keynesian economics faced a challenge from **monetarist economics,** a school of thought that emphasizes the role that changes in the money supply play in determining equilibrium real GDP and prices. The leading monetarist, Milton Friedman, had been developing monetarist theory since the 1940s, but it took several decades for his ideas to become popular. In part the shift was a product of the forcefulness of Friedman's arguments, but the relatively poor macroeconomic performance of the United States in the 1970s probably contributed to a growing disenchantment with Keynesian economics, creating an environment that was ripe for new ideas. The Economic Insight "Milton Friedman" describes how Friedman's monetarist theories became popular.

2.a. The Monetarist Model

Monetarists focus on the role of the money supply in determining the equilibrium level of real GDP and prices. In the chapter titled "Monetary Policy," we discussed monetary policy and equilibrium income. We showed that monetary policy is linked to changes in the equilibrium level of real GDP through changes in investment (and consumption). Keynesians traditionally assumed that monetary policy affects aggregate demand by changing the interest rate and, consequently, investment spending. Monetarists believe that changes in the money supply have broad effects on expenditures through both investment and consumption. An increase in the money supply pushes aggregate demand up by increasing both business and household spending and raises the equilibrium level of real GDP. A decrease in the money supply does the opposite.

Economic Insight

Milton Friedman

Milton Friedman is widely considered to be the father of monetarism. Born in 1912 in New York City, Friedman spent most of his career at the University of Chicago. Early in his professional life, he recognized the importance of developing economics as an empirical science—that is, using data to test the applicability of economic theory.

In 1957, Friedman published *A Theory of the Consumption Function*. In this book, he discussed the importance of *permanent income*, rather than current income, in understanding consumer spending. His analysis of consumption won widespread acclaim, an acclaim that would be a long time coming for his work relating monetary policy to real output and prices.

In the 1950s, Keynesian theory dominated economics. Most macroeconomists believed that the supply of money in the economy was of little importance. In 1963, with the publication of *A Monetary History of the United States, 1867–1960* (coauthored with Anna Schwartz of the National Bureau of Economic Research), Friedman focused attention on

the monetarist argument. Still, Keynesian economics dominated scholarly and policy debate.

In the late 1960s and early 1970s, the rate of inflation and the rate of unemployment increased simultaneously. This was a situation that Keynesian economics could not explain. The timing was right for a new theory of macroeconomic behavior, and monetarism, with Milton Friedman as its most influential advocate, grew in popularity. The new stature of monetarism was clearly visible in 1979, when the Fed adopted a monetarist approach to targeting the money supply.

In 1976, Milton Friedman was awarded the Nobel Prize for economics. By this time he had become a public figure. He wrote a column for *Newsweek* from 1966 to 1984, and in 1980 developed a popular public television series, *Free to Choose*, based on his book of the same title. Through the popular media, Friedman became the most effective and well-known supporter of free markets in the United States and much of the rest of the world. Many would argue that only Keynes has had as much influence on scholarly literature and public policy in economics as Milton Friedman.

> Monetarists believe that accelerating inflation is a product of efforts to increase real GDP through expansionary monetary policy.

Monetarists believe that changes in monetary policy (or fiscal policy, for that matter) have only a short-term effect on real GDP. In the long run, they expect real GDP to be at a level consistent with the natural rate of unemployment. As a result, the long-run effect of a change in the money supply is fully reflected in a change in the price level. Attempts to exploit the short-run effects of expansionary monetary policy produce an inflationary spiral, in which the level of GDP increases temporarily, then falls back to the potential level while prices rise. This is the rightward shift of the Phillips curve that we described in the chapter titled "Macroeconomic Policy: Tradeoffs, Expectations, Credibility, and Sources of Business Cycles."

2.b. The Policymakers' Role

2 | What role do monetarists believe the government should play in the economy?

Unlike Keynesian economists, monetarists do not believe that the economy is subject to a disequilibrium that must be offset by government action. Most monetarists believe that the economy tends toward equilibrium at the level of potential real GDP. Their faith in the free market (price) system leads them to favor minimal government intervention.

Monetarists often argue that government policy heightens the effects of the business cycle. This is especially true of monetary policy. To prove their point, monetarists link changes in the growth of the money supply to business-cycle fluctuations. Specifically, they suggest that periods of relatively fast money growth are followed by booms and inflation, whereas periods of relatively slow money growth are followed by recessions. The link between money growth, real GDP, and inflation has not been as visible in recent years as it was in the 1970s–1990s. The Federal Reserve used to formulate policy in terms of money growth targets, but stopped doing that a few years ago. This was a sign that the link between money growth, inflation, and real output was not a strong as it used to be. Sometimes there seem to be closer relationships than at other times. This makes it difficult to predict the effect of a particular change in monetary policy on prices or real GDP. In addition, a number of other variables influence GDP.

Monetarists favor nonactivist government policy because they believe that the government's attempts to make the economy better off by aiming monetary and fiscal policies at low inflation and low unemployment often make things worse. Why? Because economic policy, which is very powerful, operates with a long and variable lag. First, policymakers have to recognize that a problem exists. This is the *recognition lag.* Then they must formulate an appropriate policy. This is the *reaction lag.* Then the effects of the policy must work through the economy. This is the *effect lag.*

When the Federal Reserve changes the rate of growth of the money supply, real GDP and inflation do not change immediately. In fact, studies show that as much as two years can pass between a change in policy and the effect of that change on real GDP. This means that when policymakers institute a change targeted at a particular level of real GDP or rate of inflation, the effect of the policy is not felt for a long time. And it is possible that the economy could be facing an entirely different set of problems in a year or two from those that policymakers are addressing today. But today's policy will still have effects next year, and those effects may aggravate next year's problems.

Because of the long and variable lag in the effect of fiscal and monetary policies, monetarists argue that policymakers should set policy according to rules that do not change from month to month or even year to year. What kinds of rules? A fiscal policy rule might be to balance the budget annually; a monetary policy rule might be to require that the money supply grow at a fixed rate over time or that the central bank commit to following an inflation target. These kinds of rules restrict policymakers from formulating discretionary policy. Monetarists believe that when discretionary shifts in policy are reduced, economic growth is steadier than it is when government consciously sets out to achieve full employment and low inflation.

Economic policy operates with a long and variable lag.

RECAP

1. Monetarists emphasize the role that changes in the money supply play in determining equilibrium real GDP and the level of prices.

2. Monetarists do not believe that the economy is subject to disequilibrium in the labor and goods markets or that government should take an active role in the economy.

3. Because economic policy operates with a long and variable lag, attempts by government to stabilize the economy may, in fact, make matters worse.

4. Monetarists believe that formal rules, rather than the discretion of policymakers, should govern economic policymaking.

■ 3. New Classical Economics

In the 1970s an alternative to Keynesian and monetarist economics was developed: new classical economics. But before we discuss the new classical theory, let's look at the old one.

Classical economics is the theory that was popular before Keynes changed the face of economics in the 1930s. According to classical economics, real GDP is determined by aggregate supply, while the equilibrium price level is determined by aggregate demand. Figure 3, the classical aggregate demand and supply diagram, shows the classical economist's view of the world. The vertical aggregate supply curve means that the equilibrium level of output (income) is a product only of the determinants of aggregate supply: the price of resources, technology, and expectations (see the chapter titled "Macroeconomic Equilibrium: Aggregate Demand and Supply").

If the aggregate supply curve is vertical, then changes in aggregate demand, such as from AD_1 to AD_2, change only the price level; they do not affect the equilibrium level of output. Classical economics assumes that prices and wages are perfectly flexible. This rules out contracts that fix prices or wages for periods of time. It also rules out the possibility that people are not aware of all prices and wages. They know when prices have gone up and ask for wage increases to compensate.

Both Keynesians and monetarists would argue that information about the economy, including prices and wages, is not perfect. When workers and businesses negotiate wages, they may not know what current prices are, and they certainly do not know what future prices will be. Furthermore, many labor contracts fix wages for long periods of time. This means that wages are not flexible; they cannot adjust immediately to new price levels.

classical economics:
a school of thought that assumes that real GDP is determined by aggregate supply, while the equilibrium price level is determined by aggregate demand

---

FIGURE 3   The Classical Model

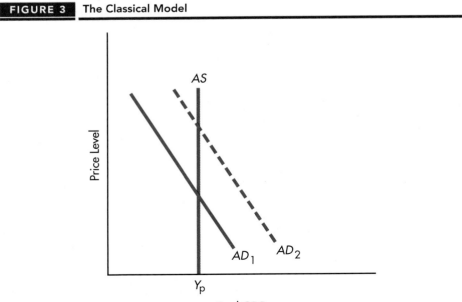

The vertical aggregate supply curve indicates that equilibrium real GDP is determined strictly by the determinants of aggregate supply.

3 | **What is new classical economics?**

new classical economics: a school of thought that holds that changes in real GDP are a product of unexpected changes in the level of prices

3.a. The New Classical Model

New classical economics was a response to the problems of meeting economic policy goals in the 1970s. New classical economists questioned some of the assumptions on which Keynesian economics was based. For instance, new classical economists believe wages are flexible, while both traditional Keynesian and new Keynesian economists assume that wages can be fixed in the short run.

New classical economics does not assume that people know everything that is happening, as the old theory did. People make mistakes because their expectations of prices or some other critical variable are different from the future reality. New classical economists emphasize rational expectations. As defined in the chapter titled "Macroeconomic Policy: Tradeoffs, Expectations, Credibility, and Sources of Business Cycles," *rational expectations* are based on all available relevant information. This was a new way of thinking about expectations. Earlier theories assumed that people formed adaptive expectations—that their expectations were based only on their past experience. With rational expectations, people learn not only from their past experience, but also from any other information that helps them predict the future.

Suppose the chairman of the Federal Reserve Board announces a new monetary policy. Price-level expectations that are formed rationally take this announcement into consideration; those that are formed adaptively do not. It is much easier for policymakers to make unexpected changes in policy if expectations are formed adaptively rather than rationally.

Another element of new classical economics is the belief that markets are in equilibrium. Keynesian economics argues that disequilibrium in markets demands government intervention. For instance, Keynesian economists define a recession as a disequilibrium in the labor market—a surplus of labor—that requires expansionary government policy. New classical economists believe that because real wages are lower during a recession, people are more willing to substitute non-labor activities (going back to school, early retirement, work at home, or leisure) for work. As the economy recovers and wages go up, people substitute away from nonlabor activities toward more working hours. The substitution of labor for leisure and leisure for labor, over time, suggests that much of observed unemployment is voluntary in the sense that those who are unemployed choose not to take a job at a wage below their reservation wage (see the chapter titled "Macroeconomic Policy: Tradeoffs, Expectations, Credibility, and Sources of Business Cycles").

3.b. The Policymakers' Role

New classical economics emphasizes expectations. Its basic tenet is that changes in monetary policy can change the equilibrium level of real GDP only if those changes are *unexpected*. Fiscal policy can change equilibrium real GDP only if it *unexpectedly* changes the level of prices or one of the determinants of aggregate supply.

Figure 4 (which is the same as Figure 4 in the chapter titled "Macroeconomic Policy: Tradeoffs, Expectations, Credibility, and Sources of Business Cycles") illustrates the new classical view of the effect of an unexpected increase in the money supply. Suppose initially the expected rate of inflation is 3 percent and the actual rate of inflation is also 3 percent. The economy is operating at point 1 in Figure 4(b), the Phillips curve diagram, with unemployment at 5 percent, which is assumed to be the natural rate of unemployment. At the natural rate of unemployment, the economy is producing the potential level of real GDP (Y_p) at price level P_1. If the central bank unexpectedly increases the money supply, pushing the inflation rate up from 3 percent to 6 percent, the economy moves from point 1 to point 2 along short-run Phillips curve I, which is based on 3 percent expected inflation. The unemployment rate is now 3 percent, which is less than the natural rate. In part (a), real GDP rises above potential income to Y_2.

FIGURE 4   New Classical Economics

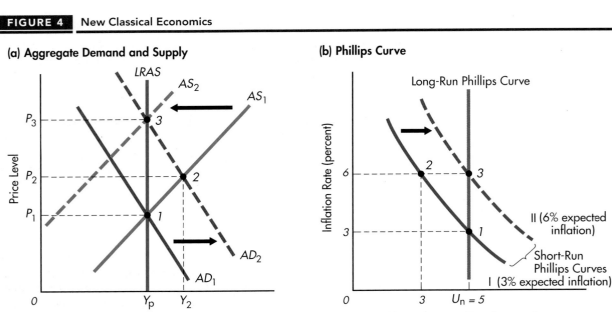

(a) Aggregate Demand and Supply

(b) Phillips Curve

New classical economists believe that government-induced shifts in aggregate demand affect real GDP only if they are un-expected. In Figure 4(a), the economy initially is operating at point 1, with real GDP at Y_p, the potential level. An unexpected increase in aggregate demand shifts the economy to point 2, where both real GDP (Y_2) and prices (P_2) are higher. Over time, as sellers adjust to higher prices and costs of doing business, aggregate supply shifts from AS_1 to AS_2. This shift moves the economy to point 3. Here GDP is back at the potential level, and prices are even higher. In the long run, an increase in aggregate demand does not increase output. The long-run aggregate supply curve (LRAS) is a vertical line at the potential level of real GDP.

In Figure 4(b), if the expected rate of inflation is 3 percent and actual inflation is 3 percent, the economy is operating at point 1, at the natural rate of unemployment (U_n). If aggregate demand increases, there is an unexpected increase in inflation from 3 to 6 percent. This moves the economy from point 1 to point 2 along short-run Phillips curve I. Here the unemployment rate is 3 percent. As people learn to expect 6 percent inflation, they adjust to the higher rate and the economy moves back to the natural rate of unemployment, at point 3. If the increase in inflation is expected, then the economy moves directly from point 1 to point 3 with no temporary decrease in the unemployment rate.

Over time, people come to expect 6 percent inflation. They adjust to the higher inflation rate, and the economy moves back to the natural rate of unemployment. At the expected rate of inflation, 6 percent, the economy is operating at point 3 on short-run Phillips curve II. As the expected rate of inflation increases from 3 to 6 percent, workers negotiate higher wages and the aggregate supply curve shifts to the left, from AS_1 to AS_2. A new equilibrium exists at point 3 in the aggregate demand and supply diagram, and real GDP drops back to its potential level.

The analysis changes dramatically if the change in the money supply is expected. Now the economy moves not from point 1 to point 2 to point 3 but from point 1 directly to point 3. This is because the shift from point 1 to point 2 is temporary, based on unexpected inflation. If the inflation is expected, the economy is on short-run Phillips curve II, where inflation is 6 percent, unemployment is at the natural rate, and real GDP is at the potential level.

> New classical economists believe that wages and prices are flexible and that people form expectations rationally, so that only unexpected changes in the price level can affect real GDP.

The lesson of new classical economics for policymakers is that managing aggregate demand has an effect on real GDP only if change is unexpected. Any predictable policy simply affects prices. As a result, new classical economists argue that monetary and fiscal policies should be aimed at maintaining a low, stable rate of inflation and should not attempt to alter real national output and unemployment. This brings new classical economists close to the monetarists, who would choose policy rules over discretionary policy.

RECAP

1. New classical economics holds that wages are flexible and that expectations are formed rationally, so that only unexpected changes in prices have an effect on real GDP.

2. New classical economists believe that markets are always in equilibrium.

3. According to new classical economic theory, any predictable macroeconomic policy has an effect only on prices.

4. New classical economists argue that monetary and fiscal policies should try to achieve a low, stable rate of inflation rather than changes in real GDP or unemployment.

■ 4. Comparison and Influence

4 | How do theories of economics change over time?

The three theories of macroeconomics we have been talking about are often treated as though they are different in every way. Yet at times they overlap and even share conclusions. Moreover, as we mentioned at the beginning of the chapter, it is an oversimplification to categorize economists by a single school of thought. Many if not most economists do not classify themselves by economic theory. Typically they take elements of each, so that their approach to macroeconomics is more a synthesis of the various theories than strict adherence to any one theory.

Macroeconomic theories have developed over time in response to the economy's performance and the shortcomings of existing theories. Keynesian economics became popular in the 1930s because classical economics did not explain or help resolve the Great Depression. Monetarist economics offered an explanation for rising unemployment and rising inflation in the United States in the 1960s and 1970s. New classical economics suggested an alternative explanation for rising unemployment and inflation that the static Phillips curve analysis used by traditional Keynesians could not explain. Each of these theories, then, was developed or became popular because an existing theory did not answer pressing new questions.

All of these theories have influenced government policy. A by-product of Keynes's work in the 1930s was the wide acceptance and practice of activist government fiscal policy. Monetarist influence was dramatically apparent in the change in monetary policy announced by the Federal Reserve in 1979. Monetarists had criticized the Fed's policy of targeting interest rates. They argued that money-growth targets would stabilize income and prices. In October 1979, Chairman Paul Volcker announced that the Fed would concentrate more on achieving money-growth targets and less on controlling interest rates. This change in policy reflected the Fed's concern over rising inflation and the belief that the monetarists were right, that a low rate of money growth would bring about a low rate of inflation. The new policy led to an abrupt drop in the rate of inflation, from more than 13 percent in 1979 to less than 4 percent in 1982.

The new classical economists' emphasis on expectations calls for more information from policymakers to allow private citizens to incorporate government plans into their outlook for the future. The Federal Reserve Reform Act (1977) and the Full Employment and Balanced Growth Act (1978) require the Board of Governors to report to Congress semiannually on its goals and money targets for the next 12 months. New classical economists also believe that only credible government policies can affect expectations. In the last chapter we discussed the time consistency of plans. For plans to be credible, to influence private expectations, they must be time consistent.

Table 1 summarizes the three approaches to macroeconomics, describing the major source of problems facing policymakers and the proper role of

| TABLE 1 | Major Approaches to Macroeconomic Policy | |

Approach	Major Source of Problems	Proper Role for Government
New Keynesian	Disequilibrium in private labor and goods markets	To actively manage monetary and fiscal policies to restore equilibrium
Monetarist	Government's discretionary policies that increase and decrease aggregate demand	To follow fixed rules for money growth and minimize fiscal policy shocks
New classical	Government's attempt to manipulate aggregate demand, even though government policies have effect on real GDP only if unexpected	To follow predictable monetary and fiscal policies for long-run stability

government policy according to each view. Only Keynesian economics supports an active role for government; the other two theories suggest that government should not intervene in the economy.

The government policy response to the financial crisis that began in 2007 incorporated ideas from the different approaches to macroeconomics. There was a huge increase in government spending financed by borrowing, a very Keynesian approach to stimulating aggregate demand. There was also an emphasis on shaping expectations of the public that fiscal and monetary policy were addressing declining incomes and output and also falling prices. If the public believes that their incomes are only temporarily depressed, they will spend more now. If the public believes that deflation will be avoided, they will be more willing to spend rather than hold on to their cash (money rises in value as prices fall), and they will not write contracts that build in expectations of falling prices and wages and further contribute to such price and wage declines. Finally, central banks around the world greatly increased the supply of money to support credit availability and spending by business firms and households. In fact, the global policy response to the financial crisis was unprecedented—which serves to emphasize the macroeconomic lessons learned by economists and government policymakers from past history and macroeconomic theory.

RECAP

1. Different economic theories developed over time as changing economic conditions pointed out the shortcomings of existing theories.

2. Keynesian, monetarist, and new classical economics have each influenced macroeconomic policy.

3. Only Keynesian economists believe that government should actively intervene to stabilize the economy.

SUMMARY

- Economists do not all agree on the determinants of economic equilibrium or the appropriate role of government policy. *Preview*

1 | What do Keynesian economists believe about macroeconomic policy?

- Keynesian economists believe that the government should take an active role in stabilizing the economy by managing aggregate demand. §1.b

2 | What role do monetarists believe the government should play in the economy?

- Monetarists do not believe that the economy is subject to serious disequilibrium, which means that they favor minimal government intervention in the economy. *§2.b*

- Monetarists believe that a government that takes an active role in the economy may do more harm than good because economic policy operates with a long and variable lag. *§2.b*

3 | What is new classical economics?

- New classical economics holds that only unexpected changes in policy can influence real GDP, so that government policy should target a low, stable rate of inflation. *§3.b*

4 | How do theories of economics change over time?

- New economic theories are a response to changing economic conditions that reveal the shortcomings of existing theories. *§4*

Key Terms

Keynesian economics *§1.a*   classical economics *§3*   new classical economics *§3.a*
monetarist economics *§2*

Exercises

1. What is the difference between traditional Keynesian and new Keynesian economics?

2. Why does monetary policy operate with a long and variable lag? Give an example to illustrate your explanation.

3. What is the difference between old classical and new classical economics?

4. Draw an aggregate demand and supply diagram for each theory of macroeconomics. Use the diagrams to explain how the government can influence equilibrium real GDP and prices.

5. What, if any, similarities are there among the theories of economics discussed in this chapter regarding the use of fiscal and monetary policies to stimulate real GDP?

6. If unexpected increases in the growth rate of the money supply can increase real GDP, why doesn't the Fed follow a policy of unexpectedly increasing the money supply to increase the growth of real GDP?

7. "The popular macroeconomic theories have evolved over time as economic conditions have changed to reveal shortcomings of existing theory." Evaluate this quote in terms of the emergence of the three theories discussed in this chapter.

For exercises 8–15, tell which school of thought would most likely be associated with the following quotes:

8. "Changes in prices and wages are too slow to support the new classical assumption of persistent macroeconomic equilibrium."

9. "The best monetary policy is to keep the money supply growing at a slow and steady rate."

10. "Frictional unemployment is a result of workers voluntarily substituting leisure for labor when wages fall."

11. "A change in the money supply will affect GDP after a long and variable lag, so it is difficult to predict the effects of money on output."

12. "Government policymakers should use fiscal policy to adjust aggregate demand in response to aggregate supply shocks."

13. "The economy is subject to recurring disequilibrium in labor and goods markets, so government can serve a useful function of helping the economy adjust to equilibrium."

14. "Since the aggregate supply curve is horizontal, aggregate demand will determine the equilibrium level of real GDP."

15. "If everyone believed that the monetary authority was going to cut the inflation rate from 6 to 3 percent, such a reduction in inflation could be achieved without any significant increase in unemployment."

You can find further practice tests in the Online Quiz at **www.cengage.com/economics/boyes**.

The Ghosts of Christmas Past Haunt Economists

Africa News **January 10, 2003**

Financial crises have come back because policy makers fail to learn earlier lessons.

In Charles Dickens' great novel, *A Christmas Carol*, the soulless businessman Ebeneezer Scrooge is tormented by a visit from the Spirit of Christmas Past. Today, economists are similarly troubled by unwanted ghosts, as they ponder the reappearance of economic ills long thought buried and dead.

From Stephen Roach at Morgan Stanley to Paul Krugman at Princeton, to the governors of the US Federal Reserve and the senior staff at the European Central Bank, to almost everyone in Japan, economists all over the world are worrying about deflation. Their thoughts retrace the economic thinking of more than 50 years ago, a time when economists concluded that the thing to do with deflation was to avoid it like the plague.

Back in 1933 Irving Fisher—Milton Friedman's predecessor atop the US's monetarist school of economists—announced that governments could prevent deep depressions by avoiding deflation. Deflation—a steady, continuing decline in prices—gave businesses and consumers powerful incentives to cut spending and hoard cash.

It reduced the ability of businesses and banks to service their debt, and might trigger a chain of big bankruptcies that would destroy confidence in the financial system, providing further incentives to hoard. Such strong incentives to hoard rather than spend can keep demand low and falling, and unemployment high and rising, for a much longer time than even the most laissez-faire-oriented politician or economist had ever dared contemplate. Hence the Keynesian solution: use monetary policy (lower interest rates) and fiscal policy (expanded government spending and reduced taxes) to keep the economy from ever approaching the precipice where deflation becomes possible.

But if this is an issue solved more than 50 years ago, why is it haunting us now? Why is this menace a matter of grave concern in Japan today, and a threat worth worrying about in the US? . . .

The truth is that economic policy makers are juggling sets of potential disasters, exchanging the one that appears most threatening for a threat that seems more distant.

In the US, the Bush administration is sceptical of the stimulative power of monetary policy and wants bigger fiscal deficits to reduce unemployment, hoping that the future dangers posed by persistent deficits—low investment, slow growth, loss of confidence, uncontrolled inflation and exchange rate depreciation—can be finessed, or will not become visible until after the Bush team leaves office.

In Europe, the European Central Bank believes the danger of uncontrolled inflation following a loss of public confidence in its commitment to low inflation, outweighs the costs of European unemployment that is far too high. . . .

The ghosts of economics' past return because the lessons of the present are always oversold. Politicians and policy makers advance their approach to economics as the One True Doctrine. But what they are doing, however, is dealing with the biggest problem of the moment, but at the price of removing institutions and policies that policymakers before them had put into place to control problems they felt to be the most pressing.

Ebeneezer Scrooge's nocturnal visitors were able to convince him of the errors of his ways. Let us hope today's economists also learn the lessons of their unwanted ghosts.

J. Bradford Delong

Macroeconomics has always been a lively field, filled with controversy over the proper approach to modeling the economy, the correct interpretation of experience, and the role that government policy can and should play. Indeed, debate in macroeconomics is as old as the field itself. The views of John Maynard Keynes, the founder of macroeconomics, were challenged by his colleague at Cambridge University, Arthur Pigou. This debate focused on the importance of the "real balance effect," whereby a fall in the price level raises real money balances (or the purchasing power of the money supply), increases wealth, and thus increases consumption. Like most debates in macroeconomics, this was more than an ivory tower exercise, since the real balance effect provides a channel by which the economy can bring itself out of a slump without government intervention.

The article indicates that in early 2003, the issue of falling prices was back again as a policy concern. The Japanese economy had experienced deflation in recent years, and some were worried that the United States could also move from low inflation to deflation. In the global recession that started in 2007, there were renewed fears of deflation, so this issue does not go away. The author claims that economists knew long ago that deflation could be avoided by expansionary fiscal and monetary policies. A monetarist-type solution would be central bank targeting of inflation. In the early 2000s, some economists were suggesting that this is what the central bank of Japan should do: Set an inflation target and aim monetary policy solely at the achievement of such a target. A Keynesian-type solution would be increasing government spending and/or reducing taxes. The Bush administration in the United States was proposing a Keynesian approach, with tax cuts to stimulate the U.S. economy. The European Central Bank was utilizing a monetarist approach of inflation targeting to achieve public confidence in its commitment to low inflation. Both of these policies may avoid deflation. However, we can never be sure of the effects of a tax cut on important variables like unemployment, interest rates, and real GDP, and the inflation target achieves only the inflation goal and may have undesirable consequences for unemployment and real GDP growth. In short, there is no magic economic solution that always provides the best mix of macroeconomic outcomes. This is a major reason for the debates that have raged in macroeconomics.

The debate between the Keynesians and the monetarists dominated the macroeconomic discourse of the 1950s and 1960s. During this period, those who identified themselves as Keynesians gave primacy to the role of fiscal policy and to the issue of unemployment; these economists had great faith in the ability of the government to fine-tune the economy through the proper application of policy, thereby ensuring stability and growth. Keynesians of this vintage also believed that changes in the money supply had little effect on the economy. In contrast, monetarists were very concerned about inflation, which they believed to be a purely monetary phenomenon. These economists also doubted that active government intervention could stabilize the economy, for they believed that policy operated only with long and variable lags.

Although outside observers may view the debate within macroeconomics as evidence of confusion, a more accurate appraisal is that the debate is a healthy intellectual response to a world in which few things are certain and much is unknown—and perhaps unknowable. The differences seen between schools of thought mask the fact that there is a great deal of consensus about a number of issues in macroeconomics. This consensus is a product of lessons learned from past debates. In a similar fashion, the controversies of today will yield tomorrow's consensus, and our knowledge of the real workings of the economy will grow.

Chapter 16

Economic Growth

Fundamental Questions

1 | What is economic growth?

2 | How are economic growth rates determined?

3 | What is productivity?

4 | What explains productivity changes?

Modern economies tend to raise living standards for the population generation after generation. This is economic growth. However, this was not always the case. Prior to the seventeenth century, economic activity involved a constant struggle to avoid starvation. Only in recent centuries has the idea of living standards being improved within a generation become common. An economist (Angus Maddison) has estimated that GDP grew at about a rate of 0.1 percent per year between the years 500 and 1500. Yet since population growth was about the same 0.1 percent per year, there was no increase in GDP per capita. He estimates that between 1500 and 1700, growth of per capita GDP increased to 0.1 percent per year, and between 1700 and 1820, it increased to about 1.6 percent per year, not too different from recent growth rates for the major industrial countries. Understanding why and how economic growth happens is a very important part of macroeconomics.

Although much of macroeconomics is aimed at understanding business cycles—recurring periods of prosperity and recession—the fact is that over the long run, most economies do grow wealthier. The long-run trend of real GDP in the United States and most other countries is positive. Yet the rate at which real GDP grows is very different across countries. Why? What factors cause economies to grow and living standards to rise?

In this chapter we focus on the long-term picture. We begin by defining economic growth and discussing its importance. Then we examine the determinants of economic growth, to understand what accounts for the different rates of growth across countries.

■ 1. Defining Economic Growth

1 | What is economic growth?

What do we mean by economic growth? Economists use two measures of growth—real GDP and per capita real GDP—to compare how economies grow over time.

1.a. Real GDP

economic growth: an increase in real GDP

Basically, **economic growth** is an increase in real GDP. As more goods and services are produced, the real GDP increases and people are able to consume more.

To calculate the percentage change in real GDP over a year, we simply divide the change in GDP by the value of GDP at the beginning of the year, and then multiply the quotient by 100. For instance, the real GDP of Singapore was approximately 56,048 million Singapore dollars in the fourth quarter of 2008 and approximately 58,411 million in the fourth quarter of 2007. This was during the global recession and the economy grew at a rate of −4.0 percent over that year:

$$\text{Percentage change in real GDP} = (\text{change over year} \times 100)/\text{beginning value}$$
$$= [(56{,}048 - 58{,}411)/58{,}411] \times 100$$
$$= -4.0\%$$

1.a.1. Compound Growth From 2000 to 2007, the industrial countries of the world showed an average annual growth rate of real GDP of 2.5 percent. Over the same period, the average annual growth rate of real GDP for developing countries was 6.5 percent. The difference between a growth rate of 2.5 percent and one of 6.5 percent may not seem substantial, but in fact it is. Growth is compounded over time. This means that any given rate of growth is applied every year to a growing base of real GDP, so any difference is magnified over time.

Small changes in rates of growth produce big changes in real GDP over a period of many years.

Figure 1 shows the effects of compounding growth rates. The upper line in the figure represents the path of real GDP if the economy grows at a rate of 6.5 percent a year. The lower line shows real GDP growing at a rate of 2.5 percent a year.

Suppose that in each case the economy originally is producing a real GDP of $1 billion. After five years, there is not much difference: a GDP of $1.08 billion at 2.5 percent growth versus $1.21 billion at 6.5 percent growth. However, the effect of compounding becomes more visible over long periods of time. After 40 years, the difference between 2.5 and 6.5 percent growth, a seemingly small difference, represents a substantial difference in output: A 2.5 percent rate of growth yields an output of $2.6 billion; at 6.5 percent, output is $11.6 billion. After 40 years, the level of output is approximately six times larger at the higher growth rate.

1.a.2. The Rule of 72 Compound growth explains why countries are so concerned about maintaining positive high rates of growth. If growth is maintained at a constant rate, we can estimate the number of years required for output to double by using the **rule of 72.** If we divide 72 by the growth rate, we find the approximate time that it takes for any value to double.

rule of 72: the number of years required for an amount to double in value is 72 divided by the annual rate of growth

Suppose you deposit $100 in a bank account that pays a constant 6 percent annual interest. If you allow the interest to accumulate over time, the amount of money

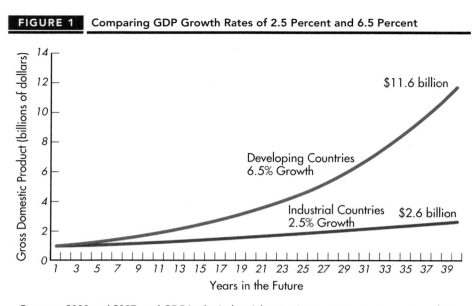

FIGURE 1 Comparing GDP Growth Rates of 2.5 Percent and 6.5 Percent

Between 2000 and 2007, real GDP in the industrial countries grew at an average annual rate of 2.5 percent, while real GDP in developing countries grew at an average annual rate of 6.5 percent. The difference seems small, but the graph shows how even a small difference is compounded over time, producing a substantial difference in real GDP.

in the account grows at a rate of 6 percent. At this rate of interest, the rule of 72 tells us that your account will have a value of approximately $200 (double its initial value) after 12 years:

$$\frac{72}{6} = 12$$

The interest rate gives the rate of growth of the amount deposited if earned interest is allowed to accumulate in the account. If the interest rate is 3 percent, the amount will double in 24 (72/3) years. The rule of 72 applies to any value. If real GDP is growing at a rate of 6 percent a year, then real GDP doubles every 12 years. At a 3 percent annual rate, real GDP doubles every 24 years.

Table 1 lists the average annual rate of growth of GDP between 2000 and 2007 and the approximate doubling times for six countries. The countries listed have growth rates ranging from a high of 10.1 percent in China to a low of 1.7 percent in Japan. If these growth rates are maintained over time, it would take just 7 years for the GDP in China to double and 42 years for the GDP in Japan to double.

1.b. Per Capita Real GDP

We've defined economic growth as an increase in real GDP. But if growth is supposed to be associated with higher standards of living, our definition may be misleading. A country could show positive growth in real GDP, but if the population is growing at an even higher rate, output per person can actually fall. Economists, therefore, often adjust the growth rate of output for changes in population. **Per capita real GDP** is real GDP divided by the population. If we define economic growth as rising per capita real GDP, then growth requires a nation's output of goods and services to increase faster than its population.

per capita real GDP: real GDP divided by the population

TABLE 1	GDP Growth Rates and Doubling Times	
Country	Average Annual Growth Rate (percent)*	Doubling Time (years)
China	10.1	7
South Korea	5.2	14
Bangladesh	5.8	12
Australia	3.3	22
United States	2.5	29
Japan	1.7	42

*Average annual growth rates from 1990 to 2007.
Source: IMF, World Economic Outlook Database, January 2009.

> *Economic growth is sometimes defined as an increase in per capita real GDP.*

Per capita GDP is often used as an indicator of economic development. In 2007, African countries had an average per capita GDP of $2,413, while the countries of the euro-zone had an average of $33,296. Although there are great differences in the levels of per capita GDP, the difference in per capita real GDP growth between low-income developing and industrial countries is much smaller than the difference in real GDP growth. The difference in growth rates between the level of output and per capita output points out the danger of just looking at real GDP as an indicator of change in the economic well-being of the citizens in developing countries. Population growth rates are considerably higher in developing countries than they are in industrial countries, so real GDP must grow at a faster rate in developing countries than it does in industrial countries just to maintain a similar growth rate in per capita real GDP. Figure 2 depicts how per capita income differs around the world. The map shows how poverty is concentrated around the world and found largely in Africa and parts of Asia.

1.c. The Problems with Definitions of Growth

Economic growth is considered to be good because it allows people to have a higher standard of living, to have more material goods. But an increase in real GDP or per capita real GDP does not tell us whether the average citizen is better off. One problem is that these measures say nothing about how income is distributed. The national economy may be growing, yet the poor may be staying poor while the rich get richer.

The lesson here is simple: Economic growth may benefit some groups more than others. And it is entirely possible that despite national economic growth, some groups can be worse off than they were before. Clearly, neither per capita real GDP nor real GDP accurately measures the standard of living for all of a nation's citizens.

> *Per capita real GDP is a questionable indicator of the typical citizen's standard of living or quality of life.*

Another reason that real GDP and per capita real GDP are misleading is that neither says anything about the quality of life. People have nonmonetary needs—they care about personal freedom, the environment, their leisure time. If a rising per capita GDP goes hand in hand with a repressive political regime or a rapidly deteriorating environmental quality, people are not going to feel better off. By the same token, a country could have no economic growth, yet reduce the hours worked each week. More leisure time could make workers feel better off, even though per capita GDP has not changed.

FIGURE 2   Differences in Per Capita Income Around the World

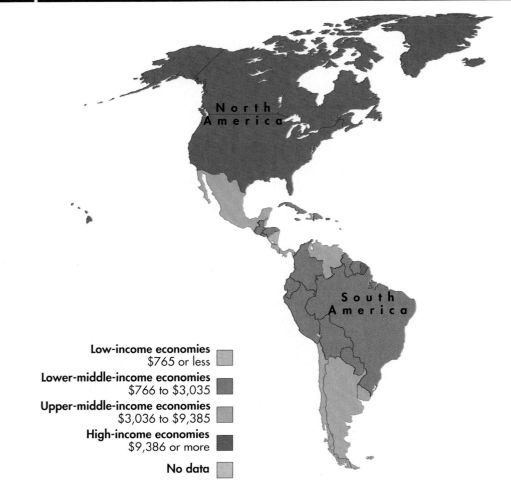

Low-income economies
$765 or less

Lower-middle-income economies
$766 to $3,035

Upper-middle-income economies
$3,036 to $9,385

High-income economies
$9,386 or more

No data

The map shows how concentrated poverty is in Africa and parts of Asia.

Once again, be careful in interpreting per capita GDP. Don't allow it to represent more than it does. Per capita GDP is simply a measure of the output produced divided by the population. It is a useful measure of economic activity in a country, but it is a questionable measure of the typical citizen's standard of living or quality of life.

RECAP

1. Economic growth is an increase in real GDP.

2. Because growth is compounded over time, small differences in rates of growth are magnified over time.

3. For any constant rate of growth, the time required for real GDP to double is 72 divided by the annual growth rate.

4. Per capita real GDP is real GDP divided by the population.

5. Per capita real GDP says nothing about the distribution of income in a country or the nonmonetary quality of life.

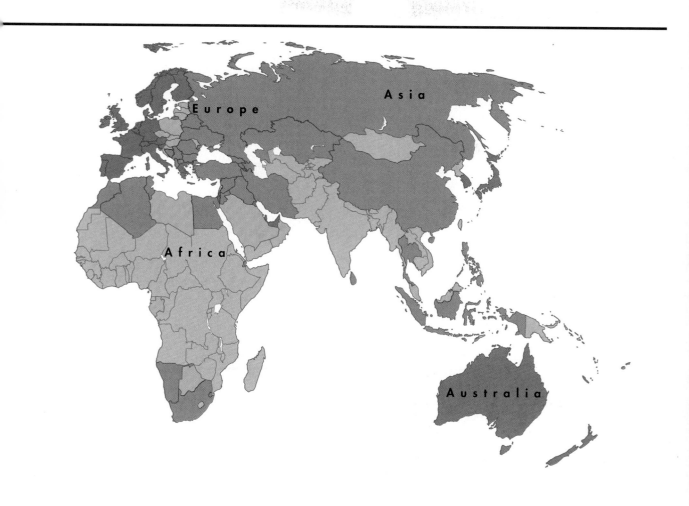

2 | How are economic growth rates determined?

Economic growth raises the potential level of real GDP, shifting the long-run aggregate supply curve to the right.

■ 2. The Determinants of Growth

The long-run aggregate supply curve is a vertical line at the potential level of real GDP (Y_{p1}). As the economy grows, the potential output of the economy rises. Figure 3 shows the increase in potential output as a rightward shift in the long-run aggregate supply curve. The higher the rate of growth, the farther the aggregate supply curve moves to the right. To illustrate several years' growth, we would show several curves shifting to the right.

To find the determinants of economic growth, we must turn to the determinants of aggregate supply. In the chapter titled "Macroeconomic Equilibrium: Aggregate Demand and Supply," we identified three determinants of aggregate supply: resource prices, technology, and expectations. Changes in expectations can shift the aggregate supply curve, but changing expectations are not a basis for long-run growth in the sense of continuous rightward movements in aggregate supply. The long-run growth of the economy rests on growth in productive resources (labor, capital, and land) and technological advances.

FIGURE 3 Economic Growth

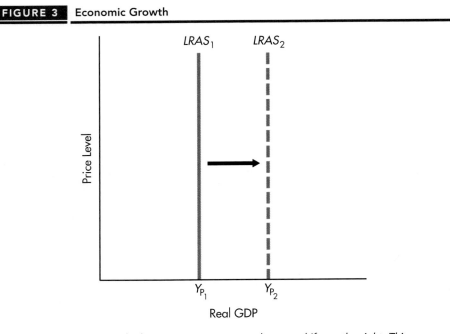

As the economy grows, the long-run aggregate supply curve shifts to the right. This represents an increase in the potential level of real GDP.

2.a. Labor

Economic growth depends on the size and quality of the labor force. The size of the labor force is a function of the size of the working-age population (16 and older in the United States) and the percentage of that population that is in the labor force. The labor force typically grows more rapidly in developing countries than in industrial countries because birthrates are higher in developing countries. Figure 4 shows the annual growth rates of the population for low-income, middle-income, and high-income countries. Between 1990 and 2006, the population grew at an average annual rate of 2.0 percent in low-income countries, 1.1 percent in middle-income countries, and 0.7 percent in high-income countries.

Based solely on growth in the labor force, it would seem that poor countries are growing faster than rich countries. But the size of the labor force is not all that matters; changes in productivity can compensate for lower growth in the labor force, as we discuss in section 3.

The U.S. labor force has changed considerably in recent decades. The most notable event of the post–World War II period was the baby boom. The children born between the late 1940s and the early 1960s made up more than a third of the total U.S. population in the early 1960s and have significantly altered the age structure of the population. In 1950, 41 percent of the population was 24 years old or younger, and 59 percent was 25 years old or older. By 1970, 46 percent of the population was in the younger group, with 54 percent in the older group. By 1990, this bulge in the age distribution had moved to where about 36 percent of the U.S. population was 24 years or younger. Over time, the bulge will move to older ranges of the population. By 2000, 35 percent of the population was 24 years or younger, with 65 percent 25 years or older.

Developing countries are playing an increasing role in the "outsourcing" of labor for firms in the industrial world. Here, workers in Bangalore, India, process data for 24/7 Customer.

The initial pressure of the baby boom fell on school systems, which were faced with rapidly expanding enrollments. Over time, as these children aged and entered the labor market, they had a large impact on potential output. The U.S. labor force grew at an average rate of about 2.5 percent a year in the 1970s, approximately twice the rate of growth experienced in the 1950s. The growth of the labor force slowed in the 1980s and 1990s as the baby boom population aged. On the basis of the size

 FIGURE 4 Average Annual Population Growth in Low-, Middle-, and High-Income Countries (percent)

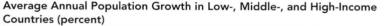

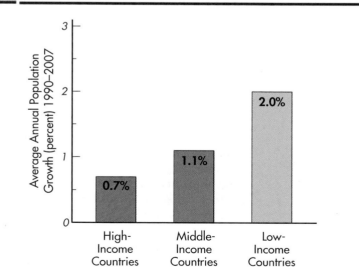

Population growth rates across countries vary considerably. Generally, population grows at a much higher rate in developing countries.
Source: Data are from World Bank, http://devdata.worldbank.org/hnpstats/query/default.html.

of the labor force, the 1970s should have been a time of greater economic growth than the 1950s and 1960s or the 1980s and 1990s. It was not. More important than the size of the labor force is its productivity.

2.b. Capital

Labor is combined with capital to produce goods and services. A rapidly growing labor force by itself is no guarantee of economic growth. Workers need machines, tools, and factories in order to work. If a country has lots of workers but few machines, then the typical worker cannot be very productive. Capital is a critical resource in growing economies.

The ability of a country to invest in capital goods is tied to its ability to save. A lack of current saving can be offset by borrowing, but the availability of borrowing is limited by the prospects for future saving. Debt incurred today must be repaid by not consuming all output in the future. If lenders believe that a nation is going to consume all of its output in the future, they will not make loans today.

The lower the standard of living in a country, the harder it is to forgo current consumption in order to save. It is difficult for a population that is living at or near subsistence level to do without current consumption. This in large part explains the low level of saving in the poorest countries.

2.c. Land

Land surface, water, forests, minerals, and other natural resources are called *land.* Land can be combined with labor and capital to produce goods and services. Abundant natural resources can contribute to economic growth, but natural resources alone do not generate growth. Several developing countries, such as Argentina and Brazil, are relatively rich in natural resources, but have not been very successful in exploiting these resources to produce goods and services. Japan, on the other hand, has relatively few natural resources, but showed dramatic economic growth until a recession in the late 1990s. The experience of Japan makes it clear that abundant natural resources are not a necessary condition for economic growth.

> *Abundant natural resources are not a necessary condition for economic growth.*

2.d. Technology

technology: ways of combining resources to produce output

A key determinant of economic growth is **technology,** or ways of combining resources to produce goods and services. New management techniques, scientific discoveries, and other innovations improve technology. Technological advances allow the production of more output from a given amount of resources. This means that technological progress accelerates economic growth for any given rate of growth in the labor force and the capital stock. A particularly dramatic example of technological change is provided in the Economic Insight "Technological Advance: The Change in the Price of Light."

> *Technological advances allow the production of more output from a given amount of resources.*

Technological change depends on the scientific community. The more educated a population, the greater its potential for technological advances. Industrial countries have better-educated populations than developing countries do. Education gives industrial countries a substantial advantage over developing countries in creating and implementing innovations. In addition, the richest industrial countries traditionally have spent 2 to 3 percent of their GNP on research and development, an investment that developing countries cannot afford. The greater the funding for research and development, the greater the likelihood of technological advances.

Technological Advance: The Change in the Price of Light

A particularly striking example of the role of technological change is provided by the change in the labor cost of providing light. An economist, William Nordhaus, estimated the effects of technological change on the labor cost of providing lighting.* Light can be measured in *lumen hours*, where a lumen is the amount of light provided by one candle. Nordhaus estimated the number of hours of work required to produce 1,000 lumen-hours of light. His estimates of the cost of providing 1,000 lumen hours of light are shown in the accompanying table.

Time	Light Source	Labor Price
500,000 BC	Open fire	58 hours
1750 BC	Babylonian lamp	41.5 hours
1800	Tallow candle	5.4 hours
1900	Filament lamp	0.2 hour
1990	Filament lamp	0.0006 hour

The choice of light is appropriate, as the desirable service provided by light, illumination, is essentially unchanged over time. What has changed dramatically is the manner in which light is produced and the cost of producing it. The example shows not only how changing technology has increased the productivity of light production, but also how the pace of technological advance has quickened in recent times. The faster technology progresses, the faster the cost of production falls.

Impeded by low levels of education and limited funds for research and development, the developing countries lag behind the industrial countries in developing and implementing new technology. Typically these countries follow the lead of the industrial world, adopting new technology developed in that world once it is affordable and feasible, given their capital and labor resources. In the next chapter we discuss the role of foreign aid, including technological assistance, in promoting economic growth in developing countries.

*William Nordhaus, "Do Real-Output and Real-Wage Measures Capture Reality? The History of Lighting Suggests Not," in *The Economics of New Goods*, ed. Timothy Bresnahan and Robert Gordon (Chicago: University of Chicago Press, 1997).

RECAP

1. Economic growth raises the potential level of real GDP, shifting the long-run aggregate supply curve to the right.

2. The long-run growth of the economy is a product of growth in labor, capital, and natural resources and advances in technology.

3. The size of the labor force is determined by the working-age population and the percentage of that population that is in the labor force.

4. The post–World War II baby boom created a bulge in the age distribution of the U.S. population.

5. Growth in capital stock is tied to current and future saving.

6. Abundant natural resources contribute to economic growth but are not essential to that growth.

7. Technology is the way in which resources are combined to produce output.

8. Hampered by low levels of education and limited financial resources, developing countries lag behind the industrial nations in developing and implementing new technology.

3 | What is productivity?

total factor productivity (TFP): the ratio of the economy's output to its stock of labor and capital

■ 3. Productivity

In the last section, we described how output depends on resource inputs like labor and capital. One way to assess the contribution that a resource makes to output is its productivity. *Productivity* is the ratio of the output produced to the amount of input. We can measure the productivity of a single resource—say, labor or capital—or the overall productivity of all resources. **Total factor productivity (TFP)** is the term that economists use to describe the overall productivity of an economy. It is the ratio of the economy's output to its stock of labor and capital.

3.a. Productivity and Economic Growth

Economic growth depends on both the growth of resources and technological progress. Advances in technology allow resources to be more productive. If the quantity of resources is growing and each resource is more productive, then output grows even faster than the quantity of resources. Economic growth, then, is the sum of the growth rate of total factor productivity and the growth rate of resources:

$$\text{Economic growth} = \text{growth rate of } TFP + \text{growth rate of resources}$$

The amount by which output grows because the labor force is growing depends on how much labor contributes to the production of output. Similarly, the amount by which output grows because capital is growing depends on how much capital contributes to the production of output. To relate the growth of labor and capital to the growth of output (we assume no change in natural resources), then, the growth of labor and the growth of capital must be multiplied by their relative contributions to the production of output. The most straightforward way to measure those contributions is to use the share of real GDP received by each resource. For instance, in the United States, labor receives about 70 percent (.70) of real GDP and capital receives about 30 percent (.30). So we can determine the growth of output by using this formula:

$$\% \Delta Y = \% \Delta TFP + .70(\% \Delta L) + .30(\% \Delta K)$$

where

$$\%\Delta = \text{percentage change in}$$
$$Y = \text{real GDP}$$
$$TFP = \text{total factor productivity}$$
$$L = \text{size of the labor force}$$
$$K = \text{capital stock}$$

The equation shows how economic growth depends on changes in productivity ($\%\Delta TFP$) as well as changes in resources ($\%\Delta L$ and $\%\Delta K$). Even if labor (L) and capital stock (K) are constant, technological innovation will generate economic growth through changes in total factor productivity (TFP).

For example, suppose TFP is growing at a rate of 2 percent a year. Then, even with labor and capital stock held constant, the economy grows at a rate of 2 percent a year. If labor and capital stock also grow at a rate of 2 percent a year, output grows by the sum of the growth rates of all three components (TFP, .70 times labor growth, and .30 times the capital stock growth), or 4 percent.

How do we account for differences in growth rates across countries? Because almost all countries have experienced growth in the labor force, percentage increases in labor forces have generally supported economic growth. But growth in the capital stock has been steadier in the industrial countries than in the developing countries, so differences in capital growth rates may explain some of the differences in economic growth across countries. Yet differences in resource growth rates alone cannot explain the major differences we find across countries. In recent years, those differences seem to be related to productivity.

3.b. Determinants of Productivity

4 | **What explains productivity changes?**

Productivity in the United States has fluctuated considerably in recent years. From 1948 to 1965, *TFP* grew at an annual average rate of 2.02 percent. In the 1970s, *TFP* growth averaged 0.7 percent per year; in the 1980s, 0.6 percent; and by the late 1990s, 1 percent. If the pre-1965 rate of growth had been maintained, output in the United States would be an estimated 39 percent higher today than it actually is. What caused this dramatic change in productivity—first down in the 1970s and 1980s, and then up in the 1990s? More generally, what determines the productivity changes for any country?

Several factors determine productivity growth. They include the quality of the labor force, technological innovations, energy prices, and a shift from manufacturing to service industries.

3.b.1. Labor Quality Labor productivity is measured as output per hour of labor. Figure 5 shows how the productivity of labor in the United States and four other countries changed between 1979 and 2007. We see that Korea has had the fastest rate of labor productivity growth and Canada the lowest over this time period. Although changes in the productivity of labor can stem from technological innovation and changes in the capital stock, they can also come from changes in the quality of labor. These changes may be a product of the level and quality of education, demographic change, and changing attitudes toward work.

Education Level The average level of education in the world has gone up over time. Table 2 lists three measures of education level for the United States.

FIGURE 5 Average Annual Percentage Change in Output per Hour of Labor

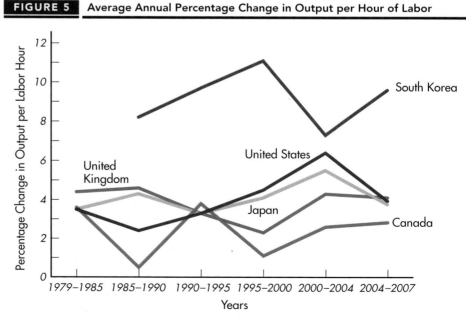

Output per labor hour is a measure of productivity.
Source: Data from Bureau of Labor Statistics, www.bls.gov/fls/home/htm.

TABLE 2	The Average Level of Education, United States, 1940–2007*							
	1940	1950	1960	1970	1980	1990	2000	2007
Median school years completed	8.6	9.3	10.6	12.1	12.5	12.7	12.9	N/A
People with at least a high school education (percent)	24.5	34.3	41.1	52.3	66.5	75.2	84.1	84.0
People with at least four years of college (percent)	4.6	6.2	7.7	10.7	16.2	20.3	25.6	27

* People 25 years of age and over.
Source: U.S. Census Bureau, www.census.gov/population/socdemo/education.

The first, median school years completed, increased from 8.6 years in 1940 to 12.9 years in 2000. From 1940 to 2007, the percentage of adults with at least a high school education rose from more than 24 percent to 84 percent, and the percentage of those with a college education rose from less than 5 percent to 27 percent. The figures seem to indicate that the level of education supports increases in U.S. productivity.

Demographic Change Changes in the size and composition of the population have an impact on the labor market. As the baby boom generation entered the labor force in the late 1960s and early 1970s, a large pool of inexperienced, unskilled workers was created. The average quality of the labor force may have fallen at this time, as reflected in some large drops in output per hour of labor. In the 1980s, the baby boom segment of the labor force had more experience, skills, and education, thus pushing the quality of the labor force up.

Another important demographic change that has affected the quality of the labor force is the participation rates of women. As more and more women entered the labor force in the 1980s, the pool of untrained workers increased, probably reducing the average quality of labor. Over time, as female participation rates have stabilized, the average quality of labor should rise as the skills and experience of female workers rise.

Finally, immigration can play a role in labor force quality. For instance, the 1970s and 1980s saw a change in the pattern of U.S. immigration. Although many highly skilled professionals immigrate to the United States as part of the "brain drain" from developing countries, recent immigrants, both legal and illegal, have generally added to the supply of unskilled labor and reduced the average quality of the labor force.

3.b.2. Technological Innovation New technology alters total factor productivity. Innovations increase productivity, so when productivity falls, it is natural to look at technological developments to see whether they are a factor in the change. The pace of technological innovation is difficult to measure. Expenditures on research and development are related to the discovery of new knowledge, but actual changes in technology do not proceed as evenly as those expenditures. We expect a long lag between funding and operating a laboratory and the discovery of useful technology. Still, a decline in spending on research and development may indicate less of a commitment to increasing productivity.

The most notable technological innovation in recent decades has been the widespread availability of cheaper and faster computers. The information technology (IT) revolution has played an important role in enhancing productivity.

One may think of the purchase of computer hardware or software as investment. The capital stock increases with such purchases. However, researchers have also found that there are increases in total factor productivity associated with the development and spread of information technology. Such gains have not been realized by all countries. Poor countries lag far behind the rich in the implementation of IT. Table 3 provides data on the number of personal computers per 100 people in selected countries in 2006. Clearly, the productivity-enhancing benefits of IT have been realized in countries like Israel, Canada, Switzerland, and the other countries at the top of the table, where the number of personal computers per 100 people is 122.1, 87.6, and 86.5, respectively.

However, in developing countries, the benefits of IT innovations are not being fully exploited as a result of poverty and lack of skills. In Table 3, the lowest level of computer ownership is 12.2 in Russia. However, in poorer countries like Bangladesh, Cambodia, and Ethiopia, the level is less than 1 computer per 100 people. This indicates an inability to implement IT widely across the economy. IT is just one example of how productivity may differ across countries as a result of differing uses of modern technology.

TABLE 3   **The Number of Personal Computers per 100 People (2006)**

Country	Personal Computers	Country	Personal Computers
Israel	122.1	Slovakia	35.8
Canada	87.6	Spain	27.7
Switzerland	86.5	Czech Republic	27.4
Netherlands	85.4	United Arab Emirates	25.6
Sweden	83.6	Latvia	24.6
United States	76.2	Kuwait	23.7
Britain	75.8	Costa Rica	23.1
Australia	75.7	Macedonia	22.2
Denmark	69.6	Malaysia	21.8
Singapore	68.2	Croatia	19.9
Japan	67.6	Lithuania	18.0
Hong Kong	61.2	Mauritius	16.9
Germany	60.6	Brazil	16.1
Norway	59.4	Hungary	14.9
France	57.5	Chile	14.1
South Korea	53.2	Mexico	13.6
Ireland	52.8	Saudi Arabia	13.6
New Zealand	50.2	Uruguay	13.6
Finland	50.0	Mongolia	13.3
Estonia	48.3	Portugal	13.3
Slovenia	40.4	Romania	12.9
Belgium	37.7	Namibia	12.3
Italy	36.7	Russia	12.2

Source: "Pocket World in Figures," based on data from the International Telecommunication Union.

3.b.3. Other Factors We have seen how changing labor quality and techno-logical innovation are related to changes in productivity. Other reasons have been offered to explain the changes in productivity across countries and over time. We examine three of them: the cost of energy, the shift from a manufactur-ing to a service-oriented economy, and the development of financial markets.

Energy Prices In 1973, 1974, and 1979, OPEC succeeded in raising the price of oil substantially. The timing of the dramatic increase in oil prices coincided with a drop in productivity growth in the United States. U.S. output per labor hour actually fell in 1974 and 1979. Higher energy prices resulting from restricted oil output should directly decrease aggregate supply because energy is an important input across industries. As the price of energy increases, the costs of production rise and aggregate supply decreases.

Higher energy prices can affect productivity through their impact on the capital stock. As energy prices go up, energy-inefficient capital goods become obsolete. Like any other decline in the value of the capital stock, this change reduces economic growth. Standard measures of capital stock do not account for energy obsolescence, so they suggest that total factor productivity fell in the 1970s. However, if the stock of usable capital actually did go down, it was the growth rate of capital, not *TFP*, that fell.

Manufacturing versus Services In recent decades, the industrial economies have seen a shift away from manufacturing toward services. Some econo-mists believe that productivity grows more slowly in service industries than in manufacturing, because of the less capital-intensive nature of providing services. Therefore, the movement into services reduces the overall growth rate of the economy.

Although a greater emphasis on service industries may explain a drop in productivity, we must be careful with this kind of generalization. It is more difficult to measure changes in the quality of services than changes in the quality of goods. If prices in an industry rise with no change in the quantity of output, it makes sense to conclude that the real level of output in the in-dustry has fallen. However, if prices have gone up because the quality of the service has increased, then output actually has changed. Suppose a hotel re-models its rooms. In effect, it is improving the quality of its service. Increased prices here would reflect this change in output.

Service industries—fast-food restaurants, airlines, hotels, banks—are not all alike. One way in which service firms compete is on the basis of the quality of service that they provide. Because productivity is measured by the amount of output per unit of input, if we don't adjust for quality changes, we may under-estimate the amount of output and so underestimate the productivity of the industry. The issue of productivity measurement in the service industries is an important topic of discussion among economists today.

Financial Market Development The evidence across countries suggests that economic growth is related to the development of financial markets. For any given amount of labor and capital, the more developed an economy's financial markets are, the more efficient should be the allocation of resources and, there-fore, the greater the productivity. A nation may have a high rate of saving and investment and a sizable capital stock, but the key to efficient production is the allocation of resources to their best use.

Financial markets facilitate the allocation of resources. This occurs through the following mechanisms:

- Financial institutions act as intermediaries between savers and borrowers and screen borrowers so that the best projects are more likely to be funded.

- Financial institutions monitor the behavior of borrowers to ensure that the borrowed funds are used as intended.

- Financial institutions lower the risk of providing funds for investment purposes, as they provide loans to different individuals and firms, and through this diversification of loans reduce the likelihood of suffering a catastrophic loss. If one borrower defaults on a loan, the financial institution does not fail, as it still has many other loans that are being repaid. This is a far different situation from the one that an individual making a single large loan may face. If you lend a large amount of your wealth to a single borrower and that borrower defaults on the loan, your living standard may be at great risk. Because of the "risk sharing" that takes place in financial institutions, the cost of borrowed funds, the interest rate, will be lower than in an environment in which there is no such pooling of loan risks.

- The more developed the financial sector of an economy, the more types of financing alternatives there are for funding investment. For instance, the typical poor country has a banking sector and a very limited stock market, if any at all. Firms in such a country must rely on bank loans. The governments in such countries often determine where banks are allowed to lend based on political considerations. As economies develop, the financial sector evolves so that alternatives to bank financing come into being. Firms in economies with well-developed financial markets can raise funds by selling shares of ownership in the stock market, by issuing debt in the form of bonds to nonbank lenders, or by borrowing from banks. The more developed a country's financial markets, the more efficient the funding sources for borrowers and the more productive the economy.

3.c. Growth and Development

Economic growth depends on the growth of productivity and resources. Productivity grows unevenly, and its rate of growth is reflected in economic growth. Although the labor force seems to grow faster in developing countries than in industrial countries, lower rates of saving have limited the growth of the capital stock in developing countries. Without capital, workers cannot be very productive. This means that the relatively high rate of growth in the labor force in the developing world does not translate into a high rate of economic growth. We use this information on economic growth in the chapter titled "Development Economics" to explain and analyze the strategies used by developing countries to stimulate output and increase standards of living.

RECAP

1. Productivity is the ratio of the output produced to the amount of input.

2. Total factor productivity is the nation's real GDP (output) divided by its stock of labor and capital.

3. Economic growth is the sum of the growth rate of total factor productivity and the growth rate of resources (labor and capital).

4. Changes in productivity may be explained by the quality of the labor force, technological innovations, energy prices, a shift from manufacturing to service industries, and financial market development.

SUMMARY

1 | What is economic growth?

- Economic growth is an increase in real GDP. *§1.a*
- Economic growth is compounded over time. *§1.a.1*
- Per capita real GDP is real GDP divided by the population. *§1.b*
- The definitions of economic growth are misleading because they do not indicate anything about the distribution of income or the quality of life. *§1.c*

2 | How are economic growth rates determined?

- The growth of the economy is tied to the growth of productive resources and technological advances. *§2*
- Because their populations tend to grow more rapidly, developing countries typically experience faster growth in the labor force than do industrial countries. *§2.a*
- The inability to save limits the growth of the capital stock in developing countries. *§2.b*
- Abundant natural resources are not necessary for rapid economic growth. *§2.c*

- Technology defines the ways in which resources can be combined to produce goods and services. *§2.d*

3 | What is productivity?

- Productivity is the ratio of the output produced to the amount of input. *§3*
- Total factor productivity is the overall productivity of an economy. *§3*
- The percentage change in real GDP equals the percentage change in total factor productivity plus the percentage changes in labor and capital multiplied by the share of GDP taken by labor and capital. *§3.a*

4 | What explains productivity changes?

- Productivity changes with changes in the quality of the labor force, technological innovations, changes in energy prices, a shift from manufacturing to service industries, and financial market development. *§3.b*

KEY TERMS

economic growth *§1.a*

rule of 72 *§1.a.2*

per capita real GDP *§1.b*

technology *§2.d*

total factor productivity (*TFP*) *§3*

EXERCISES

1. Why is the growth of per capita real GDP a better measure of economic growth than the growth of real GDP?

2. What is the level of output after four years if initial output equals $1,000 and the economy grows at a rate of 10 percent a year?

3. Use the data in the following table to determine the average annual growth rate for each country in terms of real GDP growth and per capita real GDP growth (real GDP is in billions of U.S. dollars, and population is in millions of people). Which country grew at the faster rate?

4. Suppose labor's share of GDP is 70 percent and capital's is 30 percent, real GDP is growing at a rate of 4 percent a year, the labor force is growing at 2 percent, and the capital stock is growing at 3 percent. What is the growth rate of total factor productivity?

5. Suppose labor's share of GDP is 70 percent and capital's is 30 percent, total factor productivity is growing at an annual rate of 2 percent, the labor force is growing at a rate of 1 percent, and the capital stock is growing at a rate of 3 percent. What is the annual growth rate of real GDP?

| Country | 1999 | | 2001 | |
	Real GDP	Population	Real GDP	Population
Morocco	108.0	30.1	112.0	31.2
Australia	416.2	19.2	528.0	19.5

6. Discuss possible reasons for the slowdown in U.S. productivity growth that occurred in the 1970s and 1980s, and relate each reason to the equation for economic growth. Does the growth of *TFP* or of resources change?

7. How did the post–World War II baby boom affect the growth of the U.S. labor force? What effect is this baby boom likely to have on the future U.S. labor force?

8. How do developing and industrial countries differ in their use of technological change, labor, capital, and natural resources to produce economic growth? Why do these differences exist?

9. How would an aging population affect economic growth?

10. If real GDP for China was 10,312 billion yuan at the end of 2002 and 9,593 billion yuan at the end of 2001, what is the annual rate of growth of the Chinese economy?

11. If Botswana's economy grew at a rate of 1 percent during 2006 and real GDP at the beginning of the year was 44 billion pula, then what is real GDP at the end of the year?

12. Suppose a country has a real GDP equal to $1 billion today. If this economy grows at a rate of 5 percent a year, what will be the value of real GDP after five years?

13. Is the following statement true or false? Explain your answer. "Abundant natural resources are a necessary condition for economic growth."

14. What is the difference between total factor productivity and the productivity of labor? Why do you suppose that people often measure a nation's productivity using labor productivity only?

15. How would each of the following affect productivity in the United States?
    a. The quality of education in high schools increases.
    b. A cutback in oil production by oil-exporting nations raises oil prices.
    c. A large number of unskilled immigrant laborers move into the country.

16. How does the development of financial markets enhance the productivity of a country?

You can find further practice tests in the Online Quiz at **www.cengage.com/economics/boyes**.

Riding a Surge of Technology

Federal Reserve Bank of Dallas 2003 Annual Report

Because productivity determines how well we live, Americans want to know how they're doing. In an economy as large and diverse as ours, it's a Herculean task to calculate a productivity number that sums up the efforts of 130 million workers, employed in millions of establishments that produce more than $11 trillion in output. The Bureau of Labor Statistics does the best it can in producing quarterly estimates of output per hour, derived largely from surveys of businesses.

BLS data show that U.S. productivity has grown steadily over the long haul, with output per hour rising an average 2.3 percent annually since 1870. A few percentage points a year might not sound like much, but this historical rate doubles per capita income every three decades or so.

The productivity path has been choppy due to business-cycle upturns and slowdowns as well as longer-term economic trends. From 1950 to 1973, for example, output per hour rose a healthy 2.7 percent annually. Over the next 22 years, productivity sank below its long-term trend, rising just 1.5 percent a year. The slowdown remains something of a mystery, although some economists suggest that early investments in computers and information technology didn't provide a big enough payoff.

Productivity broke out of its two-decade doldrums in the mid-1990s as computers, scanners, the Internet and other innovations finally reached critical mass in America's workplaces. Average annual productivity gains have surged at 3.2 percent since 1995.

The revival shows every sign of continuing. The economy emerged from the 2001 recession with productivity growth well above the average of the seven significant business cycles since 1960. In the first 11 quarters after employment peaked, productivity jumped 13 percent, compared with the historical norm of 8 percent. In another break with the past, the gains spread beyond manufacturing, the traditional productivity leader, and into the whole economy, including retailing and services.

Productivity's postrecession surge has been strong enough to spark controversy. The labor market has languished, with no net job creation two years into the recovery. Some see productivity as a millstone that allows companies to expand without hiring more workers. But viewing productivity as a drag on employment is myopic. Americans don't face a choice between having work and working a better way. Higher productivity raises incomes and profits, which fuels demand, boosts investment and puts more people to work, usually at new jobs.

We could dismantle our factory robots and farm equipment with the idea of hiring lots of busy hands to build cars and till the soil. We could junk our backhoes and dig ditches with shovels. Doing so would be absurd. We'd immediately see that renouncing productivity would do us great harm. Prices would be higher, wages lower and the economy smaller. Work would be harder. Living standards would be dragged backward in time, sacrificed to the false god of more jobs.

Rather than shunning productivity, we should embrace it and move forward. As the economic recovery continues, the United States may not be able to sustain the same pace of productivity growth it has the past two years. Even with a slowdown, the nation will likely build on recent years' strong productivity growth, rather than relapse into the post-1973 slump.

The bullish case for future productivity centers on the technologies that have made U.S. workplaces more efficient in recent years. The microchip revolution still has plenty of kick left in it. And as world markets integrate, we should add to our productivity gains from trade.

Further out, new generations of world-shaking technologies will impact the way we work. Take nanotechnology, the science of rearranging atoms and molecules. It promises to create new materials that are stronger, lighter and more flexible and substances with perfect insulating, lubricating and conducting properties. Biotechnology will emerge, too, as a potent force for progress.

When combined with America's entrepreneurial bent and open markets, the inventory of cutting-edge technologies should deliver rapid productivity growth for years. Healthy gains in output per hour may restore the luster of the New Economy, a concept tarnished by the dot-com implosion. The New Economy carries a powerful policy implication: With stronger productivity, the economy can grow faster without fueling inflation.

Measuring a nation's productivity has never been an easy task. As the article says, it is "a Herculean task to calculate a productivity number that sums up the efforts of 130 million workers, employed in millions of establishments that produce more than $11 trillion in output." Since business and government policymakers make important decisions on the basis of the economic data provided by government, accurate measurement is crucial.

An example of the controversy related to the measurement problems is the issue of the "New Economy." As mentioned at the end of the article, the New Economy means that with strong increases in productivity, the economy can grow faster without higher inflation. This is a world in which technological advances in computers and information technology are driving increased productivity and output.

To estimate the contribution of computers to growth, one can modify the growth equation presented in section 3.a of this chapter to allow computers to be treated apart from the rest of the capital stock:

$$\% \, \Delta Y = \% \, \Delta TFP + 0.70(\% \, \Delta L) + 0.29(\% \, \Delta K) + 0.01(\% \, \Delta COMP)$$

Note that this equation has computers accounting for 1 percent of the real GDP, and other capital for 29 percent.

The growth equation with computers treated separately from the rest of the capital stock allows us to estimate the effect of computers on growth (the product of their GDP share, 0.01, and the percentage change in the stock of computers).

A study conducted by Dale Jorgensen, Mun Ho, and Kevin Stiroh* estimated that a little less than half of the change in TFP over the period 1995–2003 can be explained by IT, compared with less than $\frac{1}{10}$ over the earlier period 1959–1973. The U.S. evidence thus indicates a clear role for IT in increasing TFP.

The article points out that productivity advances allow higher living standards and create new jobs. Countries that develop and employ new technology will have faster economic growth, less poverty, and less inflation than they would otherwise

———

*Dale W. Jorgensen, Mun S. Ho, and Kevin J. Stiroh, "Will the U.S. Productivity Resurgency Continue?" Federal Reserve Bank of New York, *Current Issues in Economics and Finance,* December 2004.

Chapter 20

© Pink

International Trade Restrictions

Fundamental Questions

1 Why do countries restrict international trade?

2 How do countries restrict the entry of foreign goods and promote the export of domestic goods?

3 What sorts of agreements do countries enter into to reduce barriers to international trade?

The Japanese government once announced that foreign-made skis would not be allowed into Japan because they were unsafe. Japanese ski manufacturers were active supporters of the ban. The U.S. government once imposed a tax of almost 50 percent on imports of motorcycles with engines larger than 700 cc. The only U.S.-owned motorcycle manufacturer, Harley-Davidson, produced no motorcycles with engines smaller than 1,000 cc and so did not care about the small-engine market. In the mid-1980s, Britain began replacing the distinctive red steel telephone booths that were used all through the country with new booths. Many U.S. residents were interested in buying an old British phone booth to use as a decorative novelty, so the phone booths were exported to the United States. However, when the phone booths arrived, the U.S. Customs Service impounded them because there was a limit on the amount of iron and steel products that could be exported from Britain to the United States. The phone booths would be allowed to enter the country only if British exports of some other iron and steel products were reduced. The British exporters protested the classification of the phone booths as iron and steel products and argued that they should be considered antiques (which have no import restrictions). The phone booths were not reclassified; as a result, few have entered the United States, and prices of old British phone booths have been in the thousands of dollars. There are many examples of government policy influencing the prices and quantities of goods that are traded internationally.

International trade is rarely determined solely by comparative advantage and the free market forces of supply and demand. Governments often find that political pressures favor policies that at least partially offset the prevailing comparative advantages. Government policy aimed at influencing international trade flows is called **commercial policy**. This chapter first examines the arguments in support of commercial policy and then discusses the various tools of commercial policy employed by governments.

commercial policy:
government policy that influences international trade flows

1 | **Why do countries restrict international trade?**

Protection from foreign competition generally benefits domestic producers at the expense of domestic consumers.

■ 1. Arguments for Protection

Governments restrict foreign trade to protect domestic producers from foreign competition. In some cases the protection may be justified; in most cases it harms consumers. Of the arguments used to promote such protection, only a few are valid. We will look first at arguments that are widely considered to have little or no merit, and then at those that may sometimes be valid.

International trade on the basis of comparative advantage maximizes world output and allows consumers access to better-quality products at lower prices than would be available in the domestic market alone. If trade is restricted, consumers pay higher prices for lower-quality goods, and world output declines. Protection from foreign competition imposes costs on the domestic economy as well as on foreign producers. When production does not proceed on the basis of comparative advantage, resources are not expended on their most efficient uses. Whenever government restrictions alter the pattern of trade, we should expect someone to benefit and someone else to suffer. Generally speaking, protection from foreign competition benefits domestic producers at the expense of domestic consumers.

1.a. Creation of Domestic Jobs

If foreign goods are kept out of the domestic economy, it is often argued, jobs will be created at home. This argument holds that domestic firms will produce the goods that otherwise would have been produced abroad, thus employing domestic workers instead of foreign workers. The weakness of this argument is that only the protected industry will benefit in terms of employment. Since domestic consumers will pay higher prices to buy the output of the protected industry, they will have less to spend on other goods and services, which could cause employment in other industries to drop. In addition, if other countries retaliate by restricting the entry of U.S. exports, the output of U.S. firms that produce for export will fall as well. Typically, restrictions to "save domestic jobs" simply redistribute jobs by creating employment in the protected industry and reducing employment elsewhere.

Table 1 shows estimates of the cost of saving U.S. jobs from foreign competition. For instance, the cost of saving 226 jobs in the U.S. luggage industry is $290 million, or $1,285,078 per worker. Studies have consistently shown that the costs of protecting domestic jobs typically outweigh the benefits. So while it is possible to erect barriers to foreign competition and save domestic jobs, restricting international trade may impose large costs on an economy. Consumers end up paying much more for the goods they buy in order to subsidize the relatively inefficient domestic producer.

TABLE 1	The Cost of Protecting U.S. Jobs from Foreign Competition		
Protected Industry	Jobs Saved	Total Cost (in millions)	Annual Cost per Job Saved
Benzenoid chemicals	216	$ 297	$1,376,435
Luggage	226	290	1,285,078
Softwood lumber	605	632	1,044,271
Sugar	2,261	1,868	826,104
Polyethylene resins	298	242	812,928
Dairy products	2,378	1,630	685,323
Frozen concentrated orange juice	609	387	635,103
Ball bearings	146	88	603,368
Maritime services	4,411	2,522	571,668
Ceramic tiles	347	191	551,367
Machine tools	1,556	746	479,452
Ceramic articles	418	140	335,876
Women's handbags	773	204	263,535
Canned tuna	390	100	257,640
Glassware	1,477	366	247,889
Apparel and textiles	168,786	33,629	199,241
Peanuts	397	74	187,223
Rubber footwear	1,701	286	168,312
Women's nonathletic footwear	3,702	518	139,800
Costume jewelry	1,067	142	132,870
Total	191,764	$44,252	
Average (weighted)			$ 231,289

Source: Federal Reserve Bank of Dallas 2002 Annual Report, "The Fruits of Free Trade," by W. Michael Cox and Richard Alm. http://dallasfed.org/fed/annual/2002/ar02f.cfm.

Table 2 shows the annual cost to the United States of import restrictions in terms of reduced GDP as estimated by an agency of the U.S. government. The total estimated amount of $14,133 million means that U.S. GDP would be over $14 billion higher without import restrictions. This estimate by the U.S. International Trade Commission incorporates estimates of all gains and losses from labor and capital income, tax revenue changes, and effects on consumption of changes in prices of goods and services. The amount of $14 billion is a very small fraction of U.S. GDP but would involve substantial changes for a few industries. For instance, in fabric mills, employment would fall by 13 percent and output by about 10 percent, and in sugar manufacturing, employment would fall by 25 percent and output by about 20 percent.

Saving domestic jobs from foreign competition may cost domestic consumers more than it benefits the protected industries.

Tables 1 and 2 demonstrate the very high cost per job saved by protection. If the costs to consumers are greater than the benefits to the protected industries, you may wonder why government provides any protection aimed at saving jobs. The answer, in a word, is politics. Protection of the U.S. textile and sugar industries means that all consumers pay a higher price for clothing and sugar. But individual consumers do not know how much of the price they pay for clothes

TABLE 2	Annual Gain in U.S. GDP if U.S. Import Restrictions Were Eliminated

Sector	GDP Gain (millions of dollars)
Simultaneous liberalization of all restraints	14,133
Individual liberalization	
Textiles and apparel	11,759
Sugar	1,089
Footwear and leather products	720
Tobacco and tobacco products	145
Canned tuna	71
Beef	66
Watches, clocks, cases, and parts	65
Ball and roller bearings	58
Ceramic wall and floor tile	50
Dairy	30
Table- and kitchenware	22
Costume jewelry	22
Glass and glass products	8
Peanuts	6
Pens, mechanical pencils, and parts	3
Cutlery and hand tools	1

Source: *The Economic Effects of Significant U.S. Imports Restraints* (U.S. International Trade Commission, Washington, D.C., 2004), hotdocs.usitc.gov/docs/pubs/332/ pub3701.pdf.

and sugar is due to protection, and consumers rarely lobby their political representatives to eliminate protection and reduce prices. Meanwhile, there is a great deal of pressure for protection. Employers and workers in the protected industries know the benefits of protection: higher prices for their output, higher profits for owners, and higher wages for workers. As a result, there will be active lobbying for protection against foreign competition.

1.b. Creation of a "Level Playing Field"

Special interest groups sometimes claim that other nations that export successfully to the home market have unfair advantages over domestic producers. Fairness, however, is often in the eye of the beholder. People who call for creating a "level playing field" believe that the domestic government should take steps to offset the perceived advantage of the foreign firm. They often claim that foreign firms have an unfair advantage because foreign workers are willing to work for very low wages. "Fair trade, not free trade" is the cry that this claim generates. But advocates of fair trade are really claiming that production in accordance with comparative advantage is unfair. This is clearly wrong. A country with relatively low wages is typically a country with an abundance of low-skilled labor. Such a country will have a comparative advantage in products that use low-skilled labor most intensively. To create a "level playing field" by imposing restrictions that eliminate the comparative advantage of foreign firms will make domestic consumers worse off and undermine the basis for specialization and economic efficiency.

Calls for "fair trade" are typically aimed at imposing restrictions to match those imposed by other nations.

Some calls for "fair trade" are based on the notion of reciprocity. If a country imposes import restrictions on goods from a country that does not have similar restrictions, reciprocal tariffs and quotas may be called for in the latter country in order to stimulate a reduction of trade restrictions in the former country. For instance, it has been claimed that U.S. construction firms are discriminated against in Japan, because Japanese construction firms do billions of dollars' worth of business in the United States each year, but U.S. construction companies rarely are seen in Japan. Advocates of fair trade could argue that U.S. restrictions should be imposed on Japanese construction firms.

One danger of calls for fairness based on reciprocity is that calls for fair trade may be invoked in cases where, in fact, foreign restrictions on U.S. imports do not exist. For instance, suppose the U.S. auto industry wanted to restrict the entry of imported autos to help stimulate sales of domestically produced cars. One strategy might be to point out that U.S. auto sales abroad had fallen and to claim that this was due to unfair treatment of U.S. auto exports in other countries. Of course, there are many other possible reasons why foreign sales of U.S. autos might have fallen. But blaming foreign trade restrictions might win political support for restricting imports of foreign cars into the United States.

1.c. Government Revenue Creation

Tariffs on trade generate government revenue. Industrial countries, which find income taxes easy to collect, rarely justify tariffs on the basis of the revenue they generate for government spending. But many developing countries find income taxes difficult to levy and collect, whereas tariffs are easy to collect. Customs agents can be positioned at ports of entry to examine all goods that enter and leave the country. The observability of trade flows makes tariffs a popular tax in developing countries, whose revenue requirements may provide a valid justification for their existence. Table 3 shows that tariffs account for a relatively large fraction of government revenue in many developing countries, and only a small fraction in industrial countries.

Developing countries often justify tariffs as an important source of government revenue.

1.d. National Defense

It has long been argued that industries that are crucial to the national defense, such as shipbuilding, should be protected from foreign competition. Even though

| TABLE 3 | Tariffs as a Percentage of Total Government Revenue |

Country	Tariffs as Percentage of Government Revenue
United Kingdom	1.2%
United States	2.1%
Canada	3.3%
Mexico	5.6%
China	6.4%
Korea	8.1%
India	31.8%
Jordan	32.6%
Lesotho	68%

Source: World Customs Organization, "Annual Survey to Determine Percentage of National Revenues Represented by Customs Duties," http://hotdocs.usitc.gov/tata/N_xxx/NCxxx/NC0013E1.pdf.

the United States does not have a comparative advantage in shipbuilding, the argument goes, a domestic shipbuilding industry is necessary, since foreign-made ships may not be available during war. This is a valid argument as long as the protected industry is genuinely critical to the national defense. In some industries, such as copper or other basic metals, it might make more sense to import the crucial products during peacetime and store them for use in the event of war; these products do not require domestic production in order to be useful. Care must be taken to ensure that the national defense argument is not used to protect industries other than those that are truly crucial to the nation's defense.

> *Industries that are truly critical to the national defense should be protected from foreign competition if that is the only way to ensure their existence.*

1.e. Infant Industries

Nations are often inclined to protect new industries on the basis that the protection will give those industries adequate time to develop. New industries need time to establish themselves and to become efficient enough that their costs are no higher than those of their foreign rivals. An alternative to protecting young and/or critical domestic industries with tariffs and quotas is to subsidize them. Subsidies allow such firms to charge lower prices and to compete with more-efficient foreign producers, while permitting consumers to pay the world price rather than the higher prices associated with tariffs or quotas on foreign goods.

> *Countries sometimes justify protecting new industries that need time to become competitive with the rest of the world.*

Protecting an infant industry from foreign competition may make sense, but only until the industry matures. Once the industry achieves sufficient size, protection should be withdrawn, and the industry should be made to compete with its foreign counterparts. Unfortunately, such protection is rarely withdrawn, because the larger and more successful the industry becomes, the more political power it wields. In fact, if an infant industry truly has a good chance to become competitive and produce profitably once it is well established, it is not at all clear that government should even offer protection to reduce short-run losses. New firms typically incur losses, but they are only temporary if the firm is successful.

1.f. Strategic Trade Policy

There is another view of international trade that regards the description of comparative advantage presented in the previous chapter as misleading. According to this outlook, called **strategic trade policy**, international trade largely involves firms that pursue economies of scale—that is, firms that achieve lower costs per unit of production the more they produce. In contrast to the constant opportunity costs illustrated in the example of wheat and cloth in the chapter "World Trade Equilibrium," opportunity costs in some industries may fall with the level of output. Such **increasing-returns-to-scale industries** will tend to concentrate production in the hands of a few very large firms, rather than many competitive firms. Proponents of strategic trade policy contend that government can use tariffs or subsidies to give domestic firms with decreasing costs an advantage over their foreign rivals.

strategic trade policy: the use of trade restrictions or subsidies to allow domestic firms with decreasing costs to gain a greater share of the world market

increasing-returns-to-scale industry: an industry in which the costs of producing a unit of output fall as more output is produced

A monopoly exists when there is only one producer in an industry and no close substitutes for the product exist. If the average costs of production decline with increases in output, then the larger a firm is, the lower its per unit costs will be. One large producer will be more efficient than many small ones. A simple example of a natural-monopoly industry will indicate how strategic trade policy can make a country better off. Suppose that the production of buses is an industry characterized by increasing returns to scale and that there are only two firms capable of producing buses: Volkswagen in Germany and Ford in the United States. If both firms produce buses, their costs will be so high that both will experience losses. If only one of the two produces buses, however, it will be able to sell buses both at home and abroad, creating a level of output that allows the firm to earn a profit.

> *Government can use trade policy as a strategy to stimulate production by a domestic industry that is capable of achieving increasing returns to scale.*

Assume further that a monopoly producer will earn $100 million and that if both firms produce, they will each lose $5 million. Obviously, a firm that doesn't produce earns nothing. Which firm will produce? Because of the decreasing-cost nature of the industry, the firm that is the first to produce will realize lower costs and be able to prevent the other firm from entering the market. But strategic trade policy can alter the market in favor of the domestic firm.

Suppose Volkswagen is the world's only producer of buses. Ford does not produce them. The U.S. government could offer Ford an $8 million subsidy to produce buses. Ford would then enter the bus market, since the $8 million subsidy would more than offset the $5 million loss it would suffer by entering the market. Volkswagen would sustain losses of $5 million once Ford entered. Ultimately, Volkswagen would stop producing buses to avoid the loss, and Ford would have the entire market and earn $100 million plus the subsidy.

Strategic trade policy is aimed at offsetting the increasing-returns-to-scale advantage enjoyed by foreign producers and at stimulating production in domestic industries that are capable of realizing decreasing costs. One practical problem for government is the need to understand the technology of different industries and to forecast accurately the subsidy needed to induce domestic firms to produce new products. A second problem is the likelihood of retaliation by the foreign government. If the U.S. government subsidizes Ford in its attack on the bus market, the German government is likely to subsidize Volkswagen rather than lose the entire bus market to a U.S. producer. As a result, taxpayers in both nations will be subsidizing two firms, each producing too few buses to earn a profit.

RECAP

1. Government restrictions on foreign trade are usually aimed at protecting domestic producers from foreign competition.

2. Import restrictions may save domestic jobs, but the costs to consumers may be greater than the benefits to those who retain their jobs.

3. Advocates of "fair trade," or the creation of a "level playing field," call for import restrictions as a means of lowering foreign restrictions on markets for domestic exports.

4. Tariffs are an important source of revenue in many developing countries.

5. The national-defense argument in favor of trade restrictions is that protection from foreign competition is necessary to ensure that certain key defense-related industries continue to produce.

6. The infant-industries argument in favor of trade restriction is to allow a new industry a period of time in which to become competitive with its foreign counterparts.

7. Strategic trade policy is intended to provide domestic increasing-returns-to-scale industries with an advantage over their foreign competitors.

■ 2. Tools of Commercial Policy

2 | How do countries restrict the entry of foreign goods and promote the export of domestic goods?

Commercial policy makes use of several tools, including tariffs, quotas, subsidies, and nontariff barriers like health and safety regulations that restrict the entry of foreign products. Since 1945, barriers to trade have been reduced. Much of the progress toward free trade may be linked to the *General Agreement on Tariffs and Trade*, or *GATT*, which began in 1947. In 1995, the *World Trade Organization*

Global Business Insight

Smoot-Hawley Tariff

Many economists believe that the Great Depression of the 1930s was at least partly due to the Smoot-Hawley Tariff Act, signed into law by President Herbert Hoover in 1930. Hoover had promised that, if elected, he would increase tariffs on agricultural products to raise U.S. farm income. Congress began work on the tariff increases in 1928. Congressman Willis Hawley and Senator Reed Smoot conducted the hearings.

In testimony before Congress, manufacturers and other special interest groups also sought protection from foreign competition. The resulting bill increased tariffs on over 12,000 products. Tariffs reached their highest levels ever, about 60 percent of average import values. Only twice before in U.S. history had tariffs approached the levels of the Smoot-Hawley era.

Before President Hoover signed the bill, 38 foreign governments made formal protests, warning that they would retaliate with high tariffs on U.S. products. A petition signed by 1,028 economists warned of the harmful effects of the bill. Nevertheless, Hoover signed the bill into law.

World trade collapsed as other countries raised their tariffs in response. Between 1930 and 1931, U.S. imports fell 29 percent, but U.S. exports fell 33 percent. By 1933, world trade was about one-third of its 1929 level. As the level of trade fell, so did income and prices. In 1934, in an effort to correct the mistakes of Smoot-Hawley, Congress passed the Reciprocal Trade Agreements Act, which allowed the president to lower U.S. tariffs in return for reductions in foreign tariffs on U.S. goods. This act ushered in the modern era of relatively low tariffs. In the United States today, tariffs are about 5 percent of the average value of imports.

Many economists believe that the collapse of world trade and the Depression were linked by a decrease in real income caused by abandoning production based on comparative advantage. Few economists argue that the Great Depression was caused solely by the Smoot-Hawley tariff, but the experience serves as a lesson to those who support higher tariffs to protect domestic producers.

(WTO) was formed to incorporate the agreements under GATT into a formal permanent international organization to oversee world trade. The WTO has three objectives: to help global trade flow as freely as possible, to achieve reductions in trade restrictions gradually through negotiation, and to provide an impartial means of settling disputes. Nevertheless, restrictions on trade still exist, and this section will review the most commonly used restrictions.

2.a. Tariffs

tariff: a tax on imports or exports

A **tariff** is a tax on imports or exports. Every country imposes tariffs on at least some imports. Some countries also impose tariffs on selected exports as a means of raising government revenue. Brazil, for instance, taxes coffee exports. The United States does not employ export tariffs, which are forbidden by the U.S. Constitution.

Tariffs are frequently imposed in order to protect domestic producers from foreign competition. The dangers of imposing tariffs are well illustrated in the Global Business Insight "Smoot-Hawley Tariff." The effect of a tariff is illustrated in Figure 1, which shows the domestic market for oranges. Without international trade, the domestic equilibrium price, P_d, and the quantity demanded, Q_d, are determined by the intersection of the domestic demand and supply curves. If the world price of oranges, P_w, is lower than the domestic equilibrium price, this country will import oranges. The quantity imported will be the difference between the quantity Q_1 produced domestically at a price of P_w and the quantity Q_2 demanded domestically at the world price of oranges.

FIGURE 1   The Effects of a Tariff

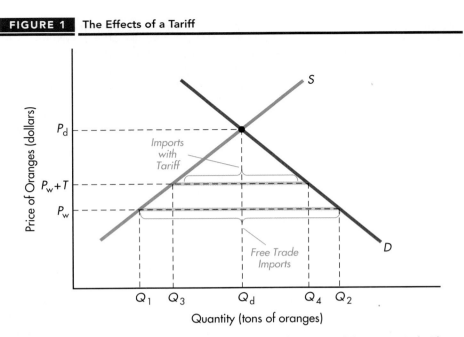

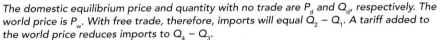

The domestic equilibrium price and quantity with no trade are P_d and $Q_{d'}$ respectively. The world price is P_w. With free trade, therefore, imports will equal $Q_2 - Q_1$. A tariff added to the world price reduces imports to $Q_4 - Q_3$.

When the world price of the traded good is lower than the domestic equilibrium price without international trade, free trade causes domestic production to fall and domestic consumption to rise. The domestic shortage at the world price is met by imports. Domestic consumers are better off, since they can buy more at a lower price. But domestic producers are worse off, since they now sell fewer oranges and receive a lower price.

Suppose a tariff of T (the dollar value of the tariff) is imposed on orange imports. The price paid by consumers is now $P_w + T$, rather than P_w. At this higher price, domestic producers will produce Q_3 and domestic consumers will purchase Q_4. The tariff has the effect of increasing domestic production and reducing domestic consumption, relative to the free trade equilibrium. Imports fall accordingly, from $Q_2 - Q_1$ to $Q_4 - Q_3$.

Domestic producers are better off, since the tariff has increased their sales of oranges and raised the price they receive. Domestic consumers pay higher prices for fewer oranges than they would with free trade, but they are still better off than they would be without trade. If the tariff had raised the price paid by consumers to P_d, there would be no trade, and the domestic equilibrium quantity, Q_d, would prevail.

The government earns revenue from imports of oranges. If each ton of oranges generates tariff revenue of T, the total tariff revenue to the government is found by multiplying the tariff by the quantity of oranges imported. In Figure 1, this amount is $T \times (Q_4 - Q_3)$. As the tariff changes, so do the quantity of imports and the government revenue.

2.b. Quotas

quantity quota: a limit on the amount of a good that may be imported

Quotas are limits on the quantity or value of goods imported and exported. A **quantity quota** restricts the physical amount of a good. For instance, for 2009, the United States allowed only 1.1 million tons of sugar to be imported. Even though the

value quota: a limit on the monetary value of a good that may be imported

United States is not a competitive sugar producer compared to other nations like the Dominican Republic or Cuba, the quota allowed U.S. firms to produce about 81 percent of the sugar consumed in the United States in 2005. A **value quota** restricts the monetary value of a good that may be traded. Instead of a physical quota on sugar, the United States could have limited the dollar value of sugar imports.

Quotas are used to protect domestic producers from foreign competition. By restricting the amount of a good that may be imported, they increase the price of that good and allow domestic producers to sell more at a higher price than they would with free trade. For example, one effect of the U.S. sugar quota is a higher sugar price for U.S. consumers. In May 2009, the world price of sugar was $0.1689 per pound, but the U.S. price was about 30 percent higher at $0.2164 per pound. Beyond the obvious effect on sugar production and consumption in the United States, there are spillover effects in related industries, such as candy manufacturing. The high price of sugar in the United States has resulted in candy manufacturers moving jobs to other countries, like Canada, where the price of sugar is about half the U.S. price. The lesson is that one must think about the total effects of trade restrictions on the economy when evaluating costs and benefits.

Figure 2 illustrates the effect of a quota on the domestic orange market. The domestic equilibrium supply and demand curves determine that the equilibrium price and quantity without trade are P_d and 250 tons, respectively. The world price of oranges is P_w. Since P_w lies below P_d, this country will import oranges. The quantity of imports is equal to the amount of the domestic shortage at P_w. The quantity demanded at P_w is 400 tons, and the quantity supplied domestically at P_w is 100 tons, so imports will equal 300 tons of oranges. With free trade, domestic producers sell 100 tons at a price of P_w.

But suppose domestic orange growers convince the government to restrict orange imports. The government then imposes a quota of 100 tons on imported oranges. The effect of the quota on consumers is to shift the supply curve to the

FIGURE 2 The Effects of a Quota

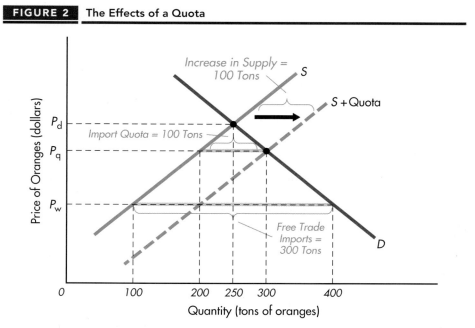

The domestic equilibrium price with no international trade is P_d. At this price, 250 tons of oranges would be produced and consumed at home. With free trade, the price is P_w, and 300 tons will be imported. An import quota of 100 tons will cause the price to be P_q, where the domestic shortage equals the 100 tons allowed by the quota.

right by the amount of the quota, 100 tons. Since the quota is less than the quantity of imports with free trade, the quantity of imports will equal the quota. The domestic equilibrium price with the quota occurs at the point where the domestic shortage equals the quota. At price P_q, the domestic quantity demanded (300 tons) is 100 tons more than the domestic quantity supplied (200 tons).

Quotas benefit domestic producers in the same way that tariffs do. Domestic producers receive a higher price (P_q instead of P_w) for a greater quantity (200 instead of 100) than they do under free trade. The effect on domestic consumers is also similar to that of a tariff: They pay a higher price for a smaller quantity than they would with free trade. A tariff generates government tax revenue; a quota does not (unless the government auctions off the right to import under the quota). Furthermore, a tariff raises the price of the product only in the domestic market. Foreign producers receive the world price, P_w. With a quota, both domestic and foreign producers receive the higher price, P_q, for the goods sold in the domestic market. So foreign producers are hurt by the reduction in the quantity of imports permitted, but they receive a higher price for the amount that they do sell.

2.c. Other Barriers to Trade

Tariffs and quotas are not the only barriers to the free flow of goods across international borders. There are three additional sources of restrictions on free trade: subsidies, government procurement, and health and safety standards. Though these practices are often entered into for reasons other than protection from foreign competition, a careful analysis reveals their import-reducing effect.

Before discussing these three types of barriers, let us note the cultural or institutional barriers to trade that also exist in many countries. Such barriers may exist independently of any conscious government policy. For instance, Japan has frequently been criticized by U.S. officials for informal business practices that discriminate against foreigners. Under the Japanese distribution system, goods typically pass through several layers of middlemen before appearing in a retail store. A foreign firm faces the difficult task of gaining entry to this system to supply goods to the retailer. Furthermore, a foreigner cannot easily open a retail store. Japanese law requires a new retail firm to receive permission from other retailers in the area in order to open a business. A firm that lacks contacts and knowledge of the system cannot penetrate the Japanese market.

The economic stimulus bill that the U.S. Congress passed in February 2009 included a "buy American" provision requiring that any steel or manufactured goods bought with federal government funds must be made in the United States. Many U.S. trade partners expressed concerns over the protectionist aspects of this policy. Such inward-looking policies in response to the financial crisis were not confined just to the United States. The level of international trade fell during the crisis and there was a fear that if many countries tried to stimulate their domestic economies at the expense of other nations, trade would not recover once the crisis passed.

export subsidies:
payments made by a government to domestic firms to encourage exports

2.c.1. Export Subsidies   **Export subsidies** are payments by a government to an exporter. These subsidies are paid in order to stimulate exports by allowing the exporter to charge a lower price. The amount of a subsidy is determined by the international price of a product relative to the domestic price in the absence of trade. Domestic consumers are harmed by subsidies in that their taxes finance the subsidies. Also, since the subsidy diverts resources from the domestic market toward export production, the increase in the supply of export goods could be associated with a decrease in the supply of domestic goods, causing domestic prices to rise.

Subsidies may take forms other than direct cash payments. These include tax reductions, low-interest loans, low-cost insurance, government-sponsored research funding, and other devices. The U.S. government subsidizes export activity through the U.S. Export-Import Bank, which provides loans and insurance to help U.S. exporters sell their goods to foreign buyers. Subsidies are more common in Europe than in Japan or the United States.

2.c.2. Government Procurement

Governments are often required by law to buy only from local producers. In the United States, a "buy American" act passed in 1933 required U.S. government agencies to buy U.S. goods and services unless the domestic price was more than 12 percent above the foreign price. This kind of policy allows domestic firms to charge the government a higher price for their products than they charge consumers; the taxpayers bear the burden. The United States is by no means alone in the use of such policies. Many other nations also use such policies to create larger markets for domestic goods. The World Trade Organization has a standing committee working to reduce discrimination against foreign producers and open government procurement practices to global competition.

2.c.3. Health and Safety Standards

Government serves as a guardian of the public health and welfare by requiring that products offered to the public be safe and fulfill the use for which they are intended. Government standards for products sold in the domestic marketplace can have the effect (intentional or not) of protecting domestic producers from foreign competition. These effects should be considered in evaluating the full impact of such standards.

As mentioned in the Preview, the government of Japan once threatened to prohibit foreign-made snow skis from entering the country for reasons of safety. Only Japanese-made skis were determined to be suitable for Japanese snow. The government of Japan certifies auto parts that are safe for use by repair shops. U.S.-manufactured parts are not certified for use, so U.S. parts manufacturers are excluded from the Japanese market. Several western European nations once announced that U.S. beef would not be allowed into Europe because the U.S. government had approved the feeding of hormones to U.S. beef cattle. In the late 1960s, France required tractors sold there to have a maximum speed of 17 miles per hour; in Germany, the permissible speed was 13 miles per hour, and in the Netherlands, it was 10 miles per hour. Tractors produced in one country had to be modified to meet the requirements of the other countries. Such modifications raise the price of goods and discourage international trade.

Product standards may not eliminate foreign competition, but standards different from those of the rest of the world do provide an element of protection to domestic firms.

RECAP

1. The World Trade Organization works to achieve reductions in trade barriers.

2. A tariff is a tax on imports or exports. Tariffs protect domestic firms by raising the prices of foreign goods.

3. Quotas are government-imposed limits on the quantity or value of an imported good. Quotas protect domestic firms by restricting the entry of foreign products to a level less than the quantity demanded.

4. Subsidies are payments by the government to domestic producers. Subsidies lower the price of domestic goods to foreign buyers.

5. Governments are often required by law to buy only domestic products.

6. Health and safety standards can also be used to protect domestic firms.

■ 3. Preferential Trade Agreements

In an effort to stimulate international trade, groups of countries sometimes enter into agreements to abolish most barriers to trade among themselves. Such arrangements between countries are known as preferential trading agreements. The European Union and the North American Free Trade Agreement (NAFTA) are examples of preferential trading agreements.

3.a. Free Trade Areas and Customs Unions

3 | What sorts of agreements do countries enter into to reduce barriers to international trade?

free trade area: an organization of nations whose members have no trade barriers among themselves but are free to fashion their own trade policies toward nonmembers

customs union: an organization of nations whose members have no trade barriers among themselves but impose common trade barriers on nonmembers

Two common forms of preferential trade agreements are **free trade areas** (FTAs) and **customs unions** (CUs). These two approaches differ with regard to the treatment of countries outside the agreement. In an FTA, member countries eliminate trade barriers among themselves, but each member country chooses its own trade policies toward nonmember countries. Members of a CU agree to both eliminate trade barriers among themselves and maintain common trade barriers against nonmembers.

The best-known CU is the European Union (EU), formerly known as the European Community and still earlier as the European Economic Community (EEC), created in 1957 by France, West Germany, Italy, Belgium, the Netherlands, and Luxembourg. The United Kingdom, Ireland, and Denmark joined in 1973, followed by Greece in 1981 and Spain and Portugal in 1986. In 1992 the EEC was replaced by the EU with an agreement to create a single market for goods and services in western Europe. On May 1, 2004, ten new members were admitted to the EU: Cyprus, Czech Republic, Estonia, Hungary, Latvia, Lithuania, Malta, Poland, Slovakia, and Slovenia. In 2007, Bulgaria and Romania were admitted to the EU. Turkey is negotiating to be included in future enlargements of the EU. In addition to free trade in goods, European financial markets and institutions will eventually be able to operate across national boundaries. For instance, a bank in any EU country will be permitted to operate in any or all other EU countries.

In 1989, the United States and Canada negotiated a free trade area. The United States, Canada, and Mexico negotiated a free trade area in 1992 that became effective on January 1, 1994. The North American Free Trade Agreement (NAFTA) lowered tariffs on 8,000 different items and opened each nation's financial market to competition from institutions in the other two nations. NAFTA does not eliminate all barriers to trade among the three nations, but it is a significant step in that direction.

The North American Free Trade Agreement stimulates trade among Mexico, Canada, and the United States. The act results in more container ships from Mexico unloading their cargo at U.S. docks. Similarly, freight from Canada and the United States will increase in volume at Mexican ports.

© Javier Fontanella/iStockphoto

3.b. Trade Creation and Diversion

Free trade agreements provide for free trade among a group of countries, not worldwide. As a result, a customs union or free trade area may make a nation better off or worse off compared to the free trade equilibrium.

Figure 3 illustrates the effect of a free trade area. With no international trade, the U.S. supply and demand curves for oranges would result in an equilibrium price of $500 per ton and an equilibrium quantity of 425 tons. Suppose there are two other orange-producing countries, Israel and Brazil. Israel, the low-cost producer of oranges, is willing to sell all the oranges the United States can buy for $150 per ton, as represented by the horizontal supply curve S_I. Brazil will supply oranges for a price of $200 per ton, as represented by the horizontal supply curve S_B.

With free trade, the United States would import oranges from Israel. The quantity demanded at $150 is 750 tons, and the domestic quantity supplied at this price is 100 tons. The shortage of 650 tons is met by imports from Israel.

Now suppose a 100 percent tariff is imposed on orange imports. The price that domestic consumers pay for foreign oranges is twice as high as before. For oranges from Israel, the new price is $300, twice the old price of $150. The new supply curve for Israel is represented as S_I + Tariff. Oranges from Brazil now sell for $400, twice the old price of $200; the new supply curve for Brazil is shown as S_B + Tariff. After the 100 percent tariff is imposed, oranges are still imported from Israel. But at the new price of $300, the domestic quantity demanded is 600 tons, and the domestic quantity supplied is 250 tons. Thus, only 350 tons will be imported. The tariff reduces the volume of trade relative to the free trade equilibrium, at which 650 tons were imported.

Now suppose that the United States negotiates a free trade agreement with Brazil, eliminating tariffs on imports from Brazil. Israel is not a member of

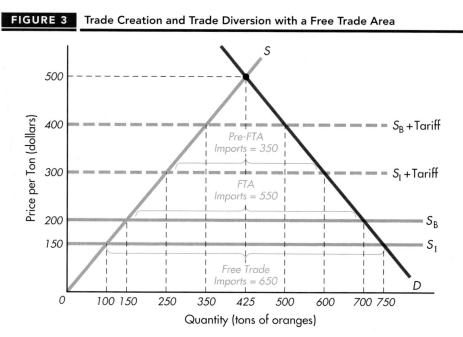

| FIGURE 3 | Trade Creation and Trade Diversion with a Free Trade Area |

With no trade, the domestic equilibrium price is $500, and the equilibrium quantity is 425 tons. With free trade, the price is $150, and 650 tons would be imported, as indicated by the supply curve for Israel, S_I. A 100 percent tariff on imports would result in imports of 350 tons from Israel, according to the supply curve S_I + Tariff. A free trade agreement that eliminates tariffs on Brazilian oranges only would result in a new equilibrium price of $200 and imports of 550 tons from Brazil, according to supply curve S_B.

the free trade agreement, so imports from Israel are still covered by the 100 percent tariff. The relevant supply curve for Brazil is now S_B, so oranges may be imported from Brazil for $200, a lower price than Israel's price including the tariff. At a price of $200, the domestic quantity demanded is 700 tons and the domestic quantity supplied is 150 tons; 550 tons will be imported.

trade diversion: an effect of a preferential trade agreement that reduces economic efficiency by shifting production to a higher cost producer

The effects of the free trade agreement are twofold. First, trade is diverted away from the lowest-cost producer, Israel, to the FTA partner, Brazil. This **trade-diversion** effect of an FTA reduces worldwide economic efficiency, since production is diverted from the country with the comparative advantage. Oranges are not being produced as efficiently as possible. The other effect of the FTA is that the quantity of imports increases relative to the effect of a tariff applicable to all imports. Imports rise from 350 tons (the quantity imported from Israel with the tariff) to 550 tons. The FTA thus has a **trade-creation** effect as a result of the lower price that is available after the tariff reduction. Trade creation is a beneficial aspect of the FTA: The expansion of international trade allows this country to realize greater benefits from trade than would be possible without trade.

trade creation: an effect of a preferential trade agreement that allows a country to obtain goods at a lower cost than is available at home

Countries form preferential trade agreements because they believe that FTAs will make each member country better off. The member countries view the trade creation effects of such agreements as benefiting their exporters by increasing exports to other member countries and as benefiting consumers by making a wider variety of goods available at a lower price. From the point of view of the world as a whole, preferential trade agreements are more desirable the more they stimulate trade creation to allow the benefits of trade to be realized and the less they emphasize trade diversion, so that production occurs on the basis of comparative advantage. This principle suggests that the most successful FTAs or CUs are those that increase trade volume but do not change the patterns of trade in terms of who specializes and exports each good. In the case of Figure 3, a more successful FTA would reduce tariffs on Israeli as well as Brazilian oranges, so that oranges would be imported from the lowest-cost producer, Israel.

RECAP

1. Countries form preferential trade agreements in order to stimulate trade among themselves.

2. The most common forms of preferential trade agreement are free trade areas (FTAs) and customs unions (CUs).

3. Preferential trade agreements have a harmful trade-diversion effect when they cause production to shift from the nation with a comparative advantage to a higher-cost producer.

4. Preferential trade agreements have a beneficial trade-creation effect when they reduce prices for traded goods and stimulate the volume of international trade.

SUMMARY

1 | Why do countries restrict international trade?

- Commercial policy is government policy that influences the direction and volume of international trade. *Preview*

- Protecting domestic producers from foreign competition usually imposes costs on domestic consumers. *§1*

- Rationales for commercial policy include saving domestic jobs, creating a fair-trade relationship with other countries, raising tariff revenue, ensuring a

domestic supply of key defense goods, allowing new industries a chance to become internationally competitive, and giving domestic industries with increasing returns to scale an advantage over foreign competitors. *§1.a–1.f*

2 | How do countries restrict the entry of foreign goods and promote the export of domestic goods?

- Tariffs protect domestic industry by increasing the price of foreign goods. *§2.a*

- Quotas protect domestic industry by limiting the quantity of foreign goods allowed into the country. *§2.b*
- Subsidies allow relatively inefficient domestic producers to compete with foreign firms. *§2.c.1*
- Government procurement practices and health and safety regulations can protect domestic industry from foreign competition. *§2.c.2, 2.c.3*

3 | **What sorts of agreements do countries enter into to reduce barriers to international trade?**

- Free trade areas and customs unions are two types of preferential trade agreements that reduce trade restrictions among member countries. *§3.a*
- Preferential trade agreements have harmful trade-diversion effects and beneficial trade-creation effects. *§3.b*

Key Terms

commercial policy *Preview*

strategic trade policy *§1.f*

increasing-returns-to-scale industry *§1.f*

tariff *§2.a*

quantity quota *§2.b*

value quota *§2.b*

export subsidies *§2.c.1*

free trade area *§3.a*

customs union *§3.a*

trade diversion *§3.b*

trade creation *§3.b*

Exercises

1. What are the potential benefits and costs of a commercial policy designed to pursue each of the following goals?
   a. Save domestic jobs
   b. Create a level playing field
   c. Increase government revenue
   d. Provide a strong national defense
   e. Protect an infant industry
   f. Stimulate exports of an industry with increasing returns to scale

2. For each of the goals listed in exercise 1, discuss what the appropriate commercial policy is likely to be (in terms of tariffs, quotas, subsidies, etc.).

3. Tariffs and quotas both raise the price of foreign goods to domestic consumers. What is the difference between the effects of a tariff and the effects of a quota on the following?
   a. The domestic government
   b. Foreign producers
   c. Domestic producers

4. Would trade-diversion and trade-creation effects occur if the whole world became a free trade area? Explain.

5. What is the difference between a customs union and a free trade area?

6. Draw a graph of the U.S. automobile market in which the domestic equilibrium price without trade is P_d and the equilibrium quantity is Q_d. Use this graph to illustrate and explain the effects of a tariff

if the United States were an auto importer with free trade. Then use the graph to illustrate and explain the effects of a quota.

7. If commercial policy can benefit U.S. industry, why would any U.S. resident oppose such policies?

8. Suppose you were asked to assess U.S. commercial policy to determine whether the benefits of protection for U.S. industries are worth the costs. Do Tables 1 and 2 provide all the information you need? If not, what else would you want to know?

9. How would the effects of international trade on the domestic orange market change if the world price of oranges were above the domestic equilibrium price? Draw a graph to help explain your answer.

10. Suppose the world price of kiwi fruit is $20 per case and the U.S. equilibrium price with no international trade is $35 per case. If the U.S. government had previously banned the import of kiwi fruit but then imposed a tariff of $5 per case and allowed kiwi imports, what would happen to the equilibrium price and quantity of kiwi fruit consumed in the United States?

11. Think of an industry in your country (if you currently have a job, use that industry). What kind of nontariff barrier could you design that would keep out foreign competitors to the domestic industry? This should be something like a health or safety standard or some other criterion that a government could use as an excuse to protect the domestic industry from foreign competition.

You can find further practice tests in the Online Quiz at www.cengage.com/economics/boyes.

Trade Group Calls for Reform to U.S. Sugar Policy

By Lorraine Heller, http://www.foodnavigator-usa.com

A sweetener industry body claims the current U.S. sugar policy is harming the nation's food and beverage industry by driving prices up and sending production overseas.

The Sweetener Users Association (SUA) last week urged members of Congress to take note of a Georgia State Senate resolution designed to encourage reform of sugar policy.

"The current system of government production controls is hurting taxpayers, consumers, and workers by distorting prices and reducing employment in the food and beverage industry. It is time for fundamental reform," said Tom Earley, an economist with Promar International who has studied the impact of the sugar program.

According to SUA, which supports manufacturers that use sweeteners, the Commerce Department last year published a study that cited the sugar program as a factor behind job losses in the food industry, especially in confectionery.

"Georgia's state senators agree with the Department of Commerce that the current sugar program is sending tens of thousands of good jobs in the food industry overseas.

We need to reform the program so we can keep those jobs in this country," the SUA quoted Earley as saying last week.

Each year, the government estimates sugar consumption and subtracts from that the amount of foreign sugar the U.S. is forced to import, while American sugar farmers supply the remainder.

According to the American Sugar Alliance, a coalition of sugar farmers and processors, this structure avoids oversupplies and shortages, resulting in sugar prices remaining stable. Consequently, this eliminates the need for government payments to farmers, said ASA.

But SUA claims that by imposing government-regulated price floors, marketing quotas, and import restrictions, domestic sugar prices are increased. This results in more and more food companies sending their production overseas where sugar is cheaper, said the group, adding that this will eventually hurt domestic producers by undermining long-term demand for their product.

SUA said the current structure of the sugar program is "increasingly incompatible" with the nation's foreign trade obligations and the changing realities of the global marketplace.

"As trade agreements like NAFTA lower trade barriers and sugar imports increase, the government will be forced to purchase more and more of the domestic supply, costing American taxpayers at least $1.3 billion over the next ten years," it said.

The SUA's announcement follows a resolution passed by Georgia's Senate urging the state's congressional delegation to work for reform of sugar policy.

The Senate had called for "the type of reasonable reform to U.S. sugar policy that will in turn stabilize our foreign trade and domestic economic policies."

Lorraine Heller

Source: foodnavigator-usa.com, 26-Mar-2007

Article online at http://www.foodproductiondaily.com/news/ng.asp?n=77360-soil-association-air-freight-food-miles

This article shows how domestic firms may seek protection from international competition even though domestic consumers and other domestic producers will be harmed by the action. In this case, the U.S. sugar quotas on imports result in a higher price for sugar in the United States than in the rest of the world. Not only do U.S. consumers pay a higher price for sugar, but U.S. producers who use sugar as an input into their products are also hurt as they must pay higher costs for sugar than their competitors in other nations. One response is for these producers to relocate their production out of the United States into other countries where sugar is cheaper than in the United States. This is not a unique situation; it is a familiar story worldwide as firms that are threatened with foreign competition seek government protection from that competition. The protectionist measure of imposing quotas or tariffs on imports saves jobs in the domestic import-competing industries, but at a great cost to consumers and, sometimes, to other producers.

The effect of reducing domestic competition with quotas can be understood using supply and demand analysis. Let's analyze the case of quotas on textile imports into the United States. In the diagram, S_1 is the domestic supply of textiles, S_2 is the sum of the domestic supply and the foreign supply allowed in by the quotas, and D is the demand for textiles. Under the quota system, the price of textiles in the United States is represented by P_q, and the quantity of textiles consumed is Q_q. If the quotas were removed, the price of textiles in the United States would equal the world price of P_w, and this lower price would be associated with an increase in the consumption of textiles to Q_w. The quota represents a cost to society in terms of both a loss of consumer welfare and a loss from the inefficient use of resources in an industry in which this country has no comparative advantage, just as Maine has no comparative advantage in the production of pineapples.

Given the costs to society of these quotas, why is there such strong support for them in Congress? An important political aspect of protectionist policies is that their benefits are concentrated among a relatively small number of people—in the case of the article, sugar beet and sugar cane growers—while their costs are diffused and spread across all consumers. Each individual import-competing producer faces very large losses from free trade, whereas the cost of a protectionist policy for each consumer is less dramatic. It is also easier to organize a relatively small number of manufacturers than to mobilize a vast population of consumers. These factors explain the strong lobby for the protection of industries like textiles and the absence of a legislative lobby that operates specifically in the interest of textile consumers.

Industrial arguments for trade protection should be seen for what they are: an attempt by an industry to increase its profits at the expense of the general public.

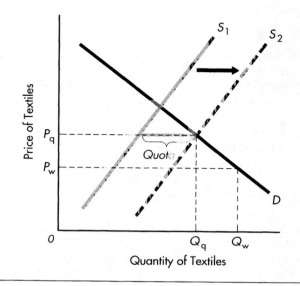

457

absolute advantage an advantage derived from one country having a lower absolute input cost of producing a particular good than another country (426)

adaptive expectation an expectation formed on the basis of information collected in the past (327)

aggregate demand curve a curve that shows the different equilibrium levels of expenditures on domestic output at different levels of prices (167)

aggregate supply curve a curve that shows the amount of real GDP produced at different price levels (171)

appreciate when the value of a currency increases under floating exchange rate, that is, exchange rates determined by supply and demand (467)

Asian tigers Hong Kong, Korea, Singapore, and Taiwan, countries that globalized in the 1960s and 1970s and experienced fast economic growth (407)

association as causation the mistaken assumption that because two events seem to occur together, one causes the other (7)

automatic stabilizer an element of fiscal policy that changes automatically as income changes (249)

autonomous consumption consumption that is independent of income (190)

average propensity to consume (*APC*) the proportion of disposable income spent for consumption (192)

average propensity to save (*APS*) the proportion of disposable income saved (192)

balance of payments a record of a country's trade in goods, services, and financial assets with the rest of the world (124)

balance of trade the balance in the merchandise account in a nation's balance of payments (125)

barter the direct exchange of goods and services without the use of money (47)

base year the year against which other years are measured (110)

bilateral aid foreign aid that flows from one country to another (393)

budget deficit the shortage that results when government spending is greater than tax revenue (90)

budget surplus the excess that results when government spending is less than tax revenue (90)

business cycles fluctuations in the economy between growth (expressed in rising real GDP) and stagnation (expressed in falling real GDP) (133)

business firm a business organization controlled by a single management (81)

capital products such as machinery and equipment that are used in production (5)

capital consumption allowance the estimated value of depreciation plus the value of accidental damage to capital stock (105)

circular flow diagram a model showing the flow of output and income from one sector of the economy to another (91)

classical economics a school of thought that assumes that real GDP is determined by aggregate supply, while the equilibrium price level is determined by aggregate demand (350)

coincident indicator a variable that changes at the same time as real output changes (136)

commercial bank loan a bank loan at market rates of interest, often involving a bank syndicate (391)

commercial policy government policy that influences international trade flows (441)

comparative advantage the ability to produce a good or service at a lower opportunity cost than someone else (426)

complementary goods goods that are used together; as the price of one rises, the demand for the other falls (54)

composite currency an artificial unit of account that is an average of the values of several national currencies (271)

consumer price index (*CPI*) a measure of the average price of goods and services purchased by the typical household (112)

consumer sovereignty the authority of consumers to determine what is produced through their purchases of goods and services (76)

consumption household spending (80)

consumption function the relationship between disposable income and consumption (187)

corporation a legal entity owned by shareholders whose liability for the firm's losses is limited to the value of the stock they own (81)

cost-of-living adjustment (COLA) an increase in wages that is designed to match increases in the prices of items purchased by the typical household (112)

cost-push inflation inflation caused by rising costs of production (161)

credit available savings that are lent to borrowers to spend (267)

crowding out a drop in consumption or investment spending caused by government spending (247)

currency substitution the use of foreign money as a substitute for domestic money when the domestic economy has a high rate of inflation (267)

current account the sum of the merchandise, services, income, and unilateral transfers accounts in the balance of payments (125)

customs union an organization of nations whose members have no trade barriers among themselves but impose common trade barriers on nonmembers (452)

deficit in a balance of payments account, the amount by which debits exceed credits (125)

demand the amount of a product that people are willing and able to purchase at each possible price during a given period of time, everything else held constant (47)

demand curve a graph of a demand schedule that measures price on the vertical axis and quantity demanded on the horizontal axis (49)

demand-pull inflation inflation caused by increasing demand for output (161)

demand schedule a table or list of prices and the corresponding quantities demanded for a particular good or service (49)

dependent variable a variable whose value depends on the value of the independent variable (16)

deposit expansion multiplier the reciprocal of the reserve requirement (281)

depreciate when the value of a currency decreases under floating exchange rates (467)

depreciation a reduction in the value of capital goods over time as a result of their use in production (105)

depression a severe, prolonged economic contraction (135)

determinants of demand factors other than the price of the good that influence demand-income, tastes, prices of related goods and services, expectations, and number of buyers (48)

determinants of supply factors other than the price of the good that influence supply-prices of resources, technology and productivity, expectations of producers, number of producers, and the prices of related goods and services (55)

devaluation a deliberate decrease in the official value of a currency (461)

direct, or **positive, relationship** the relationship that exists when the values of related variables move in the same direction (16)

discount rate the interest rate that the Fed charges commercial banks when they borrow from it (300)

discouraged workers workers who have stopped looking for work because they believe that no one will offer them a job (138)

discretionary fiscal policy changes in government spending and taxation that are aimed at achieving a policy goal (249)

disequilibrium prices at which quantity demanded and quantity supplied are not equal at a particular price (62)

ˋsposable personal income (*DPI*) personal income minus ˋrsonal taxes (107)

ˌng spending financed by borrowing or using savings (190)

double coincidence of wants the situation that exists when A has what B wants and B has what A wants (47)

double-entry bookkeeping a system of accounting in which every transaction is recorded in at least two accounts (124)

dual economy an economy in which two sectors (typically manufacturing and agriculture) show very different levels of development (390)

economic bad any item for which we would pay to have less (4)

economic good any item that is scarce (4)

economic growth an increase in real GDP (359)

equation of exchange an equation that relates the quantity of money to nominal GDP (294)

equilibrium the price and quantity at which quantity demanded and quantity supplied are equal (61)

equilibrium exchange rates the exchange rates that are established in the absence of government foreign exchange market intervention (461)

Eurocurrency market or **offshore banking** the market for deposits and loans generally denominated in a currency other than the currency of the country in which the transaction occurs (276)

European currency unit (*ECU*) a unit of account formerly used by western European nations as their official reserve asset (271)

excess reserves the cash reserves beyond those required, which can be loaned (280)

exchange rate the price of one country's money in terms of another country's money (120)

export subsidies payments made by a government to domestic firms to encourage exports (450)

export substitution the use of resources to produce manufactured products for export rather than agricultural products for the domestic market (389)

export supply curve a curve showing the relationship between the world price of a good and the amount that a country will export (429)

exports products that a country sells to other countries (84)

expropriation the government seizure of assets, typically without adequate compensation to the owners (383)

fallacy of composition the mistaken assumption that what applies in the case of one applies to the case of many (7)

Federal Deposit Insurance Corporation (*FDIC*) a federal agency that insures deposits in commercial banks (274)

federal funds rate the interest rate that a bank charges when it lends excess reserves to another bank (297)

Federal Open Market Committee (FOMC) the official policymaking body of the Federal Reserve System (290)

financial account the record in the balance of payments of the flow of financial assets into and out of a country (126)

financial intermediaries institutions that accept deposits from savers and make loans to borrowers (91)

FOMC directive instructions issued by the FOMC to the Federal Reserve Bank of New York to implement monetary policy (297)

foreign aid gifts or low-cost loans made to developing countries from official sources (393)

foreign direct investment the purchase of a physical operating unit or more than 10 percent ownership of a firm in a foreign country (391)

foreign exchange currency and bank deposits that are denominated in foreign money (119)

foreign exchange market a global market in which people trade one currency for another (119)

foreign exchange market intervention the buying and selling of currencies by a central bank to achieve a specified exchange rate (303, 460)

fractional reserve banking system a system in which banks keep less than 100 percent of their deposits available for withdrawal (279)

free good a good for which there is no scarcity (4)

free trade area an organization of nations whose members have no trade barriers among themselves but are free to fashion their own trade policies toward nonmembers (452)

fundamental disequilibrium a permanent shift in the foreign exchange market supply and demand curves such that the fixed exchange rate is no longer an equilibrium rate (468)

gains from trade the difference between what can be produced and consumed without specialization and trade and with specialization and trade (30)

GDP price index (*GDPPI*) a broad measure of the prices of goods and services included in the gross domestic product (112)

gold exchange standard an exchange-rate system in which each nation fixes the value of its currency in terms of gold, but buys and sells the U.S. dollar rather than gold to maintain fixed exchange rates (460)

gold standard a system whereby national currencies are fixed in terms of their value in gold, thus creating fixed exchange rates between currencies (459)

gross domestic product (GDP) the market value of all final goods and services produced in a year within a country (100)

gross investment total investment, including investment expenditures required to replace capital goods consumed in current production (106)

gross national product (*GNP*) gross domestic product plus receipts of factor income from the rest of the world minus payments of factor income to the rest of the world (105)

hawala an international informal financial market used by Muslims (278)

household one or more persons who occupy a unit of housing (80)

hyperinflation an extremely high rate of inflation (151)

import demand curve a curve showing the relationship between the world price of a good and the amount that a country will import (429)

import substitution the substitution of domestically produced manufactured goods for imported manufactured goods (388)

imports products that a country buys from other countries (84)

increasing-returns-to-scale industry an industry in which the costs of producing a unit of output fall as more output is produced (445)

independent variable a variable whose value does not depend on the values of other variables (16)

indirect business tax a tax that is collected by businesses for a government agency (105)

inferior goods goods for which the income elasticity of demand is negative (427)

inflation a sustained rise in the average level of prices (146)

interest rate effect a change in interest rates that causes investment and therefore aggregate expenditures to change as the level of prices changes (166)

interest rate parity (*IRP*) the condition under which similar financial assets have the same interest rate when measured in the same currency (473)

intermediate good a good that is used as an input in the production of final goods and services (100)

intermediate target an objective used to achieve some ultimate policy goal (293)

international banking facility (IBF) a division of a U.S. bank that is allowed to receive deposits from and make loans to nonresidents of the United States without the restrictions that apply to domestic U.S. banks (277)

International Monetary Fund (IMF) an international organization that supervises exchange-rate arrangements and lends money to member countries that are experiencing problems meeting their external financial obligations (460)

international reserve asset an asset used to settle debts between governments (271)

international reserve currency a currency held by a government to settle international debts (271)

international trade effect a change in aggregate expenditures resulting from a change in the domestic price level that changes the price of domestic goods relative to that of foreign goods (166)

intraindustry trade the simultaneous import and export of goods in the same industry by a particular country (434)

inverse, or negative, relationship the relationship that exists when the values of related variables move in opposite directions (16)

inventory the stock of unsold goods held by a firm (102)

investment spending on capital goods to be used in producing goods and services (81)

Keynesian economics a school of thought that emphasizes the role government plays in stabilizing the economy by managing aggregate demand (346)

labor the physical and intellectual services of people, including the training, education, and abilities of the individuals in a society (5)

lagging indicator a variable that changes after real output changes (137)

land all natural resources, such as minerals, timber, and water, as well as the land itself (5)

law of demand the quantity of a well-defined good or service that people are willing and able to purchase during a particular period of time decreases as the price of that good or service rises and increases as the price falls, everything else held constant (48)

law of supply the quantity of a well-defined good or service that producers are willing and able to offer for sale during a particular period of time increases as the price of the good or service increases and decreases as the price decreases, everything else held constant (55)

leading indicator a variable that changes before real output changes (136)

legal reserves the cash a bank holds in its vault plus its deposit in the Fed (298)

liquid asset an asset that can easily be exchanged for goods and services (266)

long-run aggregate supply curve (*LRAS*) a vertical line at the potential level of real GDP (173)

M1 money supply the financial assets that are the most liquid (268)

M2 money supply M1 plus less liquid assets (269)

macroeconomics the study of the economy as a whole (8)

marginal cost or **marginal opportunity cost** the amount of one good or service that must be given up to obtain one additional unit of another good or service, no matter how many units are being produced (29)

marginal propensity to consume (*MPC*) the change in consumption as a proportion of the change in disposable income (190)

marginal propensity to import (MPI) the change in imports as a proportion of the change in income (205)

marginal propensity to save (MPS) the change in saving as a proportion of the change in disposable income (190)

market a place or service that enables buyers and sellers to exchange goods and services (41)

microeconomics the study of economics at the level of the individual (8)

monetarist economics a school of thought that emphasizes the role changes in the money supply play in determining equilibrium real GDP and price level (347)

monetary reform a new monetary policy that includes the induction of a new monetary unit (338)

money anything that is generally acceptable to sellers in exchange for goods and services (266)

multilateral aid aid provided by international organizations that are supported by many nations (394)

multinational business a firm that owns and operates producing units in foreign countries (81)

national income (*NI*) net national product plus or minus statistical discrepancy (107)

national income accounting the framework that summarizes and categorizes productive activity in an economy over a specific period of time, typically a year (98)

natural rate of unemployment the unemployment rate that would exist in the absence of cyclical unemployment (140)

net exports the difference between the value of exports and the value of imports (85)

net investment gross investment minus capital consumption allowance (107)

net national product (*NNP*) gross national product minus capital consumption allowance (106)

new classical economics a school of thought that holds that changes in real GDP are a product of unexpected changes in the level of prices (351)

NICs newly industrialized countries (407)

nominal GDP a measure of national output based on the current prices of goods and services (108)

nominal interest rate the observed interest rate in the market (148)

normal goods goods for which demand increases as income increases (52); goods for which the income elasticity of demand is positive (427)

normative analysis analysis of what ought to be (7)

open market operations the buying and selling of government bonds by the Fed to control bank reserves, the federal funds rate, and the money supply (300)

opportunity costs the highest-valued alternative that must be forgone when a choice is made (25)

partnership a business with two or more owners who share the firm's profits and losses (81)

per capita real GDP real GDP divided by the population (360)

personal income (*PI*) national income plus income currently received but not earned, minus income currently earned but not received (107)

Phillips curve a graph that illustrates the relationship between inflation and the unemployment rate (317)

portfolio investment the purchase of securities (391)

positive analysis analysis of what is (6)

potential real GDP the output produced at the natural rate of unemployment (140)

precautionary demand for money the demand for money to cover unplanned transactions or emergencies (306)

price ceiling a situation in which the price is not allowed to rise above a certain level (65)

price floor a situation in which the price is not allowed to decrease below a certain level (65)

price index a measure of the average price level in an economy (110)

primary product a product in the first stage of production, which often serves as an input in the production of another product (388)

private property rights the rights of ownership (33, 269)

private sector households, businesses, and the international sector (80)

producer price index (*PPI*) a measure of average prices received by producers (112)

producer surplus the difference between the price firms would have been willing to accept for their products and the price they actually receive (112)

production possibilities curve (PPC) a graphical representation showing all possible combinations of quantities of goods and services that can be produced using the existing resources fully and efficiently (25)

productivity the quantity of output produced per unit of resource (58)

progressive tax a tax whose rate rises as income rises (254)

public sector the government (80)

purchasing power parity (PPP) the condition under which monies have the same purchasing power in different markets (471)

quantitative easing buying financial assets to stimulate the economy when the central bank target interest rate is near or at zero and the interest rate cannot be lowered further (302)

quantity demanded the amount of a product that people are willing and able to purchase at a specific price (47)

quantity quota a limit on the amount of a good that may be imported (448)

quantity supplied the amount that sellers are willing and able to offer at a given price during a particular period of time, everything else held constant (55)

quantity theory of money the theory that with constant velocity, changes in the quantity of money change nominal GDP (294)

"race to the bottom" the argument that with globalization, countries compete for international investment by offering low or no environmental regulations or labor standards (402)

rational expectation an expectation that is formed using all available relevant information (328)

rational self-interest the means by which people choose the options that give them the greatest amount of satisfaction (5)

real GDP a measure of the quantity of final goods and services produced, obtained by eliminating the influence of price changes from the nominal GDP statistics (108)

real interest rate the nominal interest rate minus the rate of inflation (148)

recession a period in which real GDP falls (144)

recessionary gap the increase in expenditures required to reach potential GDP (227)

required reserves the cash reserves (a percentage of deposits) that a bank must keep on hand or on deposit with the Federal Reserve (279)

reservation wage the minimum wage that a worker is willing to accept (323)

reserve currency a currency that is used to settle international debts and is held by governments to use in foreign exchange market interventions (460)

resources, factors of production, or **inputs** goods used to produce other goods, for that is, land, labor, and capital (5)

ROSCA a rotating savings and credit association popular in developing countries (277)

rule of 72 the number of years required for an amount to double in value is 72 divided by the annual rate of growth (359)

saving function the relationship between disposable income and saving (190)

scarcity the shortage that exists when less of something is available than is wanted at a zero price (4)

shock an unexpected change in a variable (333)

shortage a quantity supplied that is smaller than the quantity demanded at a given price; it occurs whenever the price is less than the equilibrium price (62)

slope the steepness of a curve, measured as the ratio of the rise to the run (20)

sole proprietorship a business owned by one person, who receives all the profits and is responsible for all the debts incurred by the business (81)

special drawing right (*SDR*) a composite currency whose value is the average of the values of the U.S. dollar, the euro, the Japanese yen, and the U.K. pound (271)

speculative attack a situation in which private investors sell domestic currency and buy foreign currency, betting that the domestic currency will be devalued (411)

speculative demand for money the demand for money created by uncertainty about the value of other assets (306)

speculators people who seek to profit from an expected shift in an exchange rate by selling the currency that is expected to depreciate and buying the currency that is expected to appreciate, then exchanging the appreciated currency for the depreciated currency after the exchange-rate adjustment (468)

spending multiplier a measure of the change in equilibrium income or real GDP produced by a change in autonomous expenditures (225)

sterilization the use of domestic open market operations to offset the effects of a foreign exchange market intervention on the domestic money supply (304)

strategic trade policy the use of trade restrictions or subsidies to allow domestic firms with decreasing costs to gain a greater share of the world market (445)

substitute goods goods that can be used in place of each other; as the price of one rises, the demand for the other rises (54)

supply the amount of a good or service that producers are willing and able to offer for sale at each possible price during a period of time, everything else held constant (55)

supply curve a graph of a supply schedule that measures price on the vertical axis and quantity supplied on the horizontal axis (56)

supply schedule a table or list of prices and the corresponding quantities supplied of a particular good or service (55)

surplus a quantity supplied that is larger than the quantity demanded at a given price; it occurs whenever the price is greater than the equilibrium price (62)

tariff a tax on imports or exports (447)

technology ways of combining resources to produce output (366)

terms of trade the amount of an exported good that must be given up to obtain an imported good (390, 427)

time inconsistent a characteristic of a policy or plan that changes over time in response to changing conditions (329)

total factor productivity (*TFP*) the ratio of the economy's output to its stock of labor and capital (368)

trade creation an effect of a preferential trade agreement that allows a country to obtain goods at a lower cost than is available at home (454)

trade credit allowing an importer a period of time before it must pay for goods or services purchased (392)

trade deficit the situation that exists when imports exceed exports (85)

trade diversion an effect of a preferential trade agreement that reduces economic efficiency by shifting production to a higher-cost producer (454)

trade surplus the situation that exists when imports are less than exports (85)

tradeoff the giving up of one good or activity in order to obtain some other good or activity (25)

transactions account a checking account at a bank or other financial institution that can be drawn on to make payments (268)

transactions demand for money the demand to hold money to buy goods and services (306)

transfer payment income or wealth earned by one person that is taken from that person by the government (in the form of taxes) and transferred or given to another person (90)

underemployment the employment of workers in jobs that do not utilize their productive potential (138)

unemployment rate the percentage of the labor force that is not working (137)

value added the difference between the value of output and the value of the intermediate goods used in the production of that output (101)

value-added tax (*VAT*) a general sales tax collected at each stage of production (257)

value quota a limit on the monetary value of a good that may be imported (449)

velocity of money the average number of times each dollar is spent on final goods and services in a year (294)

wealth the value of all assets owned by a household (195)

wealth effect a change in the real value of wealth that causes spending to change when the level of prices changes (165)

World Bank an international organization that makes loans and provides technical expertise to developing countries (160)

U.S. Macroeconomic Data for Selected Years, 1960–2008

Year	Real GDP	Consumption	Investment	Government Spending	Net Exports	GDP Growth Rate
			$ billions			%
1960	2,501.8	1,597.4	266.6	715.4	−12.7	2.5
1965	3,191.1	2,007.7	393.1	861.3	−18.9	6.4
1970	3,771.9	2,451.9	427.1	1,012.9	−52.0	0.2
1971	3,898.6	2,545.	475.7	990.8	−60.6	3.4
1972	4,105.0	2,701.3	532.1	983.5	−73.5	5.3
1973	4,341.5	2,833.8	594.4	980.0	−51.9	5.8
1974	4,319.5	2,812.3	550.6	1,004.7	−29.4	−0.5
1975	4,311.2	2,876.9	453.1	1,027.4	−2.4	−0.2
1976	4,540.9	3,035.5	544.7	1,031.9	−37.0	5.3
1977	4,750.5	3,164.1	627.0	1,043.3	−61.1	4.6
1978	5,015.0	3,303.1	702.6	1,074.0	−61.9	5.6
1979	5,173.4	3,383.4	725.0	1,094.1	−41.0	3.2
1980	5,161.7	3,374.1	645.3	1,115.4	12.6	−0.2
1981	5,291.7	3,422.2	704.9	1,125.6	8.3	2.5
1982	5,189.3	3,470.3	606.0	1,145.4	−12.6	−1.9
1983	5,423.8	3,668.6	662.5	1,187.3	−60.2	4.5
1984	5,813.6	3,863.3	857.7	1,227.0	−122.4	7.2
1985	6,053.7	4,064.0	849.7	1,312.5	−141.5	4.1
1986	6,263.6	4,228.9	843.9	1,392.5	−156.3	3.5
1987	6,475.1	4,369.8	870.0	1,426.7	−148.4	3.4
1988	6,742.7	4,546.9	890.5	1,445.1	−106.8	4.1
1989	6,981.4	4,675.0	926.2	1,482.5	−79.2	3.5
1990	7,112.5	4,770.3	895.1	1,530.0	−54.7	1.9
1991	7,100.5	4,778.4	822.2	1,547.2	−14.6	−0.2
1992	7,336.6	4,934.8	889.0	1,555.3	−15.9	3.3
1993	7,532.7	5,099.8	968.3	1,541.1	−52.1	2.7
1994	7,835.5	5,290.7	1,099.6	1,541.3	−79.4	4.0
1995	8,031.7	5,433.5	1,134.0	1,549.7	−71.0	2.5
1996	8,328.9	5,619.4	1,234.3	1,564.9	−79.6	3.7
1997	8,703.5	5,831.8	1,387.7	1,594.0	−104.6	4.5
1998	9,066.9	6,125.8	1,524.1	1,624.4	−203.7	4.2
1999	9,470.3	6,438.6	1,642.6	1,686.9	−296.2	4.5
2000	9,817.0	6,739.4	1,735.5	1,721.6	−379.5	3.7
2001	9,890.7	6,910.4	1,598.4	1,780.3	−399.1	0.8
2002	10,048.8	7,099.3	1,557.1	1,858.8	−471.3	1.6
2003	10,320.6	7,306.6	1,617.4	1,911.1	−521.4	2.7
2004	10,755.7	7,588.6	1,809.8	1,952.3	−601.3	4.2
2005	11,131.1	7,858.1	1,915.6	1,985.1	−631.9	3.5
2006	11,294.8	8,029.0	1,912.5	1,971.2	−615.7	2.8
2007	11,523.9	8,252.8	1,809.7	2,012.1	−546.5	2.0
2008	11,652.0	8,272.1	1,689.1	2,070.2	−390.2	1.1